W9-CIQ-887

Regulation of Employee Benefits: ERISA and the Other Federal Laws

Regulation of Employee Benefits: ERISA and the Other Federal Laws

by
William J. Chadwick

The statements and opinions expressed in this book are those of the author and do not necessarily represent the views or positions of the International Foundation of Employee Benefit Plans, its officers, directors or staff.

Copies of this book may be obtained from:

International Foundation of Employee Benefit Plans
P.O. Box 69
Brookfield, Wisconsin 53005 (414) 786-6700

International Foundation Members—$20.00
Non-members—$25.00

ISBN 0-89154-078-4
Printed in the United States of America

5m-778

Dedication

WLC

Acknowledgements

The preparation of this book would have been impossible without a considerable amount of assistance from other people.

A great debt of appreciation must be expressed first to the publisher of this text, the International Foundation of Employee Benefit Plans, and its staff. The contributions made by Elizabeth Hieb, who edited the manuscripts as they were submitted, members of the Composition and Design department, Mary Mayer, Kathy Schnoebelen, Rita Steele and Rosemary Leonard, who typeset the entire text, and the overall assistance of the Foundation throughout the entire publication process are beyond measure.

I have continuing debts to acknowledge to people with the firm of Paul, Hastings, Janofsky & Walker.

I would like to acknowledge my continuing debt to Barbara Raymond, a legal assistant specializing in pension and welfare plans. In one form or another, she made considerable contributions to this book from beginning to end. Her professional review of the text and her critical comments significantly improved the text.

I would also like to acknowledge Robert Hillman for editing my manuscript. I thought I was finished until he critically reviewed my product. The breadth of his knowledge made his comments invaluable.

I would further like to acknowledge June Quell, my secretary, and JoAnn Goostree, Diane Escobedo, Lorna Iverson and Mary Rydelek, of our Word Processing Center. These people typed and retyped numerous drafts of the text under continuing pressure to meet various self-imposed and other deadlines. These people worked at least as hard as I did, and they did so with unbelievable enthusiasm and energy.

Likewise, the preparation of the paper from which this book resulted would have been impossible without a considerable amount of assistance from other people. When I assumed the responsibility for the ABA, I did not anticipate much, if any, help. However, a number of people volunteered their assistance and many of the comments I received improved the original paper. I have numerous debts to acknowledge.

I would like to acknowledge my great debt of gratitude to: Lawrence Hass, Groom & Nordberg, Washington, D.C.; Robert Blum, McCutchen, Doyle, Brown & Enersen, San Francisco, California; James Hutchinson, Steptoe & Johnson, Washington, D.C.; William Kilberg, Breed, Abbott & Morgan, Washington, D.C.; Ted Rhodes, Miller & Chevalier, Washington, D.C.; and Steven Schanes, Schanes Associates, San Diego, California.

My debts to the people mentioned above are tremendous, but I must emphasize that the responsibility for the final text is mine alone.

WJC

Contents

Preface

This book is a revised version of a paper prepared by the author for the Joint Liaison Group on Employee Benefits of the American Bar Association (ABA). The paper was prepared in connection with a National Institute sponsored by the ABA for the purpose of discussing the regulation of pension and welfare plans and the other components of the plan complex.

While the National Institute would never have been sponsored but for the enactment of the Employment Retirement Income Security Act of 1974 (ERISA) 29 U.S.C. §1001, *et seq*., and the resulting regulatory difficulties, the ABA appreciated the multifaceted nature of the existing regulatory scheme. The ABA recognized that the regulation of pension and welfare plans and the other components of the plan complex involved the application of provisions contained in a number of other federal laws, as well as state laws. The ABA also recognized that the federal laws were administered and enforced by a number of federal departments and agencies. The other federal laws presented additional regulatory problems, and these problems had to be considered in connection with any evaluation of the efficiency and effectiveness of the regulatory scheme. The National Institute was held during the fall of 1977, and discussion of the regulation of pension and welfare plans has intensified as a result of increasing public awareness.

This book expands upon the author's original discussion of ERISA and the other federal laws as contained in the paper prepared for the ABA, and contains court decisions and other materials to illustrate some of the more important legal concepts. It is designed to review the applicable provisions of many of the federal laws relating to pension and welfare plans and the other components of the plan complex. Of course, the basic rules start with ERISA and the Internal Revenue Code of 1954 (the Code). However, ERISA and the Code clearly are not the only relevant federal laws. The labor, securities, equal employment and banking laws also contain provisions that have a significant impact on either the structure and content of pension and welfare plans or the administration of these plans and their interaction with the other components of the plan complex. Most issues involving pension and welfare plans require consideration of more than one of these laws.

This book summarizes many of the federal laws relating to pension and welfare plans and the other components of the plan complex. It is designed to heighten the reader's awareness of these laws and, as a result, to encourage the reader to pursue the issues further. This book does not contain an exhaustive analysis of all of the applicable laws or all of the provisions of the laws discussed. The various laws are analyzed to the extent considered necessary to illustrate their significance. State law relating to pension and welfare plans and the other components of the plan complex are not discussed.

The decision not to cover state laws was not based on the fact that these laws were considered insignificant by the author. State law and regulatory systems have an important effect on pension and welfare plans (at least until the scope of ERISA's preemption is determined). While the state laws are significant, they proved to be too numerous to analyze in this book.

William J. Chadwick
Los Angeles, California
March 1978

Introduction

Both labor and capital—the principal resources of our economy—are directly affected by the regulation of pension and welfare plans and the other components of the plan complex. The pension and welfare plans established and maintained by the private sector cover approximately 40 million people, or nearly one-half of all labor-producing persons in commerce and industry. Contributions equal to approximately $20 billion are made to these plans annually; on the average, these contributions represent 35.4% of payroll.

The contributions made to pension and welfare plans by employers and unions exceed benefit payments, and the excess is invested by trustees. It is very difficult to determine the book or fair market value of the assets held by trustees for investment, but the estimates range between $250 billion and $300 billion for pension plans alone. There is no question but that these assets constitute the largest single source of private investment capital in this country. The amounts contributed to pension and welfare plans also constitute one of the largest sources of disposable income received by a large segment of our society. Approximately $9 billion is paid out in benefits to 5.5 million people annually.

The impact of pension and welfare plans and the other components of the plan complex is determined, in large part, by the nature and extent of regulation at the federal level. The federal regulation of the plan complex shapes the structure and content of plans, the administration of plans and the relationship of plans to the other components of the plan complex. This indirect regulation of labor and capital through pension and welfare plans has increased dramatically in the past four decades.

The Employee Retirement Income Security Act of 1974 (ERISA) is by far the most comprehensive law relating to pension and welfare plans. This law establishes the base and range or scope of federal regulation of pension and welfare plans and the other components of the plan complex. Title I of ERISA governs the structure and content of plans, as well as various aspects of plan administration, such as the responsibilities of plan fiduciaries. It also governs the interaction of plans with the other components of the plan complex. For example, certain transactions between plans and related persons are strictly prohibited. ERISA will be discussed in Chapter 1.

ERISA, however, is not the only law governing pension and welfare plans. The Internal Revenue Code of 1954 (the Code) contains numerous provisions relating to pension and welfare plans. This law affects almost all activities engaged in by taxpayers and, in effect, regulates pension and welfare plans through the tax treatment accorded these plans. The Code and the other revenue laws will be discussed in Chapter 2.

The regulation of pension and welfare plans does not stop with ERISA and the Code. Numerous other laws contain provisions relating to pension and welfare plans. The labor laws, securities laws, equal employment laws and banking laws contain provisions that have a significant impact on pension and welfare plans. Historically, we have recognized the importance of some of these laws, but others have not appeared to be very significant. However, a number of recent court decisions have illustrated the significance of these laws.

The Supreme Court recently held that a pension benefit is a perquisite of seniority. *See Alabama Power Co. v. Davis,* ____ U.S. ____ (1977). This holding means that a veteran's military service must be included in computing his benefit, both for vesting and for accrued benefit purposes. Most people did not appreciate the significance of the Military Selective Service Act until this decision was handed down. The Military Selective Service Act and the other labor laws will be discussed in Chapter 3.

Another example involves the Age Discrimination in Employment Act of 1967. The Supreme Court recently ruled that an employee may be involuntarily retired pursuant to the terms of a pension plan prior to the attainment of age 65 without violating this act. *See McMann v. United Airlines,* ____ U.S. ____ (1977). This decision has heightened people's awareness of age discrimination in connection with pension plans.

Similarly, the Supreme Court's decisions in *Gilbert v. General Electric,* 429 U.S. 125 (1976) and *City of Los Angeles v. Manhart,* ____ U.S. ____ (1978) have caused people to contemplate sex discrimination issues under Title VII of the Civil Rights Act in connection with pension and welfare plans. In *Gilbert,* for example, the Court held that an employer's health or sick leave plan was not required to treat disabilities caused or contributed to by pregnancy the same as other temporary disabilities. The Supreme Court felt that a classification which differentiates between pregnant women and non-pregnant persons has no disproportionate effect on women as a protected class. These laws and the other equal employment laws will be discussed in Chapter 5.

These laws are not the only laws that have been debated recently. The Seventh Circuit's decision in *Daniel v. International Brotherhood of Teamsters,* 501 F.2d 1223 (7th Cir. 1977), *cert. granted,* has probably generated more discussion than any other decision in the past few years. In *Daniel,* the court held that an employee's interest in a collectively bargained, noncontributory pension plan is a security for purposes of the antifraud provisions contained in the security laws. This decision obviously has far-reaching implications, which will be discussed in Chapter 4.

Most of the problems resulting from the application of the laws discussed in this book to pension and welfare plans are a result of the *ad hoc* development of the law in this area. The laws have been enacted at various points in time over the past four decades, and were enacted for a number of divergent purposes. There has never been an identifiable federal policy relating to pension and welfare plans. As a result, the existing regulatory network is difficult to describe as either efficient or effective.

Predictably, the departments and agencies charged with the responsibility of administering and enforcing the various laws have published conflicting policy and legal pronouncements, which result in an inefficient utilization of our labor and capital resources. The conflicting requirements also make compliance difficult—if not impossible—and costly. Although rational arguments can be made in support of particular rules and regulations issued by a department or agency, the aggregate impact is difficult to justify. These adverse consequences are, in large part, attributable to the multifaceted regulatory system.

CHAPTER 1

Employee Retirement Income Security Act of 1974

TITLE I: PROTECTION OF EMPLOYEE BENEFIT RIGHTS

Scope

The Employee Retirement Income Security Act of 1974 (ERISA), 29 U.S.C. §1001, *et seq.*, is by far the most comprehensive federal law relating to the private employee benefit complex.

ERISA is made up of four titles.* Title I governs the structure (e.g., written form) and content (e.g., minimum participation standards) of pension and welfare plans, as well as plan administration (e.g., fiduciary responsibility) and plans' interactions with other components of the plan complex (e.g., prohibited transactions). ERISA also supersedes or preempts all state laws "relating" to covered pension and welfare plans. *See* ERISA §514.

ERISA is evidence that Congress recognized the increasingly interstate nature of the private employee benefit complex, and the impact of pension and welfare plans and the other components of the plan complex on both labor and capital.

The provisions contained in ERISA are directed at "employee benefit plans" and the numerous persons (e.g., employers and unions) involved in the establishment and maintenance of such plans. The term "employee benefit plan" includes both welfare plans and pension plans established or maintained by an employer affecting interstate commerce, or by an employee organization representing employees in commerce, or by both. *See* ERISA §4(a). (The term "commerce" is very broadly defined.)

*Title I, Protection of Employee Benefit Rights, will be discussed here and Title IV, Plan Termination Insurance, will be discussed later in this chapter. Title II, Amendments to the Internal Revenue Code (of 1954) Relating to Retirement Plans, will be discussed in Chapter 2. Title III, Jurisdiction, will be mentioned in both chapters.

Certain employee benefit plans, however, are excluded from Title I coverage. *See* ERISA §4(b). For example, governmental plans and church plans are excluded from coverage. Also excluded are plans maintained solely for the purpose of complying with workers' compensation laws or unemployment compensation or disability insurance laws, and plans maintained outside of the United States primarily for the benefit of nonresident aliens. Furthermore, certain unfunded "excess benefit plans" are also excluded from Title I coverage.

Welfare Plans

Section 3(a) of ERISA defines a "welfare plan" as:

> any plan, fund, or program . . . established or maintained by an employer or by an employee organization, or by both, to the extent that such plan, fund, or program was established or maintained for the purpose of providing for its participants or their beneficiaries, through the purchase of insurance or otherwise, (A) medical, surgical, or hospital care or benefits, or benefits in the event of sickness, accident, disability, death or unemployment, or vacation benefits, apprenticeship or other training programs, or day care centers, scholarship funds, or prepaid legal service plans, or (B) any benefit described in §302(c) of the Labor Management Relations Act (1947). . . .

Under this definition, plans which provide benefits described in clause (A) of §3(1) of ERISA and [by reason of the reference to §302(c) of the Taft-Hartley Act] plans which provide holiday, severance, or similar benefits are covered by ERISA.

The Department of Labor has adopted regulations to clarify the definition of the term "welfare plan" by identifying certain practices which do *not* constitute welfare plans under ERISA. *See* 29 C.F.R. §2510.3-1. For example, payments by an employer to an employee as compensation for services performed do not constitute a welfare plan. This particular exception from the definition of welfare plan for so-called payroll practices includes the payment of compensation at a rate in excess of the normal rate of compensation on account of the performance of duties under other than ordinary circumstances, such as overtime pay, shift premiums, holiday premiums and weekend premiums.

The fact that this particular exception from coverage is included in the regulations illustrates the perceived breadth of coverage under ERISA. The regulations also contain coverage exceptions for on-premise facilities, such as recreation facilities; hiring halls; remembrance funds; strike funds; industry advancement programs; certain group insurance programs which are not endorsed by the employer or union; and unfunded scholarship programs.

While these regulations exclude a number of benefits from the definition of welfare plan, the definition may include a wide range of practices not ordinarily thought of as welfare plans. Many of the welfare plans affected by the Internal Revenue Code and the other laws discussed in this book are arguably within the scope of the definition provided. It is critical to examine all practices to determine whether they fall within the definition of welfare plan, because ERISA coverage means that compliance with certain requirements will be necessary and that state laws will be preempted. Some of these requirements will be discussed below.

On the other hand, if a welfare plan is not subject to ERISA, compliance with certain state laws may be necessary. The court's decision in *Bell v. Employee Security Benefit Association,* 437 F.Supp. 382 (D. Kan. 1977) illustrates both the definition of welfare plan and the implications of this classification in terms of ERISA's preemption of state laws.

BELL V. EMPLOYEE SECURITY BENEFIT ASSOCIATION

437 F.Supp. 382 (D. Kan. 1977)

ROGERS, District Judge.

This case involves an interpretation of the Employee Retirement Income Security Act of 1974 (ERISA), and comes before the Court for a decision on the merits as to plaintiff's prayer for permanent injunctive relief. Jurisdiction is predicated upon 28 U.S.C. §1337, and venue is proper under 28 U.S.C. §1391(c).

Plaintiff Bell is the Commissioner of Insurance of the State of Kansas. Defendant Employee Security Benefit Association (ESBA) is an unincorporated association headquartered in Bellevue, Washington. Defendant Tresham is ESBA's president.

ESBA is (or was until this suit was filed) soliciting agents to offer to the working people of Kansas (and other States) what it terms an "employee benefit plan." On April 22, 1977, plaintiff filed a complaint seeking to enjoin ESBA's activities in Kansas until ESBA complies with the statutes and regulations governing the business of insurance in Kansas. Also on April 22, 1977, this Court granted plaintiff's request for a temporary restraining order which enjoined defendants from doing further business in Kansas until a preliminary injunction hearing could be held. On June 24, 1977, this action came before the Court for a hearing as to the merits of the action, the preliminary injunction hearing having been consolidated with the hearing on the merits pursuant to F.R.Civ.P. 65(a)(2). Despite the fact that defendants had received adequate notice of the hearing, they intentionally defaulted by failing to appear. At the hearing, plaintiff presented depositions of several of the principals of ESBA, and the Court considers the evidentiary record before it an adequate basis for the rulings which must be made.

The crux of this case involves interpretation of the provisions of ERISA, 29 U.S.C. §1001, *et seq.* Plaintiff argues that defendants' program is a program of "insurance" which is subject to regulation by the Kansas Department of Insurance. Defendants argue that ESBA's program is not "insurance," but an "employee benefit plan" which, under ERISA, is allegedly exempt from all state regulation.

FACTUAL BACKGROUND

ESBA's brochure announces that ESBA is offering "A New Concept in 'MEMBER EMPLOYEE BENEFIT PLANS.' " The brochure indicates that the program is a "Major Medical Expense and Graded Death Benefit Plan For Members and Member's Families." By way of further description, the brochure describes the program in these terms: "This is a Self-funded, Self-adjusting Employee Benefit Plan established under Public Law 93-406. 'Employee Retirement Income Security Act of 1974.' "

Article 3, Section 1 of ESBA's Articles of Association indicates that membership in ESBA is available to any employee in reasonably good health who has been employed in a common work unit for at least one month, and who pays a $10 membership fee.

Any fair evaluation of the product offered by ESBA must lead to the conclusion that this "employee benefit plan" is substantially similar to major medical and death benefit coverage offered by insurance companies generally. (*See* Quine deposition, p. 10.)

The organizers of ESBA are individuals with substantial experience in the insurance field. ESBA employs insurance agents to solicit members. ESBA markets its program through D.M.A., Inc., an agency organized by two of ESBA's officers which receives 50% of first year member contributions and 17½% of contributions on renewal of the coverage. Administrative services are provided to ESBA by Benefit Services Corporation, a corporation organized by individuals with substantial ties to the organizers of ESBA. Benefit Services Corporation receives 22% of first year and renewal member contributions as a fee for its services.

In Kansas, ESBA has enrolled as members of its plan individuals from a variety of occupations. For example, ESBA has enrolled a self-employed carpenter, an insurance agent, a domestic, a self-employed truck driver, a teacher's aide, a sewer department employee of a large city, a sole proprietor, and a contractor.

The two legal issues which we feel are of primary importance to the resolution of this dispute are: (1) What is the scope of the ERISA preemption? (2) Is ESBA's program "insurance" or an "employee benefit plan?"

I. WHAT IS THE SCOPE OF THE ERISA PREEMPTION?

As the culmination of long investigation and study, Congress passed the Employee Retirement Income Security Act of 1974, P.L. 93-406, codified at 29 U.S.C. §1001 *et seq.* ERISA was intended to make basic reforms in the area of employee pensions and other employee benefit programs.

Congress has the power, when it desires to exercise it, to occupy a field and, under the Supremacy Clause of the Constitution, preempt application of state law. *Florida Lime & Avocado Growers, Inc. v. Paul,* 373 U.S. 132, 146-147, 83 S.Ct. 1210, 10 L.Ed.2d 248 (1963).

We believe that such intent is demonstrated by the wording of 29 U.S.C. §1144:

> (a) Except as provided in subsection (b) of this section, the provisions of this subchapter and subchapter III of this chapter shall supersede any and all State laws insofar as they may now or hereafter relate to any employee benefit plan described in section 1003(a) of this title and not exempt under section 1003(b) of this title. This section shall take effect on January 1, 1975.
>
> (b)(1) This section shall not apply with respect to any cause of action which arose, or any act or omission which occurred, before January 1, 1975.
>
> (2)(A) Except as provided in subparagraph (B), nothing in this subchapter shall be construed to exempt or relieve any person from any law of any State which regulates insurance, banking, or securities.
>
> (B) Neither an employee benefit plan described in section 1003(a) of this title, which is not exempt under section 1003(b) of this title (other than a plan established primarily for the purpose of providing death benefits), nor any trust established under such a plan, shall be deemed to be an insurance company or other insurer, bank, trust company, or investment company or to be engaged in the business of insurance or banking for purposes of any law of any State purporting to regulate insurance companies, insurance contracts, banks, trust companies, or investment companies.
>
> (3) Nothing in this section shall be construed to prohibit use by the Secretary of services or facilities of a State agency as permitted under section 1136 of this title.
>
> (4) Subsection (a) of this section shall not apply to any generally applicable criminal law of a State.
>
> (c) For purposes of this section:
>
> (1) The term "State law" includes all laws, decisions, rules, regulations, or other State action having the effect of law, of any State. A law of the United States applicable only to the District of Columbia shall be treated as a State law rather than a law of the United States.
>
> (2) The term "State" includes a State, any political subdivisions thereof, or any agency or instrumentality of either, which purports to regulate, directly or indirectly, the terms and conditions of employee benefit plans covered by this subchapter.
>
> (d) Nothing in this subchapter shall be construed to alter, amend, modify, invalidate, impair, or supersede any law of the United States (except as provided in sections 1031 and 1137(b) of this title) or any rule or regulation issued under any such law.

Despite the apparently clear wording of §1144 (a), an examination of the legislative history behind it may be helpful. We believe that the legislative history indicates that this wording was meant to convey just as broad a concept of preemption as appears on the face of the statute.

The original House and Senate versions of ERI-

SA provided for preemption of state law. But the broader preemption provision which was eventually incorporated into ERISA was developed in conference committee.

The joint explanatory statement of the conference committee indicated just how broad the preemption provision was meant to be:

> *Preemption of State Laws (Sec. 514 of the bill)*
>
> Under the substitute, the provisions of title I are to supersede all State laws that relate to any employee benefit plan that is established by an employer engaged in or affecting interstate commerce or by an employee organization that represents employees engaged in or affecting interstate commerce. (However, following title I generally, preemption will not apply to government plans, church plans not electing under the vesting, etc., provisions, workmen's compensation plans, non-U.S. plans primarily for non-resident aliens, and so-called "excess benefit plans.")
>
> [1974] U.S. Code Cong. & Admin. News, p. 5162.

In introducing the conference report, Senator Harrison Williams, Chairman of the Senate Committee on Labor and Public Welfare, made the following statement:

> It should be stressed that with the narrow exceptions specified in the bill, the substantive and enforcement provisions of the conference substitute are intended to preempt the field for Federal regulations, thus eliminating the threat of conflicting or inconsistent State and local regulations, thus eliminating the threat of conflicting or inconsistent state and local regulation of employee benefit plans. This principle is intended to apply in its broadest sense to all actions of State or local governments, or any instrumentality thereof, which have the force or effect of law.
>
> [1974] U.S. Code Cong. & Admin. News, pp. 5188-89.

Senator Javits, ranking minority member of the Senate Committee on Labor and Welfare, explained the reasoning of the conference committee in broadening the preemption provision:

> Both House and Senate bills provided for preemption of State law, but—with one major exception appearing in the House bill—defined the perimeters of preemption in relation to the areas regulated by the bill. Such a formulation raised the possibility of endless litigation over the validity of State action that might impinge on Federal regulation, as well as opening the door to multiple and potentially conflicting State laws hastily contrived to deal with some particular aspect of private welfare or pension benefit plans not clearly connected to the Federal regulatory scheme.
>
> Although the desirability of further regulation —at either the State or Federal level—undoubtedly warrants further attention, on balance, the emergence of a comprehensive and pervasive Federal interest and the interests of uniformity with respect to interstate plans required—but for certain exceptions—the displacement of State action in the field of private employee benefit programs. The conferees—recognizing the dimensions of such a policy—also agreed to assign the Congressional Pension Task Force the responsibility of studying and evaluating preemption in connection with State authorities and reporting its findings to the Congress. If it is determined that the preemption policy devised has the effect of precluding essential legislation at either the State or Federal level, appropriate modifications can be made.
>
> 120 Cong.Rec. 29942 (1974).

The importance of the preemption provision was highlighted by Representative John Dent, Chairman of the Subcommittee on Labor of the House Committee on Labor and Education:

> Finally I wish to make note of what is to many the crowning achievement of this legislation, the reservation to Federal authority the sole power to regulate the field of employee benefit plans. With the preemption of the field, we round out the protection afforded participants by eliminating the threat of conflicting and inconsistent State and local regulation.
>
> . . .
>
> The conferees, with the narrow exceptions specifically enumerated, applied this principle in its broadest sense to foreclose any non-Federal regulation of employee benefit plans. Thus, the provisions of section 514 would reach any rule, regulation, practice or decision of any State, subdivision thereof or any agency or instrumentality thereof—including any professional society or association operating under color of law—which would affect any employee benefit plan as described in section 4(a) and not exempt under section 4(b).

In light of this legislative history, we conclude that federal preemption in the area of pensions and other employee benefit programs is virtually total. We are unable to agree with the decisions which apparently have applied a narrow interpretation to §1144. *See Insurers' Action Council, Inc. v. Heaton,* 423 F.Supp. 921 (D. Minn. 1976); *Dawson v. Whaland,* No. 76-266 (D. N.H. 1976).

Rather, we subscribe to the view announced by the court in *Hewlett-Packard Company v. Barnes,* 425 F.Supp. 1294, 1300 (N.D. Cal. 1977):

> Overall, the legislative history reveals both that Congress carefully considered the question of preemption, including the feasibility of enacting a more limited preemption provision, and that Congress ultimately enacted Section 514(a)

> with the express purpose of summarily preempting state regulation of ERISA-covered employee benefit plans. That the statute, standing alone or buttressed by its legislative history, was intended to supersede state regulation of benefit plans such as plaintiffs' is indisputable.

See also, Wayne Chemical, Inc. v. Columbus Agency Service Corp., 426 F.Supp. 316, 321 (N.D. Ind. 1977); *Kerbow v. Kerbow,* 421 F.Supp. 1253, 1260 (N.D. Tex. 1976); *Azzaro v. Harnett,* 414 F.Supp. 473, 474 (S.D. N.Y. 1976); *aff'd* 553 F.2d 93 (2d Cir. 1977), *petition for cert. filed,* — U.S. —, 45 U.S.L.W. 3796; *White Motor Corp. v. Malone,* 412 F.Supp. 372, 380 n. 6 (D. Minn.), *rev'd on other grounds* 545 F.2d 599 (8th Cir. 1976); *Fleck v. Spannaus,* 412 F.Supp. 366, 368 (D. Minn. 1976); Note, *Insurance Regulation—Employee Benefit Plans,* 28 Ark.L.Rev. 515, 520 (1975).

Our conclusion is bolstered by the recent statement of the House Committee on Education and Labor, which is charged with the responsibility of overseeing the implementation of ERISA:

> ERISA, among its many provisions, provides for significant adjustment in the regulatory roles of state and federal authority with respect to the various elements of the employee benefit plan field. The provisions of section 514 expressly reserve to Federal authority the regulation of employee benefit plans subject to the jurisdiction of the Act. In electing deliberately to preclude state authority over these plans, Congress acted to insure uniformity of regulation with respect to their activities. There was a recognition of the necessity for the preservation of some state activity in this field and certain limited exceptions were made to the broad preemption scheme. In general these exemptions are designed to save state law as it is applied to entities which are not employee benefit plans as defined in section 4(a) and not exempt under section 4(b), to the extent that such regulation does not relate to employee benefit plans.
>
> From the early 1970's the legislative activities which eventually produced ERISA involved various framings of preemption schemes. The Committee's hearing record prior to 1974 contains numerous discussions of the propriety of one approach or another. Once it had become clear that our policy would be the creation of uniform national standards, the problem was to extract these plans from the regulatory schemes in the several states without creating untoward side effects.
>
> A number of states had undertaken to regulate employee benefit plans as such; others had already made, or appeared ready to declare, these plans subject to state control as insurers, trust companies, or investment companies. From a drafting standpoint the difficulty arose in attempting to extricate these plans from the framework of state insurance, trust and securities regulation even though their activities might very well bring them within the sphere of conduct historically subject to such regulation. On the one hand it was clear that the plans subject to ERISA needed to be freed of the possibility of state regulation; on the other, it was important to limit the effects of preemption in order to avoid disrupting state efforts to regulate the conduct of other financial entities not subject to the federal Act.
>
> This was accomplished by articulating a broad intention to preempt; "Except as provided in subsection (b) of this section, the provisions of this title and title IV shall supersede any and all State laws insofar as they may now or hereafter relate to any employee benefit plan described in section 4(a) and not exempt under section 4(b)" [ERISA section 514(a)].
>
> *It is our understanding of this language that with respect to regulation of the activities of certain employee benefit plans (those subject to ERISA jurisdiction), federal authority has been expressly extended to occupy the field to the exclusion of state authority subject to certain exceptions.* These exceptions are designed to delineate affirmatively the limits of the "field" preempted by section 514(a), and articulate a second, but distinctly subordinate, policy within the section of preserving state authority insofar as it does not relate to any plan "... described in section 4(a) and not exempt under section 4(b)."
>
> Based on our examination of the effects of section 514, *it is our judgment that the legislative scheme of ERISA is sufficiently broad to leave no room for effective state regulation within the field preempted.* Similarly it is our belief that the Federal interest and the need for national uniformity are so great that enforcement of state regulation should be precluded. [Activity Report of the Committee on Education and Labor of the U.S. House of Representatives, House Report No. 94-1785, pp. 46-47 (1/3/77)] (emphasis added).

In sum, the preemption section of ERISA, 29 U.S.C. §1144 (quoted above) clearly preempts all state regulation of "employee benefit plans." However, the law attempts to allow the states to continue to regulate other activities, such as the sale of insurance. §1144(b)(2)(A). To preserve the distinction, ERISA also provides that a state cannot evade the preemption provision by treating an "employee benefit plan" as "insurance." §1144(b)(2)(B). *See also Hewlett-Packard Company v. Barnes, supra,* 425 F.Supp. at 1300; *Dawson v. Whaland, supra.*

Accepting the broad preemption provision of

ERISA, we must now turn to the question of whether ESBA's program constitutes "insurance" (which may be regulated by state law) or an "employee benefit plan" (which may not be regulated by state law).

II. IS ESBA'S PROGRAM "INSURANCE" OR AN "EMPLOYEE BENEFIT PLAN?"

As indicated in the previous section, under ERISA, Congress intended to prevent states from regulating in any manner "employee benefit plans." However, ERISA was not concerned with the regulation of insurance, *Dawson v. Whaland, supra,* and did not intend to preempt state laws in this regard. §1144(b)(2)(A).

Plaintiff argues that ESBA's program is "insurance," which is still subject to state regulation as provided in §1144(b)(2)(A). Defendant ESBA argues that its program is an "employee benefit plan" which, because of §1144(a), may not be regulated by states.

The Supreme Court of Kansas has defined insurance, in *State ex rel. Londerholm v. Anderson,* 195 Kan. 649, 662, 408 P.2d 864, 874 (1965), as:

> . . . any contract whereby one party promises for a consideration to indemnify the other against certain risks.

One author, after examining both statutes and case law, concluded that a good description of insurance would include five basic ingredients:

> (a) consideration (premium),
> (b) fortuitous event,
> (c) a group of people with identical interests more or less equally exposed to the same risks,
> (d) a shifting of that risk to the insurer, and
> (e) a distribution of the risk to others similarly exposed.
>
> [Duesenberg, *The Legality of Noninsured Employee Benefit Programs,* 5 B.C.Ind. & Com.L. Rev. 231, 237 (1964)]

The complicating factor in evaluating defendants' program is the fact that most employee benefit plans will meet the criteria of a general definition of insurance. Goetz, *Regulation of Uninsured Employee Welfare Plans under State Insurance Laws,* 1967 Wis.L.Rev. 319, 322; Duesenberg, *supra,* 5 B.C.Ind. & Com.L.Rev. at 237.

Even before ERISA was passed, it was realized that the mere fact that employee benefit plans, or other activities, met the broad (and often vague) definitions of insurance, did not mean that such activities should be subject to regulation by state departments of insurance. As stated in Note, *Self-Insured Employee Welfare Plans and the 501(c)(9) Trust: The Specter of State Regulation,* 43 Cinn. L.Rev. 325, 333 (1974):

> Although self-funded employee welfare plans may satisfy a vague legislative or judicial definition of insurance, it does not necessarily follow that employers providing such programs should be subject to supervision under insurance statutes.

See also State ex rel. Londerholm v. Anderson, supra, 195 Kan. at 662, 408 P.2d 864; *West & Co. of La., Inc. v. Sykes,* 515 S.W.2d 635, 637 (Ark. 1974); *Note, supra,* 28 Ark.L.Rev. at 516.

In *West & Co. of La., Inc. v. Sykes, supra,* 515 S.W.2d at 637, the court quoted a passage from an author who, after surveying the broad statutory definitions of insurance which States are prone to enacting, commented:

> Arguably these statutes should be read not as stating that every transaction having the stated characteristics is insurance but only as saying that no transaction is insurance unless it has these characteristics. [Keeton Insurance Law—Basic Text, 8.-2(a), p. 543]

Given that most employee benefit plans meet standard definitions of insurance, and that Congress meant to preempt state regulation of employee benefit plans without otherwise affecting state regulation of insurance, how are we to tell exactly what Congress meant to preempt?

The Congressional definitions of "employee benefit plans" are set out in 29 U.S.C. § 1002:

> For purposes of this subchapter:
>
> (1) The terms "employee welfare benefit plan" and "welfare plan" mean any plan, fund or program which was heretofore or is hereafter established or maintained by an employer or by an employee organization, or by both, to the extent that such plan, fund, or program was established or is maintained for the purpose of providing for its participants or their beneficiaries, through the purchase of insurance or otherwise, (A) medical, surgical, or hospital care or benefits, or benefits in the event of sickness, accident, disability, death or unemployment, or vacation benefits, apprenticeship or other training programs, or day care centers, scholarship funds, or prepaid legal services, or (B) any benefit described in section 186(c) of this title (other than pensions on retirement or death, and insurance to provide such pensions).
>
> (2) The terms "employee pension benefit plan" and "pension plan" mean any plan, fund, or program which was heretofore or is hereafter established or maintained by an employer or by an employee organization, or by both, to the extent that by its express terms or as a result of surrounding circumstances such plan, fund, or program—
>
> (A) provides retirement income to employ-

ees, or

(B) results in a deferral of income by employees for periods extending to the termination of covered employment or beyond, regardless of the method of calculating the contributions made to the plan, the method of calculating the benefits under the plan or the method of distributing benefits from the plan.

(3) The term "employee benefit plan" or "plan" means an employee welfare benefit plan or an employee pension benefit plan or a plan which is both an employee benefit plan and an employee pension benefit plan.

(4) The term "employee organization" means any labor union or any organization of any kind, or any agency or employee representation committee, association, group, or plan, in which employees participate and which exist for the purpose, in whole or in part, of dealing with employers concerning an employee benefit plan, or other matters incidental to employment relationships; or any employees' beneficiary association organized for the purpose in whole or in part, of establishing such a plan.

Defendants would have us conclude that ESBA is "any employees' beneficiary association organized for the purpose in whole or in part, of establishing such a plan" under the last phrase of §1002(4), and end the matter. However, we do not believe the solution is so simple.

Our conclusion is that just as a state cannot regulate an "employee benefit plan" by calling it "insurance," neither can defendants merchandise an insurance program, free of state regulation, by terming it an "employee benefit plan." Several factors lead to this conclusion.

First, a reading of the legislative history, including the congressional hearings, leading up to the passage of ERISA, indicates that Congress was concerned primarily with pensions and other employee benefit programs established by employers, or unions.

Further, a reading of pre-ERISA literature sheds much light on how the concept "employee benefit plan" was generally understood. Such a reading indicates that the pre-ERISA concept of an "employee benefit plan" was easily distinguished from the concept of "insurance," and was based on the premise that most "employee benefit plans" were non-profit, non-advertising, and provided by employers, or pre-existing employee groups.

One pre-ERISA discussion of "employee benefit plans" (EBPs) is located in Note, *supra,* 28 Ark. L.Rev. at 515. That article proffers the following definition of EBPs, while noting that the definition is more limited than that set out in ERISA:

> Employee benefit plans are arrangements through which employees are provided hospital, surgical, death, and disability benefits as a fringe benefit by the employer.

The article continues by discussing the early relief funds for employees established by railroad companies, and noting that they were distinguished from insurance by the following factors:

> . . . first, the funds were not open to the public; second, there was no advertising or solicitation; third, the membership was voluntary; and fourth, the fund was not operated for profit.

The Note addressed the decision of *West & Co. of La., Inc. v. Sykes, supra,* in which the Arkansas Supreme Court concluded that an employer's employee benefit plan was not subject to regulation by the Arkansas insurance authorities. At page 518, the article notes:

> In deciding that the West Plan was not insurance, the Court cited several characteristics of the plan which distinguished it from insurance. The characteristics were: first, the plan was a fringe benefit; second, it was furnished on an optional basis; third, it was substantially supported by the employer's profits; and fourth, the plan is not intended to be actuarially sound.

Finally, and perhaps most important, the articles note that the primary purposes of insurance regulation simply are not advanced by the regulation of EBPs. These objectives were stated to be:

> . . . first, to avoid overreaching by insurers; second, to assure solidity and solvency of insurers; third, to assure that rating classifications and rates are reasonable and fair. Even though not discussed by the Court, it is clear that none of these objectives would be served by the regulation of employee benefit plans. . . . There is no threat of overreaching when the given plan is provided on a non-profit basis. Any unfairness by the employer in paying out benefits would probably result in labor problems. Statutory reserve requirements would also be unnecessary since the benefit plan would only be incidental to the employer's business. Payment of benefits would normally be no more uncertain than payment of wages. Finally, since benefit plans are provided at less cost than comparable plans offered by insurers, there would be no reason for state regulation. [28 Ark.L.Rev. at 517-518]

Another such discussion of EBPs in relation to insurance appears in Duesenberg, *supra,* 5 B.C. Ind. & Com.L.Rev. That article concludes that the "primary purpose test," which has been recognized in Kansas, *State ex rel. Londerholm v. Anderson, supra,* 195 Kan. at 662, 408 P.2d 864, easily distinguishes EBPs from insurance.

> First, of course, is the proposition that programs of this kind are nothing more than inci-

> dents of the employment contract by which an employer hopes to get better service from its employees. They are a form of compensation.
>
> . . .
>
> Marketing practices are a second major distinction. They are substantially different from those normally used in selling insurance, and these dissimilarities serve to minimize the need for state regulation.
>
> Two characteristics of the programs stand out. Protection available through employee benefit plans is neither offered to the public generally nor marketed for profit. . . .
>
> . . .
>
> Non-insured employee benefit programs may be further distinguished from insurance by the inadequacy or total absence [pp. 238-240]

An important point made by Duesenberg is that while state regulation can serve to keep an insurance company solvent, no such regulation can competently protect the economic prosperity of an employer.

In Note, 43 Cinn.L.Rev., *supra,* at 334-335, it is observed that the authorities generally distinguish EBPs from insurance on these bases: (a) the employer-employee (rather than insurance company-customer) relationship; (b) the absence of a profit motive; (c) the absence of solicitation; and (d) the absence of the common reasons for insurance regulation.

Another helpful discussion of the problem, which will not be expanded upon here, appears in *Goetz,* 1967 Wis.L.Rev., *supra,* at 336-341.

Post-ERISA Congressional Reports bear out that these characterizations of EBPs are substantially what Congress had in mind when it passed ERISA. *See* Activity Report of the Committee on Education and Labor of the U.S. House of Representatives, House Report No. 94-1785 (1976).

Clearly, the EBP concept as it existed when Congress passed the preemption provisions of ERISA involved the following characteristics: (1) it was provided by an employer or homogeneous employee organization, such as a union; (2) it was non-commercial in nature; (3) it did not involve solicitation; (4) it was not intended to be actuarially sound; (5) because the employees could look only to the fund, and not to the provider of that fund, the rates were substantially lower than insurance rates. (Compare with Dept. of Labor press release, May 2, 1977.) While it is obvious from §1002(4) that Congress intended to give as broad a definition as possible to EBPs, it is also clear that it did not intend to allow companies, motivated by profit, to escape insurance regulations by setting up a program that is an EBP in name only.

Judged by the standards discussed, we believe that it is clear that ESBA's program is "insurance" and not an EBP. ESBA's program is provided by a third-party entrepreneur, not an employer or a pre-existing employee group, such as a union. When an individual purchases a plan from ESBA, neither his employer nor any of his co-employees (if any) even know about it. This ESBA plan is certainly not non-commercial; its operation provides profit-making opportunities for its marketing agency (D.M.A., Inc.) and its administrative services provider (Benefit Services Corp.), both of which have substantial ties to ESBA's organizers. ESBA's plan is apparently supposed to be actuarially sound. The evidence before the Court indicates that ESBA's rates are somewhat lower than normal insurance rates. ESBA's marketing practices are virtually indistinguishable from those of an insurance company.

We believe that this description indicates that the characteristics of ESBA's plan put it within the definition of "insurance" and outside the traditional concept of an EBP. Just as important, having examined ESBA's operation the Court can see no reason to conclude that the objectives of insurance regulation would not be well-served by application to ESBA's program. Evidence of the recent failure of similar companies attest to the need for regulation in this area.

From an examination of the broad concept of EBPs, it is our conclusion that ESBA is marketing disguised insurance. We are not alone in this conclusion. The House Activity Report, *supra,* remarked:

> It has come to our attention, through the good offices of the National Association of State Insurance Commissioners, that certain entrepreneurs have undertaken to market insurance products to employers and employees at large, claiming these products to be ERISA-covered plans. For instance, persons whose primary interest is in profiting from the provision of administrative services are establishing insurance companies and related enterprises. The entrepreneur will then argue that his enterprise is an ERISA benefit plan which is protected, under ERISA's preemption provision, from state regulation. We are concerned with this type of development, but on the basis of the facts provided us, we are of the opinion that these programs are not "employee benefit plans" as defined in Section 3(3). As described to us, these plans are established and maintained by entrepreneurs for the purpose of marketing insurance products or services to others. They are not established or

> maintained by the appropriate parties to confer ERISA jurisdiction, nor is the purpose for their establishment or maintenance appropriate to meet the jurisdictional prerequisites of the Act. They are no more ERISA plans than is any other insurance policy sold to an employee benefit plan. (p. 48)

We do not believe that the importance of this statement of the House Committee charged with overseeing the operation of ERISA can be minimized. In a recent and similar case, *Hamberlin v. VIP Insurance Trust,* 434 F.Supp. 1196 (D. Ariz. 1977), the Court quoted from this Activity Report and noted:

> While not contemporaneous legislative history, it is "virtually conclusive" as to legislative intent. *Sioux Tribe v. United States,* 316 U.S. 317, 319 (1942), 62 S.Ct. 1095, 86 L.Ed. 1501.

An examination of the specific wording of the ERISA provisions also leads us to the conclusion that ESBA's activities are not protected by the preemption provisions of ERISA because ESBA's program is not an employee benefit plan.

The term "employee benefit plan" is defined in 29 U.S.C. §1002(3) as "an employee welfare benefit plan or an employee pension benefit plan or a plan which is both . . ." Thus, if ESBA's plan is to constitute a protected EBP, it must meet the definition of an "employee welfare benefit plan" which is defined in §1002(1):

> The terms "employee welfare benefit plan" and "welfare plan" mean any plan, fund, or program which was heretofore or is hereafter established or maintained by an employer or by an employee organization, or by both, to the extent that such plan, fund, or program was established or is maintained for the purpose of providing for its participants or their beneficiaries, through the purchase of insurance or otherwise, (A) medical, surgical, or hospital care or benefits in the event of sickness, accident, disability, death or unemployment, or vacation benefits, apprenticeship or other training programs, or day care centers, scholarship funds, or prepaid legal services, or (B) any benefit described in section 186(c) of this title (other than pensions on retirement or death, and insurance to provide such pensions).

Plaintiff concedes that ESBA's program meets the second portion of this definition because the ESBA plan does provide "medical, surgical, or hospital care or benefits," etc. However, plaintiff argues that ESBA's program is not an EBP because it is not "established or maintained by an employer or by an employee organization."

[6] We have no difficulty in concluding that ESBA is certainly not an "employer." That term is defined in §1002(5):

> (5) The term "employer" means any person acting directly as an employer, or indirectly in the interest of an employer, in relation to an employee benefit plan; and includes a group or association of employers acting for an employer in such capacity.

ESBA does not employ the individuals which purchase its medical care or death benefits coverage. ESBA does not act directly as, or indirectly for the benefit of, the employer of the individuals who purchase an ESBA plan.

In *Hamberlin v. VIP Insurance Trust, supra,* the original VIP trust was a multiple employer trust insured by Old Republic Life Insurance Company. When Old Republic cancelled the group coverage, the insurance brokers, Galbraith & Green, established a new self-funded trust rather than finding another authorized insurer. The trustees were Galbraith & Green officials. Galbraith & Green sold the policies, as does ESBA, directly to individual employees who paid the entire premiums on their individual insurance policies. The Court rejected a contention that the trustees were acting as agents of employers as contemplated by 29 U.S.C. §1002(5), noting:

> The employers had no voice in the management or operation of the trust or the decision to terminate, and contributed no funds on behalf of their employees. The trustees were corporate officers of Galbraith & Green and in the operation, maintenance and ultimate termination of the plan were acting in the best and primary interest of their corporate employer. They were simply not acting as agents of or on behalf of the employers or employer groups as contemplated by 29 U.S.C. §1002(5). They were acting in the interest of and on behalf of the business of Galbraith & Green, their employer.
>
> This was purely an entrepreneurial plan put together by Galbraith & Green to protect business commissions they would have lost if the trust had not been restructured and continued after Old Republic cancelled. They also maintained business relations with customers they could have lost. Most importantly, by designating this as an ERISA plan, they hoped to escape from direct supervision and auditing by the State Insurance Department and from its coverage and reserve requirements under the theory of federal preemption.

We think it clear that ESBA is not an employer or one acting in the interest of an employer as contemplated in §1002(5).

A better argument might be made that ESBA constitutes an "employee organization," a term which is defined in §1002(4):

> The term "employee organization" means any labor union or any organization of any kind, or any agency or employee representation committee, association, group, or plan, in which employees participate and which exists for the purpose, in whole or in part, of dealing with employers concerning an employee benefit plan, or other matters incidental to employment relationships; or any employees' beneficiary association organized for the purpose in whole or in part, of establishing such a plan.

Thus, the term "employee organization" is defined in two parts. Clearly the ESBA plan does not constitute an "employee organization" as that term is defined in the portion of subsection (4) which precedes the semi-colon. For a program to meet this definition, it must be a program in which "employees participate" and the organization must exist "for the purpose, in whole or in part, of dealing with employers concerning an employee benefit plan, or other matters incidental to employment relationships."

The participation requirement of this definition is not met by ESBA. ESBA is a mere third party entrepreneur; it is not a part of any genuine employee organization. The only pretense which ESBA puts forth concerning employee participation is the provision that employees may attend, and vote at, the annual meeting. However, individuals who purchase an ESBA policy must sign a proxy appointing an ESBA official as their representative at the meeting should they not attend. In April, 1977, an annual meeting was held. Of the 3500 ESBA policyholders, none attended the annual meeting. Employee participation in the ESBA plan is a fiction.

Nor does ESBA exist for the purpose of dealing with employers concerning an employee benefit plan. There is no evidence in this case indicating that the employer of an individual who purchases an ESBA policy would have any knowledge whatsoever of ESBA. The employer of an individual who purchases an ESBA policy will in most instances no more deal with ESBA than he would deal with an insurance company which had sold a medical coverage policy to the employee. Contributions may be paid to ESBA without employer involvement, and claims and benefits are administered without any participation by the employer.

Therefore, if ESBA is to receive any comfort from this section, it must meet the requirements of the definition of an "employee organization" which is contained in the portion of §1002(4) which follows the semi-colon. This portion of the definition is very broad, indicating that an "employee organization" can be "*any* employees' beneficiary association organized for the purpose in whole or in part, of establishing such a plan." In point of fact, the Court finds this definition to be of very little help. This clause defines "employee organization" in terms of the plan provided. But if one looks to the definition of plan contained in §1002(1), that term is defined, in significant part, in terms of who provides the plan. Thus, we face a circular definition. A plan is an EBP if it meets certain requirements *and* is provided by an employee organization. An entity is an employee organization if it is organized to provide an EBP. Because of the circularity of this definitional process, we believe that it is only the first section of §1002(4)—before the semi-colon—which can be safely looked to for a useful definition of "employee organization." As noted, ESBA does not meet that definition.

Despite our reservations about the circularity of definition contained in the last clause of §1002(4), we believe that it must be analyzed, because principles of statutory construction teach that statutes should be construed in such a way as to render none of the subsections superfluous. *Stamps v. Michigan Teamsters Joint Council No. 43,* 431 F.Supp. 745 (E.D. Mich. 1977). Analysis of this clause must center on the definition of its key phrase "employees' beneficiary association."

We believe that there are a number of indications that the essential ingredients of an "employees' beneficiary association" is a commonality of interests among its employee members.

The term "employees' beneficiary association" was used in ERISA's predecessor, the Welfare and Pension Plans Disclosure Act, as amended by the Welfare and Pension Plans Disclosure Act Amendments of 1962, 29 U.S.C. §302(a)(3) (repealed effective January 1, 1975). In 1965, the Department of Labor published *The Welfare and Pension Plans Disclosure Act Interpretive Manual,* which defined the term "employees' beneficiary association" as follows:

> 315.100 CRITERIA FOR DISTINGUISHING EMPLOYEES' BENEFICIARY ASSOCIATIONS
>
> The term "employees' beneficiary association" is not defined by the Act. An analysis of the Act has led to the development of certain criteria for determining whether an organization is an "employees' beneficiary association" within the meaning of the Act:
>
> 1) The membership in the association must be conditioned on one's employment status.
>
> Examples:
>
> (a) Membership is limited to employees of

a certain employer or employers, or

(b) All members must be members of one union. Membership is tied to the union which itself is formed and maintained in large part to deal with employment relationships.

Where membership in an organization is based solely on national origin, geography, religious affiliation, or fraternal, civic, or social purposes, etc. and the employment status of the members is irrelevant, such organizations would not be employees' beneficiary associations. Examples of such organizations are the Knights of Columbus, the Elks, the Kiwanis, Rotary, Junior Chamber of Commerce, and Club of Irish-Americans. Thus, plans maintained by such organizations would not be within the scope of the WPPDA.

The importance of this construction of the term "employees' beneficiary association" is clear when it is realized that Congress, presumably aware of this interpretation [*National Lead Co. v. United States,* 252 U.S. 140, 145-146, 40 S.Ct. 237, 64 L.Ed. 496 (1920); *Helvering v. Winmill,* 305 U.S. 79, 82-83, 59 S.Ct. 45, 83 L.Ed. 52 (1938)], utilized in ERISA substantially the same definitions which had been contained in the WPPDA at 29 U.S.C. §302.2A. Sutherland on Statutory Construction §49.09, at 256 (4th ed. 1973) states:

> Where a statute has received a contemporaneous and practical interpretation and the statute as interpreted is reenacted, the practical interpretation is accorded greater weight than it ordinarily receives, and is regarded as presumptively the correct interpretation of the law.

See also Snyder v. Harris, 394 U.S. 332, 339, 89 S.Ct. 1053, 22 L.Ed.2d 319 (1969); *Brewster v. Gage,* 280 U.S. 327, 337, 50 S.Ct. 115, 74 L.Ed. 457 (1930); *State of Wyoming v. United States,* 310 F.2d 566, 580 (10th Cir. 1962).

The term "employees' beneficiary association" also appears in the Internal Revenue Code, 26 U.S.C. §501(c)(9). Again we find that interpretation of this term highlights the concept of commonality of interests among employee members. In Proposed Regulation 1.501(c)(9)—1 which appears at 34 *Fed.Reg.* 1028 (1/23/69), we find the following:

> An organization defined in section 501(c)(9) must be composed of individuals who are entitled to participate in the association by reason of their status as employees who are members of a common working unit. The members of a common working unit include, for example, the employees of a single employer, the employees of one industry, or the members of one labor union. Although membership in such an association need not be offered to all of the employees of a common working unit, membership must be offered to all of the employees of one or more classes of the common working unit, and such class or classes must be selected on the basis of criteria which do not limit membership to shareholders, highly compensated employees, or other like individuals. The criteria for defining a class may be restricted by conditions reasonably related to employment, such as, a limitation based on a reasonable minimum period of service, a limitation based on a maximum compensation, or a requirement that a member be employed on a full-time basis. The criteria for defining a class may also be restricted by conditions relating to the type and amount of benefits offered, such as, a requirement that a member meet a reasonable minimum health standard in order to be eligible for life, sick, or accident benefits.

Defendants appear to have realized the significance of the commonality requirement for an employee beneficiary association, for the ESBA by-laws, Article II, Sec. 1, define the term "common work unit" as including "all of the employees of the same employer, or all of the employees of any one industry or profession, or all of the members of a labor union."

In actual practice, the evidence indicates that ESBA largely ignores the commonality requirement and its own definition of "common work unit." In fact, defendant Tresham testified that he was not sure what the phrase "common work unit" meant (Tresham Depo., pp. 23-24). ESBA does not limit membership to one employer, one industry, or one union. Rather, ESBA will sell its program to virtually anyone who is employed. It is therefore impossible to conclude that ESBA is an "employees' beneficiary association" as that term is used in the last clause of §1002(4).

Another way in which to examine ESBA's program in relation to ERISA is to begin with the definition of "employee" in §1002(6):

> The term "employee" means any individual employed by an employer.

For purposes of ERISA, as noted earlier, §1002 (5) indicates that to be an employer one must act "in relation to an employee benefit plan." Thus, an individual would be an "employee" only if he worked for an entity which acted "in relation to an employee benefit plan." It has already been concluded that the employers of the individuals who have purchased ESBA's policies do not, in fact, act in relation to the EBP. Therefore, these policyholders are not "employees" within the meaning of ERISA.

ESBA's selling of plans to self-employed individuals is obviously contrary to ERISA for it is clear that one who is self-employed with no common law employees cannot establish a qualified plan. 29 C.F.R. §2510.3-3 (1976).

We thus find nothing in the wording of the ERISA definitions which would indicate that ESBA's program is any more deserving of the preemption protection of 29 U.S.C. §1144 than would be any other insurance company selling medical care benefits to working individuals. It is clear that under 29 U.S.C. §1144(b)(2)(A), ESBA's activities were not meant to be exempted from state regulation under ERISA. To allow ESBA to palm its insurance program off as an EBP by the use of transparent gimmickry would completely destroy the distinction between insurance and employee benefit plans which 29 U.S.C. §1144 obviously attempts to preserve. Any other decision would certainly be contrary to the policy underlying the McCarran-Ferguson Act, 15 U.S.C. §1011 *et seq.* which reserves for the various states the regulation of the industry of insurance.

IT IS THEREFORE DECLARED that the "plan" ESBA is soliciting is not an "employee welfare benefit plan," as that term is defined in 29 U.S.C. §1002;

IT IS FURTHER DECLARED that ESBA is subject to the insurance laws of the State of Kansas and to the regulations of the Kansas Insurance Commissioner;

IT IS ORDERED that defendants, and their officers, employees, agents or servants be, and are hereby, permanently enjoined from transacting any insurance business in the State of Kansas until such time as they become properly authorized to do so.

Pension Plans

Section 3(2) of ERISA defines a "pension plan" as:

> any plan, fund, or program established or maintained by an employer or by an employee organization, or by both, to the extent that by its expressed terms or as a result of surrounding circumstances such plan . . .
>
> (A) provides retirement income to employees or
>
> (B) results in a deferral of income by employees for periods extending to the termination of covered employment or beyond
>
> regardless of the method of calculating the contributions made to the plan, the method of calculating benefits under the plan or the method of distributing benefits from the plan.

The Department of Labor has adopted regulations to clarify the definition of pension plan. *See* 29 C.F.R. 2510.3-2. Typical examples of pension plans include "tax-qualified" pension, profit-sharing, stock bonus, bond purchase and annuity plans, and many "non-qualified" plans. (These types of plans will be discussed in Chapter 2, Tax Laws).

Like the definition provided for the term welfare plan, the definition of "pension plan" is very broad. The regulations clarify the limits of the definition by identifying certain specific plans, funds and programs which do not constitute pension plans for purposes of Title I of ERISA.

A review of the limited exceptions to statutory coverage provides an indication of the breadth of the pension plan concept. For example, a severance pay plan pursuant to which payments are made on account of an employee's separation from the service of an employer (other than due to retirement) is not a pension plan provided certain conditions are satisfied. All payments pursuant to the severance pay plan must be completed within one year after the employee's separation from service and the total payments made within this time period must not exceed the employee's "annual compensation level." The term "annual compensation level" is specifically defined in the regulations. Like some severance pay plans, some bonus programs, individual retirement accounts and gratuitous payments to employees will not be classified as pension plans pursuant to the regulations.

As the court's decision in *Murphy v. Inexco Oil Company,* ____ F. Supp. ____ (S.D. Tex. 1977) illustrates, not every arrangement is a pension plan.

MURPHY V. INEXCO OIL COMPANY

____F.Supp.____(S.D. Tex. 1977)

STERLING, U.S. District Judge

The Opinion of this Court dated January 19, 1977, is withdrawn and the following substituted in its place. The minor changes made are merely for clarification and in no way alter the result.

This case involves an alleged breach of an employee benefit contract, violation of the Employee Retirement Income Security Act of 1974, 29 U.S.C. §§1001, *et seq.*, and violation of ERISA's predecessor, the Welfare and Pension Plans Disclosure Act, 29 U.S.C. §§301-309. Plaintiff alleges diversity jurisdiction, federal question jurisdiction and ERISA jurisdiction, 29 U.S.C. §1132(e), to which defendants have responded with a motion to dismiss for lack of subject matter jurisdiction. The diversity allegation is without foundation from the face of the complaint. The other jurisdictional claims raise an issue which bears brief discussion because of the dearth of authority on the subject. That issue is whether the plan in this case (the Westland plan) is a "pension plan" as defined in ERISA.

Defendants, citing the Westland Royalty Participation Agreement and the complaint, accurately describe the plan as a gratuitous, supplemental compensation program. Under the Westland plan, which embodies the informal agreements of its predecessor, a defacto oil and gas royalty pool for the benefit of employees, the employer oil company assigns royalty interests to Westland Royalty Company for the benefit of the employees. The interests assigned are in a particular drilling prospect, and royalty payments are made not from the employer's funds, but from the oil well production proceeds.

The assignment of an interest in a project is discretionary, based on the employer Management Committee's and Board of Directors' assessment of the employee's contribution to the company, and is commensurate to the employee's work on the project. Finally, the interests, which vest at assignment, are assigned only while a person is employed. After a company-approved termination such as retirement, the employee is assigned no new interests but can continue to participate in the ones assigned to him before retirement.

It is undisputed that the employees receive annual payments during employment and possibly in retirement, post-employment participation depending on the continued production of the well in which an employee has an interest. Defendants contend that the annual payments are current compensation bonuses, and plaintiff argues that they are merely an incidental benefit of a pension plan. A pension plan as defined in ERISA is a

> . . . program (A) that provides retirement income to employees, or (B) results in a deferral of income by employees for periods extending to the termination of covered employment or beyond, regardless of the method of calculating the contributions made to the plan, the method of calculating the benefits under the plan or the method of distributing benefits from the plan.
> 29 U.S.C. §1002(2).

Plaintiff argues that the program provides retirement income by allowing continued participation and thus falls within §1002(2)(A), which does not expressly exclude a plan featuring current income in addition to retirement income, but the clause (B) phrase "deferral of income by employees" does exclude plans featuring current income as well as retirement income. Plaintiff would reply that clauses (A) and (B) are joined by the disjunctive conjunction "or" indicating that either one or the other is requisite, but not necessarily both, and that although the two clauses are not necessarily mutually exclusive, they are distinguishable by their applicability to different fact situations. Defendant would then contend that "or" means "or, in other words," so that (B) merely clarifies (A). Clearly one cannot resolve this issue by limiting the inquiry to the naked statutory language of §1002(2). The Regulations promulgated under ERISA must also be considered.

Defendants claim that the Westland plan is a bonus plan, expressly excluded from ERISA by Regulation 2510.3-2(c) of the Department of Labor, as amended, 40 *Fed. Reg.* 34532 (1975), which provides that a " 'pension plan' shall not include payments made by an employer to some or all of its employees as bonuses for work performed, unless such payments are systematically deferred to the termination of the covered employment or beyond, or so as to provide retirement income to employees." Before determining whether the Westland plan conforms to this Regulation, it must be determined whether this plan is in fact a bonus plan.

At paragraph 18 of the complaint, plaintiff expressly states that the plan is an inducement to lure new employees and to retain the old ones, but any benefit plan, whether bonus or pension, would have this effect. More helpful is the contract, which says that the assignments are based on length of service, job classification and special contributions to the success of the venture. Paragraph 19 of the complaint likewise states that the size of the interest assigned is "commensurate with the work that an employee did on the project." Accordingly, Regulation 2510.3-2(c) is applicable.

Regulation 2510.3-2(c) shows that the distinction between clauses (A) and (B) of §1002(2) is not deferral of income vs. retirement income but deferral to employment termination vs. deferral so as to provide retirement income. In other words, the Regulation recognizes deferral of income as being the key identifying feature of a "pension plan."

One also learns from the Regulations that generation of possible retirement income is not conclusively indicative of a "pension plan," contrary to plaintiff's suggestion. Regulation 2510.3-2(b) distinguishes a "pension plan" from a "severance pay plan," both of which involve employer payments to a retired employee. The Westland plan beneficiaries may continue to participate after employment termination, but the requisite systematic deferral of income is absent.

Unfortunately, ERISA's legislative history and purpose shed little light on the issue here. Defendants maintain that ERISA's purpose, to insure adequate funding and vesting for employee protection, bears no relation to the Westland gratuitous bonus plan for the assignment of annually payable royalty interests. This position, however, only begs the question of ERISA's applicability because the plaintiff is complaining of loss of plan benefits caused by the defendants' alleged manipulation of the interests in a certain drilling prospect. Plaintiff claims that new interests have been created in the same prospect in which plaintiff already has a vested interest and that the new interests, assigned to other people, cancel plaintiff's previously acquired interest. (Complaint, pars. 21 and 22) That, however, is a matter of contract which is in no way affected by ERISA. A plan funded by oil well royalties is by nature speculative and uncertain and is thus inherently inconsistent with ERISA's purpose of insuring that employees will have financial security and predictability in retirement.

Title 29 U.S.C. §302(a)(2), the predecessor of 29 U.S.C. §1002(2), states that the term "employee pension benefit plan" includes "any profit sharing plan which provides benefits at or after retirement." Two obvious questions, then, are whether the Westland plan is a profit sharing plan, and because §1002(2) does not specifically mention profit sharing plans, what is the effect of this omission. The answer to both questions is that the scope of §1002(2) is broader than §302(a)(2). Section 1002(2) covers any plan that "provides retirement income or results in a deferral of income by employees . . . ," including profit sharing plans that provide retirement benefits. The two sections are not inconsistent; §1002(2) subsumes §302(a)(2), and though there were no regulations promulgated under §302(a)(2), the same analysis of the "retirement income" language discussed above with respect to §1002(2) should be applicable to §302(a)(2). Neither plaintiff nor defendants have argued to the contrary.

For these reasons the Court finds that it lacks any basis for jurisdiction of this case, which boils down simply to a complaint for an alleged breach of the disclosure and possibly other provisions of the Westland Royalty Participation Agreement. The case must be dismissed, rendering it unnecessary to consider the class action allegations of the complaint.

ERISA not only focuses on pension and welfare plans, but also on the persons establishing and maintaining these plans and other persons with various relationships to them. The persons regulated under ERISA can be divided into two categories: fiduciaries and non-fiduciary parties in interest.

Fiduciary Status Defined

Section 3(21) of ERISA defines a "fiduciary" as:

> (any) person . . . with respect to a plan to the extent (i) he exercises any discretionary authority or discretionary control respecting management of (a) plan or exercises any authority or control respecting management or disposition of its assets, (ii) he renders investment advice for a fee or other compensation, direct or indirect, with respect to any monies or other property of such plan, or has any authority or responsibility to do so, or (iii) he has any discretionary authority or discretionary responsibility in the administration of such plan.

Whether a person is a fiduciary under ERISA is based on the person's authority. Thus, this definition extends beyond the common law of trusts, which focused on trustees. The ERISA definition of a fiduciary centers on the actual authority and responsibility of persons, rather than their titles. Typical examples of persons within the scope of this definition include, but are not limited to, individual and institutional trustees of plans, such as Taft-Hartley trustees, banks and insurance companies, and investment advisors.

Other persons, such as attorneys, accountants, actuaries and consultants, may, in certain cases, also be fiduciaries. *See* H.R. Rep. 93-1280, 93d Cong., 2d Sess. 323 (Joint Explanatory Statement of the Committee of Conference on ERISA). For example, there are situations where consultants to pension and welfare plans may, in effect, be exercising discretionary authority or control with respect to the management or administration of the plan or some authority or control regarding its assets. In these cases, they may be regarded as having assumed obligations within the scope of the definition of "fiduciary."

Of course, an attorney, accountant, actuary or consultant who neither exercises nor has any of the responsibilities, authority or control described in Section 3(21) of ERISA is not a fiduciary with respect to a plan. *See* 29 C.F.R. §2509.75-5, D-1. Similarly, persons who perform merely purely ministerial functions within a framework of procedures developed by others are not fiduciaries. The Department of Labor has stated that persons who do not have power to make decisions as to plan policy, interpretations, practices or procedures, but who perform certain administrative functions, such as the application of rules determining eligibility for participation or benefits, are not fiduciaries. 29 C.F.R. §2509.75-8, D-2.

The court's decision in *Hibernia Bank v. International Brotherhood of Teamsters,* ___ F. Supp. ___ (N.D. Calif. 1976), portions of which have been deleted, illustrates the scope of the term fiduciary.

HIBERNIA BANK V. INTERNATIONAL BROTHERHOOD OF TEAMSTERS
___F.Supp.___ (N.D. Calif. 1976)

. . .

The Bank's second argument is that it is entitled to sue because of its status as a "fiduciary," as defined by the statute. Section 3(21)(A) of the Act, 29 U.S.C. §1002(21)(A) provides:

> Except as otherwise provided in subparagraph (B), a person is a fiduciary with respect to a plan to the extent (i) he exercises any discretionary authority or discretionary control respecting management of such plan or exercises any authority or control respecting management or disposition of its assets, (ii) he renders investment advice for a fee or other compensation, direct or indirect, with respect to any moneys or other property of such plan, or has any authority or responsibility to do so or (iii) he has any discretionary authority or discretionary responsibility in the administration of such plan. Such term includes any person designated under section 1105(c)(1)(B) of this title.

The allegation in the complaint of the Bank's fiduciary status is purely conclusory. Here, however, even the briefs are not especially illuminating as to the Bank's argument. The Bank's original brief in opposition to the defendants' motions simply stated that "[The Bank] is a fiduciary under the plain language of the statute; Act, §3(21)(A) and 38(A) & (B), 29 U.S.C. §1002(21)(A)." In the supplemental brief, the Bank relied upon "the facts alleged in the complaint concerning Hibernia Bank's relationship with the defendant fiduciaries, and . . . the plain language of the statute. . . ." Only in responding to the arguments made by defendants did the Bank clearly state its position. The Bank argues, first, that it is a fiduciary because it has the requisite "discretionary authority [and] discretionary responsibility respecting management of such plan. . . ." 29 U.S.C. §1002 (21)(A). The Bank also claims fiduciary status because of its agency relationship with the defendant trustees, who are ERISA fiduciaries. The final argument is that ERISA gives fiduciary status to custodians of employee benefit plans, and that the Bank is such a custodian.

The Bank's first two arguments rely upon the "agency" relationship which exists between the Bank and the individual trusts because of the "letter agreement" reached between them. The Court has examined this agreement and has concluded that it simply will not support the Bank's arguments. The letter agreement sets forth seven precise duties of the Bank; no other duties are specified therein or even suggested. Items 1, 2, 3 and 7 refer to the simple maintenance of an account and the preparation of records associated therewith. Items 4, 5 and 6 refer to the payment and expenditure of moneys, but each item expressly provides that such payments and expenditures are to be made only at the direction of defendant Carlson. The Court is unable to find any evidence of the "discretionary authority and responsibility asserted by the Bank and required by the statute.

The Bank's final argument is that under Section 3(14) 29 U.S.C. §1002(14), a "custodian" of an employee benefit plan is a "fiduciary." Section 3(14) defines the phrase "party in interest" and provides in pertinent part:

> The term "party in interest" means, as to an employee benefit plan—
>
> (A) any fiduciary (including, but not limited to, any administrator, officer, trustee, or custodian), counselor, or employee of such employee benefit plan.

Obviously, a custodian *can* be a fiduciary, but only if it possesses the requisite discretionary authority and discretionary control required by Section 3(21) of ERISA. Section 3(14) in no way enlarges the definition of a fiduciary set forth in Section 3(21); it merely mentions several of the categories which might be so characterized. The Court also notes that this interpretation is consistent with an Interpretive Release, 40 *Fed.Reg.* 47491 (1975), regarding the definition of a fiduciary under ERISA issued by the Department of Labor on October 3, 1975. Therein the Department states that an entity which has "no power to make any decisions as to plan policy, interpretations, practices or procedures" and which serves such plan only for the "[c]ollection of contributions and application of contributions as provided in the plan" is *not* a fiduciary.

Accordingly, the Court concludes that the Bank is neither a fiduciary nor a beneficiary under the express provisions of ERISA and thus has no standing to bring suit under that Act.

III

Because of the Court's conclusion that the Bank lacks standing to sue under either of the federal statutes under which relief has been sought, judicial economy would not be served by the exercise of pendent jurisdiction over the state claims. *See United Mine Workers v. Gibbs*, 383 U.S. 715, 726 (1966). Because those claims are properly to be litigated in the state courts, they are hereby dismissed.

Accordingly,

IT IS HEREBY ORDERED that defendants' motions to dismiss the complaint for failure to state a claim are granted and the complaint and action herein are dismissed.

IT IS HEREBY FURTHER ORDERED that counsel for defendants shall prepare an appropriate form of judgment in accordance with this Memorandum of Opinion and Order.

IT IS HEREBY FURTHER ORDERED that the Bank's Motion for Leave to File a Second Amended Complaint is denied without hearing.

Investment Advisers as Fiduciaries

While the Department of Labor and the Department of Treasury have not adopted regulations generally relating to the definition of the term fiduciary, they have adopted regulations designed to clarify this definition as applied to persons who render investment advice to pension and welfare plans and to persons who execute securities transactions on behalf of these plans.

The regulations provide that a person renders "investment advice" to a plan only if two conditions are satisfied. *See* 29 C.F.R. §2510.3-21(c); Treas. Regs. §54.4975-9. *First,* the person must provide advice with respect to the value of securities or other property, or must make recommendations as to the advisability of purchasing or selling securities or other property. *Second,* the person must have discretionary authority or control with respect to purchasing or selling securities or other property for the pension or welfare plan; or, if the person does not have such authority or control, he must render advice on a regular basis to the plan pursuant to a mutual understanding that his advice will serve as a primary basis for investment decisions and that such advice will be related to the particular characteristics and needs of the pension or welfare plan.

While this definition at first appears to be rather broad, a careful reading reveals that it is not quite as broad as it seems. For example, there must be a "mutual understanding," among other things. In addition, a person is only a fiduciary to the extent of his discretionary authority and control. For example, if a person only provides investment advice with respect to the investment of a portion of a plan's portfolio in common stocks, that person will not be a fiduciary with respect to the investment of the other portion of the plan's portfolio in bonds.

Note that this example illustrates the possibility of limiting a person's classification as a fiduciary—and his resulting responsibility—to certain functions. The mere classification of a person as a fiduciary for one purpose does not mean that he is a fiduciary for all purposes. However, once a person is a fiduciary for any purpose, he will remain a fiduciary for purposes of the "co-fiduciary" responsibility provisions, which will be discussed below. Similarly, once a person is classified as a fiduciary, that person will remain a party in interest.

Non-Fiduciary Parties in Interest

Non-fiduciary parties in interest include a wide range of persons with various direct and indirect relationships to pension and welfare plans. Section 3(14) of ERISA defines the term "party in interest" as:

> (A) any fiduciary (including, but not limited to, any administrator, officer, trustee, or custodian), counsel, or employee of such employee benefit plan;
>
> (B) a person providing services to such plan;
>
> (C) an employer any of whose employees are covered by such plan;
>
> (D) an employee organization any of whose members are covered by such plan;
>
> (E) an owner, direct or indirect, of 50% or more of—
>
> (i) the combined voting power of all classes of stock entitled to vote or the total value of shares of all classes of stock of a corporation,
>
> (ii) the capital interest or the profits interest of a partnership, or
>
> (iii) the beneficial interest of a trust or unincorporated enterprise,
>
> which is an employer or an employee organization described in subparagraph (C) or (D);
>
> (F) a relative [as defined in paragraph (15)] of any individual described in subparagraph (A), (B), (C) or (E);
>
> (G) a corporation, partnership, or trust or estate of which (or in which) 50% or more of—
>
> (i) the combined voting power of all classes of stock entitled to vote or the total value or shares of all classes of stock of such corporation,
>
> (ii) the capital interest or profits interest of such partnership, or
>
> (iii) the beneficial interest of such trust or estate,
>
> is owned directly or indirectly, or held by persons

described in subparagraph (A), (B), (C), (D), or (E);

(H) an employee, officer, director (or an individual having powers or responsibilities similar to those of officers or directors), or a 10% or more shareholder directly or indirectly, of a person described in subparagraph (B), (C), (D), (E), or (G), or of the employee benefit plan; or

(I) a 10% or more (directly or indirectly in capital or profits) partner or joint venturer of a person described in subparagraph (B), (C), (D), (E), or (G).

This definition, which is almost identical to the definition of the term "disqualified person" in §4975(e)(2) of the Internal Revenue Code of 1954, is very broad, and it includes numerous persons with both isolated and continuous relationships to a pension or welfare plan. For example, a union whose members are covered by a pension plan is a party in interest with respect to the plan, as are the union's officers, such as the president of the local.

The court's Memorandum and Order in *Marshall v. Snyder* ___ F. Supp. ___ (E.D.N.Y. 1977) illustrates the scope of the term party in interest.

MARSHALL V. SNYDER
___ F.Supp. ___ (E.D.N.Y. 1977)

PRATT, J:

Invoking the Employee Retirement Income Security Act of 1974 (ERISA), 29 U.S.C. §§1001 *et seq.*, the Secretary of Labor has brought this action to obtain equitable relief to redress alleged violations of Title I of ERISA. Subject matter jurisdiction exists under ERISA §502(e)(1), 29 U.S.C. §1132(e)(1).

The complaint designates as defendants: General Teamsters Industrial Employees Local 806 (Local 806 or the Union); several present and former trustees of the Union's Health and Welfare Fund (the Welfare Plan), Pension and Retirement Fund (the Pension Plan), and Annuity Fund (the Annuity Plan); and 806 Record Processors, Inc. (RPI). Alleged to be a wholly owned subsidiary of the Welfare Plan, RPI performs the administrative functions of all the Plans. Some of the defendant trustees are members of the Union's Executive Board; some are officers, directors, or employees of RPI; and some are both.

In the main action, the Secretary seeks to redress past dissipation of the assets of the Plans and to prevent similar dissipation of their assets in the future. On January 25, 1977, the Secretary moved for a preliminary injunction and appointment of a receiver. Prior to the return date, the parties agreed to and submitted to the court an order for a consent disposition of the motion. On February 4, 1977 the then acting "Miscellaneous Judge" signed the consent order which provides in part:

(1) that defendant trustees of the Local 806 Welfare Fund, Pension Fund, and Annuity Fund shall not make or permit to be made any direct or indirect payments for any purpose from the assets of the respective Funds of which they are trustees to defendant George Snyder, to any of the other individual defendants, to defendant Local 806, or the benefit of any of said defendants;

(2) that defendant 806 Record Processors, Inc. shall not hereafter make or permit to be made any direct or indirect payments for any purpose from its assets to defendant George Snyder, to any of the other individual defendants, to defendant Local 806, or for the benefit of any of said defendants; with the only exception that 806 Record Processors, Inc. may continue to make salary payments for services actually rendered to defendants Clarence Clarke, Anthony Calagna, James Isola, and William Snyder in amounts not exceeding the following:

	Maximum per Week
Anthony Calagna	$750
Clarence Clarke	$300
James Isola	$825
William Snyder	$600

(3) that defendant trustees of the Welfare Fund, Pension Fund, and Annuity Fund shall make all books and records of the respective Funds and of 806 Record Processors, Inc. available for inspection and copying to the attorneys for the plaintiff or their agents, during normal business hours upon one (1) day's prior notice.

The Secretary now claims that the consent order has been violated and, asserting that the assets of the Plans are still being dissipated to the detriment of the participants and beneficiaries of the Plans, he has moved for an order (1) appointing an interim receiver to manage and control all income, assets, and disbursements of the Plans and RPI; (2) holding the defendants in contempt of the consent order of February 4, 1977; (3) enjoining RPI and the trustees of the Plans from making payments to defendants Calagna, Clarke, Isola, and William Snyder; (4) directing defendants to comply with subsequent discovery demands made by the Secretary in accordance with the Federal Rules of Civil Procedure; (5) awarding the Secretary reasonable fees and costs; and (6) granting him "such further relief as may be equitable and just."

The Secretary bases his instant claims for relief on two principal contentions. First, he asserts that defendants are permitting payments to be made to Isola, Calagna, Clarke, William Snyder and other unspecified defendants in violation of the consent order. More specifically, the Secretary contends that the Plans through RPI are making payments to those defendants either for no work at all, or for work performed for the Union, and not the Plans or RPI. Second, he asserts that defendants have frustrated his attempts to supervise their performance or non-performance of the consent order by failing to comply with his discovery requests.

With respect to the motion, defendants claim that the payments in question were for the benefit of the Plans and necessary to their operation; that even if a portion of the work done by RPI's employees was for the benefit of the Union, precisely that arrangement was contemplated by the consent order which was designed to preserve the status quo; and that defendants have cooperated with, not prevented discovery.

On April 21, 1977 an evidentiary hearing was held. Testimony was elicited from Stanley Geller, the accountant for the Union, the Plans, and RPI; Annie Craig, the medical claim processor for RPI; Constance Mavroson, the bookkeeper and office manager for the Union, the Plans, and RPI; Mary Calfee, an attorney for the Department of Labor; defendant William Snyder, recording secretary for the Union, a trustee of the Annuity Plan, and an employee of RPI; defendant James Isola, vice president of the Union and an employee of RPI; defendant Anthony Calagna, president of the Union and the president and a director of RPI; John Gonzalez, an employee of RPI; and defendant Clarence Clarke, a trustee of the Pension Plan and an employee of RPI. Twenty-five exhibits were admitted into evidence.

For the purposes of the instant motion, the court has made the following findings of fact and conclusions of law:

Findings of Fact

1. Local 806 is a union which represents approximately 2,160 member-workers organized into approximately 120 separate "shops," involving approximately 102 employers.

2. The Welfare Plan is a plan established by Local 806 for the purpose of providing the Union's members and their beneficiaries medical, unemployment, and other benefits.

3. About 10,000 potential beneficiaries, including 2,040 union members, are covered by the Welfare Plan.

4. The Pension Plan is a plan established by Local 806 to provide retirement income to the Union's members.

5. About 1,032 union members are covered by the Pension Plan. Seventy-four persons are now receiving pensions under the Plan.

6. The Annuity Plan is a plan organized by Local 806 to defer the accrual of income earned by union members.

7. The Plans are funded by employers of the Union's members pursuant to rates of payments set up in the Union's collective bargaining agreements.

8. RPI is a corporation, organized in March of 1975, which performs all the administrative functions of the Plans. For instance, it maintains all their records, it processes all claims made against them, and it collects employer contributions owing to them.

9. Defendants George Snyder and Irving Rosenzweig, as trustees of the Welfare Plan, own all of RPI's outstanding stock.

10. The Union's Executive Board currently consists of the following six persons: defendant Calagna, the Union's president; defendant Isola, the Union's vice president; defendant George Snyder, the Union's secretary-treasurer; defendant William Snyder, the Union's recording secretary; defendant Rosario Albano, a trustee of the Union; defendant George Arth, a trustee of the Union; and John Gonzalez, the third trustee of the Union. Of these individuals, only Arth and Albano are compensated directly by the Union, each at $125 per month.

11. The Welfare Plan has two trustees: George Snyder and Irving Rosenzweig, an officer of an employer under contract with a Local 806 shop.

12. The Pension Plan has two trustees: Clarke and Joseph Grippo, an officer of another "Local 806 employer."

13. The Annuity Plan has four trustees: George Snyder, William Snyder, Irving Rosenzweig, and Benjamin Petcover, who, like Rosenzweig and Grippo, is an officer of a Local 806 employer.

14. RPI's president is Calagna.

15. RPI has three directors: Calagna, Petcove, and Rosenzweig.

16. Calagna, Clarke, Isola, and William Snyder have been employed by RPI as "field representatives" since its organization in March, 1975.

17. Gonzalez is also employed by RPI as a "field representative."

18. As of February 4, 1977, Ronald Kremens was similarly employed by RPI. Sometime thereafter his employment with RPI terminated.

19. Peter DeVuone is a paid employee of RPI. He serves as the chauffeur of George Snyder who

is not an employee of RPI.

20. The Union, the Plans, and RPI share offices located at 275 Broad Hollow Road, Melville, New York. The various entities do not occupy separate space within these offices.

21. From the time the Union, the Plans, and RPI first occupied their present offices around January of 1976 until shortly after this action was filed in January of 1977, RPI had paid the entire rent for the jointly used offices.

22. The document marked as defendant's Exhibit B purports to allocate the office space rented by RPI to the various entities using the space. It assigns 43% of the space to RPI, 20% to the Welfare Plan, 20% to the Pension Plan, nothing to the Annuity Plan, and 17% to the Union.

23. Exhibit B assigns to RPI, *inter alia*, three offices which together comprise more than 10% of the leased space. These offices are used by Calagna, Isola, and William Snyder, none of whom performs appreciable in-office duties for RPI. The assignment of the three offices to RPI for purposes of rent allocation is clearly unwarranted and reflects a more general underestimation of Union use of the rented space.

24. The office space allocation document, Exhibit B, was prepared in November or December of 1976 at the earliest.

25. It is more likely than not that an increased fear of civil or criminal sanctions was the reason for the recent move toward shifting to the Union some portion of the rent for the offices occupied by it, RPI, and the Plans.

26. Overall, Exhibit B represents more of a gesture than a bona fide attempt to allocate the Melville office space among the Union, the Plans, and RPI. Exhibit B substantially underestimates the extent to which the offices are used for union as opposed to plan or RPI purposes.

27. Even though Exhibit B was prepared in November or December, 1976, as of mid-April, 1977, only one or two rental payments had been made by the Union for its "share" of the space, with the burden of the remainder of the rent resting on RPI and the Plans.

28. Geller, who is the accountant for RPI, the Plans, and the Union, and who prepared Exhibit B, testified that eventually the Union's share of the rent for the offices would be paid retroactively.

29. RPI employs at least four clerical employees, all but one (Annie Craig) of whom perform union as well as RPI duties. Nevertheless, they are all compensated by RPI and not by the Union.

30. The Union pays only one clerical employee, Constance Mavroson. She receives $320 per week and is the bookkeeper and office manager for the Union, the Plans, and RPI. Mavroson is not compensated by RPI or the Plans.

31. Aside from Mavroson, Arth, and Albano, only one other person has been on the Union payroll since February 4, 1977, namely James Kant who is retired and has been receiving $400 per month purportedly in back pay.

32. The Union's annual income consists of approximately $350,000 in dues which are deducted from members' wages by employers and paid directly to the Union.

33. The Welfare Plan's annual income consists of approximately $1,000,000 in direct employer contributions.

34. The Pension Plan's annual income consists of approximately $300,000 in employer contributions.

35. The Annuity Plan's annual income consists of approximately $75,000 in employer contributions.

36. RPI's annual income totals approximately $336,000. It receives about $300,000 from the Welfare Plan each year, about $36,000 from the Pension Plan, and nothing from the Annuity Plan.

37. During the first three months of 1977, RPI received $110,000 from the Welfare Plan and $9,000 from the Pension Plan.

38. From February 7, 1977, through April 19, 1977, RPI paid the following amounts to the indicated individuals:

	Salary	Expenses	Total
Calagna	$ 5,100	$1,500	$ 6,600
Isola	9,225	1,650	10,875
William Snyder	4,500	1,650	6,150
Clarke	2,100	1,500	3,600
Kremens	1,493	900	2,393
Gonzalez	3,458	1,430	4,888
DeVuone	1,727	737	2,464
Craig	2,000	0	2,000
Other clerical personnel	6,020	0	6,020
Totals	$35,623	$9,367	$44,990

39. Exhibit 22 provides a more detailed breakdown of the payments summarized above.

40. No salary is paid by the Union to any of the persons listed in finding #38.

41. RPI's "field representatives" do not participate in in-office processing of claims under the Plans or in any other in-office work for RPI of any significance. Clarke signs checks for RPI but does so without reviewing the claims covered by them. His function in this regard entails nothing more than signing his name to checks presented to

him by RPI's clerical staff. Any check-signing duties that the other field representatives might perform are no more significant than those performed by Clarke.

42. RPI's "field representatives," including Calagna, Clarke, Isola, William Snyder, and Gonzalez, do provide substantial services for the Union as liaisons to the members and the shops, in organizing new shops, and in renegotiating collective bargaining agreements.

43. Field representatives undoubtedly assist some members of the Union in filling out various plan-related forms; but since the forms are not complicated, problems in completing them are probably almost always solved without the direct assistance of a field representative.

44. Field representatives sometimes act as liaisons between RPI's clerical staff and union members; however, not only does this liaison function consume a small proportion of the representatives' time, it also is largely unnecessary since the clerical staff is readily available to answer questions and provide assistance to the participants.

45. When they visit the Union's shops, the representatives sometimes answer questions asked by members about the Plans.

46. In the event an employer is substantially, e.g., 60 days, delinquent in its payments to the Plans, field representatives are responsible for seeking collection of these payments; however, substantially delinquent payments are not common. At present, no more than four of the Union's 120 shops are delinquent in their plan payments.

47. Field representatives spend a significant proportion of their time preparing for and engaging in the negotiation of contracts between the Union and various employers. Normally, each shop renegotiates its contract every three years.

48. Since January of 1977, the field representatives have negotiated at least one new contract for the Union and renegotiated at least five old ones.

49. Field representatives are responsible for collecting for the Union delinquent dues payments from employers. Dues are deducted by employers directly from their employees' wages.

50. Field representatives spend a significant proportion of their time organizing new shops for the Union. Organizing a new shop can require the continual efforts of more than one representative over a two-month period.

51. Field representatives are always on call in the event of a dispute or grievance arising at one of the shops.

52. Prior to the organization of RPI, Isola was paid only by the Union and he performed essentially the same functions that he does now as a "field representative" for RPI. No evidence was elicited to show that Isola's experience in this regard differed in any way from that of the other field representatives.

53. On March 23, 1977, RPI, by and through its attorney, refused to produce certain documents and records requested pursuant to FRCP 34, pertaining to said corporation and within its possession and control, notwithstanding the fact that the consent order *inter alia* expressly provides plaintiff with access to RPI's books and records. RPI's counsel orally stated that such production was being withheld on the ground that the documents pertained to the corporation's internal-operations. The asserted ground was frivolous and appears to have been intended to delay and obstruct plaintiff's discovery.

Conclusions of Law

A. The Welfare, Pension, and Annuity Plans are "employee benefit plans" within the meaning of ERISA §3(3), 29 U.S.C. §1002(3).

B. As to each of the Plans, each of the following is a "party in interest":

The Union. 29 U.S.C. §1002(14)(D).

RPI, as a person providing services to a plan. 29 U.S.C. §1002(14)(B).

Calagna, William Snyder, Isola, Clarke, Kremens, Gonzalez, and DeVuone, as employees of RPI. 29 U.S.C. §1002(14)(B).

Calagna, Isola, William Snyder, and George Snyder, as officers of the Union. 29 U.S.C. §1002(14)(H).

C. As to the Welfare Plan, George Snyder is both a fiduciary and a party in interest by virtue of being its trustee. 29 U.S.C. §1002(14)(A).

D. As to the Pension Plan, Clarke is both a fiduciary and a party in interest by virtue of being its trustee. 29 U.S.C. §1002(14)(A).

E. As to the Annuity Plan, George Snyder and William Snyder are both fiduciaries and parties in interest by virtue of being its trustees. 29 U.S.C. §1002(14)(A).

F. The payments by RPI of salaries to Calagna, William Snyder, and Isola, who are officers of the Union, were prohibited transactions within the meaning of 29 U.S.C. §1106(a)(1)(C).

G. The payment by RPI of salary to DeVuone, a substantial part of whose work was as chauffeur for defendant William Snyder, who in turn is a party in interest as an officer of the Union, was a prohibited transaction within the meaning of 29 U.S.C. §1106(a)(1)(C).

H. The payments by RPI of salaries to Gonzalez, Kremens, and defendant Clarke, a substantial part of whose work was for the benefit of the Union, a party in interest, were prohibited transactions within the meaning of 29 U.S.C. §1106 (a)(1)(C).

I. The salaries paid by RPI to defendants Calagna, William Snyder, Isola, and Clarke since February 4, 1977 violated the consent order since a substantial portion of the services performed by them for those salaries were not actually rendered to or for the benefit of RPI or the Plans, but for the benefit of the Union.

J. To the extent that payments were made to RPI after February 4, 1977 to defendants Clarke and Isola for "accumulated vacation pay," those payments violated the terms of the consent order which prohibited RPI from making "any direct or indirect payments for any purpose from its assets . . . to any of the . . . individual defendants" except for certain salaries.

K. The salary payments made by RPI since February 4, 1977 to Messrs. Gonzalez and Kremens, who were performing substantial services for the Union, violated that part of the consent order which prohibited RPI from making "any direct or indirect payments for any purpose from its assets" either to or for the benefit of the Union.

L. Some of the clerical work done by the four clerical employees who were paid by RPI since February 4, 1977 was work done for the benefit of the Union and, therefore, violated the consent order.

M. Organizing new shops, negotiating new contracts, renegotiating renewals of contracts, handling grievances of union members, and handling other disputes by union members with employers, while all proper union functions, are not proper or appropriate activities for the Plans or RPI to engage in.

N. The best interests of the Plans' participants and beneficiaries require immediate appointment of a receiver for all three Plans and RPI pending final determination of this action.

Discussion

The Employee Retirement Income Security Act of 1974 is a comprehensive remedial statute enacted to protect "the interest of participants in employee benefit plans and their beneficiaries, . . . by establishing standards of conduct, responsibility, and obligation for fiduciaries of employee benefit plans, and by providing for appropriate remedies, sanctions, and ready access to federal courts." 29 U.S.C. 1001(2)(b). Section 1104(a)(1) of title 29 of the United States Code establishes the fundamental standard to which all fiduciaries of employee benefit plans are subject:

> a fiduciary shall discharge his duties with respect to a plan solely in the interest of the participants and beneficiaries and—
>
> (A) for the exclusive purpose of:
>
> (i) providing benefits to participants and their beneficiaries; and
>
> (ii) defraying reasonable expenses of administering the plan;
>
> (B) with the care, skill, prudence, and diligence under the circumstances then prevailing that a prudent man acting in a like capacity and familiar with such matters would use in the conduct of an enterprise of a like character and with like aims;

In this action it is claimed that the defendant trustees as fiduciaries acted, in violation of the statute, neither solely in the interest of the participants and beneficiaries nor prudently in causing or permitting the improper expenditure of plan assets, and making payments which are far in excess of any reasonable expense of administering plans of this size and kind.

Clearly the activities of RPI and the Union have been extensively intertwined. Several employee witnesses acknowledged that in their operations no work distinctions were drawn between the Union, the Plans and RPI.

The consent order represented an attempt to bring these operations in compliance with ERISA which was intended to separate the interests of the Union and its officers from those of the Plans, their participants and beneficiaries. So close are the interrelationships in this case, however, that it is apparently impossible to obtain compliance with the purposes and requirements of ERISA as long as the overlapping of duties, salaries, and interests continues.

The inherent conflict of interest and potential for self-dealing which result from the union officers' controlling both the Plans and RPI, which is the administrative agent of the Plans, coupled with the actual conduct of the defendants since the consent order, and when interpreted in the light of the serious charges of misappropriation of trust fund monies alleged in the complaint, require immediate and drastic action by the court in order to preserve from further dissipation the assets of the Plans for the benefit of their participants and beneficiaries.

The Welfare and Pension Plans pay to RPI over $300,000 a year for record keeping and administration. This constitutes nearly 25% of their total annual income, which should be used primarily for the participants and beneficiaries. On the evidence before the court, it appears that the services required for the actual administration of these Plans do not warrant such a large expenditure. The bulk of the expenditures currently being made is (a) for compensation of the field representatives, all of whom perform substantial services for the Union, but receive no compensation from the Union, and (b) for rental of the offices which are used to a substantial extent for the benefit of the Union, and which in any event are far beyond the reasonable requirements for plan administration.

Accordingly, there is need for the immediate appointment of a receiver of the Plans and of RPI, the corporation wholly owned by the Welfare Plan.

The thrust of this action is to counter past and future dissipation of the Plans' assets. As to past dissipation, the Secretary's allegations focus primarily upon: (1) the excessive compensation of defendant George Snyder, $1,239,500 in two and one-half years; (2) the extension of a $290,000 loan by the Welfare Plan to the Union via RPI, a corporation wholly owned by the Plan; and (3) the use of more than $350,000 of Pension Plan assets to refurbish the offices jointly occupied by the Union and the Plans.

The matters which are subject to this motion show a pattern of manipulation and diversion of plan assets similar to that alleged in the complaint, although here lesser amounts are involved. RPI's payments of salaries to field representatives who perform substantial services for the Union, to clerical employees who perform at least some services for the Union, and to DeVuone who serves as George Snyder's personal chauffeur, all reflect a continuing pattern of diversion of monies to or for the benefit of the Union, and, therefore, not "solely in the interest of the participants and beneficiaries." 29 U.S.C. §1104(a)(1).

This dissipation of plan assets must stop if the legitimate rights and expectations of the Plans' participants and their beneficiaries are to be protected. One of ERISA's primary objectives is to safeguard the interests of participants and beneficiaries. Even without the strict standards of ERISA, however, the court's primary concern with such trust assets would have to focus upon similarly protecting the participants and beneficiaries.

Whether the actions of the trustees of the respective Plans in permitting the transactions which have been disclosed here are sufficient to warrant their permanent removal pursuant to 29 U.S.C. §1109, is a question which will be determined after a full trial on the merits of this action. For present purposes, the trustees of each of the three Plans need only be suspended from their functions and activities as trustees pending final determination of the action. Until that final determination, all of the trustees' functions shall be performed by a temporary receiver who shall operate and administer the three Plans and defendant 806 Record Processors, Inc. in accordance with the terms of the plan instruments and the requirements of ERISA, and subject to further order of this court. All defendants are ordered to cooperate with the receiver and provide him with such information, records, and documents as he may require for the performance of his duties.

The court reserves decision on that portion of the motion that seeks to punish the defendants for contempt. The contempt defendants are admonished, however, that the court may consider the extent and effectiveness of their cooperation with the receiver as having some evidentiary weight in determining the defendants' states of mind and intentions in connection with their prior dealings with the Plans and with RPI. One of the questions bearing on contempt is whether the contempt defendants believed in good faith, although perhaps erroneously, that the intent of the consent order was to preserve a "status quo" condition even though that "status quo" constituted transactions prohibited under ERISA and perpetuated on a reduced scale a pattern of diversion of trust monies for the benefit of some of the individual defendants and the Union. Whatever may have been their belief then, the contempt defendants can no longer retain that belief in light of this decision. The conduct has clearly violated both the consent order and the prohibitions of ERISA. Prompt and willing cooperation with the court and its receiver from this point on could be viewed by the court as evidence of the defendants' good faith up to this point.

The plaintiff's motion is granted to the extent that:

A. All defendants are enjoined *pendente lite* from making or causing or permitting to be made any payments by RPI or any of the Plans to defendants Calagna, Isola, William Snyder, or Clarke; and

B. Edgar G. Brisach, Esq. of 1539 Franklin Avenue, Mineola, New York 11501 is hereby appointed receiver of Local 806 Teamsters Health and Welfare Fund, Local 806 Teamsters Pension and Retirement Fund, Local 806 Teamsters Annuity Fund, and 806 Record Processors, Inc. pending final determination of this action.

Plaintiff shall submit on notice to the defendants and the receiver a more formal order of appointment of the receiver, including therein such provisions as may be appropriate for the special circumstances of this case, as well as provision for compensation of the receiver and any professional assistance he may require. In the meantime, from the date of filing this memorandum and order, the receiver shall have all powers over the assets, liabilities, and management of the three Plans and RPI which a receiver customarily may exercise under the jurisdiction of a United States District Court.

With respect to the discovery requests by the plaintiff, defendants and their counsel are directed to comply with plaintiff's demands with a view to completing all discovery expeditiously and scheduling a prompt trial on the merits.

The receiver shall serve initially without bond, but in the more formal order to be submitted for approval by the court the plaintiff shall include an appropriate recommendation as to whether or not a bond should be required, and if so in what amount.

No formal transfer of title to the assets of the Plans and RPI shall take place until filing of the more formal order referred to above.

Defendants are enjoined until further order of this court from making or permitting any property or other transfers of assets by any of the Plans or RPI to any person, firm, or corporation (1) other than to participants or beneficiaries of the Plans for the purpose of paying benefits due under the Plans, (2) wages paid with the approval of the receiver.

On all other aspects of plaintiff's motion, including counsel fees and contempt, decision is reserved.

The principal component of the private employee benefit complex—the pension or welfare plan—and the primary classifications of persons related to the plan—fiduciaries and non-fiduciary parties in interest—are subject to numerous requirements under ERISA. Failure to satisfy these requirements may result in criminal or civil penalties.

Structure of Plans

The structure of pension and welfare plans is governed by ERISA. Many of the provisions relating to plan structure and content apply to all employee benefit plans, but some apply only to pension plans.

Mandatory Provisions

Every employee benefit plan—both pension and welfare plans—other than certain unfunded deferred compensation plans and §736 agreements, must be established and maintained in writing. *See* ERISA §402(a). The written instrument (usually the plan or trust agreement) must designate the person or persons responsible for operating the plan.

This particular requirement means that the plan must provide for "named fiduciaries" who have the authority to control and manage the plan. For example, a Taft-Hartley plan joint board of trustees is the named fiduciary with respect to a Taft-Hartley plan. 29 C.F.R. §2555.75-5, FR-2. Similarly, a corporate employer can be a named fiduciary. 29 C.F.R. §2509.75-5, FR-3. It is important to note that the Taft-Hartley plan joint board of trustees or the corporate employer does not have to be called a named fiduciary in the plan to be a named fiduciary: a person merely has to be identified in the plan as having certain fiduciary functions. 29 C.F.R. §2509.75-5, FR-1.

Funding Policy. Most plans also must provide a procedure for establishing a fund policy and method to carry out the plan objectives, and the written documents must set out the basis for contributions to and payments from the plan. Of course, a welfare plan that pays benefits solely from the general assets of the employer does not have to have a funding policy. *See* 29 C.F.R. §2509.75-5, FR-5. Pension plans and other welfare plans can establish the required funding policy by means of a discussion at a trustees' meeting, provided the discussion is recorded in the minutes of the meeting. *See* 29 C.F.R. §2509.75-5, FR-4.

Basis for Contributions and Payments. The written documents must specify the contributions to be made by the employer or employers maintaining the plan and the contributions, if any, to be made by employees covered by the plan. The basis on which payments are to be made to participants and beneficiaries also must be specified in the written documents.

Allocation and Delegation. Since it is customary for those who manage and control pension and welfare plans to allocate their responsibilities—and, within limits, to designate others to carry out the daily management of the plan—provisions contained in ERISA permit fiduciaries to allocate and delegate their responsibility. *See* ERISA §402(b). Such allocation or delegation, however, is only allowed if the plan provides for it (or provides procedures for it). Each plan must also provide a procedure for amendments and for identifying the persons who can amend the plan.

Permissive Provisions

These requirements in the form of mandatory provisions are supplemented in ERISA by a series of permissive provisions. *See* ERISA §402(c). For example, a pension or welfare plan may provide that a person may serve in more than one fiduciary capacity with respect to the plan.

A plan may also provide that certain fiduciaries may employ one or more persons to render advice with respect to fiduciary responsibility, and that a named fiduciary may appoint an "investment manager" to acquire and dispose of plan assets. An investment manager is a fiduciary who is an investment adviser (registered under the Investment Advisers Act of 1940), a bank or an insurance company, and the appointment of such a person may limit the named fiduciary's responsibility. *See* ERISA §405(c). (The Investment Advisers Act of 1940 will be discussed in Chapter 4, Securities Laws.)

While these provisions are permissive in nature, thus not specifically required, it is important to note that in the absence of these provisions in the plan documents it will not be possible to engage in these activities. For example, the joint board of trustees for a Taft-Hartley plan may not appoint an investment manager to manage plan assets in the absence of a provision in the written documents permitting them to retain such a person.

Trustees' Authority To Manage Assets

ERISA also requires that all assets of a pension or welfare plan must be held in trust by trustees and that the trustees are to manage and control these assets. *See* ERISA §403. The trustee must be either named in the written documents or appointed by the named fiduciary. The trustees have the exclusive authority and discretion to manage and control plan assets.

However, there are exceptions to both the requirement that plan assets be held in trust and to the provision that the trustees have exclusive authority to manage plan assets. *See* ERISA §403. For example, the assets of a pension or welfare plan which consist of insurance policies issued by an insurance company do not have to be held in trust. Other exceptions relate to so-called H.R. 10 plans and certain individual retirement accounts (IRAs).

There are basically two exceptions to the provision that plan trustees have exclusive management authority. *First,* the plan may provide that the trustees are subject to the direction of a named fiduciary (who is not a trustee) or, in certain cases, a participant, in which cases the trustee generally must follow proper directions given by these persons. Of course, the fiduciary's directions must be consistent with the plan and with the requirements contained in Title I of ERISA. *Second,* the authority to manage, acquire, or dispose of pension or welfare plan assets may be delegated to one or more investment managers, as discussed above. If there is such a delegation, the trustees generally are not responsible as fiduciaries for particular investment decisions.

Content of Plans

In the case of most pension plans, the general structural provisions discussed above are supplemented by rather detailed rules relating to the content of the plan. *See* ERISA §§201-211. These rules, which are usually referred to as "minimum standards," do not apply to welfare plans or to certain pension plans. *See* ERISA §201.

The minimum standards contained in ERISA are very similar to the requirements for qualification delineated in §§401-415 of the Internal Revenue Code of 1954, which will be discussed in Chapter 2. At this point, it is important to note that ERISA's minimum standards apply to both "tax-qualified" and most "non-qualified" plans. However, the requirements contained in the Internal Revenue Code of 1954 only apply to "tax-qualified" plans.

Since ERISA, in effect, applies to a greater variety of plans than the Internal Revenue Code of 1954, certain plans which are not required to comply with the Internal Revenue Code of 1954 may have to comply with ERISA. For example, certain non-qualified pension plans cannot require, as a condition of plan participation, that an employee complete a period of service with the sponsoring employer or employers extending beyond the later of the date on which the employee either attains age 25 or completes one year of service.

Once this employee becomes a participant in this plan, his benefit must accrue in a manner satisfying one of several formulas, and he must vest or attain a nonforfeitable right to the benefit within a specified period of time, which may not exceed 15 years. Of equal, if not greater importance, the plan must satisfy certain minimum funding standards. Pay-as-you-go type plans are generally prohibited.

Plan Administration: Fiduciary Responsibility

The structure and content provisions discussed above establish, among other things, certain fiduciary duties. Stated differently, these provisions also establish certain standards by which a fiduciary's conduct will be judged. *See* ERISA §404. For example, a fiduciary with respect to a pension or welfare plan must perform his duties "solely in the interest" of plan participants and beneficiaries and for the "exclusive purpose" of providing pension or welfare benefits and reducing administrative expenses. In addition, plan assets must never inure to the benefit of any employer.

It is important to note that the language used in ERISA is similar to the language contained in both the Internal Revenue Code of 1954 and the Taft-Hartley Act (which will be discussed in the Chapters 2 and 3 respectively). While the provisions in these laws are similar, they are not identical and they may not be interpreted in the same manner in every case. Yet even though there may be subtle distinctions in the standards under these different laws, they all seem to impose the same basic common law standard of undivided loyalty.

The court's decision in *Usery v. Penn,* ____ F. Supp. ____ (W.D.Okla. 1976), illustrates the "solely in the interest" and "exclusive purpose" rules. This case also illustrates the broad discretion granted to the courts to fashion remedial and equitable relief (including rescission) when a breach of these duties occurs, and the liability that may result from fiduciary breaches. The court's decision in *Bacon v. Wong,* ____ F.Supp. ____ (N.D.Calif. 1978), illustrates the "non-inurement" rule in the context of returning employer contributions made in error.

USERY V. PENN
____ F. Supp. ____ (W.D. Okla. 1976)

Findings of Fact and Conclusions of Law

The first of these actions was filed on May 25, 1976, by Glen R. Eaves and Alleen M. Eaves and others alleging violations of the Employees Retirement Income Security Act of 1974 (ERISA) and setting out additional common law causes of action against Ralph W. Penn. The Secretary of Labor filed a separate suit on June 3, 1976, alleging violations of ERISA arising out of the same transactions which were involved in the previously filed lawsuit. The Secretary of Labor named Glen R. Eaves, Alleen M. Eaves and Ralph W. Penn as defendants. The Court found the two cases to involve common issues of law and fact and ordered the cases consolidated on June 3, 1976. On that same day Glen Eaves and Alleen Eaves offered to pay $738,139.13 into the court registry pending the determination of the issues involved in this lawsuit by the Court. The offer was accepted by the Court and the sum was paid into the court registry on June 7, 1976.

On June 10, 1976, the consolidated cases came on for evidentiary hearing in regard to the application for preliminary injunction, which hearing was ended when the parties agreed to a consent order. This order was amended on November 24, 1976.

A pretrial conference was held on November 11, 1976, at which the issues for trial were narrowed. On November 23, 1976, a trial was had to the Court sitting without a jury on these issues. The Court now having heard the evidence presented, read the briefs and memoranda filed, considered the proposed findings filed by the respective parties, and considered the law applicable to the facts established by the evidence, does hereby make the following findings of fact and conclusions of law:

Findings of Fact

1. Glen's, Inc. operates a steak house, club, hickory pit and catering service on N.W. 10th Street in Oklahoma City, Oklahoma, and has done so over the past twenty-five years. Glen's restaurant is well known in Oklahoma City and the southwest area and is considered to be one of Oklahoma City's landmark restaurants.

2. From January 1, 1958, until January 16, 1976, the employees of Glen's, Inc. have participated in an employee pension benefit plan known as Glen's Profit-Sharing Plan (hereinafter the "Profit-Sharing Plan" or the "Plan") which Plan has provided retirement income to employees. On December 31, 1975, the Profit-Sharing Plan had 41 participants and beneficiaries all of whom were employees or former employees of Glen's, Inc. From its inception through December 31, 1975, the Profit-Sharing Plan received contributions from Glen's, Inc. nearly every year.

3. A primary purpose of the Profit-Sharing Plan, since its inception, has been to provide retirement income to participants. The participants of the Profit-Sharing Plan have relied on the Plan for retirement income.

4. The terms and conditions for participation in and receipt of benefits from the Profit-Sharing Plan are contained in the document known as Glen's Profit-Sharing Plan Trust Agreement. The Trust Agreement provides in relevant part, that:

a. the corporation shall make contributions to the plan each year in an amount not less than 5% of net profits;

b. contributions, forfeitures, and all income to the trust shall be allocated to participants' individual accounts each year;

c. distributions to participants shall be made in five equal annual installments in cash; and

d. the plan shall not be amended so as to impair the rights of participants without the prior specific consent of such participants;

e. the plan shall not be amended the effect of which is to permit any part of the trust fund to be used for purposes other than for the exclusive benefit of the participants or beneficiaries.

5. From 1958 until January 16, 1976, Glen R. Eaves served as trustee of the Profit-Sharing Plan. As trustee of the Profit-Sharing Plan, Glen R. Eaves had broad discretionary authority among other things to control and invest Plan assets, to provide for services to the Plan, to pursue, settle, or compromise claims on behalf of or against the Plan, and to distribute benefits payable under the Plan.

6. From 1958 until January 16, 1976, Alleen M. Eaves served as a member of the Plan Committee provided for by the terms of the Profit-Sharing Plan, which Committee had administrative responsibilities regarding the operation of the Profit-Sharing Plan. As a member of the Plan Committee, Alleen M. Eaves had the authority and the duty to participate in the final determination of all questions arising under the Plan, the supervision of the activities of the Plan trustee, and the appointment or removal of the Plan trustees.

7. On January 16, 1976, the assets of the Profit-Sharing Plan totalled $522,135.67 which included $62,738.80 cash, held in a checking account at the Capitol Hill State Bank, and a certificate of deposit issued by the Capitol Hill State Bank in the amount of $450,000 on which the accrued interest as of January 16, 1976 was $9,396.87, which annual interest was not allocated.

8. On January 16, 1976, Glen R. Eaves and Alleen M. Eaves owned 6,975 shares of Glen's, Inc., which shares constituted all of the outstanding shares of Glen's, Inc.

9. On December 17, 1975, Ralph W. Penn, Glen R. Eaves and Alleen M. Eaves executed an agreement for the sale of all of the stock of Glen's, Inc. to Penn and to the Profit-Sharing Plan. This agreement was modified by an addendum agreement and a supplemental addendum agreement also executed by Penn, Glen R. Eaves, and Alleen M. Eaves. The agreement as modified provides in relevant part:

a. that the sellers, Glen R. Eaves and Alleen M. Eaves own all of the outstanding and issued shares of the stock of Glen's, Inc.;

b. that the buyers, Ralph W. Penn and the Profit-Sharing Plan desire to purchase all of that stock;

c. that prior to closing sellers will cause the officers and directors of the Company to resign and be replaced by individuals designated by Penn;

d. that the sellers shall at closing cause the trustees of the Plan to resign and be replaced with individuals designated by Penn;

e. that Penn intends to cause the Plan to be amended to include authority to acquire employer stock at the election of the trustees;

f. that Glen's Inc. shall make a contribution to the amended Plan;

g. that Penn shall pay to sellers for 168 shares of stock the sum of $25,005.12;

h. that the Plan, as amended, shall pay to the sellers for 6,807 shares of stock the sum of $1,013,134.01; and

i. that closing will take place on January 16, 1976, at the Will Rogers Bank.

10. Pursuant to the terms of the agreement and addenda Glen R. Eaves, Alleen M. Eaves, Ralph W. Penn, and others met at the offices of the Will Rogers Bank on January 16, 1976, and executed the transactions listed below:

a. Alleen M. Eaves resigned as vice president and as a director of Glen's, Inc., and as a member of the Plan Committee of the Profit-Sharing Plan;

b. Ralph W. Penn became a member of the board of directors as did his designees Juanita Boedeker and Charlotte Robison; Penn and his designees Juanita Boedeker and Charlotte Robison also became members of the Plan Committee;

c. Glen R. Eaves resigned as president of Glen's Inc.;

d. Ralph W. Penn became vice president of Glen's Inc. and chairman of the executive committee of the board of directors;

e. Glen R. Eaves resigned as trustee of the Profit-Sharing Plan and defendant Ralph W. Penn replaced him as trustee;

f. Ralph W. Penn, as trustee of the Profit-Sharing Plan, amended the Profit-Sharing Plan by substituting in its place the Glen's Employee Stock Ownership Plan and Trust;

g. Penn, on behalf of Glen's, Inc., made an advance contribution to the amended Plan of approximately $490,998.34;

h. In consideration of 168 shares of the stock of Glen's, Inc., delivered to Penn individually by Glen R. Eaves and Alleen M. Eaves, Penn delivered to Alleen M. Eaves $24,005.12, by cashiers check no. 10276 drawn on Will Rogers Bank, and to Glen R. Eaves and Alleen M. Eaves, $1,000 by cashiers check no. 9299 drawn on Will Rogers Bank for a total consideration of $25,005.12;

i. In consideration of 6,807 shares of the stock of Glen's, Inc. delivered to Penn, as trustee for the amended Plan, by Glen R. Eaves and Alleen M. Eaves, Penn, acting as trustee for the amended Plan, endorsed and delivered to Glen R. Eaves:

(1) $238,575.44 by cashiers check no. 10278 drawn on Will Rogers Bank;

(2) $150,000 by certificate of deposit no. 4940 issued by Capitol Hill State Bank which had accrued interest on that date of $3,132.29;

(3) $450,000 by certificate of deposit no. 4941 issued by Capitol Hill State Bank which had accrued interest on that date of $9,396.87; and

(4) delivered to Alleen M. Eaves $162,029.41 by cashiers check no. 10279 drawn on Will Rogers Bank for a total consideration of $1,013,134.01.

11. The $490,998.34 advance contribution made by Penn to the amended Plan on behalf of Glen's, Inc. consisted of $215,998.34 drawn from the operating capital and liquid assets of Glen's, Inc., and $275,000 obtained by Glen's, Inc. as the partial proceeds of a loan made by the Will Rogers Bank on January 16, 1976, which loan was secured by a first mortgage on all of the real property and improvements thereon of Glen's, Inc.

12. On January 16, 1976, Penn borrowed $25,000 from Glen's, Inc., which he used to purchase his individual shares of stock of Glen's, Inc., from Glen R. Eaves and Alleen M. Eaves.

13. The total consideration paid by Ralph W. Penn from his personal assets in the sale transactions referred to above was $1,000.00

14. By virtue of his ownership of 168 shares of stock of Glen's, Inc., and his position as trustee of the Plan, Penn became chairman of the board of directors, vice president of the company and a member of the Plan Committee and exercised complete control over the affairs of Glen's, Inc., and the Plan.

15. The Plan Committee as reconstituted on January 16, 1976, did not have authority to, nor did it in fact, advise the defendant Penn with respect to the investment of Plan assets in the stock of Glen's, Inc.

16. The amended Profit-Sharing Plan provides, in relevant part, that:

a. contributions to the Plan are within the discretion of the board of directors (no contribution is required);

b. contributions to the Plan may be in shares of Glen's, Inc., or in cash; Plan assets to the extent practicable, shall be invested in shares of Glen's, Inc., as directed by the company;

c. distributions to participants shall be made in shares of Glen's, Inc., and at the discretion of the Plan Committee, in equal annual installments over a period of years not to exceed the participant's life expectancy;

d. the Plan has a right of first refusal to purchase shares of Glen's, Inc., distributed to participants (participants, however, have no right to require the Plan or Glen's, Inc. to purchase shares of Glen's, Inc. distributed to them);

e. shares of Glen's, Inc. held by the Plan trustee on behalf of the Plan shall be voted by the Plan Committee; and

f. distribution of benefits to participants may be delayed until age 65.

17. On or after January 16, 1976, Glen's, Inc. made a contribution to the Stock Ownership Plan of $1,000 which was, pursuant to the trust instrument, allocated to participants' accounts.

18. The advance contribution of $490,998.34 made to the Plan on January 16, 1976 has not been allocated to participants' accounts nor has any person who has received distributions from the amended Plan since January 16, 1976 received any distribution attributable to that advance contribution.

19. Ralph D. Sitton has been an employee of Glen's, Inc. and a participant in the Profit-Sharing Plan since the Plan was instituted in 1958. On April 23, 1976, Ralph D. Sitton terminated his employment with Glen's, Inc. On or about the date of Sitton's termination of employment he questioned officers of Glen's, Inc. and of the amended Plan about payment of his benefits under the Plan. Officers of Glen's, Inc. and officials of the amended Plan, with the knowledge and agreement of Penn, informed Sitton that he would receive his benefits over a period of 21 years. Sitton was later advised he could receive his benefits over a period of 5 years.

20. On February 5, 1976, defendant Penn negotiated on behalf of Glen's, Inc., a loan of $48,000 from the Will Rogers Bank. The purpose of the loan was to purchase shares of stock of Glen's, Inc. which had been distributed to retirees under the terms of the amended Plan.

21. The cost to Glen's, Inc. to redeem one-fifth

of the shares of stock due to eligible participants and beneficiaries under the Plan in January, 1977, valued at the price per share paid by the Plan for the stock, is approximately $74,000. Glen's, Inc. does not have sufficient cash or current assets to repurchase those shares.

22. Prior to his employment by Glen's, Inc., Penn had no substantial experience in the management or operation of a restaurant business nor had he received compensation from any employer in excess of $25,000 per year. Penn currently is compensated by Glen's, Inc. at a rate in excess of $40,000 per year.

23. In addition to the loan described in number 10 above, Penn has caused several loans to be made to himself by and from the assets of Glen's, Inc. since January 16, 1976.

24. After obtaining control of Glen's, Inc. Penn authorized four loans of $2,000 each, which were made from the assets of Glen's, Inc., to Larry W. Stacy, a business acquaintance of Penn. In February, 1976, Penn authorized a loan of $8,000 which was made from the assets of Glen's, Inc., to Roy Hackett, a business acquaintance of Penn. The loans to Stacy and Hackett were not secured.

25. In August, 1976, Penn purchased a restaurant located in Norman, Oklahoma, which is now known as Glen's Hik'ry Pit #2 and he has operated that restaurant since that time. From August 30, 1976 until November 15, 1976, Penn provided substantial quantities of food from Glen's, Inc. to the Hik'ry Pit #2 including baked goods and cooked meats prepared in the kitchens of Glen's, Inc. Until late October or November, 1976, Glen's, Inc. was paid for those shipments on the basis of the cost of the raw ingredients plus five percent; the payments did not include the costs of overhead and labor incurred by Glen's, Inc. in preparing the goods shipped. These prices were unreasonably low under the circumstances. Additionally, no consideration has been paid by Penn to Glen's, Inc. for the good will derived from the use of the name "Glen's Hik'ry Pit." The Court finds that the name of an established and well-known business is a valuable asset.

26. On October 29, 1975, the Eaves, themselves or through their attorney, received an arms-length offer to buy Glen's, Inc. for a purchase price of $896,000 which offer did not involve the use of Plan assets.

27. Prior to the sale of the stock of the Company to Penn and the Plan, the Company had $114,376 in cash, current liabilities of $88,398, marketable securities valued at $152,616, other current assets of $120,441 and long-term liabilities of $60,000; the Company enjoyed a strong and healthy financial condition.

28. As a result of the advance contribution to the Plan of $490,998.34 which was accomplished by an expenditure of Company assets of $215,998.34 and the creation of a loan liability of the Company of $300,000, the value of the Company and the shares of the Company purchased on behalf of the Plan was reduced by approximately $490,998.34.

29. The advance contribution to the Plan of $490,998.34, which is carried by the Company as an asset on its books, has no substantial value to the Company and is not properly regarded as an asset of the Company.

30. Between January 1, 1976 and September 30, 1976, Glen's, Inc. has incurred net operating losses in excess of $121,577, which losses have further impaired the value of Glen's, Inc. and the value of the shares of Glen's, Inc. held by the Plan has thus been further substantially reduced.

31. The shares of Glen's, Inc. are not publicly traded and have no ready market.

32. As of September 30, 1976, the Company had a bank overdraft of $32,964, current assets of $105,900, current liabilities of $168,517, and long-term liabilities of $362,256; the Company is in serious financial difficulty.

33. The stockholders' equity in the Company has dropped from its pre-sale value of $746,711 to a current value, discounting the value of the $490,998.34 advance contribution, to approximately $76,000.

34. The net effect of the carrying out of the agreement between Glen R. Eaves and Alleen M. Eaves and Ralph W. Penn was an impairment of the assets of the Plan.

Conclusions of Law

Jurisdiction

1. This Court has jurisdiction over the subject matter of this action and the parties thereto by virtue of ERISA Section 502(e), 29 U.S.C. 1132(e); venue of this action is properly laid in this district by virtue of ERISA Section 502(e)(2), 29 U.S.C. 1132(e)(2).

2. The Glen's Profit-Sharing Plan is an employee pension benefit plan within the meaning of ERISA Section 3(2), 29 U.S.C. 1002(2), which is maintained by an employer in an industry affecting commerce within the meaning of ERISA Section 4(a)(1), 29 U.S.C. 1003(a)(1).

3. Glen R. Eaves, Alleen M. Eaves and Ralph W. Penn were, at all times relevant to this action,

fiduciaries with respect to the Glen's Profit-Sharing Plan within the meaning of ERISA 3(21), 29 U.S.C. 1002(21).

4. The Secretary of Labor has authority to bring this action by virtue of ERISA Section 502(a)(2) and (5), 29 U.S.C. 1132(a)(2) and (5).

Liability

5. Glen R. Eaves failed to discharge his duties with respect to the Plan solely in the interest of the Plan's participants and beneficiaries and for the exclusive purpose of providing benefits to participants and their beneficiaries and defraying reasonable expenses of administering the Plan as required by ERISA Section 404(a)(1)(A), 29 U.S.C. 1104(a)(1)(A), in that, for consideration to be paid to himself and Alleen M. Eaves, he agreed with Ralph W. Penn to resign as trustee of the Plan and to cause Penn to be appointed Plan trustee, to sell to the Plan, and to commit the Plan to buy, approximately 97% of the stock of Glen's, Inc.; and he performed and accepted performance under the terms of that agreement.

6. Glen R. Eaves failed to discharge his duties with respect to the Plan solely in the interest of the Plan's participants and beneficiaries and with the care, skill, prudence, and diligence under the circumstances then prevailing that a prudent man acting in a like capacity and familiar with such matters would use in the conduct of an enterprise of a like character and with like aims, as required by ERISA Section 404(a)(1)(B), 29 U.S.C. 1104 (a)(1)(B), in that he entered into an agreement with Penn to resign as Plan trustee and to cause Penn to become Plan trustee, to allow defendant Penn to amend the Plan, to sell to the Plan approximately 97% of the stock of Glen's, Inc.; and he performed and accepted performance under the terms of that agreement without adequate attention to or assessment of the effect of those transactions on the value of the assets of the Plan and the interests of Plan participants and beneficiaries.

7. Alleen M. Eaves failed to discharge her duties with respect to the Plan solely in the interest of the Plan's participants and beneficiaries and for the exclusive purpose of providing benefits to participants and their beneficiaries and defraying reasonable expenses of administering the Plan, as required by ERISA Section 404(a)(1)(A), 29 U.S.C. 1104(a)(1)(A), in that, for consideration to be paid to herself and Glen R. Eaves, she agreed with Penn to cause Penn to be appointed Plan trustee, to sell to the Plan, and to commit the Plan to buy approximately 97% of the stock of Glen's, Inc.; and she performed and accepted performance under the terms of that agreement.

8. Alleen M. Eaves failed to discharge her duties with respect to the Plan solely in the interest of the Plan's participants and beneficiaries and with the care, skill, prudence and diligence under the circumstances then prevailing that a prudent person acting in a like capacity and familiar with such matters would use in the conduct of an enterprise of a like character and with like aims, as required by ERISA Section 404(a)(1)(B), 29 U.S.C. 1104(a)(1)(B), in that she failed to take reasonable steps to prevent the performance of Glen R. Eaves and Ralph W. Penn under the terms of their agreement for the purchase of the stock of Glen's, Inc., by the Profit-Sharing Plan.

9. Ralph W. Penn failed to discharge his duties with respect to the Plan solely in the interest of the Plan's participants and beneficiaries and for the exclusive purpose of providing benefits to participants and beneficiaries and defraying reasonable expenses of administering the Plan, as required by ERISA Section 404(a)(1)(A), 29 U.S.C. 1104 (a)(1)(A), in that, in consideration of legal ownership as trustee of the Profit-Sharing Plan of a controlling number of shares of Glen's, Inc., he entered into an agreement with Glen R. Eaves to become trustee of the Plan, and, as trustee of the Plan, to pay all of the assets of the Plan to Glen R. Eaves and Alleen M. Eaves in exchange for approximately 97% of the stock of Glen's, Inc.; and he performed and accepted performance under the terms of that agreement.

10. Ralph W. Penn failed to discharge his duties with respect to the Plan solely in the interest of the Plan's participants and beneficiaries and with the care, skill, prudence and diligence under the circumstances then prevailing that a prudent man acting in a like capacity and familiar with such matters would use in the conduct of an enterprise of a like character and with like aims, as required by ERISA Section 404(a)(1)(B), 29 U.S.C. 1104(a)(1)(B), in that he agreed with Glen R. Eaves and Alleen M. Eaves to become Plan trustee and, as trustee of the Plan, to pay all of the assets of the Plan to the Eaves in exchange for approximately 97% of the stock of Glen's, Inc.; and he performed and accepted performance under the terms of that agreement without adequate attention to or assessment of the effect of those transactions on the value of the assets of the Plan and the interests of Plan participants and beneficiaries.

11. The Court, having found these parties to have violated their fiduciary duties with respect to the Plan, has broad discretion in fashioning

remedial and equitable relief including rescission. ERISA Section 409(a), 19 U.S.C. 1109(a). The Court will mold the relief to protect the rights of the beneficiary, Bogert, *Trusts and Trustees, Second Edition*, section 861 at p. 3. Complete rescission of the sale of stock of Glen's, Inc., to the Plan, restoration of income and profits lost to the Plan and the appointment of a Plan trustee approved by the Court will best serve the goal of making whole the Plan and the interests of participants and beneficiaries.

12. Penn's suggestion that relief should be limited to recovery of excess consideration paid by the Plan or a guarantee of the benefits which were available under the Plan prior to the sale is unacceptable in that it would permit Penn to retain for himself the benefit of his unlawful scheme and fail to take into account the expectancies of the participants in their continued employment and participation under the terms of the Plan. *President and Directors of Manhattan Co. v. Kelby,* 147 F.2d 465, (2nd Cir. 1944); *Story Parchment Co. v. Paterson Parchment Co.,* 282 U.S. 555, 562-65 (1930).

13. The Court has the authority and the duty to enforce the remedy which is most advantageous to the participants and beneficiaries and most conducive to effectuating the purposes of the trust. *Restatement of Trusts, Second,* section 205 comment b.

14. In cases of a breach of trust by a fiduciary which adversely affect the interests of plan participants and beneficiaries, the appropriate goal of equitable relief should be to restore the plan participants and beneficiaries to the position in which they would have been but for the unlawful acts. *Restatement of Trusts, Second* sections 205, 206. An order of rescission, setting aside or voiding the unlawful transaction, and restoration of profit or income lost to the plan are ordinary and frequently used remedies in such cases and are appropriate in this case.

15. Glen R. Eaves, Alleen M. Eaves and Ralph W. Penn as fiduciaries of the Plan have engaged in substantial violations of their fiduciary duties and should be removed. ERISA Section 409(a); *Legislative History of the Employee Retirement Income Security Act of 1974,* 94th Cong. 2d Sess. at 1174 (1976); Bogert, *Trusts and Trustees, Second Edition,* section 861 at 7.

Attorneys' Fees

The attorneys for Glen R. Eaves, Alleen M. Eaves, Violet Cobbs, Richard Eades, Ralph Sitton and Marguirite Richards, who first brought this action have requested an award of attorneys' fees. They assert that 29 U.S.C. 1132(g) authorizes an award of attorneys' fees, and that the award should be paid from the Plan assets, based upon what is called the "common fund" theory.

The Court finds that the participation of these attorneys in the preparation and trial of these combined cases has conferred a benefit on Plan participants and beneficiaries in addition to those who are named parties. The Court further finds that any time and effort expended in this case by these attorneys on behalf of Glen R. Eaves and Alleen M. Eaves should not be paid for out of Plan assets. The Court further finds and concludes that the amount of $4,500.000 will in a conservative way compensate these attorneys for the time and effort expended on behalf of the Plan beneficiaries other than Glen R. Eaves and Alleen M. Eaves and that when considered against the benefits bestowed upon these beneficiaries and participants it is fair, equitable and just that this amount should be paid from Plan assets to these attorneys.

Conclusion

In making all such findings of fact and conclusions of law, the Court does not hold that it would be necessarily imprudent and thus unlawful in every case for a retirement plan to use its cash assets to invest primarily, or even totally, in qualified employer securities. Rather, it is the effect of such action in this particular case, and the manner in which that decision was made and carried out, which is clearly violative of the protections intended to be derived from ERISA. Indeed, this would seem to be the classic example of the abuse ERISA is intended to prevent. Rescission of the offending scheme or transaction is, in this case, the appropriate remedy for the protection of the integrity and realistic value of the Plan's assets.

The Court's order giving effect to these Findings of Fact and Conclusions of Law is being filed separately and simultaneously herewith.

Dated this 29th day of December, 1976.

Order

Having considered the evidence presented at trial and the briefs of the parties, and having found that Glen R. Eaves, Alleen M. Eaves and Ralph W. Penn have breached their fiduciary duties with respect to the Glen's Profit-Sharing Plan, in violation of the Employee Retirement Income Security Act of 1974 by the Findings of Fact and Conclusions of Law filed simultaneously herewith, and having concluded that broad equitable relief is necessary and appropriate to restore the Plan and its participants and beneficiaries to the position in which they would have been in the absence of defendants' unlawful acts, now therefore, it is,

ORDERED, ADJUDGED AND DECREED as follows:

1. All of the transactions executed by Ralph W. Penn, Glen R. Eaves and Alleen M. Eaves on January 16, 1976, pursuant to their agreement of December 17, 1975, as amended, are hereby rescinded and set aside. Those transactions include:

a. the resignation of the prior and appointment of the present directors and officers of Glen's, Inc., the trustee of the Plan and the members of the Plan Committee;

b. the advance contribution to the Plan of $490,998.34;

c. the amendment of the Plan instrument;

d. the purchase by the Plan of 6,807 shares of the stock of Glen's, Inc.;

e. the loan from Glen's, Inc. to Ralph W. Penn of $25,000;

f. the purchase by Ralph W. Penn of 168 shares of the stock of Glen's, Inc.;

g. all other transactions executed pursuant to that agreement or in furtherance of the purposes of that agreement.

The loans from the Will Rogers Bank to the Company of $300,000 made on January 16, 1976, and $48,000 made on February 5, 1976, shall remain an obligation of Glen's, Inc. All other obligations of Glen's, Inc. to third parties are unaffected by this order.

2. The Plan shall be paid an amount equal to the interest which would have been earned by the Plan assets at an annual rate of interest of 7% for the period from January 16, 1976, to the date on which such assets are restored to the Plan.

3. Lost income shall be restored to the Plan in an amount equal to the median contribution made to the Plan by Glen's, Inc. during the five-year period ending December 31, 1975.

4. Ralph W. Penn, Glen R. Eaves and Alleen M. Eaves are removed as trustees of the Plan and are barred from serving in any fiduciary capacity with respect to the Plan in the future.

5. Within five days of the date of entry of this order, Glen's, Inc. shall appoint a trustee or trustees to hold and manage the assets of the Plan which appointment shall become effective upon approval by the Court.

6. The provision of the Amended Consent Order entered in this case on November 23, 1976, requiring the payment of a sum of money by Ralph W. Penn to Glen's, Inc. is incorporated by reference and made a part of this order.

7. The monies paid into court by Glen R. Eaves, pursuant to the order of this Court of June 7, 1976, and interest accrued thereon shall be disbursed by the Clerk of the Court as follows:

a. An amount equal to $522,135.67, plus the amounts due to the Plan pursuant to paragraphs 2 and 3 of this order, less the amounts paid by Glen's, Inc. during 1976 to repurchase shares of stock distributed to Plan participants and beneficiaries under the terms of the amended Plan, and, less $4,500.00, shall be paid to the Plan trustee upon his appointment and approval pursuant to paragraph 5 of this order.

b. $4,500.000 shall be paid to Howard Wisdom and Billy Hendrix as attorneys fees; and

c. All monies in excess of the amounts referred to in a. and b. above shall be paid to Glen's, Inc.

Except as provided herein this order shall become immediately upon entry.

BACON V. WONG

____ F.Supp. ____ (N.D. Calif. 1978)

UNITED STATES DISTRICT COURT
NORTHERN DISTRICT OF CALIFORNIA

JOHN W. BACON,
A. E. LAFAYETTE,
LOUIS OTTONE, JR.,
DAVID R. COX,
WILLIAM W. WARD, JR.,
A. L. DIAMOND,
ROY MACK,
EVERETT MATZEN,
ROY BENNER,
EDWIN LABOURE, and
JAMES WHITING,
Trustees of the
CALIFORNIA BUTCHERS
PENSION TRUST FUND

Plaintiffs and
Counterdefendants,

vs.

JOHN K. WONG and
JOHNNIE B. LEE,

No. C-75-2481-CBR

MEMORANDUM OF OPINION

on behalf of themselves)
and all other persons)
similarly situated,)
)
Defendants and)
Counterclaimants.)
___________________)

This lawsuit involves the right to restitution of various employers who made mistaken contributions to the California Butchers' Pension Trust Fund ("Fund") on behalf of ineligible employees.

The Court's Memorandum of Opinion filed on December 27, 1977, sets forth the factual and procedural background of the case. The mistakenly contributing employers, who were plaintiffs in the original lawsuit and who are now and will hereinafter be referred to as defendants, exercised their leave to file their claims for restitution under California law as counterclaims to the Fund's action for restitution under §502(a)(2) of the Employee Retirement Income Security Act of 1974 ("ERISA"), 29 U.S.C. §1132(e)(1). With the case in its present posture, the Court can consider the merits of the parties' cross-motions for summary judgment. Having carefully considered the written and oral arguments of the parties, the Court concludes that defendants are entitled to restitution of all contributions made to the Fund before January 1, 1975, in the innocent and mistaken belief that the employees on whose behalf they were made were eligible for benefits from the Fund and that defendants who made such contributions on or after January 1, 1975, are not entitled to any restitution.

The major substantive dispute between the parties concerns whether ERISA or California law determines defendants' right to restitution. Section 514(a) of ERISA, 29 U.S.C. §1144(a), states that except as provided in §514(b), ERISA "shall supersede any and all State laws insofar as they may now or hereafter relate to any employee benefit plan" covered by ERISA. Subsection (a) goes on to specify that "This section shall take effect on January 1, 1975." Section 514(b)(1) explicitly provides that ERISA does not preempt "any cause of action which arose, or any act or omission which occurred, before January 1, 1975."[1]

As §§514(a), 514(b)(1), and 414(a), 29 U.S.C. §1114(a) (effective date of fiduciary standards is January 1, 1975) make clear, Congress did not intend ERISA to apply retroactively to conduct which occurred before its effective date. *Morgan v. Laborers Pension Trust Fund,* 433 F.Supp. 518, 524 (N.D. Cal. 1977); *Martin v. Bankers Trust Co.,* 417 F.Supp. 923, 925 (W.D. Va. 1976); *see Puget Sound Power & Light Co., v. FPC,* 557 F.2d 1311, 1314 (9 Cir. 1977) (no retrospective application unless Congress had that "manifest intention"). The basic issue in this case is whether the conduct which is the basis of plaintiffs' alleged liability to defendants occurred before or after that date. Section 514(b)(1) preserves state law in two situations, when the cause of action arose before January 1, 1975, and when the act or omission occurred before January 1, 1975.

There is some uncertainty under California law about when a cause of action for restitution for mistake accrues. The time of accrual is "the moment when the party owning [a cause of action] is entitled to begin and prosecute an action thereon." *Van Hook v. Southern California Waiters Alliance,* 158 Cal.App.2d 556, 565, 323 P.2d 212, 217 (1958); *Heyer v. Flaig,* 70 Cal.2d 223, 74 Cal. Rptr. 225, 230, 449 P.2d 161, 166 (1969). In the case of restitution for mistake, either the cause of action accrues when the payor discovers the mistake, *see* Cal.Civ. Code §1691 (rescission based on mistake); Cal.Civ.Proc.Code §338(4) (claim for restitution based on mistake accrues when mistake discovered), or it accrues after the payee refuses to make restitution or fails to respond within a reasonable time to the payor's demand for restitution. *Mitchell v. California-Pacific Title Insurance Co.,* 79 Cal.App. 45, 52-53 (1926); Comment, 15 Cal.L.Rev. 64, 64-65 (1926); *see* Cal.Civ. Code §1713. The issue is in essence whether California law requires the payor to try to obtain voluntary restitution from the payee before instituting suit.

The Court need not decide whether defendants' cause of action for restitution under California law arose before January 1, 1975, because defendants' mistaken contributions to the Fund were "act[s] . . . which occurred before January 1,

1. Section 514(a) and (b)(1) provides in full:

(a) Except as provided in subsection (b) of this section, the provisions of this subchapter and subchapter III of this chapter shall supersede any and all State laws insofar as they may now or hereafter relate to any employee benefit plan described in section 1003(a) of this title and not exempt under section 1003(b) of this title. This section shall take effect on January 1, 1975.

(b)(1) This section shall not apply with respect to any cause of action which arose, or any act or omission which occurred, before January 1, 1975.

1975" within the meaning of §514(b)(1). The Court assumes for the purposes of this opinion that refusal to make restitution or failure to do so within a reasonable time after the payor's demand is an element of a cause of action for restitution and that defendants' cause of action therefore accrued in March, 1975, when plaintiffs refused to make as complete restitution as defendants demanded.[2]

This lawsuit presents an example of the general case where the course of conduct on which a benefit plan's potential liability is based straddles the effective date of ERISA. Plaintiffs' refusal here to make complete voluntary restitution, an assumed element of a cause of action for restitution based on mistake, occurred after January 1, 1975, although all the other elements of defendants' state claim were complete before that date. The fact that some of the relevant acts in this lawsuit occurred before January 1, 1975, does not necessarily mean that state law controls; if the occurrence before January 1, 1975, of any act or omission relevant to a cause of action, even if it constituted an element of a multi-element cause of action, made state law controlling, the clause of §514(b)(1) concerning the accrual of a cause of action would be superfluous. Although it is not at all clear what acts and omissions Congress referred to in §514(b)(1), that clause was apparently intended to permit courts to apply state law, even if the cause of action accrued after January 1, 1975, in cases where that result most fairly accommodates the interests of all affected parties—the beneficiaries, participants, and fiduciaries of and contributors to ERISA trusts. Courts must try to phase ERISA in as rapidly as possible without judging the conduct of affected persons by standards different from those which applied when they acted.

The Court concludes that the payment of money by mistake of law is an act within the meaning of §514(b)(1) because three factors coalesce. Those factors are (1) that the subsequent acts in satisfaction of the prior demand rule which permit the institution of suit for restitution amount to an exhaustion of internal remedies, (2) that an alternative construction would impose severe hardships on the contributors, and (3) that the Court's construction does not significantly undermine the purposes of ERISA.

First, the rule that the mistaken payor must make a demand on the payee for restitution and wait a reasonable time for response before instituting suit in effect constitutes a requirement of exhaustion of private remedies to give the parties an opportunity to settle their dispute without judicial intervention. The exhaustion requirement is not designed to affect the substantive rule of liability. The state of mind which §1578 of the California Civil Code defines as a mistake of law exists at the time the payment whose restitution the payor seeks is made, which in defendants' case happened before January 1, 1975. The problem concerning the applicable law arose in this case only because the period during which the trustees had the employers' claims under submission included the effective date of ERISA. It would be anomalous if the trustees were required to apply pre-ERISA standards to claims submitted and decided before January 1, 1975, and if the applicable standards then changed overnight for claims under submission even though the conduct to which those new standards were applied was unchanged and completed. Although technically the cause of action may not accrue until the private remedies are exhausted, compliance with the exhaustion requirement should not affect the substantive liability. The purpose of §514(b)(1) is to ensure that the conduct of trustees, beneficiaries, and contributors is judged by the standards existing at the time of the conduct, and that purpose is furthered by applying state law to acts occurring before January 1, 1975, if the additional acts necessary to complete a cause of action under state law must be performed in order to satisfy a requirement of exhaustion of private remedies.

Second, the Court's construction of §514(b)(1) avoids a serious hardship for individuals who make payments to pension funds by mistake of law before January 1, 1975, but who cannot sue for restitution until after that date.

Section 403(c) prohibits fiduciaries of benefit plans from making restitution of contributions paid by mistake of law after the effective date of ERISA. The inclusion of restitution for mistake of fact among the exceptions to the general rule of §403(c)(1) prohibiting payment of trust funds to employers implies that restitution to employers would otherwise be prohibited. Under the principle of construction "expressio unius est exclusio alterius," the failure to provide for restitution for mistake of law indicates that Congress intended to ban restitution for that reason. *Cf. National Railroad Passenger Corp. v. National Ass'n. of Railroad Passengers,* 414 U.S. 453, 458 (1975) (presumption that explicit creation of certain causes of action precludes inference of others

---

2. Defendants make no claim that plaintiffs could have processed the refund applications faster than they did.

rebuttable only by "clear contrary evidence of legislative intent"). There is nothing in the legislative history of ERISA to contradict that inference. Indeed, the only example of mistakes permitting restitution included in the legislative history—arithmetical errors in calculating contributions, H.Conf.Rep. No. 93-1280, 93d Cong., 2d Sess., 1974 U.S.Code Cong. & Adm. News 5038, 5083—also suggests a narrow exception excluding restitution for mistake of law. Finally, the law has traditionally been more reluctant to permit restitution for legal than for factual mistakes, *see, e.g., Grand Trunk Western R. Co. v. Chicago & Western Indiana R. Co.,* 131 F.2d 215, 217 & n.3 (7 Cir. 1942); *Olympic S.S. Co. v. United States,* 165 F.Supp. 627, 629-631 (D.Wash. 1958), and a congressional decision to prohibit restitution based on mistake of law is consistent with this attitude.

Defendants argue that Congress could not have intended to prohibit restitution based on mistake of law, a result which they contend is unfair, out of step with current legal developments, and unnecessary to carry out the purposes of §403(c). It is unquestionably true that this interpretation of §403(c) places a heavy burden on employers to make sure that employees are eligible for benefits before they make contributions to benefit plans on their behalf. It nevertheless seems clear that Congress intended this harsh rule, and only Congress can change it.

By prohibiting restitution of money paid by mistake of law, §403(c) terminates the right under California law to restitution under those circumstances. *See* Cal.Civ.Code §§1689(b)(1) and 1692. When a legislature eliminates the remedy for the violation of a right and thereby eliminates the right itself, it must give the possessors of that right a reasonable opportunity to exercise it before they lose it. *Central Missouri Telephone Co. v. Conwell,* 170 F.2d 641, 648 (8 Cir. 1948); *Rosefield Packing Co. v. Superior Court,* 4 Cal.2d 120, 47 P.2d 716, 717 (1935); *Olivas v. Weiner,* 127 Cal.App.2d 597, 274 P.2d 476, 478 (1954). Before the enactment of ERISA on September 2, 1974, employers who made contributions to the Fund under mistake of law and who had not yet realized their mistake had a right to restitution (contingent on demand to the Fund) and faced a three-year statute of limitations which had not yet begun to run and would not start to run until after they discovered their mistake. Sections 414(a) and 514(b)(1), which made the effective date of §403(c)(2)(A) fall not quite four months after the date of its enactment, gave employers 120 days to investigate all previous contributions to the Fund, to determine whether a mistake of law had been made in any of them, to notify the Fund, and to leave the Fund a reasonable period of time to answer the request (which could itself last, as in this case, more than three months). To accomplish those tasks within 120 days is a difficult if not impossible task.[3]

The Court emphasizes that its analysis of the hardship on employers does not involve any question of the constitutional validity of a retroactive change in a substantive right to restitution. The Court therefore need not consider abstruse questions relevant to the constitutional issue, such as whether an employer's right to restitution is "vested" at the time of the mistaken payment or only when the cause of action accrues. *See generally* 2 Sutherland, Statutory Construction §41.06 (Sands ed. 1973). Even if the unfairness to employers of barring causes of action for restitution based on mistakes of law made before January 1, 1975, is not severe enough to make §514(b)(1) unconstitutional, it is severe enough to require the Court to adopt an alternative construction of which §514(b)(1) is reasonably susceptible and

3. The result would be the same if §403(c)(2)(A) is interpreted, as defendants propose, only to change the statute of limitations for actions for restitution based on mistakes of law. Under that interpretation, §403(c)(2)(A) alters the previous statute of limitations in two significant ways: it shortens the period from three years to one, and it makes the period run from the date of payment instead of the date of discovery. *Compare* §403(c)(2)(A) *with* Cal.Civ.Proc.Code §338(4). As a result of this change and given the 120-day grace period between the date of enactment and the effective date of ERISA, any employer who made a mistaken contribution to the Fund before January 1, 1974, would be faced with a one-year statute of limitations two thirds of which in effect had run instead of a three-year statute which had not yet begun to run, and the employer would have to investigate all his previous contributions and make a demand on the Fund all within the 120-day period.

A new and reduced statute of limitations can be constitutionally applied to accrued causes of action provided it gives affected parties a reasonable time to avail themselves of the remedy before the statute takes effect. *Central Missouri Telephone Co. v. Conwell, supra,* 170 F.2d at 648; *Rosefield Packing Co. v. Superior Court, supra,* 47 P.2d at 717; *Olivas v. Weiner, supra,* 274 P.2d at 478. Although an employer's cause of action in this case had technically not accrued before the effective date of the reduction of the period of limitation, the same principles apply here, and the time allowed employers to assert their cause is at most marginally reasonable.

which avoids serious constitutional questions.

The third factor that supports the Court's construction of §514(b)(1) is that it does not undercut the purposes of ERISA. The reason why §403 (c)(2)(A) prohibits restitution based on mistake of law is to encourage employers to determine the eligibility of the individuals on whose behalf the contribution is made *before* the payment to the Fund is made. That purpose could no longer be served concerning payments already made before the effective date of §403(c)(2)(A). ERISA's intent to guarantee the financial soundness of pension plans would also not be significantly impaired. Although restitution would diminish the assets of the Fund, it would also reduce the number of beneficiaries, and the contributions on behalf of eligible employees should be adequate to provide for the payments of their benefits.

For these reasons, the Court concludes that ERISA does not govern an employer's right to restitution for payments made to the Fund before January 1, 1975, by mistake of law. Because the parties agree that no federal law other than ERISA, including §§301(a) and 302(c)(5) of the Labor-Management Relations Act of 1947, 29 U.S.C. §§185(a) and 186(c)(5), define the trustees' duties under these circumstances the right to restitution of defendants and members of the defendant class who made contributions to the Fund by mistake of law before January 1, 1975, is governed by California law.

Some members of the defendant class apparently made their mistaken payments to the Fund after January 1, 1975. Their claim to restitution is governed by ERISA since their state cause of action did not accrue until after January 1, 1975, and since their payments were made after that date. ERISA's prohibition of the return of contributions to employers who paid by mistake of law, *see* pp. 6-7, *supra,* requires the Court to dismiss pursuant to Fed.R.Civ.P. 12(b)(6) the claims of these employers for failure to state a claim upon which relief may be granted.

Pursuant to the understanding reached in open court, the parties are directed to prepare an appropriate decree in accordance with the decision reached herein and submit it to the Court for execution within sixty (60) days of the date of this opinion.

Dated: February 8, 1978.

Charles B. Renfrew
United States District Judge

The Prudent Man Standard

The "solely in the interest" and "exclusive purpose" rules contained in ERISA are not the only provisions governing fiduciary conduct. One of the most important provisions contained in ERISA, and probably the provision which is most widely debated, is the "prudent man rule." Section 404(a)(1)(B) of ERISA provides:

> A fiduciary shall discharge his duties with respect to a plan solely in the interest of the participants and beneficiaries and . . . with the care, skill, prudence, and diligence under the circumstances then prevailing that a prudent man acting in a like capacity and familiar with such matters would use in the conduct of an enterprise of a like character and with like aims. . . .

The prudent man rule is based on the common law rule adopted by most states prior to ERISA, but there are some differences. For example, prior to ERISA most states required a trustee to exercise the skill a man of ordinary prudence would exercise in dealing with his own property. The courts in interpreting this rule tended to focus on each investment as opposed to the collective investments of the trust or the whole portfolio, and they concentrated on risk of loss instead of evaluating return relative to risks incurred.

In enacting ERISA, Congress recognized that the rigid interpretation of the prudent man rule as developed by the state courts might not be appropriate as applied to the various types of pension and welfare plans. The Joint Explanatory Statement of the Committee of Conference on ERISA provides the following evidence of this recognition:

> The conferees expect that the courts will interpret [the] prudent man rule . . . bearing in mind the special nature and purpose of employee benefit plans.

H.R. Rep. 93-1280, 93d Cong., 2d Sess. 302.

While this one statement may not seem to support a more flexible interpretation of ERISA's "prudent man rule" than the similar common law rules, there is additional legislative history to support this position. *See* Committee on Education and Labor, General Committee on Labor, Hearings on H.R. 1045, H.R. 1046, and H.R. 16462 (1969, 1970). These materials seem to support the position that ERISA establishes a comparative, rather than an absolute, standard of performance. The prudent man rule seems to require the fiduciary possessing investment responsibility to invest as a prudent man would invest the assets of a pension or welfare plan with a similar character and with similar aims or needs.

The prudent man rule does not mean that there

is one standard for all plans. There are different standards for large plans and small plans, and for pension plans and welfare plans. These different standards are necessary since the characteristics and needs of a pension plan are different than the characteristics and needs of a welfare plan. A pension plan trustee or investment manager may be able to justify the accumulation of bonds with medium and long term maturity dates, whereas a vacation plan trustee may have difficulty justifying such a decision in light of the plan's liquidity needs.

ERISA's prudent man rule is reinforced by a diversification requirement: a fiduciary must diversify plan investments so as to minimize the risk of large losses.

This particular provision evidences the Congressional policy decision to require the diversification of investments, but ERISA does not specify the degree of investment concentration that would violate this requirement. *But see* ERISA §407. Like the prudent man rule, the diversification requirements direct the fiduciary to consider the facts and circumstances of each case. Among other factors to be considered are (1) the purposes of the plan; (2) the amount of plan assets; (3) financial and industrial conditions; (4) the type of investment, whether mortgages, bonds or shares of stock or otherwise; (5) distribution as to geographical location; (6) distribution as to industries; and (7) the dates of maturity. *See* H.R. Rep. 93-1280, 93rd Cong. 2d Sess. 304.

The other fiduciary duty standard contained in ERISA provides that a fiduciary must act in accordance with plan documents, given that the plan documents are consistent with the provisions of ERISA. This particular standard reflects a departure from the pre-ERISA common law. Prior to ERISA, plan documents could, in many cases, authorize fiduciary conduct that would not otherwise be permitted under state law. ERISA, on the other hand, seems to be controlling with respect to pension and welfare plan fiduciaries, while the plan documents can only authorize conduct that is consistent with ERISA's provisions.

Co-Fiduciary Liability

The liability resulting from a fiduciary's breach of his own duties is not the only concern of a pension or welfare plan trustee or other fiduciary. *See* ERISA §405. ERISA provides that a fiduciary may be liable for a breach of responsibility by another trustee or other fiduciary in certain cases. Section 405(a) of ERISA provides:

> In addition to any liability which he may have under any other provision of [part 4 of Title I of ERISA], a fiduciary with respect to a plan shall be liable for a breach of fiduciary responsibility of another fiduciary with respect to the same plan in the following circumstances:
>
> (1) If he participates knowingly in, or knowingly takes to conceal, an act or omission of such other fiduciary, knowing such act or omission is a breach;
>
> (2) if, by his failure to comply with §404 (a)(1) in the administration of his specific responsibilities which gave rise to his status as a fiduciary, he has enabled such other fiduciary to commit a breach; or
>
> (3) if he has knowledge of a breach by such other fiduciary, unless he makes reasonable efforts under the circumstances to remedy the breach.

These provisions require trustees and other fiduciaries to take certain steps to prevent breaches of fiduciary responsibility by other fiduciaries. For example, in response to a question involving an apparent breach of fiduciary responsibility, the Department of Labor stated that it was incumbent upon certain trustees to take all reasonable and legal steps to prevent the breach. *See* 29 C.F.R. §2509.75-5, FR-10.

The co-fiduciary responsibility provisions mean that trustees should, among other things, adequately document discussions relating to the administration and management of pension and welfare plans. Trustees should maintain minutes of meetings, and the minutes should adequately reflect the basis for investment and other decisions. Votes on many matters should be recorded.

If a fiduciary determines that a breach of responsibility has occurred or will occur in the future, he must take some action. Mere resignation will not shield the fiduciary from co-fiduciary liability.

Prohibited Transactions

These general provisions relating to the conduct of pension and welfare plan fiduciaries and co-fiduciaries are supplemented by provisions which specifically identify certain "prohibited transactions" between the plan and a party in interest. More specifically, §406 of ERISA and §4975 (c)(1) of the Internal Revenue Code of 1954 prohibit a variety of transactions involving pension and welfare plans.[1] For example, sales or leases of real or

1. The prohibited transaction provisions contained in ERISA make certain transactions "prohibited transactions," which fiduciaries must not engage in, while the parallel provisions contained in the Internal Revenue Code of 1954 apply to "disqualified persons," not fiduciaries. The term "disqualified person" includes substan-

personal property by a party in interest to a plan or by a plan to a party in interest are prohibited. Similarly, a party in interest who lends money or extends credit to the plan, or who borrows money or receives credit from the plan, may be engaging in a prohibited transaction which is not the subject of a statutory or administrative exemption. (The statutory and administrative exemptions will be discussed below.) If a party in interest provides services to a plan, the transaction may be within the penumbra of the statutory prohibitions.

Since all of these transactions involve a transfer of plan assets—for example, the rental fee paid or received by the plan—they may be prohibited by the general transaction prohibition, which proscribes the transfer of plan assets to a party in interest. Furthermore, if a fiduciary is involved in the transaction, the fiduciary prohibitions relating to self-dealing and kickbacks may be applicable. In connection with almost any transaction involving a pension or welfare plan, it is important to determine whether a party-in-interest relationship exists between the parties and, if such a relationship does exist, whether the transaction or the fiduciary conduct is prohibited.

Relationships Examined. The first step is to determine whether a party-in-interest relationship exists. As discussed above, the term party in interest is defined quite broadly in §3(14) of ERISA [and in §4975(e)(2) of the Internal Revenue Code of 1954 (i.e., disqualified person)].

In determining whether the necessary relationship exists, one question which has arisen is whether related plans are parties in interest with respect to each other. For example, it is not uncommon for collective bargaining to result in employer contributions to both a Taft-Hartley pension plan and to a welfare plan. Although the trusts maintained in connection with these plans must be separate under §302(c)(5) of the Taft-Hartley Act, the same persons quite frequently serve as trustees for both trusts. (The Taft-Hartley Act will be discussed in Chapter 3, Labor Laws.) In this connection, the Department of Labor has stated that these plans are not parties in interest with respect to each other solely because the same employers contribute to both plans or because they have the same trustees. *See* Prohibited Transaction Exemption 76-1, Part C (Preamble), 40 *Fed. Reg.* 12740, 12745 (1976). The mere presence of common trustees does not make the two plans parties in interest with respect to each other.

If, however, one of the plans provides services to the other, the plan providing the services would be a party in interest under §3(14)(B) of ERISA. For example, a Taft-Hartley pension plan may provide administrative or recordkeeping services for a related welfare plan. This relationship, and not the presence of common sponsors and trustees, makes the pension plan a party in interest with respect to the welfare plan.

Applicable Prohibitions. If a party-in-interest relationship exists, the important point to remember is that more than one of the prohibitions contained in ERISA §406 may apply to the transaction, or to the fiduciary conduct. The application of any one of the prohibitions may result in imposition of the ERISA penalty assessments or the Internal Revenue Code of 1954 excise taxes.

If, for example, a party in interest with respect to a Taft-Hartley plan, such as the president of the union whose members are covered by the plan, rents office space to the plan on behalf of the union, several prohibitions may be applicable. As discussed above, the leasing of property to a plan by a party in interest is prohibited, as are the furnishing of facilities to a plan and the transfer of plan assets (i.e., the rent) to a party in interest. Furthermore, if the president of the union is a plan trustee (i.e., a fiduciary) there may be a violation of one or more of the self-dealing prohibitions.

The self-dealing prohibitions are illustrated by the court's decision in *Curren v. Freitag*, 432 F. Supp. 668 (S.D.Ill. 1977).

CURREN V. FREITAG
432 F.Supp. 668 (S.D. Ill. 1977)

ACKERMAN, U.S. District Judge

This case involves various charges and countercharges between two factions on the Central Laborers Pension Fund [hereinafter Fund] Board of Trustees. The Fund is a trust established in accordance with the provisions of 29 U.S.C. §186 (c)(5) which, *inter alia,* requires equal representation by employers and employees in the administration of the Fund. The Fund and its employees are subject to the provisions of the Employee Retirement Income Security Act of 1974 [hereinafter ERISA] 29 U.S.C. §§1001 *et seq.*

Plaintiffs, the trustees appointed by the employers, filed this action on May 18, 1976, alleging numerous defects in the structure and operation of the Fund and seeking to hold trustees representing the employees personally liable under ERISA provisions. The complaint survived de-

---

tially the same persons included in the term "party-in-interest." *Compare* ERISA §3(14) with IRC §4975(e)(2).

fendants' motion to dismiss for failure to state a claim on which relief can be granted. Defendants however have filed a two count counterclaim also based on alleged violations of ERISA. The matter is now before me on plaintiffs' motion to dismiss Counts I and II of the counterclaim and on defendants' motion for summary judgment on Count I as well as other motions requiring little discussion and dealt with at the end of this opinion.

Count I of the counterclaim purports to state a claim against plaintiff Curren individually alleging that Curren has violated 29 U.S.C. §§1106(b)(2) and (3), ERISA §406(b)(2) and (3), in that plaintiff Curren is actively representing certain contractors who are resisting audits ordered by the Fund and refusing to pay amounts determined owing by these contractors to the pension fund. Count II alleges that all the plaintiff trustees have violated 29 U.S.C. §1106(b)(2) through the prosecution of this lawsuit, since it allegedly is for the benefit of the employer contractors and not for the benefit of the Fund.

Central Laborers Pension Fund is a trust administering more than the $20,000,000 in assets with its principal office in Jacksonville, Illinois. The Fund was established by a trust agreement which required sixteen trustees, eight appointed by the employees' union (Laborers Local Union No. 253) and eight from the employer associations (four appointed by Associated General Contractors of Illinois and four appointed by Morgan County Contractors Association) in accord with 29 U.S.C. §186(c)(5)(B). Plaintiffs Curren, Eddy, Mantz and Keene were appointed by Associated General Contractors of Illinois (AGCI). Plaintiff Curren is employed by AGCI as Director of Labor Relations. Defendants Freitag, Ward, Bruning, Moore, Rygh, Hasty, Wierman, Dickman and Holland are trustees appointed by Local No. 253, while defendants Crabtree, Neff, Price and Moore were appointed by the Morgan County Contractors Association.

Defendants filed a motion for summary judgment on Count I of the counterclaims pursuant to Federal Rule of Civil Procedure 56 contending that the pleadings, documents and deposition of plaintiff Curren establish that there are no genuine issues of material fact and that counterplaintiffs are entitled to judgment as a matter of law. Also pending concerning Count I of the counterclaim is plaintiff's motion to dismiss pursuant to F.R.Civ.P. 12(b) for failure to state a claim upon which relief can be granted. Since I have examined matters outside the pleadings, specifically Curren's deposition, these motions will be treated as cross motions for summary judgment under F.R.Civ.P. 56 as provided in F.R.Civ.P. 12(b).

The contention in the counterclaim is that plaintiff Curren, in violation of 29 U.S.C. §§1106(b)(2) and (3), is actively representing certain contractors in resisting audit and collection efforts of the Fund and receiving a fee therefor. The statute, dealing with prohibited transactions, under ERISA, provides that:

> (b) A fiduciary with respect to a plan shall not:
>
> (2) in his individual or in any other capacity act in any transaction involving the plan on behalf of a party (or represent a party) whose interests are adverse to the interests of the plan or the interests of its participants or beneficiaries, or
>
> (3) receive any consideration for his own personal account from any party dealing with such plan in connection with a transaction involving the assets of the plan.
>
> 29 U.S.C. §1106.

More specifically, in counterplaintiffs' motion for summary judgment it is contended that contrary to Curren's duty as a trustee of the Fund to take such action as necessary to insure that employers contribute to the Fund that which they are contractually obligated to contribute, counterdefendant Curren actively represented two employers, Coggeshall Construction Company and Burlington Road Builders, in resisting audit and collection procedures brought on behalf of the Fund. Both companies are being sued by the plaintiffs in this court for allegedly delinquent payments to the Fund. Curren counseled both companies to resist Fund audits and refuse payments since, in his opinion, the audits and subsequent lawsuits were not properly authorized, but were brought merely to apply pressure during labor negotiations pending between Coggeshall and the laborers union. Curren also suggested specific legal counsel to both Coggeshall and Burlington, and held meetings concerning their defense in his office.

Further, it is alleged and counterdefendant Curren states in his deposition that he issued a "bulletin" to all AGCI members advising them that Fund auditors were not properly authorized and asking to be contacted by any members of AGCI who had any questions.

This conduct was but a portion of a continuing conflict between Curren and the defendant Arnold, a Chicago attorney, who had allegedly been improperly hired by the Fund to pursue collection efforts against individual contractors. It certainly appears that the prime motivating factor in counterdefendant Curren's actions was the belief, as plaintiffs have alleged in their complaint, that not only was Arnold using the Fund and its audit procedures to apply pressure on individual contractors for his own purposes, but that Arnold had not properly been authorized to act on behalf of the Fund at all.

Throughout the conduct complained of, Curren acted not only as a trustee for the Fund but pursuant to his duties as Director for Labor Relations for AGCI. Those duties as described in his deposition, consisted of negotiating and administering collective bargaining agreements on behalf of AGCI and its collective and individual members.

Counterplaintiff would have me believe that the actions of Curren on behalf of AGCI were "at total war" with his obligations as a trustee for the Fund, and that the state of the law is such that Curren could not perform both as trustee and as Labor Relations Director for AGCI. Admittedly, there may be an inherent conflict between the ERISA fiduciary duty and prohibited transaction provisions [29 U.S.C. §§1104 and 1106] and the provisions of the Labor Management Relations Act requiring equal representation by labor and management in the control of employee trust funds [29 U.S.C. §186(c)(5)]. However, this conflict is lessened by the language in 29 U.S.C. §1108(c)(3) which provides:

> (c) Nothing in Section 1106 of this title shall be construed to prohibit any fiduciary from . . .
>
> (3) serving as a fiduciary in addition to being an officer, employee, agent or other representative of a party in interest.

Given this statutory provision, it is not per se improper for Curren to act both as trustee and as Labor Relations Director for AGCI. Thus, the portion of the counterclaim based on 29 U.S.C. §1106 (b)(3) is unfounded since it is established by the depositions and memoranda filed that Curren received no "consideration for his personal account" other than his AGCI salary. Due to the language of 29 U.S.C. §1108(c)(3) quoted above, I believe as a matter of law that Curren's AGCI salary cannot form the basis of a complaint under §1106(b)(3).

While the elements of the counterclaim citing 29 U.S.C. §1106(b)(2) present a somewhat more difficult question, I believe the same result follows. As stated in the previous paragraphs, 29 U.S.C. §1108(c)(3) establishes that there is nothing improper about Curren acting both as a trustee and as Labor Relations Director for AGCI. A portion of Curren's responsibilities as Labor Relations Director is to advise and counsel AGCI members concerning contract negotiations. Given Curren's beliefs concerning the propriety of the Fund's auditing operation and his beliefs as to the reasons for particular audits, as seen through the allegations of this complaint, he would have been remiss in his duties as Labor Relations Director to stand mute.

Since the Act allows him to act in both capacities, it is illogical that it would require him to forego the giving of advice and assistance he would have been expected to give were he not a trustee. It certainly is not alleged that his actions would be anything but appropriate except for his status as trustee.

The question at issue then is whether counseling parties to resist audits and to refuse payment to the Fund, suggesting of specific legal counsel to them, participating in meetings concerning their legal defense and issuing a "bulletin" advising adverse parties of an allegedly improper collection effort, constitutes acting on behalf of an adverse party in any transaction involving the plan within the meaning of 29 U.S.C. §1106(b)(2).

According to the conference committee, the purpose of §1106(b)(2) is to prevent "a fiduciary from being put in a position where he has dual loyalties, and, therefore, he cannot act exclusively for the benefit of a plan's participants and beneficiaries." U.S. Code Cong. and Admin. News, 1974, pp. 4639, 5089. Clearly, however, certain dual loyalties are permissible as established by the language quoted above from §1108(c)(3). A broad reading cannot be given to both sections.

To effect the broad reading of §1106(b)(2) sought here by counterplaintiff would require a fiduciary who also serves as an employee of a party in interest as permitted by §1108(c)(3) to neither inform nor counsel his employer of his opinion of the propriety of actions taken by the fund. In short, such person would require a bifurcated personality. As a fiduciary, the actions of his co-fiduciaries must be known and acted upon but he would be required to remain silent and inactive in his capacity as an employee of a party in interest.

This construction appears to me to be unreasonable and unworkable especially in light of the provisions of the Labor Management Relations Act pursuant to which this particular fund was established which requires employees and employers to be equally represented in administering the Fund. 29 U.S.C. §186(c)(5)(B).

A preferable construction, it seems, would prevent the fiduciary from being placed in a position where he was dealing with the Fund on behalf of his employer in a matter concerning the assets of the Fund. "Dealing" in this context should mean that the fiduciary is possessed with the power to compromise the positions of his employer, or the

Fund or both. For example, the act should prohibit a fiduciary who was appointed by the contractors' association from being placed in a position which would authorize him to accept on behalf of the Fund, an amount less than the amount due the Fund in settlement of a Fund claim against an individual contractor. On the other hand, the act should not prohibit a fiduciary from counseling the individual contractor that the Fund might accept less than the full amount due in settlement of a Fund claim. In other words the act must be construed to differentiate between advocating a course of action or a solution and having the power to take that course or implement that solution.

The facts here do not show Curren possessed of this type of power. Curren's actions consisted of providing his opinion as to the propriety of fund actions, his advice as to the best way to proceed and perhaps seeking out individuals to hear his opinions and advice.

Curren's actions, of course, are in a general way adverse to the interests of the beneficiaries, since if followed it would mean at minimum, increased, collection costs for the Fund. However, the actions complained of could best be characterized as giving aid and comfort to an adverse party. Those actions, in my opinion, do not constitute acting in a transaction involving the Fund on behalf of an adverse party within the meaning of 29 U.S.C. §1106(b)(2).

In light of the foregoing, counterdefendant Curren's motion for summary judgment on Count I of the counterclaim will be granted since there are no genuine issues of material fact and since he is entitled to judgment as a matter of law.

Count II of the counterclaim names all the plaintiff trustees as counterdefendants and alleges that the bringing of this action in and of itself, violates 29 U.S.C. §1106(b)(2) since allegedly the plaintiff trustees are acting for the benefit of AGCI employers and against the interests of the Fund. Counterdefendants have moved pursuant to F.R. Civ.P. 12(b) to dismiss this count for failure to state a claim on which relief may be granted.

Given the fact that the majority of plaintiffs' complaint has survived defendants' motion to dismiss, defendants' theory on Count II of the counterclaim plainly stated, is that given an improper motivation, §1106(b)(2) prohibits fiduciaries from asserting colorable claims of breach of fiduciary duty in this or any other forum.

Congress, in ERISA Section 405(a)(3), 29 U.S.C. §1105(a)(3), provided that a fiduciary having knowledge of a breach of fiduciary duty by a co-fiduciary may be liable for that breach unless he makes "reasonable efforts under the circumstances to remedy the breach." It seems unlikely that Congress intended a fiduciary to be inhibited in his power to seek to remedy a breach of fiduciary duty, regardless of his ultimate motive.

I believe that as a matter of law, a fiduciary who seeks to remedy at least colorable breaches of fiduciary duty by his co-fiduciaries through civil litigation cannot be said to have violated 29 U.S.C. §1106(b)(2) regardless of this motivation for bringing the action. ERISA does not require a fiduciary to stand mute because calling attention to breaches of fiduciary duty would inure to the benefit of the party in interest who secured his position as a fiduciary.

Count II of the counterclaim shall be dismissed for failure to state a claim upon which relief may be granted.

As to the other pending motions in this cause, they are dealt with in summary fashion below:

(1) Counterplaintiffs' motion for summary judgment on Count I of the counterclaim is denied.

(2) Counterdefendants' motion for summary judgment on Count I of the counterclaim is granted.

(3) Counterdefendants' motion to dismiss Count II of the counterclaim is granted.

(4) Motion of Giffin, Winning, Lindner, Newkirk, Cohen and Bodewes for leave to withdraw as attorneys for plaintiff is allowed.

(5) Defendants' motion to amend counterclaim filed December 8, 1976, is allowed.

(6) Defendants' motion to amend answer filed February 1, 1977, is allowed.

Statutory Exemptions

Fortunately, ERISA also contains a number of statutory exemptions from the statutory prohibitions. *See* ERISA §408(b). There are statutory exemptions for loans to participants; services; bank deposits; purchases of insurance; bank ancillary services; conversion of securities; certain pooled investment funds; plan asset distributions; and other transactions.

However, it is important to note that the statutory exemptions do not necessarily extend to all of the applicable prohibitions. For example, §408 (b)(2) of ERISA contains an exemption for contracting with a party in interest for office space or services provided certain conditions are met. This particular exemption, however, does not extend to the self-dealing prohibitions or to the kickback prohibition. The Department of Labor regulations relating to this statutory exemption provide:

> Section 408(b)(2) of [ERISA] exempts from the prohibitions of §406(a) . . . payment by a plan to a party-in-interest, including a fiduciary, for office space or any service (or combination of services) if (1) such office space or service is necessary for the establishment or operation of the plan; (2) such office space or service is furnished under a contract or arrangement which is reasonable; and (3) no more than reasonable compensation is paid for such office space or service. However, §408(b)(2) does not contain an exemption from acts described in §406)b)(1) . . . (relating to fiduciaries dealing with the assets of plans in their own interest or for their own account), §406(b)(2) . . . (relating to fiduciaries in their individual or in any other capacity acting in any transaction involving the plan on behalf of a party (or representing a party) whose interests are adverse to the interests of the plan or the interests of its participants or beneficiaries) or §406(b)(3) . . . (relating to fiduciaries receiving consideration for their own personal account from any party dealing with a plan in connection with a transaction involving assets of the plan). Such acts are separate transactions not described in §408(b)(2).
> 29 C.F.R. §2550.408b-2(a).

As a result, the union whose members are covered by the Taft-Hartley plan, that rented office space to the plan might not be subject to penalty by reason of the statutory exemption contained in §408 (b)(2) of ERISA [and the similar exemption contained in §4975(d)(2) of the Internal Revenue Code of 1954]; but, if the president of the union was a plan trustee—a fiduciary—there may be a prohibition not covered by the exemption.

The fiduciary prohibitions are designed to supplement the other prohibitions (which relate primarily to transactions as opposed to conduct), by imposing on fiduciaries a duty of "undivided loyalty" to the plans for which they act. These prohibitions are intended to prevent fiduciaries from exercising the authority that causes their classification as fiduciaries in the first instance, in cases in which it may be difficult for them to act solely in the interest of the plan.

In the context of the statutory exemption for leasing office space, the decision in *Curren* provides support for an argument that the president of the union may make the proposal to the plan on behalf of the union and may even participate in the joint board's discussion of the matter. On the other hand, the decision implies that he should not vote. However, the *Curren* decision seems to read the fiduciary prohibition relating to adverse representation out of ERISA, by placing greater emphasis on the fiduciary prohibition relating to self-dealing.

The DOL and IRS regulations relating to the statutory exemption discussed above were not issued when the *Curren* decision was rendered, but, in light of these regulations, the Department and the Service probably disagree with the court's decision. However, as a practical matter, it may be difficult or impossible to follow a more conservative approach. If the president of the union (and, presumably, other persons appointed by the union) cannot advocate on behalf of the union or decide on behalf of the plan, the statutory exemption may be of limited value. The exclusion of these persons from the decision making process poses some serious problems under the Taft-Hartley Act. If only representatives of management can participate in the process, there may be a violation of the equal representation requirement. (The Taft-Hartley Act will be discussed in Chapter 3.)

Administrative Exemptions

Fortunately, ERISA also vests the Secretaries of Labor and Treasury with the authority to grant administrative exemptions from one or more of the applicable prohibitions. However, the Secretaries may not grant an exemption unless they find that the exemption is administratively feasible, in the interest of the plan and its participants and beneficiaries, and protective of the rights of participants and beneficiaries of the pension or welfare plan.

The Secretaries have made these findings in certain cases and have granted both individual and class exemptions. There are administrative exemptions for certain transactions involving pension and welfare plans and certain broker-dealers, reporting dealers and banks; for certain transactions in which multiemployer and multiple employer plans are involved; for mutual fund in-house plans; for plan purchases and sales of mutual fund shares; for the transfer of insurance and annuity contracts to and from plans; and for certain transactions involving insurance agents and brokers, consultants, insurance companies, investment companies, investment company principal underwriters and pension and welfare plans.

Office Space Leases. Leases of office space by plans to certain parties in interest are covered by administrative exemptions. Part C of Prohibited Transaction Exemption 76-1 provides an exemption from the transaction-oriented prohibitions if a pension or welfare plan leases office space to a contributing employer, a contributing employer association, a union whose members are covered by the plan or another Taft-Hartley plan, provided certain conditions are met. The pension or welfare plan must receive reasonable compensation (i.e., the rental fee) for the leasing of the space (but the plan does not necessarily have to make a profit). The plan must be able to terminate the lease on reasonably short notice, and the plan must maintain certain records.

However, like the statutory exemption discussed above, this administrative exemption does not provide an exemption from the fiduciary conduct prohibitions. For example, if related plans with common trustees entered into a lease pursuant to which a pension plan leased space to a welfare plan, the common trustees of both plans may be violating one of the fiduciary conduct prohibitions. While the plans may not be parties in interest with respect to each other (e.g., unless one plan provides services to the other), the common trustees may be acting on behalf of (or representing) a party whose interests are adverse to the interests of the plan. The trustees would be negotiating the terms of the lease for both the lessor and the lessee plans. While acting on behalf of the lessee plan, they would be acting on behalf of a party whose interests are adverse to those of the lessor plan.

This type of conduct prohibition, however, is the subject of another administrative exemption. Prohibited Transaction Exemption 77-10 provides an exemption from this prohibition if the plan leases office space to certain parties in interest provided certain conditions are satisfied. The conditions are similar to the conditions under Prohibited Transaction Exemption 76-1.

The important points to note are that the definition of the term "party in interest" is very broad and that a broad range of transactions involving these persons and pension and welfare plans are prohibited. More than one prohibition may be applicable to a particular transaction, and both the statutory and administrative exemptions must be carefully analyzed. Every prohibition must be covered by the exemption or the exemption will be of limited value. Of course, administrative exemptions may be applied for, but so far they have proved to be difficult to obtain.

Employer Securities and Real Property. The prohibited transaction sections of ERISA (but not the prohibited transaction provisions contained in the Internal Revenue Code of 1954) include provisions specifically relating to the acquisition and holding of employer securities and employer real property. More specifically, §406(a)(1)(E) of ERISA provides that a fiduciary must not cause a pension or welfare plan to acquire any employer security or employer real property in violation of §407(a) of ERISA, while §406(a)(2) provides that no fiduciary shall permit a plan to hold any employer security or employer real property if he knows that holding such assets violates §407(a).

Section 407(a) provides that a plan may not acquire or hold any employer securities or employer real property other than "qualifying" employer securities and employer real property. The term "employer security" is defined broadly to include any security issued by an employer (or an affiliate) of employees covered by the plan, and the term "security" has the same meaning as the term has under §2(1) of the Securities Act of 1933. (The Securities Act of 1933 will be discussed in Chapter 4, Securities Laws). "Qualifying" employer securities, however, are limited to stock and marketable obligations.

The term "employer real property" means real property which is leased to an employer (or an affiliate) of employees covered by the plan. "Qualifying" employer real property means parcels of employer real property if a substantial number of the parcels are dispersed geographically; if each parcel of real property and the improvements thereon are suitable for more than one use; and if the acquisition and retention of such property complies with §404 of ERISA (other than the diversification rules). To summarize: there must be more than one parcel of real property and the parcel must be geographically dispersed.

Section 407(a) of ERISA further provides that a plan may not acquire any qualifying employer securities or qualifying employer real property if the fair market value of the securities and property held by the plan exceeds 10% of the fair market value of plan assets. In general, this limitation only applies to certain pension plans. For example, it does not apply to certain defined contribution pension plans, such as profit-sharing plans. Section 407(b)(1) of ERISA provides that §407(a) does not apply to any acquisition or holding of qualifying employer securities or qualifying employer real property by an "eligible" individual account plan. "Eligible" individual account plans include profit-sharing, stock bonus, certain money purchase and other plans if they specifically provide for the acquisition and holding of qualifying employer securities or qualifying employer real property.

Like the other prohibited transaction provisions discussed above, the employer security and real property provisions are the subject of a statutory exemption. *See* ERISA §408(e). Similarly, the Secretaries of Labor and Treasury have the authority to grant administrative exemptions from the restrictions imposed by §407(a).

Reporting and Disclosure

Prior to ERISA, the Welfare and Pension Plans Disclosure Act (the WPPDA), 29 U.S.C. §1031, *et seq.* required pension and welfare plan administrators to file a description and an annual report of the plan with the Department of Labor. These documents were also required to be made available to employees.

During the Congressional consideration of ERISA, the commonly held view was that the WPPDA was ineffective and, as a result, this law was repealed by ERISA. ERISA contains rather comprehensive reporting and disclosure requirements. Various reports must be filed with the Department of Labor (as well as the Department of the Treasury and the Pension Benefit Guaranty Corporation) and certain documents must be disclosed to plan participants and beneficiaries either automatically or upon request, depending on the nature of the documents. The reporting and disclosure of information is intended to assist the government and participants in determining whether plans are established and maintained in accordance with the law.

Reporting to the Department of Labor

The administrator of a pension or welfare plan must file certain information describing the plan with the Department of Labor within 120 days after the plan becomes subject to ERISA's reporting provisions. *See* ERISA §104(a). This descriptive information must be filed on Form EBS-1, a type of registration statement which provides the Department with certain information relating to the administration of the plan and the plan's terms and conditions: e.g., the name of the plan administrator and the name and type of plan.

The plan administrator must also identify the various persons who perform functions for the plan and the sources and methods of determining contributions. If the plan is a pension plan, the participation, vesting and benefit accrual requirements must be provided. If the plan is a welfare plan, the type of benefits available under the plan and the requirements for benefits (e.g., the waiting period) must be indicated.

Plan Modifications. The plan administrator must also file an updated plan description at least once every five years. *See* ERISA §104(a). Any "material modification" in the terms of the pension or welfare plan and any "material changes" in information required to be contained in the Form EBS-1 must be reported on the form within 60 days after the adopting or occurrence of any "material modification" or any change that has not been incorporated in another filing.

The instructions to the Form EBS-1 broadly construe the term "material modification" to encompass changes in almost all items on the form. For example, a change in the name or address of the plan administrator or the agent for service of legal process constitutes a reportable "material modification."

Summary Plan Description. In addition to the Form EBS-1, the plan administrator of a pension or welfare plan must file a summary plan description (SPD) with the Department of Labor. *See* ERISA §104(a). Unlike the Form EBS-1, the SPD is not prepared and filed on a form; the format of the SPD is, in a sense, discretionary. However, this document must be "written in a manner calculated to be understood by the average plan participant, and [it must] be sufficiently accurate and comprehensive to reasonably apprise such participants and beneficiaries of their rights and obligations under the plan." ERISA §102(a)(1).

The Department of Labor has published regulations relating to SPDs. *See* 29 C.F.R. §2520.102-2, *et seq.* The regulations provide guidance with respect to the style and format, and contents, of the SPD. Section 2520.102-2(b) provides:

> The format of the summary plan description must not have the effect of misleading, misinforming, or failing to inform participants and beneficiaries. Any description of exceptions, limitations, reductions, and other restrictions of plan benefits shall not be minimized, rendered obscure or otherwise made to appear unimportant. Such exceptions, limitations, reductions, or restrictions of plan benefits shall be described or summarized in a manner not less prominent than the style, captions, printing type, and prominence used to describe or summarize plan benefits, the advantages and dis-advantages of the plan shall be presented without either exaggerating the benefits or minimizing the limitations. The description or summary of restrictive plan provisions need not be disclosed in the summary plan description in close conjunction with the description or summary of benefits, provided that adjacent to the benefit description the page on which the restrictions are described is noted.
>
> 29 C.F.R. §2520.102-2(b).

While the SPD must be filed with the government, its principal use is one of disclosure to participants and beneficiaries, which will be discussed below.

Annual Report. The other document required to be filed with the Department of Labor by the plan administrator is the annual financial report for each pension and welfare plan subject to the reporting provisions. *See* ERISA §104(a). This report is filed on Form 5500 (or Form 5500-C or 5500-K), and generally is to include audited financial statements for both pension and welfare plans.

With respect to welfare plans, the statement must include a statement of assets and liabilities, a statement of changes in assets held by the plan and a statement of changes in the plan's financial position. With respect to pension plans, the statement must include the statement of assets and liabilities and a statement of changes in net assets available for plan benefits, including details as to revenues and expenditures and other charges aggregated by general source and application.

In the notes to the financial statements, the accountant must disclose any significant changes in the plan, material lease commitments and contingent liabilities, any agreement or transaction with persons known to be parties in interest, information as to whether a ruling from the Internal Revenue Service concerning the tax status of the pension plan has been obtained, and any other relevant matters necessary to fairly present the financial status of the plan.

In addition to the audited financial statements, the annual report must include separate schedules showing, among other things, a statement of plan assets and liabilities aggregated by categories; a statement of receipts and disbursements; a schedule of all assets held for investment purposes, aggregated and identified by issuer, borrower, or lessee; and a schedule of each transaction involving a person known to be a party in interest.

In addition, the report must include a schedule of any loans and leases in default at the end of the year or classified during the year as uncollectible, and a schedule listing each transaction which exceeds 3% of the value of the fund. If some or all of the assets of the plan are held in a common or collective trust maintained by a bank, the annual report must include the most recent annual statement of assets and liabilities of the common or collective trust.

With respect to persons employed by the plan, the annual report must include the name and address of each fiduciary and the name of each person who receives more than minimal compensation from the plan for services rendered, along with the amount of compensation, the nature of the services, and the relationships of the employer or any other party in interest to the plan. The reasons for any changes in trustees, accountants, actuaries, investment managers, or administrators must be provided in the annual report.

Deadlines and Enforcement. The annual report for a plan has to be filed within 210 days after the close of the plan year. It is important to note that the Department of Labor may reject the filing of an annual report if it determines that the annual report is incomplete or that the opinion of the "independent qualified public accountant" or the "enrolled actuary" contains a material qualification.

If the Department of Labor rejects an annual report, the plan administrator has 45 days to submit a revised report satisfactory to the Department. If such a report is not received, the Department may: (1) retain an "independent qualified accountant" to prepare an audit; (2) retain an "enrolled actuary" to prepare an actuarial statement; (3) commence a civil action for the relief necessary to enforce the applicable ERISA provisions; or (4) take any other authorized action. The Department may also require the plan administrator to permit the "independent qualified public accountant" or the "enrolled actuary" to inspect essential books and records of the plan, and to recover from the plan the expenses of the audit or report.

Required Communications to Participants

Plan Documents. The administrator of a pension or welfare plan must provide an SPD to participants and beneficiaries when it is filed with the Department of Labor. *See* ERISA §104(b). Participants and beneficiaries covered under the plan after the filing date must receive a copy of the SPD within 90 days after either becoming participants or starting to receive benefits. The pension or welfare plan administrator must also provide participants and beneficiaries with a description of "material modifications" within 210 days after the close of the plan year in which the modification or modifications occur. *See* ERISA §104(b). New participants must also receive this document.

ERISA also requires the plan administrator to provide participants and beneficiaries with certain portions of the annual financial report. *See* ERISA §104(b). This document is called the summary annual report. In general, the plan administrator must furnish participants and beneficiaries with a copy of certain statements and schedules and such other information as is necessary to summarize the latest annual report within nine months of the end of the plan fiscal year.

The SPD and the summary of material modifications and the financial report (summary annual report) are not the only materials automatically furnished to participants and beneficiaries. For example, a pension plan administrator must provide participants who terminate their service with the employer(s) maintaining the plan, and participants who have a one year break in service, with a statement of the individual's accrued benefits under the plan and the percentage of vested or nonforfeitable benefits. *See* ERISA §209(a); *see also* ERISA §1031.

Statement of Rights. The plan administrator must also provide participants with a "statement of ERISA rights," to be distributed with the SPD. *See* ERISA §104(c). For example, participants should be told that:

> Under ERISA, there are certain steps you can take to enforce [your rights]. For instance, if you request materials from the plan and do not receive them within 30 days, you may file suit in federal court. In such a case, the court may require the plan administrator to provide the materials and pay you up to $100 a day until you receive the materials, unless the materials are not sent because of reasons beyond the control of the administrator. If you have a claim for benefits which is denied or ignored, in whole or in part, you may file suit in a state or federal court. If it should happen that plan fiduciaries misuse the plan's money, or if you are discriminated against for asserting your rights, you may seek assistance from the U.S. Department of Labor, or you may file suit in federal court.
> 29 C.F.R. §2520.102-3(t)(2).

As this portion of the regulations indicates, if a claim for benefits is wholly or partially denied, the pension or welfare plan administrator must provide the claimant with a written notice of the decision within a reasonable time after the plan receives the claim. *See* ERISA §503. This notice or statement, which, like the SPD, is required to be written in a manner calculated to be understood by the average plan participant, must include: (1) the specific reason or reasons for the denial; (2) specific references to pension or welfare plan provisions on which the denial is based; (3) a description of any additional information necessary for the participant or claimant to perfect his claim and an explanation of why such information is necessary; and (4) an explanation of the pension or welfare plan's claims review procedure. If the participant or beneficiary requests a review, the decision on review must be in writing and it must also state these specific reasons for the decision and provide additional information.

Finally, participants who separated from the employer's service during the plan year and who are entitled to deferred vested benefits must receive a statement of such benefits.

Documents to Be Furnished Upon Request

The administrator of a pension or welfare plan must provide participants and beneficiaries with copies of documents, if they are requested. These documents include: (1) the most recently filed Form EBS-1; (2) the most recently filed SPD; (3) the most recently filed Form 5500 (or Form 5500-C or 5500-K); and (4) any terminal report or collective bargaining agreement, trust agreement, contract or other documents pursuant to which the plan is established and maintained. Participants may be required to pay for copies of these documents, but in no case may such charge exceed 10¢ per page.

Upon request, but no more frequently than once a year, the administrator of a pension plan must provide a participant with a statement indicating his total benefits accrued and his vested or nonforfeitable benefits, or the earliest date on which benefits will become vested or nonforfeitable. This particular statement is due within 30 days after the request is received.

TITLE IV: PLAN TERMINATION INSURANCE

Scope and Coverage

Title IV of ERISA establishes the Pension Benefit Guaranty Corporation (the PBGC), a self-financing corporation, to provide termination insurance coverage for most "defined benefit" type pension plans. *See* ERISA §4021(a). It does not provide termination insurance coverage for defined contribution pension plans, such as profit-sharing plans, or for welfare plans. *See* ERISA §4021(b).

The purpose of the termination insurance coverage is to protect participants and beneficiaries from losing their benefits in the event their plan is terminated. The plan termination insurance provisions have a significant economic impact on the private employee benefit plan complex, but these provisions can only be touched upon here. It is important to note that the termination of a plan or the withdrawal of an employer from a plan may result in actual or potential "net worth" liability for the employer. This liability may affect the financial viability of the employer as an ongoing concern.

Since the purpose of these provisions is to "protect" participants and beneficiaries, it is interesting (and important) to note that one of the most controversial issues which has arisen to date is whether Taft-Hartley plans are "defined benefit" or "defined contribution" plans. If these plans are classified as defined benefit plans, insurance premiums will have to be paid to the PBGC and, as a result, the participants will be provided with insurance protection. On the other hand, if these plans are classified as defined contribution plans, the participants will not be protected in the event that the plan terminates and the assets available are insufficient to provide the promised benefits.

The court's order granting "summary judgment" in *Connolly v. PBGC*, 419 F.Supp. 737 (C.D. Calif. 1976), which is currently on appeal to the Ninth Circuit Court of Appeals, should be compared with the court's decision in *Defoe Shipbuilding Co. v. PBGC*, ____ F.Supp. ____ (E.D. Mich. 1978).

CONNOLLY V. PENSION BENEFIT GUARANTY CORPORATION

419 F.Supp. 737 (C.D. Calif. 1976)

Order Granting Summary Judgment

DAVID W. WILLIAMS, District Judge.

The Operating Engineers Pension Trust is a joint labor-management trust created in conformance with §302(c)(5) of the Labor-Management Relations Act of 1947, as amended in 1959 [29 U.S.C. §186(c)(5)]. It was created in 1960 by a written agreement to which several contractors associations and home builders associations were signatories as employers and the international union of operating engineers, local union No. 12, as the organization representing the employees. The individual plaintiffs are trustees of the trust who have the power to administer the Pension Fund and to administer and maintain the Pension Plan which is the subject of the trust. The purpose of the trust is to create a pension fund to which a number of employers make contributions and from which employees may draw benefits when they reach a stated age of retirement.

Congress has concerned itself over the years with the problem of employee pension funds which have terminated with financial shortages resulting in an inability of many employees to receive expected benefits upon retirement. A recent Congressional effort to bring about a cure for this problem has resulted in the enactment of the Employee Retirement Income Security Act of 1974 (ERISA). Generally, this act seeks to protect the well-being and security of the millions of employees and their dependents who are affected by benefit plans. It seeks to set safeguards for the operation of plans and to establish standards for the administration of pensions in order to minimize terminations of plans and losses to beneficiaries. Section 4002 of the Act establishes within the Department of Labor a corporate body to be known as the Pension Benefit Guaranty Corporation and its purpose is to encourage the continuation and maintenance of voluntary private pension plans so as to provide for timely and uninterrupted payment of benefits to participants. Section 4005 of the Act establishes four revolving funds which are intended to serve as insurance against the failure of the particular types of pension funds which this part of ERISA is designed to cover. The corporation is empowered to prescribe insurance premium rates which it assesses against certain employers to guarantee that the pension funds created by those employers will not suffer short-fall. In the event of a termination of a pension plan of this type, the employer could be held liable for shortages in the fund up to 30% of the net worth of the employer's business. 29 U.S.C. §1362(a) and (b). Not all types of pension plans are intended to be covered under the insurance provisions of ERISA. Section 4021 (b) of the Act provides as follows:

> (b) This section does not apply to any plan—(1) which is an individual account plan, as defined in paragraph (34) of section 1002 of this title.

Paragraph (34) of Section 3 of the Act provides as follows:

> The term "individual account plan" or "defined contribution plan" means a pension plan which provides for an individual account for each participant and for benefits based solely upon the amount contributed to the participant's account, and any income, expenses, gains and losses, and any forfeitures of accounts of other participants which may be allocated to such participant's account.

Also, Section 4021(c)(1) of the Act provides as follows:

> For purposes of subsection (b)(1) of this section, the term "individual account plan" does not include a plan under which a fixed benefit is promised if the employer or his representative participated in the determination of that benefit.

Plaintiff trustees administer a pension fund for the benefit of employees within the building industry. Defendant Pension Benefit Guaranty Corporation has taken the position that the type of pension administered by plaintiff trustees is covered by the insurance provisions of ERISA and the corporation compelled plaintiff trustees to pay a premium of $12,043 into its guaranty fund. The plaintiffs contend that their pension fund comes within the exceptions set forth in paragraph (34) of Section 3 of the Act and that they are not covered by the insurance provisions. If plaintiffs' fund is not included within the exceptions just noted, the trustees would also be limited by provisions of ERISA as to the manner in which they could administer the fund over which they are trustees. Additionally, employers who contribute to plaintiffs' fund would be subject to the liability provisions of ERISA in the event of a termination of the plan.

In short, plaintiffs contend that its plan is an "individual account plan" or "defined contribution plan" as referred to in 29 U.S.C. §1002(34) while the defendant corporation contends that plaintiffs' plan is a "defined benefit plan" as defined in Section 1002(35) and is therefore covered. Plaintiffs' trustees communicated their objections to the defendant corporation upon being required to pay premiums into the corporation's Guaranty Fund, but defendant's legal staff concluded that the Operating Engineers Pension Trust is a Defined Benefit Plan for the purposes of Section 4021(b)(1) because plaintiffs' method of computing a participant's pension benefit appeared to be a formula based on service and therefore within the class of plans called defined benefit plans rather than an individual account plan. In this litigation, which seeks to have this Court determine whether plaintiffs' plan comes within the exceptions of Section 4021(b), the defendant urges that since it is the agency charged with enforcing ERISA, its determination of coverage should be given more weight than that reached by plaintiff trustees. *Griggs v. Duke Power Co.,* 401 U.S. 424, 434, 91 S.Ct. 849, 28 L.Ed.2d 158 (1971).

Agreement Establishing the Operating Engineers Pension Trust

The 1960 agreement which established the trust administered by plaintiffs (hereinafter called the "Trust Agreement") provided that each collective bargaining agreement between the union and the employers would bind the employers to abide by the Trust Agreement and to pay a stated amount into the trust with respect to each hour worked by each employee covered by the collective bargaining agreement. Article II, Section 7 of the Trust Agreement provides as follows:

> Neither the Employers nor any Signatory Association, or officer, agent, employee or committee member of the Employers or any Signatory Association, shall be liable to make Contributions to the Fund or be under any other liability to the Fund or with respect to the Pension Plan, except to the extent that he or it may be an Individual Employer required to make Contributions to the Fund with respect to his or its own individual or joint venture operations, or to the extent he or it may incur liability as a Trustee as hereinafter provided. Except as provided in Article III hereof, the liability of any Individual Employer to the Fund, or with respect to the Pension Plan, shall be limited to the payments required by the Collective Bargaining Agreements with respect to his or its individual or joint venture operations, and in no event shall he or it be liable or responsible for any portion of the Contributions due from other Individual Employers or with respect to the operations of such Individual Employers. The Individual Employers shall not be required to make any further payments or Contributions to the cost of operations of the Fund or of the Pension Plan, except as may be hereinafter provided in the Collective Bargaining Agreements.

Article VII, Section 4 of the Plan provides as follows:

> This Pension Plan has been adopted on the basis of an actuarial calculation which has established, to the extent possible, that the contributions will, if continued, be sufficient to maintain the Plan on a permanent basis. However, it is recognized that the benefits provided by this Pension Plan can be paid only to the extent that the Plan has available adequate resources for those payments. No Individual Employer has any liability, directly or indirectly to provide the benefits established by this Plan beyond the obligation of the Individual Employer to make contributions as stipulated in any Collective Bargaining Agreement. In the event that at any time the Pension Fund does not have sufficient assets to permit continued payments under this Pension Plan, nothing contained in this Pension Plan and the Trust Agreement shall be construed as obligating any Individual Employer to make benefit payments or contributions (other than the contributions for which the Individual Employer may be obligated by any Collective Bargaining Agreement) in order to provide for the benefits established by the Pension Plan. Likewise, there shall be no liability upon the Board of Trustees, individually or collectively, or upon the Employers, Signatory Association, Individual Employer, or Union to provide the benefits established by this Plan if the Pension Fund does not have the assets to make such benefit payments.

Article VIII, Section 2 of the Plan provides:

> This Plan has been adopted on the basis of an actuarial estimate which has established (to the fullest extent possible) that the income and accruals of the Fund will be fully sufficient to support this benefit plan on a permanent basis. However, it is recognized as possible that in the future the income or liabilities of the Fund may be substantially different from those previously anticipated. It is understood that this Pension Plan can be fulfilled only to the extent that the Fund has assets available from which to make payments. Consequently, the Board of Trustees may have prepared annually an Annual Actuarial Eval-

uation of the Fund and shall take the actuarial status of the Fund into account in determining amendment or modification of this Pension Plan.

Formula for Fixing Pension Amount

The monthly amount of the pension payable to a participant who is eligible for a pension in plaintiffs' plan is determined by multiplying the numbers of his respective Prior Service Credits and Pension Credits accumulated by the appropriate Pension Factor. The Plan provides for some participants to be entitled to Prior Service Credits. It also provides for certain participants to receive Pension Credits pursuant to a prescribed formula. The Pension Factor used to determine the benefit entitlement of participants is fixed from time to time. In setting the Pension Factor, the trustees take into account the investment income, gains and losses, expenses, any forfeitures by participants, the mortality experience of the Plan and the actual anticipated employer contributions and delinquencies.

Employer Contributions

Under the Pension Trust created by its signatories in 1960 the various employers would enter into collective bargaining agreements from time to time with the union. As a part of the terms of that agreement the employer obligated himself to make certain contributions into the trust fund for each of his employees, measured by the number of hours worked and any Prior Service Credits or Pension Credits to which the employee would be entitled. The amount the employer is obligated to contribute to the fund may change from time to time. This comes about because the trustees of the Plan are authorized annually to have prepared an actuarial evaluation of the fund which shall consider the actuarial status of the fund and this is taken into account in determining which amendments or modifications shall be made to the Pension Plan. If it appears from the actuarial report that the fund is in peril, the trustees have the power at a given period to compel such additional contributions into the fund from the employers as should preserve the integrity of the fund.

By its terms as quoted hereinbefore, the Plan assures the employer that his sole obligation to the fund is to pay such contributions for each employee as from time to time the plaintiff trustees shall determine are appropriate. The agreement states in clear and concise language not subject to any ambiguity that the employer's obligation to the employee for pension benefits is ended when he pays the appropriate contribution into the fund. In no way does the employer under the structure of this agreement promise the employee a defined pension benefit. Rather, it is clear that he only promises that he will pay into the fund each pay period the contribution that is prescribed by the trustees and that his obligation to the fund is then ended.

In negotiating a collective bargaining agreement there is the possibility that a union could make a demand upon an employer to extend to the employee a defined pension benefit, but such has not been done in the contract under review. In the negotiations that attended this agreement the employer demanded that his obligation be ended once he made a contribution to the individual account of the employee and the union accepted the provision. To interpret this carefully constructed agreement as not coming within the exceptions of Section 1002(34) is to force upon the employer a greater obligation and liability than he had agreed to in his contract.

Defendant argues strenuously that plaintiffs' plan is covered by the insurance provisions of ERISA because it is not a true "individual account plan" as defined by Section 1002(34). That section defines an individual account plan as a plan which provides for an individual account for each participant and for benefits based solely upon the amount contributed to the participant's account and any income, expenses, gains and losses, and any forfeitures of accounts of other participants which may be allocated to such participant's account. Defendant states that because the contributions of the employer to the individual's account are not maintained precisely like the concept of one's savings account in a bank, but instead the money is pooled by the trustees for investment purposes, and because of the computerized method employed by the trustees in reckoning the accumulated amounts contributed to the individual's account from time to time, this destroys proper characterization of the plan as an "individual account plan" or "defined contribution plan." The legislation which must guide the consideration of this dispute is lengthy and complex and represents draftsmanship that is confusing, to say the least, but a fair reading of the Act and the legislative history which preceded the enactment leads me to conclude that the structure of plaintiffs' plan properly comes within the exceptions of Section 1002 and should be characterized as an individual account plan.

Defendant claims that plaintiffs' plan does not come within Section 1002(34) because an "individual account plan" is one which provides for an individual account for each participant and for benefits based *solely* upon the amount contributed to the participant's account, and any income, expenses, gains or losses, and any forfeitures of accounts of other participants which may be allocated to each participant's account. Defendant argues that in the instant plan, benefits are not based solely upon the amount contributed to each participant's account because a part of the retirement benefit is based on past service. The parties stipulate that a participant is entitled to a pension benefit which is determined by multiplying his "Prior Service Credits" by the current "Pension Factor." An employee earns one Prior Service Credit (up to 20) for each year of covered service in the industry prior to the establishment of the plan by the 1960 agreement.

Moreover, defendant argues, the plan provides for a monthly benefit determined by multiplying each "Pension Credit" by the appropriate "Pension Factor." A "Pension Credit" is earned whenever a participant works a given number of hours. The retirement benefits payable to a participant are based directly upon the number of hours worked by the employee and the applicable rate of contributions as reflected in his accumulated Pension Credits, as well as Prior Service Credits.

Moreover, PBGC argues that there is another reason for concluding plaintiffs' plan to be a covered plan. Section 4021(c)(1) of the Act, 29 U.S.C. §1321(c)(1) provides as follows:

> For purposes of subsection (b)(1) of this section, the term "individual account plan" does not include a plan under which a fixed benefit is promised if the employer or his representative participated in the determination of that benefit.

Defendant argues that employer representatives participated in the determination of the benefit in plaintiffs' plan.

As I see it, the employer is signatory to an agreement which sets up a joint labor-management trust which has a Board of Trustees. The Trust binds the employer to pay a stated amount to the Trust for each employee covered by the collective bargaining agreement. The trustees are the ones who made a determination of the benefits, and this scheme includes no such participation on the part of the employer as is intended in Section 4021(c)(1) of the Act.

I conclude that plaintiffs' plan is a defined contribution plan under which no fixed benefit is promised; that it comes within the exception stated in 29 U.S.C. §1321(b)(1) and that plaintiffs are entitled to summary judgment. The Court further finds that defendant should be required to return to plaintiff the sum of $12,043 plus interest thereon from the date said sum was paid to defendant and that defendant, its agents, employees and representatives are enjoined from acting in any manner inconsistent with the judgment of this Court as set forth in this memorandum which, pursuant to Rule 52(a) FRCP shall take the place of findings of fact and conclusions of law.

DEFOE V. PENSION BENEFIT GUARANTY CORPORATION

____ F.Supp. ____ (E.D.Mich. 1978)

This civil action raises significant questions as to the Employee Retirement Security Act of 1974 (ERISA).

This action is brought by the Pension Benefit Guaranty Corporation (PBGC) pursuant to Sections 4042(c) and 4048(3) of ERISA, 29 U.S.C. 1342(c) and 1348(3). Petitioner seeks a judicial determination that the pension plan in question is an "employee pension benefit plan" under Section 3(2) of ERISA, 29 U.S.C. 1002(2), that the pension plan is terminated as of January 4, 1977, and appointing the PBGC as trustee of the plan.

On August 10, 1977, this action was commenced by an "Application for Order to Show Cause." In said application, petitioner requested expedited handling under Section 4003(e)(4) of ERISA, 29 U.S.C. 1303(e)(4), for hearing at the earliest practical date. In response, defendant Defoe Shipbuilding Company moved for dismissal for lack of jurisdiction. Defendant asserts that the pension plan is exempt from ERISA under Section 4021(b) of the act, 29 U.S.C. 1321(b), because the pension plan is an "individual account plan."

The parties have presented numerous exhibits as to the nature of the pension agreement which the Court will consider on the issue of its jurisdiction.

The pension plan in question was established on July 12, 1971, pursuant to a collective bargaining agreement dated June 1, 1970, between the company and union defendants. Article XX of the collective bargaining agreement required the company to fund the plan at $.05 per every working hour. By a new collective bargaining agreement effective June 1, 1973, Defoe Shipbuilding Company was required to fund the plan at the rate of $.30 per working hour as of June 1, 1975. Section 3 of Article IV of the plan provides that the company is to have no liability under the plan except to pay over to the trustee the required contributions on the per working hour basis. Section 3 of Article IV provides further that beneficiaries of the plan and employees shall look solely to the trust fund for any payments or benefits. Benefits are to be paid based on a formula of years of credited service. However, these benefits are not strictly guaranteed under the plan. Article VIII, Section 7 provides that the benefits are to be reduced on an actuarial basis if the benefit level is not appropriate in relation to contribution level. Article XII provides for an order of preference in the payment of benefits in the event the plan is terminated.

Effective September 2, 1974, ERISA was enacted by Congress. Section 2(c) of the act, 29 U.S.C. 1001(c), provides that Congress found it necessary to enact ERISA to protect interstate commerce, the federal taxing power, and the interests of participants in private pension plans by requiring accrued benefits to vest and by requiring plan termination insurance. Subchapter III of Title IV of ERISA provides for plan termination insurance, with Section 4005 of the act, 29 U.S.C. 1305, establishing four revolving funds to be used by the Pension Benefit Guaranty Corporation to insure receipt of pension benefits. Section 4062(b) of ERISA, 29 U.S.C. 1362(b), provides that any employer who maintained a plan at the time of its termination, other than a multiemployer plan, is liable to the Pension Benefit Guaranty Corporation to the extent guaranteed plan benefits exceed assets of the plan on termination, up to 30% of the employer's net worth. However, an individual account plan is exempt under Section 4021(b)(1), 29 U.S.C. 1321(b)(1).

It is the position of defendant Defoe Shipbuilding Company that these provisions of ERISA cannot be applied to it without violation of constitutional due process. Defoe asserts that because it agreed only to fund the pension plan on a per hour worked basis, application of ERISA to it to require Defoe to guarantee the plan with up to 30% of its assets would impermissibly expand its prior contractual obligations. Defoe asserts that to avoid this constitutional deficiency, the Court should narrowly construe ERISA and find that the pension plan in question is an "individual account" plan which is exempt from Title IV of ERISA under Section 4021(b)(1), 29 U.S.C. 1321(b)(1). In support of this position, defendant relies on the case of *Connolly v. Pension Benefit Guaranty Corporation,* 419 F.Supp. 737 (C.D. Cal., 1976).

An individual account plan is defined in Section 3(34) of ERISA, 29 U.S.C. 1002(34) as a form of savings account pension plan. That subsection provides:

> The term "individual account plan" or "defined contribution plan" means a pension plan which provides for an individual account for each participant and for benefits based solely upon the amount contributed to the participant's account, and any income, expenses, gains and losses, and any forfeitures of accounts of other participants which may be allocated to such participant's account.

It is clear on the uncontroverted facts that the pension fund is not an individual account plan within the plain meaning of the statutory language. The pension plan does not provide for ". . . an individual account for each participant . . ." but is rather a pooled fund in which benefits are not fixed according to the amount of an individual's contributions. The Court also finds nothing in the legislative history of ERISA which compels an interpretation different from the plain meaning of its terms.

The district court in *Connolly v. Pension Benefit Guaranty Corporation, supra,* reached a contrary conclusion and found that a similar pension fund was an individual account plan and, therefore, was exempt from Title IV of ERISA. Although finding the legislative history to be ". . . lengthy, complex and represents draftmanship that is confusing, to say the least . . ." (419 F.Supp. at 741), the Court based its holding on ". . . a fair reading of the Act and the legislative history . . ." (419 F.Supp. at 741). However, a fair reading of the act does not suggest any support for the district court's conclusion, as the holding is contrary to the stated language.

The basis of the district court's decision is *Connolly,* and the thrust of the company's argument in this case, is that ERISA should not be interpreted in a manner that would impose potential liability on a company except to the extent the company has agreed to the same. The district court states (419 F.Supp. at 740):

> To interpret this carefully constructed agreement as not coming within the exceptions of Section 1002(34) is to force upon the employer a greater obligation and liability than he had agreed to in his contract.

This approach limiting the scope of ERISA to the extent of a contributing employer's prior agreement fails to take into consideration the purpose of the act. The primary purpose is not to hold employers liable but to require that accrued benefits vest and to provide for insurance if a plan fails. It is only as an incident of these purposes that an employer can be held liable for any deficiency in the plan, and the beneficiaries of the plan are entitled to the protection of ERISA regardless of whether the employer can be required constitutionally to fund any deficiency in the plan.

It is not necessary to determine the constitutional issue at this time. The PBGC is not requesting any seizure of any assets of defendant company but is seeking a judicial determination that the plan is terminated and to have itself appointed as trustee. If and when the PBGC petitions the Court to impose any liability on the company, the company can raise its constitutional defenses. However, the company bears a heavy burden in this regard, as a prerequisite to any finding of a constitutional deficiency based on any "taking" is a showing that Congress has excluded the normal remedy in the Court of Claims under the Tucker Act. *See Regional Rail Organization Act Cases,* 419 U.S. 102, 95 S.Ct. 335, 42 L.Ed.2d 320 (1974).

For the reasons stated, the Court finds that the pension fund in question is not an individual account plan or defined contribution plan. Instead, the plan is an employee pension benefit plan under Section 3(2), 29 U.S.C. 1002(2), which is not exempt by reason of Section 4021(b)(1), 29 U.S.C. 1321(b)(1). The plan is subject to the provisions of Title IV of ERISA, and this Court has jurisdiction over the subject matter pursuant to 29 U.S.C. 1303(e)(3), provided that the requisite nexus with interstate commerce is established.

Defendant company's motion to dismiss for lack of jurisdiction is DENIED. In order to proceed forthwith in this action, the parties shall appear before the Court for an evidentiary hearing for the remaining issues in this petition on Tuesday, March 7, 1978, at 2:00 p.m. in the Federal Building, Flint, Michigan, at which time the Court will determine finally the remaining issues, to wit:

1. Whether defendant company is an employer engaged in commerce or defendant union represents employees engaged in commerce within the meaning of 29 U.S.C. 1321 (a)(1):
2. Whether the pension plan should be adjudicated as terminated as of January 4, 1977, and the PBGC appointed as trustee.

IT IS SO ORDERED.

James Harvey

JAMES HARVEY
United States District Judge

Title IV provides for three insurance programs for covered plans. One is a mandatory insurance program guaranteeing participants' "basic" vested or nonforfeitable benefits within certain limits. *See* ERISA §4022(a). Another insurance program, which has not been established yet, will cover contingent employer liability under ERISA if a covered plan terminates with insufficient assets to pay the guaranteed benefits. *See* ERISA §4023. The third program, which may be established at the PBGC's discretion, will insure "non-basic" benefits. *See* ERISA §4022(c).

Title IV also requires the PBGC to furnish advice to individuals on the economic desirability of establishing individual retirement accounts under §§408 and 409 of the Internal Revenue Code of 1954.

Financing

PBGC's income is derived from premiums paid by covered plans, recoveries through contingent employer liability of up to 30% of the net worth of the employer and earnings on PBGC investments. *See* ERISA §4005(b). ERISA provided premium rate schedules for the first two years after enactment (September 2, 1974), after which time the PBGC was required to prescribe premium rates sufficient to generate revenue for its insurance function. Initially, ERISA set the rate for premiums at $1 per year per participant for single employer plans and 50¢ for multiemployer plans for the first and second full plan years after enactment. Effective for plan years beginning on or after January 1, 1978, single employer defined benefit pension plans must pay an annual premium per participant of $2.60. The rate for multiemployer plan participants has not been changed. The PBGC is currently trying to determine the appropriate premium.

Guaranteed Basic Benefits

In implementing its role under Title IV to define guaranteed (i.e., basic) benefits, the PBGC has decided that such definition will cover normal retirement and certain early retirement benefits, disability retirement benefits and benefits for survivors for deceased plan participants. However, payments by the PBGC to participants in defined benefit plans with an insufficiency in terms of assets to cover guaranteed benefits are limited by §4022 of ERISA. Section 4022(b)(3) provides:

> The amount of monthly benefits described in subsection (1) provided by a plan, which are guaranteed under this section with respect to a participant, shall not have an actuarial value which exceeds the actuarial value of a monthly benefit in the form of a life annuity commencing at age 65 equal to the lesser of—

> (A) his average monthly gross income from his employer during the five consecutive calendar year period, or if less, during the number of calendar years in such period in which he actively participates in the plan during which his gross income from that employer was greater than any other period with that employer determined by dividing ½ of the sum of all such gross income by the number of such calendar years in which he had such gross income or
> (B) $750 multiplied by a fraction, the numerator of which is the contribution in benefit base (determined under §230 of the Social Security Act) in effect the plan terminates, the denominator of which is such contribution and benefit base in effect in calendar year 1974.

For example, if a plan terminated during 1977, the guaranteed monthly benefit cannot exceed the actuarial value of a monthly life annuity of $937.50 starting at age 65, or 100% of a participant's highest consecutive five year average monthly gross income, whichever is less.

The statutory $750 amount has increased by virtue of the increase in the Social Security base (e.g., $750 × 16,500/13,200). In 1978 and in subsequent years, the maximum guaranteed benefit will reflect changes in the Social Security contribution and benefit base.

Termination Procedure

ERISA requires the plan administrator to notify the PBGC at least ten days prior to the proposed date of termination, and to include plan and trust identifying information plus a detailed description of the plan's status with the notice of intent to terminate. Upon filing for termination, the plan's assets and guaranteed benefit liabilities are valued. A determination is made by the PBGC within 90 days after the proposed date of termination regarding the sufficiency of assets to pay guaranteed benefits. The 90 day period may be extended by agreement by the PBGC and the plan administrator.

Where assets are sufficient to pay guaranteed basic benefits, the plan administrator is responsible for winding up the affairs of the plan. When the PBGC is unable to determine that the assets of the plan are sufficient to pay the guaranteed basic benefits, a trustee, appointed by consent of the plan administrator and the PBGC, or by a federal district court, is responsible for liquidating the plan. In all terminations, plan assets must be allocated as specified in §4044 of ERISA.

Reportable Events

Certain types of events which may reflect potential problems with respect to a plan must be reported to the PBGC within 30 days after a plan administrator learns of them. Such reportable events include loss of tax qualification; any plan amendment which may result in a decrease in benefits; a decrease in active participants by more than 20% within a plan year, or by more than 25% from the preceding plan year; a determination from the Internal Revenue Service that there has been a plan termination or partial termination for tax purposes; or a failure to meet minimum funding standards.

Contingent Employer Liability and Insurance

If a terminating plan has insufficient assets to pay the guaranteed benefits, the employer is liable to the PBGC for the payments made to provide such guaranteed benefits, up to 30% of the employer's net worth. Section 4062(b) provides:

> any employer to which this section applies shall be liable to the [PBGC], in an amount equal to the lesser of—
> (1) the excess of—
> (A) the current value of the plan's benefits guaranteed under this title on the date of termination over
> (B) the current value of the plan's assets allocable to such benefits on the date of termination, or
> (2) 30% of the net worth of the employer determined as of a day, chosen by the corporation but not more than 120 days prior to the date of termination, computed without regard to any liability under this section.

One of the more important controversies resulting from plan termination insurance coverage is the extent to which PBGC liability extends to other corporations in a controlled group. the bankruptcy judge's decision in *PBGC v. Avon Sole Company*, which is currently before the District Court for the District of Massachusetts, illustrates the importance of this issue.

PENSION BENEFIT GUARANTY CORPORATION V. AVON SOLE CO.

____ F.Supp. ____ (D. Mass. 1977)

LAVIEN, Bankruptcy Judge and Special Master

This opinion concerns itself with the possible liability of a bankrupt corporation, jointly and severally with its parent and brother-sister corporations, for pension underfunding pursuant to the Employee Retirement Income Security Act of 1974.

Prior to 1975, the Avon Sole Company (Avon) engaged in the manufacture of shoe soling material in its plant in Massachusetts. In 1973 Avon formed

Tenn-ERO Corporation (Tenn-ERO), a wholly owned subsidiary,[1] to manufacture soling material in a new plant in Tennessee. During its fiscal year ending September, 1974, Avon and Tenn-ERO (the Bankrupts) suffered consolidated operating losses of $800,000. Losses increased in the first quarter of 1975 and as a result management decided to discontinue manufacturing operations in Massachusetts. The Avon plant closed on March 25, 1975, but heavy losses continued, and on June 18, 1975 Avon and Tenn-ERO filed petitions in this Court pursuant to Chapter XI of the Bankruptcy Act, 11 U.S.C. §701 *et seq.* Subsequently, on March 22, 1976, Avon and Tenn-ERO were adjudicated bankrupts.

At the time of the closing of the Massachusetts plant, Avon was a party to a pension plan agreement, dated May 4, 1959, covering its unionized employees, all of whom worked in the Massachusetts plant. Pursuant to the Employee Retirement Income Security Act of 1974 (ERISA), P.L. 93-406, 29 U.S.C. §1001 *et seq.* Avon notified the Pension Benefit Guaranty Corporation (PBGC) of the impending discontinuance of operations in Massachusetts and the need to terminate the pension plan. Under ERISA the PBGC is charged with the administration of the pension plan termination process and the distribution of plan benefits after termination.[2]

The PBGC filed a proof of claim in the bankruptcy proceeding of Avon and Tenn-ERO on February 6, 1976, claiming that pursuant to ERISA §4062 the debtors were liable to the PBGC for an estimated $717,500.

Title IV of ERISA provides that upon the termination of a pension plan, the PBGC is to assume the plan's administration and, if necessary, to pay any guaranteed pension benefits if the plan itself has not been sufficiently funded to pay them. ERISA §4062 provides that an employer who maintains an underfunded pension plan which terminates is liable to the PBGC for an amount that is either the deficit between the plan's guaranteed benefits and its assets (in other words, the out of pocket expense of the PBGC) or 30% of the employer's net worth, whichever is less.[3]

In September, 1968, when Ouimet Corporation acquired the stock in Avon, the Avon pension plan had unfunded vested benefits in the amount of $92,000. In September, 1974, when ERISA became effective, the underfunding amounted to $606,929.53. On March 25, 1975, upon plan termination, the underfunding was reduced to $552,339.64.

The cause of the underfunding was basically threefold. First, in 1959 when the plan was instituted participants were given credit for past years of service with Avon. So the plan owed benefits before contributions even began. Second, in 1969, pursuant to a collective bargaining agreement, automatic benefit increases were written into the plan and these had not been fully amortized by the date of termination. And third, the plan's assets had been invested in certain equity and fixed-income securities, and at the date of termination the market value of these securities was approximately $75,000 less than their costs. None of these factors, on its face, represented any illegal or improper conduct on the part of Avon. In fact, ERISA, recognizing that plan underfunding for

---

1. Although separate in name, the companies were for all practical purposes one, and have so been treated by all parties throughout these proceedings.

2. On April 20, 1976, the PBGC was appointed trustee of the Avon Sole Company Pension Plan pursuant to ERISA §4041 by Judge Tauro of the U.S. District Court for the District of Massachusetts.

3. Liability of Employer

Sec. 4062. (a) This section applies to any employer who maintained a plan (other than a multiemployer plan) at the time it was terminated, but does not apply—

(1) to an employer who maintained a plan with respect to which he paid the annual premium described in Section 4006(a)(2)(B) for each of the 5 plan years immediately preceding the plan year during which the plan terminated unless the conditions imposed by the corporation on the payment of coverage under Section 4023 do not permit such coverage to apply under the circumstances, or

(2) to the extent of any liability arising out of the insolvency of an insurance company with respect to an insurance contract.

(b) Any employer to which this section applies shall be liable to the corporation, in an amount equal to the lesser of—

(1) the excess of—

(A) the current value of the plan's benefits guaranteed under this title on the date of termination over

(B) the current value of the plan's assets allocable to such benefits on the date of termination, or

(2) 30 percent of the net worth of the employer determined as of a day, chosen by the corporation but not more than 120 days prior to the date of termination, computed without regard to any liability under this section.

(c) For purposes of subsection (b)(2) the net worth of an employer is—

reasons such as these would often be the case, provides for the amortization of past underfunding over a period of thirty to forty years. ERISA §302. The reason the Avon pension plan terminated in an underfunded state in this case was because it terminated before amortization under ERISA was complete.

During February and March 1976, the PBGC examined the books and records of the Bankrupts as well as those of certain related business enterprises—Ouimet Corporation, Ouimet Stay & Leather Company, Ouimet Welting Company and the Emil R. Ouimet Wareham Trust (collectively the Ouimet Group).

At all times relevant to this case, Ouimet Corporation owned 100% of the stock of Avon/Tenn-ERO. The Ouimet Stay & Leather Company owned 100% of the stock of Ouimet Welting Company and 50% of the stock of Brockton Plastics Company. Emil R. Ouimet owned in excess of 80% of the outstanding stock of Ouimet Corporation and the Ouimet Stay & Leather Company, and 100% of the stock of the Emil R. Ouimet Wareham Trust.[4]

On March 15, 1976, the PBGC filed an amended proof of claim in the instant proceedings in the amount of $552,340 and based this figure on the treatment of the Ouimet Group as well as the Bankrupts as the plan employer for purposes of ERISA §4062.

On March 22, 1976, Ouimet Corporation and Ouimet Stay & Leather Company filed proofs of claim in the Avon and Tenn-ERO bankruptcy proceeding alleging that if Ouimet Corporation and Ouimet Stay & Leather Company were held liable to the PBGC as a result of the Avon pension plan termination, they were subrogated to the rights of the PBGC against the Bankrupts. The Trustee in Bankruptcy filed a cross claim asserting that if the PBGC's claim against the Bankrupts were allowed, the estate had a right to collect from Ouimet Corporation and Ouimet Stay & Leather Company in the amount distributed to the PBGC. Ouimet Corporation and Ouimet Stay & Leather answered the cross claim with denials.

On March 31, 1976, the PBGC commenced a civil action against the Ouimet Group in the United States District Court, pursuant to ERISA §4068(d), to collect the alleged §4062 liability of the Ouimet Group. The PBGC then filed a complaint in the Bankruptcy Court seeking relief from the automatic stay in bankruptcy in order to proceed against the Bankrupts by joining them in the District Court action.

---

(1) determined on whatever basis best reflects, in the determination of the corporation, the current status of the employer's operations and prospects at the time chosen for determining the net worth of the employer, and

(2) increased by the amount of any transfers of assets made by the employer determined by the corporation to be improper under the circumstances, including any such transfers which would be inappropriate under the Bankruptcy Act if the employer were the subject of a proceeding under that Act.

(d) For purposes of this section the following rules apply in the case of certain corporate reorganizations.

(1) If an employer ceases to exist by reason of a reorganization which involves a mere change in identity, form, or place of organization, however effected, a successor corporation resulting from such reorganization shall be treated as the employer to whom this section applies.

(2) If an employer ceases to exist by reason of a liquidation into a parent corporation, the parent corporation shall be treated as the employer to whom this section applies.

(3) If an employer ceases to exist by reason of a merger, consolidation, or division, the successor corporation or corporations shall be treated as the employer to whom this section applies.

(e) If an employer ceases operations at a facility in any location and, as a result of such cessation of operations, more than 20 percent of the total number of his employees who are participants under a plan established and maintained by him are separated from employment, the employer shall be treated with respect to that plan as if he were a substantial employer under a plan under which more than one employer makes contributions and the provisions of sections 4063, 4064, and 4065 shall apply.

4.

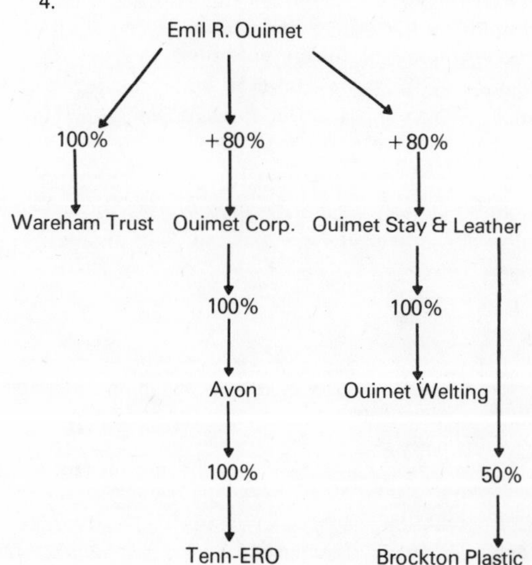

The procedural posture of the instant case embodies an objection by the Trustee in Bankruptcy to the PBGC's claim against the Bankrupts, the complaint filed by the PBGC in this Court seeking relief from the automatic stay of Bankruptcy Act §11 and Rule 401 of the Rules of Bankruptcy Procedure, and a reference to this Court as Master in the U.S. District Court action of the PBGC against the Ouimet Group. The issues as well as the role of the Court in all these matters are substantially identical, and for purposes of convenience they will be dealt with as a single proceeding to determine the validity and amount of any liability in connection with the termination of the Avon Sole Company Pension Plan.

Trial of this case began on October 19, 1976 and consumed all or part of twelve days. At least 257 pages of legal memoranda have been filed at various stages of the proceedings.

All counsel have labored diligently and competently in full recognition that this is a case of first impression, not only in this district, but, because of the novelty of the Act, in the United States. The case has important implications in bankruptcy administration as well as in the implementation of ERISA and the viability of certain concepts of corporate law.

ERISA provides for the payment to the PBGC for monies spent to pay benefits due from a terminated pension plan whose own assets were insufficient. Payment must come from the employer and the amount is limited so as not to exceed 30% of the employer's net worth. ERISA §4062. It is conceded, and the Court so finds, that Avon and Tenn-ERO, the Bankrupts, had no positive net worth at the relevant date so that unless the Ouimet Group may be included as the responsible employer, the PBGC cannot recover any of its benefit expenditures. If the Ouimet Group is included as the employer, then the question of the meaning and proper application of the waiver provision of ERISA §4004(f) must be resolved. Finally, if the Ouimet Group becomes part of the employer and waiver of liability is inappropriate, the net worth of the employer must be established in order to determine the propriety of the PBGC's claim.

I

The Pension Benefit Guaranty Corporation is a "body corporate" in the U.S. Department of Labor, ERISA §4002(a), and as such it is an agency within the meaning of §2a of the Administrative Procedure Act (APA), 5 U.S.C. §551. *See also,* Joint Explanatory Statement of the Committee of Conference, House Conference Report, No. 1280, 93rd Cong., 2d Sess. (1974). Because it involves the actions of an administrative agency, this case must be decided in light of the constraints existing both upon agency action and a court's examination of that action.

The frame work for judicial review of agency action is supplied by APA §10, 5 U.S.C. §§701, 702. That section affords a right of review to a person adversely affected by agency action "except to the extent that (1) statutes preclude judicial review; or (2) agency action is committed to agency discretion by law." The U.S. Supreme Court has enunciated the principle that only on a showing of "clear and convincing" intent to preclude court review should courts refuse to review agency action. *Dunlop v. Bachowski,* 421 U.S. 560 (1975); *Abbott Laboratories v. Gardner,* 387 U.S. 136 (1967); *Heikkila v. Barber,* 345 U.S. 229 (1953).

Professor Davis argues that this statement of the Court is somewhat more extreme than is justified by the majority of Supreme Court cases in this area; however, even he defines the general rule of the Supreme Court as establishing a presumption of reviewability to be rebutted by showing either a contrary Congressional intent or the inappropriateness of judicial consideration. 4 K. Davis, *Administrative Law Treatise* §§28.08 and 28.16-1 (1958 and Supplements) (hereinafter cited as *Davis*). Professor Jaffe concurs in this presumption of reviewability. L. Jaffe, *Judicial Control of Administrative Action* at 336 and 372-3 (1965) (hereinafter cited as *Jaffe*).

Thus, in the instant case, a finding that ERISA fails to evidence a Congressional intent, express or implied, to preclude review, together with a finding that review is not inappropriate, are enough to justify judicial review under APA §10.

In the case of ERISA, it is unnecessary to look beyond the words of the Act itself to determine the propriety of general court review. Title IV §4003(f) provides that an employer adversely affected by any action of the PBGC may bring an action in the appropriate court.[5] In the instant

5. Actually, the express words of ERISA §4003(f) are slightly confusing because of an apparent typographical error:

> Any participant, beneficiary, plan administrator, or *employee* adversely affected by any portion of the corporation [PBGC] by a receiver or trustee appointed by the corporation, with respect to a plan in which such participant, beneficiary, plan administrator or *employer* has an interest, may bring an action against the corporation, receiver or trustee in the appropriate court. (Emphasis added.)

case, the Bankrupts and the Ouimet Group, having been declared liable by the PBGC pursuant to ERISA §4062, have clearly been adversely affected by an agency action and this Court may therefore examine the validity of the PBGC's action.

Once reviewability has been established, it is necessary to define the scope of that review.

The instant case involves the assessment by an administrative agency of a monetary liability based on factual findings obtained from examination of detailed and complicated financial data. At no time prior to the assessment were the original parties offered the opportunity to appear before the agency to explain their financial records or defend their positions. Therefore, before any liability may be finally determined, such a hearing is a constitutional necessity. *Bi-Metallic Co. v. Colorado,* 239 U.S. 441 (1915); *Londoner v. Denver,* 210 U.S. 373 (1908).

Professor Davis formulates this due process hearing requirement into an adjudicative/legislative dichotomy, saying that when an agency adjudicates facts a trial type hearing is required. 1 *Davis* §7.04. Professor Jaffe speculates that categorization often confuses more than clarifies, but accepts the basic due process pronouncement:

> When a person is the object of an administrative order which will be enforced by a writ levying upon his property or person, he is at some point entitled to a judicial test of legality.
>
> *Jaffe* at 384.

This is not to say, however, that the hearing must always occur at the agency level. So long as the aggrieved party is provided a *de novo* hearing prior to the enforcement of the agency action, the constitutional requisites have been met. *Nickey v. Mississippi,* 292 U.S. 393 (1934); *Phillips v. Commissioner,* 283 U.S. 589 (1931); *Hagar v. Reclamation District,* 111 U.S. 701 (1884). Thus, when an agency assessed a tax against an individual, the U.S. Supreme Court has held that the failure of the agency to provide the taxpayer a hearing prior to the assessment did not violate the process requirements because in order to actually enforce the assessment the agency had to resort to the courts at which time a full hearing occurred. *Hagar v. Reclamation District, supra.*

The instant case is similar to those in which the Supreme Court has held that *de novo* court review of agency action satisfies due process. The PBGC, without any prior evidentiary hearing, assessed a liability against the Bankrupts and the Ouimet Group. To enforce collection of that assessment the instant court action has been necessary. ERISA §4068(d). Therefore, this Court, in offering all parties the opportunity to present their cases, must consider the evidence presented *de novo. Ewing v. Mytinger & Casselberry,* 339 U.S. 594 (1950); *Lichter v. U.S.,* 334 U.S. 742 (1948); *Nickey v. Mississippi, supra.*

In light of the *de novo* hearing requirement, the Court's scope of review of the PBGC's action is fairly broad. To the extent necessary to its decision, the Court "shall decide all relevant questions of law, interpret constitutional and statutory provisions and determine the meaning or applicability of the terms of an agency action." APA §10 (c), 5 U.S.C. §706. The Court shall set aside an agency action if it is, *inter alia,* arbitrary, capricious, contrary to constitutional right or "unwarranted by the facts to the extent that the facts are subject to a trial *de novo* by the reviewing court." *Id.*

The standards for this Court's scope of review must take into account that the agency has already acted, albeit without a hearing. Even the Court's *de novo* reception of evidence cannot ignore the agency's findings. Thus, unless the weight of the evidence presented in the *de novo* hearing supports a contrary finding, the Court must uphold the agency action. It is the burden of the aggrieved party to establish that the agency action complained of violates statutory or procedural requirements or is unwarranted according to the weight of the evidence. *Redman v. U.S.,* 507 F.2d 1007 (5th Cir. 1975).

Further, as part of the consideration of its scope of review of the agency's interpretation of a statute, the Court takes note of the deference a judicial tribunal must extend to an administrative agency's specialized expertise. The rule is venerable that a reviewing court must give great weight to the interpretation of a statute by the agency charged with its administration. *Columbia Broadcasting System, Inc. v. Democratic National Committee,* 412 U.S. 94 (1973).

It is also well established, however, that the courts are the final authorities on the issue of stat-

---

It is obvious that there is an error either in the word "employee" or "employer." Since §3(7) of ERISA defines a "participant" to include an employee, to repeat that term would be purposeless. To include employers, however, would be totally consistent with the section's obvious intent to make court review available to all those who could suffer under Title IV. It would seem, therefore, that the error lies in the word "employee," which should read "employer." The PBGC, in open court, has concurred with this interpretation.

utory construction and as such the courts are not bound by an administrative interpretation. Especially is this true when the agency interpretation creates internal statutory inconsistencies or is inconsistent with a statutory mandate, frustrates congressional policy or creates serious constitutional questions. *Morton v. Ruiz,* 415 U.S. 199 (1974); *Volkswagonwerk v. Federal Maritime Commission,* 390 U.S. 261 (1968); Annot. 39 L. Ed. 2d 942 (1975). The Court takes note in the instant case of the PBGC's youth and the consequent dearth of established agency policy and precedent that existed at the pertinent time in areas of its jurisdiction. To a certain extent this inexperience must discourage notions of agency expertise that are part of the justification for a court's deference. Furthermore, to the extent that the Court's review concerns the meaning of the words of a statute, for instance, the definition of the term "employer" or the scope of the waiver provision within ERISA, such questions are traditionally a matter of judicial competence and concern. *Jaffe* at 576 *et seq.*

II

The liability which the PBGC asserts in this case arises out of the employer liability provisions of ERISA, specifically §4062.

The PBGC claims that liability under ERISA §4062 must be assessed not only against the Bankrupt, who was the actual employer, but also against the Ouimet Group because the term "employer" as used in §4062 means all trades or businesses under common control within the terms of ERISA §4001(b).[6] The PBGC apparently maintains that in light of ERISA §4001(b), the term "employer" wherever it appears in Title IV of ERISA encompasses the control group concept.

In regulations promulgated by the PBGC pursuant to ERISA §4001(b), the PBGC adopts the regulations issued by the Treasury Department under §414(c) of the Internal Revenue Code. 29 CFR §26.12 (Supp. 1976). The Treasury Department defines "trade or business under common control" in Temp. Reg. 11.414(c). *See also,* Proposed Regs. 1.414 *et seq.* CCH Fed. Tax Rept. para. 2669F.

The Treasury Regulations delineate three groups of business relationships as common control situations. The first two, parent-subsidiary and brother-sister, are self explanatory. The third, the combined group, consists of three or more businesses where each is a member of either a parent-subsidiary or brother-sister group and at least one is *both* the parent in a parent-subsidiary group and a member of a brother-sister group. The Regulation gives the following example: A, an individual, owns substantially all the stock of ABC and DEF corporations. ABC owns substantially all the stock of subsidiary X corporation. A, ABC, X and DEF are members of a combined group since each is a member of either a parent-subsidiary or brother-sister group and ABC is both a parent in a parent-subsidiary group and a "sibling" in a brother-sister group.

In the instant case the relationship of the entities places them in the combined group category of Temp. Treas. Reg. 11.414(c).

The PBGC concedes that unless the term "employer" in the liability provision of ERISA §4062 is defined to include control group entities, the PBGC would not succeed in recouping any of the funds it may spend to pay benefits in the underfunded Avon Sole Company Pension Plan.

ERISA envisions that the PBGC will assume the administration and disbursement of a terminated pension plan whose assets are insufficient to cover all guaranteed benefits. ERISA further provides that within certain limits, the PBGC may recover from the former plan employer the funds it is forced to spend in funding the plan. The PBGC is never permitted to hold an employer liable for an amount in excess of 30% of the employer's net worth determined as of a date within 120 days of the plan termination. ERISA §4062(b). The PBGC through its own valuation has concluded that the Bankrupts had no positive net worth on the net worth valuation date, December 31, 1974. Thus, if the employer under §4062 is the Bankrupts alone, the PBGC recovers nothing and a dividend will be paid to the Bankrupts' creditors.

---

6. ERISA §4001(b) states:

An individual who owns the entire interest in an unincorporated trade or business is treated as his own employer, and a partnership is treated as the employer of each partner who is an employee within the meaning of section 401(c)(l) of the Internal Revenue Code of 1954. *For purposes of this title, under regulations prescribed by the corporation, all employees of trades or businesses (whether or not incorporated) which are under common control shall be treated as employed by a single employer and all such trades and businesses as a single employer.* The regulations prescribed under the preceding sentence shall be consistent and coextensive with regulations prescribed for similar purposes by the Secretary of the Treasury under section 414(c) of the Internal Revenue Code of 1954.

(Emphasis added.)

If, on the other hand, the employer consists of the Bankrupts and the Ouimet Group, the net worth valuation, at least according to the PBGC, increases to such a degree that the PBGC claims it can recover the entire potential out of pocket expense of $552,339.64, and the creditors of the Bankrupt would not receive a dividend.[6a]

The Bankrupts and the Ouimet Group, of course, strenuously argue that, for liability purposes under ERISA, only the Bankrupts are the employer. They further argue that even if the PBGC prevails as to the definition of "employer," ERISA §4004(f)(4) requires that all liability in this case be waived. Finally, they contend that if unwaived liability does exist, under a proper calculation of net worth that liability is considerably less than that which the PBGC demands.[7]

Because ERISA has been law for such a short period, the courts have had little opportunity to interpret its manifold and complex provisions. This Court has been unable to discover any judicial decision relating to the extent of employer liability under ERISA §4062.[8]

After careful examination of the express statutory language of ERISA, its legislative history and the public policies it is intended to advance, this Court is convinced that ERISA §4062 levies liability for the PBGC's assumption of pension plan payments only against the person or corporation acting directly as an employer in relation to an employee benefit plan, or, as provided in §4062(d), against certain successor in interest corporations when the direct plan employer attempts to avoid liability. In the instant case the employer for §4062 purposes would be the Bankrupts.

This Court in the first instance is guided by the basic principle that a statute's plain language is the primary indicator of its meaning. *Massachusetts Financial Services, Inc. v. Securities Investors Protection Corp.,* 545 F.2d 754 (1st Cir. 1976).

ERISA §4062(a)-(c) establishes a formula for determining employer liability. §4062(d) expands that liability in instances of certain corporate reorganizations. If, as the PBGC contends, ERISA §4001(b) and its control group concept applies to ERISA §4062, then §4062(d)(2) becomes superfluous. Under control group theory a parent-subsidiary relationship would already create liability in both businesses, so that the subsequent merger of the subsidiary into the parent would not affect the parent's liability. And if the control group concept of §4001(b) is extended to §4062, not only would §4062(d)(2) be superfluous, but its language would directly conflict with such concepts. §4062(d)(2) speaks of an "employer" and its "parent." But under control group theory, the word "employer" already includes both a parent and subsidiary. No reading of §4062(d)(2) can be reconciled with a simultaneous application of the control group concept.

It is an accepted principle of statutory interpretation that general provisions in one part of a statute must yield to specific provisions in another part. *MacEvoy v. U.S.,* 322 U.S. 102 (1943); *Baltimore National Bank v. State Tax Commissioner of Maryland,* 297 U.S. 209 (1936).

> Ascertainment of congressional intent with respect to the standard of liability created by a particular section . . . [of an act] . . . must therefore rest primarily on the language of that section. *Ernst & Ernst v. Hochfelder,* 425 U.S. 185, 200 (1976). *See also, Santa Fe Industries, Inc. v. Green,* ___ U.S. ___, 45 U.S.L.W. 4317 (1977).

6a. The bankrupt estate has assets of $374,000 and unsecured claims of $2,200,000. The PBGC's claim is given tax priority status, ERISA §4068(b)(2), so that after costs of administration the PBGC's priority would exhaust the assets leaving nothing for the unsecured creditors.

7. The PBGC, defining net worth in terms of fair market value and assigning a zero net worth to the Bankrupts, concludes that the net worth of the control group on the net worth valuation date was so great that 30% of that value is not exceeded by the entire $552,339.64 potential plan underfunding to be borne by the PBGC.

The Bankrupts and the Ouimet Group dispute the PBGC's conclusion. They variously contend that net worth is based on book value, that the net worth valuation date chosen by the PBGC was erroneous, that too many businesses were included in the control group and, even accepting the PBGC's position as to all of the aforementioned, that the Ouimet Group's net worth was far less than that calculated by the PBGC and that when the *negative* net worth of the Bankrupts is subtracted therefrom, the total net worth of the control group falls between $464,000 and $650,000 and that the liability is 30% of that net worth—an amount far less than $552,339.64.

8. This situation is not likely to continue much longer. Congressman John Erlenborn, one intimately involved in the drafting and enactment of ERISA, in a recent speech before the Midwest Pension Conference, pointed to a host of problems associated with the employer liability provisions of ERISA. He suggested that, as they now exist, the employer liability provisions should be renamed the employer extermination provisions. This suggests the probability, as conglomerates attempt to clarify their potential liabilities, of future litigation and possible Congressional action in this area.

The inability to reconcile ERISA §4001(b) with ERISA §4062(d)(2) is but one support of the position that the §4001(b) control group reference was intended to apply to some section other than §4062 and not as a general definition of "employer" in Title IV.

Indiscriminate application of control group theory throughout Title IV would torture the meaning of certain sections in that title. For example, under ERISA §4004(e)(4) the PBGC is given the limited authority to waive an employer's liability in certain instances when "the employer was not able, as a practical matter, to continue the plan." It is obvious that the term "employer" in the above quote refers to the direct employer who is the only one who, as a practical matter, is or is not able to continue a plan. *See also,* ERISA §§4023(d), 4044(d)(1) and 4047.

An examination of the semantic structure of §4001 reveals that while §4001 is headed "Definitions" it is subdivided into a typical definition section and a section enunciating the control group concept. If the statute meant the word "employer" wherever it appeared in Title IV to include all trades or businesses under common control it would have included the term "employer" in §4001(a) as a definition and defined it to apply throughout Title IV. Instead, the control group concept is separated in §4001(b) and states in pertinent part:

> For purposes of this title, *under regulations prescribed by the corporation* [PBGC], all employees of trades or business . . . which are under common control shall be treated as employed by a single employer and all such trades and businesses as a single employer.
> (Emphasis added.)

The PBGC's regulations under ERISA §4001(b) simply co-opt the Treasury Regulations under Internal Revenue Code §414(c). *See supra.* They define the control group but do not establish the extent of its application in Title IV. Thus, at present, it is not known to what sections in Title IV the control group concept applies. If Congress had in mind the possibility of control group liability under §4062, it left it to the PBGC to establish the proper application of that concept in light of all the various provisions in Title IV that would have to be considered in order to maintain consistency. In the interim, or permanently if the PBGC declined to promulgate regulations, the successor in interest provision of §4062(d) would prevent intercorporate abuse of the pension insurance program.

Further support for the proposition that ERISA §4062 employer liability does not comprehend the control group is the omission from Title IV of a provision for apportionment of employer liability. It is difficult to imagine that the draftors would provide for control group liability without also dealing with its apportionment. Judicial precedent on joint and several liability, if that is indeed the standard for apportionment, is neither well defined nor consistent.[9] Judicial efforts to apportion control group liability without statutory guidelines would result in inconsistency and unpredictability in a statutory scheme whose general comprehensiveness belies such a situation.

In light of the ambiguity created by ERISA §4001(b) and the unreasonable interpretation its wholesale application would bring to certain Title IV provisions, especially §4062, the Court may resort to legislative history to assist its construction. *Massachusetts Financial Services, Inc. v. Securities Investors Protection Corp., supra.*

The policy justification for holding an employer liable for the termination of an underfunded pension plan has been frequently enunciated. The intention is to "preclude abuse by [the employer] shifting the financial burden to the plan termination insurance program [and the PBGC] despite the fact that the employer had available funds to continue funding the plan." House Education & Labor Committee Report, No. 533, 93rd Cong., 2d Sess. at 15 (1973). Put another way, the employer liability provision deters "unrealistic promises" by encouraging an employer considering a pension plan to carefully determine if he can afford it, because if he can't and it is terminated he will be liable for its underfunding. Senate Finance Committee Report, No. 383, 93rd Cong., 2d Sess. at 117 (1973).

The Report of the House-Senate Conference Committee, H. Rep. No. 1280, 93rd Cong., 2d Sess. (1973), is silent as to the policy behind the assessment of employer liability generally, but since the Conference version of ERISA retained the basic framework of employer liability provided in both the House and Senate versions, it is safe to assume that the House and Senate rationale was adopted. In discussions on the floors of both the House and Senate just prior to passage of ERISA the above stated policy was outlined in support of the employer liability provisions of the

9. Compare, for example, *Lorimer v. Julius Knack Coal Co.,* 246 Mich. 214, 224 N.W. 362 (1929) with *United States Fidelity and Guaranty Co. v. Naylor,* 237 F. 314 (8th Cir. 1916).

Conference Bill. 120 Cong. Rec. H. 1126—H. 1175 and S. 15737—S. 15774 (1974).

In the early House and Senate versions of ERISA no mention is made of control group theory in the employer liability provisions. *See,* 3 U.S. Code Cong. & Admin. News 4639 *et seq.* (1974). On the other hand, in these versions, each contains the precursor to present §4062(d). *See* House Education & Labor Committee Report, No. 533, 93rd Cong., 2d Sess. (1973); Senate Labor & Public Welfare Committee Report, No. 127, 93rd Cong., 2d Sess. (1973); Senate Finance Committee Report, No. 303, 93rd Cong., 2d Sess. (1973). The Senate Finance Committee Report offers a clear explanation:

> Under the bill, a successor employer is treated as the employer to which the liability rules apply —whether the change has come about because of a reorganization which involves a mere change in identity, form, or place of organization, or by reason of a liquidation into a parent corporation, or by reason of a merger or consolidation. In other words, a potential liability cannot be avoided where the employer is bought out by another company and ceases to exist because it is merged into the other company.
>
> S. Rep. No. 383, 93rd Cong., 2d Sess. at 118 (1973).

The legislative history of the control group concept of ERISA §4001(b) is, unfortunately, not so clear. As has been stated, no comparable provision may be found in any version of ERISA prior to the House-Senate Conference's final draft.[10] In the Joint Explanation of the Committee on Conference accompanying the final draft of ERISA, under the section headed "Employer Liability," the Conference Committee describes the liability provision and states that in determining the employer who may be liable, all trades or businesses under common control are to be treated as a single employer. H. Conf. Rep. No. 1280, 93rd Cong., 2d Sess. at 169 (1974). No mention is made of the successor in interest provision [now §4062(d)]. In light of the inconsistency between the two provisions, it is possible that the Conference Committee intended to substitute control group liability for successor in interest liability, but this is unknown. What is known is that the successor in interest provision remains in §4062 while the control group provision has found its way into the opening section of Title IV thus apparently rendering the Conference Committee's above-cited comment dubious.

The express purpose for requiring employer liability in case of termination of an underfunded pension plan, and the logical purpose as well, is to discourage employers, irresponsible or malicious, from establishing pension benefits more generous than they can afford to fund or from terminating plans which they can afford to maintain, knowing that the PBGC stands ready to take up the plan administration.[11] In this light the successor in interest provisions of §4062(d) close an obvious loophole—overextension of plan benefits, unjustified termination and then pro forma corporate reorganization to escape liability. The control group concept, on the other hand, not only doesn't advance the purpose of ERISA §4062, it may impede it. A solvent employer who knows it will be held liable if its pension plan terminates in an underfunded state will strive for a fiscally responsible plan. Query: whether the same incentive exists for an employer who knows that in certain situations its liability may be assumed by its parent and even sister corporations, the latter possibly with a deeper pocket yet in any business sense often completely unrelated to the employer.

The legislative history of ERISA points to one further basis upon which to rest a finding that ERISA §4062 does not comprehend control group liability, namely, that the drafters did not intend to assess plan termination liability against an insolvent employer.

Early drafts of ERISA contain specific provision limiting employer liability to solvent employers. 3 U.S. Code Cong. & Admin. News 4664 and 4879 (1974). *See also,* House Education & Labor Com-

10. This fact in itself seems to present a serious obstacle to the assertion that control group theory applies to ERISA §4062. 2 U.S.C. §190C(a) states:

> In any case in which a disagreement to an amendment in the nature of a substitute has been referred to conferees, it shall be in order for the conferees to report a substitute on the same subject matter; *but they may not include in the report matter not committed to them by either House.* They may, however, include in their report in any such case matter which is a germane modification of subjects in disagreement.
>
> (Emphasis added.)

11. The employer liability provisions of ERISA are not intended as a primary revenue raising measure for the PBGC who has to pay the pension benefits of underfunded plans. Under ERISA §4006, the PBGC is to prescribe insurance premiums to be paid periodically by all plan employers "to provide sufficient revenues to the . . . [PBGC fund] . . . to carry out its functions under this title."

mittee Report, *supra,* §405; Senate Labor & Public Welfare Committee Report, *supra,* §405.

Although the enacted version of ERISA contains no specific prerequisite of solvency prior to assessment of employer liability, the spirit of that provision lingers in the present §4062 in its limitation of liability to a percentage of net worth. It may very well have been that the express provision applying employer liability to solvent employers was deleted because the limitation of liability to 30% of net worth was felt to accomplish the same result. An insolvent company by definition would have little or no net worth and thus little or no termination liability.

Despite the fact that there is no express statement limiting employer liability to solvent employers, remarks made on the floors of both houses of Congress during debate on the final version of ERISA indicate that such a limitation should be implied.

> Obviously the purpose of plan termination insurance is to protect the participants and beneficiaries from any loss of benefits and where the employer contributing to the plan which terminates is insolvent, there is no claim against the employer for the amount of funds expended by the [PBGC].
>
> 120 Cong. Rec. H1137 (1974) (remarks of Congressman Gaydos).
>
> Since there would be a possibility of abuse by solvent employers who terminate a plan and shift the financial burden to the insurance program notwithstanding their own financial ability to continue funding such plan, the Conference Bill imposes liability on employers whose plans terminate . . .
>
> 120 Cong. Rec. S15740 (1974) (remarks of Senator Williams) *See also,* Comment, *The Employee Retirement Income Security Act of 1974; Policies and Problems,* 16 Syracuse L.R. 539 at 552 (1975).

The concept of control group liability advocated by the PBGC is inconsistent with ERISA's policy of limiting liability to solvent employers. No better example of this fact exists than the case at bar in which the PBGC asserts liability against the Bankrupts as part of the control group which would result in exhausting the bankruptcy estate and depriving the unsecured creditors of any dividend, when it admittedly could made no such assertion against the Bankrupts alone.[12]

In light of the Bankruptcy Act policy of ratable distribution of a bankrupt's property to his creditors, is it reasonable to assume that unsecured creditors who provide credit on the basis of a borrower-employer's financial condition, when in the case of a solvent borrower-employer they would normally be subject to a loss no greater than 30% of the borrower's net worth on termination of an underfunded pension plan, now, because the borrower is bankrupt, would not only suffer severe losses as a result of the bankruptcy but would lose even the small bankruptcy dividend because the dumping of the bankrupt into a control group creates an unanticipated liability that completely consumes the bankruptcy estate?

Congress was aware of the Bankruptcy Act when it drafted and passed ERISA. For example, ERISA §4068(b)(2) provides that an employer's liability for underfunded plan termination be treated for bankruptcy priority purposes as a tax due and owing to the United States. Congress appeared to be aware of the difference that would result in cases of the bankruptcy of the terminating employer and expressly provided that in such cases where net worth would not be an appropriate measure of ERISA liability that the PBGC claim be given tax claim priority. *See also,* ERISA §4042.

Before presuming a construction of ERISA that alters long established bankruptcy policy, an unequivocal expression of Congressional intent to do so should be evident. All that is evident in fact is that Congress intended to give the ERISA claim a priority status not to appropriate the entire estate by the unrestricted use of the control group concept.

In light of the express statutory language, the legislative history and its policies, this Court believes that when ERISA provides for liability to be borne by an employer whose pension plan has

12. It may be posited that this last argument against control group liability is not really broad enough and merely supports the removal of the insolvent employers from the control group and the assessment of liability against the solvent remainder. Such a position would be ludicrous and points up more clearly the inapplicability of control group concepts to the employer liability provisions of ERISA. To absolve the insolvent employer directly responsible for the underfunded plan and the one solely to whom the policies behind liability apply, but to indiscriminately hold liable its corporate relatives, is to completely ignore elementary tenents of business incorporation. It may be that in a given situation the interrelatedness of the corporate entities mandates some sort of control group liability upon entities other than the terminating employer. Such situations would be susceptible to control group theory through the regulations that ERISA §4001(b) requires of the PBGC, and in any case are often covered by ERISA §4062(d).

terminated in an underfunded state, that employer must be the direct employer and not some stranger to the plan beneficiaries who becomes the employer through control group theory. In the instant case the employer for purposes of ERISA §4062 are the Bankrupts, the Avon Sole Company and its wholly owned subsidiary Tenn-ERO Corporation.

III

Assuming arguendo, that for purposes of employer liability under ERISA §4062, control group theory does apply and thus in the instant case, since the control group has some positive net worth, a liability may be assessed, that liability would still be subject to possible waiver under ERISA §4004(f).[13]

An employer with potential liability for termination under ERISA §4062 may escape liability if the plan is terminated (1) within the first 270 days after enactment of ERISA, (2) the employer as a practical matter could not continue the plan, and (3) an assessment of liability would result in unreasonable hardship to that employer. ERISA §4004(f)(4).

The PBGC argues that the Bankrupts and the Ouimet Group are not eligible for liability waiver under §4004(f)(4) because although the plan terminated within the 270 day period, a waiver of liability was not requested within that 270 day period. A requirement that the employer request waiver within the 270 day period is nowhere a part of §4004(f), nor is its implication logical, equitable or consistent with the obvious intent of the section to alleviate hardship in certain cases of plan termination during the first nine months of ERISA's operation. It is conceivable, for instance, that in accordance with ERISA §§4042 and 4048 (2), the PBGC's termination of a plan could have occurred on the 270th day of the 270 day period. ERISA §4004(f)(4) cannot be read to preclude an employer, who may otherwise be eligible, from seeking waiver of liability merely because it failed to so request within the few hours or minutes remaining of the 270th day.

Assuming then, that liability existed in this case and, since the Avon Sole Company Pension Plan terminated during the 270 day period, that those liable would be eligible for waiver of liability, it would remain to be determined whether the other criteria for waiver under ERISA §4004(f)(4), namely, undue hardship and impracticality of continuation, have been satisfied. Since the statutory scheme seems to have left this determination to the discretion of the PBGC, the Court in the first instance would feel compelled to defer to the agency for such findings.

Thus, in the event that control group theory applied to ERISA §4062 on liability, before that liability could be finally approved by a Court, the PBGC would have to consider and decide the possibility of waiver in accordance with ERISA §4004(f)(4).

IV

The instant case has been decided without a judgment of liability against any of the parties defendant. It should be pointed out, however, that a contrary conclusion on the definition of "employer" in ERISA §4062 and a finding of some employer liability, would cause to surface doubt as to the constitutionality of ERISA §4062.

Prior to the enactment of ERISA, no law existed that required pension plans to be fully funded, that is, to be able to pay all vested benefits if the plan were to suddenly terminate. Employers were constrained only by whatever annual contribution requirements they may have contracted for in a plan or collective bargaining agreement, and if they claimed an income tax deduction for plan contributions, by the requirements of the Internal Revenue Code. None of these constraints required full funding and one of the prime functions of ERISA was to introduce this requirement. Statement of President Gerald R. Ford upon signing ERISA, September 2, 1974. ERISA generally requires all plan funding from the effective date onward to be adequate to cover current liabilities *and* if the plan dates from before the Act and is

13. ERISA §4004(f) provides:

In addition to its other powers under this title, for only the first 270 days after the date of enactment of this Act the corporation may—

(1) contract for printing without regard to the provisions of chapter 5 of title 44, United States Code,

(2) waive any notice required under this title if the corporation finds that a waiver is necessary or appropriate.

(3) extend the 90-day period referred to in section 4041(a) for an additional 90 days without the agreement of the plan administrator and without application to a court as required under section 4041(d), and

(4) waive the application of the provisions of sections 4062, 4063, and 4064 to, or reduce the liability imposed under such sections on, any employer with respect to a plan terminating during that 270 day period if the corporation determines that such waiver or reduction is necessary to avoid unreasonable hardship in any case in which the employer was not able, as a practical matter, to continue the plan.

underfunded, amortization of that past liability over a period of years. ERISA §302. It is to advance this objective that ERISA §4062 makes a monetary assessment on an employer whose terminated plan is underfunded.

But in a case where a pension plan is underfunded because it was established prior to ERISA, when the law in no way prohibited underfunding, to subsequently hold the employer liable for this innocent past act is a retroactive application of the law that may violate the Fifth Amendment to the U.S. Constitution, and possibly Article I section 10 as well. *Darlington, Ind. v. Federal Housing Administration,* 142 F.Supp. 341 (E.D. S.C. 1956) rev'd on other grounds 352 U.S. 977 (1957); C. Hockman, *The Supreme Court and the Constitutionality of Retroactive Legislation,* 73 Harv. L.R. 692 (1960).

It is well established that retroactive liability is not alone sufficient to void an act on constitutional grounds. The retroactivity must be irrational or otherwise violative of due process. *Usery v. Turner Elkhorn Mining Co.,* 49 L.Ed.2d 752 (1976). In *Usery,* a recent and definitive case on this issue, Justice Marshall, writing for the Supreme Court, sets forth certain factors to be considered in determining the constitutionality of a retrospective law. It is in light of these factors that the constitutional doubts arise in the instant case.

ERISA contains no transition period after its enactment during which employer liability is not assessed.[14] *Usery, supra,* at 763. Its liability provision to a great extent is founded on considerations of deterrence and blameworthiness,[15] yet the *Usery* Court held that in order to justify retroactive imposition of liability on grounds of deterrence or blameworthiness, it should be shown that, had the retroactive law in fact been in existence all along, those sought to be held liable would have still failed to comply. *Usery, supra,* at 767, citing *Welch v. Henry,* 305 U.S. 134 (1938). In the instant case this translates into a showing that, had there always been a law against inadequate pension plan funding, Avon would nevertheless have continued to underfund its plan. The PBGC has made no such showing, nor in all probability could it. Furthermore, any attempt to justify ERISA liability as the *Usery* Court justified the statute in that case, namely, as a device to spread costs to employers who have profited by the fruits of their employees' labor, *Usery, supra,* at 768, fails in light of the attempted imposition of liability on entities like sister corporations having no relation whatever to the Avon pension plan, its underfunding or its beneficiaries.

And finally, the Supreme Court in *Usery,* after upholding the retroactive legislation in that case, specifically distinguishes that situation from one similar to the instant case. The Court points out that the legislation in question in *Usery* related to a specific need created by dangerous working conditions saying that retroactive legislation relating to pension benefits and the need to supplement a former employee's salary may not be constitutional. *Usery, supra,* at 768-9, citing *Railroad Retirement Board v. Alton R. Co.,* 295 U.S. 330 (1935).

The potential constitutional infirmity of ERISA §4062 grows larger if, as the PBGC asserts, the retroactive liability is imposed not only on the direct plan employer, but on related entities in the control group. The related entities, never mind whether or not the pension plan's underfunding was legal at the time, may have had no control whatever, or even knowledge, of the plan underfunding. *cf. State v. A.S. Nye Kristianberg,* 84 F.Supp. 775 (D.C. Md. 1949).

In the instant case the Ouimet Group had no employer-employee relationship with the pension beneficiaries. It could not compel the Bankrupts to make benefit contributions, control labor contracts or influence the pension fund investments, whose subsequent depreciation in value partly accounted for the plan underfunding.

And of course the creditors relied, as they had a right to, on the balance sheets of the companies that would not and could not reflect ERISA liability magnified by a control group concept.

The potential constitutional infirmity brought about by interpreting ERISA §4062 to include control group concepts militates strongly against such an interpretation. It is a "cardinal principle" that a statutory construction inconsistent with the Constitution be avoided if an alternative, consistent construction may be ascertained. *Pernell v. Southall Realty,* 416 U.S. 363, 365 (1974).

Internal conflicts and constitutional questions are eliminated or greatly reduced while the act remains consistent with its legislative history and avoids a disruption of the traditional rights of unsecured creditors if in the instant case the control group concept is not used as a definition of employer for purposes of liability under §4062.

In light of the foregoing, it is this Court's con-

14. The waiver provision of ERISA §4004(f)(4) could assume this role but for the extremely narrow interpretation given it by the PBGC.

15. See discussion of legislative history, *supra.*

clusion, pursuant to Title IV of ERISA, that liability for the terminated underfunded Avon Sole Company Pension Plan exists solely with the actual employers, namely, the Bankrupts, the Avon Sole Company and Tenn-ERO Corporation, and that because the Bankrupts had no positive net worth on the net worth valuation date, there is no liability pursuant to ERISA §4062. It is unnecessary to further prolong these findings by considering the issue of the actual net worth of the control group.

In its role as a Court of Bankruptcy, the PBGC's request for relief from the automatic stay in bankruptcy is denied and its claim against the Bankrupts is disallowed.

In its role as Special Master, the above findings of fact and conclusions of law are submitted for approval of the District Court and a decision in favor of the Defendants, in C.A. No. 76-1314-T, is recommended.

ORDER

In accordance with the Court's Memorandum of May 13th, 1977, it is

ORDERED

That the claim of the Pension Benefit Guaranty Corporation in the above-captioned case is disallowed, and it is further

ORDERED

That relief from the automatic stay is denied. No action shall be brought seeking to enforce against the Bankrupts any liability under the Employee Retirement Income Security Act in any court other than the Bankruptcy Court.

Entered at Boston, in said District, this 13th day of May, 1977.

HAROLD LAVIEN
Bankruptcy Judge

The PBGC must provide insurance for coverage of an employer's contingent liability. (As in the basic benefit program, the PBGC will prescribe premium rates sufficient to fund such coverage.) Such coverage, however, will not be applicable until premiums are paid for five years. The PBGC may arrange for private insurers to participate in this program.

Withdrawal of Substantial Employer

On "withdrawal" from a plan to which more than one employer contributes, a "substantial employer" is liable to the PBGC for the proportionate share of the plan's unfunded liability in the event the plan terminates during the ensuing five years. Section 4001(a)(2) defines the term "substantial employer" as:

> . . . an employer . . . who has made contributions to or under a plan under which more than one employer makes contributions for each of—
>
> (a) the two immediately preceding plan years, or
>
> (b) the second and third preceding plan years,
>
> equal or exceeding 10% of all employer contributions paid to or under the plan for each such plan year. . . .

Thus, for any plan to which more than one employer contributes, it is important to determine whether a given employer contributes 10% or more of all contributions. If the employer makes 10% or more of the contributions, the next question is whether certain events will constitute a "withdrawal." Unfortunately, ERISA does not define this term, and the PBGC has not published regulations. However, it would seem that a "withdrawal" from a multiemployer plan is analogous to a "partial termination."

The "partial termination" concept was developed by the Internal Revenue Service prior to the enactment of ERISA. The pre-ERISA section of the Internal Revenue Code of 1954 [§401(a)(7)] under which it published interpretations relating to partial terminations was reenacted as §411(d)(3) of the Internal Revenue Code of 1954 and in so doing, Congress implicitly endorsed the previously issued interpretations.

These interpretations provide that whether or not a partial termination has occurred is a function of the "facts and circumstances." It seems fairly clear that the relevant facts and circumstances relate to the reduction in participants and contributions resulting from certain events. For example, if an employer contributing to a multiemployer plan ceased operations at a certain facility and, as a result, decreased its contributions to the multiemployer plans substantially, such an event may constitute a withdrawal.

Liability Limits. In the event of a withdrawal, the employer's liability will be determined under §4063(b) of ERISA. This section provides that the substantial employer's liability:

> . . . shall be computed on the basis of an amount determined by the [PBGC] to be the amount described in §4062 for the entire plan, as if the plan had been terminated by the [PBGC] on the date of the employer's withdrawal, multiplied by a fraction—
>
> (1) the numerator of which is the total amount required to be contributed to the plan by such employer for the last five years ending prior

to the withdrawal, and

(2) the denominator of which is the total amount to be contributed to the plan by all employers for such last five years.

In effect, the substantial employer's potential liability as a result of ceasing operations at a facility is determined by the PBGC as if the plan terminated, but the substantial employer is only potentially liable for a portion of the total amount, based on its percentage of total plan contributions made during the last five years. However, this potential liability is limited to the lesser of the excess of guaranteed benefits over plan benefits or 30% of the substantial employer's net worth.

Section 4062(c) of ERISA defines the term "net worth." The definition provides that the substantial employer's net worth will be increased by the amount of any transfers of assets made by the substantial employer if the PBGC determines that the transfer was improper. In general, the PBGC has the authority to increase the substantial employer's net worth for the purpose of determining its maximum liability by the amount of any transfers of assets made for the purpose of reducing net worth (and, therefore, the substantial employer's maximum liability).

Bonding. In the event of a withdrawal from a multiemployer plan by a substantial employer, the substantial employer will be required either to pay the PBGC an amount equal to its potential liability or to furnish a bond to the PBGC in an amount not exceeding 150% of its liability. If the plan is not terminated within the five year period commencing on the date of the withdrawal, the substantial employer's liability is abated and the amount paid, which is held in escrow, shall be refunded without interest, or the bond will be canceled.

If the multiemployer plan terminates within the five year period, the PBGC will either hold the amount in escrow for the benefit of the plan or realize on the bond. If a substantial employer is liable to the PBGC and neglects or refuses to pay the amount of its liability, there is a lien in favor of the PBGC upon all property and rights to property, whether real or personal, belonging to the substantial employer.

Reporting

Like Title I of ERISA, Title IV requires the filing of certain documents with the PBGC. The "reportable events" requirement was discussed above. In addition, the administrator of a covered pension plan must file a premium payment declaration report on Form PBGC-1, together with the required premiums. *See* ERISA §4007.

The Form PBGC-1 provides the PBGC with information relating to the number of participants. Premium payment declaration (Form PBGC-1) is supplemented by premium reconciliation: the administrator of a defined benefit pension plan must file Form PBGC-1 with respect to reconciliation of premiums.

The Form PBGC-1 also includes an annual report (Schedule A). This report requires the administrator to indicate whether any reportable events occurred during the plan year; whether a substantial facility closed; and whether a substantial employer withdrew from the plan. Of course, the plan administrator must finally file a detailed notice with the PBGC that the plan is to be terminated on a proposed date, which date may be no sooner than ten days after the date of the filing.

CHAPTER 2

Tax Laws

INTERNAL REVENUE CODE OF 1954

Scope

The Internal Revenue Code of 1954 (the Code), 26 U.S.C. §1, *et seq.*, regulates almost all activities engaged in by taxpayers. Prior to ERISA, it was the most comprehensive federal law relating to the private employee benefit complex.

Title II of ERISA contains amendments to the Code, which increase the scope of federal regulation of certain pension plans and the other components of the plan complex. The Code governs the structure (e.g., written form) and content of plans (e.g., minimum participation standards), as well as plan administration (e.g., exclusive benefit rule) and plans' interactions with the other components of the plan complex (e.g., prohibited transactions). This law does not supersede or preempt state law and, in some cases, the requirements contained in the Code are based on state law.

The Code regulates pension and welfare plans through the tax treatment accorded these plans. The tax consequences are determined by the form and substance of the plan.

Certain plan designs will result in tax consequences which are generally considered favorable to the components of the plan complex. For example, if an employer establishes and maintains a tax-qualified pension or profit-sharing plan, contributions to a trust pursuant to the terms of the plan are deductible from income (within certain limits) for the taxable year when paid, rather than in a subsequent year when distributed to employees. *See* IRC §404(a)(1)-(3). The employer is entitled to deduct contributions currently even though no distribution is made to its employees. However, the amount contributed does not have to be included in income by the employees on whose behalf the contribution is made until the amount is distributed or made available to the employee or his beneficiary. *See* IRC §402(a). Similarly, earnings on the amounts set aside for eventual distribution are not taxable to the trust, and the employees do not have to include investment earnings in gross income until there is a distribution to them. *See* IRC §501(a).

When the amounts contributed by the employer and investment earnings thereon are distributed to the employees, they may receive favorable tax treatment. The employee's total income at the time of distribution—and, therefore, the applicable tax rate—probably will be lower than during the employee's working years. If the employee receives his benefit in a lump sum rather than in installments, he may be entitled to special tax treatment that mitigates the effect of receiving a large amount of income in one year. *See* IRC §402(e). These income tax advantages are supplemented by estate and gift tax advantages. *See* IRC §§2039(c), 2517.

This favorable tax treatment encourages employers to establish tax-qualified plans as opposed to other types of plans. For example, if an employer establishes and maintains a non-qualified plan, contributions may be deductible from income, but only in the taxable year in which the contributions are includable in the gross income of employees participating in the plan. *See* IRC §404(a)(5). Employees must include employer contributions in gross income for the taxable year in which their interest in such contributions is no longer subject to a substantial risk of forfeiture. *See* IRC §§83, 402(b). If there is a substantial risk of forfeiture, the employer is not entitled to a deduction and the employee is not required to include the amounts in income. When the employee's interest is no longer forfeitable, the employer is entitled to a deduction, but, if more than one employee is a participant, the deduction is only available if separate accounts are maintained.

The favorable tax treatment accorded tax-qualified plans and certain welfare plans results in a revenue loss to the government. The federal budget for fiscal 1977 includes this favorable tax treatment as an item of tax expenditure (i.e., revenue loss) estimated at approximately $9 billion.

The revenue loss justifies the regulation of these plans under the Code. It is argued that if the federal government is, in effect, to subsidize plans with tax benefits, these plans should meet specified federal standards. Favorable tax consequences historically have only resulted from plans satisfying certain requirements contained in the revenue laws. For example, the Revenue Act of 1921 included a tax exemption for trusts "... created by an employer as part of a stock bonus or profit-sharing plan for the *exclusive benefit* of some or all of his employees. . . ." (Emphasis added.)

This requirement was interpreted in later Treasury Regulations [§101, Art. 165-1(a), which were issued under the Revenue Act of 1938] to mean that the trust must benefit all or a large percentage of the total number of the employer's clerks or workmen as distinguished from persons in authority. While this interpretation was incorporated into the Internal Revenue Code of 1939, there was still Congressional concern with the proliferation of plans covering only a small percentage of employees or only the highly compensated. This concern led to amendments to the Internal Revenue Code of 1939 changing the standards governing tax-qualified plans. For example, plans had to meet one of two alternative coverage tests, a percentage test or a classification test. These tests, which are currently in the Code, will be discussed below. Over the years, the standards governing tax-qualified plans have become more comprehensive.

Most persons think of the Code in terms of the tax treatment accorded tax-qualified plans. However, the Code also affects virtually every arrangement pursuant to which employee benefits are provided to employees, as well as other components of the plan complex including employers, employer associations, employees, employee organizations, asset managers (such as banks and insurance companies), investment advisers, and persons providing other services to plans, such as attorneys, accountants, actuaries, administrators and consultants.

Pension Plans

The provisions contained in the Code affect both tax-qualified and non-qualified plans. For example, Section 401(a) of the Code provides that certain trusts created in the United States and forming part of a pension, profit-sharing or stock bonus plan which satisfies certain requirements, shall constitute qualified trusts, which are tax-exempt under Section 501. [It is important to note that group trusts may be qualified trusts under Section 401(a) and tax-exempt under Section 501, while common trust funds are exempt under Section 584 of the Code. *See* Rev. Rul. 56-267, 1956-1 Cum. Bull. 206; Rev. Rul. 67-301, 1967-2 Cum. Bull. 146. Common investment funds will be discussed in Chapter 6, Banking Laws.] This classification results in favorable tax treatment. Favorable tax treatment is also associated with annuity and bond purchase plans, among others.[1] *See* IRC §§403, 405.

Plans which do not satisfy the requirements relating to these types of plans (and other similar plans) are usually referred to as non-qualified plans, and do not receive the same tax treatment accorded tax-qualified plans.

Tax-Qualified Plans

Other than by reason of the applicable requirements, tax-qualified pension, profit-sharing and stock bonus plans are not defined in the Code. However, the Internal Revenue Service has published regulations defining the terms used in the Code. *See generally* Treas. Regs. §1.401-1.

A *tax-qualified pension plan* is a plan established and maintained by an employer to provide systematically for the payment of definitely determinable benefits to its employees over a period of years after retirement. Pension contributions and benefits must not depend upon the employer's profits. Forfeitures of benefits by terminating employees may not increase the benefits of the remaining employees; instead, they must reduce future employer contributions. A pension plan may provide for a disability pension and for incidental death benefits. However, it may not provide layoff benefits or benefits for sickness, accidents, hospitalization or, except in certain circumstances, medical expenses.

1. Although purchases of annuities referred to in Section 403(b) of the Code, individual retirement accounts, annuities and bonds referred to in Sections 408-409 of the Code and certain stock options referred to in Sections 421-425 of the Code are usually not referred to as tax-qualified plans, these arrangements do receive favorable tax treatment and, consequently, must satisfy certain Code requirements. The Code requirements applicable to these plans are not the same as the requirements discussed in this chapter.

A pension plan may be either the money purchase type, in which contributions are fixed and benefits equal the amount in the employee's account, or the defined benefit type, in which benefits are fixed and contributions are equal to the amount necessary to fund those benefits. Most Taft-Hartley pension plans are considered to be of the defined benefit type, although, as the *Connolly* decision indicates, at least one court feels that Taft-Hartley plans are of the defined contribution type. (The *Connolly* case was discussed in Chapter 1.)

A *tax-qualified profit-sharing plan* is defined in the regulations as one established and maintained by an employer to enable its employees to participate in its profits pursuant to a definite formula for allocating contributions and distributing accumulated assets. However, contributions do not have to be made pursuant to a definite formula—the formula may be discretionary.

It is important to distinguish a definite allocation formula from a definite contribution formula, since only the former is generally required.[2] An allocation formula establishes the shares that the participants will have in the employer's contributions (and investment earnings). A contribution formula, on the other hand, establishes the contributions that must be made. If the profit-sharing plan contains a definite contribution formula, e.g., 10% of net profits, contributions must be made according to this formula in order for the plan to maintain its tax-qualified status. If the plan has a discretionary formula, such as an annual specification by the employer of the portion of net profits to be contributed, contributions must be made with some regularity or the Internal Revenue Service will consider that a permanent discontinuance of contributions has occurred, resulting in full vesting.

Contributions allocated to the account of a participating employee may be used to provide incidental life or accident or health insurance, and distributions from the plan may be made prior to retirement, for various reasons. For example, distributions may be made after a fixed number of years, the attainment of a stated age, or the prior occurrence of some events such as layoff, illness, disability, retirement, death or severance from employment. The term "fixed number of years" means at least two years.

Revenue Ruling 71-295, 1971-2 Cum. Bull. 184, illustrates this aspect of this profit-sharing plan definition.

2. It is important to note that the Fair Labor Standards Act and the Equal Pay Act, both of which are discussed in Chapter 3 may require an employer to contribute to a plan pursuant to a definite contribution formula.

REVENUE RULING 71-295

1971-2 Cum. Bull. 184

The purpose of this Revenue Ruling is to update and restate under the current statute and regulations, Revenue Ruling 54-231, C.B. 1954-1, 150. The question presented is whether a profit-sharing plan may be qualified if it permits an employee to withdraw his employer's contributions under the circumstances described below.

The profit-sharing plan permits an employee to withdraw any portion of his employer's contribution 18 months after it is made. There is no other condition in the plan on the employee's right to withdraw.

Section 401(a) of the Internal Revenue Code of 1954 prescribes the requirements that must be met for qualification of a trust forming part of a pension, profit-sharing, or stock bonus plan.

Section 1.401-1(b)(1)(ii) of the Income Tax Regulations provides that a profit-sharing plan must provide a definite predetermined formula for allocating the contributions made to the plan among the participants and for distributing the funds accumulated under the plan after a fixed number of years, the attainment of a stated age, or upon the prior occurrence of some event such as layoff, illness, disability, retirement, death, or severance of employment.

The term "fixed number of years" is considered to mean at least two years.

Accordingly, it is held that a plan which permits any employee to withdraw any portion of his share of the employer's contribution 18 months after it has been made without regard to the attainment of a stated age or the occurrence of some event such as layoff, illness, disability, retirement, death, or severance of employment is not a profit-sharing plan within the purview of section 401(a) of the Code.

Revenue Ruling 54-231, is hereby superseded since the position stated therein is restated under the current law and regulations in this Revenue Ruling.

It is interesting to note that the definitions provided for the terms "pension plan" and "profit-sharing plan" create some curious distinctions. For example, if the employer maintaining the plan earns profits, there is virtually no distinction between a money purchase pension plan that provides for annual contributions equal to 10% of each employee's compensation and a profit-sharing plan that provides for annual contributions equal to 10% of each employee's compensation out of profits. However, while the words "out of profits" may make very little practical difference to either the employer or the employee, their addition changes the requirements for qualification. For example, with this phrase, benefits may be distributed before retirement, forfeitures may be applied to increase benefits, the contribution formula may be discretionary, and accident or health insurance may be provided for employees.

Another distinction arises out of the requirement that a profit-sharing plan provide for the participation of employees in the employer's profits. One type of tax-qualified plan in common use is a so-called thrift plan, under which each employee has the option to contribute a percentage of his salary to the plan. The employer then contributes an amount equal to a percentage of the employee's contributions. Usually, the amounts contributed under a thrift plan may be withdrawn before retirement in the case of emergencies, such as large medical expenses. Since benefits cannot be paid prior to retirement under pension plans, thrift plans are drafted to meet the requirements applicable to profit-sharing plans. In the case of a profit-earning employer, however, there is no real profit sharing. Employees will receive the same benefits whether profits are high or low.

The regulations define a *tax-qualified stock bonus plan* as one established and maintained by an employer to provide benefits similar to those of a profit-sharing plan, except that the contributions of the employer do not necessarily depend upon profits and benefits must be distributed in stock of the employer. Stock bonus plans are governed by essentially the same rules as profit-sharing plans, but contributions are not necessarily profit related. For example, an employer who wishes to adopt a tax-qualified plan that requires fixed contributions independent of profits and permits distributions prior to retirement can do so only through a stock bonus plan, which must provide for the distribution of benefits in stock of the employer company. If the combination of fixed contributions and early distributions is acceptable in a plan that distributes benefits in employer stock, it would seem that the combination also should be acceptable in plans that distribute benefits by other means, but this is not the case.

Non-Qualified Plans

Unlike tax-qualified plans, non-qualified plans are not specifically defined in either the Code or the regulations. The easiest way to describe non-qualified plans is to say that these plans do not satisfy the requirements applicable to tax-qualified plans: their failure (either intentional or unintentional) to satisfy these requirements results in their classification as non-qualified plans. Since these plans generally do not receive favorable tax treatment under the Code, no (or significantly limited) requirements are imposed. There is no justification for tax regulation since these plans do not receive favorable tax treatment.

Non-qualified plans include a wide variety of arrangements pursuant to which employee benefits are provided to employees. The term embraces all arrangements other than tax-qualified plans by which the payment of compensation to employees for services is postponed to some future date.

In this regard, use of the term "plan" is somewhat misleading. For example, an employer and a highly compensated employee may execute a deferred compensation contract designed to facilitate the attainment of particular tax-economic objectives by the employee. Such a contract would constitute a non-qualified plan, even though the plan only provides benefits to one employee. A strong argument can be made that such an arrangement would not be classified as a pension plan under ERISA.

In general, there are two types of non-qualified plans: funded and unfunded plans. A *funded plan* is an agreement or arrangement pursuant to which an employer makes contributions for the benefit of an employee. The amounts contributed by the employer are placed beyond the control of the employer, and are not available to its creditors. (It is important to note that most funded plans must satisfy the requirements contained in ERISA.)

An *unfunded plan* is a promise by an employer to provide a benefit to an employee at some point in the future. The promise usually is not assignable or secured. The employer may or may not make an informal allocation of assets to fund its ultimate liability, but any assets so segregated usually remain subject to the claims of the employer's creditors. [It is important to note that many unfunded plans must satisfy ERISA's reporting and disclosure provisions. However, if the plan falls within the exception contained in ERISA for unfunded plans maintained for the purpose of providing deferred compensation for a select group of management or highly compensated employees, ERISA's other requirements are not applicable. *See* ERISA

§§201(2), 301(a)(3), 401(a)(1). It may prove difficult to fall within the scope of this particular exception.]

Typical examples of non-qualified plans include deferred compensation contracts, pension, profit-sharing, stock bonus and other similar plans which do not satisfy the requirements for qualification, and "phantom" and "shadow" stock plans.

Welfare Plans

Like the term non-qualified plan, "welfare plan" is not defined in either the Code or the regulations. However, provisions contained in the Code relate to arrangements usually thought of as welfare plans and to arrangements that would be classified as welfare plans under ERISA.

The Code determines whether employers may deduct expenses, such as amounts paid for dismissal wages, unemployment benefits or vacations and amounts paid to a sickness, accident, hospitalization, medical expense, recreation, or similar welfare plan. *See* IRC §162; Treas. Regs. §1.162-10. These expenses are deductible provided they are "ordinary and necessary" expenses. Provisions of the Code also determine whether such amounts paid constitute income to the employee. *See, e.g.,* IRC §§61(a), 79. Similarly, provisions of the Code determine whether amounts received by employees constitute income. *See, e.g.,* IRC §§101, 104, 105, 120.

Like trusts maintained in connection with tax-qualified plans, certain employee organizations providing welfare benefits may be tax exempt. *See* IRC §501(c)(9), (17), (18), (20). Certain welfare plans receive tax treatment which is considered favorable to various components of the plan complex and, therefore, these welfare plans must satisfy requirements contained in the Code. Other types of welfare plans do not have to satisfy Code requirements.

Fiduciaries and Other Disqualified Persons

The Code not only focuses on pension and welfare plans, but also on persons establishing and maintaining these plans and the other persons with various relationships to them. The persons regulated under the Code, like those regulated under ERISA, can be divided into two categories: fiduciaries (except if they are acting only as fiduciaries) and non-fiduciary disqualified persons. However, unlike ERISA, regulation under the Code generally extends only to persons with relationships to tax-qualified plans.

Section 4975(e)(3) of the Code defines a fiduciary in the same manner as the term is defined in §3(21) of ERISA. Similarly, §4975(e)(2) of the Code defines the term "disqualified person" in substantially the same manner as the term "party in interest" is defined in §3(14) of ERISA.

Tax-Qualified Plans

Structure of Plans

The structure of tax-qualified plans is governed by the Code as well as by ERISA. Most of the provisions relating to plan structure apply to pension, profit-sharing, stock bonus, annuity, bond purchase and other similar plans, but some of the provisions apply only to pension or profit-sharing or stock bonus plans. Some of these provisions are discussed below.

Every tax-qualified plan must be a definite written program setting forth all of the plan provisions necessary to satisfy the requirements for qualification delineated in §401 of the Code. *See* Treas. Regs. §1.401-1(a)(2). (The qualification or content requirements will be discussed below.) The requirement that the plan must be in writing is similar to the written instrument requirement under ERISA.

In addition to the written plan, in the case of a trusteed plan, there must be a valid existing trust, complete in all respects and recognized as a valid trust under the applicable local law. However, this does not mean that the trust must have assets prior to the close of the employer's taxable year. If only the trust corpus is lacking at the close of the first taxable year, the trust will be considered to be in effect for the taxable year provided the employer is an accrual basis taxpayer and the corpus is furnished no later than the due date of the employer's return. Of course, the trust must be evidenced by an executed written document setting forth its terms. Revenue Ruling 69-231, 1969-1 Cum. Bull. 118 illustrates this requirement.

REVENUE RULING 69-231
1969-1 Cum. Bull. 118

The purpose of this Revenue Ruling is to update and restate, under the current statute and regulations the position set forth in Mimeograph 6394, C.B. 1949-1, 118. This ruling relates to whether an oral agreement is sufficient to establish a valid trust for purposes of section 401(a) of the Internal Revenue Code of 1954.

The directors of a corporation had been discussing the creation of a pension plan during the fiscal year ending June 30, 1968. At a special meeting on June 3, 1968, the directors orally agreed to put such a plan into effect as of June 30, 1968. Pursuant to this agreement contributions were deposited in a separate account prior to the end of the fiscal year. On November 19, 1968, the agreement was first reduced to writing and the formal plan and trust were executed.

Section 401(a)(2) of the Code and section 1.401-2(a)(2) of the Income Tax Regulations provide that a trust forming part of a pension, profit-sharing, or stock bonus plan shall constitute a qualified trust only if, in addition to meeting the other requirements of section 401, under the trust instrument it is impossible, at any time prior to the satisfaction of all liabilities with respect to the employees and their beneficiaries under the trust, for any part of the corpus or income to be used for, or diverted to, purposes other than for the exclusive benefit of the employees or their beneficiaries.

It is recognized that, in many jurisdictions, an oral agreement may be a sufficient basis for the establishment of a valid trust. However, section 1.401-2(a)(2) of the regulations provides that the phrase "under the trust instrument it is impossible" means that the trust instrument must definitely and affirmatively make it impossible for the non-exempt diversion or use to occur. Furthermore, section 1.401-1(c) of the regulations provides that a qualified status must be maintained throughout the entire taxable year of the trust in order for the trust to obtain any exemption for such year. Moreover, contributions are deductible within specified limits under section 404(a)(1) or (3) of the Code for a taxable year only if such taxable year ends within or with a taxable year of the trust for which the trust is exempt under section 501(a).

Thus, all of the following conditions must be met prior to the end of the taxable year in order that contributions may be deductible under section 404(a)(1), (3), or (7) of the Code for such year: (1) there must be a valid trust recognized as such under the law prevailing in the jurisdiction to which the trust is subject; (2) the trust must be evidenced by an executed "instrument"; and (3) the instrument must definitely and affirmatively preclude the prohibited diversion.

The term "trust instrument," as used in section 401(a)(2) of the Code and section 1.401-2(a)(2) of the regulations, means a document or documents clearly setting forth the terms of the trust. The "instrument" evidencing the trust agreement must be in writing, containing sufficient words to make the prohibited diversion impossible, and signed before the end of the taxable year under consideration by persons competent to bind the parties. The Internal Revenue Service will not follow the decision in the case of *Hill York Corporation et al. v. United States,* 64-2 U.S.T.C. 9654; 14 A.F.T.R. 2d 5160, which reached a contrary conclusion.

The trust instrument is not required to be in a specified form but must be in such form that the provisions of the trust agreement can be enforced on the basis of such written evidence alone. See, however, Revenue Ruling 57-419, C.B. 1957-2, 264, which holds that a trust complete in all respects under the local law, except that it had no corpus on the last day of the taxable year, will be deemed to have been in existence and in effect on the last day of such year if the accrual basis employer paid the required corpus into the trust within the time prescribed by law for filing the return for such taxable year.

Accordingly, it is held that the oral agreement was not sufficient to establish a valid trust for purposes of section 401(a) of the Code.

Mimeograph 6394 is hereby superseded, since the position stated therein is restated under the current law in this Revenue Ruling.

The plan and the trust must be communicated to the employees. One method is to furnish each employee with a copy of the plan or with a booklet summarizing the plan. However, if a booklet is used, it must state clearly that a copy of the complete plan may be inspected at a designated place on the employer's premises during reasonable time (which must also be stated). *See* Rev. Rul. 71-90, 1971-1 Cum. Bull. 115.

The plan communicated to employees must be a funded plan. Typically, contributions are made to a trust, which is tax exempt, but contributions also may be made under a custodial account, or may be used to pay premiums on insurance contracts, to purchase face-amount certificates, or to buy retirement bonds. However, a qualified plan must not provide for direct payments by an employer to his employees. For example, a so-called pay-as-you-go pension plan is not a tax-qualified plan. The court's decision in *Trebotich v. Commissioner,* 492 F.2d 1018 (9th Cir. 1974) illustrates this requirement.

TREBOTICH V. COMMISSIONER
492 F.2d 1018 (9th Cir. 1974)

SNEED, Circuit Judge:

In November of 1961, the Pacific Maritime Association (PMA), an organization of West Coast shipping industry employers formed for the primary purpose of negotiating and administering maritime union labor contracts, and the International Longshoremen's and Warehousemen's Union (ILWU), a labor organization representing West Coast dock workers, entered into a Memorandum of Agreement on Mechanization and Modernization in order to revise and amend provisions in existing labor contracts so as to permit the mechanization of operations throughout the West Coast shipping industry. In exchange for ILWU's consent to mechanization, the Memorandum of Agreement stipulated that PMA would establish a fund to provide certain enumerated benefits for those ILWU workers facing either a reduction in working hours or removal from the work force because of the resulting changes.

To effect the Memorandum of Agreement, PMA and ILWU also entered into a Supplemental Agreement of Mechanization and Modernization. Under the Supplemental Agreement, the employers agreed to make periodic contributions to a "mechanization fund," which was to be collected and administered by PMA. Pursuant to the scheme envisioned under the Supplemental Agreement, PMA was to transfer funds from the mechanization fund to three separate trusts established for the benefit of the dock workers: (1) a "vesting benefit trust," which was to distribute supplemental retirement benefits; (2) a "welfare trust," which was to distribute death and disability benefits; and (3) a "supplemental wage benefit trust," which was to supplement the earnings of those workers whose wages were reduced below certain minimum levels due to mechanization. Upon the expiration of the 1961 Supplemental Agreement in 1966, PMA and ILWU entered into an Amended Supplemental Agreement which, except for the deletion of the supplemental benefit trust and an adjustment in the aggregate employer contribution, essentially extended the scheme as initially designed.

Both the 1961 and 1966 Supplemental Agreements provided that individual employers were required to contribute to the mechanization fund in amounts based on the type and tonnage of cargo which they moved. While this allowed the actual amount of each employer's contribution to float, the annual aggregate contribution to the fund from all employers was fixed.[1] However, this fixed aggregate contribution was subject to reduction in the event that there were unauthorized work stoppages or certain other enumerated violations of the Agreement. PMA was also empowered to decrease the rate of contributions if at any time it appeared that the amount being contributed would exceed the immediate needs of the various trusts. In addition, if the total contributions which were called for under the Supplemental Agreement proved insufficient to meet the various benefit payments required under the Agreement, PMA and ILWU were authorized to decrease, defer, or eliminate any or all of those benefits.

The Supplemental Agreement envisioned that PMA would assume a dual function in administering the plan. In its relationship with the employer group, its status was designated as a "collecting agent" and as such it was given the authority to take any necessary action to compel defaulting employers to make their required contributions to the fund. In its relationship with ILWU, its status was designated as being that of a "conduit" for the transfer of funds to the respective trusts. As a "conduit," PMA was authorized to use the fund for payment of payroll taxes incurred by the employers as a result of the transfers to the trusts. But the Supplemental Agreement also provided that PMA was neither to commingle contributions to the mechanization fund with any other funds under its control, nor to act as a repository for contributions beyond such time as was reasonably necessary to perform the banking and accounting functions essential to the plan's effectuation.

Under the terms of the Supplemental Agreement, neither ILWU nor the employees had any "right, title or interest, or any claim whatsoever, legal or equitable" in the mechanization fund. Nor did the trustees or trusts have any such right, title, interest or claim in the fund beyond that specifically provided by the Agreement. With respect to funds which were to be transferred from the Mechanization Fund into the vesting benefit trust, the Supplemental Agreement specifically provided that PMA

> . . . shall not, in any event, transfer from the Mechanization Fund any moneys to the Trustees of the ILWU-PMA Vesting Benefit Trust,

1. The 1961 Supplemental Agreement provided that the employers were required to contribute a total of $29,000,000 into the fund at a rate of $6,500,000 in 1961, $5,000,000 in each of the next four years, and $2,500,000 during the first six months of 1966. The 1966 Amended Supplemental Agreement increased the aggregate contribution to $38,053,308.40 and made according adjustments in the annual rate.

> which are not required by said Trustees for immediate payment of such obligations, administration expenses or taxes which are currently due and owing by said Trustees.
>
> . . . Upon receipt of such moneys from the Association, said Trustees shall immediately use the same for payment of such obligations, administration expenses or taxes which are currently due and owing by said Trustees.

In order to implement the above provision, the trust indenture expressly limited the power of the trustees by permitting them only to deposit the funds in a bank account until they were to be disbursed. There was no provision in the indenture authorizing them to invest any of the trust funds which they had received.

This appeal from the Tax Court raises the question of how payments made to employees from the vesting benefit trust should properly be taxed. Taxpayer, Thomas Trebotich, was a longshoreman covered by the 1966 Supplemental Agreement. Under the provisions of that Agreement, he was entitled to receive benefits totaling $13,000, less applicable payroll and withholding taxes, subject of course to the power retained by PMA and ILWU to decrease, defer or eliminate the amount of his vesting benefits. At the time of his retirement, Taxpayer applied for the benefits to which he was then entitled. He received two monthly payments of $270.84 (less payroll and withholding taxes) and then exercised his option to accelerate by applying to have the balance then due paid in a single lump sum.

On or about August 25, 1967, the trust paid over to Taxpayer the sum of $12,291.66, which he reported on his federal income tax return for that year as long-term capital gain. In so doing, Taxpayer treated the lump-sum payment as being a distribution from a trust which was qualified under Section 401(a) of the Code, 26 U.S.C. §401(a), hence subject to capital gains treatment pursuant to Section 402(a)(2), 26 U.S.C. §402(a)(2).[2] The Commissioner subsequently determined that the lump-sum payment was taxable as ordinary income because the vesting benefit trust failed to satisfy the requirements of Section 401(a), 26 U.S.C. §401(a), and asserted a deficiency. On appeal to the Tax Court, the Commissioner's determination was sustained on the ground that Section 401(a), 26 U.S.C. §401(a), implicitly required that a trust must be "funded" to be qualified, and that the vesting benefit trust at issue here was not funded within the proper meaning of that term.

[1] This appeal raises two interrelated issues. First, is whether a trust must be "funded" in order to be a "qualified trust" under Section 401(a) of the Internal Revenue Code of 1954, 26 U.S.C. §401(a). In particular, we are asked to determine whether there must be a systematic setting aside of funds, either by the employer or the employee, during the course of employment to provide a source of payment for future benefits under a pension plan or other type of deferred compensation plan before it will be deemed "qualified."[3] Second, if such a requirement exists, we are asked to determine whether the PMA-ILWU vesting benefit trust, created and operated as an integral part of the Mechanization and Modernization Agreement, is "qualified" under Section 401(a) so that a longshoreman receiving early retirement benefits is entitled to treat the receipt of a lump-sum benefit payment as a long-term capital gain under Section 402(a)(2).

Section 401(a) establishes a series of requirements which must be met before a trust which is a part of a stock bonus, pension or profit sharing plan will be deemed qualified.[4] Although referring

2. Section 402(a)(2), as in effect for 1967, provided that if the total distributions payable to an employee from a trust which qualified under Section 401(a) were paid within one year following the employee's separation from service, such distributions were taxable as long-term capital gain. Section 402(a) has since been amended by Section 515(a)(1) of the Tax Reform Act of 1969, 83 Stat. 487, 643-644, to limit the long-term capital gain treatment of such qualified trust distributions.

3. In this regard, a "funded" plan is to be distinguished from a "pay-as-you-go" type plan under which the employer agrees to pay benefits when they become due without presently setting aside funds for payment of future benefits.

4. In order for a trust to qualify under the express language of the Code, it must be a domestic trust established and maintained by the employer as a part of a stock bonus, pension or profit sharing plan for the exclusive benefit of his employees. Contributions made by the employer or his employees must be "for the purpose of distributing to such employees or their beneficiaries the corpus and income of the fund accumulated by the trust in accordance with such plan." Section 401(a)(1). The trust instrument must prohibit the trust funds from being "used for, or diverted to, purposes other than the exclusive benefit of [the] employees or their beneficiaries" at any time prior to the satisfaction of all liabilities owed employees under the plan. Section 401(a)(2). The plan itself must be so structured as not to discriminate in favor of employees who are officers, shareholders or supervisors, or in favor of other highly-compensated employees. Section 401(a)(3), (4) and (5). The plan must provide that the rights of em-

to the accumulation of funds in a trust, neither the literal language of the Code nor the regulations thereunder require that a qualified pension plan be funded. However, both the Commissioner's revenue rulings[5] and scholarly commentators[6] uniformly have taken the position that funding is a prerequisite to qualification. The issue before us is thus whether there is support in the legislative history of Section 401 to permit a judicially imposed gloss upon its proper construction.

Prior to 1921, there were no specific provisions in the revenue laws dealing with the treatment of employee pension trusts. The general rule appears to have been that employer contributions were deductible only where the employer made contributions to a pension fund which was not within his control. *See* O.D. 110, 1 Cum.Bull. 224 (1919); Art. 136 Regs. 33. Trust income was taxable under the general provisions applicable to trusts, Rev.Act of 1918, §219, 40 Stat. 1057, 1071-1072, and the tax consequences to employee-beneficiaries were determined under the constructive receipts doctrine. *See* 4A Mertens, Law of Federal Income Taxation, §25B.02, p. 3 (1966). With the passage of the Revenue Act of 1921, the tax consequences of distributions from stock bonus or profit sharing plans were changed to provide that such distributions would not be taxable until actually received by the employee.[7] And in 1926, this provision was expanded to include pension trusts,[8] thereby resulting in the basic provisions which have been carried into the present Section 401(a)(1).

Neither the 1921 nor the 1926 Revenue Acts contained an express provision dealing with the deductibility of contributions to a pension trust. Under the general provision dealing with the deductibility of business expenses, however, the regulations did limit employer deductions to contributions made into a plan under which the employer himself did not hold the funds. *See* Section 214(a), Art. 109, Regs. 65, 69. And, in following the general thrust of the regulations, the Board of Tax Appeals denied deductions where the employer utilized a reserve account rather than making contributions into an independent trust. *See Merrill Trust Co.,* 21 B.T.A. 1409 (1931); *Lemuel Scarbrough,* 17 B.T.A. 317 (1929).

The basic distinction between pension funds held by the employer and those placed in a qualified pension trust outside the employer's control was carried through into the Revenue Act of 1928. Employer contributions to a qualified pension trust were, by statute, made presently deductible if for present services and deductible over a ten-year period if for past services. Rev.Act. of 1928, §23(q), 45 Stat. 791, 802. A review of the legislative history underlying the above provision clearly indicates that this favorable tax treatment was intended to be accorded only where the pension funds were not held by the employer.[9]

---

ployees which have accrued, to the extent then funded, or the amounts which have been credited to the employers' accounts must be non-forfeitable upon any termination or complete discontinuance of contributions under the plan. Section 401(a)(8). Where the plan involves trusts benefiting self-employed individuals and owner-employees, certain additional requirements not relevant here must also be satisfied. Section 401(a)(9) and (10). *See generally* 26 C.F.R. §1.401-1.

5. *See* Rev.Rul. 71-91, 1971-1 Cum.Bull. 116; Rev. Rul. 69-421, 1969-2 Cum.Bull. 59; Rev.Rul. 65-178, 1965-2 Cum.Bull. 94; Rev.Rul. 61-157, 1961-2 Cum.Bull. 67.

6. *See e.g.,* Collins, Federal Income Taxation of Employee Benefits, §502 [9], p. 5-178; Holzman, Guide to Pension and Profit Sharing Plans 6 (1969); Montgomery's Federal Taxes 3-23 (39th ed. 1964); 2 Rabkin & Johnson, Federal Income, Gift and Estate Taxation, ch. 15.01, p. 1504 (1972); Rothman, Establishing & Administering Pension & Profit Sharing Plans & Trust Funds 107 (1967); Wood & Cerny, Tax Aspects of Deferred Compensation 234 (2d ed.); Duncan & Chaice, "Relative Merits of Funded & Unfunded Plans" in Sellin, Taxation of Deferred Employee and Executive Compensation 258 (1960).

As used in Judge Simpson's opinion below, the concept of "funding" is used to describe the accumulation of contributions in an entity beyond the employer's control prior to the payment of benefits. While such a definition is narrower than that used by some commentators, who consider any plan which contemplates prior accumulation as "funded" and designate as "advance funding" a scheme utilizing an outside entity, *see* Rothman, *supra* at 105, we have adopted Judge Simpson's approach in our analysis. Thus for purposes of this opinion, the term "funding" will refer to the advance accumulation of funds in an individual or entity independent of the employer.

7. The Revenue Act of 1921 provided in pertinent part that the income of "[a] trust created by an employer as a part of a stock bonus or profit sharing plan . . . to which contributions are made by such employer, or employees, or both, for the purpose of distributing to such employees the earnings and principal of the fund accumulated" was not taxable until actually distributed to the employee. Rev.Act of 1921, §219(f), 42 Stat. 227, 247.

8. Rev.Act of 1926, §219(f), 44 Stat. 9, 33.

9. The provision allowing a deduction for contributions relating to past services was added by the Senate Finance Committee. The Senate Report accompanying

[2,3] As fully amplified in Judge Simpson's opinion below, the subsequent legislative history dealing with the tax treatment of qualified pension plans involved provisions designed to insure that the funds set aside for such purposes would actually benefit the employees concerned.[10] While Congress has never explicitly required that a qualified plan must be funded, it has repeatedly referred to the accumulation of principal or corpus in a trust; and the provisions relating to qualified plans appear to have been enacted on the assumption that pension funds would be accumulated, either in a trust or in an individual other than the employer, prior to payment to the employees.[11] As Judge Simpson's opinion demonstrates:

> The statutory provisions relating to qualified plans establish special and favorable tax treatment for participants in such plans. As stated by a Presidential committee, "[t]he purpose of tax concessions granted by the Federal Government to qualified pension plans is to encourage the growth of sound plans which supplement the public retirement security system." The President's Committee on Corporate Pension Funds and Other Private Retirement and Welfare Programs, Public Policy and Private Employee Retirement Plans 50-51 (1965). The interests of the employees are furthered by having an employer set aside, while the employees are working, the funds to be distributed to them when they retire. In that manner, the employees' retirement funds are protected from the misfortunes that may occur to the employer. The diversion of funds accumulated for the retirement of employees is specifically prohibited. We cannot assume that Congress would have extended the favorable tax treatment to plans in which funds were not accumulated in an independent trust or similar manner for the benefit of employees. Thus, we think that it is fair to conclude from the legislative history that Congress expected qualified plans to be funded.

[4] Viewing the vesting benefit trust in this case, whether considered alone or in conjunction with the mechanization fund held by PMA, in light of the requirement that a trust must be "funded" to qualify under Section 401(a), we have concluded that Taxpayer is not entitled to treat his early retirement benefits as capital gains. Our decision is based on the belief that the plan as structured was not intended to be, nor did it operate as a funded trust such that capital gains treatment is available under Section 402(a)(2).

While admittedly the overall plan does embody certain attributes which might suggest characterization as a funded medium, these attributes are outweighed by the elements which clearly contemplate a conduit design. As presently structured, the actual operation of the plan, regardless of the label applied, does not envision the accumulation of funds over a substantial period of time. Certain of the contractual provisions do provide for ag-

---

the bill clearly indicates that the committee was aware that funds held by the employer were non-deductible, and that the provision was designed to allow a deduction, spread over a ten-year period, if such funds were transferred to a qualified pension trust. S.Rept. No. 960, to accompany H.R. 1 (P.L. 562), 70th Cong., 1st Sess., pp. 21-22 (1928). In explicitly recognizing the existence of various forms of pension plans, the Senate Report is particularly noteworthy in its determination that favorable tax treatment was to be given only to those plans which provided that funds, were not to be held by the employer. *See Caxton Printers, Ltd.,* 27 B.T.A. 1110 (1933).

10. *See generally* Rev.Act of 1938, §165(a), 52 Stat. 477, 518; H.Rept. No. 1860, to accompany H.R. 9682 (P.L. 554), 75th Cong., 3d Sess., p. 46 (1938); H.Rept. No. 2333, 77th Cong., 2d Sess., (1942), 1942-2 Cum.Bull. 373, 413.

11. The primary purpose behind the legislation relating to qualified plans appears to have been to prescribe the time at which employers could deduct their contributions and employees would be required to include the various forms of deferred compensation in their taxable income. Absent such provisions, employer deductions would be governed by the general requirements regarding timing of deductions, and constructive receipt principles would be applied to the realization of income by employees. With a qualified trust, the employer is assured of a deduction at the time his contributions are made and the employee is not held to have realized income until such contributions are either distributed or made available for distribution. *Compare* Sections 404(a)(1) and 402(a) *with* Sections 402(b) and 404(a)(5). Under a non-funded plan, however, there is no issue of timing to be resolved since the time of payment and receipt is essentially the same for both the employer and the employee.

In addition, the provisions allowing capital gains treatment for certain lump-sum distributions of benefits from a qualified trust exempt under Section 501 clearly suggest a funding requirement. *See* Section 402(a)(2). The conceptual basis for such treatment—i.e., that the payment represents the distribution of funds accumulated over an extended period of time—is applicable only to a funded plan. With an unfunded plan, there is no accumulation of deferred compensation at any time prior to the actual distribution of funds to the employee.

gregate contributions in a fixed overall amount, and the fund has been insulated from direct employer control; however, a careful reading of the entire Supplemental Agreement makes it quite clear that it has been designed primarily for pass-through rather than for accumulative purposes. Such accumulation as may occur appears to be the product of error in actuarial computations concerning the projected payout rate, and not a part of a plan to create a *res* which would generate capital for future payments.

Under the express terms of the 1966 Supplemental Agreement, the vesting benefit trust was to receive only such funds as were immediately necessary to meet its obligations to employees, pay administrative expenses and pay taxes currently due and owing. Although it is not entirely clear as to the precise length of time the trust would hold funds under the Agreement, a complementary provision required that the trustees disburse funds from the trust "immediately" upon receipt from the mechanization fund. In addition, it is very significant that there was no provision empowering the trustees to invest funds in their possession. These provisions argue strongly that the vesting benefit trust was merely a conduit for transfer of funds from PMA to the employees covered under the Agreement. As pointed out in Judge Simpson's opinion below, it is clear that the Agreement did not contemplate that the trust would hold any substantial funds for a significant period of time and thus the arrangement does not constitute a funded trust as required under Section 401(a).

[5-8] Nor do we feel that the employers' contractual obligation to contribute a set aggregate dollar amount to the mechanization fund, even absent the provisions for reduction of this amount in the event of unauthorized work stoppages or other violations of the PMA-ILWU Agreement, should alter the plan's characterization as being either funded or unfunded. The crucial determinant in this area is whether the employer has systematically set aside funds presently, as benefits accrue, to provide for these benefits when they become due in the future. Whether or not the employer is contractually obligated to pay pension benefits is irrelevant to our determination, in that the protections provided under the qualified trust provisions of the Code are geared, not to the employer's legal obligation to continue a plan, but to the existence of a continuing program under which funds, already contributed, are protected from direct or indirect diversion contrary to the interests of the employees. As we have indicated, the statute envisions the actual setting aside of funds in a protected trust, and not merely the existence of a promise, whether enforceable or not, to pay benefits when they become due.[12]

The issue remains, however, as to whether the mechanization fund, acting in conjunction with the vesting benefit trust, has satisfied the funding requirement for qualification under Section 401(a). A careful review of the Supplemental Agreement reveals that while the Agreement provided that PMA was to collect contributions to the mechanization fund from employers at a predetermined annual rate, which might initially suggest the accumulation of funds, the overall structure of the plan seems clearly to counter such a view of its design.

PMA's status under the Supplemental Agreement was simply that of a "collecting agent acting for and on behalf of Employers in accumulating their respective Contributions to the Mechanization Fund." While PMA was empowered to enforce each employer's obligation to make contributions, there is nothing in the Agreement to indicate that PMA was to function either independently of the employers or as a fiduciary with respect to the union or the employees. Neither the union, the employees or the trusts and their trustees had any "right, title or interest, or any claim whatsoever, legal or equitable, in or to any portion of the Mechanization Fund" until actually paid

12. While a promise under seal to contribute to a pension plan can constitute a *res* of a trust, Rev.Rul. 55-640, 1955-2 Cum.Bull. 231. *Cf. Tallman Tool & Machine Corp.,* 27 T.C. 372 (1956); 555 Inc., 15 T.C. 671 (1950) *aff'd per curiam* 192 F.2d 575 (8th Cir. 1951), a trust must have more than a *res* to be funded. While cases have held that contributions are deductible when, and only when, a trust has been found because of the existence of such a *res, West Virginia Steel Corp.,* 34 T.C. 851 (1960); *Tallman Tool & Machine Corp., supra; Abingdon Potteries, Inc.,* 19 T.C. 23 (1952); *Crow-Burlingame Co.,* 15 T.C. 738 (1950) *aff'd per curiam* 192 F.2d 574 (8th Cir. 1951); 555 Inc., *supra,* such cases deal solely with when the trust was actually created. No issue was raised as to whether the trust qualified under Section 401. In the instant case, it seems clear that the rights of the trust under the 1966 Agreement constituted a *res* and that a trust existed; the question for determination here is whether that trust is funded so that the plan was qualified.

over by PMA into the trusts. The only persons with any interest in the fund were the employers, to the extent of their *pro rata* share of undistributed contributions, and PMA was authorized to reduce the rate of these contributions if funds were received at a greater rate than necessary to meet the obligations of the trusts.

Particularly when coupled with the language in the Agreement which also designated PMA as "a conduit for transferring the whole, or portions, of the Mechanization Fund received by it to the respective trusts," the provisions of the Agreement which forbid PMA to act as a repository of funds, except insofar as necessary to perform banking transactions, clearly suggests that funds were not to be accumulated in a substantial amount over any extended period of time. Indeed, if the initial actuarial computations were correct, there would be no accumulation necessary except possibly at the end of each aggregation period. PMA was to pay out funds only when the needs of the trusts required, and to reduce the rate of contribution when those requirements fell short of the rate which had been stipulated in the Agreement.[13]

[9] However, even if substantial funds were accumulated by PMA, such accumulation would still not constitute the type of funding contemplated by Section 401. While under the Agreement the trust was given certain contractual rights, and it may be that under California law PMA had certain duties imposed upon it with respect to its handling of the funds, these rights and duties were insufficient to impress a trust upon the money held by PMA. Under the Agreement, PMA was an agent of the employers rather than a fiduciary,[14] and thus the arrangement was clearly analogous to an accumulation by the employers in a reserve account, established and controlled by them, which does not constitute the funding of a qualified plan. *See Reginald H. Parsons,* 15 T.C. 93 (1950); *Claxton Printers, Ltd.,* 27 B.T.A. 1110 (1933); *Merrill Trust Co.,* 21 B.T.A. 1409 (1931); *Spring Canyon Coal Co.,* 13 B.T.A. 189 (1928) *aff'd* 43 F.2d 78 (10th Cir., 1930), *cert. denied* 284 U.S. 654, 52 S.Ct. 33, 76 L.Ed. 555 (1931).

In light of the above, we find ourselves compelled to agree with Judge Simpson's holding that:

> For their own reasons, the employers arranged to have their agent, the PMA, hold the funds until they were needed by the vesting benefit trust. The effect of the arrangement was as if the employers merely set aside the funds in a reserve account which they maintained. We cannot ignore the specific provisions of the agreement; we must conclude that in effect the funds were not transferred to the vesting benefit trust to be held by it for any substantial period of time, and that the plan was not funded as contemplated by Section 401.

Therefore, the judgment below is affirmed.

---

13. Testimony at trial also indicated that any accumulation was the result of actuarial error rather than as a part of a plan to fund future benefits.

> Q. You mean to say that the agreement expired and it was renegotiated [referring to the 1965 renegotiation and Agreement]?
>
> A. Right.
>
> Q. Were the benefits increased at that time?
>
> A. The benefits were increased from $8,000 approximately up to $13,000 and there was also a carryover in the funds. There were some funds that were available out of the original program because there wasn't the amount of deaths and disabilities that the actuary figured and that money was set into the new program, more or less as seed money to perpetrate the fund and take care of the liabilities of the fund until new funds would be coming in under the newly negotiated agreement.

14. The fact that the Agreement did not give PMA the power to either invest the funds it collected, or pay any interest on funds it might hold, only bolsters the conclusion that no substantial accumulation of funds was contemplated and that PMA was not to function as other than an agent for the employers.

In addition, the Supplemental Agreement expressly provided that:

> The Association [PMA], on account of the respective Employers, may use that portion of the Mechanization Fund required for payment of such payroll taxes as the respective Employers may incur either by reason of the transfer by the Association of their Respective Contributions to the Mechanization Fund to any of the Trusts employed to effectuate the Plan or by payment of benefits by said trusts.

This provision appears to negate the express requirements of Section 401(a)(2)—i.e., in order to qualify the trust instrument must provide that it is impossible for *any part* of the corpus or income to be diverted to purposes other than for the exclusive benefit of employees or their beneficiaries prior to the satisfaction of all liabilities with respect to such employees or their beneficiaries—which further undermines the view that the mechanization fund in conjunction with the vesting benefit trust constituted a qualified plan.

The Code also contains requirements relating to the structure of the trust. For example, a trust maintained in connection with a tax-qualified plan must be organized or created in the United States and maintained at all times as a domestic trust. *See* IRC §401(a); Treas. Regs. §1.401-1(a)(3)(i). However, a foreign situs trust which satisfies all of the requirements for qualification delineated in §401(a) of the Code other than the domestic situs requirement, may result in the same tax consequences to the components of the plan complex. *See* IRC §§402(c), 404(a)(4). The contributions to the trust must be made by the employer or its employees (or both).

Content of Plans

Tax-qualified plans not only must satisfy the definitional and structural requirements discussed above, but they also must satisfy certain content requirements. The requirements for qualification, which are usually referred to as "minimum standards," are very similar to the standards contained in ERISA. However, it is important to note that ERISA's minimum standards apply to both tax-qualified and non-qualified plans, while the standards contained in the Code only apply to tax-qualified plans. The requirements contained in the Code relate to participation, vesting, funding and other matters. Some of these requirements are discussed below.[3]

Participation. Section 401(a)(3) provides that a tax-qualified plan must satisfy the minimum participation standards contained in §410 of the Code. Under §410, a plan is not a tax-qualified plan unless the plan satisfies, among other requirements, (1) minimum age and service requirements, (2) maximum age requirements, and (3) minimum coverage requirements.

The *minimum age and service requirements* preclude a tax-qualified plan from providing, as a condition of participation in the plan, that an employee complete a period of service with the employer(s) maintaining the plan which extends beyond the later of age 25 or the date on which an employee completes one year of service. (It is important to note that there are special rules for, among others, plans providing for 100% nonforfeitability or vesting after not more than three years of service and for plans maintained by certain educational institutions.)

The minimum age and service requirements may affect plan provisions which do not directly impose age and service requirements. Plan provisions which have the effect of imposing an age or service requirement with the employer or employers maintaining the plan will be treated as if they impose an age or service requirement. *See* Treas. Regs. §1.410(a)-3(e). For example, a plan covering only retired employees would not satisfy the minimum age and service requirements.

The *maximum age requirement* precludes a tax-qualified plan from excluding an employee from participation on account of age unless the plan is a pension plan or a target benefit plan and the employee begins employment with the employer after the employee has attained an age specified by the plan which is not more than five years before normal retirement age. For example, a pension plan which defines normal retirement age as the later of age 65 or completion of ten years of service would not satisfy this requirement: no employee could ever be hired within five years of his normal retirement age. *See* Treas. Regs. §1.410(a)-4(a)(2) (Example 2).

The *minimum coverage requirements* have a long history under the Code. The court's decision in *Commissioner v. Pepsi-Cola Niagara Bottling Corporation*, 399 F.2d 390 (2d Cir. 1968), illustrates the minimum coverage requirements as well as the requirements prohibiting discrimination in contributions or benefits, which are contained in §401(a)(4) of the Code.

COMMISSIONER V. PEPSI-COLA NIAGARA BOTTLING CORPORATION

399 F.2d 390 (2d Cir. 1968)

FRIENDLY, Circuit Judge:

This petition by the Commissioner of Internal Revenue to review a decision of the Tax Court, 48 T.C. 75, annulling his determination of deficiencies in the income tax of Pepsi-Cola Niagara Bottling Corporation for 1961, 1962 and 1963, raises a nice, thougn narrow, question of the interpretation of §401(a) of the Internal Revenue Code defining what pension, profit-sharing and stock bonus plans qualify for deduction of contributions as provided in §404. The statute, so far as here rele-

3. The requirements discussed herein are generally applicable to all tax-qualified plans, but plans maintained by proprietorships, partnerships and so-called Subchapter S corporations must satisfy additional requirements. *See* IRC §§401(a)(9), (10), (17), (18), 401(c)-(3), 401(j), 1379.

vant, is set out in the margin.[1]

In November 1960 the Bottling Corporation, an enterprise of moderate size, established a profit-sharing and retirement plan for its salaried employees and a trust to receive contributions thereunder. The Corporation was to contribute 40% of its annual net profits in excess of $4,000 but not exceeding 15% of the compensation of all participants. Eligibility was limited to all regular salaried employees who had completed three years of continuous service on December 31, 1961, or any anniversary date of the plan. Benefits were distributed on the basis of a formula which credited each covered employee with one unit for each $100 of compensation and one unit for each year of continuous employment; no deduction was made for the portion of compensation, $4800 in the years in question, constituting "wages" for which Social Security contributions were made, 26 U.S.C. §3121(a)(1).[2] Omitting temporary and seasonal employees on an hourly wage basis whose exclusion is not claimed by the Commissioner to disqualify the plan, the Corporation had six salaried employees who were covered and eight hourly wage employees who were not; their names and compensation are shown in the margin.[3]

The Corporation did not seek a determination of the plan's qualification until December 1963; the District Director of Internal Revenue denied this on the ground that the plan was discriminatory in favor of "highly paid" employees within the meaning of §401(a)(3)(B) and (4). The Chief of the Pension Trust Branch sustained this, the Corporation then amended the plan as of January 1, 1965, to make all permanent employees eligible for coverage, and the District Director accepted the plan as so amended. Consistently with these rulings of his subordinates, the Commissioner determined income tax deficiencies for 1961, 1962 and 1963 based on disallowance of contributions of $5,831, $5,381 and $8,080, respectively. The Tax Court annulled this determination on the basis that persons receiving the modest compensation of all the participants save the president of the Corporation could not rationally be regarded as "highly paid," particularly when the differential between them and the uncovered employees was so small, see fn. 3.

1. §401(a) *Requirements for qualification.*—

A trust created or organized in the United States and forming a part of a stock bonus, pension, or profit-sharing plan of an employer for the exclusive benefit of his employees or their beneficiaries shall constitute a qualified trust under this section—

. . . . .

(3) if the trust, or two or more trusts, or the trust or trusts and annuity plan or plans are designated by the employer as constituting parts of a plan intended to qualify under this subsection which benefits either—

(A) 70 percent or more of all the employees, or 80 percent or more of all the employees who are eligible to benefit under the plan if 70 percent or more of all the employees are eligible to benefit under the plan, excluding in each case employees who have been employed not more than a minimum period prescribed by the plan, not exceeding 5 years, employees whose customary employment is for not more than 20 hours in any one week, and employees whose customary employment is for not more than 5 months in any calendar year, or

(B) such employees as qualify under a classification set up by the employer and found by the Secretary or his delegate not to be discriminatory in favor of employees who are officers, shareholders, persons whose principal duties consist in supervising the work of other employees, or highly compensated employees; and

(4) if the contributions or benefits provided under the plan do not discriminate in favor of employees who are officers, shareholders, persons whose principal duties consist in supervising the work of other employees, or highly compensated employees.

2. Other features of the plan, not significant as to the issue here presented, are set forth in the Tax Court's opinion.

3. A. Salaried Employees Covered Under Plan.

Name	Salaries 1961	1962	1963
H. Winter	$28,000.00	$28,000.00	$30,000.00
P. Seereiter	10,710.00	11,180.00	11,813.41
J. Gunetta	9,410.00	9,620.00	9,880.00
R. Lambrecht	8,515.50	8,880.00	9,223.50
B. Riggs	7,595.40	8,060.00	8,580.00
K. Rowland	5,615.00*	5,720.00	2,990.00
P. Cahill	n.e.**	n.e.**	3,430.00*

B. Permanent Hourly Paid Employees Not Covered Under Plan.

Name	Wages 1961	1962	1963
R. Mitchell	$ 6,626.02	$ 7,128.93	$ 7,342.94
H. Holt	6,452.27	6,745.47	7,071.47
R. Roth	5,255.01	5,662.86	5,812.61
R. Riggs	1,110.99	5,601.81	6,060.14
A. Grose	5,405.80	5,544.50	5,604.28
J. Berhalter	4,823.83	5,287.93	5,509.87
M. Bowers	4,715.12	5,240.47	5,553.81
H. Kendall	3,968.96	4,160.00	4,420.00

* Not eligible under three-year requirement

** Not employed

We can readily agree that a plan like the Bottling Corporation's was untypical of the "mischief and defect," Heydon's Case, 3 Co. 72 (1584), for which the Revenue Code's pension trust sections had failed to provide until 1942 when they were placed in substantially their present form, 56 Stat. 798, 862-63. We do not, however, accept the Tax Court's result; a legislature seeking to catch a particular abuse may find it necessary to cast a wider net.

The movement for reform of the deduction for pension, profit-sharing and bonus plans had begun with a message to Congress from President Roosevelt on June 1, 1937. This incorporated a letter from the Secretary of the Treasury stating that the exemption "has been twisted into a means of tax avoidance by the creation of pension trusts which include as beneficiaries only small groups of officers and directors who are in the high income tax brackets." 81 Cong.Rec. 5125, 75th Cong., 1st Sess. After investigating and deciding that correction was indeed in order, Congress had to determine in what manner to move from the agreed general purpose to legislation that could be practically applied to the thousands of varying situations with which the Internal Revenue Service would be faced. Congress adopted a two-fold approach. Plans would qualify if a sufficient proportion of the firm's employees were eligible or participated. If, however, a plan's coverage provisions were not so broad as to include the minimum percentage of employees prescribed in §401(a)(3)(A), they were to be subjected to a more intensive scrutiny by the Treasury Department whose nature the legislature could prescribe only in a more generalized way. Restrictive plans were to qualify only if the Secretary or his delegate were to find that the eligibility requirements were not "discriminatory" in favor of officers, shareholders, supervisors, or "highly paid employees." The legislative history suggests that Congress did not believe itself equipped to give more content to the two phrases we have quoted. The original House Bill sought to define more precisely the characteristics of plans that discriminated in favor of the "highly paid," at least with regard to a companion provision, §401(a)(4), which guarded against the danger that highly paid employees would gain a disproportionate share of pension benefits despite the fact that eligibility requirements were not found discriminatory under §401(a)(3). It stated that the "benefits or contributions" required under the plan shall "not have the effect of discriminating in favor of *any* employee whose compensation is greater than that of *other* employees." H.R. 7378, §144(a)(4), 77th Cong., 2d Sess. (1942) (emphasis supplied). A literal reading of this provision would unequivocally have made fairness to the lowest paid employee covered by the plan the test of qualification. This formulation, however, was apparently believed to be unduly rigid, for when the tax bill was returned from the Ways and Means Committee to which it had been referred for reconsideration, §401(a)(4) had been amended to correspond with the more general language of §401(a)(3)(B), simply banning discrimination in favor of the "highly paid."

The Commissioner found himself confronted with problems in administering the statute similar to those that Congress had encountered in drafting it. While there are attractions in the idea that a plan can be rejected under §§401(a)(3) and (4) only if it discriminates in favor of employees who would generally be regarded as "highly paid," it poses difficulties of administration which the Tax Court did nothing to resolve. Words like "high" and "highly" clamor for a referent. A 500 foot hill would look high in Central Park but not among the Grand Tetons or even at Lake Placid. Apparently the Tax Court regarded the president of the Bottling Corporation with a $28,000-$30,000 salary as "highly paid," and we assume he would be so considered in Niagara Falls, but he hardly would be in Hollywood. More to the point, while we would not regard Bernard J. Riggs, with a salary of $7595-$8580 from the Bottling Corporation as "highly paid," that might not be the view of Helen Kendall whose wages ranged from $3969 to $4420 in the same period, see fn. 3. Considerations such as these led the Commissioner to rule in 1956:

> In order for the plan to meet the coverage requirements, there must be sufficient participation by the lower paid employees to demonstrate that in practice the plan does not discriminate in favor of the high paid employees. . . . The terms "highly compensated" and "lower compensated" are relative, and the distinction between them must be based upon the circumstances of each case. Rev.Rul. 56-497, 1956-2 Cum.Bull. 284, 286.[4]

---

4. The Commissioner cites as further persuasive evidence of the propriety of his relative interpretation §§406-07 which were added to the Internal Revenue Code as part of the Revenue Act of 1964, 78 Stat. 19, 58-63. In prescribing the method by which a domestic corporation may include in its pension plan United States citizens working abroad for a foreign subsidiary the statute directs, §406(b)(1)(B) that

> (B) the determination of whether such individual is a highly compensated employee shall be made by treating such individual's total compensation . . . as

[1-2] We cannot say that in thus reading "highly" as "more highly" and taking the compensation of non-covered employees as the standard, the Commissioner went beyond the powers Congress conferred upon him by §401(a)(3). When Congress has used a general term and has empowered an administrator to define it, the courts must respect his construction if this is within the range of reason. *Gray v. Powell,* 314 U.S. 402, 411-413, 62 S.Ct. 326, 86 L.Ed. 301 (1941); *N.L.R.B. v. Hearst Publications, Inc.,* 322 U.S. 111, 130-132, 64 S.Ct. 851, 88 L.Ed. 1170 (1944). That requirement was met here and it was not for the Tax Court to substitute its reading for that of the administrator on the firing line.[5]

The Tax Court's decision likewise cannot be sustained on the basis that, given the Commissioner's reading of the statute, the facts did not fairly support his determination of non-compliance. While use of the phrase "found by the Commissioner," §401(a)(3)(A), does not preclude meaningful judicial review, it does suggest an intention that the Commissioner's finding be given a shade more than its usual substantial weight. Compare *Grenada Industries, Inc. v. C.I.R.,* 17 T.C. 231, 255, *aff'd,* 202 F.2d 873 (5 Cir.), *cert. denied,* 346 U.S. 819, 74 S.Ct. 32, 98 L.Ed. 345 (1953). In two of the three years every one of the covered eligible employees received higher compensation than any of the non-covered employees, although the differential between the lowest of the covered group and the highest of the uncovered group was only in the neighborhood of $1000; and even in 1962 only one non-covered employee received more than one covered employee. The median salary of the covered group was around $9000; the median wage of the non-covered group was less than $6000. Averages would produce a larger discrepancy. Just how high a penetration of the covered group by the uncovered group would require the Commissioner to find the taint removed is an issue not here before us.

We add only that the Corporation's case is not aided by §401(a)(5). While that subsection says that a plan shall not be considered discriminatory "merely because it is limited to salaried or clerical employees," this is quite different from saying that no plan covering all salaried employees can be discriminatory. *See Fleitz v. C.I.R.,* 50 T.C. No. 35 (1968).

The judgment is reversed, with directions to the Tax Court to sustain the Commissioner's determination.

---

compensation paid by such domestic corporation and by *determining such individual's status with regard to such domestic parent corporation.* (Emphasis added.)

. . . . . .

The same rule applies with respect to foreign-based employees of domestic subsidiaries of domestic parent corporations. Section 407(b)(1)(B), Internal Revenue Code of 1954.

5. We were told at the argument that the sparsity of reported cases dealing with the problem here considered is due to the general practice of obtaining advance clearance of plans.

Although the amendments to the Code contained in Title II of ERISA modified the minimum coverage requirements in effect at the time of the court's decision in the *Pepsi-Cola* case, the requirements currently in effect are substantially identical. Section 410(b)(1) of the Code provides:

> A trust shall not constitute a qualified trust under §401(a) unless the trust . . . benefits either—
>
> (A) 70 percent or more of all employees, or 80 percent or more of all employees who are eligible to benefit under the plan if 70 percent or more of all employees are eligible to benefit under the plan, excluding in each case employees who have not satisfied the minimum age and service requirements, if any, prescribed by the plan as a condition of participation, or
>
> (B) such employees as qualify under a classification set up by the employer and found by the Secretary [of Treasury] not to be discriminatory in favor of employees who are officers, shareholders, or highly compensated.

Clause (A) is referred to as the "percentage test," while clause (B) is referred to as the "classification test." The percentage test is objective in its application, while the classification test is more subjective in its approach. However, in applying either test, certain employees may be excluded from consideration. For example, employees not included in the plan who are included in a unit of employees covered by a collective bargaining agreement may be excluded if retirement benefits were the subject of good faith bargaining between the employer or employers maintaining the plan and the representative of their employees. *See* IRC §410(b)(2)(A). It is also possible to exclude certain air pilots and nonresident aliens. *See* IRC §410(b)(2)(B), (C).

These exclusions make satisfaction of the minimum coverage requirements possible in cases where such a possibility did not exist prior to the amendment of the Code by Title II of ERISA. For example, prior to ERISA, if bargaining unit employees selected an increase in wages or another form of employee benefits as opposed to coverage under a pension plan, the employer might have been unable to establish a plan for other employees since the percentage test could not be satisfied without the bargaining unit employees. The employer would have to satisfy the classification test. This test was very difficult to satisfy in some cases if the non-bargaining unit employees were relatively highly compensated. Congress perceived this result as inequitable and, therefore, amended the Code to provide for the exclusion of bargaining unit employees in certain cases. [It is important to note that provision of the bargaining unit employees exclusion in a plan may lead to violations of the National Labor Relations Act, which will be discussed in Chapter 3. *See* Tappan Co. 228 NLRB 176 (1977).]

Vesting. Section 401(a)(7) provides that a tax-qualified plan must satisfy the minimum vesting standards contained in §411 of the Code. Section 411 of the Code contains both vesting requirements and accrued benefit requirements. Every tax-qualified plan must satisfy the vesting requirements, but only certain plans, such as pension plans, must satisfy the accrued benefit requirements.

The *vesting standards* require the plan to provide that the employee's rights in his accrued benefits derived from his own contributions must be 100% vested or nonforfeitable at all times, and that the employee's rights in his accrued benefits derived from employer contributions must be nonforfeitable pursuant to schedules providing for vesting or nonforfeitability over a period of time, which may not exceed 15 years.

One of the statutory schedules provides for full vesting after ten years of service. If every employee who has at least ten years of service has a 100% vested or nonforfeitable right to his accrued benefit derived from employer contributions, vesting under the plan is adequate.

The second statutory schedule provides for "graded" vesting. To satisfy this standard, an employee who has completed at least five years of service must have a nonforfeitable right to at least 25% of his accrued benefit derived from employer contributions. From the fifth through tenth year of service, at least an additional 5% a year must be vested in the employee; from the tenth through fifteenth year, at least 10% a year more must vest. The employee must be fully vested after no more than 15 years of service.

The third schedule, which is referred to as the "Rule of 45," allows an employer maintaining a plan to provide for vesting according to the employee's age and years of service. Under this schedule, each employee must have a vested or nonforfeitable right to at least 50% of his accrued benefit when the sum of his age and years of service equals or exceeds 45. If the employee continues in the service of the employer maintaining the plan, every year of service thereafter will entitle him to at least an additional 10% of vested benefits.

It is important to note that these three statutory schedules establish "minimum" standards. A plan may contain almost any vesting schedule provided the schedule satisfies all of the requirements of a particular statutory schedule with respect to all of an employee's years of service. For example, a plan could provide for 100% vesting or nonforfeitability after five years of service since this would satisfy the ten year-100% vesting schedule with respect to all of an employee's years of service.

The vesting requirements relating to an employee's rights in his accrued benefit derived from employer contributions are supplemented by the requirement that an employee's right to his normal retirement benefit must be 100% vested or nonforfeitable upon and after the attainment of normal retirement age. For example, if normal retirement age under the plan is age 65, an employee must be 100% vested in his accrued benefit derived from employer contributions upon the attainment of age 65 even though the employee would not otherwise be 100% vested pursuant to the vesting schedule. For example, if an employee commenced participation in a pension plan at age 57 and the plan provided for ten year-100% vesting, the employee must be 100% vested at age 65 even though he would have only eight years of service.

In the case of defined benefit plans, such as pension plans, the viability of the vesting requirements is dependent on the *accrued benefits* to which these minimum vesting percentages are applied. Therefore, the Code also establishes three alternative standards for the computation of accrued benefits.

Under a "3% test," for each year of participation at least 3% of the benefit payable under the plan must accrue to a participant who begins participation at the earliest possible entry age and serves continuously until age 65 or normal retirement age under the plan, whichever is earlier. Under a "133⅓% test," a plan qualifies if the accrual rate for any participant for any later years is not more than 133⅓% of his accrual rate for the current year. Finally, under a "pro rata test," the benefit is computed as though the employee will continue to earn the same rate of compensation annually that he earned during the years that would have been taken into account under the plan, if the employee retired on the date in question. This amount is then to be multiplied by a fraction whose numerator is the employee's total years of active participation in the plan, up to the date for which the computation is being made, and whose denominator is the total number of years of active participation he would have had, had he continued his employment until normal retirement age.

Joint and Survivor Annuity. Section 401(a)(11) requires a tax-qualified plan to provide for the payment of benefits in the form of a joint and survivor annuity, if the plan provides for the payment of benefits in the form of an annuity. The Internal Revenue Service has interpreted this requirement as only applying to plans which provide for payment of benefits in any form of a "life annuity." *See* Treas. Regs. §1.401(a)-11. The term "life annuity" means an annuity that provides retirement payments and requires the survival of the participant or his spouse as one of the conditions for any payment or possible payment under the annuity. For example, annuities that make payments for ten years or until death, whichever occurs first or whichever occurs last, are life annuities. Any plan providing benefits in this form must also provide a joint and survivor annuity.

The term "joint and survivor annuity" means an annuity for the life of the participant with a survivor annuity for the life of his spouse which is neither less than one-half of, nor greater than the amount of, the annuity payable during the joint lives of the participant and his spouse. The joint and survivor annuity requirements are rather complex, since §401(a)(11) contains a number of rules relating to the time during which the joint and survivor annuity must be available and the rights of the participant to elect to receive or not to receive his benefit in the form of a joint and survivor annuity.

Merger. Section 401(a)(12) and §414(l) require a tax-qualified plan to provide that, in the case of any merger or consolidation of the plan with any other plan or any transfer of assets or liabilities to any other plan, each participant in the plan would (if the plan then terminated) receive a benefit immediately after the merger, consolidation, or transfer which is equal to or greater than the benefit he would have been entitled to receive immediately before the merger, consolidation, or transfer (if the plan had then terminated).

It is important to note that this requirement applies to Taft-Hartley plans only to the extent determined by the Pension Benefit Guaranty Corporation.

Anti-Assignment. Section 401(a)(13) requires a tax-qualified plan to provide that benefits under the plan may not be assigned or alienated. However, this requirement does not preclude any voluntary and revocable assignment of 10% or less of any benefit payment made by any participant who is receiving benefits under the plan, provided the assignment of alienation is not made for purposes of defraying plan administrative costs.

Benefit Commencement. Section 401(a)(14) requires a tax-qualified plan to provide that the payment of benefits to the participant must commence (unless the participant elects otherwise) no later than the sixtieth day after the close of the plan year in which the latest of the following events occurs:

1. The participant attains age 65 (or any earlier normal retirement age specified under the plan);
2. Ten years have elapsed from the time the participant commenced participation in the plan; or
3. The participant terminates his service with the employer.

The Internal Revenue Service has interpreted this requirement as permitting the plan to require that a participant file a claim for benefits before payment of benefits will commence. *See* Treas. Regs. §1.401(a)-14. The Regulations also contain a retroactive payment rule. *See* Treas. Regs. §1.401 (a)-14(d). If the amount of the payment required to commence on the date determined under the rules discussed above cannot be ascertained by such date, or if it is not possible to make the payment at that time because the plan administrator is unable to locate the participant, a payment retroactive to such date may be made no later than 60 days after the earliest date on which the amount of the payment can be ascertained or the date on which the participant is located.

Social Security Decreases. Section 401(a)(15) provides that a tax-qualified plan must not reduce benefits on account of increases in the benefits payable under Title II of the Social Security Act or increases in the wage base under Title II, if the increase takes place after the earlier of the date the participant first began to receive benefits or the date the participant separated from service.

Limits on Benefits and Contributions. Section 401(a)(16) states that a tax-qualified plan must not provide for benefits or contributions which exceed the limitations contained in §415. Section 415 contains limitations for defined benefit plans, such as pension plans, and limitations for defined contribution plans, such as profit-sharing plans. This section also contains limitations for any case in which an individual is a participant in both a defined benefit plan and a defined contribution plan maintained by the same employer.

In the case of a pension plan, the benefits with respect to a participant must not exceed the lesser of $90,150 or 100% of the participant's average compensation for his high three years. In the case of a defined contribution plan, contributions and other additions with respect to a participant must not exceed the lesser of $30,050 or 25% of the participant's compensation. The Secretary of the Treasury must increase these dollar amounts for increases in the cost of living. In the case of a participant in both a defined benefit plan and a defined contribution plan maintained by the employer, his total benefits and contributions must not exceed the sum of his benefits under the defined benefit plan and his contributions and other additions under the defined contribution plan by more than 40%.

Funding. The Code also contains minimum funding standards. *See* IRC §412. These standards apply to defined benefit plans, such as pension plans, but not to most defined contribution plans, such as profit-sharing and stock bonus plans.

Each plan subject to §412 of the Code must establish and maintain a "funding standard account." Each plan year, this account must be credited and charged with certain amounts. For example, the funding standard account must be *charged* with (1) the normal cost of the plan for the plan year; (2) the amounts necessary to amortize in equal annual installments (a) the unfunded past service liability over a period of 40 years and (b) the net experience loss or gain over a period of 20 or 30 plan years, respectively; and (3) the amount necessary to amortize certain funding deficiencies over 15 plan years. The funding standard account is *credited* with (1) the amount considered contributed by the employer for the plan year and (2) the amount necessary to amortize in equal annual installments (a) the net decrease in unfunded past service liabilities over 40 years and (b) the net experience gain over 20 or 30 years.

These minimum standards were designed to ensure the presence of assets sufficient to satisfy liabilities, and they are closely related to the plan termination insurance provisions contained in ERISA (discussed in Chapter 1).

Administration of Plans

Fiduciary Responsibility. The structure and content provisions discussed above established the basic framework for tax-qualified plans. The Code also contains provisions relating to the administration of these plans and their relationship to the other components of the plan complex.

Section 401(a) provides that a qualified trust must form part of a pension, profit-sharing or stock bonus plan maintained by an employer for the exclusive benefit of his employees, and, under the trust agreement, it must be impossible for any part of the trust corpus or income to be used for purposes other than for the exclusive benefit of the employer's employees. Section 4975(c) identifies certain "prohibited transactions" between the plan and a disqualified person.

The "exclusive benefit" rule, like the "exclusive purpose" rule and the "solely in the interest" rule contained in ERISA, relates to investments made by the trust. However, the exclusive benefit rule contained in the Code has not been interpreted literally: neither the courts nor the Internal Revenue Service has interpreted the exclusive benefit rule as precluding others from deriving some benefit from a transaction with the trust. *See, e.g., Time Oil Co. v. Commissioner,* 458 F.2d 237 (9th Cir. 1958).

The word "exclusive" has generally been interpreted by the Internal Revenue Service as meaning "primary." For example, a sale of securities to a qualified trust benefits the seller, but if the purchase price is not in excess of the fair market value of the securities at the time of the sale and if certain criteria are satisfied, the investment will be consistent with the "exclusive benefit" rule. Revenue Ruling 69-494, 1969-2 Cum. Bull. 88, illustrates the application of the exclusive benefit rule by the Internal Revenue Service to an investment in employer securities.

REVENUE RULING 69-494
1969-2 Cum. Bull. 88

The purpose of this Revenue Ruling is to update and restate, under the current statute and regulations, the position set forth in PS No. 49, dated June 16, 1945, relating to the requirements an exempt employees' trust must comply with in order to invest funds in the stock or securities of an employer corporation.

An exempt employees' trust maintained by a corporate employer invests trust funds in the stock and securities of the employer. These investments are permitted under the trust instrument and under local law.

Section 1.401-1(b)(5)(i) of the Income Tax Regulations states that no specific limitations are provided in Section 401(a) of the Code with respect to investments that may be made by the trustees of a trust qualifying under Section 401(a). Generally, the contributions may be used by the trustees to purchase any investments permitted by the trust agreement to the extent allowed by local law. However, such a trust will be subject to tax under Section 511 of the Code with respect to any "unrelated business taxable income" (as defined in Section 512) realized by it from its investments. Furthermore, the tax-exempt status of the trust will be forfeited if the investments made by the trustees constitute "prohibited transactions" within the meaning of Section 503 of the Code. See also the regulations under those sections.

Section 1.401-1(b)(5)(ii) of the regulations provides that, where trust funds are invested in stock or securities of the employer or other person described in Section 503 of the Code, full disclosure must be made of the reasons for such arrangement and the conditions under which such investments are made in order that a determination may be made whether the trust serves any purpose other than constituting part of a plan for the exclusive benefit of employees. The trustee shall report any of such investments on the return that it is required to file and shall with respect to any such investment furnish the information required by such return.

Section 1.6033-1(a)(3) of the regulations provides that every employees' trust described in Section 401(a) of the Code and exempt from Federal income taxation under Section 501(a) shall file an annual return on Form 990-P, including the information required by Section 1.401-1 of the regulations.

The primary purpose of benefiting employees or their beneficiaries must be maintained with respect to investments of the trust funds as well as with respect to other activities of the trust. This requirement, however, does not prevent others from also deriving some benefit from a transaction with the trust. For example, a sale of securities at a profit benefits the seller, but if the purchase price is not in excess of the fair market value of the securities at the time of sale and the applicable investment requisites have been met, the investment is consistent with the exclusive-benefit-of-employees requirement. These requisites are: (1) the cost must not exceed fair market value at time of purchase; (2) a fair return commensurate with the prevailing rate must be provided; (3) sufficient liquidity must be maintained to permit distributions in accordance with the terms of the plan, and (4) the safeguards and diversity that a prudent investor would adhere to must be present. However, the requirement set forth in item (2) with respect to a fair return is not applicable to obligatory investments in employer securities in the case of a stock bonus plan. *See* Rev. Rul. 69-65, C.B. 1969-1, 114. Upon compliance with these requisites, if the trust instrument and local law permit investments in the stock or securities of the employer, such investments are not deemed to be inconsistent with the purposes of Section 401(a) of the Code.

In view of the foregoing, it is concluded that the trustee in this case must notify the District Director of Internal Revenue of the investment of trust funds in the stock and securities of the employer so that a determination may be made whether the trust serves any purpose other than constituting a plan for the exclusive benefit of employees. This notification is to be made as part of the annual information return, Form 990-P, unless an advance determination letter is requested. If an advance determination letter is requested, the notification is to be made as part of the request. The notification is to include the information called for under the appropriate provisions of Section 4 of Revenue Procedure 69-4, C.B. 1969-1, 391, and is to be certified by the accounting or other responsible officer.

The filing of the required information does not automatically render the trust part of a plan for the exclusive benefit of employees. It is merely a means of enabling the District Director to make a determination with respect thereto. Neither is such a determination, nor the absence of a disapproval of the contemplated investment, to be construed as an opinion as to whether or not the purchase of the employer's stock or securities constitutes a good investment. In such matters the trustee should be guided by the trust instrument, local law, and his own judgment as a reasonably prudent investor.

PS No. 49 is hereby superseded since the position stated therein is restated under current law in this Revenue Ruling.

If the criteria established in Revenue Ruling 69-494 are satisfied, investments in the stock or securities of the employer maintaining the plan will not be inconsistent with §401(a) of the Code, provided the trust agreement and local law also permit this type of investment. However, the Internal Revenue Service must be notified if assets are invested in stock or securities of, or loaned to, the employer so that a determination may be made whether the trust serves any purpose other than constituting part of a plan for the exclusive benefit of employees. *See* §1.401-1(b)(5)(ii).

It is important to note that much of the language used in the Code is similar to language contained in both ERISA and the Taft-Hartley Act. While the provisions in these laws are similar, they are not identical and they may not be interpreted in the same manner in every case. However, even though there may be subtle differences in the standards under these different laws, they all seem to impose the same basic common law standard of undivided loyalty.

Section 401(a)(2) contains the prohibition against diversion of assets to the employer or employers maintaining the plan pursuant to which the trust is established. *Compare* IRC §401(a)(2) *with* ERISA §403(c). This section requires that the trust agreement must definitely and affirmatively make it impossible for diversion to occur. Treas. Regs. §1.401-2(a)(2).

However, this requirement does not preclude conditional payments and certain other reversions. For example, a provision in a newly established plan permitting the return of employer contributions only in the event that the Internal Revenue Service rules that the plan is not qualified does not prevent qualification of the plan and the trust. *See* Rev. Rul. 60-276, 1960-2 Cum. Bull. 150. It is only as a result of the Internal Revenue Service's determination that the plan does not qualify that a return of employer contributions made prior to such determination is possible. Similarly, employer contributions may be returned to the employer if a surplus exists because of an actuarial error.

Prohibited Transactions. Section 4975 of the Code is similar to §§406 and 408 of ERISA. Section 4975(a) and (b) provides that an initial 5% excise tax and an additional 100% excise tax are imposed on each "prohibited transaction" between a plan and a "disqualified person." Section 4975(c) defines the term "prohibited transaction" in the same manner as the term is defined in ERISA, with certain exceptions. The prohibited transaction provisions contained in the Code do not prohibit a fiduciary from acting in a transaction on behalf of an adverse party. This prohibition is not contained in the Code because of the perceived difficulty involved in calculating the amount of the excise tax. The Code also does not contain the prohibitions relating to the acquisition and holding of employer securities and employer real property.

The excise taxes imposed under the Code must by paid by any "disqualified person" who participated in the prohibited transaction (other than a fiduciary acting only as a fiduciary). The term "disqualified person" includes substantially the same persons included in the definition of the term "party in interest." *Compare* IRC §4975(e)(2) *with* ERISA §3(14). The statutory exemptions contained in the Code are also substantially identical to the statutory exemptions contained in ERISA, and the Secretary of Treasury has the authority to grant administrative exemptions.

Reporting and Disclosure

Like ERISA, the Code contains rather comprehensive reporting requirements. Various reports must be filed with the Internal Revenue Service (as well as with the Department of Labor and the Pension Benefit Guaranty Corporation). In many cases, the information required to be filed with the Internal Revenue Service is substantially identical to the information required to be filed with the Department of Labor. The Internal Revenue Service and the Department of Labor (as well as the Pension Benefit Guaranty Corporation) have consolidated many of the important filing requirements.

An employer maintaining a tax-qualified plan (or the plan administrator) must file certain financial information with the Internal Revenue Service. *See* IRC §6058(a). This information is filed on Form 5500 (or Form 5500-C or 5500-K), which was developed with the Department of Labor. While the deadline for filing the Form 5500 with the Internal Revenue Service originally was different than the deadline for filing with the Department of Labor, the Internal Revenue Service and the Department of Labor have agreed to a single filing date.

The administrator of certain tax-qualified plans must also file an annual registration statement with the Internal Revenue Service. The registration statement must provide various identifying information regarding the plan, the administrator and certain participants, and must specify the nature, amount and form of deferred vested benefit to which any such participants are entitled. *See* IRC §6057(a)(2).

Any plan administrator required to file this statement must notify the Internal Revenue Service of: (1) any change in the plan's name; (2) any change in the name or address of the plan administrator; (3) the termination of the plan; or (4) the plan's merger or consolidation with any other plan or its division into two or more plans. IRC §6057(b). Certain actuarial statements also must be filed. *See* IRC §6058(b), §6059.

Non-Qualified Plans

While the structure and content of non-qualified plans is not governed by the Code, the provisions contained in the Code influence the shape of these plans. Sections 61, 83, 402 and 405 determine the tax consequences to the employer and the employees participating in the plan or arrangement.

The shape of the plan or arrangement will have a bearing on the resulting tax consequences. For example, whether the arrangement is funded or unfunded will, in part, determine whether the employer is entitled to deduct contributions or payments, and the taxable year in which the deduction is available. Similarly, the funded or unfunded nature of the plan or arrangement will determine the taxable year in which the employee has to include contributions or payments in his income.

Welfare Plans

While the term "welfare plan" is not defined in either the Code or the regulations, provisions contained in the Code affect welfare plan structure and content, as well as plan administration and the interaction of welfare plans with the other components of the plan complex. The Code provisions relating to prepaid legal services plans and voluntary employees' beneficiary associations illustrate the applicability of the Code provisions to these arrangements.

Prepaid Legal Plans

Section 120 of the Code provides that an employer may establish a prepaid legal services plan for its employees and their beneficiaries and, if the plan satisfies certain requirements, employer contributions to the plan will be excludable from the gross income of the employee. The value of legal services actually provided under the plan is also excludable by the recipient of the services.

The requirements relate to the structure and content of the plan. A prepaid legal services plan must be a separate written plan of an employer for the exclusive benefit of its employees, and the plan must specify the benefits that will be furnished through prepayment of all or part of the legal fee incurred. The plan must provide benefits for employees who qualify under a classification set up by the employer and found by the Internal Revenue Service not to be discriminatory in favor of certain classes of employees. Similarly, contributions or benefits provided under the plan must not discriminate in favor of certain classes of employees. These requirements are similar to the requirements applicable to tax-qualified plans.

Amounts contributed under the plan must be paid only to certain persons, such as insurance companies. The plan must give notice to the Internal Revenue Service that it is applying for recognition of status as a prepaid legal services plan.

Voluntary Employees' Associations

Section 501(c)(9) provides that voluntary employees' beneficiary associations, which provide for the payment of life, sickness, accident or other benefits to the members of the association or their beneficiaries, can qualify for tax exemption. Supplemental unemployment compensation benefit plans may also qualify under §501(c)(9). *See* Rev. Rul. 58-442, 1958-2 Cum. Bull. 194. If the employees' association satisfies certain structure and content requirements, it is accorded a form of favorable tax treatment.

First, the association must be an association of employees. That is, it must be composed of individuals who are entitled to participate in the association through their status as employees who are members of a common working unit. *See* Treas. Regs. §1.501(c)(9)-1(b)(1)(i). Members of a common working unit include the employees of a single employer, the employees of a union or the employees of one industry. Second, membership of the employees in the association must be voluntary. An association is not a voluntary association if the employer unilaterally imposes membership in the association on the employee as a condition of his employment and the employee incurs a detriment (e.g., deductions from his salary) because of his membership in the association. *See* Treas. Regs. §1.501(c)(9)-1(b)(2). Third, the organization must be operated only for the purpose of providing for the payment of life, sickness, accident, or other benefits to its members or their dependents. The term "life benefits" includes life insurance benefits or similar benefits payable on the death of the member, made available to members for current protection only. *See* Treas. Regs. §1.501(c)(9)-1(b)(3)(iii). For example, term insurance is an acceptable benefit. The term "sickness and accident benefits" means an amount furnished in the event of illness or personal injury to a member. *See* Treas. Regs. §1.501(c)(9)-1(b)(3)(iv). For example, a sickness and accident benefit includes a benefit provided under a plan to reimburse a member for amounts he expends because of illness or injury, or for premiums he pays to a medical benefit program such as Medicare. Sickness and accident benefits may also be furnished in non-cash form: e.g., clinical care, services by visiting nurses and transportation furnished for medical care. Fourth, no part of the net earnings of the organization may inure (other than through the payment of acceptable benefits) to the benefit of any private shareholder or individual. This requirement, in effect, relates to the administration of the plan. For example, the disposition of property to, or the performance of services for, any person for less than its cost to the association will constitute prohibited inurement. *See* Treas. Regs. §1.501(c)(9)-1(b)(4). Fifth, the association is subject to the tax on unrelated business income. *See* IRC §§511-515.

The applicability of these sections to employees' beneficiary associations affects the relationship of the association with the other components of the plan complex. Certain activities, if engaged in by the association, will result in taxation of its income.

SECOND LIBERTY LOAN ACT

The Second Liberty Loan Act (the Loan Act), 31 U.S.C. §757(c)(2), authorizes the Secretary of the Treasury to offer for sale bonds of the United States designated as United States Retirement Plan Bonds. This law provides the Secretary of the Treasury with the authority to promulgate rules and regulations governing the terms and conditions of issuance and redemption of these bonds.

The Secretary of the Treasury exercises this authority by making these bonds available for investment by tax-qualified pension and profit-sharing plans and by bond purchase plans. *See* Treas. Regs. §§341.0-341.15. The regulations describe the bonds, including their investment yield (interest), their term and the denomination in which the bonds will be available, and provide for the purchase of the bonds over the counter or by mail from the Federal Reserve Banks and branches and from the Office of the Treasurer of the United States.

TAX REDUCTION ACT OF 1975

The Tax Reduction Act of 1975 (the Tax Reduction Act), 26 U.S.C. §1, *et seq*., contains numerous amendments to the Code, including an increase in the investment tax credit. Section 301(a) of the Tax Reduction Act, which amends Section 46 of the Code, provides for an election by a corporate taxpayer of an 11% investment tax credit for 1975-1976 (instead of the generally available 10%) if an amount equal to 1% of the tax credit is contributed to a plan referred to in the Tax Reduction Act as an "employee stock ownership plan." The employee stock ownership plan must satisfy certain requirements delineated in Section 301(d) of the Tax Reduction Act. It is important to note that this section does *not* amend the Code and, therefore, the requirements are not contained in the Code.

Like the favorable tax treatment accorded tax-qualified plans if the plan satisfies certain requirements, Section 301(d) of the Tax Reduction Act contains numerous structure and content requirements which must be satisfied by the plan in order for the employer to be entitled to the additional investment tax credit. The employee stock ownership plan must be a profit-sharing, stock bonus, or stock bonus and money purchase pension plan which is established in writing and which is designed to invest primarily in common stock issued by the corporation establishing the plan.

All common stock transferred to or purchased by the plan must be allocated to the account of each participant in proportion to compensation. Once the stock is allocated to the account of a particular participant, the participant must be 100% vested in the stock allocated to his account. However, the stock cannot be distributed to the participant or his beneficiary for seven years, except in certain cases.

TAX REFORM ACT OF 1976

The Tax Reform Act of 1976 (the Tax Reform Act), 26 U.S.C. §1, *et seq*., also contains numerous amendments to the Code, including an increase in the investment tax credit. Section 801 of the Tax Reform Act extends the additional tax credit provided under the Tax Reduction Act amendments to the Code through 1980, provided the corporate taxpayer contributes an amount equal to 1% of the tax credit to an employee stock ownership plan. The employee stock ownership plan must satisfy the non-Code structure and content requirements delineated in Section 301(d) of the Tax Reduction Act. The Tax Reform Act also expands upon the Tax Reduction Act by providing for an extra ½% investment tax credit if the corporation's additional contribution is matched by employees.

TRADE ACT OF 1974

The Trade Act of 1974 (the Trade Act), 19 U.S.C. §2101, *et seq*., authorizes the Secretary of Commerce to guarantee loans made to private borrowers by private lending institutions in connection with projects in trade-impacted areas. When considering whether to guarantee a loan by a private lending institution to a corporation, Section 2373(f)(1) directs the Secretary of Commerce to give preference to a corporation which agrees to contribute 25% of the principal amount of the loan to an employee stock ownership plan established and maintained by the corporation.

Like the favorable tax treatment accorded tax-qualified plans which satisfy certain requirements, Section 2363(f)(2) of the Trade Act contains numerous structure and content requirements which the plan must satisfy for the corporation to be afforded preferential treatment by the Secretary of Commerce. The employee stock ownership plan must provide that the amount contributed by the corporation will be used to purchase common stock issued by the corporation establishing the plan. The plan must be designed to amortize the loan on behalf of the corporation out of amounts contributed by the corporation and, during the amortization period, the plan must allocate the common stock held by the plan to the accounts of each participant. The plan also must satisfy the requirements delineated in Title I of ERISA and in Sections 401(a) and 4975(e)(7) of the Code.

CHAPTER 3

Labor Laws

NATIONAL LABOR RELATIONS ACT

The National Labor Relations Act of 1935 (the NLRA), 29 U.S.C. §151, *et seq.*, was designed to promote collective bargaining between employers and representatives of their employees. Unlike many of the other laws discussed in this book, the NLRA does not contain numerous provisions relating to pension and welfare plans, nor does it contain provisions relating to plan structure and content or administration. However, like the Internal Revenue Code of 1954, the NLRA has contributed to a legal environment that has led to the proliferation of pension and welfare benefit plans.

An early court decision interpreting the NLRA held that employee benefits were a mandatory subject of collective bargaining. Specifically, through the conjunction of §§8(a)(5) and 9(a), the NLRA requires employers in interstate commerce "to bargain collectively with representatives of [its] employees . . ." with respect to ". . . rates of pay, wages, hours of employment or other conditions of employment . . ."

In *Inland Steel Co. v. N.L.R.B.*, 170 F.2d 247 (7th Cir. 1948), *cert. denied* 336 U.S. 960, the Seventh Circuit Court of Appeals held that employee benefit plans were within the scope of the term "wages" and the phrase "other conditions of employment." Consequently, an employer presented with a proper demand cannot refuse to bargain with respect to an employee benefit plan for its employees. However, according to the Supreme Court in the case of *Allied Chemical Workers v. Pittsburgh Plate Glass Co.*, 404 U.S. 157 (1971), retired employees are not "employees" within the meaning of the NLRA. This decision stands for the proposition that the employer's duty to bargain does not extend to retired employees.

INLAND STEEL CO. V. N.L.R.B.
170 F.2d 247 (7th Cir. 1947)

MAJOR, Circuit Judge:

These cases are here upon petition (in No. 9612) of Inland Steel Company (hereinafter called the Company), to review and set aside an order issued by the National Labor Relations Board on April 12, 1948, against the company, pursuant to Sec. 10(c) of the National Labor Relations Act,[1] following the usual proceedings under Sec. 10 of the Act, and upon petition (in No. 9634) of the United Steel Workers of America, C.I.O. (hereinafter called the Union), to review and set aside a condition attached to the Board's order.

In the beginning, it seems appropriate to set forth that portion of the Board's order which gives rise to the questions here in controversy. The order requires the Company to

> Cease and desist from:
>
> (a) Refusing to bargain collectively with Local Unions Nos. 1010 and 64, United Steelworkers of America (CIO), with respect to its pension and retirement policies if and when said labor organization shall have complied within thirty (30) days from the date of this Order, with Section 9(f), (g), and (h) of the Act, as amended, as the exclusive bargaining representative of all production, maintenance, and transportation workers in the [peti-

---

1. The National Labor Relations Act, 49 Stat. 449, 29 U.S.C.A. §151 *et seq.* (hereinafter referred to as the Act), was amended by the Labor Management Relations Act, 1947, effective August 22, 1947, 61 Stat. 136, 29 U.S.C.A. §141 *et seq.* (hereinafter referred to as the amended Act). The unfair labor practices found by the Board herein occurred, in part, prior to the effective date of the amendment and, in part, thereafter.

tioner's] Indiana Harbor, Indiana, and Chicago Heights, Illinois, plants, excluding foremen, assistant foremen, supervisory, office and salaried employees, bricklayers, timekeepers, technical engineers, technicians, draftsmen, chemists, watchmen, and nurses;

(b) Making any unilateral changes, affecting any employees in the unit represented by the Union, with respect to its pension and retirement policies without prior consultation with the Union, when and if the Union shall have complied with the filing requirements of the Act, as amended, in the manner set forth above.

The Company, in case No. 9612, attacks that portion of the order which requires it to bargain with respect to its retirement and pension policies. The Union has been permitted to intervene and joins the Board in the defense of this part of the order. The Union, in case No. 9634, attacks the condition attached to the order, which requires as a prerequisite to its enforcement that the Union comply with Sec. 9(h) of the Act. Obviously, if the Company's position is sustained, the Union's petition need not be considered. On the other hand, if the Company's contention is denied, we will be confronted with the question raised by the Union.

We shall, therefore, first consider the question presented on the Company's petition for review. In doing so, we do not overlook the board's contention that we are without authority to consider such question on the ground that the Company is not aggrieved until there has been compliance by the Union with the condition attached to the order. We think this contention is without merit and need not be discussed.

There is no question as to jurisdiction and no dispute of any consequence as to the facts in either case. The Company's refusal to bargain concerning a retirement and pension plan is based solely on its contention that it is not required to do so under the terms of the Act. The Union has refused to comply with the condition attached to the order insofar as Sec. 9(h) is concerned, on the ground that the paragraph is unconstitutional. Thus, a question of law is presented in each case.

The collective bargaining requirement in the original Act was embraced mainly in Secs. 8(5) and 9(a).[2] No question is raised as to any change in the status of the parties because of the amended Act. It seems, therefore, that the original Act is of importance only as an aid in construing the amended Act wherein Congress employed the identical language, so far as pertinent to the instant question, which it had originally used.

The Company relates in lengthy detail the complicated nature of its retirement and pension plan, for the purpose, as we understand, of showing that it is impossible, or at any rate highly impractical, for it to bargain relative thereto with the multiplicity of bargaining units which the Board has established in its plant. It states in its brief:

> Retirement and pension plans such as the petitioner's cannot be dealt with through the processes of compulsory collective bargaining required by the National Labor Relations Act, which entail bargaining within units of the character established by Section 9(a) and (b) of that Act.

The Company concedes that "Congress could have established a requirement of compulsory collective bargaining upon any subject which a representative of the employees chose to present for that purpose," and we understand from some parts of its argument that it tacitly concedes that some retirement and pension plans may be within the scope of the bargaining requirement. However, we find in the Company's reply brief, in response to the Board's argument, what appears to be the inconsistent statement that "Congress intended to exclude from the compulsory bargaining requirement of the Act all industrial retirement and pension plans. The law is a law for all and it is the same law." We agree, of course, with the last sentence of this quotation. We also are of the view that the Bargaining requirements of the Act include all retirement and pension plans or none. Otherwise, as the Board points out, "Some employers would have to bargain about pensions and some would not, depending entirely upon the unit structure in the plant and the nature of the pension plan the employer has established or desires to establish." Such a holding as to the Act's requirements would supply the incentive for an employer to devise a plan or system which would be sufficiently comprehensive and difficult to remove it from the ambit of the statute, and success of such an effort would depend upon the ingenuity of the formulator of the plan. We are satisfied no such construction of the Act can reasonably be made.

It is, therefore, our view that the Company's retirement and pension plan, complicated as it is asserted to be, must be treated and considered the

2. These sections were reenacted in Secs. 8(a)(5) and 9(a) of the amended Act, without material change so far as the present issue is concerned. The Board found that retirement and pension matters were subjects of compulsory collective bargaining under the Act and that they remained so under the amended Act.

same as any other such plan. It follows that the issue for decision is, as the Board asserts, whether pension and retirement plans are part of the subject matter of compulsory collective bargaining within the meaning of the Act. The contention which we have just discussed has been treated first, and perhaps somewhat out of order, so as to obviate the necessity for a lengthy and detailed statement of the Company's plan.

Briefly, the plan as originally initiated on January 1, 1936, provided for the establishment of a contributory plan for the payment of retirement annuities pursuant to a contract between the Company and the Equitable Life Assurance Society. Only employees with earnings of $250.00 or more per month were eligible to participate. Effective December 31, 1943, the plan was extended to cover all employees regardless of the amount of their earnings, provided they had attained the age of 30 and had five years of service. The plan from the beginning was optional with the employees, who could drop out at any time, with rights upon retirement fixed as of that date. On December 28, 1945, the Company entered into an agreement with the First National Bank of Chicago, wherein the Company established a pension trust, the purpose of which was to augment the Company's pension program by making annuities available to employees whose period of service had occurred largely during years prior to the time when participation in the retirement plan was available to them. These were employees whose retirement date would occur so soon after the establishment of the plan that it would not afford them adequate retirement annuity benefits. The employees eligible to participate in the pension trust were not required to contribute thereto, but such fund was created by the Company's contributions.

An integral and it is asserted an essential part of the plan from the beginning was that employees be compulsorily retired at the age of 65. (There are some exceptions to this requirement which are not material here.)

The Company's plan had been in effect for five and one-half years when, because of the increased demands for production and with a shortage of manpower occasioned by the war, it was compelled to suspend the retirement of its employees as provided by its established program. In consequence there were no retirements for age at either of the plants involved in the instant proceeding from August 26, 1941 to April 1, 1946. This temporary suspension of the compulsory retirement rule was abrogated, and it was determined by the Company that no retirements should be deferred beyond June 30, 1946. By April 1, 1946, all of the Company's employees, some 224 in number, who had reached the age of 65, had been retired. Thereupon, the Union filed with the Company a grievance protesting its action in the automatic retirement of employees at the age of 65. The Company refuses to discuss this grievance with the Union, taking the position that it was not required under the Act to do so or to bargain concerning its retirement and pension plan, and particularly concerning the compulsory retirement feature thereof. Whereupon, the instant proceeding was instituted before the Board, with the result already noted.

This brings us to the particular language in controversy. Sec. 8(5) of the Act requires an employer "to bargain collectively with the representative of his employees, subject to the provisions of Sec. 9(a)," and the latter section provides that the duly selected representative of the employees in an appropriate unit shall be their exclusive representative "for the purposes of collective bargaining *in respect to rates of pay, wages, hours of employment, or other conditions of employment. . . .*" (Italics supplied.) The instant controversy has to do with the construction to be given or the meaning to be attached to the italicized words; in fact, the controversy is narrowed to the meaning to be attached to the term "wages" or "other conditions of employment."

The Board found and concluded that the benefits accruing to an employee by reason of a retirement or pension plan are encompassed in both categories. As to the former it stated in its decision:

> With due regard for the aims and purposes of the Act and the evils which it sought to correct, we are convinced and find that the term "wages" as used in Section 9(a) must be construed to include *emoluments of value,* like pension and insurance benefits, which may accrue to employees out of their employment relationship. . . . Realistically viewed, this type of wage enhancement or increase, no less than any other, becomes an integral part of the entire wage structure, and the character of the employee representative's interest in it, and the terms of its grant, is no different than in any other case where a change in the wage structure is effected.

(1) The Board also found and concluded that in any event a retirement and pension plan is included in "conditions of employment" and is a matter for collective bargaining. After a careful study of the well written brief with which we have been favored, we find ourselves in agreement with the Board's conclusion. In fact, we are

convinced that the language employed by Congress, considered in connection with the purpose of the Act, so clearly includes a retirement and pension plan as to leave little, if any, room for construction. While, as the Company has demonstrated, a reasonable argument can be made that the benefits flowing from such a plan are not "wages," we think the better and more logical argument is on the other side and certainly there is, in our opinion, no sound basis for an argument that such a plan is not clearly included in the phrase, "other conditions of employment." The language employed, when viewed in connection with the stated purpose of the Act, leads irresistibly to such a conclusion. And we find nothing in the numerous authorities called to our attention or in the legislative history so strongly relied upon which demonstrates a contrary intent and purpose on the part of Congress.

The opening sentence in the Company's argument is as follows: "Sections 8(5) and 9(a) of the Act do not refer to industrial retirement and pension plans, such as that of the petitioner, in haec verba." Of course not, and this is equally true as to the myriad matters arising from the employer-employee relationship which are recognized as included in the bargaining requirements of the Act but which are not specifically referred to. Illustrative are the numerous matters concerning which the Company and the Union have bargained and agreed, as embodied in their contract of April 30, 1945. A few of such matters are: a provision agreeing to bargain concerning nondiscriminatory discharges; a provision concerning seniority rights, with its far reaching effect upon promotions and demotions; a provision for the benefit of employees inducted into the military service; a provision determining vacation periods with pay; a provision concerning the safety and health of employees, including clinic facilities; a provision for in-plant feeding, and a provision binding the Company and the Union to bargain, in conformity with a Directive Order of the National War Labor Board concerning dismissal or severance pay for employees displaced as the result of the closing of plants or the reduction in the working force following the termination of the war. None of these matters and many others which could be mentioned are referred to in the Act "in haec verba," yet we think they are recognized generally, and they have been specifically recognized by the Company in the instant case as proper matters for bargaining and, as a result, have been included in a contract with the Union. Some of the benefits thus conferred could properly be designated as "wages," and they are all "conditions of employment." We think no common sense view would permit a distinction to be made as to the benefits inuring to the employees by reason of a retirement and pension plan.

The Company in its brief states the reasons for the establishment of a uniform fixed compulsory retirement age for all of its employees in connection with its retirement annuity program, among which are (1) "The fixed retirement age gives the employee advance notice as to the length of his possible service with the Company and enables him to plan accordingly," (2) "The fixed retirement age prevents grievances that otherwise would multiply as the question of each employee's employability arose," (3) "A fixed retirement age gives an incentive to younger men," and (4) "It is unfair and destructive of employee morale to discriminate between types of jobs or types of employees in retiring such employees from service." These reasons thus stated for a compulsory retirement age demonstrate, so we think, contrary to the Company's contention, that the plan is included in "conditions of employment."

The Supreme Court, in *National Licorice Co. v. N.L.R.B.,* 309 U.S. 350, 360, 60 S.Ct. 569, 84 L.Ed. 799, held that collective bargaining extends to matters involving discharge actions and, as already noted, the Company in its contract with the Union has so recognized. We are unable to differentiate between the conceded right of a Union to bargain concerning a discharge, and particularly a nondiscriminatory discharge, of an employee and its right to bargain concerning the age at which he is compelled to retire. In either case, the employee loses his job at the command of the employer; in either case, the effect upon the "conditions" of the person's employment is that the employment is terminated, and we think, in either case, the affected employee is entitled under the Act to bargain collectively through his duly selected representatives concerning such termination. In one instance, the cessation of employment comes perhaps suddenly and without advance notice or warning, while in the other, his employment ceases as a result of a plan announced in advance by the Company. And it must be remembered that the retirement age in the instant situation is determined by the Company and forced upon the employees without consultation and without any voice as to whether the retirement age is to be 65 or some other age. The Company's position that the age of retirement is not a matter for bargaining leads to the incongruous result that a proper bargaining matter is presented if an employee is suddenly discharged on the day before he reaches the age of 65, but that the next day, when he is subject to compulsory retirement, his Union is without right to bargain concerning such retirement.

The Company, however, attempts to escape the force of this reasoning by arguing that the retirement provision affects tenure of employment as distinguished from a condition of employment. The argument, as we understand, rests on the premise that the Act makes a distinction between "tenure of employment" and "conditions of employment," and attention is called to the use of those terms in Secs. 8(3) and 2(9) of the Act. Having thus asserted this distinction, the argument proceeds that tenure of employment is not embraced within the term "conditions of employment." Assuming that the Act recognizes such distinction for some purposes, it does not follow that such a distinction may properly be made for the purpose of collective bargaining, as defined in Sec. 9(a). "Tenure" as presently used undoubtedly means duration or length of employment. The tenure of employment is terminated just as effectively by a discharge for cause as by a dismissal occasioned by a retirement provision. And in both instances alike, the time of the termination of such tenure is determined by the Company. As already shown, a termination by discharge is concededly a matter for collective bargaining. To say that termination by retirement is not amenable to the same process could not, in our judgment, be supported by logic, reason or common sense. In our view, the contention is without merit.

The Company also concedes that seniority is a proper matter for collective bargaining and, as already noted, has so recognized by its contract with the Union. It states in its brief that seniority is "the very heart of conditions of employment." Among the purposes which seniority serves is the protection of employees against arbitrary management conduct in connection with hire, promotion, demotion, transfer and discharge, and the creation of job security for older workers. A unilateral retirement and pension plan has as its main objective not job security for older workers but their retirement at an age predetermined by the Company, and we think the latter is as much included in "conditions of employment" as the former. What would be the purpose of protecting senior employees against lay-off when an employer could arbitrarily and unilaterally place the compulsory retirement age at any level which might suit its purpose? If the Company may fix an age at 65, there is nothing to prevent it from deciding that 50 or 45 is the age at which employees are no longer employable, and in this manner wholly frustrate the seniority protections for which the Union has bargained. Again we note that discharges and seniority rights, like a retirement and pension plan, are not specifically mentioned in the bargaining requirements of the Act.

The Company in its brief as to seniority rights states that it "affects the employee's status every day." In contrast, the plain implication to be drawn from its argument is that an employee is a stranger to a retirement and pension plan during all the days of his employment and that it affects him in no manner until he arrives at the retirement age. We think such reasoning is without logic. Suppose that a person seeking employment was offered a job by each of two companies equal in all respects except that one had a retirement and pension plan and that the other did not. We think it reasonable to assume an acceptance of the job with the company which had such plan. Of course, that might be described merely as the inducement which caused the job to be accepted, but on acceptance it would become, so we think, one of the "conditions of employment." Every day that such an employee worked his financial status would be enhanced to the extent that his pension benefits increased, and his labor would be performed under a pledge from the company that certain specified monetary benefits would be his upon reaching the designated age. It surely cannot be seriously disputed but that such a pledge on the part of the company forms a part of the consideration for work performed, and we see no reason why an employee entitled to the benefit of the plan could not upon the refusal of the company to pay, sue and recover such benefits. In this view, the pension thus promised would appear to be as much a part of his "wages" as the money paid him at the time of the rendition of his services. But again we say that in any event such a plan is one of the "conditions of employment."

The Company makes the far fetched argument that the contributions made to a pension plan "differ in no respect from a voluntary payment that might be made to each employee on his marriage, or on the birth of a child, or on attaining the age of 50, or on enlisting in the armed forces in time of war or on participating as a member of a successful company baseball team," but we think there is a vast difference which arises from the fact that such hypothetical payments are not made as the result of a promise contained in a plan or program. They represent nothing more than a gift. Assume, however, that such supposed payments were made to employees as a result of a company obligation contained in a plan or program. Such an obligation would represent a part of the consideration for services performed, and payments made in the discharge of such obligation would, in our view, be "wages" or included in "conditions of employment."

The Board cites a number of authorities wherein the term "wages" in other fields of law has been broadly construed in support of its conclusion in the instant case that the term includes retirement and pension benefits for the purpose of collective bargaining. While we do not attach too much importance to the broad interpretation given the term in unrelated fields, we think they do show that a broad interpretation here is not unreasonable. For instance, the Board has been sustained in a number of cases where it has treated for the purpose of remedying the effects of discriminatory discharges, in violation of Sec. 8(3) of the Act, pension and other "beneficial insurance rights of employees as part of the employees' real wages and, in accordance with its authority under Sec. 10(c), to order reinstatement of employees with . . . back pay," and has required the employer to restore such benefits to employees discriminated against. *See Butler Bros., et al. v. N.L.R.B.,* 7 Cir., 134 F.2d 981, 985; *General Motors Corp. v. N.L.R.B.,* 3 Cir., 150 F.2d 201, and *N.L.R.B. v. Stackpole Carbon Co.,* 3 Cir., 128 F.2d 188. In the latter case, the court stated (128 F.2d at page 191) that the Board's conclusion "seems to us to be in line with the purposes of the Act for the insurance rights in substance were part of the employee's wages."

In the Social Security Act, 49 Stat. 642, Sec. 907, 42 U.S.C.A. §1107, the same Congress which enacted the National Labor Relations Act defined taxable "wages" as embracing "all remuneration . . . [for services performed by an employee for his employer], including the cash value of all remuneration paid in any medium other than cash. . . ." This definition has been construed, as the Supreme Court noted, in *Social Security Board v. Nierotko,* 327 U.S. 358, 365, 66 S.Ct. 637, 90 L.Ed. 718, 162 A.L.R. 1445 (note 17), as including "vacation allowances," "sick pay," and "dismissal pay."

In the field of taxation, pension and retirement allowances have been deemed to be income of the recipients within the Internal Revenue Act definition of wages as "compensation for personal services." 26 U.S.C.A. Int. Rev. Code §22(a). Thus, in *Hooker v. Hoey,* D.C., 27 F.Supp. 489, 490, *affirmed,* 2 Cir., 107 F.2d 1016, the court said: "It cannot be doubted that pensions or retiring allowances paid because of past services are one form of compensation for personal service and constitute taxable income. . . ."

The Company in its effort to obtain a construction of Sec. 9(a) favorable to its contention devotes much of its brief to the legislative history of the Act which it is claimed demonstrates that Congress did not intend to subject retirement and pension plans to the bargaining process. In view of what we have said, this argument may be disposed of without extended discussion. It is sufficient to note that we have studied this legislative history and, while there are some portions of it which appear to support the Company's position, yet taken as a whole it is not convincing. It would, in our judgment, require a far stronger showing of congressional intent than exists here before we would be justified in placing a construction upon the provision in question which would do violence to the plain words of the statutory requirement and which would result in an impairment of the purpose of the Act. It may be true, as argued by the Company, that retirement and pension plans were employed only to a limited extent in 1935, when the original Act was passed. Such provisions, however, were being generally used at the time of the passage of the amended Act in 1947. And we doubt the validity of the argument that the language of the latter Act cannot be given a broader scope even though Congress used the same phraseology. We do not believe that it was contemplated that the language of Sec. 9(a) was to remain static. Congress in the original as well as in the amended Act used general language, evidently designed to meet the increasing problems arising from the employer-employee relationship. As was said in *Weems v. United States,* 217 U.S. 349, 373, 30 S.Ct. 544, 551, 54 L.Ed. 793, 19 Ann. Cas. 705:

> Legislation, both statutory and constitutional, is enacted, it is true, from an experience of evils, but its general language should not, therefore, be necessarily confined to the form that evil had theretofore taken. Time works changes, brings into existence new conditions and purposes. Therefore a principle to be vital must be capable of wider application than the mischief which gave it birth.

The Company places great stress upon the bargaining language used in the Railway Labor Act of 1926, 45 U.S.C.A. §151 *et seq.,* on the theory that the instant Act is in pari materia. It points out that numerous retirement and pension plans were put into effect by the railroads and that they were never subjected to the process of collective bargaining. This showing is made for the purpose of demonstrating that Congress in the enactment of the legislation now before us did not intend to include such matters. In this connection, we think it is pertinent to note that in the Railway Labor Act the bargaining language was quite different from that of the instant legislation. There, it read, "rates of pay, rules, or working conditions." Here, it reads, "rates of pay, wages, hours of employment, or other conditions of employment." A comparison of the language of the two Acts shows that Congress in the instant legislation must have intended a bargaining provision of broader scope than that contemplated in the Railway Labor Act. Certainly the term "wages" was intended to include something more than "rates of pay." Otherwise, its use would have served no purpose. Congress in the instant legislation used the phrase, "other conditions of employment," instead of the phrase, "working conditions," which it had previously used in the Railway Act. We think it is obvious that the phrase which it later used is more inclusive than that which it had formerly used. Even though the disputed language of the instant Act was open to construction, we think a comparison of the language of these two Acts is of no benefit to the Company.

The Company places much reliance upon a statement from the opinion in *J. I. Case Co. v. N.L.R.B.,* 321 U.S. 332, 339, 64 S.Ct. 576, 88 L.Ed. 762. While the court was not considering a question such as that with which we are now concerned, we think it must be conceded that the language furnishes some support for the Company's position, and if this case stood alone as the sole expression of the Supreme Court relative to the question before us it would at least cause us to hesitate; however, in a later case, *United States v. United Mine Workers of America,* 330 U.S. 258, 286, 287, 67 S.Ct. 677, 91 L.Ed. 884, the court made a statement which indicates a view contrary to the Company's present position. Again, however, the question here presented was not before the court and we do not regard either of these cases as an expression of the view of the Supreme Court upon the instant question. The support which the Company professes to find in the *Case* case is at least offset by the court's statement in the *United Mine Workers* case.

It is our view, therefore, and we so hold that the order of the Board, insofar as it requires the Company to bargain with respect to retirement and pension matters, is valid, and the petition to review, filed by the Company in No. 9612, is denied.

This brings us to the Union's position for review of the order in No. 9634. Upon issuance of the same, the Union satisfied the condition attached thereto insofar as it pertained to Sec. 9(f) and (g) of the Act, but failed and refused to comply with Sec. 9(h).

On May 14, 1948, the Union filed with the Board a document entitled, "Return by United Steel Workers of America to Conditional Order of National Labor Relations Board," in which the Union requested the Board to amend its order by making it unconditional. In this document, the Union alleged "that it had not complied with the requirement of Sec. 9(h) of the Act, as amended, because the Union believes that Sec. 9(h) is unconstitutional and void." The Board by its order entered May 17, 1948, denied the request, saying:

> Upon due consideration of the matter, the Board believes that the Union's request for an amendment rendering the Board's order unconditional must be, and it hereby is, denied. In the absence of authoritative judicial determination to the contrary, the Board assumes the constitutional validity of the provisions of the amended Act.

Thus, we have presented the important and perplexing problem as to the constitutionality of Sec. 9(h), the relevant portion of which provides:

> No investigation shall be made by the Board . . ., no petition . . . shall be entertained, and no complaint shall be issued pursuant to a charge made by a labor organization . . . unless there is on file with the Board an affidavit executed contemporaneously or within the preceding twelve-month period by each officer of such labor organization and the officers of any national or international labor organization of which it is an affiliate or constituent unit that he is not a member of the Communist Party or affiliated with such party, and that he does not believe in, and is not a member of or supports any organization that believes in or teaches, the overthrow of the United States Government by force or by any illegal or unconstitutional methods. The provisions of section 35 A of the Criminal Code shall be applicable in respect to such affidavits.

The Union attacks the constitutionality of Sec. 9(h) on the ground that it is violative of the Constitution in numerous respects. It asserts (1) that the provision invades the political freedom of Philip Murray (petitioner), as well as that of other officials of the Union of which he is the head, and of the members of such Union, in violation of the First, Ninth and Tenth Amendments; (2) that it constitutes a bill of attainder within the meaning of Article I, Sec. 9, Clause 3; (3) that it deprives the Union, its officials and members of liberty and property without due process of law and arbitrarily discriminates against them in violation of the Fifth Amendment, and (4) that it is unconstitutional because of its vagueness, indefiniteness and uncertainness. The constitutionality of the provision has also been attacked by the National Lawyers Guild in a brief which we have permitted to be filed as amicus curiae.

The Board defends the constitutional power of Congress to require as a condition to the compulsory right of a labor organization to bargain collectively that each of its officers make the required affidavit. It is argued (1) that the withholding of such benefits does not impinge on the constitutional right to self-organization; (2) that the condition imposed and the congressional policy which it effectuates does not invade rights of freedom of speech or freedom of the press, or deny freedom of political belief, activity or affiliation; (3) that Congress could reasonably believe that the policies of the Act, and the security interests of the nation, would not be fostered by the extension of the benefits of the Act to labor organizations whose officers are Communists or supporters of organizations dominated by Communists; (4) that the means adopted by Congress to accomplish such purpose are appropriate; (5) that the language of the provision is sufficiently definite and certain to escape constitutional impairment, and (6) that it does not constitute a bill of attainder.

The constitutionality of Sec. 9(h) has been sustained in *National Maritime Union v. Herzog,* D.C., 78 F.Supp. 146, and by the District Court for the Southern District of New York, in *Wholesale and Warehouse Workers' Union, etc. v. Douds,* 79 F.Supp. 563. Each of these cases was decided by a three-Judge statutory court in proceedings wherein it was sought to enjoin the Labor Board from giving effect to the provision in controversy. In the *Herzog* case the court rendered a lengthy opinion in support of its position, which was approved in the *Douds* case. In each of the cases there was a dissenting opinion in which the dissenting Judge viewed the provision as unconstitutional. In the *Herzog* case the court also sustained the constitutionality of Sec. 9(f) and (g). On appeal, the Supreme Court in a Per Curiam order entered June 21, 1948, 334 U.S. 854, S.Ct. 1529, affirmed the statutory court as to these two paragraphs but found it unnecessary to consider the validity of Sec. 9(h).

I find myself in disagreement with my associates. Judge Kerner has written an opinion, concurred in by Judge Minton, upholding the constitutionality of the section. I think to the contrary. Among many Supreme Court cases cited and discussed by the respective parties, there are none which present an analogous situation; in fact, the section is unique in the annals of the entire legislative and judicial field. The cases do teach, however, in unmistakable fashion, especially in recent times, the broad interpretation given the First Amendment and the zealous protection which the Supreme Court has afforded it from impairment or encroachment.

As illustrative, a few cases may be noted. "That priority gives these liberties a sanctity and a sanction not permitting dubious intrusions. And it is the character of the right, not of the limitation, which determines what standard governs the choice." *Thomas v. Collins,* 323 U.S. 516, 530, 65 S.Ct. 315, 322, 89 L.Ed. 430. "For the First Amendment does not speak equivocally. It prohibits any law 'abridging the freedom of speech, or of the press.' It must be taken as a command of the broadest scope that explicit language, read in the context of a liberty-loving society, will allow." *Bridges v. California,* 314 U.S. 252, 263, 62 S.Ct. 190, 194, 86 L.Ed. 192, 159 A.L.R. 1346. "If there is any fixed star in our constitutional constellation, it is that no official, high or petty, can prescribe what shall be orthodox in politics, nationalism, religion, or other matters of opinion or force citizens to confess by word or act their faith therein. If there are any circumstances which permit an exception, they do not now occur to us." *West Virginia State Board of Education v. Barnette,* 319 U.S. 624, 642, 63 S.Ct. 1178, 1187, 87 L.Ed. 1628, 147 A.L.R. 674. "The freedom of speech and of the press guaranteed by the Constitution embraces at the least the liberty to discuss publicly and truthfully all matters of public concern without previous restraint or fear of subsequent punishment." *Thornhill v. Alabama,* 310 U.S. 88, 101, 60 S.Ct. 736, 744, 84 L.Ed. 1092.

The Board in substance concedes that the section cannot be justified by what the Supreme Court has characterized the "clear and present danger" rule. *Bridges v. California, supra,* 314 U.S. at page 263, 62 S.Ct. at page 194; *Thornhill v. Alabama, supra,* 310 U.S. 88, at page 104, 60 S.Ct. 736. Rather, the Board attempts to uphold its validity on the reasoning of the *Herzog* case that Congress, having bestowed upon labor organizations certain benefits and privileges, had a right to attach as a condition to their enjoyment the requirement contained in Sec. 9(h). The Board in its brief states and restates that the purpose of Congress was to eliminate from the bargaining process Communist-dominated Unions. Its position is stated thus:

> We turn then to the precise questions which may here properly be presented, whether denial of the benefits of the Act to labor organizations whose officers are Communists or members of Communist dominated organizations, or who believe in, or support organizations which advocate violent overthrow of the government, is reasonably related to the objectives which Congress legitimately sought to promote by enactment of the statute, and whether the methods utilized to promote these objectives are appropriate means for their effectuation.

Referring to the opinion in the *Herzog* case, the Board states:

> The Court concluded that the consequences upon self-organizational activity of willful noncompliance by a union with conditions which Congress was entitled to impose could not be attributed to Congress or to the Board, but solely to the union itself, and that denial of the benefits of the Act to labor organizations which refused to comply could therefore not be said to deprive those labor organizations of their constitutional right to freedom of association.

Thus, the fallacious premise is laid for the Board's argument that Congress, having endowed labor organizations with certain benefits, was justified in imposing a condition that such benefits should not be enjoyed by Communist-dominated organizations. A hypothetical situation is created which bears no resemblance either to the requirements of the section or to the benefits bestowed by the Act. Sec. 9(h) imposes no obligation upon a Union, Communist-dominated or otherwise; in fact, a Union is without power to comply with the condition which Congress has imposed. This is in marked contrast with Sec. 9(f) and (g), which require the Unions to file certain factual reports as a prerequisite to their right to act as a bargaining agent. The instant section is directed at the individual officers of this far-flung labor organization, each of whom has been empowered to stymie the entire bargaining process and thus deprive the Union of its right to act as bargaining agent. And a single official can do this very thing by refusing to make the affidavit for any reason or no reason. He may refuse solely because of an arbitrary or capricious attitude, because the terms of the statute are so vague as to make it uncertain whether the affidavit can be truthfully made, or because he belongs to the proscribed class. Thus, the section gathers within its devastating reach a Union all of whose officials save one are willing and able to make the affidavit.

The impact which this section has upon employees represented by the Union is even more pronounced. As illustrative, the Union in the instant situation has been duly selected by some 12,000 employees of an appropriate bargaining unit as their agent. The Board minimizes, in fact almost ignores, their predicament. Their interest is disposed of on the erroneous theory that their rights stem from Congress, and what Congress has given it can take away.

It is well to keep in mind, however, what the Board appears to overlook, that is, that employees have certain constitutional rights irrespective of any benefit bestowed by the Wagner Act or its successor. It has been held that the right "to organize for the purpose of securing redress of grievances and to promote agreements with the employers relating to rates of pay and conditions of work" is a constitutional right, and that the right of employees to self-organization and to select representatives of their own choosing for collective bargaining or other material protection is fundamental. Further, that employees have as clear a right to organize and select their representatives for a lawful purpose as an employer has to organize its business and select its own officers and agents. *National Labor Relations Board v. Jones & Laughlin Steel Corp.,* 301 U.S. 1, 33, 57 S.Ct. 615, 627, 81 L.Ed. 893, 108 A.L.R. 1352. And it has been held that the right of workmen or of Unions "to assemble and discuss their own affairs is as fully protected by the Constitution as the right of business men, farmers, educators, political party members or others to assemble and discuss their affairs and to enlist the support of others." *Thomas v. Collins,* 323 U.S. 516, 539, 65 S.Ct. 315, 327, 89 L.Ed. 430. And as employees have a constitutional right to organize, to select a bargaining agent of their own choosing and, if members of a Union, to elect the officials of such Union, so I would think that the bargaining agent when so selected had a right of equal standing to represent for all legitimate purposes those by whom it had been selected. The employees in the instant situation have availed themselves of constitutional rights in selecting the Union as their bargaining agent and in the election of its officials.

At this point it is pertinent to observe that the Wagner Act was enacted primarily for the benefit of employees and not for Unions. The latter derive their authority from the employees when selected as their bargaining agent, rather than from the law. The very heart of the Act is contained in Sec. 7, which provides: "Employees shall have the right to self-organization, to form, join, or assist labor organizations, to bargain collectively through representatives of their own choosing. . . ." This was not a Congress-created right but the recognition of a constitutional right, which Congress provided the means to protect. This is clearly shown by the declared policy of the Act that commerce be aided "by encouraging the practice and procedure of collective bargaining and by protecting the exercise of workers of full freedom of association, self-organization, and designation of representatives of their own choosing, for the purpose of negotiating the terms and conditions of their employment or other mutual aid or protection."

In my view, the condition attached to the Board's order in the instant case is a direct and serious impairment upon these constitutional rights of both the employees and the Union. The rights of the former to organize, select a bargaining agent of their own choosing and elect officers of the Union have been reduced to a state of meaningless gesture. *See Texas & N.O.R. Co. v. Brotherhood of Ry. & S. S. Clerks,* 281 U.S. 548, 570, 50 S.Ct. 427, 74 L.Ed. 1034, and *National Labor Relations Board v. Jones & Laughlin Steel Corp., supra,* 301 U.S. 1, at page 34, 57 S.Ct. 615.

In order to comply with the condition of the Board's order, they must select a bargaining agent not of their own choosing but one which conforms to the pattern which Congress has prescribed. The fundamental right to elect officers of their Union, untrammeled and unfettered, has been made subservient to the congressional edict as to the character of officials which will be tolerated. Not only does the section represent an intrusion by Congress in the internal affairs of a Union and its members, but it is legislative coercion expressly designed to compel Union members to forego their fundamental rights. "Freedom of speech, freedom of the press, and freedom of religion all have a double aspect—freedom of thought and freedom of action. Freedom to think is absolute of its own nature; the most tyrannical government is powerless to control the inward workings of the mind." Murphy, J., dissenting in *Jones v. City of Opelika,* 316 U.S. 584, 618, 62 S.Ct. 1231, 1249, 86 L.Ed. 1691, 141 A.L.R. 514, subsequently a majority opinion of the court in 319 U.S. 103, 63 S.Ct. 890, 87 L.Ed. 1290.

Contrast this philosophy with that which the Board attributes to the Act, as evidenced by the following statement: "The assumption is that if the facts are known through this filing procedure, union members . . . will soon remove Communists from leadership rather than allow themselves to be precluded from enjoying the benefits of the Act." *Northern Virginia Broadcasters, Inc.,* 75 N.L.R.B. No. 2.

But it is argued that employees have in their own hands the means of obtaining compliance by the selection of a bargaining representative whose officers are able and willing to make the affidavit. Assuming that employees are always members of a Union which acts as their bargaining agent, which is not the case, it is a shallow and unrealistic argument. How can employees when they select a Union as their bargaining agent know that each of its officers will be able and willing to make the affidavit? And how can they compel such officers to do so subsequent to their election? How could the members rid their Union of an officer who refused to make the affidavit, for good reason or no reason? The record before us does not disclose who or how many officers refused to make the affidavit. Assuming, however, that it was Philip Murray, president of a national labor organization of which the instant Union is an affiliate, how long, I wonder, would it take the 12,000 employees of the bargaining unit here involved to replace him with an officer who would comply? The Act provides that no election shall be directed in any bargaining unit wherein a valid election has been held within the preceding twelve-month period. Sec. 159(c)(3). I do not think that the constitutional rights of the employees or the Union can be suspended in mid-air for a time of such dubious and uncertain length.

The upshot of the whole situation is that employees when members of a Union are under a continuing compulsion to elect officers who will meet the congressional prescription in order that their Union may remain in the good graces of the Board, and they must do this even though it be contrary to their belief, conscience and better judgment. Experience, ability, honesty and integrity of candidates for official positions in the Union must be cast aside.

For similar reasons, the section also affects, and I think seriously impairs, the fundamental rights of Union officials. The affidavit prescribed is directed at the belief entertained by the affiant in contrast to conduct, behavior or action. Assuming arguendo, however, that it has no effect upon the constitutional right of an officer who refuses to make it, what about the effect upon those who comply? The right of the officers of a Union to manage and control its affairs is a basic right and

I would suppose to be exercised in accordance with the principle of majority rule. The section, however, limits the rights of the officers of a Union by making them dependent upon the affirmative action of each officer. The officers who make the affidavit, even though in the majority, are no better off than if they had refused. More than that, the affidavit, particularly in view of its vague and uncertain terms, is calculated to create in the mind of the maker a continuous apprehension lest the affiant make some expression, perform some act, have some association or indulge in conduct which might later be used as evidence to show that the affidavit was false. As was said in the dissenting opinion in *Minersville School District v. Gobitis,* 310 U.S. 586, 606, 60 S.Ct. 1010, 1018, 84 L.Ed. 1375, 127 A.L.R. 1493:

> The Constitution expresses more than the conviction of the people that democratic processes must be preserved at all costs. It is also an expression of faith and a command that freedom of mind and spirit must be preserved, which government must obey, if it is to adhere to that justice and moderation without which no free government can exist.

In my view, Congress has attempted to do indirectly what it could not do directly under the Constitution. "In approaching cases, such as this one, in which federal constitutional rights are asserted, it is incumbent on us to inquire not merely whether those rights have been denied in express terms, but also whether they have been denied in substance and effect." *Oyama v. California,* 332 U.S. 633, 636, 68 S.Ct. 269, 270.

Many cases are cited and relied upon in support of the argument that Congress was reasonably justified in attaching the condition contained in Par. (h) as a prerequisite to the right of employees to compulsory bargaining. Without attempting to mention all of such cases, a few may be noted as typical. *Turner v. Williams,* 194 U.S. 279, 24 S.Ct. 719, 48 L.Ed. 979; *Hawker v. New York,* 170 U.S. 189, 18 S.Ct. 573, 42 L.Ed. 1002; *Hamilton v. Board of Regents,* 293 U.S. 245, 55 S.Ct. 197, 79 L.Ed. 343; *United Public Workers v. Mitchell,* 330 U.S. 75, 67 S.Ct. 556, 91 L.Ed. 754. The strongest of these cases, in my judgment, is the *Mitchell* case. There, the question involved was the constitutionality of the Hatch Act, now 18 U.S.C.A. §594 *et seq.,* which forbade government employees to engage in political activity, admittedly a right protected by the First Amendment. There, the favor bestowed by Congress was governmental employment, and an employee had the choice between accepting the favor and foregoing his right to engage in political activity, or in declining the governmental favor and exercising such right. This is quite a contrast to the instant situation where the grant is bestowed upon the employees with the power lodged in a third person to prevent them from obtaining the benefit.

Turner v. Williams, supra, is of no benefit to the Board's position. There, it was held that Congress could properly make the privilege of immigration turn upon the political beliefs of the immigrant. As later pointed out in *Bridges v. Wixon,* 326 U.S. 135, 161, 65 S.Ct. 1443, 1455, 89 L.Ed. 2103, "Since an alien obviously brings with him no constitutional rights, Congress may exclude him in the first instance for whatever reason it sees fit." In other words, an alien, at least in the first instance, is not entitled to the benefits of the Bill of Rights. In the *Hawker* case, *supra*, it was held that a State could constitutionally prevent persons who had previously been convicted of a felony from practicing medicine. The decision goes no further than holding that the State under its police power had the authority to fix the standards to be met by one who sought the privilege of administering to the health and well being of its citizens. In *Hamilton v. Board of Regents, supra,* it was held that the State might properly bar from its colleges persons who refused to attend classes in military training. Again, the condition attached to the privilege could be met at the discretion of the person who sought to become the recipient of the State's favor.

A more relevant pronouncement is that contained in *Frost Trucking Co. v. Railroad Commission,* 271 U.S. 583, 46 S.Ct. 605, 70 L.Ed. 1101, 47 A.L.R. 457. There, the court held that Congress was without constitutional power to do indirectly what it was prohibited from doing directly in a matter wherein it had attached a condition to be performed as a prerequisite to the receipt of a benefit. The court 271 U.S. on page 593, 46 S.Ct. on page 607 stated:

> May it stand in the conditional form in which it is here made? If so, constitutional guaranties, so carefully safeguarded against direct assault, are open to destruction by the indirect, but no less effective, process of requiring a surrender, which, though, in form voluntary, in fact lacks none of the elements of compulsion. Having regard to form alone, the act here is an offer to the private carrier of a privilege, which the state may grant or deny, upon a condition which the carrier is free to accept or reject. In reality, the carrier is given no choice, except a choice between the rock and the whirlpool—an option to forego a privilege which may be vital to his

> livelihood or submit to a requirement which may constitute an intolerable burden.

The Board reviews at length the congressional history and other data for the purpose of demonstrating that Congress was reasonably justified in attaching the condition as a prerequisite to the enjoyment of the benefits which it had provided. As already pointed out, however, it did not give such beneficiaries the option of compliance or noncompliance. The result of the congressional inquiry is summarized in the Board's brief as follows:

> Congress was not unaware that Communist officers of labor organizations sometimes effectively represent the economic interests of members in collective bargaining, and in grievance adjustment, and that to this extent their activities do tend to effectuate the policies of the Act. But Congress believed that whatever public value Communist leadership of labor unions might have in this respect was clearly outweighed by the danger that they might, on other occasions, utilize their power and influence for purposes inimical to the policies of the Act and to national security.

Thus, notwithstanding this congressional recognition that some labor organizations with Communist officials were willing and able to cooperate in effectuating the policies of the Act, it placed such Unions in the same category with those whose officials were unwilling to do so, and denied to each class alike the benefits and facilities which Congress had provided. By the same token, the rights of loyal and patriotic employees, as well as Union officials, were made to rest upon the affirmative act of "each" officer of the Union. So, if employees of a bargaining unit are willing to submit to the pressure which Par. (h) engenders and are fortunate enough to select a bargaining agent, each of whose officers will make the affidavit, such employees receive the benefits of the Act. Employees, however, who insist on maintaining their fundamental right to select a bargaining agent, or who for any reason have not succeeded in selecting a bargaining agent "each" officer of which is willing to comply, are deprived of the congressional grant. The same comparison may be made between competing Unions. One Union is permitted to represent its employees and the other is not. In my view, a statute which creates such a situation, especially considered in connection with its vague and indefinite requirements, is so arbitrarily discriminatory as to violate the due process clause of the Fifth Amendment. As was said in *Hurtado v. California,* 110 U.S. 516, 535, 4 S.Ct. 111, 121, 292, 28 L.Ed. 232:

> It is not every act, legislative in form, that is law. Law is something more than mere will exerted as an act of power. It must be not a special rule for a particular person or a particular case. . . .

See also Nichols v. Coolidge, 274 U.S. 531, 47 S.Ct. 710, 71 L.Ed. 1184, 52 A.L.R. 1081, and *United States v. Lovett,* 328 U.S. 303, 66 S.Ct. 1073, 90 L.Ed. 1252.

According to the Board's argument, the congressional target was Communist-dominated Unions. The legislative fire, however, was not directed merely at those whom it intended to disable. The range included a scope of far greater area. It encompassed what it recognized as good Communists as well as the bad. And of more importance it included countless patriotic employees and Union officials who carried no taint of Communism. All alike were made to suffer the same fate and required to answer for the sins of a few, even one. From a practical aspect, it is not unlike throwing a barrel of apples in the river in order to get rid of one that is rotten. From a legal viewpoint, it has the effect of arbitrarily singling out for legislative action a particular person or group because of the personal belief of their associates. As was said in *Schneiderman v. United States,* 320 U.S. 118, 136, 63 S.Ct. 1333, 1342, 87 L.Ed. 1796:

> . . . under our traditions beliefs are personal and not a matter of mere association, and that men in adhering to a political party or other organization notoriously do not subscribe unqualifiedly to all of its platforms or asserted principles.

That the section is void because of its vague and uncertain language appears plain. This is so both as to the persons within its scope and the subject matter of the required affidavit. There must be ascertainable standards of guilt. Men of common intelligence cannot be required to guess at the meaning of the enactment. The vagueness may be from uncertainty in regard to persons within the scope of the Act, *Lanzetta v. New Jersey,* 306 U.S. 451, 59 S.Ct. 618, 83 L.Ed. 888, or in regard to the applicable tests to ascertain guilt. *Winters v. New York,* 333 U.S. 507, 515, 68 S.Ct. 665, 670.

The section applies to "each officer of such labor organization and the officers of any national or international labor organization." Such officers are neither enumerated nor defined, either in the section in controversy or otherwise in the Act. While the record does not purport to disclose a list of such officers, it does show that the agreement between the Union and the Company was signed by six officials of the national organization, including Philip J. Murray, as president, and by nine officers of the local Union. From the agreement it is discernible that there are twenty members of the grievance committee with authority to negotiate on the part of the Union, twenty assistant members of the grievance committee, and a safety committee of equal number authorized to represent the Union in its dealings with the Company concerning safety matters. I assume that there are hundreds of officers between the bottom and the top of this vast labor organization. The importance of the word "officer" is evident, particularly in view of the fact that "each officer" is given the power by refusal to make the affidavit to paralyze a Union and its members.

That those who come within the scope of the word "officer" have been left in a state of uncertainty and doubt is well illustrated by an opinion of the Labor Board, *In The Matter of Northern Virginia Broadcasters, Inc., etc., and Local Union No. 1215, in the National Brotherhood of Electrical Workers,* page 11, volume 75, Decisions and Orders of the N.L.R.B. In that case, the Regional Director, following instructions of the General Counsel of the Labor Board, dismissed the proceeding for failure of compliance with Sec. 9(h) by the American Federation of Labor, with which the local Union was affiliated. The Board held that compliance by officials of the national organization was not required, on the ground that such a construction would make the section unworkable. There was a concurring and a dissenting opinion. The point is that the Board itself had great difficulty in deciding who were included in the term "officer," and the decision when made was by a divided Board. This emphasizes the difficult problem presented to officers of a Union in attempting to determine whether they are within the scope of persons required to make the affidavit.

The facts required to be stated in the affidavit are of such an uncertain and indefinite nature as to afford little more than a fertile field for speculation and guess. What is meant by a "member of the Communist party or affiliated with such party?" How and when does a person become a member of that party, or any other party for that matter? And what does it mean to be "affiliated?" The Supreme Court, in *Bridges v. Wixon, supra,* devoted several pages to the meaning to be attributed to the word "affiliation," as used in the deportation statute. The court's discussion is convincing that its meaning would be quite beyond the reach of the ordinary citizen. As close as the court came to defining the term was (326 U.S. at page 143, 65 S.Ct. at page 1447): "It imports, however, less than membership but more than sympathy." The court pointed out that cooperation with Communist groups was not sufficient to show affiliation with the party.

What does the word "supports" include? Does a person by voting for the candidates of a party or by attending its meetings and making contributions, or by buying its literature or books, become a supporter thereof? And how can the ordinary person possibly be expected to make an affidavit that he is not a member of any organization that believes in or teaches the overthrow of the United States Government "by any illegal or unconstitutional methods?" These are matters which perplex the Bench and the Bar, and the diversity of opinion among Judges as to what is illegal and unconstitutional often marks the boundary line between majority and dissenting opinions.

See the recent case of *United States v. Congress of Industrial Organizations,* 335 U.S. 106, 68 S.Ct. 1349 and particularly the concurring opinion by four members of the court, which held unconstitutional Sec. 313 of the Federal Corrupt Practices Act of 1925, as amended by Sec. 304 of the instant Act, 2 U.S.C.A. §251, because of the vagueness and uncertainty of the phrase, "a contribution or expenditure in connection with any election. . . ." The discussion is quite relevant to the instant situation. On page 153 of 335 U.S., on page 1372 of 68 S.Ct. it is stated:

> Vagueness and uncertainty so vast and all-pervasive seeking to restrict or delimit First Amendment freedoms are wholly at war with the long-established constitutional principles surrounding their delimitation. They measure up neither to the requirement of narrow drafting to meet the precise evil sought to be curbed nor to the one that conduct proscribed must be defined with sufficient specificity not to blanket large areas of unforbidden conduct with doubt and uncertainty of coverage. In this respect the Amendment's policy adds its own force to that of due process in the definition of crime to forbid such consequences. . . . Only a master, if any, could walk the perilous wire strung by the section's criterion.

The Board makes no serious argument but that the section is vague and uncertain as charged. It attempts to excuse its infirmities by contending (1) that its vagueness is cured by Sec. 35-A of the Criminal Code, now 18 U.S.C.A. §1001, and (2) that the rule against vagueness and uncertainty is not applicable because the statute is not compulsory. No authorities are cited which sustain either proposition.

The substance of the argument in favor of the first proposition is that an officer of a Union need not be too much concerned about the truthfulness of the affidavit which he makes because he can only be convicted under Sec. 35-A of the Criminal Code for "knowingly and willfully" making a false affidavit. In the Board's own words, "Clearly, no affiant could successfully be prosecuted under this section for filing a false affidavit under Sec. 9(h) unless it could be proven that he knowingly lied in making the averments contained in his affidavit." This statement, so I think, could be made concerning every prosecution for perjury. The Board makes the further puerile suggestion that an affiant need not be afraid of a groundless prosecution because "our law provides adequate modes of redress to victims of malicious prosecution."

To me, this argument is shocking and should be repudiated in no uncertain terms. Bluntly stated, it means that an officer of the Union who makes the affidavit need not be concerned with the sanctity of his oath because of the unlikelihood of conviction in case of a prosecution for perjury. He need not be afraid because the only danger which he assumes is the hazard of a prosecution which when unsuccessful leaves him as the possessor of a damage suit against his accuser in an action for malicious prosecution. This argument is a persuasive indication that the section should be invalidated because of its vagueness and uncertainty.

Neither do I think there is any merit in the suggestion that the authorities as to vagueness and uncertainty are inapplicable because the making of the affidavit is voluntary. In reality, the making of the affidavit is indispensable if the Union is to survive and the rights of its members protected. It is made at the invitation of Congress, and I can discern no reason why the rule as to uncertainty and vagueness should not be applied. The reason for the rule, as the authorities show, is that persons of ordinary intelligence may not be required to guess or speculate at the meaning of a statute, and every reason of which I can think which entitles the maker of a compulsory affidavit to such information exists in the instant situation. The need for this information is emphasized from the fact that the section serves notice that one who makes a false affidavit is subject to prosecution for perjury.

I would hold Sec. 9(h) unconstitutional and direct the elimination of the condition which the Board has attached to its order.

ALLIED CHEMICAL V. P.P.G. CO.
404 U.S. 157 (1971)

Mr. Justice Brennan delivered the opinion of the Court.

Under the National Labor Relations Act, as amended, mandatory subjects of collective bargaining include pension and insurance benefits for active employees,[1] and an employer's mid-term unilateral modification of such benefits constitutes an unfair labor practice.[2] This cause presents the question whether a mid-term unilateral modification that concerns, not the benefits of active employees, but the benefits of already retired employees also constitutes an unfair labor practice. The National Labor Relations Board, one member dissenting, held that changes in retired employees' retirement benefits are embraced by the bargaining obligation and that an employer's unilateral modification of them constitutes an unfair labor practice in violation of §§8(a)(5) and (1) of the Act. 177 NLRB 911 (1969).[3] The Court of Appeals for the Sixth Circuit disagreed and refused to enforce the Board's cease-and-desist order, 427 F.2d 936 (1970). We granted certiorari, 401 U.S. 907, 27 L.Ed. 2d 804, 91 S.Ct. 867 (1971). We affirm the judgment of the Court of Appeals.

I

Since 1949, Local 1, Allied Chemical and Alkali Workers of America, has been the exclusive bargaining representative for the employees "working" on hourly rates of pay at the Barberton, Ohio, facilities of respondent Pittsburgh Plate Glass Co.[4] In 1950, the Union and the Company negotiated

1. *See, e.g., N.L.R.B. v. Black-Clawson Co.,* 210 F.2d 523 (C.A.6 1954) (dictum); *N.L.R.B. v. General Motors Corp.,* 179 F.2d 221 (C.A.2 1950); *W. W. Cross & Co. v. N.L.R.B.,* 174 F.2d 875 (C.A.1 1949); *Inland Steel Co. v. N.L.R.B.,* 1970 F.2d 247 (C.A.7 1948).

2. *See e.g., N.L.R.B. v. Scam Instrument Corp.,* 394 F.2d 884 (C.A.7 1968). Of., *e.g., N.L.R.B. v. Huttig Sash & Door Co.,* 377 F.2d 964 (C.A.8 1967); *C & S Industries, Inc.,* 158 N.L.R.B. 454 (1966). *See also N.L.R.B. v. Katz,* 369 U.S. 736, 8 L.Ed. 2d 230, 82 S.Ct. 1107 (1962).

3. The Board has since adhered to its decision in: *Union Carbide Corp.-Linde Div.,* 76 LRRM 1585 (1971); *Westinghouse Electric Corp.,* 76 LRRM 1451 (1971); *Union Carbide Corp.,* 75 LRRM 1548 (1970); and *Hooker Chemical Corp.,* 75 LRRM 1357 (1970).

4. The Labor Board's direction of election described the bargaining unit as: "all employees of the Employer's plant and limestone mine at Barberton, Ohio, *working* on hourly rates, including group leaders who *work* on hourly rates of pay, but excluding salaried employees

an employee group health insurance plan, in which, it was orally agreed, retired employees could participate by contributing the required premiums, to be deducted from their pension benefits. This program continued unchanged until 1962, except for an improvement unilaterally instituted by the Company in 1954 and another improvement negotiated in 1959.

In 1962 the Company agreed to contribute two dollars per month toward the cost of insurance premiums of employees who retired in the future and elected to participate in the medical plan. The parties also agreed at this time to make 65 the mandatory retirement age. In 1964 insurance benefits were again negotiated, and the Company agreed to increase its monthly contribution from two to four dollars, applicable to employees retiring after that date and also to pensioners who had retired since the effective date of the 1962 contract. It was agreed, however, that the Company might discontinue paying the two-dollar increase if Congress enacted a national health program.

In November 1965, Medicare, a national health program, was enacted, 79 Stat. 291, 42 U.S.C. §1395 *et seq.* The 1964 contract was still in effect, and the Union sought mid-term bargaining to renegotiate insurance benefits for retired employees. The Company responded in March 1966 that, in its view, Medicare rendered the health insurance program useless because of a non-duplication-of-benefits provision in the Company's insurance policy, and stated, without negotiating any change, that it was planning to (a) reclaim the additional two-dollar monthly contribution as of the effective date of Medicare; (b) cancel the program for retirees; and (c) substitute the payment of the three-dollar monthly subscription fee for supplemental Medicare coverage for each retired employee.[5]

The Union acknowledged that the Company had the contractual right to reduce its monthly contribution, but challenged its proposal unilaterally to substitute supplemental Medicare coverage for the negotiated health plan. The Company, as it had done during the 1959 negotiations without pressing the point, disputed the Union's right to bargain in behalf of retired employees, but advised the Union that upon further consideration it had decided not to terminate the health plan for pensioners. The Company stated instead that it would write each retired employee, offering to pay the supplemental Medicare premium if the employee would withdraw from the negotiated plan. Despite the Union's objections the Company did circulate its proposal to the retired employees, and 15 of 190 retirees elected to accept it. The Union thereupon filed unfair labor practice charges.

The Board held that although the Company was not required to engage in mid-term negotiations, the benefits of already retired employees could not be regarded as other than a mandatory subject of collective bargaining. The Board reasoned that "retired employees are 'employees' within the meaning of the statute for the purposes of bargaining about changes in their retirement benefits. . . ." 177 NLRB, at 912. Moreover, "retirement status is a substantial connection to the bargaining unit, for it is the culmination and the product of years of employment." *Id.,* at 914. Alternatively, the Board considered "bargaining about changes in retirement benefits for retired employees" as "within the contemplation of the statute because of the interest which active employees have in this subject . . ." *Id.,* at 912. Apparently in support of both theories, the Board noted that "[b]argaining on benefits for workers already retired is an established aspect of current labor-management relations." *Id.,* at 916. The Board also held that the Company's "establishment of a fixed, additional option in and of itself changed the negotiated plan of benefits" contrary to §§8(d) and 8(a)(5) of the Act. *Id.,* at 918. Accordingly, the Company was ordered to cease and desist from refusing to bargain collectively about retirement benefits and from making unilateral adjustments in health insurance plans for retired employees without first negotiating in good faith with the Union. The Company was also required to rescind, at the Union's request, any adjustment it had unilaterally instituted and to mail and post appropriate notices.[6]

---

and supervisors . . ." (Emphasis supplied.) The Union was recertified in 1970, after the Board's decision in this case, with the same unit description embracing only employees working on hourly rates.

5. Hospital benefits under Medicare provided automatically to any Social Security annuitant 65 or over. Medical benefits are optional and, at the relevant time period, required a monthly three-dollar payment per person.

6. The Board found that the Company had violated not only §8(a)(5) but §8(a)(1), and the Board framed its cease-and-desist order accordingly. Section 8(a)(1) makes it an unfair labor practice for an employer "to interfere with restrain, or coerce employees in the exercise of the rights guaranteed in" §7, which include "the right to self-organization . . . [and] to bargain collectively through representatives of their own choosing . . ." 49 Stat. 452, as amended, 29 U.S.C. §§158(a)(1),

II

Section I of the National Labor Relations Act declares the policy of the United States to protect commerce "by encouraging the practice and procedure of collective bargaining and by protecting the exercise by workers of full freedom of association, self-organization, and designation of representatives of their own choosing, for the purpose of negotiating the terms and conditions of their employment . . ." 49 Stat. 449, as amended, 29 U.S.C. §151. To effectuate this policy, §8(a)(5) provides that it is an unfair labor practice for an employer "to refuse to bargain collectively with the representatives of his employees, subject to the provisions of section" 9(a). 49 Stat. 453, as amended, 29 U.S.C. §158(a)(5). Section 8(d), in turn, defines "to bargain collectively" as "the performance of the mutual obligation of the employer and the representative of the employees to meet at reasonable times and confer in good faith with respect to wages, hours, and other terms and conditions of employment. . . ." 61 Stat. 142, 29 U.S.C. §158(d). Finally, §9(a) declares: "Representatives designated or selected for the purposes of collective bargaining by the majority of the employees in a unit appropriate for such purposes, shall be the exclusive representatives of all the employees in such unit for the purposes of collective bargaining in respect to rates of pay, wages, hours of employment, or other conditions of employment. . . ." 49 Stat. 453, as amended, 29 U.S.C. §159(a).

Together, these provisions establish the obligation of the employer to bargain collectively, "with respect to wages, hours, and other terms and conditions of employment," with "the representatives of his employees" designated or selected by the majority "in a unit appropriate for such purposes." This obligation extends only to the "terms and conditions of employment" of the employer's "employees" in the "unit appropriate for such purposes" that the Union represents. *See, e.g., Mine Workers v. Pennington,* 381 U.S. 657, 666, 14 L.Ed. 2d 626, 634, 85 S.Ct. 1585 (1965); *N.L.R.B. v. Borg-Warner Corp.* 356 U.S. 342, 2 L.Ed. 2d 823, 78 S.Ct. 718 (1958); *Packard Co. v. N.L.R.B.,* 330 U.S. 485, 91 L.Ed. 1040, 67 S.Ct. 789 (1947); *Phelps Dodge Corp. v. N.L.R.B.,* 313 U.S. 177, 192, 85 L.Ed. 1271, 1282, 61 S.Ct. 845, 133 ALR 1217 (1941) (dictum); *Pittsburgh Glass Co. v. N.L.R.B.,* 313 U.S. 146, 85 L.Ed. 1251, 61 S.Ct. 908 (1941). The Board found that benefits of already retired employees fell within these constraints on alternative theories. First, it held that pensioners are themselves "employees" and members of the bargaining unit, so that their benefits are a "term and condition" of their employment.[7]

The Court of Appeals, in contrast, held "that retirees are not 'employees' within the meaning of Section 8(a)(5) and . . . the Company was under no constraint to collectively bargain improvements in their benefits with the Union." 427 F.2d, at 942. The court reasoned, first, "[r]etirement with this Company, as with most other companies, is a complete and final severance of employment. Upon retirement, employees are completely removed from the payroll and seniority lists, and thereafter they perform no services for the employer, are paid no wages, are under no restrictions as to other employment or activities, and have no rights or expectations of re-employment," *id.,* at 944; and second, "[i]t has repeatedly been held that the scope of the bargaining unit controls the extent of the bargaining obligation. . . . [And] the unit certified by the Board as appropriate was composed . . . only of presumably active employees. . . ." *Id.,* at 945. For the reasons that follow we agree with the Court of Appeals.

FIRST. Section 2(3) of the Act provides:

> The term "employee" shall include any employee, and shall not be limited to the employees of a particular employer, unless this subchapter explicitly states otherwise, and shall include any individual whose work has ceased as a consequence of, or in connection with, any current labor dispute or because of any unfair labor practice, and who has not obtained any other regular and substantially equivalent employment. . . .

49 Stat. 450, as amended, 29 U.S.C. §152(3).

We have repeatedly affirmed that the task of determining the contours of the term "employee" "has been assigned primarily to the agency created by Congress to administer the Act." *N.L.R.B. v. Hearst Publications,* 322 U.S. 111, 130, 88 L.Ed.

157. However, the §8(a)(1) violation derives from the alleged §8(a)(5) misconduct and, therefore, presents no separate issues.

7. The Court of Appeals below seems to have read the Board's decision as holding that retirees might be considered "employees" under the Act, but not as finding that the retirees in this case were. *See* 427 F.2d, at 944 n. 14. We do not read the Board's decision that way. The Board said: "For the reasons stated above, the 'underlying economic facts' of this case persuade us that Congress intended to confer employee status on retired employees with respect to health insurance plans affecting them." 177 N.L.R.B. 911, 914.

1170, 1184, 64 S.Ct. 851 (1944). *See also Iron Workers v. Perko,* 373 U.S. 701, 706, 10 L.Ed. 2d 646, 649, 83 S.Ct. 1429 (1963); *N.L.R.B. v. Atkins & Co.* 331 U.S. 398, 91 L.Ed. 1563, 67 S.Ct. 1265 (1947). But we have never immunized Board judgments from judicial review in this respect. "[T]he Board's determination that specified persons are 'employees' under this Act is to be accepted if it has 'warrant in the record' and a reasonable basis in law." *N.L.R.B. v. Hearst Publications, supra,* at 131, 88 L.Ed. at 1185.

In this cause we hold that the Board's decision is not supported by the law. The Act, after all, as §1 makes clear, is concerned with the disruption to commerce that arises from interference with the organization and collective bargaining rights of "workers"—not those who have retired from the work force. The inequality of bargaining power that Congress sought to remedy was that of the "working" man, and the labor disputes that it ordered to be subjected to collective bargaining were those of employers and their active employees. Nowhere in the history of the National Labor Relations Act is there any evidence that retired workers are to be considered as within the ambit of the collective bargaining obligations of the statute.

To the contrary, the legislative history of §2(3) itself indicates that the term "employee" is not to be stretched beyond its plain meaning embracing only those who work for another for hire. In *N.L.R.B. v. Hearst Publications, supra,* we sustained the Board's finding that newsboys were "employees" rather than independent contractors. We said that "the broad language of the Act's definitions, which in terms reject conventional limitations on such conceptions as 'employee,' . . . leaves no doubt that its applicability is to be determined broadly, in doubtful situations, by underlying economic facts rather than technically and exclusively by previously established legal classifications." The term "employee" must be understood with reference to the purpose of the Act and the facts involved in the economic relationship." 322 U.S., at 129, 88 L.Ed. at 1184. Congress reacted by specifically excluding from the definition of "employee" "any individual having the status of an independent contractor." The House, which proposed the amendment, explained:

> An "employee," according to all standard dictionaries, according to the law as the courts have stated it, and according to the understanding of almost everyone . . . means someone who works for another for hire. But in the case of *National Labor Relations Board v. Hearst Publications, Inc.* . . ., the Board . . . held independent merchants who bought newspapers from the publisher and hired people to sell them to be "employees." The people the merchants hired to sell the papers were "employees" of the merchants, but holding the merchants to be "employees" of the publisher of the papers was most far reaching. It must be presumed that when Congress passed the Labor Act, it intended words it used to have the meanings that they had when Congress passed the Act, not new meanings that, 9 years later, the Labor Board might think up. In the law, there always has been a difference, and a big difference, between "employees" and "independent contractors." "Employees" work for wages or salaries under direct supervision. . . . It is inconceivable that Congress, when it passed the act, authorized the Board to give to every word in the Act whatever meaning it wished. On the contrary, Congress intended then, and it intends now, that the Board give to words not far-fetched meanings but ordinary meanings.
>
> HR Rep. No. 245, 80th Cong., 1st Sess., 18 (1947) (emphasis added). *See also* 93 Cong. Rec. 6441-6442; HR Conf. Rep. No. 510, 80th Cong., 1st Sess., 32-33 (1947).

The 1947 Taft-Hartley revision made clear that general agency principles could not be ignored in distinguishing "employees" from independent contractors. *N.L.R.B. v. United Insurance Co.,* 390 U.S. 254, 256, 19 L.Ed. 2d 1083, 1086, 88 S.Ct. 988 (1968). Although *Hearst Publications* was thus repudiated, we do not think its approach has been totally discredited. In doubtful cases resort must still be had to economic and policy considerations to infuse §2(3) with meaning. But, as the House comments quoted above demonstrate, this is not a doubtful case. The ordinary meaning of "employee" does not include retired workers; retired employees have ceased to work for another for hire.

The decisions on which the Board relied in construing §2(3) to the contrary are wide of the mark. The Board enumerated "unfair labor practice situations where the statute has been applied to persons who have not been initially hired by an employer or whose employment has terminated. Illustrative are cases in which the Board has held that applicants for employment and registrants at hiring halls—who have never been hired in the first place—as well as persons who have quit or whose employers have gone out of business are 'employees' embraced by the policies of the Act." 177 NLRB, at 913 (citations omitted). Yet all of these cases involved people who, unlike the pensioners here, were members of the active work force available for hire and at least in that sense could be identified as "employees." No decision under the Act is cited, and none to our knowledge exists, in which an individual who has ceased work without expectation of further employment has been held to be an "employee."

The Board also found support for its position in decisions arising under §302(c)(5) of the Labor Management Relations Act, 61 Stat. 157, 29 U.S.C. §186(c)(5). Section 302 prohibits, *inter alia,* any payment by an employer to any representative of any of his employees. Subsection (c)(5) provides an exemption for payments to an employee trust fund established "for the sole and exclusive benefit of the employees of such employer" and administered by equal numbers of representatives of the employer and employees. The word "employee," as used in that provision, has been construed to include "current employees and persons who were . . . current employees but are now retired." *Blassie v. Kroger Co.,* 345 F.2d 58, 70 (C.A.8 1965).[8] The Board considered that it would be anomalous to hold "that retired employees are not 'employees' whose ongoing benefits are fit subjects of bargaining under Section 8(a)(5), while under [§302(c)] they are 'employees' for the purpose of administering the same health insurance benefits. It would create the further anomaly that a union would not be entitled to act as the representative of retired employees under Section 8(a)(5), while subject to an explicit statutory duty to act as their representative under [§302(c)]." 177 NLRB, at 915.[9]

Yet the rationale of *Blassie* is not at all in point. The question there was simply whether under §302(c)(5) retirees remain eligible for benefits of trust funds established during their active employment. The conclusion that they do was compelled by the fact that the contrary reading of the statute would have made illegal contributions to pension plans, which the statute expressly contemplates in subsections (A) and (C).[10] No comparable situation exists in this case.

Furthermore, there is no anomaly in the conclusion that retired workers are "employees" within §302(c)(5) entitled to the benefits negotiated while they were active employees, but are not "employees" whose ongoing benefits are embraced by the bargaining obligation of §8(a)(5). Contrary to the Board's assertion, the Union's role in the administration of the fund is of a far different order from its duties as collective bargaining agent. To accept the Board's reasoning that the Union's §302(c)(5) responsibilities dictate the scope of the §8(a)(5) collective bargaining obligation would be to allow the tail to wag the dog.[11]

SECOND. Section 9(a) of the Labor Relations Act accords representative status only to the labor organization selected or designated by the majority of employees in a "unit appropriate" "for the purposes of collective bargaining." Section 9(b) goes on to direct the Labor Board to

8. *See also Garvison v. Jensen,* 355 F.2d 487 (C.A.9 1966); *Local No. 688, Int'l Bro. of Teamsters v. Townsend,* 345 F.2d 77 (C.A.8 1965). Section 501(3) of the Labor Management Relations Act provides that the term "employee" as used in that legislation has the same meaning as when used in the National Labor Relations Act. 61 Stat. 161, 29 U.S.C. §142(3).

9. Although the Board referred to §302(b) rather than §302(c), it is clear from the context of the Board's discussion that the latter citation was the one intended.

10. Section 302(c)(5) provides an exemption:

With respect to money or other thing of value paid to a trust fund established by such [employee] representative, for the sole and exclusive benefit of the employees of such employer, and their families and dependents . . .: *Provided,* That (A) such payments are held in trust for the purpose of paying . . . for the benefit of employees, their families and dependents, for medical or hospital care, *pensions on retirement or death of employees,* compensation for injuries or illness resulting from occupational activity or insurance to provide any of the foregoing, or unemployment benefits or life insurance, disability and sickness insurance, or accident insurance; . . . and (C) *such payments as are intended to be used for the purpose of providing pensions or annuities for employees are made to a separate trust which provides that the funds held therein cannot be used for any purpose other than* paying such *pensions or annuities* . . ." (Emphasis supplied.)

The express reference to pensions in subsections (A) and (C) requires that the phrase "for the sole and exclusive benefit of the employees of such employer" in the introductory clause to §302(c)(5) be read to include retirees.

11. The Board adds an argument in its brief for construing "employee" in §§302(c)(5) and 8(a)(5) in pari materia. Not to read the term that way, the Board contends, "would frequently interject into welfare plan negotiations the troublesome threshold question whether particular proposals involved the administration of the written agreement, in which case the union would be entitled to represent retired employees, or its renegotiation, in which case . . . it would not." However, nothing we hold today precludes permissive bargaining over the benefits of already retired employees. Moreover, to the extent that "the troublesome threshold question" posited by the Board may arise, it is no different from the task of distinguishing the distinct functions of contract application and contract negotiation which employers and labor organizations are already accustomed to addressing.

"decide in each case whether, in order to assure to employees the fullest freedom in exercising the rights guaranteed by this subchapter, the unit appropriate for the purposes of collective bargaining shall be the employer unit, craft unit, plant unit, or subdivision thereof . . ." 49 Stat. 453, as amended, 29 U.S.C. §159(b). We have always recognized that, in making these determinations, the Board is accorded broad discretion. *See N.L.R.B. v. Hearst Publications,* 322 U.S., at 132-135, 88 L.Ed. at 1185, 1186; *Pittsburgh Glass Co. v. N.L.R.B.,* 313 U.S. 146, 85 L.Ed. 1251, 61 S.Ct. 908 (1941). Moreover, the Board's power in respect of unit determinations are not without limits, and if its decision "oversteps the law," *Packard Co. v. N.L.R.B.,* 330 U.S., at 491, 91 L.Ed. at 1050, it must be reversed.

In this cause, in addition to holding that pensioners are not "employees" within the meaning of the collective bargaining obligations of the Act, we hold that they were not and could not be "employees" included in the bargaining unit. The unit determined by the Board to be appropriate was composed of "employees of the Employer's plant . . . working on hourly rates, including group leaders who work on hourly rates of pay. . . ." Apart from whether retirees could be considered "employees" within this language, they obviously were not employees "working" or "who work" on hourly rates of pay. Although those terms may include persons on temporary or limited absence from work, such as employees on military duty, it would utterly destroy the function of language to read them as embracing those whose work has ceased with no expectation of return.

In any event, retirees could not properly be joined with the active employees in the unit that the Union represents. "As a standard, the Board must comply . . . with the requirement that the unit selected must be one to effectuate the policy of the Act, the policy of efficient collective bargaining." *Pittsburgh Glass Co. v. N.L.R.B., supra,* at 165, 85 L.Ed. at 1265. The Board must also exercise care that the rights of employees under §7 of the Act "to self-organization . . . [and] to bargain collectively through representatives of their own choosing" are duly respected. In line with these standards, the Board regards as its primary concern in resolving unit issues "to group together only employees who have substantial mutual interests in wages, hours, and other conditions of employment." 15 NLRB Ann. Rep. 39 (1950). Such a mutuality of interest serves to assure the coherence among employees necessary for efficient collective bargaining and at the same time to prevent a functionally distinct minority group of employees from being submerged in an overly large unit. *See Kalamazoo Paper Box Corp.,* 136 NLRB 134, 137 (1962).

Here, even if, as the Board found, active and retired employees have a common concern in assuring that the latter's benefits remain adequate, they plainly do not share a community of interests broad enough to justify inclusion of the retirees in the bargaining unit. Pensioners' interests extend only to retirement benefits, to the exclusion of wage rates, hours, working conditions, and all other terms of active employment. Incorporation of such a limited-purpose constituency in the bargaining unit would create the potential for severe internal conflicts that would impair the unit's ability to function and would disrupt the processes of collective bargaining. Moreover, the risk cannot be overlooked that union representatives on occasion might see fit to bargain for improved wages or other conditions favoring active employees at the expense of retirees' benefits.[12]

But we need not rely on our own assessment of the probable consequences of including retirees in the bargaining unit to conclude that the resulting unit would be inappropriate. The Board itself has previously recognized that retirees do not have a sufficient interest to warrant participation in the election of a collective bargaining agent. In *Public Service Corp. of New Jersey,* 72 NLRB 224, 229-230 (1947), for example, the Board stated:

> We have considerable doubt as to whether or not pensioners are employees within the meaning of Section 2(3) of the Act, since they no longer perform any work for the Employers, and have little expectancy of resuming their former employment. In any event, even if pensioners were to be considered as employees, we believe that

12. The Board argues in its brief that retirees will be at a greater disadvantage if they are required to bargain individually with the employer than if they are represented by the union. The argument assumes that collective bargaining over the benefits of already retired employees would be a one-way street in their favor. The assumption, however, is not free from doubt, as the Board itself recognized in its opinion, *see* 177 NLRB, at 917, in declining to take a position on the question. Compare *Elgin, J. & E. R. Co. v. Burley,* 325 U.S. 711, 89 L.Ed. 1886, 65 S.Ct. 1282 (1945), adhered to on rehearing, 327 U.S. 661, 90 L.Ed. 928, 66 S.Ct. 721 (1946), with §9(a) of the National Labor Relations Act. In any event, in representing retirees in the negotiation of retirement benefits, the union would be bound to balance the interests of all its constituents, with the result that the interests of active employees might at times be preferred to those of retirees. *See* Recent Developments, 68 Mich. L.Rev. 757, 766-767, 772-773 (1970).

they lack a substantial community of interest with the employees who are presently in the active service of the Employers. Accordingly, we find that pensioners are ineligible to vote in the election.[13]

The Board argues, however, that the pensioners' ineligibility to vote is not dispositive of their right to membership in the bargaining unit, since the franchise and the right to membership depend upon different levels of interest in the unit.[14] Yet in *W. D. Byron & Sons of Maryland, Inc.*, 55 NLRB 172, 174-175 (1944), which the Board found controlling in *Public Service Corp. of New Jersey, see* 72 NLRB, at 230 n. 10, the Board not merely held ineligible to vote, but expressly excluded from the bargaining unit pensioners who had little expectation of further employment. In any event, it would be clearly inconsistent with the majority rule principle of the Act to deny a member of the unit at the time of an election a voice in the selection of his bargaining representative.[15] The Board's own holdings thus compel the conclusion that a unit composed of active and retired workers would be inappropriate.

THIRD. The Board found that bargaining over pensioners' rights has become an established industrial practice. But industrial practice cannot alter the conclusions that retirees are neither "employees" nor bargaining unit members. The parties dispute whether a practice of bargaining over pensioners' benefits exists and, if so, whether it reflects the views of labor and management that the subject is not merely a convenient but a mandatory topic of negotiation.[16] But even if industry commonly regards retirees' benefits as a statutory subject of bargaining, that would at most, as we suggested in *Fibreboard Corp. v. N.L.R.B.*, 379 U.S. 203, 211, 13 L.Ed. 2d 233, 238, 85 S.Ct. 398, 6 ALR 3d 1130 (1964), reflect the interests of employers and employees in the subject matter as well as its amenability to the collective bargaining process; it would not be determinative. Common practice cannot change the law and make into bargaining unit "employees" those who are not.

III

Even if pensioners are not bargaining unit "employees," are their benefits, nonetheless, a mandatory subject of collective bargaining as "terms and conditions of employment" of the active employees who remain in the unit? The Board held, alternatively, that they are, on the ground that they "vitally" affect the "terms and conditions of employment" of active employees principally by influencing the value of both their current and future benefits. 177 NLRB, at 915.[17] The Board

---

13. *See also J. S. Young Co.*, 55 NLRB 1174 (1944). The Board indicates in its brief that it adheres to these decisions. Indeed, we are informed by the Company that the Board excluded retirees from the representation election that it conducted following its decision in this case. *See* n. 4, *supra.*

14. The Board on that theory at one time withheld the right to vote from certain employees who were, nonetheless, acknowledged unit members. *See, e.g., H. P. Wasson & Co.*, 105 NLRB 373 (1953). However, that policy was subsequently abandoned. *See Post Houses, Inc.*, 161 NLRB 1159, 1160 n. 1, 1172 (1966).

15. Section 7 of the Act declares that "[e]mployees shall have the right . . . to bargain collectively through representatives of their own choosing. . . ." Section 9(a), in turn, provides that "[r]epresentatives designated or selected . . . by the majority of the employees in a unit. . . ." The majority rule principle that the Act thus establishes was adopted after considerable public controversy. Both the House and the Senate committees that reported out the Wagner bill were at pains to explain that the principle not only was necessary for the effective functioning of collective bargaining but was sanctioned by the philosophy of democratic institutions. Moreover, they carefully reviewed the provisions that the Act establishes to protect minority groups within the bargaining unit, such as the prohibition on discrimination in favor of union members. *See* H.R. Rep. No. 972, 74th Cong. 1st Sess., 18-20 (1935); S. Rep. No. 573, 74th Cong. 1st Sess., 13-14 (1935). The language of §§7 and 9(a), coupled with this legislative history, makes plain that all unit members are enfranchised.

This is not to say that the Board is without power to develop reasonable regulations governing who may vote in Board-conducted elections. The House committee expressly indicated that the Board may "make and publish appropriate rules governing the conduct of elections and determining who may participate therein." H.R. Rep. No. 972, *supra,* at 20. Thus, the Board may, for example, withhold the ballot from employees hired after the election eligibility date. As Member Zagoria explained in his dissent from the Board's decision below, that rule "provides an administrative cutoff date for convenience in conducting elections, and to prevent payroll padding and other possible abuses." 177 NLRB, at 919.

16. The Company also contends that the record is barren of any evidence to support the Board's findings on industry experience. Even if that is the case, the evidence cited by the Board may have properly been officially noticed. But we need not decide that question in view of our conclusion that the industrial practice that the Board found to exist does not validate its holdings.

17. The additional interests that the Board found active employees have in pensioners' benefits were properly dealt with by the Court of Appeals below and do not need extended consideration here. The Board stated

explained: "It is not uncommon to group active and retired employees under a single health insurance contract with the result that . . . it is the size and experience of the entire group which may determine insurance rates." *Ibid.* Consequently, active employees may "benefit from the membership of retired employees in the group whose participation enlarges its size and might thereby lower costs per participant." *Ibid.* Furthermore, the actual value of future benefits depends upon contingencies, such as inflation and changes in public law, which the parties cannot adequately anticipate and over which they have little or no control. By establishing a practice of representing retired employees in resolving those contingencies as they arise, active workers can insure that their own retirement benefits will survive the passage of time. This, in turn, the Board contends, facilitates the peaceful settlement of disputes over active employees' pension plans. The Board's arguments are not insubstantial, but they do not withstand careful scrutiny.

Section 8(d) of the Act, of course, does not immutably fix a list of subjects for mandatory bargaining. *See, e.g., Fibreboard Corp. v. N.L.R.B., supra,* at 220-221, 13 L.Ed. 2d at 243, 244 (Stewart, J., concurring); *Richfield Oil Corp. v. N.L.R.B.,* 97 U.S. App. D.C. 383, 389-390, 231 F.2d 717, 723-724 (1956). But it does establish a limitation against which proposed topics must be measured in general terms, the limitation includes only issues that settle an aspect of the relationship between the employer and employees. *See, e.g., N.L.R.B. v. Borg-Warner Corp.,* 356 U.S. 342, 2 L.Ed. 2d 823, 78 S.Ct. 718 (1958). Although normally matters involving individuals outside the employment relationship do not fall within that category, they are not wholly excluded. In *Teamsters Union v. Oliver,* 358 U.S. 283, 3 L.Ed. 2d 312, 79 S.Ct. 297 (1959), for example, an agreement had been negotiated in the trucking industry, establishing a minimum rental that carriers would pay to truck owners who drove their own vehicles in the carriers' service in place of the latter's employees. Without determining whether the owner-drivers were themselves "employees," we held that the minimum rental was a mandatory subject of bargaining, and hence immune from state anti-trust laws, because the term "was integral to the establishment of a stable wage structure for clearly covered employee-drivers." *United States v. Drum,* 368 U.S. 370, 382-383, n. 26. 7 L.Ed. 2d 360, 368, 82 S.Ct. 408 (1962).[18] Similarly, in *Fibreboard Corp. v. N.L.R.B., supra,* at 215, 13 L.Ed. 2d at 241, we held that "the type of 'contracting out' involved in this case—the replacement of employees in the existing bargaining unit with those of an independent contractor to do the same work under similar conditions of employment—is a statutory subject of collective bargaining. . . ." As we said there, *id.,* at 213, 13 L.Ed. 2d at 240, "the work of the employees in the bargaining unit was let out piecemeal in *Oliver,* whereas here the work of the entire unit has been contracted out."

---

that "the Union and current employees have a legitimate interest in assuring that negotiated retirement benefits are in fact paid and administered in accordance with the terms and intent of their contracts. . . ." 177 NLRB, at 915. That interest is undeniable. But Congress has specifically established a remedy for breaches of collective bargaining agreements in §301 of the Labor Management Relations Act. 61 Stat. 156, 29 U.S.C. §185. *See, e.g., Upholsterers' Int'l Union v. American Pad & Textile Co.,* 372 F.2d 427 (C.A.6 1967). Similarly, Congress has expressly provided for employee representation in the administration of trust funds under §302(c)(5) of that Act. In any event, the question presented is not whether retirement rights are enforceable, but whether they are subject to compulsory bargaining.

The Board also noted "that changes in retirement benefits for retired employees affect the availability of employer funds for active employees." 177 NLRB, at 915. That, again, is quite true. But countless other employer expenditures that concededly are not subjects of mandatory bargaining, such as supervisors' salaries and dividends, have a similar impact. The principle that underlies the Board's argument sweeps with far too broad a brush. The Board does suggest in its brief that pensioners' benefits are different from other employer expenses because they are normally regarded as part of labor costs. The employer's method of accounting, however, hardly provides a suitable basis for distinction. In any case, the impact on active employees' compensation from changes in pensioners' benefits is, like the effect discussed in the text of including retirees under the same health insurance plan as active employees, too insubstantial to bring those changes within the collective bargaining obligation.

18. Specifically, we noted in *Oliver,* 358 U.S. at 294, 3 L.Ed. 2d at 320:

> [The collective bargaining agreement constitutes] . . . a direct frontal attack upon a problem thought to threaten the maintenance of the basic wage structure established by the . . . contract. The inadequacy of a rental which means that the owner makes up his excess costs from his driver's wages not only clearly bears a close relation to labor's efforts to improve working conditions but is in fact of vital concern to the carrier's employed drivers; an inadequate rental might mean the progressive curtailment of jobs through withdrawal of more and more carrier-owned vehicles from service.

The Board urges that *Oliver* and *Fibreboard* provide the principle governing this cause. The Company, on the other hand, would distinguish those decisions on the ground that the unions there sought to protect employees from outside threats, not to represent the interests of third parties. We agree with the Board that the principle of *Oliver* and *Fibreboard* is relevant here; in each case the question is not whether the third-party concern is antagonistic to or compatible with the interests of bargaining unit employees, but whether it vitally affects the "terms and conditions" of their employment.[19] But we disagree with the Board's assessment of the significance of a change in retirees' benefits to the "terms and conditions of employment" of active employees.

The benefits that active workers may reap by including retired employees under the same health insurance contract are speculative and insubstantial at best. As the Board itself acknowledges in its brief, the relationship between the inclusion of retirees and the overall insurance rate is uncertain. Adding individuals increases the group experience and thereby generally tends to lower the rate, but including pensioners, who are likely to have higher medical expenses, may more than offset that effect. In any event, the impact one way or the other on the "terms and conditions of employment" of active employees is hardly comparable to the loss of jobs threatened in *Oliver* and *Fibreboard.* In *Fibreboard,* after holding that "the replacement of employees in the existing bargaining unit with those of an independent contractor to do the same work under similar conditions of employment" is a mandatory subject of bargaining, we noted that our decision did "not encompass other forms of 'contracting out' or 'subcontracting' which arise daily in our complex economy." 379 U.S., at 215, 13 L.Ed. 2d at 241. The inclusion of retirees in the same insurance contract surely has even less impact on the "terms and conditions of employment" of active employees than some of the contracting activities that we excepted from our holding in *Fibreboard.*

The mitigation of future uncertainty and the facilitation of agreement on active employees' retirement plans, that the Board said would follow from the Union's representation of pensioners, are equally problematical. To be sure, the future retirement benefits of active workers are part and parcel of their overall compensation and hence a well-established statutory subject of bargaining. Moreover, provisions of those plans to guard against future contingencies are equally subsumed under the collective bargaining obligation. Under the Board's theory, active employees undertake to represent pensioners in order to protect their own retirement benefits, just as if they were bargaining for, say, a cost-of-living escalation clause. But there is a crucial difference. Having once found it advantageous to bargain for improvements in pensioners' benefits, active workers are not forever thereafter bound to that view or obliged to negotiate in behalf of retirees again.[20] To the contrary, they are free to decide, for example, that current income is preferable to greater certainty in their own retirement benefits or, indeed, to their retirement benefits altogether. By advancing pensioners' interests now, active employees, therefore, have no assurance that they will be the beneficiaries of similar representation when they retire. The insurance against future contingencies that they may buy in negotiating benefits for retirees is thus a hazardous and, there-

19. This is not to say that application of *Oliver* and *Fibreboard* turns only on the impact of the third-party matter on employee interests. Other considerations, such as the effect on the employer's freedom to conduct his business, may be equally important. *See Fibreboard Corp. v. N.L.R.B., supra,* at 217, 13 L.Ed. 2d at 242 (Stewart, J. concurring). But we have no occasion in this case to consider what, if any, those considerations may be.

20. Since retirees are not members of the bargaining unit, the bargaining agent is under no statutory duty to represent them in negotiations with the employer. Nothing in *Railroad Trainmen v. Howard,* 343 U.S. 768, 96 L.Ed. 1283, 72 S.Ct. 1022 (1952), is to the contrary. In *Howard* we held that a union may not use the powers accorded it under law for the purposes of racial discrimination even against workers who are not members of the bargaining unit represented by the union. The reach and rationale of *Howard* are a matter of some conjecture. *See* Cox, The Duty of Fair Representation, 2 Vill. L. Rev. 151, 157-159 (1957). But whatever its theory, the case obviously does not require a union affirmatively to represent nonbargaining unit members or to take into account their interests in making bona fide economic decisions in behalf of those whom it does represent. This does not mean that when a union bargains for retirees—which nothing in this opinion precludes if the employer agrees—the retirees are without protection. Under established contract principles, vested retirement rights may not be altered without the pensioner's consent. *See generally* Note, 70 Col. L. Rev. 909, 916-920 (1970). The retiree, moreover, would have a federal remedy under §301 of the Labor Management Relations Act for breach of contract if his benefits were unilaterally changed. *See Smith v. Evening News Assn.,* 371 U.S. 195, 200-201, 9 L.Ed. 2d 246, 251, 83 S.Ct. 267 (1962); *Lewis v. Benedict Coal Corp.,* 361 U.S. 459, 470, 4 L.Ed. 2d 442, 449, 80 S.Ct. 489 (1960).

fore, improbable investment, far different from a cost-of-living escalation clause that they could contractually enforce in court. *See* n. 20, *supra.* We find, accordingly, that the effect that the Board asserts bargaining in behalf of pensioners would have on the negotiation of active employees' retirement plans is too speculative a foundation on which to base an obligation to bargain.

Nor does the Board's citation of industrial practice provide any ground for concluding otherwise. The Board states in its brief that "[n]either the bargaining representative nor the active employees . . . can help but recognize that the active employees of today are the retirees of tomorrow —indeed, such a realization undoubtedly underlies the widespread industrial practice of bargaining about benefits of those who have already retired . . . and explains the vigorous interest which the Union has taken in this case." But accepting the Board's finding that the industrial practice exists, we find nowhere a particle of evidence cited showing that the explanation for this lies in the concern of active workers for their own future retirement benefits.

We recognize that "classification of bargaining subjects as 'terms [and] conditions of employment' is a matter concerning which the Board has special expertise." *Meat Cutters v. Jewel Tea,* 381 U.S. 676, 685-686, 14 L.Ed. 2d 640, 646, 647, 85 S.Ct. 1596 (1965). The Board's holding in this case, however, depends on the application of law to facts, and the legal standard to be applied is ultimately for the courts to decide and enforce. We think that in holding the "terms and conditions of employment" of active employees to be vitally affected by pensioners' benefits, the Board here simply neglected to give the adverb its ordinary meaning. *Cf. N.L.R.B. v. Brown,* 380 U.S. 278, 292, 13 L.Ed. 2d 839, 849, 85 S.Ct. 980 (1965).

IV

The question remains whether the Company committed an unfair labor practice by offering retirees an exchange for their withdrawal from the already negotiated health insurance plan. After defining "to bargain collectively" as meeting and conferring "with respect to wages, hours, and other terms and conditions of employment," §8(d) of the Act goes on to provide in relevant part that "where there is in effect a collective bargaining contract covering employees in an industry affecting commerce, the duty to bargain collectively shall also mean that no party to such contract shall terminate or modify such contract" except upon (1) timely notice to the other party, (2) an offer to meet and confer "for the purpose of negotiating a new contract or a contract containing the proposed modifications," (3) timely notice to the Federal Mediation and Conciliation Service and comparable state or territorial agencies of the existence of a "dispute," and (4) continuation "in full force and effect [of] . . . all the terms and conditions of the existing contract . . . until [its] expiration date . . ." The Board's trial examiner ruled that the Company's action in offering retirees a change in their health plan did not amount to a "modification" of the collective-bargaining agreement in violation of §8(d), since the pensioners had merely been given an additional option that they were free to accept or decline as they saw fit. The Board rejected that conclusion on the ground that there were several possible ways of adjusting the negotiated plan to the Medicare provisions and the Company "modified" the contract by unilaterally choosing one of them. The Company now urges, in effect, that we adopt the views of the trial examiner. We need not resolve, however, whether there was a "modification" within the meaning of §8(d), because we hold that even if there was, a "modification" is a prohibited unfair labor practice only when it changes a term that is a mandatory rather than a permissive subject of bargaining.

Paragraph (4) of §8(d), of course, requires that a party proposing a modification continue "in full force and effect . . . all the terms and conditions of the existing contract" until its expiration. Viewed in isolation from the rest of the provision, that language would preclude any distinction between contract obligations that are "terms and conditions of employment" and those that are not. But in construing §8(d), " 'we must not be guided by a single sentence or member of a sentence, but look to the provisions of the whole law, and to its object and policy.' " *Mastro Plastics Corp. v. N.L.R.B.,* 350 U.S. 270, 285, 100 L.Ed. 309, 321, 76 S.Ct. 349 (1956) (quoting *United States v. Boisdore's Heirs,* 8 How. 113, 122, 12 L.Ed. 1009, 1013). *See also N.L.R.B. v. Lion Oil Co.,* 352 U.S. 282, 288, 1 L.Ed. 2d 331, 337, 77 S.Ct. 330 (1957). Seen in that light, §8(d) embraces only mandatory topics of bargaining. The provision begins by defining "to bargain collectively" as meeting and conferring "with respect to wages, hours, and other terms and conditions of employment." It then goes on to state that "the duty to bargain collectively shall also mean" that mid-term unilateral modifications and terminations are prohibited. Although this part of the section is introduced by a "proviso" clause, *see* n. 21, *supra,* it quite plainly is to be construed in pari materia with the preceding definition. Accordingly, just as §8(d) defines the obligation to bargain to be with respect to mandatory terms alone, so it prescribes the duty to maintain only mandatory terms without unilateral modification for the duration of the collective bargaining agreement.[21]

The relevant purpose of §8(d) that emerges from the legislative history of the Act together with the text of the provision confirms this understanding. The section stems from the 1947 revision of the Act, an important theme of which was to stabilize collective bargaining agreements. The Senate Bill, in particular, contained provisions in §§8(d) and 301(a) to prohibit unilateral mid-term modifications and terminations and to confer federal jurisdiction over suits for contract violations. *See* S. 1126, 80th Cong. 1st Sess., §§8(d), 301(a). The bill also included provisions to make it an unfair labor practice for an employer or labor organization "to violate the terms of a collective bargaining agreement." *Id.,* §§8(a)(6), 8(b)(5). In conference the Senate's proposed §§8(d) and 301(a) were adopted with relatively few changes. *See* HR Conf. Rep. No. 510, *supra,* at 34-35, 65-66. The provisions to make contract violations an unfair labor practice, on the other hand, were rejected with the explanation that "[o]nce parties have made a collective bargaining contract the enforcement of that contract should be left to the usual processes of the law and not to the National Labor Relations Board." *Id.,* at 42. The purpose of the proscription of unilateral mid-term modifications and terminations in §8(d) cannot be, therefore, simply to assure adherence to contract terms. As far as unfair-labor-practice provisions that were rejected in favor of customary judicial procedures, *see Dowd Box Co. v. Courtney,* 368 U.S. 502, 510-513, 7 L.Ed. 2d 483, 488-490, 82 S.Ct. 519 (1962).

The structure and language of §8(d) point to a more specialized purpose than merely promoting general contract compliance. The conditions for a modification or termination set out in paragraphs (1) through (4) plainly are designed to regulate modifications and terminations so as to facilitate agreement in place of economic warfare. Thus, the party desiring to make a modification or termination is required to serve a written notice on the other party, offer to meet and confer, notify mediation and conciliation agencies if necessary, and meanwhile maintain contract relations. Accord-

21. Section 8(d) reads in full:

For the purposes of this section, to bargain collectively is the performance of the mutual obligation of the employer and the representative of the employees to meet at reasonable times and confer in good faith with respect to wages, hours, and other terms and conditions of employment, or the negotiation of an agreement, or any question arising thereunder, and the execution of a written contract incorporating any agreement reached if requested by either party, but such obligation does not compel either party to agree to a proposal or require the making of a concession: Provided, That where there is in effect a collective bargaining contract covering employees in an industry affecting commerce, the duty to bargain collectively shall also mean that no party to such contract, unless the party desiring such termination or modification—

(1) serves a written notice upon the other party to the contract of the proposed termination or modification sixty days prior to the expiration date thereof, or in the event such contract contains no expiration date, sixty days prior to the time it is proposed to make such termination or modification;

(2) offers to meet and confer with the other party for the purpose of negotiating a new contract or a contract containing the proposed modifications;

(3) notifies the Federal Mediation and Conciliation Service within thirty days after such notice of the existence of a dispute, and simultaneously therewith notifies any State or Territorial agency established to mediate and conciliate disputes within the State or Territory where the dispute occurred, provided no agreement has been reached by that time; and

(4) continues in full force and effect, without resorting to strike or lock-out, all the terms and conditions of the existing contract for a period of sixty days after such notice is given or until the expiration date of such contract, whichever occurs later:

The duties imposed upon employers, employees, and labor organizations by paragraphs (2)-(4) of this subsection shall become inapplicable upon an intervening certification of the Board, under which the labor organization or individual, which is a party to the contract, has been superseded as or ceased to be the representative of the employees subject to the provisions of section 159(a) of this title, and the duties so imposed shall not be construed as requiring either party to discuss or agree to any modification of the terms and conditions contained in a contract for a fixed period, if such modification is to become effective before such terms and conditions can be reopened under the provisions of the contract. Any employee who engages in a strike within the sixty-day period specified in this subsection shall lose his status as an employee of the employer engaged in the particular labor dispute, for the purposes of sections 158 to 160 of this title, but such loss of status for such employee shall terminate if and when he is reemployed by such employer.
29 U.S.C. §158(d).

ingly, we think we accurately described the relevant aim of §8(d) when we said in *Mastro Plastics Corp. v. N.L.R.B., supra,* at 284, 100 L.Ed. at 321, that the provision "seeks to bring about the termination and modification of collective bargaining agreements without interrupting the flow of commerce or the production of goods. . . ."

If that is correct, the distinction that we draw between mandatory and permissive terms of bargaining fits the statutory purpose. By once bargaining and agreeing on a permissive subject, the parties, naturally, do not make the subject a mandatory topic of future bargaining. When a proposed modification is to a permissive term, therefore, the purpose of facilitating accord on the proposal is not at all in point, since the parties are not required under the statute to bargain with respect to it. The irrelevance of the purpose is demonstrated by the irrelevance of the procedures themselves of §8(d). Paragraph (2), for example, requires an offer "to meet and confer with the other party for the purpose of negotiating a new contract or a contract containing the proposed modifications." But such an offer is meaningless if a party is statutorily free to refuse to negotiate on the proposed change to the permissive term. The notification to mediation and conciliation services referred to in paragraph (3) would be equally meaningless, if required at all.[22] We think it would be no less beside the point to read paragraph (4) of §8(d) as required continued adherence to permissive as well as mandatory terms. The remedy for a unilateral mid-term modification to a permissive term lies in an action for breach of contract, *see* n. 20, *supra,* not in an unfair-labor-practice proceeding.[23]

As a unilateral mid-term modification of a permissive term such as retirees' benefits does not, therefore, violate §8(d), the judgment of the Court of Appeals is affirmed.

Since employee benefits for employees (but not retired employees) are a mandatory subject of collective bargaining, collectively bargained plans cover employees in numerous industries and trades and crafts. These plans are the result of negotiations between employers, who cannot discriminate between union and non-union members solely on the basis of union membership, and employee representatives, who must fairly represent employees in their unit.

LABOR-MANAGEMENT RELATIONS ACT

The Labor-Management Relations Act of 1947 (the Taft-Hartley Act), 29 U.S.C. §1, *et seq.*, an amendment to the NLRA, was intended to remedy certain deficiencies in labor-management relations. For example, Section 302(a) of the Taft-Hartley Act amended the NLRA to prohibit payments by employers engaged in interstate commerce to representatives of its employees. Payments to employee organizations, such as unions, and the organization's officers and employees are prohibited, and any person willfully making or receiving such payments may be guilty of a misdemeanor and subject to a fine of not more than $10,000 or to imprisonment for not more than one year, or both. The purpose of Section 302 is to preserve the integrity of the labor-management relationship by prohibiting bribery, extortion and similar forms of dishonesty between the employer and representatives of its employees.

The Taft-Hartley Act, unlike the NLRA, contains provisions specifically relating to plan structure and content. This law also contains provisions that may affect plan administration.

Section 302(c) of the Taft-Hartley Act contains an exception from the broad prohibitions stated in Section 302(a). Section 302(c)(5) provides that:

> The provisions of Section 302 shall not be ap-

22. In coming to a contrary conclusion, the trial examiner mistakenly relied on *Brotherhood of Painters, Local Union No. 1385,* 143 NLRB 678 (1963), where the Board held that a union violated §8(d) by refusing to execute a written contract containing a permissive term to which it had previously agreed. "The parties did discuss the provision," the Board reasoned, "and for us to hold that the Employers in this case may not insist on the inclusion of this provision in their contract would upset, if not undo, the stabilizing effects of the agreement which was reached after several negotiation meetings." *Id.,* at 680. The union was required to sign the contract at the employers' request, not because §8(d) reaches permissive terms, but because the union's refusal obstructed execution of an agreement on mandatory terms. Cf. *N.L.R.B. v. Katz, supra,* n. 2.

23. The notification required by paragraph (3) is "of the existence of a dispute." Section 2(9) of the Act defines "labor dispute" to include "any controversy concerning terms, tenure or conditions of employment, or concerning the association or representation of persons in negotiating, fixing, maintaining, changing, or seeking to arrange terms or conditions of employment. . . ." 49 Stat. 450, as amended, 29 U.S.C. §152(9). Since controversies over permissive terms are excluded from the definition, a paragraph (3) notice might not be required in the case of a proposed modification to such a term even if §8(d) applied.

> plicable . . . (5) with respect to money or other things of value paid to a trust fund established by such representative, for the sole and exclusive benefit of the employees of such employer, and their families and dependents. . . .

For a payment by an employer to a representative of its employees to be within the scope of this exception to Section 302(a), a number of structure and context requirements must be satisfied. The basis on which payments are to be made by the employer or employers must be specified in a written agreement between the employer and the representative(s) of his employees. The payments must be held in trust for the purpose of providing certain benefits to employees, and pension trusts must be separate from health and welfare trusts. The trust or trusts in which the payments are held must be jointly administered by employers and employees, who must be equally represented. Joint administration, in many cases, means that the trustees are appointed in equal number by management (i.e., the employers contributing to the plan) and labor (i.e., the union representing the employees of the contributing employers). The trustees must act for the exclusive benefit of the employees, and must not act in an arbitrary or capricious manner.

It is important to note that the language used in the Taft-Hartley Act is similar to the language contained in ERISA and the Internal Revenue Code of 1954, which were discussed in Chapters 1 and 2, respectively. The court's decision in *Kroger Co. v. Blassie,* 225 F.Supp. 300 (E.D. Mo. 1964) illustrates these requirements.

KROGER CO. V. BLASSIE
225 F.Supp. 300 (E.D.Mo. 1964)

HARPER, Chief Judge.

The "Wholesale Meatcutters and Butcher Workmen, Local 88 and Metropolitan St. Louis Meat Dealers' Welfare Fund" was established by the original Trust Agreement in January of 1953. Subsequently, the name was changed to "Local 88 Meat and Related Industries Welfare Trust Fund" (hereinafter referred to as the 88 Welfare Trust). The provisions of the original trust agreement were thereafter amended on numerous occasions. The last amendment of substance was made in December, 1958, when the entire agreement and declaration of trust was rewritten (Plaintiffs' Exhibit 2). Such amendment purported to be a compilation of previous amendments. Thereafter, there was only one amendment (October 15, 1959), the purpose of which was to strike out the word "pensions," prior to the beginning of the trial.

Initially, only the employees of wholesalers in the meat industry were covered by the trust agreement, but plaintiffs and other retail employers began making payments into the 88 Welfare Trust in December of 1953 for the benefit of their employees who were members of Local 88 of the Meatcutters and Butcher Workmen of America, AFL, pursuant to an amendment of the trust agreement, which actually was not effective until May, 1955.

The plaintiffs in this action are three employers committed by contract to make payments to the trustees of the 88 Welfare Trust for the benefit of certain of their employees referred to above. The plaintiffs, three of the 279 contributing employers, made annual contributions to the 88 Welfare Trust amounting to in excess of $200,000.00, which is more than twenty-five percent of the total contributions. The 88 Welfare Trust is subject to the requirements of 29 U.S.C.A. §186 (hereinafter sometimes referred to as "the Act").

The plaintiffs charge the defendants, the trustees of the 88 Welfare Trust, who will be more fully described hereinafter, with violating the provisions of 29 U.S.C.A. §186 in a number of particulars, and question whether the 88 Welfare Trust meets the requirements of 29 U.S.C.A. §186(c)(5) and (6). Basically, the Act forbids an employer from paying money to employee representatives, but permits the payment of money to a trust fund, provided the trust fund meets certain conditions.

The plaintiffs seek herein a determination as to whether the 88 Welfare Trust meets the requirements of the Act, but in the event that it does not, do not seek the abolishment of said trust or to cause any material interruption in the primary medical benefits to which the employees are entitled under the 88 Welfare Trust, but, rather, request that the court by injunction prohibit any activities which do not meet the requirements of the Act.

The defendants are Nicholas M. Blassie, Otto Etzel, Edward J. Schnuck, Albert Wagenfuehr, Rt. Rev. Monsignor John W. Miller and James Mathews, trustees of the 88 Welfare Trust. At the time the suit was instituted Blassie and Etzel were trustees of the 88 Welfare Trust, being the representatives of the employees covered by said trust. In addition, the defendant Blassie was chairman of the board and financial secretary and treasurer of the Meatcutters and Butcher Workmen of America AFL, Local 88 (hereinafter referred to as Local 88), and was at the time and has been for many years the business agent and actual dominant leader in Local 88.

Defendant Etzel, the second trustee for the employees covered by the 88 Welfare Trust, was the recording secretary and business representative of Local 88 at the time the suit was filed.

Defendant Mathews, a first alternate trustee on behalf of the employees, was president of Local 88 when the suit was filed.

Defendant Schnuck at the time the suit was filed, and at the time of the trial, was one of the two employer trustees of the 88 Welfare Trust, and so recognized by the other trustees. Schnuck was an officer of Schnuck Giant Value Markets, Inc., one of the contributing employers to the 88 Welfare Trust.

Defendant Wagenfuehr was purportedly designated by a majority of the contributing employers as an employer trustee in July of 1960, but prior to the filing of this suit had not been recognized by trustees Blassie and Etzel as trustee, and had not been permitted to participate as a trustee in the operation of the 88 Welfare Trust until shortly before the trial, when the situation changed, as will be hereinafter referred to.

The defendant, Rt. Rev. Monsignor Miller, at the time the suit was filed and at the time of the trial, was the designated public trustee, chairman of the board of trustees, and so recognized, having been appointed in the latter part of 1959. Monsignor Miller is director of Catholic Charities of the Archdiocese of St. Louis.

During the week before the trial commenced, the International Union removed Blassie, Etzel and Mathews as officers of Local 88 and as trustees of the 88 Welfare Trust, and placed in their stead as employee trustees Harry R. Poole and Frank X. Davis.

Immediately thereafter, a meeting of the trustees of the 88 Welfare Trust was held, and at that time, for the first time, Wagenfuehr was duly recognized by the other trustees as a trustee and permitted to act as such. During the trial the attorney for defendants Blassie, Etzel and Mathews stipulated as follows: "We would like also to make it plain that we stipulate, we concede, that the five gentlemen, including Mr. Wagenfuehr, who are now serving as the board of trustees, replacing in part Mr. Blassie, Mr. Etzel and Mr. Mathews, are a legally constituted board of trustees, and we want them to function." (Tr. 269)

The attorney further said: "We do not question in any respect the legality of the board or any party on it. As a matter of fact, we have nothing to do with it any more and we don't intend to question it in this lawsuit or elsewhere. If anyone else does, that is their business." (Tr. 272-3)

Initially, the purpose of the Trust was to "provide group insurance benefits for the participants who were eligible to receive such benefits." (Plffs' Ex. 2.) The present purposes of the trust agreement have been broadly expanded to those which now appear in Article I and Article IV, Section 2(i) of the Trust Agreement (Plffs' Ex. 2.) The purposes of the Trust as set forth in Article I of the Trust Agreement, as amended (adopted in December, 1958) are to pay

> . . . either from principal or income, or both, for the benefit of employees as hereinafter defined, their families and dependents, for medical or hospital care, *pensions on retirement or death of employees,* compensation for injuries or illness resulting from occupational activity, or insurance to provide any of the foregoing, or life insurance, disability and sickness insurance, or accident insurance; and to build, erect, maintain, equip, manage and operate a non-profit health and medical center or hospital, camp or other installation, as is more fully provided in Article IV, Section 2(i). . . .

(Note: The italicized above, i.e., pensions on retirement or death of employees, was subsequently deleted by amendment in 1959.)

Article IV, Section 2(i) states that the Board of Trustees shall use the Fund:

> To build, erect, maintain, equip, manage and operate a non-profit health and medical center, camp, hospital or other similar installation and to furnish or provide medical (including preventive) surgical, and dental care and attention and hospital services in any form for the benefit of the classes of persons named as employees and beneficiaries in Article I of the agreement and Declaration of Trust; such health and medical center, camp, hospital, or other similar installation to be operated in accordance with such plan or directions as the Trustees shall from time to time establish and Trustees shall have the full power and authority to purchase, hold and otherwise acquire and deal with property, real and personal, in connection with such health and medical center, camp, hospital, or other similar installation and to employ directors, superintendents, doctors, nurses, and such subordinate employees as may be necessary for the proper conduct of such institution; and to do generally anything and everything necessary, expedient or incidental to the operation of a health and medical center, camp, hospital, or other similar installation including, but not limited to making contracts and incurring liabilities which may be appropriate to enable such health and medical center, camp, hospital, or other installation to accomplish any or all of the foregoing purposes, to borrow money

> for such purposes, at reasonable rates of interest, to issue notes and other obligations and to secure any of its obligations by mortgage, pledge, or deed of trust of all or any of its properties. By way of example and not by way of limitation, said program of medical care shall at the discretion of the trustees include a competently-staffed convalescent home and center, an occupational therapy workshop, erection and maintenance of dormitories and cottages where group therapy may be applied in camp surroundings, a day nursery (with dietary kitchen) for infants, stressing instruction for parents as to proper child care, erection and maintenance under the supervision of professionally qualified personnel of a swimming pool, water facilities, athletic fields and gymnastic equipment to be used in rehabilitating persons recovering from diseases and to be used in supervised physical education for employees and their dependents, classrooms and a movie projection room where classes and movies on preventive medical care can be held, . . . and everything necessary, expedient or incidental to the operation of a health and medical center, camp, hospital, or other similar institution in all its phases.

Article I further provides that "the Union and/or Board of Trustees shall be considered Employers within the scope and purview of Article I, if they choose to make contributions and otherwise to bring members within this agreement . . . their employees shall be treated in every respect the same as other employers and their employees with identical and corresponding rights, obligations and duties."

The 88 Welfare Trust operation at this time may be roughly divided into three categories: (1) a group insurance program, which includes medical benefits, weekly disability benefits and life insurance; (2) a Medical Institute; and (3) a recreational area in Jefferson County, Missouri.

The insurance program is under the direct supervision of George Marklin, a trustee employee, who operates from an office located in a building owned by the Benevolent Society of Local 88. Local 88 has its offices in the same building, and also located in the building are the offices of Local 88's Benevolent Society and Credit Union, the 88 Insurance Agency, and another union.

All contributions to the Trust are paid through Marklin's office and his office pays all premiums for group insurance and routes the funds expended by other phases of the Trust.

Currently, contributions by employers amount to $35.70 per month per employee working more than twenty-three hours per week. Of this amount the group insurance premium paid by the Trust is $12.37-½ per month per employee (Tr. 794).

Defendant Blassie has been the broker from whom insurance was purchased by the Trust. Through the years he has collected over $38,000.00 in commissions. As early as 1959 the propriety of the acceptance of such commissions was raised by a fellow-trustee, but Blassie continued to take such commissions (Tr. 96-7 and Plffs' Ex. 7: 10-15-59 Minutes of Trustees).

The insurance benefits to which beneficiaries are entitled are described in a booklet (Plaintiffs' Exhibit 12). As a condition precedent to participation in the insurance program each member is required to sign a subrogation agreement under which the Trust becomes subrogated to the claims of a participant against third persons from whom recovery is made of amounts paid by the Trust.

The Medical Institute, located at 4488 Forest Park Boulevard, was completed in 1958. It is staffed by medical personnel, headed by a chief of staff, the staff including physicians and surgeons in various specialized categories, all of whom are on a salary basis with the Trust (Tr. 763-64; Plffs' Exhibit 48, p. 6).

The facilities of the Medical Institute include a pharmacy where beneficiaries may purchase drugs at reduced prices. This facility has been made available to members of other unions, who have no connection with the Trust.

The Trust owns some 586 acres of land in Jefferson County, Missouri, which was acquired late in 1958 from a corporation owned and controlled by defendants Blassie and Etzel. Details of the acquisition of this land are reflected in the Minutes of the Trustees (Plffs' Ex. 6: Minutes of Trustees: 4-17-58, 5-15-58, 6-19-58, 7-17-58, 8-21-58, 9-18-58, 10-16-58 and 11-29-58), and in the testimony of Blassie and Etzel and other witnesses.

When the area was first acquired it was called "Local 88 Recreational, Educational and Convalescent Area." It presently carries the name of "Local 88 Retreat for Convalescing and Geriatrics" (Tr. 208 and Plffs' Ex. 7: 121-60 Minutes of Trustees).

The plaintiffs raise a number of questions, in that they challenge benefits afforded persons who have lost their status as employees of contributing employers, benefits afforded to employees of Local 88 and of the 88 Welfare Trust, the acquisition and intended use of the land in Jefferson County, Missouri, and a number of acts which pertain to the day-by-day administration of the 88 Welfare Trust. Before discussing some of these matters in detail, and others by general reference, one must turn to the law under which the 88 Welfare Trust must operate to be a legal trust. In order to understand the conditions under which the 88 Welfare Trust must operate, we must first turn to the statute itself.

29 U.S.C.A. §186 is divided into several subsections and provides, in part, as follows:

> (a) It shall be unlawful for any employer or association of employers . . . to pay, lend, or deliver, any money or other thing of value—
>
> (1) to any representative of any of his employees who are employed in an industry affecting commerce; or
>
> (2) to any labor organization, or any officer or employee thereof, which represents, seeks to represent, or would admit to membership, any of the employees of such employer who are employed in an industry affecting commerce. . . .

Subsection (b) is the counterpart of subsection (a), and provides: "It shall be unlawful for any person to request, demand, receive, or accept, or agree to receive or accept, any payment, loan, or delivery of any money or other thing of value prohibited by subsection (a). . . ."

Subsection (c) provides that the prohibitions of subsections (a) and (b) shall not be applicable with respect to certain enumerated payments which, for the purposes of this litigation, are covered in subsection (c)(5)(A), (B) and (C), and subsection (c)(6). (Note: Subsection (c)(6) amended 29 U.S. C.A. §186, in 1959.)

Subsection (c)(5) provides that the prohibition of subsections (a) and (b) shall not be applicable "with respect to money or other thing of value paid to a trust fund established by such representative for the sole and exclusive benefit of the employees of such employer, and their families and dependents (or of such employees, families, and dependents jointly with the employees of other employers making similar payments, and their families and dependents)," provided certain conditions are met:

> First: A trust must be established to hold the payments.
>
> Second: The payments must be for the sole and exclusive benefit of the employees and families or dependents (or of such employees, families and dependents jointly with the employees of other employers making similar payments, and their families and dependents).
>
> Third: The trust must provide for payment out of principal or income, or both, for: (1) Medical or hospital care; (2) pensions on retirement or death of employees; (3) compensation for injuries or illness resulting from occupational activity or insurance to provide any of the foregoing; or (4) unemployment benefits or life insurance; (5) disability and sickness insurance; or (6) accident insurance; (7) pooled vacation, holiday, severance or similar benefits, or defraying costs of apprenticeship or other training programs. [(7) was added in 1959 by 29 U.S.C.A. §186(c)(6).]

Subsection (c)(5)(B) prescribes further rules governing the allowed trusts:

> 1) The detailed basis of the payments by the employer must be specified in a written agreement with the employer.
>
> 2) The employees and the employers must be equally represented in the administration of the trust fund.
>
> 3) There may be provision for a neutral person to act as a trustee in the administration of the fund; or, in the absence of any provision for such a neutral person, selection to be made of such neutral person in the case of a deadlock, with recourse to the District Court if no agreement can be reached on the appointment of a neutral person.
>
> 4) There must be provision for an annual audit of the trust fund, and the statement of the results of that audit must be made available to interested persons at the principal office of the trust fund and at such other places as may be provided in the trust fund agreement.

With relation to pensions or annuities, it is provided, in subsection (c)(5)(C), that payments made for the purpose of providing pensions or annuities must be made to a separate trust.

29 U.S.C.A. §186(d) provides that any person who willfully violates any of the provisions of Section 186 shall, upon conviction thereof, be guilty of a misdemeanor and subject to fine of not more than $10,000.00, or imprisonment for not more than one year, or both.

29 U.S.C.A. §186(e) provides that the District Court shall have jurisdiction to restrain violations of Section 186. This court is vested with jurisdiction in this cause by virtue of subsection (e), in that plaintiffs seek to restrain violation 29 U.S. C.A. §186, and to obtain such other relief as shall be proper under the proof.

There have been a number of district and appellate court decisions dealing with 29 U.S.C.A. §186, based upon various sets of facts, but said decisions for the most part are of little help to the court in deciding the questions presented in this case, other than as to the question of day-by-day administration. The Supreme Court in *Arroyo v. United States*, 359 U.S. 419, 79 S.Ct. 864, 3 L.Ed.2d 915, dealt with a problem concerning the Act and laid down what to this court seems to be very clear and controlling standards by which welfare trusts subject to this Act are controlled. The court in that case, 359 U.S.1.c. 426, 79 S.Ct. at pages 868-869, 3 L.Ed.2d 915, had this to say:

> Congress believed that if welfare funds were established which did not define with specificity the benefits payable thereunder, a substantial danger existed that such funds might be employed to perpetuate control of union officers, for political purposes, or even for personal gain, ...To remove these dangers, specific standards were established to assure that welfare funds would be established only for purposes which Congress considered proper and expended only for the purposes for which they were established. . . . Continuing compliance with these standards in the administration of welfare funds was made explicitly enforceable in federal district courts by civil proceedings under §302(e). The legislative history is devoid of any suggestion that defalcating trustees were to be held accountable under federal law, except by way of the injunctive remedy provided in that subsection. (Section 302 is 29 U.S.C.A. §186.)

Before turning to the specific problems with which the court is confronted in this case, it is worth noting that while the trust provides it shall be governed by five trustees (two representing the employees, two representing the employers, and one public trustee), the activities of this trust, since its inception, has been dominated by and subject to the whims of one trustee—Blassie. He has dominated every aspect of it and its activities have been the result of his desires, an examination of which would indicate little regard for the real purpose of the 88 Welfare Trust, but rather, to foster in every aspect the welfare of Local 88 and his personal aggrandizements, and with almost seemingly utter contempt for the law.

Under the original Trust Agreement the only beneficiaries (called participants) of the trust were union member employees of the contributing employers (Plffs' Ex. 2, p. 2). The purpose of the trust was to provide group insurance benefits for such participants.

Retired persons became beneficiaries of the trust by an amendment passed at a trustees' meeting on March 28, 1957. The amendment was adopted to include as beneficiaries: ". . . and members of Local 88 . . . who were insured under this agreement, but who have retired and whose annual earnings do not exceed $1,200.00 per year." (Tr. p. 75; Plffs' Ex. 6: 3/28/57 Minutes of Trustees; Plffs' Ex. 2, pp. 36-38.)

This original program was put into operation on June 1, 1957, with seventy-four members participating. The program was self-insured, with the retired members and the 88 Welfare Trust sharing the cost. In October, 1961, the monthly contribution of each retired member was raised from five to ten dollars because of the rising cost of the program (Plffs' Ex. 48). Both of these figures are well below the amount contributed by contributing employers for the benefit of participating employees.

The provision, adopted on March 28, 1957, establishing retired persons as beneficiaries was deleted by amendment on August 21, 1958 (Plffs' Ex. 2, p. 45). The trustees subsequently reinstated retired persons as proper participants or beneficiaries of the welfare trust. On January 15, 1959, the trustees purportedly adopted "Regulation No. 4," which purported to permit retired union members who maintained their union membership to to use the facilities of the Medical Institute after retirement, upon payment by them of such amounts as should be specified by the trustees. "Regulation No. 4" is not mentioned in the minutes of the trustees' meeting of January 15, 1959; however, on May 11, 1960, the trustees amended "Regulation No. 4," eliminating Union membership as a prerequisite to participation in the program for retired persons, referred to as the "Senior Membership" program (Plffs' Ex. 7, 5/11/60 Minutes of Trustees' meeting). It should be noted that the present time "Senior members" are eligible for the same Medical Institute benefits accorded other full benefit members as well as Local 88 Retreat benefits (Tr. 80), plus the group insurance benefits (*See* Plffs' Ex. 48).

At the beginning of the "Senior Members' Program," membership was available to all retired meatcutters, regardless of whether they had ever been covered by the trust, and others. Now, there are fixed standards of eligibility, including the requirement that the member must have been covered by 88 Welfare Trust (that is, his employer must have made monthly contributions for him) from the inception of the program. Although this objective test is one of the rules governing the Senior Members' Program, it is not followed, as the evidence shows that as of May 31, 1963, there were one hundred one persons covered under the program, of which eight had never been covered by the trust program prior to retiring (Plffs' Ex. 48, pp. 10, 11).

It should also be noted that although the trustees, on May 11, 1960, eliminated union membership as a prerequisite to participation in the Senior Members' Program, Marklin testified that union membership is necessary for participation.

The plaintiffs contend that it is illegal under subsection (c)(5) of the Act to provide the benefits of the 88 Welfare Trust to retired persons, since they have lost their "employee" status. The defendants contend that the Act permits certain benefits to be set up for retired persons. An examination of the Act discloses defendants' contention to be true, in that it provides in substance that trusts may be established for the payment of pensions on retirement or death of employees, but the Act (29 U.S.C.A. §186(c)(5)(C)) further provides that payments made for the purpose of providing pensions on annuities must be made to a separate trust, which is separate from a welfare trust, and in this instance (88 Welfare Trust) we are dealing with a welfare trust. In other words, the Act specifically provides for the establishment of two types of trusts, one for the benefit of employees, the other for the benefit of retired employees. Congress did not intend welfare trusts to include pensions or annuities as benefits of such trusts. As stated in the *Arroyo* case, supra, Congress established specific standards with respect to welfare trusts. As stated in the Act, a welfare trust is established "for the sole and exclusive benefit of the employees (emphasis added) of such employer, and their families, and dependents (or of such employees, families, and dependents jointly with the employees of other employers making similar payments, and their families and dependents): . . ."

Retired personnel are not employees of the contributing employers and cannot legally be included as beneficiaries under the 88 Welfare Trust. What has occurred with respect to this activity of the trust clearly indicates the desires of Blassie, in that not only has 88 Welfare Trust included persons who before retirement were beneficiaries of the 88 Welfare Trust, but has been expanded to include union members who were never beneficiaries of the 88 Welfare Trust before retirement. Also, in a further effort to promote the union activities, provisions of 88 Welfare Trust have required that all retired members who were permitted to participate in the benefits of the trust must be union members (subsequently deleted but still required), and further must be personally passed upon by Blassie, who would determine personally whether or not they would be permitted to share in the benefits of the trust.

The plaintiffs have challenged the inclusion of the employees of the 88 Welfare Trust as beneficiaries under the trust. Turning to this problem, the testimony discloses that in December, 1957, a regulation was adopted to permit the trust itself to be considered an "employer." The regulation was passed at a meeting where only three trustees were present. The employees of the trust were thereafter accorded the privilege of becoming beneficiaries under the trust (Tr. 83, 84; Plffs' Ex. 6: 12/9/57 minutes).

In December, 1958, a complete rewrite of the trust agreement was prepared by Harlin Heath, an employee of the trust. It was intended that such rewrite was to include no new matter, but was to include only all amendments passed in earlier meetings (and names of new trustees). However, the provisions of the regulation adopted in 1957, relating to the trust as an employer, were incorporated in the rewrite (Plffs' Ex. 16: 12/18/58 Minutes of trustees, Plffs' Ex. 2, p. 54).

Although Heath testified that he intended to include only amendments in the composite trust agreement (of 1958), it is clear that the regulation was included as a part of the trust agreement.

By bookkeeping transfers within the trust, the trust made payments to itself for those employees of the trust who became union members of Local 88 (a prerequisite), and such employees were thereafter considered beneficiaries. These employees of the trust who became beneficiaries became entitled to benefits on the same basis and subject to the same limitations as the active employees of contributing employers.

Defendants contend that there is little reason to be concerned about participation in the programs of the trust, as beneficiaries, by employees of the trust. Defendants argue that no bribery, extortion or abuse of power is likely to result because of such participation. Further, defendants contend that such participation is simply part of the compensation of trust employees and nothing in 29 U.S.C.A. §186 states or implies that trust funds may not be used for this purpose.

Possibly, defendants are correct in assuming that no bribery, extortion or abuse of power is likely to result because of such participation. However, it is not the function of this court to make such determination, as was made quite clear by the United States Supreme Court in *Arroyo v. United States*, 359 U.S. 419, 79 S.Ct. 864, 3 L.Ed. 2d 915 (1959). Clearly, if Congress had thought employees of such trustees should be included they could have done so. They did not, however.

Further reasons compel the court to hold that the employees of the 88 Welfare Trust in particular should not participate in the 88 Welfare Trust's benefits. In the case at bar, there are no payments or contributions made on behalf of the employees of the 88 Welfare Trust except by the trust itself. 29 U.S.C.A. §186(c)(5) clearly provides that the trust fund must be for the sole purpose of employees of contributing employers. This requirement cannot be satisfied simply by bookkeeping transfers within the trust itself. The requirement was obviously put into the Act so that employees of contributing employers would be protected. If the requirement was absent, dishonest trustees could easily make payments to employees of the trust who actually were not full time employees, etc., of the trust. This could give power and control to union leaders who were also trustees.

Plaintiffs challenge the validity of the inclusion of officers and employees of the union as beneficiaries of the 88 Welfare Trust. From the very inception of the Local 88 Welfare Trust the officers of the union have been included as beneficiaries, with payments made on their behalf by the Union (Tr. 55). The original trust agreement contained no provision for their inclusion.

In December, 1957, a "regulation" was adopted that permitted the union to be considered an employer so that employees of the union could thereafter be considered beneficiaries under the trust (Tr. 83, 84; Plffs' Ex. 6: 12/9/57). (See the facts discussed, supra, under the section concerning employees of the trust.)

The plaintiffs contend that officers and employees of Local 88 cannot be regarded as employees and, therefore, cannot be validly considered beneficiaries of the 88 Welfare Trust under 29 U.S.C.A. §186(c)(5).

Defendants contend that since a union can be an employer, then its employees can rightfully receive benefits of the trust if Local 88 (acting as an employer) makes similar payments (compared with plaintiffs' payments) into the trust fund.

29 U.S.C.A. §186(c)(5) states that employees of contributing employers may be made beneficiaries "jointly with the employees of other employers making similar payments." Defendants contend that the union made like contributions just as any other employer.

29 U.S.C.A. §152(2) provides that "[t]he term 'employer' . . . shall not include . . . any labor organization (other than when acting as an employer). . . ." The statutory definition indicates that a labor organization in its capacity as an employer is an "employer" within the meaning of the statute, 29 U.S.C.A. §152(a), is applicable to 29 U.S.C.A. §186 via 29 U.S.C.A. §142(3). *See Office Employees International Union Local No. 11, A.F.L.-C.I.O. v. N.L.R.B.,* 353 U.S. 313, 77 S.Ct. 799, 1 L.Ed.2d 846 (1957), where the Supreme Court held that when a labor union takes on the role of an employer, the statute applies to its operations just as it would any employer. The court decided that the Teamsters union was an employer of office-clerical workers employed in the Teamsters Building. The court was interpreting 29 U.S. C.A. §152(2) at the time.

Defendants contend that because "employers" includes labor organizations, that 29 U.S.C.A. §186(c)(5) allows officers and employees of the union to be included as beneficiaries of the trust. Defendants also point out that "[t]he term 'employee' shall include any employee, and shall not be limited to the employees of a particular employer, unless the Act explicitly states otherwise. . . ." 29 U.S.C.A. §152(3) applied to 29 U.S. C.A. §186 via 29 U.S.C.A. §142(3).

The court is of the opinion that the United States Supreme Court in *Office Employees International Union, Local No. 11, A.F.L.-C.I.O. v. N.L.R.B., supra*, did not hold that a union could be considered an "employer" as related to "officers" of the union. The facts of the case and the court's holding clearly show that the court considered a union an "employer" of clerks, secretaries, and the like, and did not hold that a union was an employer of its officers. If officers were considered employees of the union, and if such officers would organize among themselves and bargain with their employer-union, a situation would exist where such officers would be bargaining with themselves. Such a situation would be untenable.

Although it is well established that a union can be an employer, the court holds that a union cannot be an employer under the terms of 29 U.S. C.A. §186(c)(5) as applied to the 88 Welfare Trust. To hold otherwise would be to defeat the primary purpose of 29 U.S.C.A. §186. One of the primary purposes of the Act was to alleviate the substantial danger that welfare funds might be employed to perpetuate control of union officers. *Arroyo v. United States, supra*. To allow Local 88 to be an employer under the 88 Welfare Trust would be to give union leaders an opportunity to funnel welfare benefits to union employees at the union leaders' discretion.

To hold that a union was an employer for the purposes of this trust would be to say that the union would have the right to participate in the selection of employer trustees. This would be contra to 29 U.S.C.A. §186(c)(5)(B), which requires that "employees and employers are equally represented in the administration of such fund. . . ."

In this connection, it might well be that the challenge by Blassie and Etzel of Wagenfuehr as a trustee was in their capacity as representatives of an employer (Local 88), although the court is of the opinion they opposed Wagenfuehr because he would not be subjected to economic pressure by Blassie in union dealings since he employed no meatcutters.

Another question for the court is that pertaining to the 586 acres of land owned by the 88 Welfare Trust in Jefferson County, Missouri, which was acquired in 1958 from a corporation owned and controlled by defendants Blassie and Etzel. The details on the acquisition of this land as reflected in the minutes of the trustees' meeting and the testimony of various witnesses are not clear, but this is a matter with which we are not concerned at this point. When the area was first acquired it was called "Local 88 Recreational, Educational and Convalescent Area." At the time of the trial it was called "Local 88 Retreat for Convalescing and Geriatrics."

The testimony clearly shows that at the time this property was acquired, it was so acquired as a purportedly joint venture on behalf of the 88 Welfare Trust and Local 88. A reading of the Act clearly discloses that no joint venture under any circumstances could ever be legal. All the money for the purchase and development of the area has been provided for from trust funds and the union disappeared from the project in the early stages.

The testimony discloses that it was called to the attention of the trustees that this was probably an illegal venture on the part of the 88 Welfare Trust, and it was suggested that a lawsuit be brought to determine whether or not the 88 Welfare Trust could hold the property for the purposes for which it was acquired and the use to which it was to be put. Such a lawsuit was filed in the Circuit Court of Jefferson County, Missouri. The lawsuit was dismissed when it was determined that this was a matter that could only be passed on by the federal courts, and the lawsuit was not refiled in the federal court. There can be no question under the record but what the area was acquired for recreational purposes and it has never been used in any respect for any other purpose. Thousands of dollars have been spent under the supervision of Blassie and Mathews in the development of the area for recreational purposes. The use of the area which has been made has been limited to the good weather months, with little or no use during the winter. The area has been used by persons and groups who have no connection with the 88 Welfare Trust, such as Local 88, the St. Louis Food Council, Boy Scouts, Cedar Hill Fire Department, a speech defect group, church groups, and others. Members of Local 88 are permitted to take guests to the recreational area without limitation, either as to the number of guests or as to whether or not the union member is a beneficiary under the trust.

The defendants Blassie, Etzel and Mathews contend that the use of the property was never intended to be limited to recreation; that the recreational program was only secondary to the medical and health master plan. These defendants further argue that the reason the facilities for medical and health programs have not been established is due to lack of funds, but the testimony discloses without question that the entire development of the property to this point has been for recreation alone; that trust money has been spent in having elaborate plans prepared with respect to the use of the property, which plans have dealt almost entirely with recreation. One of such plans referred to as a "master plan" (Pliffs' Ex. 5) was prepared by the Layton firm; another study was made by one James Heath; and both of these dealt with recreation, covering many phases of recreation, ranging from spots designated on which to play mumble-peg, to other areas set aside for the location of a ski lift.

On cross-examination, Blassie, the mastermind of this area, stated that all types of recreation were intended to be provided, and that if anything concerning recreation had been forgotten, "We want to include that too" (Tr. 528). He was quite proud of the barbecue pit, purportedly the world's largest, which he had had built for the trust on the grounds. In passing, however, Blassie did indicate that it would not include a golf course as he did not play golf. During the trial it was interesting to note that after Blassie had expounded so voluminously on the recreational aspects to which the area would be put, a recess was taken, and that immediately after the recess his testimony was changed to some extent to indicate that recreation was only a secondary purpose of the area, and that the primary purpose was one of providing an area which would benefit the health of the beneficiaries of the 88 Welfare Trust.

The Act prior to 1959 clearly did not allow trust fund moneys to be used for recreational purposes. In 1959, the Landrum-Griffin amendments to the Act included among the benefits authorized the following: pooled vacation, holiday, severance or similar benefits, or defraying costs of apprenticeship or other training programs. The court holds that even under the Landrum-Griffin amendments to the Act trust fund moneys may not be used for recreational purposes. Clearly, the past and present use of this area has been for recreational purposes alone. Several hundred thousand dollars, which should have been spent to provide medical benefits in the form of medical care or insurance for the participating employees under this 88 Welfare Trust, have been misused. Had it been properly used, there is no reason why substantially more insurance and other benefits should not have been accorded to these participating employees. In a trust such as the 88 Welfare Trust, which does not deal with pensions, there is no valid reason to have more than a normal amount of cash for emergencies in reserve. The rest should be used to secure benefits for which the trust was set up, as authorized by the Act.

The acquisition of the land in Jefferson County was in violation of the Act, and the money which has been spent on it and with respect to it, equally so. The Supreme Court in the *Arroyo* case, *supra*, clearly set out that Congress was concerned with the possible abuse by union officers of the power which they might achieve if welfare funds were left to their sole control. No better example can be given of such abuse than the acquisition of this land for this purpose, clearly in the face of the statute.

It was contended that this property would eventually be used as a part of a medical and health master plan, primarily for the benefit of convalescent employees covered by the 88 Welfare Trust, and retired personnel. Blassie testified that if he had not had to be present to testify in the case that he would have been with a group in Sweden who were exploring how programs are set up for retired personnel, such housing to be on property near this area, and the area developed for the use of retired personnel who would live nearby, which of course, would mean primarily a recreational development, and in addition perhaps the establishment of a small sausage factory to help supplement the income of retired personnel. As the court reads the Act and follows the guide laid down in the *Arroyo* case, it is the court's opinion that under the past and present use of the property it is in violation of the Act, and even the purported use of the property for convalescing and retired personnel's use is in violation of the Act. The court would not want to leave the impression in holding that the 88 Welfare Trust cannot carry on this activity that the court is limiting it to recreation alone, as this opinion has previously dealt at length with respect to retired personnel.

The testimony discloses, as previously mentioned, that at the Medical Institute, one of the facilities of the 88 Welfare Trust, is a pharmacy which is operated so that beneficiaries of the trust may purchase drugs at reduced prices. In the operation of the pharmacy its use has been made available to members of Local 88 and other unions who have no connection whatever with and are not covered by the trust agreement. As previously stated, the 88 Welfare Trust is for the benefit of employees, their families and dependents, in whose behalf contributing employers have made payments for such purpose, and such purpose alone, and the operation of a pharmacy for the benefit of others is in violation of the statute.

The testimony, as previously indicated, discloses that Marklin's office is located in a building owned by the Benevolent Society of Local 88, and that in the same building, Local 88, Local 88's Benevolent Society and Credit Union, the 88 Insurance Agency, and another union, are located. In the spirit in which the Act was written, as set out in the *Arroyo* case, *supra*, the trustees will seek other convenient quarters away from the building wherein Local 88 and various facets of the union are located. A similar order was entered by the court in *American Bakeries Company v. Barrick*, D.C., 162 F.Supp. 882, 885.

Initially, the question was raised as to whether there was equal representation of employers and employees in the 88 Welfare Trust. A provision in the trust agreement had been made for alternate trustees for the trustees representing the employees, but there was no provision for alternate trustees for trustees representing the employers. This question is moot at this time because during the trial the provisions for alternate trustees for employee trustees were eliminated. Defendant Miller's Exhibit 3 contains an amendment to that effect, being the minutes of the trustees' meeting on May 27, 1963. In the same amendment the trustees eliminated the requirement that the removal of employer trustees could only be for substantial cause. While these matters are moot at this time, the court is of the opinion that such amendments are proper, and had the amendments not been passed the court would have required that the same standards with respect to alternate trustees must apply to both sets of trustees, as the Act provides that the representation of employers and employees with respect to the operation of the trust shall be equal. The court would have also required the removal provision regarding employer trustees be deleted.

The plaintiffs challenge various acts as to which there was considerable testimony concerning the day-to-day administration of the trust funds. Plaintiffs, to support such allegations and the testimony with respect thereto, contend that this court has authority to exercise more general equity powers over welfare funds than just the mere authority to forbid the payments into welfare funds, in violation of 29 U.S.C.A. §186. A number of cases have been cited by plaintiffs to support such broad jurisdictional power. *Upholsterers' International Union of North America v. Leathercraft Furniture,* D.C., 82 F.Supp. 570; *Copra v. Suro*, 1 Cir., 236 F.2d 107; *In re Bricklayers' Local No. 1, etc.,* D.C., 159 F.Supp. 37; *American Bakeries Company v. Barrick,* D.C., 162 F.Supp. 882.

On the other hand, a number of cases reject the claim that the statute vests the federal courts with broad equity jurisdiction of welfare funds. *Moses v. Ammond,* D.C., 162 F.Supp. 886; *Employing Plasterers' Ass'n of Chicago v. Journeymen Plasterers' Protective and Benev. Soc. of Chicago, Local No. 5,* 7 Cir., 279 F.2d 92; *American Bakeries Company v. Barrick,* D.C., 162 F.Supp. 882; *Sanders v. Birthright,* D.C., 172 F.Supp. 895. It will immediately be noted that the *American Bakeries Company* case, *supra*, has been cited as supporting both sides of this matter, and as the court reads the case it may be so interpreted.

The court is of the opinion that while plausible arguments may be advanced for both sides of the question, the court is persuaded that the better reasoning is set forth in the *Employing Plasterers' Ass'n* case, *supra*, a Seventh Circuit decision, wherein the court discusses the matter at some length, and in dicta 279 F.2d at page 97 indicates that the Seventh Circuit is of the opinion that the "Act does not create jurisdiction . . . to entertain . . . claims based solely on the alleged diversion or conversion of . . . welfare funds."

This reasoning in the court's opinion is in line with what the Supreme Court had to say in the *Arroyo* case, *supra*, 359 U.S. 427, 79 S.Ct. at page 869, 3 L.Ed. 2d 915: "The legislative history is devoid of any suggestion that defalcating trustees were to be held accountable under federal law, except by way of the injunctive remedy provided in that subsection."

It would seem to this court that the Supreme Court clearly indicates that while activities in the day-to-day administration of the trust may be subject to control by the courts, that it is the state courts, who from day-to-day deal with the administration of trust funds, in trusts of all kind, description and character, who must deal with those activities in trusts of this type. It is this court's opinion that 29 U.S.C.A. §186 is aimed primarily at the prevention of possible abuse and not at providing a remedy for abuse actually perpetrated in the operation of the trust. The Act grants jurisdiction to district courts to enjoin violation of 29 U.S.C.A. §186(a) and (b). Nothing is mentioned about giving federal courts jurisdiction over welfare trusts and trustees except where violations of the Act occur. If the conduct is legal under the Act, then this court has no jurisdiction, but rather, jurisdiction is that of the state court.

The plaintiffs' brief contends that defendants Blassie and Mathews should be enjoined permanently from acting as trustees of the 88 Welfare Trust. It should be noted that the plaintiffs' complaint does not specifically ask for any such relief. It should further be noted that at the time of the trial the question of the removal of Blassie and Mathews, and for that matter, Etzel, was moot, because as previously indicated, these men were removed as trustees shortly before the trial commenced by the International, and as previously indicated, their attorney stipulated that at the time of the trial they did not question the legality of the board or any part of it. The plaintiffs' challenge, and testimony was produced regarding a number of instances of conduct with respect to the activity of the trustees in the performance of their fiduciary duties. Abundant evidence exists with respect to some of these matters, such as Blassie's interference with the selection of employer trustees, his position that employer trustees should not be appointed unless they were acceptable to the union, his participation in the purchase of property for the 88 Welfare Trust owned by himself and Etzel, his acting as broker for the insurance and the receiving of commissions over the years for the sale of insurance to the 88 Welfare Trust, the making of a movie regarding the trust primarily for the union's benefit, and other activities which the court shall not enumerate. The reason is, that, as previously stated, the court is of the opinion that the federal district courts do not have jurisdiction to review the administration of a welfare trust except where violation of the Act occurs, because such matters are not violations of the Act, but fall within the activities of the day-to-day administration of the trust. In view of this finding by the court, it would serve no useful purpose for this court to discuss the matters pertaining to administration of the trust, for those are matters for a state court's consideration.

The court accordingly finds that the trustees of the 88 Welfare Trust who were defendants at the time the case was instituted and tried, those trustees who were substituted for Blassie and Etzel, and any successor trustees, are enjoined from expending trust funds for the benefit of retired employees of the contributing employers to the 88 Welfare Trust, retired employees who were not formerly beneficiaries under the trust, employees of the 88 Welfare Trust, and officers and employees of Local 88.

They are further enjoined from expending money toward the proposed facilities to be erected on the land in Jefferson County, Missouri, except for normal upkeep, until within a reasonable time said land must be disposed of.

They are further enjoined from the operation of a pharmacy at the Medical Institute except for the benefit of the legal participants of the 88 Welfare Trust.

They are further directed to remove the office occupied by George Marklin from its present location and to secure quarters for Marklin's office in a location completely removed from any union activities.

This memorandum opinion is adopted by the court as its findings of fact and conclusions of law, and the attorneys for the plaintiffs are directed to prepare the proper judgment and submit to the court for entry.

It is clear that Section 302(c)(5) affects the structure and content of collectively bargained pension and welfare plans. The more difficult question is the extent to which Section 302(c)(5) relates to the administration of the plans. Other than the "sole and exclusive benefit" language, the Taft-Hartley Act does not explicitly relate to the administration of the plan by its trustees, or the interaction of the plan with other components of the plan complex. Some courts, however, have concluded that the Taft-Hartley Act implicitly relates to such matters. There are two distinct lines of authority, for example, on the issue of the extent to which trustees of jointly administered trusts may represent the interests of the parties that appointed them (i.e., labor or management).

In *Blankenship v. Boyle,* 329 F.Supp. 1089 (D. D.C., 1971) the court concluded that the trustees of such a trust are not free to act as representatives of the parties that appointed them. According to the court, Section 302(c)(5) was enacted to "reinforce 'the most fundamental duty owed by the trustee': the duty of undivided loyalty to the beneficiaries."

Other courts have concluded, however, that Section 302(c)(5)'s equal representation language allows the trustees to consider the interests of the parties they represent. *See, e.g., Toensing v. Brown,* 374 F.Supp. 191 (N.D. Cal., 1974), *affirmed* 528 F.2d 69 (1975). These courts conclude that the administration of the Taft-Hartley trust is, to a certain extent, an extension of the collective bargaining process. The ultimate resolution of this issue is important because of the potential conflict between the Taft-Hartley Act and ERISA.

BLANKENSHIP V. BOYLE
329 F.Supp. 1089 (D.D.C. 1971)

GESELL, District Judge.

This is a derivative class action brought on behalf of coal miners who have a present or future right to benefits as provided by the United Mine Workers of America Welfare and Retirement Fund of 1950. Plaintiffs have qualified under Rule 23.2 of the Federal rules of Civil Procedure. Jurisdiction is founded on diversity and on the general jurisdiction of this Court, 11 D.C. Code §521, in effect at the time suit was filed.

Defendants are the Fund and its present and certain past trustees; the United Mine Workers of America; and the National Bank of Washington and a former president of that Bank.

Plaintiffs seek substantial equitable relief and compensatory and punitive damages for various alleged breaches of trust and conspiracy. Defendants oppose these claims on the merits and in addition interpose defenses of laches and the statute of limitations. The issues were specified at pretrial conferences, and after extensive discovery the case was tried to the Court without a jury. Following trial, the case was fully argued and detailed briefs were exchanged. This Opinion constitutes the Court's findings of fact and conclusions of law on the issues of liability and equitable relief.

I. Background

A. Organization and Purpose of the Welfare Fund.

The Fund was created by the terms of the National Bituminous Coal Wage Agreement of 1950, executed at Washington, D.C., March 5, 1950, between the Union and numerous coal operators. It is an irrevocable trust established pursuant to Section 302(c) of the Labor-Management Relations Act of 1947, 29 USC §186(c), and has been continuously in operation with only slight modifications since its creation.

The Fund is administered by three trustees: one designated by the Union, one designated by the coal operators, and the third a "neutral party designated by the other two." The Union representative is named Chairman of the Board of trustees by the terms of the trust. Each trustee, once selected, serves for the term of the Agreement subject only to resignation, death or an inability or unwillingness to serve. The original trustees named in the Agreement were Charles A. Owen for the Operators, now deceased; John L. Lewis for the Union, now deceased; and Miss Josephine Roche. The present trustees are W. A. (Tony) Boyle, representing the Union; C. W. Davis, representing the Operators; and Roche, who still serves.[2]

Each coal operator signatory to the Agreement (there are approximately fifty-five operator signatories) is required to pay a royalty (originally thirty cents, and now forty cents per ton of coal mined) into the Fund. These royalty payments represent in excess of ninety-seven percent of the total receipts of the Fund, the remainder being income from investments. In the year ending June 30, 1968, royalty receipts totalled $163.1 million and investment income totalled $4.7 million. Total benefit expenditures amounted to $152 million.

In general, the purpose of the Fund is to pay various benefits, "from principal or income or both," to employees of coal operators, their families and dependents. These benefits cover medical and hospital care, pensions, compensation for work related injuries or illness, death or disability, wage losses, etc. The trustees have considerable discretion to determine the types and levels of benefits that will be recognized. While prior or present membership in the Union is not a prerequisite to receiving welfare payments, more than ninety-five percent of the beneficiaries were or are Union members.

The Fund has maintained a large staff based mainly in Washington, D.C., which carries out the day-to-day work under policies set by the trustees. Roche, the neutral trustee, is also Administrator of the Fund serving at an additional salary in this full-time position. Thomas Ryan, the Funds' Comptroller, is the senior staff member next in line.

The trustees hold irregular meetings, usually at the Fund's offices. Formal minutes are prepared and circulated for approval. In the past, a more detailed and revealing record of discussions among the trustees has been prepared and maintained in the files of the Fund by the Fund's counsel, who attended all meetings. The Fund is regularly audited, and a printed annual report summarizing the audit and other developments was published and widely disseminated to beneficiaries, Union representatives, and coal operators, as well as to interested persons in public life.

From the outset the trustees contemplated that the Fund would operate on a "pay-as-you-go" basis—that is, that the various benefits would be paid out largely from royalty receipts rather than solely from income earned on accumulated capital. Always extremely liquid, the Fund vested some of its growing funds in United States Government securities and purchased certificates of deposit. It also purchased a few public utility common stocks, and in very recent years invested some amounts in tax-free municipal securities. The chart appended as Exhibit A reflects in a general way the growth of the Fund's assets and its investment history until June 30, 1969.

From its creation in 1950, the Fund has done all of its banking business with the National Bank of Washington. In fact, for more than twenty years it has been the Bank's largest customer. When this lawsuit was brought, the Fund had about $28 million in checking accounts and $50 million in time deposits in the Bank. The Bank was at all times owned and controlled by the Union which presently holds 74 percent of the voting stock. Several Union officials serve on the Board of Directors of the Bank, and the Union and many of its locals also carry substantial accounts there. Boyle, President of the Union, is also Chairman of the Board of Trustees of the Fund and until recently was a Director of the Bank.[3] Representatives of the Fund have also served as Directors of the Bank, including the Fund's house counsel and its Comptroller. The Fund occupies office space rented from the Union for a nominal amount, located in close proximity to the Union's offices.

B. The Responsibilities of the Trustees.

The precise duties and obligations of the trustees are not specified in any of the operative documents creating the Fund and are only suggested by the designation of the Fund as an "irrevocable trust." There appears to have been an initial recognition by the trustees of the implications of this term. Lewis, who was by far the dominant factor in the development and administration of the Fund, stated at Board meetings that neither the Union's nor the Operators' representative was responsible to any special interest except that of the beneficiaries. He declared that each trustee should act solely in the best interests of the Fund,

2. Lewis and Boyle have been the only Union trustees. There has been a succession of Operator trustees. Owen served until 1957, followed in sequence by Henry Schmidt, George Judy, Guy Farmer and C. W. Davis.

3. Boyle resigned from the Bank board after the record in this case was closed and following his indictment for other alleged misconduct.

that the day-to-day affairs of the Fund were to be kept confidential by the trustees, that minutes were not to be circulated outside the Fund, and that the Fund should be soundly and conservatively managed with the long-term best interests of the beneficiaries as the exclusive objective. While he ignored these strictures on a number of occasions, as will appear, his view is still accepted by counsel for the Fund in this action, who took the position at oral argument that the duties of the trustees are equivalent to the duties of a trustee under a testamentary trust. Counsel stated, "You can't be just a little bit loyal. Once you are a trustee, you are a trustee, and you cannot consider what is good for the Union, what is good for the operators, what is good for the Bank, anybody but the trust." (Tr. 2590).

This view, which corresponds with plaintiffs' position, is not accepted by all parties. While acknowledging that a trustee must be "punctilious," counsel for some of the parties urge that trustees as representatives of labor or management may properly operate the Fund so as to give their special interests collateral advantages (e.g., managing trust funds so as to increase tonnage of Union-mined coal), and that this is not inconsistent with fiduciary responsibility since such actions ultimately assist beneficiaries by raising royalty income. But there is nothing in the Labor-Management Relations Act or other federal statutes or in their legislative history which can be said to alleviate the otherwise strict common-law fiduciary responsibilities of trustees appointed for employee welfare or pension funds developed by collective bargaining. Indeed, the statute under which the 1950 Fund is organized was designed expressly to isolate such welfare funds from labor-management politics. In *Lewis v. Seanor Coal Co.,* 382 F.2d 437, 442 (3d Cir. 1967), the court indicated that Congress was motivated by the example of the UMWA's pre-1950 Fund:

> This provision was written into the statute because the special concern of Congress over the welfare fund of the United Mine Workers of America, which already was in existence and which Senator Taft described as administered without restriction by the Union so that "practically the fund became a war chest . . . for the union."

See also United States v. Ryan, 350 U.S. 299, 304-305, 76 S.Ct. 400, 100 L.Ed. 335 (1956).

It is true that trustees are allowed considerable discretion in administering a trust as large and complex as the Fund. In determining the nature and levels of benefits that will be paid by a welfare fund and the rules governing eligibility for benefits, the trustees must make decisions of major importance to the coal industry as well as to the beneficiaries, and their actions are valid unless arbitrary or capricious. *E.g., Roark v. Lewis,* 130 U.S.App.D.C. 360, 402 F.2d 425, 426 (1968); *Kosty v. Lewis,* 115 U.S.App.D.C. 343, 319 F.2d 744, 747 (1963). On these matters, trustee representatives of the Union and the Operators may have honest differences in judgment as to what is best for the beneficiaries. Congress anticipated such differences in enacting §302(c) of the Labor-Management Relations Act, and sought to temper them by the anticipated neutrality of the third trustee. The congressional scheme was thus designed not to alter, but to reinforce "the most fundamental duty owed by the trustee": the duty of undivided loyalty to the beneficiaries. 2 Scott on Trusts §170 (3d ed. 1967). This is the duty to which defendant trustees in this case must be held.

C. Conduct of the Trustees.

Before dealing with the specific breaches of trust alleged, a general comment concerning the conduct of the trustees is appropriate to place the instances of alleged misfeasance into proper context. It has already been noted that the trustees did not hold regular meetings but only met subject to the call of the chairman. There was, accordingly, no set pattern for deciding policy questions, and often matters of considerable import were resolved between meetings by Roche and Lewis without even consulting the Operator trustee.

The Fund's affairs were dominated by Lewis until his death in 1969. Roche never once disagreed with him. Over a period of years, primarily at Lewis' urging, the Fund became entangled with Union policies and practices in ways that undermined the independence of the trustees. This resulted in working arrangements between the Fund and the Union that served the Union to the disadvantage of the beneficiaries. Conflicts of interest were openly tolerated and their implications generally ignored.[4] Not only was all the money of the Fund placed in the Union's Bank without any consideration of alternative banking services and facilities that might be available, but Lewis felt no scruple in recommending that the Fund invest in securities in which the Union and Lewis, as trustee for the Union's investments, had an interest. Personnel of the Fund went on the Bank's

4. In one instance, Roche was momentarily troubled by Ryan's going on the Bank board, but when she took this up hesitantly with Lewis he "just smiled," and Roche let the matter drop.

board without hindrance, thus affiliating themselves with a Union business venture. In short, the Fund proceeded without any clear understanding of the trustees' exclusive duty to the beneficiaries, and its affairs were so loosely controlled that abuses, mistakes and inattention to detail occurred.

II. Accumulation of Excessive Cash

A. The Breach of Trust.

The major breach of trust of which plaintiffs complain is the Fund's accumulation of excessive amounts of cash. A basic duty of trustees is to invest trust funds so that they will be productive of income. *E.g., Barney v. Saunders,* 57 U.S. (16 How.) 535, 542, 14 L.Ed. 1047 (1853); *Spruill v. Ballard,* 36 F.Supp. 729, 730 (D.D.C. 1941); *In re Hubbell's Will,* 302 N.Y. 246, 97 N.E.2d 888, 892 (1951); 2 Scott on Trusts §181 (3d ed. 1967). It is contended that the trustees failed to invest cash that was available to generate income for the beneficiaries, and in total disregard of their duty allowed large sums to remain in checking accounts at the Bank without interest.

It is further claimed that this breach of trust was carried out pursuant to a conspiracy among certain trustees, the Union, and the Bank through its President, and that all these parties are jointly liable for the fund's loss of income resulting from the failure to invest.

That enormous cash balances were accumulated and held at the Bank over the twenty-year period is not disputed. The following figures are representative.

Fiscal Year	Amount of Cash in Demand Deposits at End of Year	Percentage of Cash To the Fund's Total Resources
1951	$29,000,000	29%
1956	30,000,000	23
1961	14,000,000	14
1966	50,000,000	34
1967	75,000,000	44
1968	70,000,000	39
1969	32,000,000	18

The significance of these huge sums has greater import when two factors are considered.

First, not only did the trustees have a duty to invest but the early minutes of the Fund clearly reflect the trustees' knowledge that income could be earned by investment in Government securities without sacrificing desired liquidity. The safety and practicality of using excess cash in this manner were also fully appreciated. Yet the money remained at the Bank on demand to the Bank's advantage but earning nothing for the Fund. This practice continued in spite of suggestions from successive Operator trustees that the money should be used to earn income for the beneficiaries.

Second, the Fund could easily have met its obligations with only a fraction of the cash maintained in its checking accounts, as the most cursory examination of its accounts clearly shows. The income and outgo were constant and unusual demands on the Fund could in any event always be anticipated sufficiently to liquidate Government securities should this have been unexpectedly necessary. Over the years the Fund paid out monthly approximately $10 million to $14 million for medical and pension benefits and administrative expenses. Against these obligations the Fund had a predictable steady income in the form of monthly royalty payments which, for each month in the years 1967, 1968 and to the date of the complaint in 1969, always totaled from $10 million to $14 million. In addition, there was regular predictable investment income in the range of $2 million to $3 million per annum. Plaintiffs' Exhibit No. 1627, appended hereto as Exhibit B, charts the cash which was held in the general Pension and Administrative checking accounts by month from 1953 to June 1969, and reflects the regularity of the Fund's income and outgo. It will be immediately noted that cash balances greatly in excess of the Fund's day-to-day needs were permitted to accumulate from the outset. Even the formula of having two to two-and-one-half times monthly expenditures in cash, a formula urged by the trustees as appropriate but without apparent justification, was ignored in practice.

The beneficiaries were in no way assisted by these cash accumulations, while the Union and the Bank profits; and in view of the fiduciary obligation to maximize the trust income by prudent investment, the burden of justifying the conduct is clearly on the trustees. Cf. *Pepper v. Litton,* 308 U.S. 295, 306, 60 S.Ct. 238, 84 L.Ed. 281 (1939).

Three explanations were seriously presented in justification of the cash accumulations: the trustees' general concern as to the future course of labor relations and other developments in the coal industry which might make it necessary to have money readily at hand on short notice; tax factors; and what was characterized as inadvertence or accident. None of these explanations will withstand analysis.

(a) *Uncertainty about the future.* Prior to 1950,

strikes and labor disputes had caused mine shutdowns, placing heavy demands on the then-existing welfare programs. Any repetition of these or similar conditions would have shut off royalty payments, perhaps for a considerable period. While this factor could therefore justify the trustees in maintaining a substantial, highly liquid reserve, it affords no justification for the failure of the trustees to put the large accumulations of excess cash to work for the beneficiaries. Roche testified that she favored maintaining an amount equal to several months' expenditures in cash because "that is the only way you can be sure." Such naivete by a trustee is unacceptable, particularly in light of the trustees' knowledge that short-term Government securities, which the evidence showed were redeemable on one-half hour notice, for example, were readily available and would have generated substantial income for the Fund while still assuring maximum liquidity.

This reliance on future uncertainty must also be weighed in the light of conditions existing in the coal industry in the latter years of the Fund's history under review. These were succinctly epitomized by a Union economist at the trial. In brief, it appears that beginning around 1960 the industry was profitable and increasingly stable, with encouraging prospects for the future, all of which was reflected in the increasing amount of coal mined and the favorable progress of the Union in its effort to organize increasing numbers of miners for work at the Union scale. Prosperous conditions made any recurrence of the pre-1950 experience far less likely.

(b) *Tax considerations.* The Fund has from the beginning been competently advised by experienced outside tax counsel. Naturally its return was examined by field audit from time to time. The Fund first sought an exemption from income tax as a charitable trust. This was denied in 1954, after a long delay while the requested ruling was being processed at the Treasury Department. This negative ruling was prospective, and thereafter the Fund understood that it would have to pay taxes on any amount of investment income that exceeded its administrative expenses. In fact, investment income never exceeded administrative expense and indeed was usually well below. In one year the spread was $2.4 million. It was obvious that even if income exceeded expenses and taxes became due on the excess, the Fund would have profited to the extent of its after-tax income.

An additional latent worry was apparently the possibility that royalties would be treated by the Internal Revenue Service as income, which would have been disastrous for the Fund. Tax counsel advised that royalties were not income, and they were so reported. The Internal Revenue Service agents conducting audits seemed interested in the point, but took no action. The Fund never asked for a ruling, preferring to let the Internal Revenue Service make the first move. When the question arose as to another welfare fund, the Anthracite Fund, the IRS eventually ruled that royalties were not income. Significantly, the Fund's representatives, although familiar with the Anthracite Fund's problem, were not sufficiently concerned even to inquire as to the final ruling of the IRS in the matter.

Thus none of these tax considerations can justify the trustees' failure to invest.

(c) *Accident or inadvertence.* There was no proof to support this desperate theory which the Fund itself does not advance and which in any event is in effect an admission of failure to adhere to minimum fiduciary standards of care and skill in administering the trust. 2 Scott on Trusts §174 (3d Ed. 1967). The Fund's Comptroller stoutly denies accident or inadvertence, and the proof shows that the trustees well knew at all times that cash was steadily accumulating.

Under the most charitable view, this accident theory can help to account only for the staggering accumulations of cash in the period 1966 to 1968, when Lewis was in failing health and the trustees met infrequently. However, as is clear from the discussion of the conspiracy aspects of this case, infra, these accumulations were only an extension of a conscious, longstanding policy of the trustees.

The following testimony by Roche is revealing:

> Mr. Lewis felt very strongly, sir, the necessity of having a good deal beyond what we could invest without raising the taxation problem, keeping it very much in a situation where we could get at it at once. He did not feel enthusiastic for a long time over tax-exempt securities such as municipals.
>
> I talked to him frequently about it personally, aside from the general discussions we had. And I finally in '67-'68 realized how strongly I probably had been mistaken myself on anything that had to do with minute fiscal things. And I said, you know, Tom Ryan we both have the utmost confidence in, and he feels we ought to get some of his money out, make it earn money. Now let's think again about municipals. And he did . . . And finally he definitely agreed in '68, he said, Yes, we better go ahead, go ahead.
>
> . . . . .
>
> So it was really a long-delayed decision which really probably, and I know completely from the

> point of view of a financial expert, that there is no excuse perhaps for it at all. To us who had felt that need, too, but felt these other things so terribly imminent, it is not the brightest chapter that we have, but we did some other things that perhaps made up for it a little bit.
>
> . . . . .
>
> [T]he fiscal requirements certainly didn't justify what we had on deposit. I know that perfectly well.

(Transcript pp. 957-60).

Considering this testimony, and the enormous cash balances which existed in 1966 through 1968, the following excerpt from "A Statement by United Mine Workers of America Welfare and Retirement Fund," printed in the United Mine Workers Journal on May 1, 1969, in answer to growing criticism of the trustees' policies, takes on special significance:

> *The criticism:* "Large" bank deposits drawing no interest.
>
> *The record:* At most times during our existence, our bank balances were not nearly so high as we would like to have them in relation to our monthly expenditures.
>
> In January of 1965 the Trustees made substantial improvements in the benefit programs which had the effect of increasing our expenditures by over $45 million annually. As a consequence, as income permitted, our cash balance was allowed to build up somewhat. Our cash balance on June 30, 1968, was actually no greater in relation to our monthly and annual expenditures than it had been at times in the past when expenditures were at a lower level.
>
> With the conclusion of negotiations for a new three-year contract between the Union and the operators in October, 1968, the potential need for cash reserves has lessened and these balances have been reduced considerably.

This statement was signed by Roche, Ryan, and Well K. Hopkins, General Counsel of the Fund. It is not only lacking in candor, as was much of Ryan's testimony at trial, but actually misleads.

The trustees well knew that cash deposits at the Bank were unjustified. It was a continued and serious violation of the trustees' fiduciary obligation for them to permit these accumulations of cash to remain uninvested. It remains to be determined whether the Union, the Bank, or certain individual defendants are also responsible for the breach of trust.

B. The Conspiracy as to Cash Deposits.

Plaintiffs contend that the Union and the Bank conspired with the trustees to maintain the excessive cash at the Bank for their respective benefit. On this phase of the case the applicable law is well established and need here only be briefly summarized.

A conspiracy is an agreement between two or more persons to accomplish an unlawful object or to accomplish a lawful object in an unlawful manner. *American Tobacco Co. v. United States,* 328 U.S. 781, 809, 66 S.Ct. 1125, 90 L.Ed. 1575 (1946); *Edwards v. James Stewart & Co.,* 82 U.S.App. D.C. 123, 160 F.2d 935, 937 (1947). The gist of a civil conspiracy, however, is not the agreement itself, but the civil wrong alleged to have been done pursuant to the agreement; the allegation of conspiracy bears only upon evidentiary and other formal matters. *Edwards v. James Stewart & Co., supra,; Ewald v. Lane,* 70 App.D.C. 89, 90, 104 F.2d 222, 223 (1939); *Martin v. Ebert,* 245 Wis. 341, 13 N.W.2d 907, 908 (1944). The civil wrong here is a breach of trust; and it is settled that where a third person "has knowingly assisted the trustee in committing a breach of trust, he is liable for participation in the breach of trust." 4 Scott on Trusts §326 (3d ed. 1967); *See Jackson v. Smith,* 254 U.S. 586, 41 S.Ct. 200, 65 L.Ed. 418 (1921). If the third person's participation in or inducement of the breach is pursuant to an agreement with one or more of the trustees, he is liable as a conspirator.

That there was opportunity to conspire as to the cash balances cannot be doubted. There is, however, no direct evidence of an agreement, no unguarded admissions of conscious impropriety. Lewis, the dominant actor in these events, is dead and the named individual defendants contest charges of conspiratorial participation. Plaintiffs rely on documents, circumstantial evidence and inference to support the claim.

Despite the denials, there is clear and convincing proof that there was an agreement among Lewis, Roche, and Colton made contemporaneously with the creation of the Fund and the Union's acquisition of a controlling interest in the Bank, to use the Bank as the sole depository of Fund moneys and to maintain large sums in interest-free accounts at the Bank without regard to the Fund's needs. Late in 1949, Lewis, through an agent, solicited Colton to become president of the Union's newly acquired Bank. At their second meeting, Lewis discussed with Colton the transfer of both the Union and the Fund accounts from previous depositories to the National Bank of Washington. As early as April 30, 1950, the Fund had over $36 million on deposit in checking accounts at the Bank, and the balance remained near or about this level for more than a year thereafter. Over the next twenty years the trustees' decision to leave cash in the Bank without interest greatly benefited the Bank and the Union as the Bank's majority shareholder. At all times these sums well exceeded the immediate cash needs of the Fund, as the previous discussion has shown.

This banking arrangement met strong objection from the Operators' trustee, Owen, who at a trustees' meeting as early as August, 1950, demanded that all moneys of the Fund be withdrawn from the National Bank of Washington. He stated:

> It is undoubtedly the law that trustee should not deposit trust funds in a bank which he controls or in which he has a substantial participation. Amongst other criticism, he may cause the dividends upon his stock to be enhanced by the Bank's use of a large deposit of his trust's funds for loan purposes. Also, conflicting interests may arise; or, losses may occur.

The trustees' minutes through 1950 and 1951 reflect that Lewis and Roche, rather than replying to Owen's repeated complaints on this score, ignored his protests altogether and Lewis even equivocated as to his interest as a trustee holding bank stock for the Union.[5] In March of 1951, Owen included the Fund's relationship with the Bank as one of four matters on which he believed his proposals had been rejected, "utterly without justification," by Lewis and Roche "acting jointly."

The formal minutes of the Fund reflect practically none of this crucial discussion held at trustee meetings. Mitch, the Fund's attorney, attended the meetings, however, and thereafter prepared what he designated a stenographic draft of the proceedings based on copious contemporary notes. The stenographic drafts are in evidence. These were viewed by Roche and possibly others and a truncated, far less informative formal minute was developed. Roche struck out most of the informative detail. No satisfactory explanation was offered as to why this was done, and the inference is unavoidable that Lewis and Roche had a conscious desire to conceal the actual embarrassing discussions that had taken place.

Lewis and Roche chose, without taking legal advice in the face of strong objection to the legality of their actions, to advance the interests of the Union and the Bank in disregard of the paramount interest of the beneficiaries who were entitled to receive the benefit of prudent investment of their funds.

The Union urges that Lewis kept his own conscience, acted solely as a trustee and after 1960, when he became President Emeritus, an honorary position, was wholly removed from any executive authority in the Union's affairs. Hence, it is claimed, the Union cannot be held responsible for Lewis' actions, neither prior to nor especially after 1960. This position cannot be squared with the facts. Lewis totally dominated the Union both before 1960 and to a large extent thereafter, especially as to financial matters, including the Fund. Other Union officers knew of Lewis' actions with regard to the Fund and the Bank, but uttered not a word of protest. While Boyle, in the period after 1960, often suggested that Lewis raise pensions, which would have had the effect of reducing the Fund's bank balances, neither Boyle nor any other officer sought to break the longstanding practice of retaining Fund moneys in non-interest-bearing checking accounts at the Bank rather than in investments. When the Welfare Fund agreement was renegotiated in 1964, 1966 and 1968, the Union could have designated another representative to act as trustee, had it been unwilling to accept the benefits of the course that Lewis had so obviously set.

The inference is also unavoidable that Lewis made more than a mistake of judgment as a trustee. He acted to benefit the Bank and to enhance its prestige and indirectly the prestige of the Union, not simply to keep money needed by the Fund in a safe place. The minutes show that he knew the large demand deposits were unnecessary for any legitimate purpose of the Fund. Moreover, he was not lacking in financial sophistication. He had been president of a bank himself and the record shows his many financial dealings and the manner in which, as President of the Union, he utilized the considerable financial resources of the Union for the Union's benefit. The conclusion is clear that Lewis, in concert with Roche, used the Fund's resources to benefit the Union's Bank and to enhance the Union's economic power in disregard of the paramount and exclusive needs of the beneficiaries which he was charged as Chairman of the Board of Trustees to protect.

Lewis acted for the Union when he entered into the conspiracy.[6] A conspiracy once formed is presumed to continue; to escape continuing liability,

5. The stock of the Bank owned by the Union was held by the three Union officers named trustees for the Union. Lewis and later Boyle were each a trustee during their respective service as President of the Union.

6. The Union claims that it cannot be held liable for the acts of Lewis except upon "clear proof" that the membership of the Union actually participated in, authorized, or ratified his actions. This position is based

a party must affirmatively withdraw from the conspiracy and seek to avoid its effects. *See Hyde v. United States,* 225 U.S. 347, 369, 32 S.Ct. 793, 56 L.Ed. 1114 (1912); *South-East Coal Co. v. Consolidation Coal Co.,* 434 F.2d 767, 784 (6th Cir. 1970). The Union did not withdraw from the conspiracy; it had full power to end this breach of trust, yet it knowingly perpetuated the breach and continued to reap the benefits thereof.

Any doubt as to Lewis' motivation is fully dissipated by other evidence showing respects in which the Fund was used to benefit the Union during Lewis' chairmanship, to be discussed later. There is no suggestion that Lewis personally benefited, but he allowed his dedication to the Union's future and penchant for financial manipulation to lead him and through him the Union into conduct that denied the beneficiaries the maximum benefits of the Fund. A finding of conspiracy to maintain excessive cash at the Bank, justifying an award of damages against the Union in favor of the beneficiaries, is required.

The Bank, for its part, contends it played no conscious role in these arrangements and that it merely acted as a responsible banker handling the Fund's business in accordance with sound conservative banking practice. To be sure, the Bank did not overreach in any manner. It treated the Fund fairly. It performed extensive services for the Fund free of charge. There is no showing that the Bank conducted its business on the premise that the cash would not be summarily withdrawn. It was always highly liquid—indeed more liquid than other comparable banking institutions. Moreover, it did not receive any pressure from the Union to increase dividends for the Union's benefit, and dividend levels were in accord with the general parsimony that conservative bankers usually display toward shareholders at dividend time. There is no evidence that the Union or anyone connected with the Fund ever required the Bank to loan money to a friend or associate without adequate security and no such loans were made. Nor did the Bank show any favoritism toward the Union or the Fund contrary to proper banking standards.

upon Section 6 of the Norris-LaGuardia Act, 29 U.S.C. §106. Section 6, however, applies only to actions taken in the course of a labor dispute. By no view of the facts in this case can the management of the Welfare Fund by its trustees be termed a "labor dispute" as that phrase is defined in 29 U.S.C. §113(c). *See Columbia River Packers Ass'n. v. Hinton,* 315 U.S. 143, 146-147, 62 S.Ct. 520, 86 L.Ed. 750 (1942).

While the measure of the benefits the Bank received from this relationship is unclear, and certainly not as monumental as the size of the deposits suggests, the Bank was in a position to make money on the Fund's large demand deposits and in fact did just that. The deposits enhanced the Bank's earnings and its prestige and position in the banking community.

It is likely that the initial agreement among the Union (acting through Lewis), Roche, and the Bank (acting through Colton), to maintain trust accounts in a bank substantially owned by a Union whose president was a trustee, and the losses of income to the beneficiaries caused thereby, are sufficient without more to hold the Bank liable in conspiracy for damages under the special circumstances of this case.[7] This was not the theory on which plaintiffs proceeded, however, and the Court need not make such a finding.

The Bank recognizes, as does the Court, that the above facts, plus a showing of actual knowledge on its part that the funds maintained by the trustees in non-interest-bearing accounts were substantially in excess of the Fund's need for cash, will render it liable. The Bank vigorously denies that any such actual knowledge may be inferred from the facts established at trial. A review of those facts leads the Court to a contrary conclusion.

The Bank knew, from the time of the 1950 meeting between Lewis and Colton, that the ac-

7. This theory of the case would present the question whether it was a breach of trust for the trustees to deposit any money whatsoever in the Union's bank. There is a conflict among the cases as to whether a trustee may under any circumstances deposit trust funds in a bank in which he has a substantial interest. See the full discussion in 2 Scott on Trusts §§170.18, 170.19 (3d ed. 1967); compare *Caldwell v. Hicks,* 15 F.Supp. 46 (S.D.Ga. 1946) (deposit improper), with *In re Sexton,* 61 Misc. 569, 115 N.Y.W. 973 (1908) (deposit proper). It is universally held, however, that any such deposits will be subjected to the closest scrutiny for signs of self-dealing or negligence where the bank fails or the funds are left on deposit uninvested for an excessive period of time. *See, e.g., In re Culhane's Estate,* 269 Mich. 68, 256 N.W. 807, 811 (1934). And where the bank has notice that the trustee is acting in breach of trust in allowing such deposits to be made, it is liable along with the trustee for losses to the trust. *See Olin Cemetery Ass'n. v. Citizens Savings Bank,* 222 Iowa 1053, 270 N.W. 455, 459 (1936). Where the initial deposits are upwards of thirty million dollars and form a substantial percentage of the bank's business, as in the case of the Fund, it would be an extreme principle which would absolve the bank from any responsibility for resulting losses to the trust.

counts came to the Bank without solicitation at the initiative of the Chairman of the Board of Trustees of the Fund who was also President of the controlling shareholder of the Bank. The Bank knew that these were trust accounts, and from its own extensive experience in acting as trustee knew of the high standards governing the conduct of trustees. The Bank knew the actual dollar amounts in the fund's various interest-free accounts, and the percentage of the Fund's total assets that these accounts represented. The offices of the Bank, the Union, and the Fund were in close physical proximity. There were a number of interlocking relationships among the Union, the Bank, and the Fund throughout the twenty-year period.[8] Colton, the President of the Bank, was well aware of the propensity of the Union to use the Bank for Union objectives, as witnessed by his remarkable personal financial dealings with the Union, the Bank's loans to coal operators backed by Union collateral, and the unusual financial relationships between the Union and Cyrus Eaton, which the Bank aided.

The Bank strongly urges that it was ignorant of the terms of the trust agreement, the needs of the Fund for liquidity, or the possible tax consequences of enlarging the Fund's investment income, and hence that it had no way of knowing whether or not the obvious failure of the trustees to invest constituted a breach of trust.[9] Any inquiry into these matters would, of course, have revealed their total irrelevance to the startling size of the cash deposits continuously maintained by the trustees over almost twenty years. In the face of its full knowledge as to the size of the deposits and the relationship between the Union and the Fund, the Bank could hardly have assumed that the deposits were justified by any such possibilities. Its lack of inquiry into these suspicious matters is only further evidence of the Bank's awareness of the real reason for the deposit benefits it was receiving year after year.

Never in this entire period, Colton testified, did he ever discuss the Fund's accounts with anyone, inquire as to the Fund's needs or plans, or question the propriety of what was taking place. Not even casual inquiries were addressed to the interlocking directors and the nature of future prospects of the account were never mentioned at a single Board meeting. Since the Fund's business with the Bank accounted for over twenty percent of the Bank's time deposits and grew to over thirty percent of its demand deposits, this disinterest in the Bank's principal account is indeed more than remarkable. Perhaps this may be accounted for by incompetence, but Colton did not exhibit this characteristic on the stand. His explanations are unacceptable. In the light of all the facts and circumstances this silence and disinterest buttress the sole inference permissible on the totality of all the facts: that the Bank knowingly accepted and participated in a continuing breach of trust that redounded substantially to its own benefit.

This conclusion draws strong support from the cases which hold that where a bank enters into a transaction with a trustee, with actual or constructive knowledge that the transaction is in breach of the trustee's fiduciary duty, the bank may be held liable for the resulting loss to the trustee. *See, e.g., Union Stock Yards Bank v. Gillespie,* 137 U.S. 411, 416, 11 S.Ct. 118, 34 L.Ed. 724 (1890); *Anacostia Bank v. United States Fidelity & Guaranty Co.,* 73 U.S. App.D.C. 388, 119 F.2d 455 (1941); *American Surety Co. v. First National Bank,* 141 F.2d 411 (4th Cir. 1944); Restatement of Restitution §138 (1937); 4 Scott on Trusts §§324 *et seq.,* (3d ed. 1967). It is true, as the Bank suggests, that the Uniform fiduciaries Act, 21 D.C. Code §1701 *et seq.,* modifies the law in this juris-

8. In considering the interlocks between the Bank and the fund, two individuals involved occupied positions of special significance. Ryan, the fund's comptroller, knew full well that the cash deposits were excessive and, in effect, at one stage had so advised the trustees. He was named to the Advisory Board at the Bank in 1963, and became a director in 1965. He was also an honorary member of the Union. Hopkins, initially inside general counsel of the Union and later inside general counsel of the Fund, was a director of the Bank and of course fully familiar with the provisions of the trust and the legal responsibilities of the trustees. He attended trustee and Bank meetings. The knowledge of Ryan and Hopkins, insofar as it arose from their duties at the Fund, is not strictly imputable to the Bank. *See Arlington Brewing Co. v. Bluethenthal & Bickart,* 36 App.D.C. 209 (1916); 3 Fletcher, Cyclopedia of Corporations §§793, 808 (Rev. ed. 1965). Their knowledge was, however, continuously available to the Bank throughout the period.

9. The only reference in the testimony to any communication on these matters between Lewis and the Bank is the following from the cross-examination of Colton:

Q: Did Mr. Lewis ever tell you anything about the need of substantial balance in the fund accounts?

A: It seems to me that in the early '50s they had some difficulties and Mr. Lewis made the statement to me in one of our meetings that he would like to feel that the fund always had sufficient funds on hand to protect several monthly payments to miners so they shouldn't be in the position of being short of money. [Transcript p. 197.]

diction to limit a bank's liability for transactions with a trustee to cases in which the bank has actual knowledge of a breach of trust or knowledge of such facts that its action amounts to bad faith. In *Colby v. Riggs National Bank,* 67 U.S.App.D.C. 259, 92 F.2d 183 (1937), the Act was construed to require "actual knowledge of misappropriation," and misappropriation was taken to mean "wrong appropriation, or the use of a fund to a different purpose from that for which it was created; but not necessarily a dishonest purpose." 67 App. D.C. 259, 270 92 F.2d 183, 194. As the foregoing discussion demonstrates, the Bank knew that the money deposited in the Fund's checking accounts was being used for an improper purpose over a twenty-year period.

The Bank and the Union seek support from *United States v. Falcone,* 311 U.S. 205, 61 S.Ct. 204, 85 L.Ed. 128 (1940), and *Direct Sales Co. v. United States,* 319 U.S. 703, 63 S.Ct. 1265, 87 L.Ed. 1674 (1943). Both those cases dealt with the sufficiency of the evidence to support an inference of conspiracy. The decisions and, at the most, for the proposition that the act of selling morphine in large quantities to a doctor known to be selling drugs illegally is sufficient to support a finding of conspiracy to violate the narcotics acts; while the act of selling sugar in large quantities to a known bootlegger is not necessarily sufficient to support a finding of conspiracy to violate the alcoholic beverages acts. This distinction, which counsel for the Union correctly labeled "a question of how bad the fish smell," is irrelevant in this case; for it is not only the nature and size of the deposits involved, but also the close and interlocking relationships among the Fund, the Union, and the Bank, the evidence of the original understanding between Lewis and Colton, and the long course of dealing to mutual advantage that irresistibly support a clear inference of conspiracy here.[10]

To summarize this aspect of the case, the Court finds: an agreement among Lewis, Colton and Roche to maintain on deposit at the Bank substantial sums in interest-free accounts, without relation to the real needs of the Fund for liquidity or otherwise, for the benefit of the Union and the Bank and in disregard of the best interests of the beneficiaries; knowing participation in the breach of trust by the Union and the Bank, beginning in 1950 and continuing at least until this lawsuit was filed; and resulting injury to the beneficiaries measured by the loss of income on funds wrongfully maintained in interest-free accounts.

10. The finding of an agreement between Lewis and Colton in 1950 is not an essential element of the cause of action against the Bank and Colton as to the later years of the period under review. For whatever the nature of the understanding at the time the account was opened, the continuous maintenance of huge sums of money in demand deposits over the years was more than sufficient to convey to Colton and the Bank knowledge that the Bank was benefiting from a breach of trust.

III. OTHER BREACHES OF TRUST

Plaintiff specified at pretrial six categories of conduct, in addition to the excessive cash balances, allegedly constituting breaches of trust and claimed that as to each the Union, the Bank, and the individual defendants conspired. Some of these claims were abandoned in whole or in part as proof developed in the course of the trial, and only those fiduciary issues remaining at the end of trial need to be considered in this opinion. The Court is satisfied that plaintiffs have by clear and convincing evidence established conduct which violates the trustees' fiduciary duty to the beneficiaries in all respects still urged, except with regard to the claim that the trustees failed to collect or properly to determine delinquent royalty payments. The Bank and Colton are not shown to have conspired as to any of these breaches, and no participation by the Union was proved except as hereinafter indicated.

A. Withholding Health Cards.

The proof on this issue reflects a serious impropriety by the then-trustees of the Fund which has now apparently been rectified. Coal miners entitled to benefits are issued health cards which are used to obtain appropriate medical and hospital services directly from local physicians. When certain marginal coal operators in some sections of the country failed to account properly for royalties, and hence were in flagrant violation, the health cards of miners employed by those operators were revoked by the trustees, apparently on the theory that this action would lead the operators to pay up to avoid wildcat strikes. This practice was highly improper for the benefits owed the miners as qualified beneficiaries could not, under the terms of the Fund, be cancelled solely because their particular employer was in default on his royalty payments. This policy was of limited duration. Initiated in 1962, it was terminated by 1966 and affected some 7,000 card holders. It was arbitrary and capricious, and hence constituted a breach of trust. There is no proof, however, that this action was taken by the trustees to assist the Union in the conduct of labor disputes, nor is there any other proof of conspiracy on this aspect of the case.

B. Use of Misleading Application Forms.

The proof showed that the Fund called on Union locals to assist beneficiaries and potential beneficiaries of the Fund in preparing pension applications, and to carry out other administrative functions. It should be understood that the Fund as a practical matter is required to work through the locals in processing applications. The expense of establishing field offices exclusively for the Fund would be enormous, and in any event information from Union records may be required as a cross-check on the applicant's representations. This arrangement, however, has been seriously abused, and the trustees must be held at least partially responsible.

The trustees sponsored an application form which incorrectly implies that Union membership and Union approval is necessary before an application will be processed. The Application for Pension, for example, carries at its foot a space for certification by the local and by the district that the applicant "is currently a member of Local Union No. ____" and "is a member of District No. ____." There is ample documentary and testimonial evidence that applicants were improperly led by this form and by the locals to believe that Union membership was a prerequisite for eligibility, and were often forced to make substantial payments, sometimes running into hundreds of dollars, as "back dues" to reinstate their Union membership. The full extent of illegal collection of back dues by the Union through this device is unknown.

There is no proof that the trustees had actual knowledge of these improper practices by Union locals. In delegating certain functions to the Union local and district offices, however, they should have recognized the potential for abuse of the benefit application process where non-Union member beneficiaries were concerned. In continuing to use patently misleading forms which encouraged applicants to believe that a paid-up Union membership was a prerequisite to receiving benefits, the trustees were grossly negligent, to an extent that constitutes breach of trust. The trustees have apparently not acted decisively even to this date to terminate use of these misleading forms.

No cause of action was pleaded against the Union for fraud in collecting back dues from individual beneficiaries. Although the Union knowingly used the trustees' neglect to its own advantage, damages are recoverable only by individual beneficiaries who were defrauded, not by the trust itself. Since this action is only derivative, relief on this aspect of the case will be limited to an injunction to terminate the improper use of application forms in the future.

C. Investment in Utility Stock.

This issue relates to the Fund's purchases of stock of certain electric utility companies, principally Cleveland Electric Illuminating Company and Kansas City Power & Light Company. While these stocks are on the list approved for trustees, the propriety of these investments is challenged on the ground that they were made primarily for the purpose of benefitting the Union and the operators, and assisting them in their efforts to force public utilities to burn Union-mined coal. The investments have declined in value and are said to have been in violation of the trustees' duty of undivided loyalty to the beneficiaries.

In the late 1950's and early 1960's, the Union was engaged in a vigorous campaign to force public utility companies to purchase Union-mined coal. Public relations and organizational campaigns to this end were pressed vigorously in several cities. Lewis, then a trustee, worked closely with Cyrus S. Eaton, a Cleveland businessman. It is undisputed that between February and April 1955 the Fund purchased 30,000 shares of Cleveland Electric, and in March of that year the Union loaned Eaton money to enable him to buy an additional 20,000 shares. Eaton then went on the Board of Directors of Cleveland Electric. Similarly, between January and March 1955 the Fund purchased 55,000 shares of Kansas City Power & Light, and in June of the same year the Union loaned Eaton money to buy an additional 27,000 shares. In each of the years from 1956 to 1965 the Fund gave a general proxy for all of its shares in Cleveland Electric and Kansas City Power & Light to Eaton. The Union and Eaton were pressing the managements of each company to force them to buy Union-mined coal. The Fund purchased both Cleveland Electric and Kansas City Power & Light stock on the recommendation of Lewis, who was then fully familiar with the Union's activities affecting these companies and proxies were given to the Union by the Fund at Lewis' request.

Schmidt, who became a trustee of the Fund in 1958, was president of the principal coal operator standing to benefit from Cleveland Electric's additional purchases of Union-mined coal. He was acquainted with the activities of the Fund and of the Union with respect to Cleveland Electric, and actively encouraged them. When the Union's campaign to push Union-mined coal focused on Cleveland Electric in 1962 and 1963, the Fund purchased an additional 90,000 shares, with the hearty approval of Schmidt.

Further indication that these particular challenged stock purchases were made primarily for the collateral benefits they gave the Union is found in a general course of conduct. Lewis and Widman, the Union man spearheading the efforts to force utilities to buy Union-mined coal, discussed some seventy utility companies on the Fund's investment list, looking toward the possibility of obtaining proxies from fifteen. Proxies were in fact given the Union by the Fund not only on Cleveland Electric and Kansas City Power & Light, but on the shares the Fund held in Union Electric, Ohio Edison, West Penn Electric, Southern Company and Consolidated Edison. The intimate relationship between the Union's financial and organizing activities and the utility investment activities of the trustees demonstrates that the Fund was acting primarily for the collateral benefit of the Union and the signatory operators in making most of its utility stock acquisitions. These activities present a clear case of self-dealing on the part of trustees Lewis and Schmidt, and constituted a breach of trust. Roche knowingly consented to the investments, and must also be held liable. The Union is likewise liable for conspiring to effectuate and benefit by this breach of trust.

D. Collection of Royalties.

The Fund followed a set routine to make sure royalties were current and fully paid. Reports filed by operators with state and federal authorities were carefully checked and correlated with any information available from the Union. Delinquency notices were sent to any operator in arrears, and if payments were not brought into line the matter was referred to counsel. Numerous suits were filed when the controversies could not be resolved by negotiation. Collection techniques were vigorous and persistent.

It was inevitable over a twenty-year period that some operators would fail to pay royalties on time. This was particularly likely in the case of marginal operators confronting financial difficulties of one kind or another, but occasionally larger operators were also in default. Some delinquencies reflected honest differences as to the amount owing. There was never a time, however, when overdue royalty payments represented more than a small fraction of the operators' royalty obligations. Royalties were delinquent in amounts ranging from $5 million to a high of $9 million per annum. These figures contrast with annual royalty receipts in the range of $1780 million to $185 million. Moreover, collection efforts were in progress on many of these delinquencies.

Two specific situations were highlighted by the proof. Plaintiffs leveled particular criticism at arrangements made by the trustees to collect royalties from some small operators by dealing with associations representing those operators, and also at the Fund's failure promptly to collect royalties from West Kentucky Coal Co., a large operator controlled by the Union in conjunction with Cyrus Eaton and Defendant Colton, then President of the Bank. Admittedly the trustees had to make difficult business judgments in each of these situations, but the evidence of breach of trust is not clear. In the first instance the actions of certain locals[11] and the inadequacy of available records of coal mined made effective collection impractical. The cost of pursuing some of these small operators would undoubtedly have exceeded the royalty sums, if any, that would by legal or other means ultimately have been collected.

In the instance of West Kentucky, a substantial dollar delinquency, as high as $700,000 in 1961, was tolerated over a period of time. This company, a large but marginal operator, in 1963 eventually made its royalty payments current with aid of an ear-marked loan from the Union, and its royalty payments to the Fund eventually exceeded $40 million. Difficult judgments had to be made by the Fund's representatives during the period of deficiency, but these were made honestly and the decision temporarily to tolerate substantial nonpayment ultimately redounded to the benefit of the Fund.

The Union's heavy stock interest in West Kentucky (acquired as early as 1954) should have disqualified Lewis from any participation as a trustee in decisions involving royalty collections from that company. He wholly ignored the conflict of interest. The fund was placed in an indefensible position of having to deal with a Union-controlled operator. The royalties were eventually paid, however, and no substantial dispensations were grant-

11. In the period 1959-1964, the trustees were hobbled in collecting royalties from some 16 to 18 small operators because Union organizers had told the mines they didn't have to pay full royalties. This practice by the Union organizers was improper, but the evidence failed to show complicity by the trustees of the Fund.

ed West Kentucky which were not granted other flagrantly delinquent operators. Thus the West Kentucky episode reflects the loose standards of fiduciary responsibility which governed Lewis' conduct rather than a breach of trust by any other trustee.

E. Pension Increase.

One of the principal subjects of inquiry at the trial involved the circumstances under which monthly pensions were raised from $115 to $150 on June 24, 1969. This $35 increase was not without consequences, since it involved an additional annual disbursement from the Fund of approximately $30 million. Plaintiffs do not seek a rollback of the pension increase, but assert that the motives for which it was made, and the manner in which it was made, are grounds for removal of Boyle as a trustee, and for monetary relief from Boyle, Judy, and the Union for any injuries the Fund may suffer as a result of the action. A full discussion of the incident is required.

Roche broke her hip early in June, 1969, and for most of that month was recuperating at the Washington Hospital Center. She was nonetheless in frequent contact with her office by telephone and although immobile was otherwise fully functional. Lewis, still a trustee, was at home in Alexandria where he had remained more or less continuously for many months. He was alert but his health was failing. No trustee meeting had been held since February, 1969. Schmidt, the Operator trustee, had resigned on that date and a vacancy existed. On June 4, 1969, defendant Judy was installed as Schmidt's successor at a brief semi-social meeting held at Lewis' home. Roche, already hospitalized, knew of the meeting and approved of Judy's designation, but could not attend.

Lewis died on June 11, 1969, and Boyle, who had been president of the Union since 1963, was designated as the Union's trustee representative, and hence chairman of the Board of Trustees of the Fund, at a meeting of Union officials on June 23. Boyle had received some general information concerning the Fund's operations which led him to feel that a sizable pension increase could be financed. As an energetic Union leader, he was confident that if additional money were needed, the operators could be forced to increase their royalty payments when the next collective bargaining agreement was negotiated. He felt the unexpended balance of the Fund was far too large, and that a pension increase was long overdue. Indeed, at Union meetings and elsewhere he had promised that if he ever had anything to do with the matter he would increase pensions at the earliest possible opportunity. Boyle had urged Lewis to raise the amount of the pension but Lewis had refused to act.

When Lewis died and Boyle was named trustee, an election contest for presidency of the Union was looming.[12] Boyle undoubtedly recognized that if he delivered on his pension promises to the rank and file, his position would be strengthened in the campaign. These election considerations account for the timing of his actions, but they were not the primary factor motivating Boyle. He genuinely believed that a pension increase should be made in the interests of the miner beneficiaries. Boyle knew that Roche was opposed to a pension increase, but with her hospitalized, he was in a position to force the issue with Operator trustee Judy, and undoubtedly felt that the end—that is, the increase in pensions—justified the means. Even if Judy refused to go along, the Union's position in subsequent bargaining would be strengthened. Thus, Boyle decided to see if he could bully it through. As soon as he was designated trustee, Boyle called a meeting of the trustees for the next day at his offices at the Union.

Judy approved the increase in a private session with Boyle immediately before the formal meeting, under circumstances which will be mentioned later. The increase was formally approved a few minutes later and an announcement was thereafter sent out over Boyle's name to all pensioners and potential beneficiaries.

This action was taken in unnecessary haste. The trustees did not adequately consider the implications of their action, and while the increase was not wholly irresponsible it was not approached with adequate regard for the trustees' fiduciary obligations. Roche was not consulted or even advised of the action in advance, and in fact continued vigorously to oppose the pension increase. No detailed projections of the Fund's long-term ability to pay were made, nor were possible alternative changes in benefit payments considered.[13] The trustees took no contemporaneous steps par-

12. Joseph Yablonski had announced his candidacy on May 29, 1969. Boyle had relieved him of his position with the Union's Nonpartisan League on June 9.

13. The range of alternative increases in benefits was indicated by Ryan in a report to the Union's Executive Board on March 14, 1968. Besides a pension hike, Ryan noted that the following changes were among those being urged on the trustees: broadening eligibility for pensions to include totally disabled miners with ten years' service, regardless of age; making miners' wid-

tially to offset the added payout by eliminating unnecessary administrative expenses or by investing cash in income-producing securities. In short, the increase was handled as an arrangement between labor and management with little recognition of its fiscal and fiduciary aspects.

Prior to June 24, Judy had never attended a meeting of the trustees except for the pro forma session at Lewis' home earlier that month. He was president of the BCOA and well familiar with the negative attitudes of some operators toward higher benefits. He had some general knowledge of the Fund's fiscal position. Before he entered the meeting he had been warned by the Association's lawyer that matters of substance might be raised by Boyle, and it had been suggested he not act without further consultation. He failed to call Roche for her views or to question Boyle as to his representations, and after making some hasty mental calculations, proceeded on the basis of his own generally favorable attitude. At the trial he took the position that money to support a pension increase was available, that the miners deserved the increase, and that he approved of it on the merits. He testified that he had no obligation to consult the operators, pointing out that his predecessor had never consulted them.

After the action had been taken, however, he was called on the carpet by the operators, some of whom violently opposed the pension increase. He made little, if any, effort to justify his action on the merits. He rather argued that he had simply been placed in an impossible position at the meeting because Boyle had advised him that he, Boyle, had Roche's proxy and that the neutral trustee was in Boyle's pocket.

Thus two explanations are suggested for Judy's conduct: that he voted to increase pensions because he believed it was the correct thing to do, and that he voted for the increase because he was led to believe Boyle and Roche were for it.

While Judy undoubtedly felt that the miners needed a pension increase and that there was money available to pay it, this was not solely why he acted. Judy would not have voted for the increased pensions at the June 24 meeting on the spur of the moment, without advance warning, against the advice of counsel, knowing that the royalty payments of the coal operators might be affected, if he had not been falsely led to believe by Boyle that Boyle had Roche's proxy. It was a serious error of judgment for Judy to have accepted Boyle's representations and for Judy not to have checked with Roche, at least by telephone. While Judy was forced to resign under pressure a few days later when the operators learned that Boyle did not have Roche's proxy, and while he was but a passing participant, his conduct fell below the standard of care and skill required of a trustee. He acted hastily and without taking the normal precautions requisite for responsible fiduciary actions.

Boyle of course also proceeded without regard to his fiduciary obligations in pushing through the pension increase. He failed even to notify the neutral trustee of the meeting or of the contemplated pension increase, which was itself in neglect of the duty of a co-trustee. *See Wilmington Trust Co. v. Coulter,* 41 Del.Ch. 548, 200 A.2d 441, 451 (1964); Bogert, Trusts & Trustees §554 (2d ed. 1960). He brought about the action by a hasty power play, fortifying his position by falsely indicating that Roche supported his proposal. Unlike Judy, Boyle remains a trustee. It has been shown by testimony and by Boyle's demeanor at the trial that he considers the fund in effect the property of the Union to be used in whatever manner the immediate and long-term objectives of the Union warrant. As Boyle's conduct in this instance demonstrates, such compulsions of militant Union leadership are inconsistent with the dictates of prudent trusteeship.

The most revealing document in this entire episode is the full text of the press release which the Fund's public relations man issued on the day of the pension increase. It reads as follows:

> Washington, D.C.—W.A. "Tony" Boyle, President of the United Mine Workers of America, succeeded John L. Lewis today as the Chief Executive Officer and Trustee of the Union's Welfare and Retirement Fund, and immediately boosted the pension of retired soft coal miners from $115 to $150 monthly.
>
> The new pension rate will be effective August 1. It was voted at the first session of the Trustees attended by the Union chief. He was chosen trustee at a meeting of the International Executive Board yesterday, and as chief executive officer of the Fund, as set forth under the UMWA contract with the bituminous coal industry, called a meeting of the trustees, and the pension boost was adopted. Other trustees are George Judy, for the coal operators, and Josephine Roche,

ows eligible for medical care benefits until the age of 65; providing additional medical benefits for incapacitated children of miners; paying Medicare premiums for beneficiaries over the age of 65; extending benefits for unemployed or disabled miners; and increasing widows' and survivors' benefits. According to Ryan's estimates, the additional cost of these modifications would eventually amount to over $35 million annually.

> also director of the fund, as the neutral.
>
> Pensions now are going to approximately 70,000 retired soft coal miners. Last year, the Fund paid out $96 million in this benefit alone. Other benefits are complete hospital care for miners and their families, and death benefits to widows and survivors.
>
> Chairman Boyle also called for an immediate in-depth study of all benefits of the 23 year-old Fund, with complete analysis of the entire program of miners, their widows and families. He has received scores of suggestions for possibly improving the benefits at a series of rallies in the coal fields of West Virginia, Pennsylvania and Illinois in recent months.
>
> The new chief executive of the Fund, like his predecessor, will accept no pay for serving as Trustee.

Nothing could more blatantly expose the realities of what had occurred in this instance and had been occurring for some time. However correct or incorrect the pension increase decision may have been, it reflected the Union influence over fund policy and the loss of independence that the Fund's continuous deferences to the Union's self-interest had by this time achieved.

IV. THE INDIVIDUAL DEFENDANTS

Before considering the involvement of each of the named individual defendants, a brief statement of the applicable legal standards is required. The elements of conspiracy or participation in breach of trust discussed earlier with respect to the Union and the Bank are equally applicable to the individual defendants. An officer of a corporation or other entity found to have participated in a breach of trust is not liable simply by reason of his officership, but an officer is liable if he personally knows of the breach of trust and participates therein or fails to take action to correct it. *See Strauss v. United States Fidelity & Guaranty Co.,* 63 F.2d 174 (4th Cir. 1933); 4 Scott on Trusts §326.3 (3d ed. 1967). It is not necessary to prove that the individual personally profited from the transaction. And one who knowingly joins a conspiracy "even at a later date takes the conspiracy as he finds it, with or without knowledge of what has gone on before." *Myzel v. Fields,* 386 F.2d 718, 738 n. 12 (8th Cir. 1967), *cert. denied,* 390 U.S. 951, 88 S.Ct. 1043, 19 L.Ed.2d 1143 (1968).

Josephine Roche: Roche had a distinguished public career before joining the Fund, and she has played a unique role in the affairs of the Fund since its inception. She has been both the neutral trustee and the Administrator, a full-time salaried position. While she has had a long interest and commitment to the welfare objectives of the Fund and has contributed substantially to many of its unique welfare successes, her business experience was more limited. She did not profit personally in any way by any of the actions taken. She idolized John L. Lewis and felt entirely confident to follow his leadership in financial matters, apparently without independent inquiry. She was an active participant in each breach of trust except the pension increase. Indeed, without her affirmative approval they probably would not have occurred. She accepted without question the accumulations of excessive cash at the Union's Bank even when the propriety of depositing these balances was raised at trustee meetings, and in the face of advice that the cash could be invested without impairing the liquidity of the Fund. Perhaps she failed wholly to recognize the full implications of her actions, but naivete and inattention cannot excuse her conduct. She violated her duty as trustee in all the respects previously discussed, and she must be said to have knowingly furthered the conspiracies as to the cash and the utility company investments.

W. A. (Tony) Boyle: Boyle was not a party to the original conspiracy, and never adopted its ends. He was not responsible for the accumulation of excessive cash at the Bank, although he knew about it. From the moment he became President of the Union in 1963, and indeed earlier, he sought to persuade Lewis to have the Fund pay out larger benefits, which would have had the effect of reducing cash balances. Boyle also insisted that various loans and other financial involvements engineered on behalf of the Union by Lewis in cooperation with the Fund and the Bank be terminated, and this was done. This did not disentangle the Union from the conspiracy as to the cash balances, but it is action inconsistent with individual participation by Boyle in any conspiracy. The failure of the Union to supplant Lewis after Boyle became president cannot, on the evidence before the Court, be considered sufficient to hold Boyle as an individual conspirator, although the agreement was renegotiated after 1963 and Lewis could have been removed.

Boyle, however, violated his duty as trustee in several particulars. His actions in forcing through the pension increase, partly by misrepresentation, in haste and without consulting the neutral trustee, reflect an insensitivity to fiduciary standards. In addition, he continued to serve as director of the Bank and member of its Executive Committee after becoming trustee, a relationship which conflicted with that degree of independence required of a trustee under the circumstances of this case. He took only limited action to modify the inappropriate application forms that encouraged improper cash levies by the Union on applicants as a condition precedent to receiving pension benefits.

George L. Judy: Judy is guilty of poor judgment but not of conduct that violated his duty as trustee. He should have consulted the independent trustee before acting hastily at Boyle's insistence and without adequate information in approving a pension increase which had substantial effect upon the long-term operations of the Fund. No relief is required as to Judy, since he is no longer a trustee and there is no likelihood he will be one in the future. He was a trustee for only six weeks, and did not participate in any conspiracy. The case as to him is dismissed.

Barnum L. Colton: Colton was a party to the original conspiratorial agreement to place excessive cash in the Bank, and as the chief executive of the Bank he participated in carrying out that breach of trust. His collaboration with the Union was far more than that which followed merely from his office.

C. W. Davis: Davis, the trustee representative of the Operators, is a nominal defendant named to assure proper implementation of any equitable relief against the Fund. He is not shown to have engaged in any improper conduct. All the events here reviewed occurred prior to his designation as trustee.

V. RELIEF

All defendants contend that the doctrine of laches bars any relief for the claimed breaches of trust, and alternatively that the statute of limitations bars any claim for damages by reason of events occurring more than three years prior to the filing of this suit. Plaintiffs assert that laches, not the statute of limitations, is applicable to all causes of action herein, and urge that they have not been guilty of any unreasonable delay which would bar relief.

It is clear that an action to redress a breach of trust sounds in equity, and that the statute of limitations is inapplicable to such a suit in the District of Columbia. *See Naselli v. Millholland,* 88 App.D.C. 237, 188 F.2d 1005 (1951); *Haliday v. Haliday,* 56 App.D.C. 179, 11 F.2d 565, 569 (1926); *Nedd v. Thomas,* 316 F.Supp. 74, 77 (M.D.Pa. 1970); 3 Scott on Trusts §219 (3d ed. 1967). Nor is the statute of limitations strictly applicable to the cause of action against the Union or the Bank, for it is the breach of trust they conspired to carry out, not the conspiracy itself, which is the gist of the action. See cases cited page 1099 *supra;* Restatement of Trusts 2d §327(a), Comment K. It is true that courts customarily follow the statute of limitations even in equity cases where essentially legal relief, such as damages or an accounting, is sought. *Columbian University v. Taylor,* 25 App. D.C. 124, 131 (1905). This rule, however, is not strictly followed in this jurisdiction. *Haliday v. Haliday, supra,* 56 App.D.C. 179, 11 F.2d 565, 569 (1926). The guiding principle is that "laches is not like limitation, a mere matter of time; but principally a question of the inequity of permitting the claim to be enforced. . . ." *Holmberg v. Armbrecht,* 327 U.S. 392, 396, 66 S.Ct. 582, 584, 90 L.Ed. 743 (1946).

The Court is mindful of several factors which bear upon the equity of awarding damages for the excessive cash accumulations at the Bank going back to 1950. The actual size of the deposits was never concealed, but was regularly reported in the annual reports of the Fund which were widely distributed. The relationships of the Union and the Fund with the Bank were mentioned on numerous occasions in the Mine Workers Journal and elsewhere. Certainly by reasonable diligence most, though not all, of the relevant facts as to the cash deposits could have been readily ascertained. The delay has prejudiced the defendants in that some of the major participants in these events are now dead, and if damages were assessed for the Fund's loss of investment income over the full twenty years, both the Union and the Bank, whose resources will necessarily feel the major impact of the judgment, would be seriously injured. In assessing the reasonableness of the delay, however, the Court must consider the impecunious nature of the beneficiaries, the obstacles of Union discipline which could well have intervened, the fact that the class of beneficiaries was continually changing, and the fact that as late as May, 1969, the Fund through a statement in the Union newspaper disingenuously represented that the large cash balances were necessary for the operation of the Fund. Thus the delay is not inexcusable, but it must be taken into account in determining the period for which damages will be assessed.

Moreover, the Court notes that while the beneficiaries have suffered as a result of the Fund's loss of investment income, they have benefited to some extent from the Union's activities over the past twenty years. In the longer view of matters, the Union's strength protects the interests of the beneficiaries, past and prospective; the Union should not be weakened to a point where its stance at the bargaining table will be substantially impaired.

Balancing these facts, and recognizing the similarity between this action in equity and one at law for damages, the Court will adopt the three-year limitation provided by 13 D.C.Code §301(8) as to the damages aspect of this case.

No considerations of equity intervene to bar prospective remedies for mismanagement of the Fund by its trustees. The Fund has been seriously compromised. It has failed to develop a coherent investment policy geared to immediate or long-term goals. It has collaborated with the Union contrary to the trustees' fiduciary duties, and has left excessive sums of money on deposit with the Union's Bank in order to assist the Union. In their day-to-day decisions the trustees have overlooked their excessive obligation to the beneficiaries by improperly aiding the Union to collect back dues and by cutting off certain beneficiaries unfairly.

Alongside these serious deficiencies must be placed the pioneer role of the Fund, which by constant effort has led in the development of a broad program of welfare benefits for a distressed segment of the working population. The many beneficial and well-motivated actions cannot, however, excuse the serious lapses which have resulted in obvious detriments to many beneficiaries. There is an urgent need for reformation of policies and practices, which only changes in the composition of the Board of Trustees, an adjustment of its banking relationship, and other equitable relief can accomplish.

Further proceedings must be conducted on the measure of damages, but as the Court indicated before trial, it is desirable at this stage to establish the nature of equitable relief which must be taken for the protection of the beneficiaries. Equitable relief shall take the following form.

Neither Boyle nor Roche shall continue to serve as a trustee. Each shall be replaced by June 30, 1971, under the following procedures. A new trustee must first be named by the Union. Consonant with the provisions of the Agreement, the new Union trustee and the existing trustee representing the Operators shall then select a new neutral trustee. The neutral trustee shall be designated on or before June 15, 1971, and the designation will then be submitted for approval by this Court before the new trustee takes office on June 30.

The newly constituted Board of Trustees selected as required by the decree shall then immediately determine whether or not Roche shall continue as Administrator of the Fund. No trustee shall serve as Administrator after June 30, 1971.

Upon the selection of a replacement for Boyle and the neutral trustee, the newly constituted Board of Trustees shall be required to obtain independent professional advice to assist them in developing an investment policy for creating maximum income consistent with the prudent investment of the Fund's assets, and such a program shall be promptly put into effect.

The Fund shall by June 30, 1971, cease maintaining banking accounts with or doing any further business of any kind with the National Bank of Washington. Following termination of this relationship, the Fund shall not have any account in a bank in which either the Union, any coal operator or any trustee has controlling or substantial stock interest. No employee, representative or trustee of the Fund shall have official connection with the bank or banks used by the Fund after June 30, 1971. The Fund shall not maintain non-interest-bearing accounts in any bank or other depository which are in excess of the amount reasonably necessary to cover immediate administrative expenses and to pay required taxes and benefits on a current basis.

A general injunction shall be framed enjoining the trustees from the practices here found to be breaches of trust and generally prohibiting the trustees from operating the Fund in a manner designed in whole or in part to afford collateral advantages to the Union or the operators.

Counsel are directed to confer and prepare a proposed form of decree carrying out the equitable relief here specified. This proposed decree shall be presented to the Court and any disagreements as to form settled on May 13, 1971, at 4:00 p.m. On May 21, 1971, plaintiffs shall furnish the Court and defendants with a precise statement of the amounts of compensatory damages and attorneys' fees and expenses claimed in light of this Opinion, a statement of the method used to compute the claims, and a list of witnesses to be called at the damages phase of this proceeding. No punitive damages will be awarded. A hearing as to compensatory damages is set forth June 21, 1971, at 9:30 a.m.

TOENSING V. BROWN

374 F.Supp. 191 (N.D. Calif. 1974)

RENFREW, District Judge.

The named plaintiffs, retired carpenters eligible for retirement benefits from the Carpenters Pension Trust Fund for Northern California, have brought this suit as a class action under Rule 23, Federal Rules of Civil Procedure, challenging the administration of that Trust Fund by defendants, current and former trustees of the Trust Fund. Plaintiffs invoke this Court's jurisdiction under 29 U.S.C. §186(e) and 28 U.S.C. §1337, and also under the doctrine of pendent jurisdiction.

Plaintiffs have stated two causes of action. First, they complain that the trustees decided, on or about July 1, 1971 (actually July 23, 1971), to increase the pensions of those carpenters retiring on or after July 1, 1971, more than the pensions of carpenters who retired before that date.[1] Plaintiffs attack this action as grossly discriminatory, arbitrary and capricious, and an abuse of the trustees' authority which has raised the serious possibility of a depletion of the Pension Trust Fund. Plaintiffs assert that defendants' action violates 29 U.S.C. §186(c)(5) which requires monies paid to such a trust fund to be "for the sole and exclusive benefit" of the employees of the contributing employer. Second, plaintiffs charge that defendants' action constitutes a violation of their fiduciary responsibility as established by California state law. Plaintiffs ask this Court to order defendants to rescind their decision on the differential pension increases and to make across-the-board increases so that pensions for persons retiring before July 1, 1971, will equal pensions for those retiring on or after that date. They also ask for an order awarding plaintiffs the amount of money they would have received if the initial decision had been for equal pension increases and also awarding damages, costs, and attorneys' fees.

Defendants moved for summary judgment on July 20, 1973. That motion was heard on August 29, 1973, and was taken under submission. Subsequently, the Court determined that a hearing should be held on the question of whether the action should be allowed to proceed as a class action. At that hearing, on December 19, 1973, the Court ordered that the action was maintainable as a class action. A class notice was sent to those persons falling within the class represented by the named plaintiffs,[2] and an opportunity was given those persons to choose to be excluded from the class.[3] Plaintiffs have now also moved for summary judgment. Another hearing was held on February 22, 1974, on both motions for summary judgment.

I. SOLE AND EXCLUSIVE BENEFIT OF THE EMPLOYEES

The essential legal question posed by these motions is the proper interpretation of 29 U.S.C. §186 (c)(5).[4] That provision excepts from the general prohibition of payments of money by an employer to a representative of his employees[5] those payments made to a trust fund "for the sole and exclusive benefit of the employees" of the employer. The trust fund to which such payments are allowed must be constituted so that the employer and employees are equally represented.[6] The legal basis of plaintiffs' action is that this provision must be interpreted to mean that the motivation or considerations of the trustees in carrying out their responsibilities must be only the benefit of the employee beneficiaries, and that any other purpose or intention is an illegitimate consideration. Plaintiffs argue that the trustees must be completely independent in administering the trust funds and that they should not consider the recommendations of the collective-bargaining parties binding or obligatory.

The general principles stated by plaintiffs are not an accurate and complete interpretation of §186(c)(5). They ignore the complexity and the varied purposes which the statutory scheme pursues. The purpose was not simply to establish a trust fund with independent trustees:

> Those members of Congress who supported [§186] were concerned with corruption of collective bargaining through bribery of employee representatives by employers, with extortion by

1. The increase was from $9.00 to $15.00 each month per year of pension credit for all pension awards effective on or after July 1, 1971 (except for minimum pensions) and for a 5% across-the-board increase for all pension awards effective prior to July 1, 1971 (again excepting minimum pensions).

2. The class is comprised of all those persons including pensioners, beneficiaries, or recipients under joint and survivor options, who have received or are receiving pension payments as the result of pension awards effective prior to July 1, 1971.

3. There were 7,294 notices mailed; 1,935 were returned because addressees were deceased or not at address, 22 notices are outstanding, 2,510 chose exclusion from the class, leaving 2,838 members of the class.

4. The pertinent portion of §186 reads as follows:

> . . . (c) The provisions of this section shall not be (5) with respect to money or other thing of value paid to a trust fund established by such representative, for the sole and exclusive benefit of the employees of such employer, and their families and dependents (or of such employees, families, and dependents jointly with the employees of other employers making similar payments, and their families. . . .

5. *See* 29 U.S.C. §186(a), (b).

6. 29 U.S.C. §186(c)(5)(B).

employee representatives, and with the possible abuse by union officers of the power which they might achieve if welfare funds were left to their sole control. Congressional attention was focussed particularly upon the latter problem because of the demands which had then recently been made by a large international union for the establishment of a welfare fund to be financed by employers' contributions and administered exclusively by union officials. *See United States v. Ryan,* 350 U.S. 299 [76 S.Ct. 400, 100 L.Ed. 335].

Congress believed that if welfare funds were established which did not define with specificity the benefits payable thereunder, a substantial danger existed that such funds might be employed to perpetrate control of union officers, for political purposes, or even for personal gain. [citations omitted] To remove these dangers, specific standards were established to assure that welfare funds would be established only for purposes which Congress considered proper and expended only for the purposes for which they were established.

Arroyo v. United States, 359 U.S. 419, 425-426, 79 S.Ct. 864, 868, 3 L.Ed.2d 915 (1959). *See also United States v. Ryan,* 350 U.S. 299, 305, 76 S.Ct. 400, 100 L.Ed. 335 (1956).

As indicated in *Arroyo, supra,* Congress did not rely solely upon the appointment of neutral, non-employer, non-employee trustees, and the application of traditional law governing trusts and fiduciary relationships. Instead it directed that employers and employees be equally represented among the trustees, that "the detailed basis on which . . . payments are to be made [be] specified in a written agreement with the employer," that there be a way for resolving deadlocks among the trustees, that there be an annual audit of the trust fund, and that the results of the audit be available "for inspection by interested persons. . . ." 29 U.S.C. §186(c)(5)(B). These structural provisions were the statutory devices provided for the protection of the beneficiaries.

But plaintiffs argue that the trustees must still be completely independent from the collective-bargaining parties. Indeed the implication of plaintiffs' position seems to be that if the trustees' actions are clearly consistent with and further the interests of the union and employers, those actions are suspect even if they are actuarially sound and otherwise consistent with the interests of the beneficiaries of the trust fund. If only such complete independence of the trustees had been sought, however, Congress would not have enacted §186(c)(5) in its present form. That section requires that employees and employers be equally represented in the administration of the trust fund. It does not prohibit a person from serving both as collective-bargaining representative and as trustee of the trust fund. Congress intentionally placed the trust fund provisions within the collective-bargaining context, believing that the trust fund was best managed when the contending views of employer and union were resolved in the best interests of the beneficiaries:

It is a commonplace of modern industrial relations for employers to provide security for employees and their families to enable them to meet problems arising from unemployment, illness, old age or death. While employers in many other industries assume this burden directly, this welfare fund was jointly created by the coal industry and the union for that purpose. Not only has Benedict [the employer] entered into a long-term relationship with the union in this regard, but in compliance with [§186(c)(5)(B)] it has assumed equal responsibility with the union for the management of the fund. In a very real sense Benedict's interest in the soundness of the fund and its management is in no way less than that of the promisee union.

Lewis v. Benedict Coal Co., 361 U.S. 459, 468-469, 80 S.Ct. 489, 495, 4 L.Ed.2d 442 (1960) (emphasis added).

Language used in a recent decision by the Supreme Court differentiating the meaning of the term "employees" when used in §186(c)(5) from its meaning when used in 29 U.S.C. §158(a)(5) also suggests that trustees were not intended by §186(c)(5) to reside in a noumenal world apart from the difficult realities of the collective-bargaining process:

[T]here is no anomaly in the conclusion that retired workers are "employees" within [§186 (c)(5)] entitled to the benefits negotiated while they were active employees, but are not "employees" whose ongoing benefits are embraced by the bargaining obligation of [§158(a)(5)]. Contrary to the Board's assertion, the union's role in the administration of the fund is of a far different order from its duties as collective-bargaining agent. To accept the Board's reasoning that the union's [§186(c)(5)] responsibilities dictate the scope of the [§158(a)(5)] collective-bargaining obligation would be to allow the tail to wag the dog.

Chemical Workers v. Pittsburgh Glass, 404 U.S. 157, 170-171, 92 S.Ct. 383, 393, 30 L.Ed.2d 341 (1971).

The metaphor used by the Supreme Court suggests that collective bargaining does, at least to some extent, affect the scope of the administrative decisions of the trustees. *See also* 404 U.S. 157, at 171, n. 11, 92 S.Ct. 383, 30 L.Ed.2d 341.

And clearly the collective-bargaining parties do determine the amount of resources that flow into the fund through the employer's contributions.

[3] That the trust fund and collective-bargaining process are not completely separate and independent institutions does not mean that the trustees have no fiduciary responsibilities. It does mean that they may look to the collective-bargaining agreements as guides and, under appropriate circumstances, adopt the terms of those agreements. If, for instance, the union in bargaining with the employer has represented both active and retired employees, it would be odd indeed for the trustees to ignore the changes in payments of pension benefits from the trust fund provided for in the new agreement. If the union did not purport to represent the retired employees, the trustees would have to give full consideration to their interests before accepting the terms of the newly negotiated agreement.[7] But the trustees are not required to provide the same benefits for all beneficiaries. Active workers can properly be given higher benefits than retired workers. *See Chemical Workers v. Pittsburgh Glass,* 404 U.S. 157, 173, n. 12, 92 S.Ct. 383, 30 L.Ed.2d 341 (1971); *Jensen v. Garvison,* 274 F. Supp. 866, 869 (D.Or. 1967). The trustees must also certainly consider the impact which the changes would have on the long-term viability of the trust fund. But it would be anomalous to impose upon trustees, as representatives of the employer and union, a duty to ignore the terms agreed upon by the employer and union. Indeed it could place the trustees personally in untenable, conflicting roles. The law does not require such schizophrenic duties.

Plaintiffs have cited out of context statements in a number of reported cases which they claim support the extreme type of independence which they demand of defendants. But when analyzed in light of their facts and specific holdings, it is clear that the cases do not support plaintiffs' interpretation of §186(c)(5). The district court did state in *Lewis v. Scanor Coal Company*, 256 F.Supp. 456, 461 (W.D.Pa. 1966), *aff'd*, 382 F.2d 437, 143 (3 Cir. 1967), *cert. denied*, 390 U.S. 947, 88 S.Ct. 1035, 19 L.Ed.2d 1137 (1968), that "[i]t was the intent of Congress that such trusts under [§186(c)(5)] be separate and apart from the union and employer creating the trust." But that general language was used in holding that an oral modification of the written terms of a trust violated §186(c)(5)(B), an explicit structural requirement. In *Blankenship v. Boyle*, 329 F.Supp. 1089, 1113 (D.D.C. 1971), *motion denied*, 145 U.S.App. D.C. 111, 447 F.2d 1280 (1971), *opinion supplemented*, 337 F.Supp. 296 (D.D.C. 1972), the court did enjoin "the trustees from operating the Fund in a manner designed in whole or in part to afford collateral advantages to the Union or the operators," but the injunction was given in the context of "practices . . . found to be breaches of trust. . . ." The court was not describing the general obligations of trustees under §186(c)(5). The language in *United Marine Division v. Essex Transportation Co.*, 216 F.2d 410, 412 (3 Cir. 1954), that certain trustees were not representatives of the employees, was used in holding that a promise to make payments to the trustees of a welfare trust by an employer which was not a party to the trust fund was not within the prohibition of §186(a) and (b). In *American Bakeries Company v. Barrick,* 162 F.Supp. 882, 884 (N.D.Ohio 1958), *aff'd by order*, 285 F.2d 426 (6 Cir. 1960), the question posed was "whether the court should declare the complete separation and *physical divorcement* of the trust fund offices from the Union offices. . . ." (emphasis added). This was a structural, physical question rather than one of the complete intellectual independence of the trustees from the collective-bargaining context.

Plaintiffs also suggest that the motivation of the trustees is critical: If their primary motivation is directed toward objectives other than the "sole and exclusive benefit" of the beneficiaries, then their action is unlawful. Plaintiffs place too much reliance in their arguments on the slippery concept of motivation and not enough on the question of type and sufficiency of proof of improper action. §186(c)(5) is clearly directed against the payment of funds to persons other than the beneficiaries and also against the use of funds supplied by one employer for the benefit of the employees of other employers. *Bey v. Muldoon*, 223 F.Supp. 489, 495-496 (E.D.Pa. 1963), *aff'd per curiam,* 354 F.2d 1005 (3 Cir. 1966), *cert. denied,* 384 U.S. 987, 86 S.Ct. 1888, 16 L.Ed.2d 1004 (1966). Trustees are indeed held to high standards of honesty and good faith, and they are called upon to resist bad faith efforts by the union or employer to utilize the trust fund for their own ends. *See Insley v. Joyce,* 330 F.Supp. 1228, 1234 (N.D. Ill. 1971):

7. Retirees' benefits are not a mandatory subject of bargaining. *Chemical Workers v. Pittsburgh Glass,* 404 U.S. 157, 92 S.Ct. 383, 30 L.Ed.2d 341 (1971). But bargaining over retirees' benefits is permissible. 404 U.S. at 171, n. 11, 92 S.Ct. 383. When bargaining covers benefits payable to both active and retired employees, the union must "balance the interests of all its constituents," a duty of fair representation. 404 U.S. at 173, n. 12, 92 S.Ct. at 394.

> If the purposes *and effects* behind this provision are thus primarily to benefit the union and penalize employees, we clearly are presented with a trust fund that possesses the structural deficiency of not being solely for the benefit of employees. (emphasis added)

Indeed, as in the case of one's struggle for salvation, good motives are not enough. Thus, even if the primary motivation of one trustee is his belief that a pension increase would be in the interest of the beneficiaries, his decision to "bully" the increase through, in a "hasty power play," with the increase "handled as an arrangement between labor and management with little recognition of its fiscal and fiduciary aspects," makes that increase one not for the "sole and exclusive benefit" of the beneficiaries. *Blankenship v. Boyle,* 329 F.Supp. 1089, 1108-1109 (D.D.C. 1971). The court in *Blankenship* found, moreover, that Boyle "considers the fund in effect the property of the Union to be used in whatever manner the immediate and long-term objectives of the Union warrant." 329 F.Supp. 1089, at 1109.

[5,6] Though the trustees are held to high standards, they were not intended to be subjected by §186(c)(5) to a court's speculation as to their motivation behind a decision in the absence of substantial evidence showing that they have neglected or subverted the interests of the beneficiaries. The standard of review which a court must follow in considering a challenged action of the trustees in whether it is arbitrary or capricious. *Lee v. Nesbitt,* 453 F.2d 1309, 1311 (9 Cir. 1972); *Roark v. Lewis,* 130 U.S. App. D.C. 360, 401 F.2d 425, 427 (1968). That standard is not met by merely showing that the trustees adopted the recommendation of the collective-bargaining parties. The trustees have a wide discretion in determining what action would be in the best interests of the beneficiaries. Cf., *Kosty v. Lewis,* 115 U.S. App. D.C. 343, 319 F.2d 744, 748-749 (1963), *cert. denied*. 375 U.S. 964, 84 S.Ct. 482, 11 L.Ed. 2d 414 (1964).

Therefore, the plaintiffs' proposed interpretation of §186(c)(5) must be rejected. The next question is whether, considering their factual showings, either side is entitled, under the Court's view of §186(c)(5), to summary judgment.

II. THE PARTIES' FACTUAL OFFERINGS

Defendants' moving papers included affidavits and exhibits which were offered as showing the factual background of the trustees' decision on July 23, 1971, to give a larger pension increase to pensioners retiring on or after July 1, 1971, than to those retiring before that date. C. Bruce Sutherland, secretary to the Board of Trustees, gave the following history of the policy that formed the basis of that decision, supplemented by the minutes of the various Board meetings. The Pension Trust Fund was established by a trust agreement as of August 19, 1958. At a Board meeting on December 17, 1962, the Martin E. Segal Company, Inc., consultants and actuaries to the Pension Trust Fund, had proposed three alternative benefit increases, one of which would have given a pension increase to all active carpenters but not to any retired carpenters. That alternative was not adopted by the Board. At the December 17, 1965, meeting of the Board the consultants proposed as one alternative a similar differential; it was not adopted.[8] At the Board meeting on June 28, 1966, the following motion was passed: "that all pensions, including minimum pensions, be increased by 5% effective July 1, 1966, that any benefit increases which may be effected in the future apply only to those carpenters who retire after the effective date of each such benefit increase, whether such increases result from favorable actuarial experience or increased contribution rates. . . ."

On September 17, 1968, the Board modified its 1966 decision so that those carpenters already retired "shall benefit by way of interest or yield increment but not by subsequent Collective Bargaining changes. . . . On June 17, 1969, the Board increased the pension rate per year of pension credit for pensioners whose awards would first become effective on or after September 1, 1969, from $8.40 to $9.00 and for pensioners whose awards were effective prior to September 1, 1969, from $8.40 to $8.80.

Therefore, the uncontroverted facts[9] demonstrate that the Board had a history of approving a

---

8. The Board adopted the following provision:

> That all other Pensions [other than minimum pensions] be increased by 60%, with recognition by the Trustees that any further benefit increases which result solely from increased contribution rates are to be applied only to those carpenters who retire after the date of any such benefit increase. However, in the event that benefit increases may be effected as a result of the fund's favorable actuarial experience in the future, such benefit changes may, in the discretion of the Trustees, be applied to the existing pensioners as well as prospective pensioners.

9. Plaintiffs have tried to raise a factual dispute with respect to this history. They claim that prior to 1971 the Board never followed a policy of restricting future benefits, from any source, to future retirees. But defendants do not dispute this. Such a policy was proposed in 1966, but was modified in 1968. See text, *supra.* Indeed, in

differential in pension benefits prior to the action in question here.

At its meeting on June 15, 1971, the Board again discussed benefit increases. Alfred A. Figone, an employee trustee, proposed *inter alia* a 5% across-the-board increase in benefits for all pensioners then on the pension rolls and a revision of the unit value per year from $9.00 to $10.00. After an "Employer Caucus," the employer trustees "indicated that in view of the fact that labor negotiations were presently in process and that undoubtedly additional funds and commensurate additional benefits would be shortly forthcoming, the Employer Trustees would prefer not to make any changes in the plan pending final result of said negotiations, at which time the total amount available from a contribution standpoint, would be known to the Trustees and that at that time definitive judgment could be reached with respect to the entire package and that certain adjustments in the benefit level, could, if proper, be applied retroactively." Figone's proposal failed to carry because of a tie vote, with the seven employee trustees voting in favor and the seven employer trustees voting against. Provision was made for calling another meeting on twenty-four hours' notice after a collective-bargaining agreement was executed.

The next meeting was held on July 23, 1971. The minutes of the meeting state the following:

> Mr. Figone discussed with the Board the recently concluded negotiations between the Collective Bargaining Parties with respect to fringe contributions and collateral issues considered in the course of those negotiations. In this respect Mr. Figone noted the recommendation of the Collective Bargaining Parties to the Trustees that consideration be given to a $15.00 unit value and that this will benefit liberalization previously discussed, it being noted that said revised unit value and liberalization were based upon actuarial calculations previously made available, not only to the Board of Trustees, but to the Collective Bargaining Parties.

A motion was unanimously carried which adopted *inter alia* a provision for a 5% increase across the board for all pensioners whose pensions were effective before July 1, 1971 (the increase to be effective August 1, 1971) and a provision for an increase from $9.00 to $15.00 for the unit value per year of pension credit for all pension awards effective on or after July 1, 1971.

Defendants also submitted the affidavit of Berton Jacobson, executive vice president of the Martin E. Segal Company, Inc. He states that his company had never advised the Board of Trustees that the $6.00 increase in unit value for pension awards effective on or after July 1, 1971, was excessive and endangered the fiscal stability of the Pension Trust Fund.[10] He also states "that said increase is not in fact too high and does not endanger the stability of the Fund."[11]

Plaintiffs have not submitted evidence which would raise a triable dispute as to the actuarial soundness of the increase from $9.00 to $15.00 per year of pension credit.

Plaintiffs have offered the following factual evidence. Four of the employee trustees who voted to adopt the increases in 1971 retired after July 1, 1971. E. A. Brown retired effective January, 1972; Gail Gordon retired effective February, 1972; Dave Williams and Alfred A. Figone retired effective June, 1972. Defendants do not dispute these retirement dates, although they do dispute any inference to be drawn from them that the higher increase for those retiring on or after July 1, 1971, was designed specifically to benefit these four trustees.

Plaintiffs assert that at least two, and perhaps three, of the employee trustees approving the 1971 increases had also participated in the collective-bargaining negotiations prior to the Board meeting on July 23, 1971.[12] Defendants do not dispute this fact.

Plaintiffs point to a conflict or confusion in the deposition testimony of Larry W. Null and Alfred A. Figone, both employee trustees at the time of the 1971 decision, concerning the manner in which the union membership was consulted about the increase in pension benefits.[13] Plaintiffs have also offered an affidavit of Wilfred J. Stone who states that he attended a few union meetings from January 1, 1971, through March 1, 1971, and that

---

1971, those retiring prior to July 1, 1971, also received an increase.

10. Defendants also submitted the affidavit of Beverly Heywood, vice president of the Martin E. Segal Company, Inc., who states that she attended one meeting of the Board of Trustees of the Fund which Jacobson had missed and that she had not advised, and to her knowledge no one else at her company had ever advised, the Board that the $6.00 increase was excessive or dangerous for the Fund's stability.

11. See also his testimony at his deposition taken on August 22, 1973, at pp. 45-47, in which he states that he advised the trustees before the increase was approved that it would be actuarially sound.

12. See the deposition of C. Bruce Sutherland, August 22, 1973, at p. 20.

13. See the deposition of Larry W. Null, August 23, 1973, pp. 6-13, and the deposition of Alfred A. Figone, August 23, 1973, pp. 8-14.

he never heard nor was informed "that negotiations were being held with the employers for a new contribution rate to the retirement fund, and that the increase in the rate would be used to increase the pension for post-July 1, 1971 retirees from $9.00 to $15.00 for each unit of credit." In another affidavit submitted by plaintiffs, Vivien Paul Kaufenberg states that he attended several meetings of a local during the period of January, 1971, to July, 1971, and that he also heard nothing of the proposed increase.

This evidence concerns the manner in which the union consulted its rank and file about the proposed increase. This issue, however, is not material to any of plaintiffs' claims in this action. It would perhaps be material to a claim that the union failed to follow its prescribed procedures in collective bargaining and that it unfairly represented some union members. But those claims have not been made here, and, apart from that fact, the record does not support any inference that those claims would be at all colorable.

The testimony of Null and Figone, however, does establish that the collective-bargaining parties did recommend the pension increases subsequently adopted by the Board on July 23, 1971, and that Null and Figone, two of the fourteen trustees approving the increases, felt "obligated" or "bound" to follow that recommendation if actuarially sound.[14]

Plaintiffs have offered the affidavit of Ernest T. Quick to show that the Trustees allowed at least one person who had submitted an application for retirement prior to July 1, 1971, to receive the $15.00 rate. Quick states that one Orban Hudson had had his pension approved effective June, 1971, but that Hudson had told him that he was allowed to receive the new rate, although he had to forego his first check for June, 1971. Plaintiffs offer the affidavit of Luther H. Curry to establish that he was a participant in the collective-bargaining negotiations and had advised members of his local not to apply for a pension until after the conclusion of those negotiations because pension benefits were to be increased for future retirees. Curry states: "During the time that the negotiations were taking place I repeatedly informed members of Local 1622 who approached me concerning applying for their pension that they should not do so because there was going to be an increase effective July 1, 1971 and I was not sure they would get it if they applied before then." Vivien Paul Kaufenberg also stated in his affidavit that he overheard one union officer tell a secretary who was giving Kaufenberg his pension application that a person named Paul should be told to "wait a while to see what the pension is going to amount to." Plaintiffs have also offered the affidavits of Albert Maddox and Kaufenberg to show that at least two persons, who retired effective June, 1971, would have waited if they had known of the possibility of the higher increase in benefits for persons retiring on or after July 1, 1971.

---

14. Deposition of Larry W. Null, August 23, 1973, at pp. 17-19:

Q. And was it your understanding that as a member of the Board of Trustees, you were bound by that recommendation?

A. Only if it was actuarially sound.

Q. But aside from the actuarial considerations, was it your understanding that you were bound by that recommendation?

A. Not that we were bound by it, that we were obligated.

Q. You were obligated?

A. Right.

Q. To vote a 9 to $15 increase in the unit value for retirees who became eligible effective July 1st, 1971; is that correct?

. . . .

Q. Would it be a fair statement to say that the provision for five percent increase across the Board came about as a result of the independent exercise of judgment by the Board of Trustees of the Pension Trust Fund?

A. Based upon actuarial facts, I would say that was probably correct.

Q. Without regard to any recommendations by the collective bargaining parties?

A. Not to my knowledge.

Q. Would it be a fair statement to say that you felt, as a member of the Board of Trustees, bound to institute the 9 to $15 increase if it was actuarially sound because of the recommendation of the collective bargaining parties?

A. I think that would be our duty.

. . . .

Deposition of Alfred A. Figone, August 23, 1973, at p. 16:

. . . Do you recall whether or not you, as a Trustee, felt bound by that recommendation of the collective bargaining parties?

A. As a Trustee, I felt that by virtue of the actuarial data that was given to us, that it was a prudent move, yes.

Q. But did you feel bound by the fact it was actuarially sound and the fact that the collective bargaining parties made the recommendation that you should vote on it?

A. When I indicate they made the recommendation, I am indicating they made the recommendation that the money went in and would support these benefits.

Defendants deny that there was a secret policy of allowing some persons to take advantage of the higher increase for future retirees despite the fact that they had retired prior to July 1, 1971, or of informing some persons to wait until after July 1, 1971, to retire. They offer the affidavit of C. Bruce Sutherland, secretary to the Board of Trustees, who states:

> That as previously alleged the meeting of the Board of Trustees at which the motion was passed to increase the amount payable per year of pension credit from $9.00 to $15.00 was held on July 23, 1971. When the Board of Trustees did act, the Administrative Office under the direction and supervision of affiant immediately prepared and mailed notice of that action to all those whose applications were still being processed or whose retirement payments had not in fact commenced. These were people whose pensions could have otherwise been effective prior to July 1, 1971 and whose pensions had been approved by the Pension Approval Committee on July 15, 1971. These approvals of the Committee were up for ratification by the full Board of Trustees at the same July 23, 1971 meeting. These individuals were given an election between the earlier retirement date they had chosen with the 5% increase to come on August 1, 1971 and a change in the retirement date to the later date of July 1, 1971 with the higher $15.00 amount for all pensions effective July 1, 1971 and after.

Sutherland states, and documents submitted by defendants establish, that Orban Hudson was one of those persons given an election who chose to take the $15.00 unit value effective July 1, 1971. Sutherland states: "All those in a position similar to Mr. Hudson's were treated in precisely the same manner."

III. SUMMARY JUDGMENT FOR DEFENDANTS

To obtain summary judgment, a party must demonstrate that there is no genuine issue of material fact and that under the uncontroverted facts it is entitled to a judgment as a matter of law. *Adickes v. Kress & Co.,* 398 U.S. 144, 158-161, 90 S.Ct. 1598, 26 L.Ed.2d 142 (1970); Rule 56(c), Federal Rules of Civil Procedure. The moving party has the burden of conclusively showing by factual evidence "that the facts upon which [the opposing party] relied to support his allegation were not susceptible of the interpretation which he sought to give them." *First Nat. Bank v. Cities Service,* 391 U.S. 253, 289, 88 S.Ct. 1575, 1593, 20 L.Ed.2d 569 (1968). The factual material presented by a moving party "must be viewed in the light most favorable to the opposing party." *Adickes v. Kress & Co.,* 398 U.S. 144, at 157, 90 S.Ct. 1598, at 1608, 26 L.Ed.2d 142. *See also United States v. Diebold, Inc.,* 369 U.S. 654, 655, 82 S.Ct. 993, 8 L.Ed.2d 176 (1962).

Plaintiffs' complaint raises essentially five legal claims, each of which, they contend, demonstrates that the trustees' decision to increase pension benefits more for pensioners retiring on or after July 1, 1971, than for those retiring before that date was arbitrary or capricious. As to each claim, the Court finds that there is no genuine dispute as to a material question of fact and that defendants are entitled to summary judgment as a matter of law.

A. Union, Employer Interests

Plaintiffs claim that the trustees' decision "was done for the purpose of fortifying the position of the unions with their active union member carpenters and to better the relationship between the employer groups and the active union member carpenters." They also claim that decision "grossly discriminates" against those persons retiring before July 1, 1971.

Even if the trustees had the purposes alleged by plaintiffs, their decision would not be in violation of §186(c)(5) as arbitrary and capricious. Plaintiffs have not claimed that pensioners retiring prior to July 1, 1971, were unfairly represented by the union in the collective bargaining negotiations. They have not alleged that the union's conduct toward those pensioners was "arbitrary, discriminatory, or in bad faith." *Vaca v. Sipes,* 386 U.S. 171, 190, 87 S.Ct. 903, 916, 17 L.Ed.2d 842 (1967). Since increased support of the union by its active members would be a natural consequence of a differential in benefits favoring those members, the fact of such increased support cannot itself be sufficient evidence of a violation of the trustees' duties. Cf., Note, 68 Mich.L.Rev. 757, 766-767 (1969-70). A contrary view would greatly undermine the collective-bargaining process as now constructed and would conflict with "the faith of Congress in free collective bargaining between employers and their employees when conducted by freely and fairly chosen representatives of appropriate units of employees." *Ford Motor Co. v. Huffman,* 345 U.S. 330, 337, 73 S.Ct. 681, 686, 97 L.Ed. 1048 (1953). "Inevitable differences arise in the manner and degree to which the terms of any negotiated agreement affect individual employees and classes of employees. The mere existence of such differences does not make them invalid. The complete satisfaction of all who are represented is hardly to be expected. A wide range of reasonableness must be allowed a statutory bargaining representative in serving the unit it represents, subject always to complete good faith and honesty of purpose in the exercise of its discretion." 345 U.S. 330, at 338, 73 S.Ct. 681, at 686, 97 L.Ed. 1048. *See also Motor Coach Employees v. Lockridge,* 403 U.S. 274, 299, 301, 91 S.Ct. 1909, 29 L.Ed.2d 473 (1971); *Humphrey v. Moore,* 375 U.S. 335, 349-350, 84 S.Ct. 363, 11 L.Ed.2d 370 (1964). A purpose to fortify its strength among its active members does not imply bad faith on the part of a union. The strength of a union, and hence its ability to represent effectively all its members, including those retired, depends upon its strength in the workplace. No evidence in the record here indicates any basis for a finding of bad faith by the union in bargaining.[15] Thus, "in representing retirees in the negotiation of retirement benefits, the union would be bound to balance the interests of all its constituents, with the result that the interests of active employees might at times be preferred to those of retirees." *Chemical Workers v. Pittsburgh Glass,* 404 U.S. 157, 173, n. 12, 92 S.Ct. 383, 394, 30 L.Ed.2d 341 (1971).

The acceptance by the trustees of the recommendation of the collective-bargaining parties as to benefit increases and differentials is not arbitrary or capricious unless it can be shown that the interests of the beneficiaries were neglected or subverted. The trustees' decision in 1971 was based upon advice by experts that it would be actuarially sound. There is no claim or evidence that all beneficiaries were not fairly represented during the collective-bargaining negotiations or that the union was ignoring the interests of the beneficiaries and following, for instance, the personal interests of union leaders. Cf. *Blankenship v. Boyle,* 329 F.Supp. 1089, 1107-1110 (D.D.C. 1971).

Similarly, employers may legitimately seek to strengthen their relationship with currently employed union members:

> Congress obviously contemplated payments to union welfare funds would be made by employers for the benefit of their employees, in the expectation that such payments further legitimate interests of the employers. If an individual employer establishes an individual plan for the "benefit of the employees of such employer" his legitimate interest may well lie in confining retirement benefits to his employees.
>
> *Roark v. Boyle,* 141 U.S. App.D.C. 390, 439 F.2d 497, 502 (1970).

Therefore plaintiffs could not succeed on this claim even if their allegations as to the union and employer's purposes were proven true.

Since plaintiffs have not alleged or offered evidence of unfair representation or of improper purpose behind the collective-bargaining recommendation, the Court does not find the trustees' decision grossly discriminatory or unreasonably discriminatory.[16] The fact that two employee trustees believed the recommendation by the collective-bargaining parties "obligatory" or "binding"[17] upon them if actuarially sound is neither surprising nor evidence of anything unlawful. As the Court expressed in the first section of this opinion,[18] §186(c)(5) contemplates a close relationship between collective bargaining and the management of a trust fund formed under its aegis. Unless the uncontroverted allegations or undisputed facts show a course of conduct by the trustees clearly not "for the sole and exclusive benefit" of the trust-fund beneficiaries, the actions of the trustees in following the recommendation of the collective-bargaining cannot be held to be arbitrary and capricious.

B. Actuarial Soundness

Plaintiffs also complain that "the actions of the trustees of raising the benefits of retired persons [those who retired on or after July 1, 1971] $6.00 per month was an abuse of authority on the part of the trustees and has placed the fund in serious danger of being depleted thus adversely affecting the plaintiffs and members of their class." They also allege that the actuaries advised the trustees of this danger prior to their decision.[19]

The facts are undisputed[20] and are completely contrary to this claim. The Trust Fund's actuarial consultants have stated that the decision did not endanger the Fund and that the trustees were never advised that it would.

15. There is some uncertainty in the record as to how and to what extent union members were consulted by the union negotiators about the pension plan terms being negotiated, but there is no indication that retired members were treated differently than active members in this respect. See pp. 190-200, *supra.*

16. The Agreement establishing the Pension Trust Fund prohibits trustees' decisions which are "unreasonably discriminatory under the provisions of the Internal Revenue Code, or under any other applicable law or regulation." Art. VII, Section 8, p. 20.

17. *See* p. 200, *supra.*

18. *See* pp. 194-198, *supra.*

19. Plaintiffs have not pursued this claim on their cross-motion for summary judgment.

20. *See* pp. 199-200, *supra.*

C. Retiring Trustees

Plaintiffs' third claim is that the trustees approved the higher benefits for pensioners retiring on or after July 1, 1971, in order to give higher benefits to several employee trustees who retired shortly thereafter. Four employee trustees have retired since the decision was made. Two retired five to seven months after the decision, and the other two ten to eleven months afterward.

Defendants have offered evidence of the history of the trustees' policy of differential benefit increases favoring prospective retirees.[21] They also point to the uncontestable fact that, since the decision was made on July 23, 1971, to be effective retroactively to July 1, 1971, any trustee who had not retired prior to the decision and who did retire subsequently would receive the higher monthly rate of $15.00 per credit year.

The Court finds that these facts give sufficient support to defendants' motion for summary judgment to require plaintiffs to present factual evidence which would show a genuine issue for trial. *See* Rule 56(e), Federal Rules of Civil Procedure. Plaintiffs, however, point solely to the fact that four employee trustees did retire after the effective date of the higher pension benefits. This fact, which is not disputed, does not support plaintiffs' claim of a violation by the trustees of their fiduciary duties. It does not, by itself, support an inference that the trustees were motivated by a desire to benefit the retiring trustees, especially when the policy basis of the differential in increases had been under consideration for nearly a decade. Because the only evidence proffered by plaintiffs of a motivation to benefit the retiring trustees would not entitle plaintiffs to a judgment as a matter of law, it is not sufficient to prevent a granting of summary judgment to defendants. *First Nat. Bank v. Cities Service,* 391 U.S. 253, 288-290, 88 S.Ct. 1575, 20 L.Ed.2d 569 (1968); *McGuire v. Columbia Broadcasting System, Inc.,* 399 F.2d 902, 905-906 (9 Cir. 1968).[22]

Therefore, defendants have demonstrated that the facts are not in genuine dispute as to this claim and that under those facts they are entitled to a summary judgment that their action was not arbitrary or capricious.

D. Secret Information to Some Retirees

Plaintiffs' fourth claim is that the trustees "secretly inform[ed] persons who were to retire prior to July 1, 1971, that they should wait until after July 1, 1971, to retire to receive the new benefits. This action was taken before the trustees had voted on the new increase." Defendants deny this claim and also contend that it is not material to this lawsuit. They have presented evidence that the Board of Trustees had adopted the policy (and given notice to the persons affected) of allowing those retirees whose pensions would have been effective prior to July 1, 1971, but were still being processed at the time of the July 23, 1971, meeting to elect to have their pensions made effective as of July 1, 1971.[23] Plaintiffs' evidence on this issue consists of the affidavits of Curry and Kaufenberg[24] to the effect that persons *other than trustees* informed carpenters preparing to retire to postpone their decisions. They also have offered affidavits of two retirees who attest that they would have waited until after July 1, 1971, to retire if they had known of the prospective increase for future retirees.

Defendants' evidence establishes that the trustees adopted and implemented a policy of allowing some retirees to take advantage of the higher post-July 1, 1971, benefits. The Court finds this policy to have been reasonable resolution of a difficult and thorny problem of line-drawing. Indeed, the policy recognized and softened the impact of the decision upon those whose pension had not been finally approved at the time of the decision. Unavoidably, some individuals fell just short of this line and were not allowed to elect the higher benefits.

Plaintiffs' evidence fails to support their allegations. Since there is no genuine issue of material fact, defendants are entitled to summary judgment on this claim. *First Nat. Bank v. Cities Service,* 391 U.S. 253, 288-291, 88 S.Ct. 1575, 20 L.Ed.2d 569 (1968); *McGuire v. Columbia Broadcasting System, Inc.,* 399 F.2d 902, 905-906 (9 Cir. 1968).

---

21. *See* pp. 198-199, *supra.*

22. Plaintiffs rely upon *Poller v. Columbia Broadcasting,* 368 U.S. 464, 473, 82 S.Ct. 486, 7 L.Ed.2d 458 (1962). But the Supreme Court in *Poller* found that there was "no conclusive evidence supporting respondents' [the moving parties] theory." 368 U.S. 464, at 473, 82 S.Ct. 486, at 491, 7 L.Ed.2d 458. Here the moving parties have demonstrated sufficient evidence to support their theory. In addition, in *Poller*, the Court found "substantial factual evidence" supporting the allegations of the complaint. *First Nat. Bank v. Cities Service,* 391 U.S. 253, 285, 88 S.Ct. 1575, 20 L.Ed.2d 569 (1968). Plaintiffs have failed to present substantial factual evidence here.

23. *See* p. 201, *supra.*

24. Kaufenberg's statement on this point is hearsay and cannot be considered with respect to a motion for summary judgment. Rule 56(e), Federal Rules of Civil Procedure.

E. Allowing Reapplications by Some Retirees

Plaintiffs' final claim is that "in several instances . . . persons who had put in for their retirement prior to July 1, 197[1] and thus would have been entitled only to the 5% increase were allowed to withdraw their previous application and reapply after the July 1, 1971 date and receive the new and substantially higher benefits."

Defendants' evidence here is, again, their policy of allowing certain pension applicants to elect the higher benefits. Plaintiffs have offered evidence of one person who was allowed to withdraw his application and reapply. But that evidence consists of hearsay statements by affiant Quick and as such cannot be considered with respect to a motion for summary judgment. Rule 56(e), Federal Rules of Civil Procedure. Moreover, defendants have conclusively shown that that individual was one who was allowed to elect the higher benefits.[25]

Defendants are entitled to summary judgment on this issue.

IV. Pendent State Claim

Plaintiffs' second cause of action is based entirely on state law and the pendent jurisdiction doctrine. Since defendants will be awarded summary judgment on plaintiffs' federal cause of action, there is no good reason for the Court to retain jurisdiction over this state claim. "Certainly, if the federal claims are dismissed before trial, even though not insubstantial in a jurisdictional sense, the state claims should be dismissed as well." *Mine Workers v. Gibbs,* 383 U.S. 715, 726, 86 S.Ct. 1130, 1139, 16 L.Ed.2d 218 (1966). The second cause of action will therefore be dismissed for lack of jurisdiction.

It is hereby ordered, adjudged, and decreed that summary judgment is granted defendants on plaintiffs' first cause of action and that judgment be entered for defendants as to that cause of action.

It is hereby further ordered, adjudged, and decreed that plaintiffs' motions for summary judgment on both causes of action are denied.

It is hereby further ordered, adjudged and decreed that plaintiffs' second cause of action is dismissed for lack of jurisdiction.

---

25. *See* p. 201, *supra.*

LABOR-MANAGEMENT REPORTING AND DISCLOSURE ACT

The Labor-Management Reporting and Disclosure Act (the LMRDA), 20 U.S.C. §401, *et seq.*, like the Taft-Hartley Act, was intended to remedy certain deficiencies in labor-management relations. The LMRDA, however, does not contain provisions which govern the structure and content of pension and welfare plans or the administration of plans. The provisions contained in the LMRDA which relate to the private employee benefit complex primarily affect unions.

The LMRDA requires every employee organization or union to adopt a constitution and bylaws and to file copies of these documents with the Secretary of Labor. These documents must be accompanied by a report containing certain information. Section 431(a) provides that the report must contain:

> (5) Detailed statements, or references to specific provisions of documents filed under this subsection which contain such statements, showing the provisions made and procedures followed with respect to. . . . (C) participation in insurance or other benefit plans. . . .

This requirement is supplemented by the requirement imposed on every employee organization to file an annual report with the Secretary of Labor. In this report, the Secretary of Labor requires the employee organization to indicate whether it has employee benefit plans. If the employee organization has such a plan—for example, an unfunded dues financed plan or a plan which pays benefits out of the employee organization's general assets—the plan administrator must file an annual report for the trust formed as part of the plan.

VIETNAM ERA VETERANS READJUSTMENT ASSISTANCE ACT OF 1974 (MILITARY SELECTIVE SERVICE ACT)

The Vietnam Era Veterans Readjustment Assistance Act of 1974 (the Vietnam Era Assistance Act), 38 U.S.C. §2021, *et seq.*, which is a recodification of the Military Selective Service Act, sets out the rules governing the status of an employee after serving in the armed forces of the United States.

Section 2021 of the Vietnam Era Assistance Act provides that any person who enters the armed forces and who leaves a position in the employ of an employer in order to perform service and who subsequently makes an application for reemployment must be restored by such employer to a position of "like seniority, status, and pay." This section further provides that the employee must be entitled to participate in insurance or other benefits offered by the employer pursuant to the established rules and practices relating to employees on furlough or leave of absence. The returning employee must be treated as if he occupied his position continuously during the war. *See Fishgold v. Sullivan Drydock & Repair Corp.*, 328 U.S. 275 (1946).

Section 2021 affects the structure and content of pension and welfare plans, although many persons were unaware of its impact until the Supreme Court decided the case of *Alabama Power Co. v. Davis*, ____ U.S. ____ (1977). This case involved an employee who was inducted into the Armed Forces during World War II, served for approximately 30 months and then resumed his job. During the time that Davis was in the service, Alabama Power established a "defined benefit" type pension plan. The amount of benefits paid under the plan depended on an employee's "accredited service." "Accredited service" was defined in the plan as including both "future service" and "past service." Future service was not credited for leaves of absence without pay, or for military leaves.

Davis sued Alabama Power under Section 9 of the Military Selective Service Act, which has been recodified as §2021 of the Vietnam Era Assistance Act, claiming that Alabama Power was required to give him credit towards his pension for his military service time. Alabama Power argued, however, that pension benefits were compensation for services rendered rather than perquisites of seniority.

The issue before the Supreme Court was whether pension benefits, provided by an employer and computed on the basis of an employee's total years of service with the employer, are perquisites of seniority toward which a returning veteran is entitled to credit for his time in the military service, or whether they are deferred compensation. The Court held that the pension was a reward for length of service (i.e., a perquisite of seniority) and, therefore, a seniority privilege.

ALABAMA POWER CO. V. DAVIS

____ U.S. ____ (1974)

Mr. Justice Marshall delivered the opinion of the Court.

Respondent Davis became a permanent employee of petitioner Alabama Power Co. on August 16, 1936, and continued to work until March 18, 1943, when he left to enter the military. After serving in the military for 30 months, he resumed his position with Alabama Power, where he worked until he retired on June 1, 1971. Davis received credit under the company pension plan for his service from August 16, 1937[1] until the date of his retirement, with the exception of the time he spent in the military and some time spent on strike. Davis claimed that §9 of the Military Selective Service Act, 50 U.S.C. App. §450(b) (1970)[2] requires Alabama Power to give him credit toward his pension for his period of military service. With the assistance of the United States Attorney,[3] he sued to vindicate that asserted right. The District Court, 383 F.Supp. 880 (N.D. Ala. 1973), and the Court of Appeals for the Fifth Circuit, 542 F.2d 650 (1976), agreed with Davis. Because of the importance of the issue and a conflict among the circuits,[4] we granted certiorari, ____ U.S. ____.[5] We affirm.

I

The Military Selective Service Act provides the mechanism for manning the Armed Forces of the United States. Section 9 of the Act evidences Congress' desire to minimize the disruption in individuals' lives resulting from the national need for military personnel. It seeks to accomplish this goal by guaranteeing veterans that the jobs they had before they entered the military will be available to them upon their return to civilian life. Specifically, §9 requires that any qualified person who leaves a permanent position with any employer to enter the military, satisfactorily completes his military service, and applies for re-employment within 90 days of his discharge from the military,

> be restored by such employer or his successor in interest to such position or to a position of like seniority, status, and pay . . . unless the employer's circumstances have so changed as to make it impossible or unreasonable to do so.
> 50 U.S.C. App. §459(b)(B)(i) (1970).

Moreover, any person so restored to such a position

> shall be considered as having been on furlough or

1. Employees do not become eligible to participate in the plan until they have worked for one year. *See* p. 9, *infra*.

2. Section 459(b) has been recodified, without substantial change, as 38 U.S.C. §2021 (Supp. V. 1975).

3. *See* 50 U.S.C. App. §459(d), now codified at 38 U.S.C. §2022 (Supp. V. 1975).

4. Compare *Jackson v. Beech Aircraft Corp.*, 517 F.2d 1322 (CA. 10 1975) and *Litwicki v. Pittsburgh Plate Glass Industries, Inc.*, 505 F.2d 189 (CA. 3 1974) (denying pension credit), with *Smith v. Industrial Employers and Distributors Assn.*, 546 F.2d 314 (CA. 9 1976) (granting past service credit and denying future service credit).

5. The grant of certiorari was limited to the first question presented, excluding the issue of the applicability of the Alabama statute of limitations.

> leave of absence during his period of training and service in the armed forces, shall be so restored without loss of seniority, shall be entitled to participate in insurance or other benefits offered by the employer pursuant to established rules and practices relating to employees on furlough or leave of absence in effect with the employer at the time such person was inducted into such forces, and shall not be discharged from such position without cause within one year after such restoration.
>
> *Id.*, §459(c)(1).

In our first confrontation with the predecessor of §9,[6] we held that the statutory protection against discharge within a year of re-employment did not protect a veteran from being laid off while nonveterans with greater seniority retained their jobs. *Fishgold v. Sullivan Drydock & Repair Corp.*, 328 U.S. 275 (1946). In reaching this conclusion, we announced two principles that have governed all subsequent interpretations of the re-employment rights of veterans. First, we stated that under the Act, the veteran

> does not step back on the seniority escalator at the point he stepped off. He steps back on at the precise point he would have occupied had he kept his position continuously during the war.
>
> *Id.*, at 284-285.

Congress incorporated this doctrine in succeeding re-enactments of the re-employment provision. *See* 50 U.S.C. App. §450(c)(2).[7]

The second guiding principle we identified was that

> This legislation is to be liberally construed for the benefit of those who left private life to serve their country in its hour of great need. . . . And no practice of employers or agreements between employers and unions can cut down the service adjustment benefits which Congress has secured the veteran under the Act.
>
> 328 U.S., at 285.

Our next cases were also concerned with the extent of the protection afforded rights that were clearly within the Act's scope. *Trailmobile Co. v. Whirls,* 331 U.S. 40 (1947); *Aeronautical Industrial Dist. Lodge 727 v. Campbell,* 337 U.S. 521 (1949); *Oakley v. Louisville & N. R. Co.,* 338 U.S. 278 (1949). More recently, however, our efforts have been directed at determining whether a particular right claimed by a veteran is an aspect of the "seniority" which the Act protects. We have been unable to rely on either the language or the legislative history of the Act when making these determinations, for neither contains a definition of "seniority."

We first faced this problem in *McKinney v. Missouri-K.-T. R. Co.,* 357 U.S. 265 (1958). McKinney had been reemployed at a higher level than he had attained when he left for military service, with seniority in his new position dating from his return to work. When his job was abolished, he claimed that his seniority at the higher level should have dated from the time he would have been eligible to reach that level had he not served in the military. This Court rejected his claim because of the contingent nature of his expectation of being promoted from the job he previously held. That promotion, the Court found, depended "not simply on seniority or some other form of automatic progression, but on the exercise of discretion on the part of the employer." *Id.,* at 272. Since the promotion would not have come automatically had McKinney continued to ride the seniority escalator, the Court concluded that neither the promotion nor a seniority date calculated as of the time he might have been promoted were incidents of the "seniority" protected by the Act.[8]

Eight years later, the Court again considered whether a veteran was entitled to a seniority date calculated as if he had obtained a higher level position while in the military. *Tilton v. Missouri Pac. R. Co.,* 376 U.S. 169 (1964). Tilton had been promoted before he left the railroad to enter the military, but he had not worked enough days to complete the probationary period necessary to obtain permanent status and begin accumulating seniority in the higher level job. When he returned to the

---

6. The Selective Training and Service Act of 1940, c.720, §8(b), 54 Stat. 885, 890.

7. "It is declared to be the sense of the Congress that any person who is restored to a position in accordance with the provisions of paragraph (A) or (B) of subsection (b) of this section should be so restored in such manner as to give him such status in his employment as he would have enjoyed if he had continued in such employment continuously from the time of his restoration to such employment."
This provision is now codified at 38 U.S.C. §2021(b)(2) (Supp. V. 1975).

8. "[Section] 9(c) does not guarantee the returning serviceman a perfect reproduction of the civilian employment that might have been his if he had not been called to the colors. Much there is that might have flowed from experience, effort, or chance to which he cannot lay claim under the statute. Section 9(c) does not assure him that the past with all its possibilities of betterment will be recalled. Its very important but limited purpose is to assure that those changes and advancements in status that would necessarily have occurred simply by continued employment will not be denied the veteran because of his absence in the military service." 357 U.S., at 271-272.

railroad, he successfully completed the remainder of the probationary period. The company set his seniority date as of the time he actually finished the probationary period; he claimed that the date should have been fixed as of the time he would have satisfied the probationary work requirement had it not been for his military service.

This Court agreed. Unlike in *McKinney,* we found that the only management discretion involved was the decision to allow Tilton to assume probationary status in the higher level position, and that discretion had been exercised before he entered the military. Tilton's satisfactory completion of the probationary period after he was reinstated by the railroad was sufficient indication that he would have completed that period earlier if his tenure had not been interrupted by his service to his country. The mere possibility that his ride on the escalator might have been interrupted by some other circumstance could not be allowed to deny him the status he almost certainly would have obtained:

> In every veteran seniority case the possibility exists that work of the particular type might not have been available; that the veteran would not have worked satisfactorily during the period of his absence; that he might not have elected to accept the higher position; or that sickness might have prevented him from continuing his employment. In light of the purpose and history of this statute, however, we cannot assume that Congress intended possibilities of this sort to defeat the veteran's seniority rights.
> *Id.,* at 180-181.

In *McKinney* and *Tilton*, the Court decided whether the veterans' promotions were incidents of the "seniority" protected by the Act, but in both cases, the benefit claimed by the veterans earlier seniority dates was clearly "seniority." Our most recent cases have involved claims to benefits that could not be so easily classified. These cases have required us to consider not only the relative certainty of the benefit's accrual but also the nature of the benefit itself.

We first encountered this added complexity in *Accardi v. Pennsylvania R. Co.,* 383 U.S. 225 (1966), a case involving a claim to severance pay. The petitioners in *Accardi* were tugboat firemen who had left their jobs for military service and had later been restored with appropriate seniority credit. When technological change led to the elimination of the position of tugboat fireman, the railroad agreed to provide severance pay, with the amount of the payment dependent on the employee's length of "compensated service." Since Accardi and his colleagues had not received compensation from the company during their military service, the railroad did not give them credit for that time when calculating their severance payments.

This Court ruled in favor of the firemen. It was clear that had the petitioners remained on their jobs, they would have received severance pay credit for the years they spent in the military. Therefore, the reasonable certainty criterion established in *McKinney* and *Tilton* was satisfied. The company argued, however, that the payment was not based on, and so an incident of, seniority, but rather was based on total actual service to the railroad. While questioning the company's argument because of the "bizarre results possible under the definition of 'compensated service,' " *id.*, at 230[9] we rejected it because the "real nature" of the payments was compensation for the lost rights and expectations that accrued as the employees' longevity on the job increased. *Ibid.* That nature could not be disguised by use of a "compensated service" formula to calculate the amount of the payments. Accordingly, we concluded that

> the amount of these allowances is just as much a perquisite of seniority as the more traditional benefits such as work preference and order of lay off and recall.
> *Ibid.*

Failing to credit the veterans with their military service time when calculating their payments therefore violated the Act's requirement that they be reinstated without loss of seniority.[10]

Most recently, in *Foster v. Dravo Corp.,* 420 U.S. 92 (1975), we dealt with another claim for payment because of time spent in military service. Foster had worked for his private employer for seven weeks in 1967, spent 18 months in the military, and returned to work for the last 13 weeks of 1968. He claimed that he was entitled to vacation

9. It was possible for an employee to receive credit for a full year of "compensated service" by working only seven well-timed days during the year. The company defined a month of "compensated service" as any month during which the employee worked one or more days, and a year of "compensated service" was defined as 12 such months, or a major portion thereof.

10. The Court also held that whatever the full scope of the statutory language governing "other benefits" contained in §459(c), *see* p. 2-3, *supra,* that language was intended to add to the protections afforded the veteran's seniority rights, not to lessen those protections. 383 U.S. at 231-232. The Court's conclusion that the severance payments were perquisites of seniority therefore made unnecessary consideration of the "other benefits" provision.

pay for both years, although the collective-bargaining agreement granted full vacation benefits only for 25 weeks of work in a calendar year.

Again focusing on the nature of the benefit at issue, we rejected Foster's claim. Vacation benefits, we held, are "intended as a form of short term compensation for work performed" *id.,* at 100, not as a reward for longevity with an employer.[11] In reaching this conclusion, we noted the work requirement imposed by the collective-bargaining contract, the proportionate increase in vacation benefits that resulted from overtime work, and the availability of pro rata benefits if an employee was laid off before he had worked the required number of weeks. These facts, however, were sufficient only to "lend substantial support," *id.,* at 100, to the employer's argument that the vacation benefits were a form of pay for work done. The nature of the benefits—"the common conception of a vacation as a reward for and respite from a lengthy period of labor," *id.,* at 101—was decisive.

Thus, our cases have identified two axes of analysis for determining whether a benefit is a right of seniority secured to a veteran by §9. If the benefit would have accrued, with reasonable certainty, had the veteran been continuously employed by the private employer, and if it is in the nature of a reward for length of service, it is a "perquisite of seniority." If, on the other hand, the veteran's right to the benefit at the time he entered the military was subject to a significant contingency, or if the benefit is in the nature of short term compensation for services rendered, it is not an aspect of seniority within the coverage of §9. We evaluate respondent Davis' right to pension credit for his years in the military in light of these principles.

II

Alabama Power established its pension plan on July 1, 1944, during the time Davis was in the military. The plan, which is funded entirely by the company, covers all "full-time regular employee[s]" who have completed one year of continuous service with the company and are at least 25 years old. App. 58-59. Under the labor agreements and practices of the company, a full-time regular employee is one who, with limited exceptions,[12] works a 40-hour week. A covered employee has no vested right to any benefit from the plan until he has completed 20 years of service, which for this purpose includes time spent in the military, or has completed 15 years of service and attained the age of 50. App. 90-91.[13] Normal retirement age under the plan is 65, but an employee with 20 years of "accredited service" can elect to retire any time after he has reached the age of 55. App. 43-44. Davis chose the early retirement option.

The concept of "accredited service" is a major determinant of the amount of benefits paid and is the source of the present controversy. The plan defines "accredited service" as the period of "future service" together with the period of "past service." App. 34-35. These terms, in turn, are defined as an employee's period of service after the initiation of the pension plan and his inclusion within it ("future service") and his period of service prior to that date ("past service"). App. 35. Future service is credited to an employee "for service rendered to the Company" as a full-time, regular employee and for periods of authorized leave of absence with pay. Employees on leave of absence without regular pay, and persons serving in the military, are not credited with future service during their absence from the company. App. 40.[14] Retirement benefits are calculated by use of formulas in which years of accredited service are multiplied by an earnings factor.[15] Had Davis re-

11. Under the collective-bargaining agreement in *Foster,* the length of an employee's vacation increased with his length of continuous employment with the firm. The company conceded that the employee's time in military service had to be counted in determining the length of his vacation. 420 U.S., at 101 n. 9.

12. The established exceptions include annual vacations, paid holidays, 10 days of annual sick leave, which may be accumulated up to a maximum of 30 days, and up to three days leave in case of a death in the employee's immediate family. In addition, longtime employees may be allowed up to nine months of extended sick leave.

13. The Employee Retirement Income Security Act of 1974, §203, 88 Stat. 832, 854, 29 U.S.C. §1053 (Supp. V. 1975), establishes vesting requirements more favorable to employees than those described in text. This law, which generally requires vesting within 10 to 15 years, did not affect respondent and, insofar as is relevant to the question presented in this case, does not alter the nature of pension plans.

14. A limited exception to this rule, *see* App. 61-62, was not applicable to Davis.

15. Davis' pension payment is calculated under §V.4 (b)(ii) of the plan. That section provides:

> The minimum Retirement Income payable after January 1, 1966 to an employee included in the Plan retiring from the service of the Company after January 1, 1966, at his Early Retirement Date (before adjustment for Provisional Payee designation, if any) shall be an amount equal to 1% of his monthly earnings on his Early Retirement Date multiplied by his years of Accredited Service, rendered by [specified amounts]. App. 70.

ceived accredited service for the time he spent in the military, his monthly pension payment would have been \$216.06 rather than the \$198.95 to which the company said he was entitled.

It is clear that the reasonable certainty requirement of *McKinney* and *Tilton* is satisfied in this case. Respondent's work history both before and after his military tour of duty demonstrates that if he had not entered the military, he would almost certainly have accummulated accredited service for the period between March 18, 1943, and October 8, 1945. Unpredictable occurrences might have intervened, but "we cannot assume that Congress intended possibilities of this sort to defeat the veteran's seniority rights." *Tilton v. Missouri Pac. R. Co., supra,* at 181.

Alabama Power contends, however, that pension payments should be viewed as compensation for service rendered, like the vacation payments in *Foster*, rather than as a perquisite of seniority like the severance payments in *Accardi.* The company argues that the definition of accredited service in terms of full-time service to the company is a bona fide, substantial work requirement which, under *Foster*, "is strong evidence that the benefit in question was intended as a form of compensation." 420 U.S. at 99. Since §9 does not grant veterans the right to compensation for work they have not performed, Alabama Power concludes that Davis is not entitled to his claimed pension increase.

As we noted in our discussion of *Foster,* that case turned on the nature of vacation benefits, not on the particular formula by which those benefits were calculated. Even the most traditional kinds of seniority privileges could be as easily tied to a work requirement as to the more usual criterion of time as an employee. Yet, as we held in *Fishgold,* "no practice of employers . . . can cut down the service adjustment benefits which Congress has secured the veteran under the Act." 328 U.S. at 285. We must look beyond the overly simplistic analysis suggested by Alabama Power to the nature of the payments.

"Normal retirement income" under the plan is calculated by reference to specified percentages of an employee's earnings, exclusive of overtime, during his years with the company. App. 65-68, 73. The amount to which an employee would be entitled under the "normal retirement income" formula has, however, been periodically adjusted upward by formulas which, like the formula applicable to Davis, call for multiplication of a percentage of recent earnings by the number of years of accredited service. *See* App. 74-84.

It is obvious that pension payments have some resemblance to compensation for work performed. Funding a pension program is a current cost of employing potential pension recipients, as are wages. The size of pension benefits is a subject of collective bargaining,[16] and future benefits may be traded off against current compensation.[17] The same observations, however, can be made about any benefit and therefore are of little assistance in determining whether a particular benefit recompenses labor or rewards longevity with an employer.

Other aspects of pension plans like the one established by petitioner[18] suggest that the "true nature" of the pension payment is a reward for length of service. The most significant factor pointing to this conclusion is the length period required for pension rights to vest in the employee. It is difficult to maintain that a pension increment is deferred compensation for a year of actual service when it is only the passage of years in the

16. *Inland Steel Co. v. N.L.R.B.,* 170 F.2d 247 (CA.7 1948), *cert. denied* on this issue. 336 U.S. 960 (1949), aff'd on other grounds, 339 U.S. 382 (1950). The company contends that *Inland Steel* holds that pensions are "wages" and that they must therefore be classified as "other benefits," *see* n. 10, *supra,* under the Military Selective Service Act. *Inland Steel* concluded, however, only that pensions are a mandatory subject of relative bargaining under the National Labor Relations Act (NLRA) because they are either wages "or other conditions of employment." 170 F.2d at 249-255. Even if pensions are "wages" for the purposes of the NLRA, that classification would not control their treatment under the very different statute at issue in this case.
Cf. United States v. Embassy Restaurant, 359 U.S. 29, 33 (1959) (payments to union welfare fund may be "wages" under NLRA but not under the Bankruptcy Act).

17. *Cf.* S. Slichter, J. Healy, E. Livernash, The Impact of Collective Bargaining on Management 373 (1960) (pension plans encouraged during World War II by difficulty of obtaining general wage increases).

18. Petitioner's plan is a "defined benefit" plan under which the benefits to be received by employees are fixed and the employer's contribution is adjusted to whatever level is necessary to provide those benefits. The other basic type of pension is a "defined contribution" plan, under which the employer's contribution is fixed and the employee receives whatever level of benefits the amount contributed on his behalf will provide. *See* 29 U.S.C. §1002 (34), (35): Note, Fiduciary Standards and the Prudent Man Rule Under the Employee Retirement Income Security Act of 1974, SS Harv. L. Rev. 960, 961-963 (1975). We intimate no views on whether defined contribution plans are to be treated differently from defined benefit plans under the Military Selective Service Act.

same company's employ, and not the service rendered, that entitles the employee to that increment. Moreover, because of the vesting requirement and the use of payment formulas that depend on earnings at the time of retirement, both the cost to the employer and the payment to the employee for each year of service depend directly on the length of time the employee continues to work for that employer. Periodic adjustments of the benefit formulas to account for unanticipated increases in living costs, *see* App. 74-84, emphasize the dissociation of payment levels from the work that Alabama Power claims the payments compensate.

The function of pension plans in the employment system also supports respondent's claim. A pension plan assures employees that by devoting a large portion of their working years to a single employer, they will achieve some financial security in their years of retirement. By rewarding lengthy service, a plan may reduce employee turnover and training costs and help an employer secure the benefits of a stable work force. *See* D. McGill, Fundamentals of Private Pensions 21-23 (3d ed. 1975). In addition, by providing economic security in retirement, pension plans encourage longtime employees whose working efficiency may be on the decline to retire and make way for younger workers. *Id.*, at 21-22; S. Slichter, J. Healy, E. Livernash, The Impact of Collective Bargaining on Management 374 (1960). The relationship between pension payments and passage of time as an employee is central to both of these functions.

We conclude, therefore, that pension payments are predominantly rewards for continuous employment with the same employer. Protecting veterans from the loss of such rewards when the break in their employment resulted from their response to the country's military needs is the purpose of §9. That purpose is fulfilled in this case by requiring Alabama Power to pay Davis the pension to which he would have been entitled by virtue of his lengthy service if he had not been called to the colors. Accordingly, the judgment below is affirmed.

It is difficult to determine the extent to which this decision will affect agreements under which pension benefits are provided to employees. For example, the Court specifically declined to offer its views on whether defined contribution pension plans are to be treated differently from defined benefit plans. The Court did not focus on Taft-Hartley plans, either.

However, the Court's decision in *Foster v. Dravo Corp.*, 420 U.S. 92 (1975) supports the position that most welfare plans will not be affected. For example, vacation benefits are "intended as a form of short term compensation for work performed," not as a reward for longevity with an employer. Most other welfare benefits should not be treated as perquisites of seniority, either.

FOSTER V. DRAVO CORP.
420 U.S. 92 (1975)

Opinion of the Court by Mr. Justice Marshall, announced by Mr. Chief Justice Burger.

Through the Military Selective Service Act, Congress has sought to protect veterans returning to civilian jobs from being penalized for having served in the Armed Forces. Section 9 of the Act, 62 Stat. 614, as amended, 50 U.S.C. App. §459 [50 U.S.C.S. Approx. §459], ensures a returning serviceman the right to be restored to his job with the same levels of seniority, status, and pay that he would have enjoyed if he had held the job throughout the time he was in the military.[1] This

---

1. Section 9(b) provides a right to re-employment for any serviceman who "has left or leaves a position . . . and . . . makes application for reemployment within ninety days after he is relieved from such training and service." Section 9(b)(B)(i) adds that if the serviceman is "still qualified to perform the duties of such position, [he shall] be restored by such employer . . . to such position or to a position of like seniority, status, and pay." Section 9(c), which governs the rights of those restored to positions after return from the service, provides in relevant part:

(1) Any person who is restored to a position in accordance with the provisions of . . . this section shall be considered as having been on furlough or leave of absence during his period of training and service in the armed forces, shall be so restored without loss of seniority, shall be entitled to participate in insurance or other benefits offered by the employer pursuant to established rules and practices relating to employees on furlough or leave of absence in effect with the employer at the time such person was inducted into such forces, and shall not be discharged from such position without cause within one year after such restoration.

(2) It is declared to be the sense of the Congress that any person who is restored to a position in accordance with the provisions of . . . this section should be so restored in such manner as to give him such employment continuously from the time of his entering the armed forces until the time of his restoration to such employment.

case presents the question whether the statute entitles a veteran to vacation benefits when, because of his departure for military service, he has failed to satisfy a substantial work requirement upon which the vacation benefits are conditioned.

I

Petitioner, Earl R. Foster, began working full time for respondent Dravo Corp. in 1965. He worked 22 weeks for the company during that year and earned 20 hours of paid vacation eligibility.[2] In 1966, he worked the entire year and earned the standard second-year vacation benefits,[3] for which he subsequently accepted payment.

In March of the following year, petitioner took a military leave of absence from his job. Before leaving, he worked the first seven weeks of 1967 for the company, and upon his return some 18 months later he worked the last 13 weeks in 1968. Because the collective-bargaining agreement between petitioner's union and Dravo required employees to work a minimum of 25 weeks in each calendar year in order to earn full vacation benefits,[4] Foster was not awarded any benefits for either year. Since that time, he has continued to work full time for Dravo and has received full vacation benefits from the company for each year of his employment.

Unhappy with the denial of vacation benefits for 1967 and 1968, petitioner brought suit against Dravo in the District Court for the Western District of Pennsylvania.[5] He sought credit for full vacation benefits in both years, claiming that since he would have earned two vacations if he had worked for respondent throughout the time he was in the service, §9 of the Military Selective Service Act requires that he be credited with the benefits even though he failed to meet the 25-week work requirement in either year.

The District Court held that since the vacation benefits in question did not accrue automatically with continued employment, it did not violate the statute to deny them to employees on military leave of absence. The Court of Appeals for the Third Circuit agreed with the District Court that petitioner had no statutory right to full vacation benefits. From its examination of the contract and other related factors, the court concluded that the vacation right in dispute was not a perquisite of seniority but an earned benefit, and was thus unavailable to a returning serviceman who had not satisfied the work requirement. Noting that a limited pro rata vacation provision in the collective-bargaining agreement might provide an alternative basis for petitioner to receive some vacation benefits for 1967 and 1968, the court remanded the case to the District Court for further proceedings on that narrow question. 490 F.2d 55 (1973). We granted certiorari, 419 U.S. 823, 42 L.Ed.2d 46, 95 S.Ct. 38 (1974), because of an apparent conflict with the decisions of the Courts of Appeals for the Seventh and Ninth Circuits. *See Ewert v. Wrongth Washer Mfg. Co.,* 477 F.2d 128 (Ca.7 1973); *Locaynia v. American Airlines,* 457 F.2d 1253 (Ca.9), *cert denied* 409 U.S. 982, 34 L.Ed.2d 246, 93 S.Ct. 317 (1972). We affirm.

II

The Selective Training and Service Act of 1940, 54 Stat. 885, 890, which was very similar to the present 50 U.S.C. App. §459(c)(1),[6] [50 U.S.C.A.

2. The collective-bargaining agreement between Dravo and petitioner's union, the Industrial Union of Marine and Shipbuilding Workers of America, AFL-CIO, governed the eligibility conditions for vacation benefits. In his first year with the company, petitioner was eligible for four hours of paid vacation for each month worked, up to a maximum of 40 hours. Art. XIV, §1.

3. Under the collective-bargaining agreement, the length of the vacation earned each year increases with the employee's seniority. The ordinary second-year vacation is seven days' leave with pay. After the second year, the vacation increases by one day per year, for the first five years with the company, and then by one week for each five years of "continuous employment," to a maximum of five weeks. Art. XIV, §1.

4. The agreement provides that after the first year an employee can qualify for a vacation if he has received earnings in at least 25 work weeks during the calendar year. A vacation earned in one year can be taken during the next year at a time designated by the company. When an employee is laid off prior to taking his earned vacation, the company gives him his vacation pay at that time, regardless of when his vacation was scheduled. Art. XIV, §1.

5. Petitioner has been represented by the Government throughout this action. By statute, the United States Attorney is charged with representing claimants under §9 of the Military Selective Service Act, if the claimant reasonably appears entitled to the benefits in dispute. 50 U.S.C. App. §459(d) [50 U.S.C.S. Appx. §459(d)].

6. The 1940 Act was essentially reenacted in the Selective Service Act of 1948, 62 Stat. 604. The name of the Act was changed in 1951 to the Universal Military Training and Service Act, 65 Stat. 75. In 1967 it was renamed the Military Selective Service Act of 1967, 81 Stat. 100. It was given its present name, the Military Selective Service Act, in 1971, 85 Stat. 348. The present §§9(b) and 9(c)(1) have remained largely unchanged

Appx. §459(c)(1)], provided that any person leaving a civilian job to enter the military would be entitled to be restored to a position of "like seniority, status, and pay" upon his return unless circumstances had so changed "as to make it impossible or unreasonable to do so." The statute further required that the veteran be restored "without loss of seniority" and be considered "as having been on furlough or leave of absence" during the period of his military service.

On the first of several encounters with the Act, this Court interpreted the guarantee against loss of seniority rights to mean that the veteran's time in the service must be credited toward his seniority with his employer just as if he had remained on the job throughout. *Fishgold v. Sullivan Drydock & Repair Corp.* 328 U.S. 275, 285, 90 L.Ed. 1230, 66 S.Ct. 1105, 165 ALR 110 (1946). To deny him credit for time spent in the military would mean that the veteran would lose ground by reason of his absence. This, the Court stated, would violate the statutory principle that the serviceman "does not step back on the seniority escalator at the point he stepped off. He steps back on at the precise point he would have occupied had he kept his position continuously during the war." *Id.,* at 284-285, 90 L.Ed. 1230. *See also Oakley v. Louisville & Nashville R. Co.* 338 U.S. 278, 283, 94 L.Ed. 87, 70 S.Ct. 119 (1949).

After the *Fishgold* decision, Congress reenacted the statute, adding language that expressly codified the holding in that case. The amendment provided that a veteran must be restored to his position with the status that "he would have enjoyed if he had continued in such employment continuously from the time of his entering the armed forces until the time of his restoration." 62 Stat. 604, 615-616, 50 U.S.C. App. §459(c)(2) [50 U.S.C.S. Appx. §459(c)(2)].

In subsequent cases, the Court has consistently applied the statute to assure that benefits and advancements that would necessarily have accrued by virtue of continued employment would not be denied the veteran merely because of his absence in the military service. *McKinney v. Missouri-Kansas-Texas R. Co.* 357 U.S. 265, 272, 2 L.Ed.2d 1305, 78 S.Ct. 1222 (1958). On the other hand, where the claimed benefit requires more than simple continued status as an employee, the Court has held that it is not protected by the statute. *See Id.,* at 273, 2 L.Ed.2d 1305; *Tilton v. Missouri Pacific R. Co.* 376 U.S. 169, 181, 11 L.Ed.2d 590, 84 S.Ct. 595 (1964).

In *Accardi v. Pennsylvania R. Co.,* 383 U.S. 225, 15 L.Ed. 2d 717, 86 S.Ct. 768 (1966), the Court applied these principles for the first time to a benefit not traditionally considered a seniority right. The dispute in that case concerned a veteran's eligibility for a severance payment. Under the applicable collective-bargaining agreement, the amount of severance pay due each employee depended on the length of the employee's "compensated service" with the respondent railroad. The railroad argued that the Act was inapplicable because the amount of the severance payment did not depend directly on seniority. The Court, however, took a broader view. Looking beyond the narrow characterization of seniority rights in the collective-bargaining agreement, the Court concluded that the severance payments were not intended as a form of deferred compensation for work done in the past, but rather as a means of compensating employees for the loss of rights and benefits accumulated over a long period of service. Accordingly, the Court held that the severance payments in that case were "just as much a perquisite of seniority as the more traditional benefits such as work preference and order of layoff and recall." *Id.,* at 230, 15 L.Ed. 2d 717.

Two years later, in *Eagar v. Magma Copper Co.,* 389 U.S. 323, 19 L.Ed. 2d 557, 88 S.Ct. 503 (1967), the Court applied the statute to a vacation and holiday pay provision in the collective-bargaining agreement. The petitioner in that case had satisfied all the work requirements for the benefits in question, but he had not met the further conditions that he be employed on the one-year anniversary date of his starting work with the company, and that he be on the payroll for the three months preceding each paid holiday.

In a per curiam opinion, the Court reversed the judgment for the company on the authority of *Accardi.* Since the petitioner had met all the contractual work requirements and would have been eligible for the contested benefits if he had simply remained on the company payroll, it was unnecessary to consider whether the work requirements would have barred veterans who had not met them. On the facts before the Court, the decision fell within the principle that a returning serviceman must be treated as if he had kept his job con-

---

since 1940, and §9(c)(2) has been preserved in its current form since the reenactment of 1948. The reemployment provisions of the Act apply not only to those drafted under the provisions of the Act, but also to men and women who enlist voluntarily in the Armed Forces, as long as the period of service does not exceed four, or in certain cases, five years. 50 U.S.C. App. §459(g)(1) [50 U.S.C.S. Appx. §459 (g)(1)].

tinuously throughout the period of his military service.[7]

III

Petitioner argues that under *Accardi* and *Eagar* the vacation benefits in this case must be granted to him as a returning serviceman because the entitlement to a vacation is not closely correlated to the amount of work actually performed by the employee. Under the collective-bargaining agreement, a Dravo employee theoretically could earn full vacation benefits by doing as little as one hour's work in each of 25 weeks during the year. From this, petitioner concludes that the agreement really conditions vacation benefits only on continued employment, and that Dravo therefore could not legally deny him full vacation benefits for either 1967 or 1968.

This approach would extend the statute well beyond the limits set out in our prior cases. Generally, the presence of a work requirement is strong evidence that the benefit in question was intended as a form of compensation. Of course, as in the *Accardi* case, the work requirement may be so insubstantial that it appears plainly designed to measure time on the payroll rather than hours on the job; in that event, the Act requires that the benefits be granted to returning veterans. But where the work requirement constitutes a bona fide effort to compensate for work actually performed, the fact that it correlates only loosely with the benefit is not enough to invoke the statutory guarantee.

We agree with the Court of Appeals that, unlike the severance payments in *Accardi,* the vacation benefits in this case were intended as a form of short-term compensation for work performed. Although Dravo employees who work for 25 weeks receive the same paid vacation rights as those who work a full year, the collective-bargaining agreement provides additional vacation credit for employees who work overtime for a substantial period. The benefits under the overtime vacation provision increase with the amount of overtime worked. In addition, the agreement provides that if an employee is laid off during the year and does not work the requisite 25 weeks, he will be awarded vacation benefits on a pro rata basis.

These provisions lend substantial support to respondent's claim that the vacation scheme was intended as a form of deferred compensation. Petitioner's observation that an employee could in theory earn a vacation under the collective-bargaining agreement with only a few carefully spaced hours of work is not enough to rebut the plain indication that a full vacation was intended in most cases to be awarded for a full year's work.[8]

On petitioner's theory of the case, the company would be required to provide full vacation benefits to a returning serviceman if he worked no more than one week in each year; indeed, following this approach to its logical limits, a veteran who served in the Armed Forces for four years would be entitled to accumulate vacation benefits for all four years upon his return. This result is so sharply inconsistent with the common conception of a vacation as a reward for and respite from a lengthy period of labor that the statute should be applied only where it clearly appears that vacations were intended to accrue automatically as a function of continued association with the company. Since no such showing was made here, and since petitioner has not met the bona fide work requirement in the collective-bargaining agreement, we conclude that §9 did not guarantee him full vacation rights for the two years in question.[9]

IV

In the alternative, petitioner asserts that the

7. The dissenters in *Eagar v. Magma Copper Co.* argued that the statute's protection applied only to rights associated with seniority. 389 U.S., at 323, 325, 19 L.Ed.2d 557, 88 S.Ct. 503 (1967) (Douglas J., joined by Harlan and Stewart, J. J., dissenting). They would have distinguished between eligibility based upon being on the payroll on a particular date or for a particular period from eligibility based upon length of service with the company. The majority implicitly rejected this distinction.

8. Petitioner's reliance on the treatment of the work requirement in *Accardi* is misplaced. The Court there concluded that the severance payments were based primarily on the employees' length of service with the railroad, not on the actual total service rendered. The putative "work requirement" in that case, the Court concluded, did not disguise the true nature of the payments as compensation for the loss of jobs. The *Eagar* case provides even less support for petitioner since that case did not involve an unsatisfied work requirement.

9. In contrast to the conditions of eligibility for a vacation are the terms governing the length of the vacation to which an employee is entitled. As noted above, the length of vacation increases with the employee's length of "continuous employment" with Dravo, which is defined in the collective-bargaining agreement as "continuous seniority." Art. XIV, §§1, 2. Respondent concedes that the employee's time in the service must be counted in determining the length of the vacation that is earned; for the years in which petitioner has worked the 25 weeks required to earn a vacation, the length of his vacation has been calculated as if he had been continuously employed with the company since 1965.

statute entitles him at least to pro rata vacation benefits for the time he served Dravo during 1967 and 1968. If he is denied even a pro rata share of vacation benefits, petitioner claims he will in effect be penalized for taking a military leave of absence, a result that the Act was expressly intended to prevent.

We can find nothing in the statute, independent of the rights conferred in the collective-bargaining agreement, that would justify such a Solomonic solution. The statute requires that a returning veteran be treated the same as an employee "on furlough or leave of absence," 50 U.S.C. App. §459(c)(1) [50 U.S.C.S. Appx. §459 (c)(1)], but petitioner's suggestion would grant pro rata vacation rights to veterans regardless of whether any other class of employees would be similarly treated.

Although we reject petitioner's statutory theory, the potential availability of pro rata vacation rights enters the case in a somewhat different way. The collective-bargaining agreement provides pro rata vacation rights to those employees who were unable to accumulate the minimum of 25 weeks of employment because of layoffs. Art. XIV, §2. In light of this provision, the Court of Appeals noted that petitioner might have a claim for pro rata benefits under the agreement. It therefore remanded the case to the District Court to determine whether petitioner had adequately preserved that point before the District Court and, if so, whether he was entitled to some vacation benefits.[10]

We agree with the Court of Appeals that because it was not litigated at the trial level, this question should be remanded to the District Court for further proceedings. Accordingly, we affirm the judgment of the Court of Appeals.

---

10. Even if petitioner is not eligible for vacation benefits as a purely contractual matter, he may be entitled to pro rata benefits under the "other benefits" provision of §9(c)(1) of the Act, read in conjunction with the collective-bargaining agreement. Since the statute requires that vacation benefits be granted to returning veterans on the same basis as they are to those on furlough or leave of absence, petitioner would be entitled to pro rata benefits if the layoff referred to in the collective-bargaining agreement includes a furlough or leave of absence, or is found to be the equivalent of either.

SERVICE CONTRACT ACT

The Service Contract Act of 1965 (the Service Contract Act), 41 U.S.C. §351, *et seq.*, pertains to contracts for services entered into by the United States or the District of Columbia. Such contracts must contain certain provisions relating to the structure and content of pension and welfare plans. For example, under Section 351 of the Service Contract Act, every contract must contain a provision specifying the minimum wages and fringe benefits to be furnished to various employees engaged in the performance of the contract. The wages and fringe benefits must be in accordance with prevailing rates paid similar employees in the locality. The necessary fringe benefits are defined in Section 351(a)(2) to include:

> . . . medical or hospital care, pension on retirement or death, compensation for injuries or illness resulting from occupational activity, or insurance to provide any of the foregoing, unemployment benefits, life insurance, disability and sickness insurance, accident insurance, vacation and holiday pay, cost of apprenticeship and other similar programs and other bona fide fringe benefits. . . .

The obligation to provide such fringe benefits may be discharged by furnishing any equivalent combination of fringe benefits, or by making equivalent or differential payments in cash under rules and regulations established by the Secretary of Labor.

These required provisions are supplemented by a requirement that any person who enters into a contract with the federal government must pay his employees the minimum wage specified under Section 206(a)(1) of the Fair Labor Standards Act. (The Fair Labor Standards Act will be discussed in Chapter 5.) Section 355 of the Service Contract Act, however, provides that the determination of an employee's overtime pay, which determination is made with reference to the employee's regular or basic hourly rate of pay, may be made without including any fringe benefit payments which may be excluded from the regular rate under §207(d) of the Fair Labor Standards Act. Among the excludable payments are employer contributions to a "bona fide profit-sharing plan or trust" and payments to a bona fide plan for providing "old age, retirement, life, accident, or health insurance or similar benefits."

The Service Contract Act affects the structure and content of pension and welfare plans. If, for example, a pension plan maintained by an employer contracting with the federal government does not satisfy the structure and content requirements relating to a "bona fide profit-sharing plan or trust" under the Equal Pay Act amendments to the Fair

Labor Standards Act, the employer's contributions to such plan may not be excluded from the employee's regular or basic hourly rate of pay for purposes of determining any overtime pay to which the employee is entitled. These requirements will be discussed in Chapter 5.

DAVIS-BACON ACT

The Davis-Bacon Act, 40 U.S.C. §276a, pertains to construction contracts entered into by the United States or the District of Columbia. This law relates to the structure and content of employee benefit plans in the same way as does the Service Contract Act. In general, every covered contract must provide for wages that are prevailing for the corresponding class of employees employed on projects of a similar character in a similar area. In determining the minimum wages, the Secretary of Labor must consider both the regular or basic hourly rate of pay and the contributions made to pensions and welfare plans providing certain benefits.

The Davis-Bacon Act affects the structure and content of pension and welfare plans. For example, under regulations, a contractor or a subcontractor who makes payments to a "bona fide" fringe benefit program could credit those payments toward discharging the prevailing wage obligation only if the fringe benefit was of a type found to be prevailing by the Secretary of Labor. If there was no fringe benefit found to be prevailing in a particular category, no credit was given for any fringe benefit payments in that category; but if a fringe benefit was found prevailing, then a contractor could fully offset all such fringe benefit payments, even to the extent of decreasing the basic hourly rate.

This regulation, however, recently has been overturned by the Labor Department's Wage Appeals Board. In the case of *In re Collinson Construction Company,* 23 WH Cases 189 (1977), the Wage Appeals Board determined that a construction contractor may deduct the cost of a fringe benefit from its wage obligation even if the benefit is not found to be prevailing.

CHAPTER 4

Securities Laws

SECURITIES ACT OF 1933

Scope

The Securities Act of 1933 (the '33 Act), 15 U.S.C. §77a, *et seq.*, regulates transactions in securities. This law requires disclosure, primarily through a registration statement and a prospectus, of pertinent information concerning securities publicly offered and sold in interstate commerce or through the mails. The purpose of the disclosure provisions, which are commonly referred to as the registration provisions, is to provide potential investors with an adequate basis by which to judge whether a security represents a good investment. The '33 Act also makes unlawful certain fraudulent practices in the sale of securities, without regard to whether the securities are required to be registered. The purpose of the antifraud provisions is to provide a remedy for misrepresentation, deceit and other fraudulent practices in connection with the sale of securities.

As a preliminary matter, it is important to distinguish between the two aspects of regulation under the '33 Act: (1) disclosure and (2) antifraud. Certain activities engaged in by pension and welfare plans and the other components of the plan complex may be subject to both the disclosure and the antifraud provisions, while others may only be subject to the antifraud provisions.

The '33 Act contains provisions that affect the administration of pension and welfare plans and the interaction of plans with the plan complex. Numerous activities engaged in by pension and welfare plans may be subject to the '33 Act. For example, the establishment of a pension or welfare plan and the distribution of interests therein to employees in the form of their participation may involve the sale of securities to employees. In another example, the '33 Act may be applicable to a contribution of its securities by the employer(s) maintaining the plan, or to the employer's contribution of cash which is used by the plan to purchase securities from the employer. Alternatively, the plan might use cash contributed by the employer(s) maintaining the plan to purchase securities of the employer from someone other than the employer, either in the market or in a negotiated transaction. Pension and welfare plans not only purchase the securities of the employers maintaining the plan, but they also may sell those securities to the employer(s) maintaining the plan and to other persons, either in the market or in negotiated transactions. A further example of transactions engaged in by pension and welfare plans which require consideration of the provisions of the '33 Act involves a plan's distribution of securities to employees. Some pension plans, such as stock bonus plans, are required to distribute employer securities to participants, and other plans make "in kind" distributions to employees. Subsequently, these securities may be disposed of by the participant. These types of activities, among others, require consideration of both the disclosure and the antifraud provisions.

"Security" Defined

In considering the applicability of the '33 Act to the establishment of a pension or welfare plan and the distribution of interests therein to employees in the form of their participation, the first question is whether such activity involves a "security" as the term is defined in the '33 Act. Section 2(1) of the '33 Act provides:

> When used in this title, unless the context otherwise requires, the term "security" means . . . any

> ... certificate of interest or participation in any profit sharing agreement, ... investment contract ... or, in general, any interest or instrument commonly known as a "security"....

The legislative history of the '33 Act indicates that the term "security" is defined broadly to include "the many types of instruments that in our commercial world fall within the ordinary concept of a security." H.R. Rep. No. 73-85, 73d Cong., 1st Sess. 11 (1933).

The Securities and Exchange Commission and the Supreme Court have historically been inclined to interpret the term "security" rather broadly. The Court's decision in *SEC v. Howey*, 328 U.S. 293 (1946), in which the Court focused on the inclusion of "investment contracts" within the statutory definition of "security," established the traditional test applied by the courts. This test recently was reiterated in *United Housing Foundation, Inc. v. Forman*, 421 U.S. 837 (1975).

SEC V. HOWEY CO.

328 U.S. 293 (1946)

Securities Regulation, §1—sales of interests in citrus groves.

1. The provisions of the Securities Act of 1933 for registration with the Securities and Exchange Commission of securities offered for sale to the public apply to the offering for sale of units of a citrus grove development, which are conveyed by deed to the purchaser, who is also offered a contract for cultivating, marketing, and remitting the net proceeds, even though contracts for servicing may be, and sometimes are, made with others than the company controlled by the seller.

[*See annotation references,* 1 and 2.]

Securities Regulation, §1—investment contract—what is.

2. An investment contract for purposes of the Securities Act of 1933 means a contract, transaction, or scheme whereby a person invests his money in a common enterprise and is led to expect profits solely from the efforts of the promoter or a third party, it being immaterial whether the shares in the enterprise are evidenced by formal certificates or by nominal interests in the physical assets employed in the enterprise.

[*See annotation reference,* 2.]

Securities Regulation, §1—sale of interests in nonspeculative enterprise.

3. The requirements of the Securities Act of 1933 must be met even though the enterprise interests in which are offered to the public as investments is not speculative or promotional in character and the tangible interest which is sold has intrinsic value independent of the success of the enterprise as a whole, so long as the scheme involves an investment of money in the common enterprise with profits to come solely from the efforts of others.

[*See annotation reference,* 2.]

[No. 843.]

Argued May 2, 1946. Decided May 27, 1946. Rehearing denied October 14, 1946.

ON WRIT of Certiorari to the United States Circuit Court of Appeals for the Fifth Circuit to review a judgment affirming a judgment of the District Court of the United States for the Southern District of Florida denying an injunction against the use of the mails and instrumentalities of interstate commerce in the offer and sale of securities, sought on the ground that such offer and sale was in violation of §5(a) of the Securities Act of 1933. Reversed.

See same case below, 151 F.2d 714, aff'g 60 F.Supp. 440.

Roger S. Foster, of Washington, D.C., argued the cause, and, with Solicitor General McGrath, Robert S. Rubin, and Alexander Cohen, also of Washington, D.C., filed a brief for petitioner:

The broad definition of "security" as including an "investment contract" is not an innovation introduced by the federal statute. In §2(1) of the Act, 15 U.S.C.A. §77b(1), 4 FCA title 15, §77b(1), Congress merely followed the pattern of many state "blue sky" laws which give the term wide scope to prevent evasion of the statutory purposes. The term "investment contract" appears in at least thirty state statutes, in addition to the Federal Act, and has been recognized by the courts as affording the investing public a full measure of protection, whether the transaction takes one of the more orthodox forms of a security or whether the promoter clothes the transaction with the appearance of a sale of some species of real or personal property.

The term "investment contract" is not defined by state or Federal statutes; but, in adopting the definition of a security from the "blue sky" laws, Congress must be deemed to have intended also

---

Annotation References

1. As to what constitutes stock, securities, or investment contracts within contemplation of state and Federal statutes regulating sale of securities, see annotation in 163 ALR 1050.

2. As to Federal Securities Acts, see annotation in 85 L.ed. 506.

to adopt that construction of the term which was uniformly followed by the state courts. Following such construction, the Federal courts have defined the phrase "investment contract," in §2(1) of the Act, to include any transaction in which the investor looks solely to the efforts of the promoter of the enterprise for the success of his investment. *See, e.g., Atherton v. United States* (CCA 9th) 128 F.2d 463, 465; *Penfield Co. v. Securities & Exch. Commission* (CCA 9th) 143 F.2d 746, 750, 751, 154 ALR 1027, *writ of certiorari denied* in 323 U.S. 768, 89 L.ed. 614, 65 S.Ct. 121; *Securities & Exch. Commission v. Universal Serv. Asso.* (CCA 7th) 106 F.2d 232, 237, *writ of certiorari denied* in 308 U.S. 622, 84 L.ed. 519, 60 S.Ct. 378.

In the present case, also, the undisputed facts make it clear that investors were offered land in combination with service contracts, making the arrangement one wherein the investor laid out his money on the expectation of profits to be derived solely through the efforts of the promoters. In the light of all the relevant circumstances, it can hardly be said that these were ordinary land transactions—i.e., that purchasers were buying citrus groves, per se. Rather, the arrangement contemplated was one whereby customers invested their money, converted into the form of an interest in land, in a large citrus enterprise managed and partly owned by respondents. The "economic inducements held out to the prospect" included the expectation of substantial profits from respondents' highly skilled managerial efforts; it was represented that profits of 20% in a particular year, and 10% over a ten-year period could be expected. Respondents' prospective customers—some 6,000 tourists and vacationists from all parts of the United States and Canada—were not in their own citrus businesses. Rather, they were predominantly lawyers, doctors, manufacturers and the like—residents of distant localities—who could be persuaded to invest their money with respondents only under an arrangement such as that offered here.

The question is not at all affected by the fact that the purchaser of a unit of citrus acreage is not required to enter into a service contract with respondents, but may have his unit serviced by another company. All investors are offered land and service contracts in combination, and 85% of the acreage sold during the period involved was sold under this arrangement. Indeed, the emphasis in the sales literature upon expected profits of 20% in a particular year and 10% per year average profits, was based on the hypothesis of service by respondents. The statute prohibits the offer as well as the sale of unregistered, nonexempt securities, and the fact that some purchasers chose not to accept the full offer of an "investment contract" is hardly relevant to the question whether unlawful offers are made. Likewise, the possibility that the service contract may not be renewed at the expiration of the ten-year term, or may be cancelled by the parties, is no more significant than the fact that any investment contract may be modified or terminated.

In broadly defining "security" to include any "investment contract," Congress intended to afford safeguards to investors in business enterprises whether established or promotional, speculative or nonspeculative, and irrespective of the method of distributing profits or of the intrinsic value of property incidentally acquired. The existence of such special factors as were stressed by the court below is not an adequate substitute for, and hence cannot render inapplicable, the statutory provisions for protection of the investor against fraud and inadequate disclosures.

To hold, as did the court below, that the Commission must establish the speculative character of the enterprise before it is entitled to such notification would be to make such an appraisal virtually impossible, as a matter of overall administration, by denying to the Commission an opportunity even to be notified of the pendency of the transaction, let alone its nature. The Commission's test, on the other hand, requires no detailed financial study; the Commission must be able to show only, on the basis of facts which are not hard to come by, that the proposed transaction involves an investment of capital in an enterprise whose promotor's efforts are alone relied upon for the production of profit for the investor.

C. E. Duncan, of Tavares, Florida, and George C. Bedell, of Jacksonville, Florida, argued the cause and filed a brief for respondents:

> Reduced to simple terms, the question to be determined is whether the transactions carried on by the Howey Company and the Service Company, which share the same offices and are directed by common control, utilizing the same facilities and personnel, bring the business of the companies within the control of the Securities and Exchange Commission. The form of the transaction is of little consequence if in fact the transactions carried on are in substance a marketing of securities. If in fact the transactions carried on are not in substance a marketing of securities, the Commission is without jurisdiction. *Securities & Exch. Commission v. C. M. Joiner Leasing Corp.* 320 U.S. 351, 88 L.Ed. 93, 64 S.Ct. 120.

We attribute no great importance to the fact that there are two companies rather than one. Were there no service company officered and controlled by the owners and officers of the Howey Company, no doubt some other company not officered and owned would be rendering similar services. The determinative fact, as we see it, is that the two companies were engaged in the development and marketing of fruit-producing land and not in the uttering and marketing of written obligations.

The Howey Company sells to persons who do not use the Service Company as their caretaker and the Service Company services trees on land not purchased from the Howey Company and solicits service contracts from others than purchasers from the Howey Company. Sales of acreage by the Howey Company are not conditioned upon the purchaser's entering into service agreements with the Service Company and the caretaking agreements are not conditioned upon the purchase of acreage from the Howey Company.

Prospective customers have opportunity to learn that there are numerous competing service companies of high standing operating in the vicinity whose business is to service property owned by others. Such competitors post signs by the land serviced by them, which are visible from the highway.

The Howey Company is not trafficking in options, licenses, or precarious leaseholds. The contract, Exhibit "A," is not a device to attract capital but is an out and out contract for conveyance of described land by a warranty deed conveying merchantable title. Under the laws of Florida upon the execution and delivery of such a contract the vendor becomes the holder of the legal interest in trust for its vendee as security for the deferred purchase price due from the latter to the former. Were the Howey Company and the Service Company identical and the possession retained by it, the sales contract would operate to transfer the equitable title to the purchaser. This is clearly stated in the leading Florida case on this subject: "We do not think that the retention of possession of the land by the vendor . . . makes any material difference in his status as owner. . . . He had the right to stipulate . . . for the retention of possession until the purchase money was paid, but this did not render the transaction any the less an unqualified sale of the property on his part." *Insurance Co. of N. A. v. Erickson,* 50 Fla. 419, 428, 39 So. 495, 498, 2 LRA (NS) 512, 111 Am. St. Rep. 121, 7 Ann. Cas. 495; *Reed v. American Ins. Co.* 128 Fla. 549, 175 So. 224.

The business of the Service Company is in no sense a profit-sharing arrangement. Its compensation is rated at so much per acre, per year, according to the age of the trees. Under that arrangement, the owner pays, dollar for dollar, the market price delivered at the described property of pruning, dusting, dusting material, spraying, spraying material, special treatment, seed for cover crop, sowing of same, fertilizer, replacement of any trees which may die, and watering trees when and as performed or applied in accordance with the best judgment of the Service Company.

The Service Company is bound to discharge its obligation diligently and in good faith, and is legally responsible in damages if it fails to do so. *Griffing Bros. Co. v. Winfield,* 53 Fla. 589, 43 So. 687.

Some point is made of the fact that possession of the premises is granted the Service Company, but its purpose is strictly limited by the third clause to the purpose of maintenance of the grove and the payment of the net proceeds from the sale of the fruit, and assures to the owner the fealty of a tenant. *Ibid.*

Mr. Justice Murphy delivered the opinion of the Court.

Headnote 1

This case involves the application of §2(1) of the Securities Act of [May 27] 1933[1] to an offering of units of a citrus grove development coupled with a contract for cultivating, marketing and remitting the net proceeds to the investor.

The Securities and Exchange Commission instituted this action to restrain the respondents from using the mails and instrumentalities of interstate commerce in the offer and sale of unregistered and non-exempt securities in violation of §5(a) of the Act, 15 U.S.C.A. §77e, 4 FCA title 15, §77e. The District Court denied the injunction, 60 F.Supp. 440, and the Fifth Circuit Court of Appeals affirmed the judgment. 151 F.2d 714. We granted certiorari on a petition alleging that the ruling of the Circuit Court of Appeals conflicted with other federal and state decisions and that it introduced a novel and unwarranted test under the statute which the Commission regarded as administratively impractical.

Most of the facts are stipulated. The respondents, W. J. Howey Company and Howey-in-the-Hills

*[295]

1. 48 Stat. 74, c. 38, 15 U.S.C.A. §77b(1), 4 FCA title 15, §77b(1).

Service, *Inc., are Florida corporations under direct common control and management. The Howey Company owns large tracts of citrus acreage in Lake County, Florida. During the past several years it has planted about 500 acres annually, keeping half of the groves itself and offering the other half to the public "to help us finance additional development." Howey-in-the-Hills Service, Inc., is a service company engaged in cultivating and developing many of these groves, including the harvesting and marketing of the crops.

Each prospective customer is offered both a land sales contract and a service contract, after having been told that it is not feasible to invest in a grove unless service arrangements are made. While the purchaser is free to make arrangements with other service companies, the superiority of Howey-in-the-Hills Service, Inc., is stressed. Indeed, 85% of the acreage sold during the 3-year period ending May 31, 1943, was covered by service contracts with Howey-in-the-Hills Service, Inc.

The land sales contract with the Howey Company provides for a uniform purchase price per acre or fraction thereof, varying in amount only in accordance with the number of years the particular plot has been planted with citrus trees. Upon full payment of the purchase price the land is conveyed to the purchaser by warranty deed. Purchases are usually made in narrow strips of land arranged so that an acre consists of a row of 48 trees. During the period between February 1, 1941, and May 31, 1943, 31 of the 42 persons making purchases bought less than 5 acres each. The average holding of these 31 persons was 1.33 acres and sales of as little as 0.65, 0.7 and 0.73 of an acre were made. These tracts are not separately fenced and the sole indication of several ownership is found in small land marks intelligible only through a plat book record.

*[296]

*The service contract, generally of a 10-year duration without option of cancellation, gives Howey-in-the-Hills Service, Inc., a leasehold interest and "full and complete" possession of the acreage. For a specified fee plus the cost of labor and materials, the company is given full discretion and authority over the cultivation of the groves and the harvest and marketing of the crops. The company is well established in the citrus business and maintains a large force of skilled personnel and a great deal of equipment, including 75 tractors, sprayer wagons, fertilizer trucks and the like. Without the consent of the company, the land owner or purchaser has no right of entry to market the crop;[2] thus there is ordinarily no right to specific fruit. The company is accountable only for an allocation of the net profits based upon a check made at the time of picking. All the produce is pooled by the respondent companies, which do business under their own names.

The purchasers for the most part are non-residents of Florida. They are predominantly business and professional people who lack the knowledge, skill and equipment necessary for the care and cultivation of citrus trees. They are attracted by the expectation of substantial profits. It was represented, for example, that profits during the 1943-1944 season amounted to 20% and that even greater profits might be expected during the 1944-1945 season, although only a 10% annual return was to be expected over a 10-year period. Many of these purchasers are patrons of a resort hotel owned and operated by the Howey Company in a scenic section adjacent to the groves. The hotel's advertising mentions the fine groves in the vicinity and the attention of the patrons

*[297]

is drawn to the *groves as they are being escorted about the surrounding countryside. They are told that the groves are for sale; if they indicate an interest in the matter they are then given a sales talk.

It is admitted that the mails and instrumentalities of interstate commerce are used in the sale of the land and service contracts and that no registration statement or letter of notification has ever been filed with the Commission in accordance with the Securities Act of 1933 and the rules and regulations thereunder.

Section 2(1) of the Act defines the term "security" to include the commonly known documents traded for speculation or investment.[3] This defi-

---

2. Some investors visited their particular plots annually, making suggestions as to care and cultivation, but without any legal rights in the matters.

3. "The term 'security' means any note, stock, treasury stock, bond, debenture, evidence of indebtedness, certificate of interest or participation in any profit-sharing agreement, collateral-trust certificate, preorganization certificate or subscription, transferable share, investment contract, voting-trust certificate, certificate of deposit for a security, fractional undivided interest in oil, gas, or other mineral rights, or, in general, any interest or instrument commonly known as a 'security,' or any certificate of interest or participation in, temporary or interim certificate for, receipt for, guarantee of, or warrant or right to subscribe to or purchase, any of the foregoing." [As amended June 6, 1934, 48 Stat. 881, 905, c. 404, 15 U.S.C.A. §77b(1), 4 FCA title 15, §77 b(1).]

nition also includes "securities" of a more variable character, designated by such descriptive terms as "certificate of interest or participation in any profit-sharing agreement," "investment contract" and "in general, any interest or instrument commonly known as a 'security.' " The legal issue in this case turns upon a determination of whether, under the circumstances, the land sales contract, the warranty deed and the service contract together constitute an "investment contract" within the meaning of §2(1). An affirmative answer brings into operation the registration requirements of §5(a), unless the security is granted an exemption under §3(b), 15 U.S.C.A. §77c, 4 FCA title 15, §77c. The lower courts, in reaching a negative answer to this problem, treated the contracts and

*[298]

deeds *as separate transactions involving no more than an ordinary real estate sale and an agreement by the seller to manage the property for the buyer.

The term "investment contract" is undefined by the Securities Act or by relevant legislative reports. But the term was common in many state "blue sky" laws in existence prior to the adoption of the federal statute and, although the term was also undefined by the state laws, it had been broadly construed by state courts so as to afford the investing public a full measure of protection. Form was disregarded for substance and emphasis was placed upon economic reality. An investment contract thus came to mean a contract or scheme for "the placing of capital or laying out of money in a way intended to secure income or profit from its employment." *State v. Gopher Tire & Rubber Co.* 146 Minn. 52, 56, 177 NW 937, 938. This definition was uniformly applied by state courts to a variety of situations where individuals were led to invest money in a common enterprise with the expectation that they would earn a profit solely through the efforts of the promoter or of someone other than themselves.[4]

By including an investment contract within the scope of §2(1) of the Securities Act, Congress was using a term the meaning of which had been crystallized by this prior judicial interpretation. It is therefore reasonable to attach that meaning to the term as used by Congress, especially since such a definition is consistent with the statutory aims. In other words, an investment contract for purposes of the Securities Act means a

Headnote 2

*[299]

contract, transaction *or scheme whereby a person invests his money in a common enterprise and is led to expect profits solely from the efforts of the promoter or a third party, it being immaterial whether the shares in the enterprise are evidenced by formal certificates or by nominal interests in the physical assets employed in the enterprise. Such a definition necessarily underlies this Court's decision in *Securities & Exch. Commission v. C. M. Joiner Leasing Corp.* 320 U.S. 344, 88 L.Ed. 88, 64 S.Ct. 120, and has been enunciated and applied many times by lower federal courts.[5] It permits the fulfillment of the statutory purpose of compelling full and fair disclosure relative to the issuance of "the many types of instruments that in our commercial world fall within the ordinary concept of a security." H. Rep. No. 85, 73d Cong. 1st Sess. p. 11. It embodies a flexible rather than a static principle, one that is capable of adaptation to meet the countless and variable schemes devised by those who seek the use of the money of others on the promise of profits.

The transactions in this case clearly involve investment contracts as so defined. The respondent companies are offering something more than fee simple interests in land, something different from a farm or orchard coupled with management services. They are offering an opportunity to contribute money and to share in the profits of a large citrus fruit enterprise managed and partly owned by respondents. They are offering this opportunity to persons who reside in distant localities

*[300]

and who lack the equipment *and experience

4. *State v. Evans,* 154 Minn. 95, 191 NW 425, 27 ALR 1165; *Klatt v. Guaranteed Bond Co.* 213 Wis. 12, 250 NW 825; *State v. Heath,* 199 N.C. 135, 153 SE 855; *Prohaska v. Hemmer-Miller Development Co.* 256 Ill. App. 331; *People v. White,* 124 Cal. App. 548, 12 P.2d 1078; *Stevens v. Liberty Packing Corp.* 111 N.J. Eq. 61, 161 A. 193. *See also Moore v. Stella,* 52 Cal. App.2d 766, 127 P.2d 300.

5. *Atherton v. United States* (CCA 9th) 128 F.2d 463; *Penfield Co. v. Securities & Exch. Commission* (CCA 9th) 143 F.2d 746; *Securities & Exch. Commission v. Universal Serv. Asso.* (CCA 7th) 106 F.2d 232; *Securities & Exch. Commission v. Crude Oil Corp.* (CCA 7th) 93 F.2d 844; *Securities & Exch. Commission v. Bailey* (DC) 41 F.Supp. 647; *Securities & Exch. Commission v. Payne* (DC) 35 F.Supp. 873; *Securities & Exch. Commission v. Bourbon Sales Corp.* (DC) 47 F.Supp. 70; *Securities & Exch. Commission v. Wickham* (DC) 12 F.Supp. 245; *Securities & Exch. Commission v. Timetrust, Inc.* (DC) 28 F.Supp. 34; *Securities & Exch. Commission v. Pyne* (DC) 33 F.Supp. 988. The Commission has followed the same definition in its own administrative proceedings. Re Natural Resources Corp. 8 SEC 635.

requisite to the cultivation, harvesting and marketing of the citrus products. Such persons have no desire to occupy the land or to develop it themselves; they are attracted solely by the prospects of a return on their investment. Indeed, individual development of the plots of land that are offered and sold would seldom be economically feasible due to their small size. Such tracts gain utility as citrus groves only when cultivated and developed as component parts of a larger area. A common enterprise managed by respondents or third parties with adequate personnel and equipment is therefore essential if the investors are to achieve their paramount aim of a return on their investments. Their respective shares in this enterprise are evidenced by land sales contracts and warranty deeds, which serve as a convenient method of determining the investors' allocable shares of the profits. The resulting transfer of rights in land is purely incidental.

Thus all the elements of a profit-seeking business venture are present here. The investors provide the capital and share in the earnings and profits; the promoters manage, control and operate the enterprise. It follows that the arrangements whereby the investors' interests are made manifest involve investment contracts, regardless of the legal terminology in which such contracts are clothed. The investment contracts in this instance take the form of land sales contracts, warranty deeds and service contracts which respondents offer to prospective investors. And respondents' failure to abide by the statutory and administrative rules in making such offerings, even though the failure result from a bona fide mistake as to the law, cannot be sanctioned under the Act.

This conclusion is unaffected by the fact that some purchasers choose not to accept the full offer of an investment contract by declining to

*[301]

enter into a service contract with *the respondents. The Securities Act prohibits the offer as well as the sale of unregistered, non-exempt securities.[6] Hence it is enough that the respondents merely offer the essential ingredients of an investment contract.

We reject the suggestion of the Circuit Court of Appeals, 151 F.2d at 717, that an investment contract is necessarily missing where the enterprise is not speculative or promotional in character and where the tangible interest which is sold has intrinsic value independent of the success of the enterprise as a whole. The test is whether the scheme involves an investment of money in a common enterprise with profits to come solely from the efforts of others. If that test be satisfied, it is immaterial whether the enterprise is speculative or nonspeculative or whether there is a sale of property with or without intrinsic value. *See Securities & Exch. Commission v. C. M. Joiner Leasing Corp. supra* (320 U.S. 352, 88 L.Ed. 93, 64 S.Ct. 120). The statutory policy of affording broad protection to investors is not to be thwarted by unrealistic and irrelevant formulae.

Headnote 3

Reserved.

Mr. Justice Jackson took no part in the consideration or decision of this case.

Mr. Justice Frankfurter dissenting.

"Investment contract" is not a term of art; it is a conception dependent upon the circumstances of a particular situation. If this case came before us on a finding authorized by Congress that the facts disclosed an "investment contract" within the general scope of §2(1) of the Securities Act, 48 Stat. 74, c. 38, 15 U.S.C.A. §77b(1), 4 FCA Title 15, §77b(1), the Securities and Exchange Commission's finding would govern, unless, on the record, it was wholly unsupported. But

*[302]

*that is not the case before us. Here the ascertainment of the existence of an "investment contract" had to be made independently by the District Court and it found against its existence. 60 F.Supp. 440. The Circuit Court of Appeals for the Fifth Circuit sustained that finding. 151 F.2d 714. If respect is to be paid to the wise rule of judicial administration under which this Court does not upset concurrent findings of two lower courts in the ascertainment of facts and the relevant inferences to be drawn from them, this case clearly calls for its application. *See Allen v. Trust Co. of Ga.* 326 U.S. 630, ante, 367, 66 S.Ct. 389. For the crucial issue in this case turns on whether the contracts for the land and the contracts for the management of the property were in reality separate agreements or merely parts of a single transaction. It is clear from its opinion that the District Court was warranted in its conclusion that the record does not establish the existence of an investment contract:

> . . . the record in this case shows that not a single sale of citrus grove property was made by the Howey Company during the period involved in this suit, except to purchasers who actually inspected the property before purchasing the

6. The registration requirements of §5 refer to sales of securities. Section 2(3) defines "sale" to include every "attempt or offer to dispose of, or solicitation of an offer to buy," a security for value.

> same. The record further discloses that no purchaser is required to engage the Service Company to care for his property and that of the fifty-one purchasers acquiring property during this period, only forty-two entered into contracts with the Service Company for the care of the property.
>
> 60 F.Supp. at 442.

Simply because other arrangements may have the appearances of this transaction but are employed as an evasion of the Securities Act does not mean that the present contracts were evasive. I find nothing in the Securities Act to indicate that Congress meant to bring every innocent transaction within the scope of the Act simply because a perversion of them is covered by the Act.

Pension Plan Interest as a "Security"

The breadth of the statutory definition of the term "security" and the Supreme Court decision in *Howey* and other cases provide the basis for the conclusion that, for example, an employee's interest in a pension plan may be a security. The position that an employee's interest in a pension plan is a security may rest on the inclusion within the statutory definition of "investment contract."[1]

The term "investment contract" is not itself defined in the '33 Act, but it has been defined on numerous occasions by state courts considering the applicability of state "blue sky" laws. These state court decisions served as the basis for the Supreme Court's decision in the *Howey* case. In *Howey,* the Supreme Court defined "investment contract" as including "an investment in a common venture premised on a reasonable expectation of profits to be derived from the entrepreneurial or managerial effort of others."

An analysis of this definition indicates that several elements must be present in order for the court to find that an "investment contract," and thus a "security," exists. There must be (1) an investment of money (2) in common enterprise (3) with the expectation of profits (4) as a result of the efforts of third parties.

The possibility that an employee's interest in a pension plan may constitute an investment contract and thus a security became a reality in *Daniel v. International Brotherhood of Teamsters,* 501 F.2nd 1223, *cert. granted.* In *Daniel,* the Seventh Circuit Court of Appeals has held that an employee's interest in a collectively bargained, noncontributory pension plan is an investment contract and, therefore, such interest constitutes a security for purposes of the antifraud provisions. Other courts have reached the same conclusion. Although the Seventh Circuit did not hold that such an interest constitutes a security for purposes of the disclosure or registration provisions, the Securities and Exchange Commission has traditionally taken this view. However, based on the rationale that no sale is involved, registration has not been necessary. (It is important to note that the court found the "no sale" rationale "no longer viable even as to the registration provisions.")

DANIEL V. INTERNATIONAL BROTHERHOOD OF TEAMSTERS

561 F.2d 1223 (7th Cir. 1977)

CUMMINGS, Circuit Judge.

Plaintiff is a resident of Illinois and has been a member of defendant Local Union 705 of the International Brotherhood of Teamsters, Chauffeurs, Warehousemen and Helpers of America since 1951. He also purports to serve as the representative of the class of all members of all affiliate locals of the Teamsters International who have "purchased and acquired an interest in a Teamsters' pension fund." The original defendants were Local 705, the International Brotherhood, three classes (Teamster local unions with pension funds similarly situated to Local 705, trustees of such pension funds and all officers of locals with such pension funds), and Louis Peick, an officer of Local 705 and a trustee of its pension fund. Additional defendants added by amendment are Local 705's Pension Fund and seven individuals representing that pension fund and all other Teamster pension funds.

According to the complaint, the Teamsters locals negotiate labor contracts with companies across the United States for the benefit of their members who are employees of such companies. Under these contracts, Teamster members agree to provide their services as employees of the companies in return for wages and various other forms of consideration. Since 1955, most of those labor contracts negotiated by the Teamsters have provided for the establishment of pension funds for their union members. Under the labor contracts, the employing companies make set payments into the pension funds for Teamster members "as part consideration for the labor services provided by such union members" (Complaint par. 12).

---

1. It is also possible to argue that, if such interests are not securities, the exemption in Section 3(a)(2) is not necessary. This exemption will be discussed below.

These payments are held in trust and invested by pension trust fund trustees who are equally divided between employer and union representatives. Therefore, the Teamster member employees contribute their labor services in return for their participating interest in the pension trust funds and their wages and fringe benefits.

Again, according to the complaint, the Teamsters' pension plans do not differ *inter se* in any material respect for the purposes of this case. Each was a defined benefit pension plan where employees are offered various benefits if they meet certain eligibility requirements. Actuarial assumptions based on estimated union member turnover, mortality and the rate of return on fund capital are used to determine the amount the employer must contribute so that the pension fund will be able to pay the promised benefits to union members as they retire without jeopardizing the payment of benefits to future and antecedent retirees. The pension trust funds have lengthy vesting periods. If a Teamster member does not meet the length of service requirement of the vesting period, the entire contribution paid into the trust fund for him is forfeited, thereby extinguishing his interest in the fund. Local 705's pension fund had a twenty-year vesting period, a typical provision.

In addition to the lengthy plan-vesting periods, most of the Teamsters' pension plans require continuity of employment with employers who have entered into labor contracts with the Teamsters.[1] Under this continuity or "break-in-service" rule, no pension benefit is available to a Teamster union member who has been employed by covered employers for the full vesting period but whose employment with covered employers is not continuous and uninterrupted. Employer-paid contributions are also forfeited when the union member cannot meet the break-in-service requirement of his pension plan's vesting rule.

The monies contributed to the pension funds are invested by the trustees thereof, and it is alleged that each trust fund "over the long run [is] reasonably expected to grow through the accumulation of dividends, interest and other earnings" (Complaint par. 15). Failure to meet the length or continuity requirements of the pension fund's vesting provision also causes the forfeiture of a union member's participating interest in these accumulated earnings. When the complaint was filed in 1974, plaintiff had worked for covered employers for 22½ years, but his service was interrupted by an involuntary four-month break in service from December 1960 to April 1961.[2] Because of this interruption in service, Local 705 has refused to pay plaintiff any pension benefits whatsoever and the employer contributions paid on his behalf and the earnings accumulated therefrom had been forfeited.

Count I of the complaint asserts that beginning in 1955 and continuing to the present, defendants misrepresented certain material facts and omitted to make other material facts by making misleading statements which in general related to the value of a member's participating interest in his local pension fund. The misrepresentations concerned misleading statements as to the length and continuity requirements of the pension plan's vesting provision. Defendants are said to have made omissions of material facts by failing to inform the members that they would receive no pension benefits whatsoever if they did not meet the length or continuity requirements of the vesting provision and that, upon failing to satisfy these requirements, the contributions made on their behalf into the fund and the earnings accumulated therefrom would be forfeited. Defendants allegedly also omitted to state that the fund's actuarial basis was arbitrary. Other omissions are said to be the failure to disclose pertinent information needed to disclose the actuarial basis upon which the funds were grounded and the actuarial likelihood that a union member will not receive any pension benefits at all. Finally, plaintiff alleged a failure to state that the defendants have unlawfully diverted pension funds for the benefit of persons other than the pension trust beneficiaries.

Plaintiff claims in Count I that although he purchased an interest in the pension fund by providing labor service to an employer with a labor contract with the Teamsters, he sustained sub-

1. A survey of 32 pension plans representing over half of the Teamster membership disclosed no other plan which would have absolutely disqualified a man in Daniel's circumstances. Most plans have continuity requirements but involuntary breaks in service are usually remediable upon satisfaction of certain requirements. Local 705's continuity requirement has been so modified for a break in service occurring after 1970 (International Br. at 9 n. 12).

2. According to plaintiff's supporting affidavit, from April 1961 to July 5, 1961, his employer's bookkeeper embezzled the employer's contributions to the Local 705 Pension Fund. Plaintiff reported this embezzlement to Local 705. It subsequently treated his break in service as a seven-month interruption, although it had assured him at the time of his report to it about the lapse vis-a-vis his pension rights that it "would take care of whatever had to be done on account of the embezzlement" (App. 95a).

stantial losses which were a direct and proximate result of a violation of Section 10(b) of the Securities Exchange Act of 1934 and Rule 10b-5 thereunder by the defendants. Besides requesting class relief, plaintiff requested the district court to find that defendants violated Section 10(b) and Rule 10b-5 and to reform the pension fund agreements by deleting the length and continuity requirements of the vesting provision. The plaintiff also sought a judgment requiring defendants to pay pension benefits unlawfully withheld from plaintiff and his class. In addition, a judgment was sought in the amount of any interests which had been diverted from their proper purposes.

Count II of the complaint sought similar relief under Section 17(a) of the Securities Act of 1933. However, neither this nor any other count of the complaint charged that the registration requirements of that Act were applicable.[3]

Plaintiff's Affidavit

Four months after the docketing of his complaint, plaintiff filed an affidavit which we treat as part of the pleadings for purposes of our review of the order below denying the motion to dismiss. The affidavit showed that he had only an elementary school education and had joined Local 705 in April 1950 when he became a truck driver with an employer who had a collective bargaining agreement with that Union. He worked continuously as a truck driver with Local 705 contracting employers from April 1950 through November 1973, except for an interruption from December 5, 1960, until April 1961, when he was involuntarily laid off wholly because of the adverse economic condition of his employer.[4] Plaintiff tried unsuccessfully to find any trucker's work during this time period. He retired because of cataracts on December 1, 1973, at the age of 63. Since his retirement, Daniel has not worked at all.

In 1955, plaintiff learned of Local 705's pension fund and understood that as a Local 705 member he would be eligible to receive retirement benefits upon completing 20 years of employment with Local 705 covered employers. He believed that employer contributions to the Local 705 pension fund would finance the retirement payments which he would receive after 20 years of employment. This retirement plan was a material factor in his continuing employment with Local 705 covered employers. If he had known that Local 705 would interpret the pension plan as requiring uninterrupted service of 20 years, he would have sought employment elsewhere with an adequate retirement plan. The communications he received from Local 705 did not disturb his understanding that he would receive a pension after 20 years of employment with covered employers.[5]

In June 1971, plaintiff received a letter from defendant Peick stating that after 20 years of covered service and at 60 years of age or over, a retired employee would receive a monthly pension of $400. He expected to receive such a pension on his retirement. One of Local 705's booklets advised him that the purpose of the pension fund was to take care of him and his family in case of retirement and that the funds afforded protec-

3. The original complaint contained three additional counts, and a fourth was added by amendment on February 7, 1975. The plaintiff thereby seeks relief for the defendants' alleged breach of their duty of fair representation under Section 9(a) of the National Labor Relations Act ("NLRA"), 29 U.S.C. 159(a), and for the failure of the pension fund to be established for the "sole and exclusive benefit of the employees," as required by Section 302(c)(5) of the NLRA, 29 U.S.C. §186(c)(5). Finally, the plaintiff seeks to recover under common law theories of breach of fiduciary duty, fraud and deceit. Since they are not involved in this appeal, the additional counts will not be discussed further herein.

4. *See* note 2 *supra.*

5. Pension plan booklets describing pension plans are often designed "to sell the plan . . .," D. McGill, Fulfilling Pension Expectations 17 (1962) (Institute for Public Interest Representation's Br. at 12.) For example, these materials do not forthrightly disclose in terms understandable to a truck driver with a limited education the "minimum length of time considered to constitute a break-in-service in the Local 705 Pension Fund 20 years continuous service vesting rule; such materials do not disclose that all contributions made on behalf of a Local 705 member into the Local 705 Pension Fund (and all accumulated earnings on the aggregate of such contributions) will be forfeited following any proscribed break in service; and such materials do not disclose either the actuarial bases on which the Local 705 Pension Fund has been established or the likelihood that any Local 705 member will ever receive a pension benefit" (Pl. Br. at 5).

Indeed, one *amicus* siding with defendants admits that this lack of disclosure is rampant generally in the pension field:

> Thus employees are often not aware of the fact that the actual realization of benefits depends upon meeting certain benefit eligibility conditions, depends upon prudent management of the retirement fund, depends upon contributions by their employer sufficient to pay retirement benefits as they come due, and depends upon their employer remaining in business.

(ERISA Regulations Industry Committee's Br. at 19-20).

tion to him, his wife and unmarried children under 18 years of age. He relied on such assurances that the fund would provide for financial security in his old age.

He did not learn until December 1973 that his involuntary 4-month layoff caused the Draconian result of total forfeiture of his pension. He never learned of the success or failure of the trustees' management of the Local 705 pension fund, nor was he advised of the type of investments being made by the trust fund. During several months prior to his December 1, 1973, retirement, he visited Local 705's office on five to eight occasions to arrange for his pension and was not then advised that he was ineligible to receive it. After Daniel's retirement, he was told for the first time that his 4-month involuntary break in service made him ineligible to receive any pension benefits. On December 26, 1973, and on March 28, 1974, he appeared before the Local 705 trustees, but they refused to reverse the prior denial of his pension. He and his fellow Local 705 members had always had the common understanding that they would receive a retirement benefit after 20 years of covered employment and that no employer contributions could be forfeited. Other members of Local 705 were shocked to learn that a Local 705 member with Daniel's record of employment could be denied all pension benefits because of a temporary break in service. Indeed neither the defendants nor the *amici* who support their position dispute that this is "unfair in the extreme, shocking to the conscience" (Secretary of Labor's Br. at 21).

Local 705, Peick and the International Brotherhood of Teamsters filed motions to dismiss Counts I and II of the complaint on the ground that the court lacked subject matter jurisdiction and that they failed to state a claim upon which relief could be granted.[6] Local 705 and Peick also maintained that the action under Counts I and II was barred by the limitations provisions of the Securities Act of 1933 and the Illinois Statute of Limitations.[7] On March 1, 1976, the district judge handed down a memorandum opinion and order denying the motions to dismiss as to all counts and holding the anti-fraud provisions of the securities laws applicable. This opinion is reported in 410 F.Supp. 541. The effect of the opinion is to require defendants, when offering a defined pension plan to a member, to disclose the actuarial probability, here perhaps as low as 8% (410 F.Supp. at 551), that a member actually will receive pension benefits, and factors such as risk of loss, breaks in service, death before retirement age, and plan termination, that can cause this member to be deprived of his benefits, or otherwise defendants must face fraud liability under the securities acts. Subsequently, the court entered an order denying defendants' motions to reconsider its refusal to dismiss Counts I and II but certified their application for interlocutory appeal under 28 U.S.C. §1292(b). The certification was limited to Counts I and II of the complaint. The controlling question of law certified to this Court can be easily identified by the district court's careful circumscription of its holding below with respect to Counts I and II, *viz.:*

> The Court makes no finding here beyond the narrow holding that the complaint alleges the sale of a security for purposes of application of the anit-fraud provisions of the Securities Acts, and that the complaint alleges violations of those provisions. The Court makes no finding with respect to applicability of any other sections of those Acts to employee pension plans such as the one here litigated.
>
> 410 F.Supp. at 553.

Thereafter we granted permission to appeal.[8] Three *amici curiae* have filed briefs urging reversal and four urge affirmance.[9] We affirm.

Modality of Analysis

The securities cases in the Supreme Court's 1976 October Term have underscored its recently expressed methodology in interpreting the securities laws. *See, e.g., Piper v. Chris-Craft Industries, Inc.,* 430 U.S. 1, 97 S.Ct. 926, 51 L.Ed.2d 124; *Santa Fe Industries, Inc. v. Green,* 430 U.S. 462, 97 S.Ct. 1292, 51 L.Ed.2d 480. Analysis be-

6. Local 705 and Peick included additional defenses in their motion to dismiss as to Counts I and II as well as some defenses directed at the other Counts of the complaint. The International answered the complaint and subsequently filed a motion to dismiss Counts I and II only, based on an asserted lack of subject-matter jurisdiction and failure to state a claim.

7. On appeal, the limitations defense has been abandoned.

8. The district court has not yet ruled upon plaintiff's and defendants' respective motions for class action certification.

9. Those favoring affirmance are the Securities and Exchange Commission (SEC), the Gray Panthers, the Institute for Public Interest Representation (IPIR) and the Teamsters for a Democratic Union. Opposed are the Secretary of Labor, the ERISA Regulations Industry Committee (ERIC) and the National Coordinating Committee for Multiemployer Plans. The General Counsel of the SEC and a representative of the Secretary of Labor participated in the oral argument.

gins with the relevant statutes themselves. After a study of their language and any court-added gloss, attention shifts to the statutes' legislative history. Additional considerations weigh in the balance. The history of the SEC's administration of the securities laws often can add a substantive gloss of its own which is entitled to the usual administrative deference (*Investment Company Inst. v. Camp,* 401 U.S. 617, 626-627, 91 S.Ct. 1091, 28 L.Ed.2d 367) so long as it does not become law-making. *Ernst & Ernst v. Hochfelder,* 425 U.S. 185, 212-214, 96 S.Ct. 1375, 47 L.Ed.2d 668. And to the extent that these more cogent interpretive tools are not dispositive of the statutes' meaning, additional considerations of policy may tip the scales. *Id.* at 214 n. 33, 96 S.Ct. 1375; *Blue Chip Stamps v. Manor Drug Stores,* 421 U.S. 723, 737 S.Ct. 1917, 44 L.Ed. 2d 539. We shall use this methodology in our analysis of this case.

Statutes

Both of the major anti-fraud portions of the federal securities laws are relied upon in this complaint. Count I charges a breach of Section 10(b) of the Securities Exchange Act of 1934 [15 U.S. C. §78j(b)][10] and Rule 10b-5 thereunder [17 C.F.R. §240.10(b)(5)][11] while Count II alleges a violation of Section 17(a) of the Securities Act of 1933 [15 U.S.C. §77q(a)].[12] This being an appeal from an order denying a motion to dismiss, the allegations concerning the use of the jurisdictional means and the making of material misrepresentations, the omissions to state material facts or the use of manipulative or fraudulent devices are treated as true by defendants. Their argument is based upon the phrase "in connection with the purchase or sale of any security" in Section 10(b) and Rule 10b-5 and the phrase "sale of any securities" in Section 17(a). Defendants assert that these anti-fraud provisions are inapplicable on their face on the ground that plaintiff's interest in the pension fund is not a "security" and was not acquired by him in a "sale."

Plaintiff's Interest in the Pension Fund Is a "Security"

The term "security" is defined in Section 2(1) of the 1933 Act [15 U.S.C. §77b(1)][13] and in Section 3(a)(10) of the 1934 Act [15 U.S.C. §78c

---

10. Section 10(b) provides:

It shall be unlawful for any person, directly or indirectly, by the use of any means or instrumentality of interstate commerce or of the mails, or of any facility of any national securities exchange—

(b) To use or employ, in connection with the purchase or sale of any security registered on a national securities exchange or any security not so registered, any manipulative or deceptive device or contrivance in contravention of such rules and regulations as the Commission may prescribe as necessary or appropriate in the public interest or for the protection of investors.

11. Rule 10b-5 provides:

It shall be unlawful for any person, directly or indirectly, by the use of any means or instrumentality of interstate commerce, or of the mails or of any facility of any national securities exchange,

(1) to employ any device, scheme, or artifice to defraud,

(2) to make any untrue statement of a material fact or to omit to state a material fact necessary in order to make the statements made, in the light of the circumstances under which they were made, not misleading, or

(3) to engage in any act, practice, or course of business which operates or would operate as a fraud or deceit upon any person, in connection with the purchase or sale of any security.

12. Section 17(a) provides:

It shall be unlawful for any person in the offer or sale of any securities by the use of any means or instruments of transportation or communication in interstate commerce or by the use of the mails, directly or indirectly—

(1) to employ any device, scheme, or artifice to defraud, or

(2) to obtain money or property by means of any untrue statement of a material fact or any omission to state a material fact necessary in order to make the statements made, in the light of the circumstances under which they were made, not misleading, or

(3) to engage in any transaction, practice, or course of business which operates or would operate as a fraud or deceit upon the purchaser.

13. Section 2(1) of the 1933 Act provides:

When used in this title, unless the context otherwise requires—

(1) The term "security" means any note, stock, treasury stock, bond, debenture, evidence of indebtedness, certificate of interest or participation in any profit-sharing agreement, collateral-trust certificate, preorganization certificate or subscription, transferable share, *investment contract,* voting-trust certificate, certificate of deposit for a security, fractional undivided interest in oil, gas, or other mineral rights, or, in general, any interest or instrument commonly known as a "security," or any certificate of interest or participation in, temporary or interim certificate for, receipt for, guarantee of, or warrant or right to subscribe to or purchase, any of the foregoing. (Emphasis supplied.)

(a)(10)].[14] In each statute, the definition of "security" includes any "investment contract."[15] Since the same Congress which passed both the 1933 and 1934 Acts clearly indicated that its definition of "security" in the 1934 Act was intended to be " 'substantially the same . . .' " as in the 1933 Act, cases construing either definition can be used interchangeably. *United Housing Foundation, Inc. v. Forman,* 421 U.S. 837, 847 n. 12, 95 S.Ct. 2051, 44 L.Ed.2d 621; *Tcherepnin v. Knight,* 389 U.S. 332, 336, 342, 88 S.Ct. 548, 19 L.Ed.2d 564. Therefore we need not break out separate lines of analysis in order to determine the existence of a security under Section 10(b) of the 1934 Act and Section 17(a) of the 1933 Act.

[1] In construing the statutory term "security," guidance is provided by two overriding principles. First, as remedial legislation the securities acts should be construed broadly to effectuate their purposes. Congress purposely defined the term "security" broadly, and it has been construed liberally by the Supreme Court in order to protect the public from speculative or fraudulent schemes. *Tcherepnin v. Knight,* 389 U.S. 332, 336, 338, 88 S.Ct. 548. Secondly, in searching for content in the term "security," "form should be disregarded for substance and the emphasis should be on economic reality." *Id.* at 336, 88 S.Ct. at 553.

[2] With this background, attention can now focus on whether plaintiff's interest in the Teamsters' pension fund is an investment contract. An investment contract was defined by the Supreme Court in *SEC v. W. J. Howey Company,* 328 U.S. 293, 298-299, 66 S.Ct. 1100, 1103, 90 L.Ed. 27, to mean

> a contract, transaction or scheme whereby a person invests his money in a common enterprise and is led to expect profits solely from the efforts of the promoter or a third party, it being immaterial whether the shares in the enterprise are evidenced by formal certificates or by nominal interests in the physical assets employed in the enterprise.

In *United Housing Foundation, Inc. v. Forman,* 421 U.S. 837, 852, 95 S.Ct. 2060, the Supreme Court reiterated this rule and stated that

> [t]his test, in shorthand form, embodies the essential attributes that run through all of the Courts' decisions defining a security. The touchstone is the presence of an investment in a common venture premised on a reasonable expectation of profits to be derived from the entrepreneurial or managerial efforts of others.
>
> . . . . .
>
> What distinguishes a security transaction [from every other form of commercial dealing] is an investment where one parts with his money in the hope of receiving profits from the efforts of others, and not where he purchases a commodity for personal consumption or living quarters for personal use.
>
> *Id.* at 858, 95 S.Ct. at 2063.[16]

As demonstrated below, the elements of the *Howey* rule are present here, for under the Local 705 Pension Fund, money is invested in a common enterprise, the management of which is committed to a third party, and from which profits and income are reasonably expected.

The Union Member as an Investor

In the present case, the money invested in the pension fund came from employer contributions paid on behalf of the employee. The local defendants maintain that non-contributing beneficiaries of a fund cannot be conceptualized as investing in the fund, citing *SIPC and SEC v. Morgan, Kennedy & Cox, Inc.,* 533 F.2d 1314 (2d Cir. 1976).

---

14. Section 3(a)(10) of the 1934 Act provides:

> When used in this title, unless the context otherwise requires—
>
> (10) The term "security" means any note, stock, treasury stock, bond, debenture, certificate of interest or participation in any profit-sharing agreement or in any oil, gas, or other mineral royalty or lease, any collateral-trust certificate, preorganization certificate or subscription, transferable share, *investment contract,* voting-trust certificate, certificate of deposit, for a security, or in general, any instrument commonly known as a "security" or any certificate of interest or participation in, temporary or interim certificate for, receipt for, or warrant or right to subscribe to or purchase, any of the foregoing; but shall not include currency or any note, draft, bill of exchange, or banker's acceptance which has a maturity at the time of issuance of not exceeding nine months, exclusive of days of grace, or any renewal thereof the maturity of which is likewise limited.
>
> (Emphasis supplied.)

15. Plaintiff does not seriously press the theory that he had a "certificate of interest or participation in any profit-sharing agreement" but rather relies on the "investment contract" theory. Since we find merit in the "investment contract" theory, we have no occasion to express a view on the adequacy of the "certificate" theory under the facts of this case where Daniel has no document which evidences his interest in the Local 705 Pension Fund.

16. The International's argument that a union member is not an investor "in any sense understood by Congress when it was protecting investors in the securities markets" (Br. 12) is addressed *infra.*

In *Morgan, Kennedy,* the Second Circuit was asked "to determine whether the one hundred and eight employee-beneficiaries of a trust created under a profit-sharing plan qualify as 'customers' of a bankrupt broker-dealer for the purpose of receiving compensation for losses available to such customers under the Securities Investor Protection Act of 1970 (SIPA), 15 U.S.C. §78aaa *et seq.*" *Id.* at 1315. The statutory definition of "customer" read in pertinent part "persons (including persons with whom the debtor deals as principal or agent) who have claims on account of securities *received, acquired* or *held* by the debtor from or for the *account of such persons . . .*" (emphasis supplied). *Id.* at 1316. Prior Second Circuit law had used investor and customer status interchangeably. *Id.* at 1317. In *Morgan, Kennedy* it was the trust as an entity as represented by the trustees, rather than its beneficiaries, who were the customers of the debtor broker-dealer. The account was held in the trustees' names and the individual beneficiaries' identities were totally unknown to the broker-dealer. Moreover, control over investment decisions was exercised exclusively by the trustees. "The employee-beneficiaries . . . made no purchases, transacted no business, and had no dealings whatsoever with the broker-dealer in question respecting the trust account." *Id.* at 1318. Common sense mandated the conclusion that the individual beneficiaries were not customers of the broker-dealer. Because of the *sui generis* definition of customer/investor under the Securities Investor Protection Act of 1970, *Morgan, Kennedy* is irrelevant to the question whether the union members have made an investment within the meaning of the 1933 and 1934 Acts.

More relevant is the recent case of *Klamberg v. Roth*, 425 F.Supp. 440 (S.D.N.Y. 1976). There the court held that the plaintiff as beneficiary in an employee pension plan had standing to bring an anti-fraud action against the plan trustees:

> Fraud perpetrated by a trustee in the purchase or sale of securities on behalf of the trust has a tangible impact on each beneficiary, no matter how many beneficiaries are thereby affected and regardless of the precise purposes of the trust. The policies behind the *Birnbaum* rule are not undermined.
>
> *Id.* at 443.[17]

The employer contributions to the plan's pension fund constitute a sector of the total employee compensation structure. *Inland Steel Co. v. National Labor Relations Board,* 170 F.2d 247 (7th Cir. 1948), *certiorari denied,* 336 U.S. 960, 69 S.Ct. 887, 93 L.Ed. 1112. "Regardless of the form they take, the employer's share of the cost of these plans or the benefits the employers provide are a form of compensation." Welfare and Pension Plans Disclosure Act of 1958, S.Rep. No. 1440, 85th Cong., 2d Sess. (1958), reprinted in 3 U.S. Code Cong. and Admin. News, pp. 4137, 4139. This thesis is accepted by the courts, *see, e.g., Lewis v. Benedict Coal Co.,* 361 U.S. 459, 469, 80 S.Ct. 489, 4 L.Ed.2d 442; *Employing Plasterers' Assoc. v. Journeymen Plasterers' Protective and Benevolent Soc'y,* 279 F.2d 92, 99 (7th Cir. 1960), and the commentators alike. P. Drucker, The Unseen Revolution 8, 34 (1976); Note, Legal Problems of Private Pension Plans, 70 Harv.L.Rev. 490, 494 (1957). Indeed the International Brotherhood has conceded[18] these pension funds "constitute a form of compensation for an employee's labor" (Br. 12).[19] Realistically speaking, employers are putting money into a fund for an employee's future use which he would otherwise be getting in his paycheck. Mundheim and Henderson, Applicability of the Federal Securities Laws to Pension and Profit-Sharing Plans, 29 Law & Contemp. Prob. 795, 803-804 (1964).

[3] The International maintains that employees do not even have an interest in the pension plan except in the attenuated sense that they have a contingent expectancy of receiving pension payments at a future date. But mere contingent expectancies are the rule rather than the exception in the equity markets. Profits in an equity security require that the market value plus accrued dividends of a stock be greater than the stockholder's cash basis. Thus profits are contingent on the successful operation of the common enterprise, there the issuing corporation. Whether an em-

17. *Birnbaum v. Newport Steel Corp.,* 193 F.2d 461 (2d Cir. 1952), *certiorari denied,* 343 U.S. 956, 72 S.Ct. 1051, 96 L.Ed. 1356, confined recoveries under Section 10(b) of the Securities Exchange Act of 1934 and Rule 10b-5 thereunder to buyers and sellers of securities.

18. In the district court, the International Brotherhood did not challenge that an "investment contract" was involved here. Even now all the defendants agree that "the SEC has consistently taken the position that interests in some pension plans are "securities" (Joint Rep. Br. at 2).

19. The International Brotherhood argues that the employee, once employed, has no individual control over either the fact or amount of the contributions to the fund. Such issues of investment autonomy are best addressed in the context of the existence of a sale. Consequently we defer the bulk of our discussion on these issues until our discussion of whether a sale of an instrument found to be a security can be said to have occurred.

ployee is found to have covered employment before his benefits vest or a stockholder is forced to sell his stock at a net loss does not eject his interest in the respective common enterprises from the bounds of the *Howey* definition of security. Realizing this analogy is not exact, we think that a right to receive benefits, received as a form of compensation and not subject to unilateral withdrawal by the pension trustee or the employer, is a sufficient interest to constitute a security, even though it will only mature upon the happening of certain events in the future.

The Local defendants attempt to erect a dichotomy between wages *per se* and the fringe benefits of employment which together make up an employee's total compensation by referring to sections of the Bankruptcy Act, the Internal Revenue Code, the Social Security Act, the Fair Labor Standards Act and the Sherman Act which purportedly raise such a distinction for the purposes of those Acts. The existence of a wage/compensation dichotomy in other unrelated statutes is wholly irrelevant to whether a union member has made an investment under the *Howey* rule. The *Howey* test only requires that the employer-paid contributions to the pension fund can be properly considered to be economic compensation to the employee. This proposition is universally accepted by the courts and commentators. Accordingly, the investment of money prong of the *Howey* rule has been satisfied.[20]

The Pension Fund as a Common Enterprise

[4] Under *Howey,* it is "immaterial whether the shares in the enterprise are evidenced by formal certificates or by nominal interests in the physical assets employed in the enterprise." 328 U.S. at 299, 66 S.Ct. at 1103. As a result, the common enterprise can properly take the form of a trust fund investing in the capital markets where the beneficiaries' common relationship with the enterprise is an undivided interest in such a trust without the beneficiaries having certificates evidencing their interest or the power to transfer their interests in the trust. *See Collins v. Rukin,* 342 F.Supp. 1282, 1286 (D.Mass. 1972). Presumably, an investor who purchases a minority block of stock from a close corporation whose shares have restraints on their alienation may still sue for fraud under the securities laws. *Holdsworth v. Strong,* 545 F.2d 687 (10th Cir. 1976) (*en banc*). Here the enterprise is common to all of the Local 705 members. The pension fund trustees self-admittedly exercise exclusive control over the common enterprise and the investment of its assets. The pension fund which receives the union members' investments is a common enterprise under *Howey.*

Profits from the Efforts of Others

The Local defendants point principally to *United Housing Foundation v. Forman,* 421 U.S. 837, 95 S.Ct. 2051, 44 L.Ed.2d 621, in arguing that the pension fund does not generate profits in the *Howey* sense.[21] In *Forman,* profits were defined as follows:

> By profits, the Court has meant either capital appreciation resulting from the development of the initial investment, as in *Joiner* [*S.E.C. v. C. M. Joiner Leasing Corp.,* 320 U.S. 344, 64 S.Ct. 120, 88 L.Ed. 88] (sale of oil leases conditioned on promoters' agreement to drill exploratory well), or a participation in earnings resulting from the use of investors' funds, as in *Tcherepnin v. Knight, supra* (dividends on the investment based on savings and loan association's profits). In such cases the investor is "attracted solely by the prospects of a return" on his investment. *Howey, supra,* 328 U.S. at 300, 66 S.Ct. [1100] at 1103.
>
> *Id.* at 852, 95 S.Ct. at 2060.

It is conceded that the expected payout to a beneficiary will exceed the contributions made by the employer on the employee's behalf (the union member's investment). The resulting gain would commonly be termed a profit. Black's Law Dictionary. However, the Local defendants attempt to discredit this gain as a *Forman* "profit" because, on an amortized basis, some of the gain may be attributable to "pooled" contributions of all participating employers, forfeitures of employees whose pension rights do not vest or to increased contributions negotiated by the union.

Initially it may be noted that gain relative to a security can derive from sources other than the direct efforts of the managers of the common enterprise. In both *SEC v. Koscot Interplanetary,*

20. The International makes the overly facile analogy to *Forman, supra,* that just as the "shareholders" in *Forman* decided whether to live in a particular place, the union members made the decision whether to work for a Teamster shop. It is clear that the union member does not intend to purchase a commodity or realty for personal use; rather he parts with his money in the hope it, through the management of others, can fund his retirement.

21. Defendants do not contest that whatever is expected from the common venture will be solely derived from the efforts of persons other than the venture's investors.

Inc., 497 F.2d 473 (5th Cir. 1974), and *SEC v. Glenn W. Turner Enterprises, Inc.,* 474 F.2d 476 (9th Cir. 1973), *certiorari denied,* 414 U.S. 821, 94 S.Ct. 117, 38 L.Ed.2d 53, the gain present for any particular investor in those pyramid sales schemes had as its source a substantial fraction of the investment of another investor in the scheme. Similarly, the payout to a maturing annuitant in *SEC v. Variable Annuity Life Ins. Co.,* 359 U.S. 65, 79 S.Ct. 618, 3 L.Ed.2d 640, was more likely to derive from investments of new annuitants than from a return on his original investment and the compounded income earned on it.[22] Moreover, realizing a profit from a non-transferable stock option given in exchange for services would depend upon the investor having enough money to exercise the option. *Collins v. Rukin,* 342 F.Supp. 1282 (D.Mass. 1972). Yet in all of these cases the investor's interest was still characterized as a security.

In any event, only a portion of the gain can even arguably derive from non-investment sources. A substantial part of the gain (which even defendants concede to be at least 25%, International Br. at 10-11) will derive from traditional return on the pension fund participant's investment, a dollar-profit element in the form of capital gains, interest, dividends, and other accumulated earnings realized from the trustees' management of the pension fund.[23] For example, the current weekly contribution to the Local 705 pension fund of $24 invested at the current maximum bank interest rate of 7 ½ percent per annum on a compounded basis generates a substantial sum of money. At this rate, over a 20-year career, almost $25,000 is invested and if earnings are accumulated on a tax-deferred basis pursuant to Section 401 of the Internal Revenue Code (26 U.S.C. §401), the profit over capital contribution will be over $33,000. An increase of 1% in return on a pension fund's capital can allow benefits to be increased by 20% (SEC Br. at 11). It is precisely this promise of retirement benefits far in excess of the pensioner's investment that forms the economic inducement to invest in a pension fund.[24]

Recently the district court for the District of Columbia has decided that surviving spouses and dependents of deceased coal miners, who claimed a right to permanent health care coverage by the United Mine Workers, did not have an interest in the United Mine Workers of America 1950 Benefit Plan and Trust, which provides health benefits for active and retired miners, their families, dependents and survivors, that could be deemed to be a "security" under the 1933 or 1934 Acts. *Robinson v. United Mine Workers of America Health and Retirement Funds et al.,* 435 F.Supp. 245, (D.D.C. 1977). Although conceding that the district court's opinion in *Daniel* was distinguishable from his case (435 F.Supp. at 246 n. 1), Judge Gesell in *dicta* disagreed with the reasoning of Judge Kirkland in *Daniel.*

The *Robinson* opinion was based squarely on the gloss *United Housing Foundation v. Forman,* 421 U.S. 837, 95 S.Ct. 2051, 44 L.Ed.2d 621, gives to the term "investment contract" appearing in the securities acts' definitions of "security." Judge Gesell's "reluctance" to find the *Robinson* plaintiffs' interest to be an investment contract was based entirely upon his view that *Forman* foreclosed such a result (435 F.Supp. at 246). *Robinson* is not applicable here.

In no sense could the spouses and dependents of the deceased coal miners in *Robinson* be viewed as investing in the fund since they contributed nothing to the employers in return for the employers' payment of per-tonnage royalties into the trust fund on behalf of and in return for the services of the union miners. The *Robinson* plaintiffs were donees instead of purchasers, so that the requisite *Blue Chip* sale (421 U.S. 723, 95 S.Ct. 1917, 44 L.Ed.2d 539) was lacking.

Unlike *Daniel,* where Local 705 members could affect the employers' payments into the pension

22. Both *Turner* and *Variable Annuity* were cited in *Forman.* The Supreme Court did not speak disapprovingly of either case. 421 U.S. at 852 n. 16 and 857 n. 24, 95 S.Ct. 2051.

23. That this profit element is fixed because pension payments are set at specific levels from time to time is wholly immaterial to gain being profit in the *Forman* sense. A number of instruments which all would concede to be securities (bonds, debentures, etc.), are fixed return.

24. The district court also noted "there is no warranty that the trust will be able to fund the supposedly fixed benefits due to members of the plaintiff class." 410 F. Supp. at 551. This resulting risk was deemed to generate "risk capital" return under *Silver Hills Country Club v. Sobieski,* 55 Cal.2d 811, 13 Cal.Rptr. 186, 361 P.2d 906 (1961). Some doubt as to the validity of the risk capital approach exists. *See Forman,* 421 U.S. at 857 n. 24, 95 S.Ct. [2051] at 2063. Since traditional profits are present in our case, we need not explore the risk capital theory beyond noting that pensioners are far from taking "no risk in any significant sense." *Id.; El Khadem v. Equity Securities Corp.,* 494 F.2d 1224 (9th Cir. 1974), *certiorari denied,* 419 U.S. 900, 95 S.Ct. 183, 42 L.Ed.2d 146.

fund or the allocation of contributions between pension fund payments and current wages by failing to ratify a given contract with set contribution levels, the *Robinson* plaintiffs were powerless to increase or decrease payments or convert them to their personal use. Additionally, there was no expectation of profit in *Robinson,* because benefits were to be paid out of the employers' current contributions to the trust rather than depending on the fund's capital. In *Daniel,* however, funding of the benefit program was crucially dependent on profits from the investment of the fund capital. Further, all the assets of the pension fund not committed to pay out current benefits were invested at risk for profit.

Although the UMW Benefit Plan included retirement benefits for retired miners and lump-sum death benefits to their heirs, only the length of time health care coverage was to be extended to the plaintiffs was in issue in *Robinson.* That case therefore involved merely the consumption of "free" medical care rather than, as in *Daniel,* an actual dollar financial return on investment, *i.e.,* "an expectancy of dollar benefits," which the investor could then use to purchase anything he chose. 421 U.S. at 852-853, 95 S.Ct. 1917.

To declare the *Robinson* plaintiffs' interest in the benefit plan to be a "security" would indeed have required "a degree of creativity unwarranted by the realities of the transactions and the function and purpose of the securities laws" (435 F.Supp. at 246). As already shown, to declare Daniel's interest to be a security does not require such an attempt "to stretch the securities laws beyond their traditional scope" (435 F.Supp. at 247). Finally, the legislative history relied upon in *Robinson* concentrates on the registration provisions of the securities laws rather than the anti-fraud provisions, as discussed more fully *infra.*

Economic Reality

[5] The literal passage of the *Howey* test is only the first hurdle. The definitional sections herein involved are introduced with the phrase "unless the context otherwise requires." This context is, of course, economic reality in view of the surrounding factual circumstances. *Emisco Industries, Inc. v. Pro's, Inc.,* 543 F.2d 38 (7th Cir. 1976). As Mr. Justice Powell explained in *Forman:*

> The primary purpose of the Acts of 1933 and 1934 was to eliminate serious abuses in a largely unregulated securities market. The focus of the Acts is on the capital market of the enterprise system: the sale of securities to raise capital for profit-making purposes, the exchanges on which securities are traded, and the need for regulation to prevent fraud and to protect the interest of investors. Because securities transactions are economic in character Congress intended the application of these statutes to turn on the economic realities underlying a transaction, and not on the name appended thereto. Thus, in construing these Acts against the background of their purpose, we are guided by a traditional canon of statutory construction:
>
> > [A] thing may be within the letter of the statute and yet not within the statute, because not within its spirit, nor within the intention of its makers. *Church v. the Holy Trinity v. United States,* 143 U.S. 457, 459 (1892).
>
> 421 U.S. at 849, 95 S.Ct. at 2059.

If an interest is not a security in economic reality, abuses should be remedied by Congress rather than by an over-liberal extension of the securities laws. *Id.* at 859 n. 26, 95 S.Ct. 2051.

However, the economic inducement for plaintiff's interest in the pension fund was investment for a profit to provide wherewithal in his retirement. This plaintiff's interest in the fund embodies many of the significant characteristics typically present in the instruments concededly covered by the securities acts. *Id.* at 851, 95 S.Ct. 2051. Plaintiff has an undivided interest in the Local 705 Pension Fund consisting of the aggregate of all monies invested on behalf of Local 705 union members by covered employers for whom those members worked. Those monies are managed and invested by the pension fund trustees in stocks, bonds, mortgages and other investments for the sole benefit of Local 705 members. As such, the Local 705 Pension Fund resembles a mutual fund, *viz.,* a pool of money invested for the benefit of the mutual fund shareholder by the fund manager. The amount of payout to any particular member would depend upon his length of service in covered employment, the extent of funding in the plan and the monthly pension determined by the trustees. Their success in money management will be one of the most important factors in determining the amount of payout. A Local 705 member invests $1,248 per year through his employer contributions into that fund. Since an interest in a mutual fund is a security, the interest in a pension fund should also be considered a security. *See* Testimony of SEC Commissioner Purcell. Hearings on Proposed Amendments to the Securities Act of 1933 and the Securities Exchange Act of 1934 before the House Committee on Interstate and Foreign Commerce, 77th Cong., 1st Sess. 895 (1941). Otherwise the trustees of private pension plans with annual employer contributions of $23 billion for the benefit of 30 million employees[25] will be able to mislead their beneficiaries with immunity from the anti-fraud provisions of the 1933 and 1934 Acts.

Not only is plaintiff's interest like an interest in a mutual fund, it is also like an interest in a variable annuity contract. Variable annuity contracts have been held to be securities within the securities laws. *SEC v. Variable Annuity Life Insurance Co.,* 359 U.S. 65, 79 S.Ct. 618, 3 L.Ed.2d 640; *SEC v. United Benefit Life Ins. Co.,* 387 U.S. 202, 87 S.Ct. 1557, 18 L.Ed.2d 673. The securities in *VALIC* and *United Benefit* were investment vehicles designed to provide a return on capital upon retirement. Even though the annuity contract in *VALIC* contained several elements of traditional life insurance and although the flexible fund annuity in *United Benefit* contained a minimum insurance type guarantee, the Court separated the conventional life insurance attributes from the security involved. *See e.g., United Benefit, supra,* at 207, 87 S.Ct. 1557. Similarly, the employment fringe benefit aspect of a pension can be separated from its security aspects. Plaintiff can be both an investor and employee. *See e.g., SEC v. Koscot Interplanetary, Inc.,* 497 F.2d 473, 476 (5th Cir. 1974); *Collins v. Rukin,* 342 F.Supp. 1282 (D.Mass. 1972). As in *VALIC* and *United Benefit,* a Local 705 member is entitled to full disclosure of the material of the enterprise in which his money is put so that he can intelligently appraise the risks involved.

Reduced to fundamentals, economic reality mandates the realization of the immense importance of private pension plans to the American capital markets. As a Senate Report has disclosed:

> In 1940, an estimated four million employees were covered by private pensions; in 1950, the figure had more than doubled to 9.8 million; in 1960, over 21 million employees were covered; and in 1973, approximately *30 million workers participated.* Currently, *one-half* of the industrial work force in the United States are members and participants of private pension plans. It is projected that by 1984, 42.3 million workers will be covered by private pension plans. The growth of the assets owned or controlled by pension funds has closely paralleled this expansive growth. Total estimate assets of pension plans have accelerated from $2.4 billion in 1940 to *$150 billion in 1973* and are increasing at a rate projected to exceed $250 billion by 1980. (Emphasis added.)
>
> S.Rep. No. 93-127, 93rd Cong., 2d Sess. 2-3 (1973).

Because of favorable tax provisions and economies of scale, pension funds are the most efficient way for an employee to invest. N. Ture, The Future of Private Pension Plans 3 (1976). On a relative scale, his pension plan will probably be a Teamster member's largest investment. On an aggregate basis, private pension funds control a huge amount of the capital markets. At the end of 1972, they held 11% in value of all New York Stock Exchange listed stocks and in the same year they accounted for over 23% of the dollar value of all shares traded there. If the sole investment vehicles for tens of millions of Americans which in the aggregate control a quarter or more of the entire capital market are exempt from the anti-fraud provisions of the securities laws, then policing of the capital markets is significantly neutralized.

Legislative History and SEC Interpretation

Not only do the cases support considering this interest as an investment contract, but so do the legislative history and the SEC's interpretation of the securities acts. The legislative history of the 1933 and 1934 Acts themselves is silent on the question of pension plans. However, subsequent legislative action[26] and accompanying SEC interpretation[27] do provide a measure of guidance in construing the 1933 and 1934 Acts.

Thus in 1934, the Senate adopted an amendment to the 1933 Act to exempt from registration

> an offering made solely to employees of an issuer or of its affiliates in connection with a *bona fide plan for the payment of extra compensation* or stock-investment plan for the exclusive benefit of such employees.
>
> 78 Cong.Rec. 8708 (1934). (Emphasis supplied.)

The amendment was eliminated in conference in order to protect participants in such plans who

> may be in as great need of protection afforded by availability of information concerning the issuer for which they work as are most other members of the public.

25. Skolnick, Private Pension Plans, 1950-74, 39 Social Security Bulletin 34 (June 1976).

26. As to the significance of subsequent congressional expressions with respect to the meaning of earlier statutes, *see National Labor Relations Board v. Bell Aerospace Co.,* 416 U.S. 267, 274-275, 94 S.Ct. 1757, 40 L.Ed.2d 134; *Red Lion Broadcasting Co. v. FCC,* 395 U.S. 367, 380-81, 89 S.Ct. 1794, 23 L.Ed.2d 371.

27. As to the significance of subsequent SEC administrative practice with respect to the meaning of the securities laws, *see United States v. National Ass'n of Securities Dealers,* 422 U.S. 694, 725, 95 S.Ct. 2427, 45 L.Ed.2d 436; *Chemehuevi Tribe of Indians v. FPC,* 420 U.S. 395, 409-410, 95 S.Ct. 1066, 43 L.Ed.2d 279.

H.R.Rep. No. 1838, 73d Cong., 2d Sess. at 41 (1934).[28]

In 1941, SEC Commissioner Purcell commented on the 1934 rejection of the Senate amendment as requiring the SEC to interpret the 1933 Act as applying to employee pension funds which involve the sale of securities as "investment contracts."[29] In his view, this included any

> plan under which employees are given the opportunity to place part of their earnings in a fund which is to be invested for their benefit and returned to them at a later date. . . .
>
> 1941 Hearings at 895-896.

Commissioner Purcell also noted that the 1940 Congress was aware of the economic congruence between employee pension plans and ordinary mutual funds because it defined an "employees' security company" as one type of "investment company" in Section 2(a)(13) of the Investment Company Act of 1940. 1941 Hearings at 895. Consequently, an employee pension plan is regulated by the 1940 Act unless it falls within an exemption from registration. *See e.g.,* 15 U.S.C. §§80a-3 (c)(11) and -6(b).

Similarly, the opinion of the Assistant General Counsel of the SEC in 1941 was that "security" within the definition of the 1933 Act included employee pension plans.[30] More recently, former Chairman Cohen of the SEC also has testified on the basis of his own expertise as to the common understanding of a number of institutional investors that interests in a pension plan fall within the definition of a security in the 1933 Act.[31] Like Commissioner Purcell, he explained that is why they had to be specifically exempted from the Investment Company Act of 1940 [15 U.S.C. §80a-3(c)(11)]. Additionally, he commented on the similarities between a pension fund and a mutual fund investment. Accordingly, Professors Mundheim and Henderson have characterized the SEC's interpretation of "security" as used in the securities laws as including an interest in employee pension plans as that "traditionally taken."[32]

[6,7] Congress has evidenced agreement with the SEC's position that interests in pension funds are securities by way of the Investment Companies Amendments Act of 1970. Recognizing that interests in employee pension funds are "securities," in 1970 Congress decided to exempt them from the registration requirements of Section 5 of the 1933 Act (15 U.S.C. §77e) if the employee pension fund was maintained by a bank or in a separate account maintained by an insurance company [15 U.S.C. §77c(a)(2)(A)].[33]

---

28. Since the 1934 Act was passed by the same Congress that passed the 1933 Act, this legislative history is tantamount to being actual 1933 Act history and should be credited accordingly. *Techerepnin v. Knight,* 389 U.S. 332, 336, 342, 88 S.Ct. 548, 19 L.Ed.2d 564.

Recently, class action suits against employee profit-sharing plans have charged that the managers of these plans have failed in their responsibilities by investing too much in the employer's own stocks. "Employees' Wrath Hits Profit-Sharing Plans," *Bus. Week,* July 18, 1977 at 25.

29. Hearings on Proposed Amendments to the Securities Act of 1933 and the Securities Exchange Act of 1934 before the House Committee on Interstate and Foreign Commerce, 77th Cong., 1st Sess. 895-896 (1941) (1941 Hearings).

30. Opinion of Assistant General Counsel of SEC [41-44 Transfer Binder] CCH Fed.Sec.L. Rep. ¶75,195 (1941).

31. Hearings on S. 3598 before the Subcommittee on Labor of the Senate Committee on Labor and Public Welfare, 92 Cong., 2d Sess. 231 (1972). In those hearings, Mr. Cohen included Ch. VII of the Summary Volume of the SEC's 1971 *Institutional Investor Study* which states that interests of participants in employee pension plans meet the definition of security in the 1933 Act. *See also* Interim Report, Senate Committee on Labor and Public Welfare S.Rep.No. 92-634, 92nd Cong., 2d Sess. 96 (1972). The defendants concede the SEC has treated interests in pension funds as securities since 1971 (Rep. Br. at 5).

32. Mundheim and Henderson, Applicability of the Federal Securities Laws to Pension and Profit Sharing Plans, 29 Law and Contemp. Prob. 795, 811 (1964). The defendants and some *amici* rely on comments by Congressman Wolverton, a member of the House Committee that reported the 1933 and 1934 Acts, sitting on the Committee before which Commissioner Purcell was testifying, that he did not believe Congress intended to regulate pensions under the securities laws. 1941 Hearings, at 870-871, 878, 888, 913. Although the 1934 Congress did not specifically focus on pension funds, the 1934 abortive Senate amendment does show Congress did have some forms of employee security plans in mind. Certainly, the definition of security adopted is broad enough to include the plans.

Moreover, the statements by Congressman Wolverton deal with "supervision" or "regulation" under the 1933 Act, *viz.,* registration. But as we show in the opinion, the registration provisions of the 1933 Act do not apply to securities consisting of interests in pension plans. It might be that a realization of this fact will calm concerns about undue "regulation of employee benefit plans." Statement of Representative Dent, 174 D.L.R. at A-6 (BNA, Sept. 7, 1976).

33. The exemption comprehends, in pertinent part:

> Except as hereinafter expressly provided, the provisions of this title shall not apply to any of the following classes of *securities:*
>
> . . . . .

This exemption was to codify the long established administrative practice of the Commission in exempting certain pension funds from the registration requirements of the 1933 Act. H.R.Rep. No. 91-1631, 91st Cong., 2nd Sess. 31 (1970). U.S. Code Cong. & Admin. News 1970, p. 4897, 4943. A similar exemption amendment was provided with respect to the 1934 Act. 15 U.S.C. §78c(a)(12).[34] This action of course shows that Congress considered such pension funds to be securities that would not exempt from registration absent the 1970 Amendments. Therefore, if the Local 705 Pension Fund is being maintained by a bank,[35] the interests involved here would be securities exempt from registration. However, exemption from registration and reporting requirements does not mean exemption from Section 17(a) of the 1933 Act, Section 10(b) of the 1934 Act and Rule 10b-5 thereunder, as the House Committee on Interstate and Foreign Commerce realized in its report.[36] *See also* 15 U.S.C. §77q(c).

Defendants and the *amici* who support their

---

any interest or participation in a single or collective trust fund maintained by a bank or in a separate account maintained by an insurance company which interest or participation is issued in connection with (A) a stock bonus, pension, or profit-sharing plan which meets the requirements for qualification under section 401 of Title 26, or (B) an annuity plan which meets the requirements for the deduction of the employer's contribution under section 404(a)(2) of Title 26, *other than* any plan described in clause (A) or (B) of this paragraph (i) the contributions under which are held in a single trust fund maintained by a bank or in a separate account maintained by an insurance company for a single employer and under which an amount in excess of the employer's contribution is allocated to the purchase of securities (*other than interests or participations in the trust or separate account itself*) issued by the employer or by any company directly or indirectly controlling, controlled by or under common control with the employer or (ii) which covers employees some or all of whom are employees within the meaning of section 401(c)(1) of Title 26. The Commission, by rules and regulations or order, shall exempt from the provisions of section 77e of this title any interest or participation issued in connection with a stock bonus, pension, profit-sharing, or annuity plan which covers employees some or all of whom are employees within the meaning of section 401(c)(1) of Title 26, if and to the extent that the Commission determines this to be necessary or appropriate in the public interest and consistent with the protection of investors and the purposes fairly intended by the policy and provisions of this subchapter.

(Emphasis supplied).

34. The 1934 Act provision provides:

The term "exempted security" or "exempted securities" includes—

any interest or participation in a collective trust fund maintained by a bank or in a separate account maintained by an insurance company which interest or participation is issued in connection with (A) a stock-bonus pension, or profit-sharing plan which meets the requirements for qualification under section 401 of Title 26, or (B) an annuity plan which meets the requirements for the deduction of the employer's contribution under section 404(a)(2) of Title 26, other than any plan described in clause (A) or (B) of this paragraph which covers employees some or all of whom are employees within the meaning of section 401(c)(1) of Title 26; and such other securities (which may include, among others, unregistered securities the market in which is predominantly intrastate) as the Commission may, by such rules and regulations as it deems necessary or appropriate in the public interest or for the protection of investors, either unconditionally or upon specified terms and conditions or for stated periods, exempt from the operation of any one or more provisions of this chapter which by their terms do not apply to an "exempted security" or to "exempted securities."

This provision specifically exempts only interests in collective trust funds while the 1933 Act exemption includes interests in single funds. However, the final clause of the exemption quoted above gives the SEC plenary authority to exempt other securities from the reporting requirements of the 1934 Act. The comments of the General Counsel of the SEC speaking for the Commission in argument before us suggest the SEC in the exercise of this power has decided that interests in pension funds are "exempted securities" under the 1934 Act.

However, under the 1933 Act the SEC's interpretative and quasi-legislative powers are limited by Section 3(b) which provides "no issue of securities shall be exempted under this subsection where the aggregate amount at which such issue is offered to the public exceeds $500,000" [15 U.S.C. §77c(b)]. Accordingly, in order to achieve exempted status for securities such as interests in pension funds under the 1933 Act, Congress could not rely on SEC administrative practice being binding as it could under the 1934 Act. Thus the wording differences between the 1933 and 1934 Act represent a need to codify the administrative practice under the 1933 Act.

35. A large portion of Local 705's Pension Fund is maintained by the trust departments of major Chicago banks. *See* note 61, *infra.* Plaintiffs represent that "because most employee pension plans are bank maintained, registration is not required for most employee pension plans" (Pl. Br. at 37-38).

36. Report of the House Committee on Interstate and Foreign Commerce on the Investment Company Amendments Act of 1970. H.Rep. No. 91-1382, 91st Cong., 2d Sess. 10, 43 (1970).

position seek to downplay the importance of the 1970 Amendments by arguing that the 1970 exemption relates only to the sale of interests in certain bank collective trust funds and insurance company separate accounts for pension funds, claiming that the sale to employees of interests in the underlying pension fund is entirely outside the scope of the 1970 Act. However, these arguments relate to legislative history concerning an earlier version of the Act which referred only to "collective" trust funds. A close study of the legislative history shows that the version of the Act which was finally adopted contemplated the interests sold to employees in the underlying pension fund.

The principal stimulus for the amendment to the 1933 Act in 1970 was to settle the legal status of certain commingled investment accounts maintained by banks and insurance companies.[37] As a result the early versions of the bill only exempted:

> any interest or participation in a *collective* trust fund maintained by a bank or in a separate account maintained by an insurance company which interest or participation is issued in connection with . . . a stock bonus, pension, or profit-sharing plan which meets the requirements for qualification under section 401 of the Internal Revenue Code of 1954
> (emphasis added).

See e.g., S. 34, 91st Cong., 1st Sess. 65 (1969), reprinted in S. Comm. on Banking and Currency, *Analysis of S. 34,* 91st Cong., 1st Sess. 119 (1969). After the Senate passed a bill containing this language, the General Counsel of the Sperry-Rand Corporation wrote a letter to the House Subcommittee considering the legislation, pointing out that the bill did not exempt interests in single trust funds. Hearings Before a Subcommittee of the House Committee on Interstate and Foreign Commerce, 91st Cong., 1st Sess., Part 2 at 929-931. His suggestion was to add the language "or any employees' stock bonus, pension or profit-sharing trust" after "separate account maintained by an insurance company."

In response to this suggestion, the Subcommittee reported out a bill with the added phrase "single or" to precede the phrase "collective trust fund maintained by a bank." This version, later passed by the House, thereby altered the focus of the exemption to encompass interests in the underlying pension funds. The Conference Report went along with the House version:

> The Senate bill exempted from the registration requirements of the 1933 Act certain collective trust funds maintained by a bank or in a separate account maintained by an insurance company.
>
> The House amendment would have codified a long established administrative practice of the Commission by making it clear that this exemption applied not only to collective trust funds, but also to single trust funds.
>
> The conference agreement follows the House version.
>
> H.R.Rep. No. 91-1631, 91st Cong., 2d Sess. 31 (1970), U.S.Code Cong. & Admin. News 1970, p. 4947.

Two subsequent changes in the language of the exemption show the shift to include interests in the underlying plans. Although the Conference Committee generally adopted the House version, it did include a small modification. Since the House provision exempted interests in all pension funds, it was contrary to the SEC's administrative position that non-registration of pension interests did not apply in all situations. In particular, the SEC required registration where an amount in excess of the employer's contribution to a pension fund is allocated to the purchase by the fund of securities issued by the employer. In order to conform the exemption, a provision was included to exclude the above situation from exemption. *Id.* at 24.

This exclusion generated another legislative fillip. The exclusion applied when the excess was used to purchase securities issued by the employer. Since interests in pension funds are themselves securities, the exclusion could potentially be interpreted to require registration of all pension plans where any money is contributed to the pension plan directly by employees, since they could be conceptualized as buying securities.[38] Accordingly, Section 3(a)(2) of the 1933 Act was amended one week after the passage of the 1970 Amendments to make it clear that the term "security issued by the employer" did not include the secu-

37. "Banks maintaining these collective funds would solicit money from various institutional investment vehicles, including pension funds, and would promise to commingle the funds to take advantage of the economies of size that could be gained in the securities market and the investment expertise of the bank's analysts. Since an interest in such collective funds held by an individual pension fund is a security and the bank collective fund an investment company, efforts were made to exempt this security from the registration provisions of the Securities Act and the collective fund from the Investment Company Act." (SEC Br. 32 n. 40).

38. "In particular, there was concern that where an insurance company maintained a separate account to fund pension benefits for its own employees, interests in such an account might be considered securities issued by the employer" (SEC Br. 34 n. 44).

rities consisting of the interests in the pension fund. *See* 116 Cong.Rec. 40608 (Dec. 9, 1970).

Therefore the 1970 Amendments show that Congress intended to conform the 1933 Act to the SEC's administrative view that, although interests in pension funds did not need to be registered in most cases, they are nonetheless securities. *See* 116 Cong.Rec. 33287 (Sept. 23, 1970). When conjoined with the above-detailed legislative history and SEC interpretation, the 1970 Amendments provide substantial support for the proposition that an interest in an employee pension fund is a security.

Policy

Perhaps the main reason that pension plans are not specifically mentioned in the legislative history of the 1933 and 1934 Acts themselves is the fact that in the early 1930's pension plans were still a rarity. In the early decades of the 20th century, only 38% of invested capital was invested indirectly, and of this amount only 1/10 of 1% was invested in pension funds. By 1962, the indirect sector of the capital markets had jumped to 83% and pensions constituted 27% of this amount. Hearings Before the Subcommittee on Fiscal Policy, U.S. Cong. Joint Economic Committee, 91st Cong., 2d Sess. 17-18 (1970). Since 1955, the asset value of pension plans has exceeded the total accumulated by the other three major institutional investors: mutual funds, life insurance companies and property and liability insurance companies. We are informed by an *amicus curiae* that the book value of private pension plan assets is $216.9 billion, the largest single source of private investment capital in the economy.

Because employee pension plans are now the major, if not sole, form of investment for most American workers to provide for their old age and because of the now crucial role that such plans play in today's capital markets, they are just the sort of investment vehicle that the securities acts were passed to regulate. To proclaim that the securities laws encompass securities consisting of interests in pension plans is "quite consistent with the congressional enactment and with the role of the federal judiciary in interpreting it. . . ." *Blue Chip Stamps v. Manor Drug Stores,* 421 U.S. 723, 737, 95 S.Ct. 1917, 1926, 44 L.Ed.2d 539. The type of fraud allegedly perpetrated on the plaintiff is among those the securities laws were passed to prevent and remedy.

Of course, the normal scheme of the securities acts require registration as well as providing antifraud remedies. However, as demonstrated above, the 1970 Amendments codified the SEC's practice of exempting pension funds from the registration requirements of the 1933 Act. Thus declaring an interest in a pension fund to be a security will not subject any plans to registration which are not already so subject. Consequently, since the antifraud provisions do not impose an undue burden on anyone, they should be available to employees to remedy fraud. Mundheim and Henderson, *supra,* at 814. The proper inquiry then is not whether interests in employee pension plans are securities but rather why such a vital investment vehicle should be nevertheless excluded from the protection of the securities laws. We now turn to this inquiry.

Plaintiff's Security Was Acquired in a "Sale"

[8] Defendants maintain that even if the plaintiff's interest is a security, his cause of action is defeated because he did not acquire it in a sale.

The 1933 Act defines "sale" as including

> every . . . disposition of a security or interest in a security, for value
> [15 U.S.C. §77b(3)]

and the 1934 Act defines "sale" as including "any contract to sell or otherwise dispose of" [15 U.S.C. §78c(a)(14)]. Accordingly, in both Acts, a "sale" of an interest in a pension fund depends upon whether there has been a disposition of it. Here plaintiff acquired an interest in the Local 705 Pension Fund, and as shown, that interest is a security. Therefore, there necessarily has been a disposition of a security to plaintiff within the scope of the two Acts. The 1933 Act also requires that the disposition be "for value." Here plaintiff's giving of his services and the employer's contribution on behalf of the employee constitutes value, thereby meeting the "for value" requirement. *See* S.Rep. No. 1440, 85th Cong., 2d Sess. 4 (1958), U.S.Code Cong. & Admin. News, p. 4137. From the employee's viewpoint, the contributions to the pension fund are part of his compensation and the value flows from him to that extent.[39] From the employer's viewpoint, the con-

39. Union spokesmen for both the United Auto Workers and the Teamsters have testified that pensions are deferred wages which are given high priority in collective bargaining. As to the UAW, *see* Hearings before the Senate Subcommittee on Private Pension Plans of the Committee on Finance, 93d Cong., 1st Sess. 467 (1973). As to the Teamsters, *see* Hearings before the Special Subcommittee on Labor, House Committee on Education and Labor, 87th Cong., 1st Sess. 225 (1961). This was the recurrent theme emerging from the ERISA

tribution flows from the employer, constituting a part of the employee's compensation package. In either event, value has been given for a security, so that erection of a direct-indirect dichotomy is unwarranted. *SEC v. Harwyn Industries Corp.,* 326 F.Supp. 943, 954-955 (S.D.N.Y. 1971, Mansfield, J.); *see also Hector v. Wiens,* 533 F.2d 429, 431-433 (9th Cir. 1976); *cf. Pete v. United Mine Workers,* 170 U.S.App.D.C. 1, 517 F.2d 1275, 1287 (D.C.Cir. 1976).

The defendants maintain there is a controlling conceptual distinction between "non-contributory" plans and plans where the employee first receives cash and then pays over such cash into the pension fund. We refuse to subscribe to undue literalism. An employee's performance of services satisfies the for value requirement of the 1933 Act. *See Collins v. Rukin,* 342 F.Supp. 1282 (D.Mass. 1972); *SEC v. Addison,* 194 F.Supp. 709 (N.D.Tex. 1961); *Lawrence v. SEC,* 398 F.2d 276 (1st Cir. 1968); *see also Truncale v. Blumberg,* 88 F.Supp. 677 (S.D.N.Y. 1950); *Hector, supra,* at 432. Recent SEC interpretations also support the view that an interest in a non-contributory plan is gained for value. *Oklahoma National Gas Co.* [71-72 Transfer Binder] CCH Fed.Sec.L.Rep. ¶78,583 (1971); *Allis-Chalmers Corp.* [72-73 Transfer Binder] CCH Fed.Sec.L.Rep. ¶78,803; *Keene Corp.* [71-72 Transfer Binder] CCH Fed. Sec.L.Rep. ¶78,475; *Missouri Research Laboratories, Inc.* [72-73 Transfer Binder] CCH Fed. Sec.L.Rep. ¶79,036.

[9] Defendants argue that there can be no sale because the contribution to the pension fund is compulsory. However, the definitions of "sale" in the 1933 and 1934 Acts do not require volition. In any case, volition is present to the extent that Local 705 members voted whether or not to accept the collective bargaining contract containing this pension fund and whether to ratify subsequent agreements governing the level of employer contributions into the fund or seek dismissal of union officers or the unlikely radical measure of decertification of the Union.[40] Similarly, in the corporate merger context (where a vote by the shareholders to merge is binding notwithstanding any individual shareholder's vote to the contrary), cases under the anti-fraud provisions have held that a sale occurs where there is no voluntary action by the alleged purchaser. *Vine v. Beneficial Finance Co.,* 374 F.2d 627, 635 (2d Cir. 1967); *Zeller v. Bogue Electric Manufacturing Corp.,* 476 F.2d 795 (2d Cir. 1973); *International Controls Corp. v. Vesco,* 490 F.2d 1334 (2d Cir. 1974), *certiorari denied,* 417 U.S. 932, 94 S.Ct. 2644, 41 L.Ed.2d 236. The volition argument in a no-sale conclusion in the merger context, which was used only in the registration milieu, was derived from SEC Rule 133 [33 C.F.R. §230-133 (1964)] but it was rescinded in 1972. In rescinding that rule, the Commission characterized that rationale as "only correct in the formalistic sense" in that it "overlooks the reality of the transaction." As the SEC pointed out, the "corporate action . . . is not some type of independent fiat, but is only the aggregate effect of the voluntary decisions made by the individual stockholders. . . ." 37 Fed.Reg. 23631, 23632 (Nov. 7, 1972). To like effect, the Local 705 Pension Fund contributions are not an independent employer fiat but rather represent the aggregate effect of the union members.

[Employment Retirement Income Security Act] hearings as well:

> An important theme which emerged from Subcommittee hearings related to the basic dichotomy in the rationale for a pension plan. Repeatedly, witnesses volunteered testimony that they regarded their pension benefits as deferred wages. Since labor negotiations resulting in wage increases through collective bargaining invariably include some consideration of pension benefits, employees believe that had pensions not been included in the settlement package, they would have received higher wage commitments.
>
> S.Rep. No. 92-634, Interim Report of Activities of the Pension Welfare and Pension Plan Study, 1971, 92d Cong., 2d Sess. 75 (1972).

40. The Teamsters maintain that a local whose constitution requires member ratification of pension plan agreements such as 705's is a rarity. Be that as it may, in our mobile society, an employee will be faced with a number of employment decisions during his career, and as he ages, such shifts will be more and more affected by the pension plan offered by a prospective employer. Accordingly, an employee may be faced with a meaningful decision even in the case of a compulsory plan whether to acquire interests in the pension fund. *See* Note, *supra,* 70 Harv.L.Rev. at 494. Needless to say, this construct does not render the individual employee a party to the bargain with the employer in the technical labor law sense. In this sense, the Union remains the exclusive agent.

Amicus ERIC suggests that if ratification is the doctrinal reed upon which a finding of volition is hung, unions will quickly eliminate ratification votes. First, we have shown that volition can exist even if ratification does not. But in any event, volition is not necessary for a sale under the securities acts. Even in a worst-case analysis, movement away from contract ratification would probably be limited. Elimination would require constitutional amendment which would presumably be difficult to achieve, requiring, in effect, a vote to weaken union democracy.

Also, plaintiff's affidavit shows that he would not have worked for a Local 705 covered employer if he had been advised about the continuous nature of the 20-year requirement before receiving a pension. When an employee decides to retain his job, his decision results in his continuing to give value in the future and in his further acquisition of interests in the pension fund.

In its brief as *amicus curiae,* the SEC has persuasively shown why it formerly reached a different result for the purposes of the 1933 Act's registration provisions in the case of plans that are either non-contributory or compulsory. It was reasoned that there was no sale involved for a non-contributory plan because there was no direct investment of money by the employee, consistent with the then current legal view that the employer's contributions were gifts. Although the SEC recognized that an individual had a choice whether to become or remain an employee, it was thought that the choice would never turn on representation concerning the pension plan.[41] Therefore compulsory plans were not considered to involve sales. Testimony of Commissioner Purcell, 1941 Hearings at 896-897; Opinion letter of the Assistant General Counsel of the SEC, 1 CCH Fed. Sec. L.Rep. ¶2105.53; Testimony of Chairman Cohen, Hearings on Amendment No. 438 to S. 1659 Before the Senate Committee on Banking and Currency, 90th Cong., 1st Sess., part 3, at 1326 (1967). *See also* 3 SEC Institutional Investor Study 980 quoted in Rep. Br. at 7-8.

These positions were never taken as to the anti-fraud provisions and are no longer viable even as to the registration provisions because non-contributory pensions are no longer viewed as a mere gift. Even though the Commission had in the past applied a no-sale rule to pension trusts as to the registration requirements of the 1933 Act, that rule was not administratively and should not be judicially applied to the anti-fraud provisions of both Acts. *SEC v. National Securities, Inc.,* 393 U.S. 453, 465-466, 86 S.Ct. 564, 21 L.Ed.2d 668. The purposes of the registration and anti-fraud provisions differ (*The Exchange National Bank of Chicago v. Touche Ross & Co.,* 544 F.2d 1126, 1139 [2d Cir. 1976]), so that a narrow view of "sale" would be most inappropriate as to fraudulent activity. *Collins v. Rukin,* 342 F.Supp. 1282, 1287-1288 (D.Mass. 1972). Since "sale" as used in the two securities laws is not limited to transactions covered by the commercial law of sales but is to be broadly construed in view of the need for anti-fraud protection,[42] we conclude that the present disposition to plaintiff falls within the definitions of sale in the two statutes. *See Dasho v. Susquehanna Corp.,* 380 F.2d 262, 266-267, 269 (7th Cir. 1967).[43]

---

41. This is invalid in our case because Daniel's affidavit reveals material reliance on pension benefits in retaining his job. Moreover, now that pension benefits have become such an important part of the total wage package, this conclusion has little, if any, general application. *See* S.Rep. No. 1734, Welfare and Pension Plan Investigation, 84th Cong., 2d Sess. 11-13 (1956); Hearings before the Special Subcommittee on Labor, House Committee on Education and Labor, 87th Cong., 1st Sess. 32 (1961); Hearings before the Subcommittee on Labor, Senate Committee on Labor and Public Welfare, 92d Cong., 2d Sess. 99 (1972). Pensions are second only to wages as a reason for membership rejection of settlement proposals and are well ahead of such factors as vacations, hours and overtime, working conditions and seniority. Simkin, Union Membership Rejection of Contract Settlements, Labor Relations Yearbook 332, 342 (IPIR Br. at 13).

42. As one industry spokesman has testified:

> The magnitude of the investment employers make in pension benefits for employees, encourages the tendency to present the plan in the most positive terms possible so that a return in positive employee attitudes can be realized on the investment. This leads to over simplification and an advertising sales approach. When, as is so often the case, the communication material is prepared by persons not thoroughly cognizant of the technical and legal nature of plan provisions, the result can easily become a document subject to criticism as incomplete and misleading.

Testimony of Ernest Griffes on behalf of the American Society for Personnel Administration, Hearings before the Subcommittee on Labor, Senate Committee on Labor and Public Welfare, 93d Cong., 1st Sess. 765 (1973).

43. *Blue Chip Stamps v. Manor Drug Stores,* 421 U.S. 723, 95 S.Ct. 1917, 44 L.Ed.2d 539 on which defendants rely, reaffirmed the *Birnbaum* rule (note 17 *supra*) that liability under Section 10(b) of the 1933 Act and Rule 10b-5 requires a purchaser and seller. It does not weaken our holding in *Dasho* that "sale" in the securities laws is a comprehensive term not to be narrowly construed. Similarly, *Alabama Power Co. v. Davis,* —U.S.—, 97 S.Ct. 2002, 52 L.Ed.2d 595, is not contrary to the opinion below. That case merely categorizes pension plans as a compensation for length of service rather than for daily services rendered as required under the prevailing conceptualization on employee rights given returning veterans under the Military Selective Service Act. Although *Hurn v. Retirement Trust Fund,* 424 F.Supp. 80 (C.D.Ca. 1977), and *Wiens v. International Brotherhood of Teamsters,* BNA Sec. Reg. and L.Rep. No. 397 at A-13 (C.D.Ca. 1977) (where the district judge gave his ruling from the bench), support defendants, neither contains an in-depth discussion and we respectfully decline to follow them.

Section 17(a) of the 1933 Act Creates a Private Cause of Action

[10,11] It is now well settled that Section 10(b) of the 1934 Act and Rule 10b-5 give rise to a private right of action for the breach of its substantive terms. *Blue Chip Stamps v. Manor Drug Stores,* 421 U.S. 723, 730-731, 95 S.Ct. 1917, 44 L.Ed.2d 539. The existence of a private right of action under Section 17(a) of the 1933 Act is not as universally admitted. *Id.* at 733 n. 6, 95 S.Ct. 1917. Since we proceed on the assumption that the operative provisions of the anti-fraud sections of the 1933 and 1934 Acts are identical for the purposes of this lawsuit, the validity of our unitary analysis requires that we deem Section 17(a) of the 1933 Act as creating a private action under the facts of this case.

As a preliminary matter, Judge Kirkland rejected Local 705's and Peick's argument that Section 17(a) of the Securities Act of 1933 does not create a private cause of action, 410 F.Supp. at 546. In the court below and in its principal brief here, no argument was presented by the International Brotherhood as to the existence or non-existence of a private cause of action under Section 17(a). The language of Section 17(a) [15 U.S.C. §77q(a)] is certainly broad enough to imply such a right. In fact, Section 17(a) is more specific than Section 10(b) of the Securities Exchange Act of 1934 [15 U.S.C. §78j(b)] under which private rights of action have been commonly approved. *See Blue Chip Stamps v. Manor Drug Stores,* 421 U.S. 723, 730, 95 S.Ct. 1917, 44 L.Ed.2d 539. Accordingly in another opinion by the same district court as below, Judge McGarr also held that Section 17(a) impliedly calls for a private right of action. *Local 734 Trust v. Continental Illinois National Bank & Trust Co.,* [73-74 Transfer Binder] CCH Fed.Sec.L.Rep. ¶94,565 at 95,963 (N.D.Ill. 1974). After noting that various courts have expressly recognized the existence of such a remedy while others have assumed it, the *Local 734 Trust* court concluded "there seems to be little practical value in denying the existence of a private action under §17 once [as here] it is established that a plaintiff has an action under §10(b) of the 1934 Act."[44]

44. For similar rulings by the court below, *see Freed v. Szabo Food Service, Inc.,* [61-64 Transfer Binder] CCH Fed.Sec.L.Rep. ¶91,317 (N.D.Ill. 1964); *Schaefer v. First National Bank of Lincolnwood,* 326 F.Supp. 1186, 1190 (N.D.Ill. 1970), *affirmed in this respect,* 509 F.2d 1287, 1293 (1975); *contra, Reid v. Mann,* 381 F.Supp. 525, 526-528 (N.D.Ill. 1974), noting the divergence of opinion on the subject.

In *Surowitz v. Hilton Hotels Corp.,* 342 F.2d 596, 604 (7th Cir. 1965), reversed on other grounds, 383 U.S. 363, 86 S.Ct. 845, 15 L.Ed.2d 807, we first assumed there was a private cause of action under Section 17(a), for Judge Major stated "[t]he plain language of that Section convinces us that any cause of action arising under that Section is a right of the person injured by the acts and practices therein proscribed." In *Schaefer v. First National Bank of Lincolnwood,* 509 F.2d 1287, 1293 (7th Cir. 1975), this Court squarely held that Section 17(a) permits a private cause of action, stating:

> Since [as here] fraud as well as negligence has been alleged and the section 10(b) claim established, plaintiffs' section 17 claim will be allowed to stand.[45]

[12,13] In Local 705's main brief before us, the Section 17(a) point is only mentioned in passing (Br. 21). Similarly, in their joint reply brief, defendants do "not particularize with respect to the non-applicability of [Section 17(a)]" (Reply Br. 8 n. 19). Defendants there observed that the 1933 Act relates to the initial issuance of securities and the 1934 Act relates to the resale market and then reasoned that Section 17(a) is the only anti-fraud provision even possibly applicable here.[46] Finally, the reply brief states that defen-

45. In *Globus v. Law Research Service, Inc.,* 418 F.2d 1276, 1283-1284 (2d Cir. 1969), *certiorari denied,* 397 U.S. 913, 90 S.Ct. 913, 25 L.Ed.2d 93, the Second Circuit decided there was a cause of action under Section 17(a) because there was "little practical point in denying the existence of an action under §17 once it is established that an aggrieved buyer has a private action under §10(b) of the 1934 Act." The court cited many authorities upholding a private right of action for a violation of Section 17(a).

46. As Judge Friendly has noted, *"courts have shrunk from a literal reading that* would extend the reach of the statutes beyond what could reasonably be thought to have been intended in these two great pieces of legislation and *would produce a seemingly irrational difference in the scope of their anti-fraud provisions." Exchange Nat. Bank, supra,* at 1133. (Emphasis supplied.) Here the security is plaintiff's interest in the pension plan. These interests generically arose when the pension plan was first formed for the benefit of Local 705 members. This was the primary distribution of the securities. Since Daniel was a member of Local 705 at this time, he has standing to sue for fraud in the primary distribution under Section 17(a) of the 1933 Act. Each year Daniel paid more value into the fund and from time to time plan amendments were effected which Daniel claims contributed to his being defrauded. This is the conceptual predicate for finding a secondary distribution under Section 10(b) of the 1934 Act.

dants "raise but do not argue the absence of an implied right of private action under Section 17(a)" (*ibid.* n. 9). In sum, defendants either do not contest or only weakly contest the existence of a private right of action under Section 17(a) where a "sale" of a "security" is present. Having decided that the definitions of a "sale" and "security" have been met by this complaint, we reaffirm *Schaefer* and therefore hold that Section 17(a) permits Count II to proceed.[47]

The Anti-fraud Provisions of the Federal Securities Laws Have Not Been Preempted by ERISA

[14] The defendants[48] and the *amici* who support their position urge that the Employee Retirement Income Security Act of 1974 (ERISA) has repealed the anti-fraud provisions of the 1933 and 1934 Acts insofar as they apply to union pension funds. Since we have concluded that the securities laws apply to a union member's interest in his pension fund, preemption may only be declared in the face of an explicit repealer provision or the most cogent repugnancy between the securities and pension regulatory schemes. *Cf. Gordon v. New York Stock Exchange,* 422 U.S. 659, 682-683, 95 S.Ct. 2598, 45 L.Ed.2d 463. Neither of these triggering conditions for preemption of the securities laws is present in this case.

Section 514(d)[49] of ERISA [29 U.S.C. §1144 (d)] is a general savings clause which provides that ERISA shall not be construed to supersede any federal law or rule thereunder. At the same time, Congress preserved state securities laws [29 U.S.C. §1144(b)(2)(A)] in Section 514(b)(2)(A)[50] and they generally do not exempt pension interests from their anti-fraud provisions.[51] Thus ERISA's own savings clause by its own terms strongly suggests that preemption was not intended.

The defendants attempt to counter the statute's explicit terms by arguing that since it was universally believed pension funds were outside the scope of the securities acts, Congress saw no need to explicitly exempt a truism. But *see Jones v. Alfred H. Mayer Co.,* 392 U.S. 409, 416 n. 20, 437, 88 S.Ct. 2186, 20 L.Ed.2d 1189. Defendants strain for support in the legislative history of the various pension regulatory acts. But all of the sources cited by the defendants[52] support only the proposition that

> Pension and profit sharing plans are exempt from coverage under the Securities Act of 1933 (15 U.S.C. 77 *et seq.*), unless the plan is a voluntary contributory pension plan and invests in the securities of the employer company an amount greater than that paid into the plan by the employer. A voluntary contributory plan is one to which both the employee and the employer contribute and in which employees voluntarily participate. If the plan's investment in the employer's securities exceeds the employer's contribution, both the employer's securities and the interest in the plan must be *registered* under the Securities Acts with the SEC.
>
> Interim Report of the Private Welfare and Pension Plan Study, 1971, S.Rep. No. 92-634 of the 92d Cong., 2d Sess. 96 (emphasis supplied).

Herein lies the defendants' quintessential error. They confuse the requirements of the 1933 Act's

---

47. In *Sanders v. John Nuveen & Co., Inc.,* 554 F.2d 790 (7th Cir. 1977), we found it unnecessary to decide whether a private right of action exists under Section 17(a) when it is not accompanied by a viable Rule 10b-5 claim (at 795). Where, as here, the Section 17(a) count accompanies a viable Rule 10b-5 count, *Sanders* requires proof of *scienter* under Section 17(a) (at 795).

48. In the court below, the International Brotherhood conceded that ERISA does not exempt "employee pension plans from the Federal Securities Laws, either expressly or by implied repeal." International's Sup. Memo. in support of Its Motion to Dismiss at 4 (Oct. 9, 1975).

49. Section 514(d) provides in pertinent part:

> Nothing in [ERISA] . . . shall be construed to alter, amend, modify, invalidate, impair, or supersede any law of the United States . . . or any rule or regulation issued under any such law.

50. Section 514(b)(2)(A) provides in pertinent part:

> [N]othing in this title shall be construed to exempt or relieve any person from any law of any State which regulates . . . securities.

51. The Illinois Securities Law of 1953 defines a security, for our purposes, in terms identical to the federal acts. 1975 Ill.Rev.Stat. Ch. 121½, Section 137.2-1. Pension interests are covered by the definition since "securities issued by or pursuant to . . . employee pension trusts or plans" are freed from registration requirements. 1975 Ill.Rev.Stat. Ch. 121½, Section 137.30. A similar definition of security and exemption from registration is included in the Uniform Securities Act which has been adopted in 32 jurisdictions. 7 Uniform Laws Ann., Uniform Securities Act §§501(1) and 402(a)(11) (1970) and Cumulative Annual Pocket Part at 342 (1976).

52. S.Rep. No. 1440, 85th Cong., 2d Sess. reprinted in 3 U.S.Code Cong. & Admin. News p. 4145 (1958); Welfare and Pension Plans Investigation, Hearings before the Senate Subcomm. on Labor and Public Welfare, 84th Cong., 1st Sess. 943-945 (1955); S.Rep. No. 1734, 84th Cong., 2d Sess. 57, 60 (1956); 3 U.S.Code Cong. & Admin. News, 93d Cong., 2d Sess. pp. 4649, 4863 (1974); *id.* at 4641-4643, 4840-4842, 4847. *See Mundheim* and *Henderson, supra,* at 837.

registration provisions with the anti-fraud provisions of the 1933 and 1934 Acts. The registration provisions are designed to assure that investors will be furnished with all material information concerning an informed investment decision. The mechanism to implement this objective includes filing of a registration statement and the delivery of a prospectus containing detailed information about the security and its issuer. In contradistinction, the anti-fraud provisions do not establish an affirmative disclosure system requiring the filing of documents. Rather the anti-fraud provisions are essentially a generalized self-executing prohibition against fraudulent activity. There is no invitation "to create a federal common law governing the management of pension plans." *Lugo v. Employers Retirement Fund,* 529 F.2d 251, 255 (2d Cir. 1976), *certiorari denied,* 429 U.S. 826, 97 S.Ct. 81, 50 L.Ed.2d 88.

The fact that the SEC has historically advocated[53] a hands-off approach to the regulation of pension plans with respect to disclosure requirements holds no brief for exempting pension plans from the anti-fraud provisions of the securities acts. Nor does the fact that ERISA provides for disclosure of a plethora of information after its effective date of January 1, 1975,[54] and that it heavily regulates the pension industry *ipso facto* dictate that pension funds should enjoy a blanket exemption from the anti-fraud sections. Although banks and life insurance companies are subject to stringent regulation, bank securities and insurance variable annuities and flexible funds are subject to the anti-fraud rules of the securities acts, even though they are sometimes exempt from the registration regulations of the acts. *Tcherepnin v. Knight,* 389 U.S. 332, 88 S.Ct. 548, 19 L.Ed.2d 564; *SEC v. Variable Annuity Life Insurance Co.,* 359 U.S. 65, 87 S.Ct. 1557, 18 L.Ed.2d 673; *SEC v. United Benefit Life Ins. Co.,* 387 U.S. 202, 87 S.Ct. 1557, 18 L.Ed.2d 673; *SEC v. National Securities, Inc.,* 393 U.S. 453, 89 S.Ct. 564, 21 L.Ed.2d 668.

Reading the anti-fraud provisions of the securities laws to be complementary to the requirements of ERISA makes good sense. The requirements of ERISA do not substitute for the protections afforded by the anti-fraud provisions because the securities laws require that all material facts, including, of course, risk of loss, be disclosed prior to the investment decision (*TSC Industries, Inc. v. Northway, Inc.,* 426 U.S. 438, 96 S.Ct. 2126, 48 L.Ed.2d 757) while ERISA disclosure limits itself to the plan provisions[55] without a particularizing of how or how likely benefits may be lost [ERISA Section 102 (29 U.S.C. §1022)] and

---

53. The Senate Report on the 1958 pension act explained:

> Serious consideration was given earlier to placing the administration of the bill with the Securities and Exchange Commission on the basis of its past experience in the administration of disclosure type legislation. However, as the official representatives of the Securities and Exchange Commission clearly indicated that they did not feel they were the proper agency to handle the administration of this type of legislation, and as they felt that the taking on of this function might interfere with their presently established functions, this consideration was abandoned.
>
> S.Rep. No. 1440, 85th Cong., 2d Sess., reprinted at 3 U.S.Code Cong. & Admin. News, pp. 4137, 4156 (1958). *See also* 1957 Hearings at 107, 119.

The SEC's decision not to accept a regulatory role to enforce disclosure of material investment information was largely based on the conclusion that:

> Inasmuch as welfare and pension plan beneficiaries generally have no individual choice as to the securities to be purchased by a welfare or pension fund, the type of meaningful information to be furnished to them as to the management, investments and transactions of their funds may involve quite different criteria from those presently employed by the Commission under the various Federal Securities Acts.
>
> *Id.* at 119.

The SEC did not apparently object to being given plenary jurisdiction over individual retirement accounts. ERISA Leg. Hist., Vol. III at 4605. Nor was the Congress that enacted ERISA unaware that the SEC considered interests in pension funds to be securities under the 1933 Act unless excepted. *See* note 31 *supra.*

54. It should be noted that the defendants concede that certain voluntary and contributory pension plans are subject to both the securities laws' registration requirements and ERISA (Rep. Br. 206). The securities laws apparently have not torpedoed such plans. This seems to follow from the continuing registration of such plans. In fact, the disclosure requirements are becoming complementary as the SEC in its revisions of Form S-8 attempts to avoid duplication of, but not defer to the ERISA requirements. Form S-8, Sec. Act Release No. 33-5488 (1974), CCH Fed.Sec.L.Rep. ¶7197; Sec. Act Release No. 5767 (Nov. 22, 1976), [76-77 Transfer Binder] CCH Fed.Sec.L.Rep. ¶80,809; *SEC v. Garfinkle* [74-75 Transfer Binder] CCH Fed.Sec.L.Rep. ¶95,020 (S.D.N.Y. 1975).

55. ERISA has other *post-hoc* disclosure times. Thus the amended provisions of a pension plan need not be disclosed until after adopted ERISA Section 104(b)(1)(B) (29 U.S.C. §1024(b)(1)(B)) and then only summaries of the changed provisions are given until five years later when they must be incorporated into the integrated plan summary. In the establishment of a new plan, disclosure can occur within four months of adoption. *Id.*

may be made 90 days subsequent to the investment commitment.[56] ERISA Section 104(b)(1)(A) [29 U.S.C. §1024(b)(1)(A)]. Defendants have not shown that ERISA would provide relief to persons who have acquired an interest in a pension fund where false or misleading representations have been made at inception or during subsequent ratifications or upon a job offer.[57] Affirmance of the judgment below will supplement ERISA by providing a self-executing compulsion to disclose adequate information at such times, including a statistically determinable risk that many employees covered by a plan will never receive their pension benefits.[58] Thus the anti-fraud provisions of the securities acts will protect the interests of an investor before he makes an investment decision, while ERISA serves employees who have been employed for a substantial period of time at a job covered by a pension plan, protecting them from losing benefits through ignorance of the plan provisions. Consequently, we conclude it would be unwarranted to impute an intent on the part of Congress for ERISA to override the federal or state securities laws, *SEC v. Garfinkle* [74-75 Transfer Binder] CCH Fed. Sec.L. Rep. ¶95,020 (S.D.N.Y. 1975), where protections offered by ERISA do not fully overlap those of the anti-fraud provisions of the securities acts. *Cf. Califano v. Sanders,* 430 U.S. 99, 97 S.Ct. 980, 51 L.Ed.2d 192.

Judge Kirkland's disposition is not repugnant to the regulatory scheme outlined by ERISA. Although the defendants assert any remedy given plaintiff would contravene Section 203(b)(1)(F) of ERISA [29 U.S.C. §1053(b)(1)(F)][59] because that Section permits pension plans to disregard nonforfeitable years of service before the September 2, 1974, effective date of that statute if, as here, the employee would not have been entitled to benefits because of a break in continuous service under his pension plan, the district court can fashion relief to avoid a conflict with ERISA if plaintiff should prevail on the merits. Judge Kirkland has not, contrary to ERISA, held defendant's twenty-year continuous service rule invalid. His opinion merely holds that it and other essential matters had to be disclosed, and defendants will doubtless attempt to show at trial that plaintiff was aware of that and other key requirements.

Effect on Labor-Management Relations

[15] Even if ERISA does not exempt pension plans from the securities acts, it is argued that a resultant devastating effect on labor-management relations in and of itself should require an exemption in the absence of specific inclusory language in the securities acts. But holding the anti-fraud provisions to be applicable here will not destroy labor-management relations as defendants and the *amici* who support their position insist, for the anti-fraud provisions only probe fraudulent conduct such as the making of false or misleading representations. They do not require any complex filings. Moreover, most pension plans have been specifically exempted from the registration re-

56. Circumscribing the utility of ERISA disclosure further are the widespread disclaimers of liability for incorrect plans description or analysis which are contained in most post-ERISA summary plan description booklets. Under Section 14 of the 1933 Act and Section 29 of the 1934 Act, waivers of liability regarding securities are ineffective. *See Wilko v. Swan,* 346 U.S. 427, 74 S.Ct. 182, 98 L.Ed. 168; *Weissbuch v. Merrill Lynch, Pierce, Fenner & Smith Inc.,* 558 F.2d 831 (7th Cir. 1977).

57. Moreover the denial of pension benefits to John Daniel occurred before the effective date of ERISA. Section 502(a) of ERISA, 29 U.S.C. §1132(a), provides a right of action for a pension fund beneficiary "to obtain . . . appropriate equitable relief . . . to redress . . . violations" of any provision of Title I of ERISA ("Protection of Employee Benefit Rights"), 29 U.S.C. §§1001-1144. However, there is no provision of Title I which generally prohibits the making of false or misleading representations to an employee concerning the pension fund.

58. "ERISA §102(b) [29 U.S.C. §1022(b)] requires that summary plan descriptions include a statement of 'circumstances which may result in disqualification, ineligibility, or denial or loss of benefits.' In theory, employees should be able to infer from this information in the plan description that there is a risk of loss, and perhaps the nature of that risk. The Department of Labor has interpreted the statutory language very narrowly, however, in proposed rules issued on June 9, 1975, 40 Fed.Reg. 24654, on which the Department has stated plan administrators may rely. 41 Fed.Reg. 16957 (April 23, 1976). Plan administrators are permitted to describe the benefits of the plan in positive language, leaving the employee to deduce the negatives implicit in the affirmative language" (IPIR Br. at 21 n. *).

59. Section 203(b)(1)(F) provides:

(b)(1) In computing the period of service under the plan for purposes of determining the nonforfeitable percentage under subsection (a)(2) of this section, all of an employee's years of service with the employer or employers maintaining the plan shall be taken into account, except that the following may be disregarded:

(F) years of service before this part first applies to the plan if such service would have been disregarded under the rules of the plan with regard to breaks in service, as in effect on the applicable date.

quirements of the 1933 Act. 15 U.S.C. §77c(a)(2)(A). Since a sale triggering the anti-fraud provisions would normally occur when an employee decides to accept or continue in a job, the holding below would not be disruptive of the collective bargaining process. Indeed, the application of the anti-fraud provisions of the securities laws should enhance federal labor policy by augmenting the unchallenged statutory right of workers to be fairly represented by their union (Local 705 Br. 14 n. 31; 29 U.S.C. §185; *Vaca v. Sipes,* 386 U.S. 171, 87 S.Ct. 903, 17 L.Ed.2d 842). And as *amicus* Gray Panthers point out, such an application will further the purpose of Section 302(c)(5) of the Labor Management Relations Act [29 U.S.C. §186(c)(5)] by letting each employee know to what he is entitled under a union pension fund. 2 NLRB, Legislative History of Labor Management Relations Act of 1947, 1305 (1948). The only negative effect on unions *qua* unions will be in preventing them from defrauding their rank and file with impunity. *See Walsh v. Schlecht,* 429 U.S. 401, 410, 97 S.Ct. 679, 58 L.Ed.2d 641.

In sum, Congress has nowhere provided that the anti-fraud provisions of the securities acts should not apply to pension funds. The Secretary of Labor's arguments that affirmance will undermine a union's authority as exclusive bargaining agent for its employees vis-a-vis the employer or will disrupt the bargaining process are specious. Of course a finding of liability implies nothing about the entirely separate and not uncomplicated question of the form of relief which is a matter for the trial court, and the construction of formulae giving the measure of damages is for the trial court in the first instance. *Mills v. Electric Auto-Lite Co.,* 396 U.S. 375, 386, 90 S.Ct. 616, 24 L.Ed. 2d 593; *Shapiro v. Merrill Lynch, Pierce, Fenner & Smith, Inc.,* 495 F.2d 228, 241 (2d Cir. 1974). Furthermore, as *amicus* Institute for Public Interest Representation has shown, current employees need not be disadvantaged because of the generous amortization and waiver provisions contained in Sections 302, 303 and 304 of ERISA (29 U.S.C. §§1082-1084). It is for the district court to construct a remedy which properly balances the needs of plaintiff against those of other fund participants.

The Parade of Horribles

The parade of horribles offered by defendants and the *amici* who support their position (including their predictions of $200 billion liabilities) results mainly from their zeal as advocates and should not distract a court from enforcing the Congressional policies contained in the anti-fraud provisions of the securities laws.[60] Finally, we wish to emphasize that we are not holding the registration requirements of the 1933 Act or the reporting requirements of the 1934 Act to be applicable to these pension funds.[61] We do not require the filing of any document or establish judicial control over pension fund operations. There should be no undue burden caused by the type of disclosure the anti-fraud provisions would encourage because all of the material information will be readily available to the plan trustees since their actuaries needed all of the information in order to set up the plan in the first place.

Moreover, plan liability, given the fact that employees' interests in pension funds are covered by the anti-fraud provisions of the securities acts, is still limited by a number of factors. Particular employees must show, in light of all the ambient circumstances, justifiable reliance on a material misrepresentation or omission causing them injury. If all material facts are disclosed in a manner comprehensible to the average worker, as in any other securities fraud case, no damage causation will exist under the securities laws. *Sundstrand Corp. v. Sun Chemical Corp.,* 553 F.2d 1033, 1049-1051 (7th Cir. 1977), *certiorari denied* ___ U.S. ___, 98 S.Ct. ___, 53 L.Ed.2d ___. Thus if the plan documents sent to a plan beneficiary understand-

60. *See Northern Securities Co. v. United States,* 193 U.S. 197, 351-352, 24 S.Ct. 436, 48 L.Ed. 279 (plurality opinion).

61. Because of the longtime and consistent administrative practice, these pension funds might be deemed beyond the scope of the registration requirements even if they are not already exempted by 15 U.S.C. §77c(a)(2)(A). The SEC maintains 96% of all pension plans are so exempted apparently because most funds, including Local 705's, are invested by the trust departments of major banks. (Hansen Ex. 1, App. 184a at 14-15):

> There is only one affirmative condition—qualification under Section 401 of the Internal Revenue Code—that a pension plan must meet in order to qualify for this exemption. It has been estimated that 96% of pension plans satisfy this condition. *See* S.Rep. No. 92-1150, 92d Cong., 2d Sess. 110 (1972). There is also a negative condition; the exemption is lost if the plan invests an amount greater than the employer's contributions in securities of the employer.
> (SEC Br. at 59 n. 81).

Because the seller is the pension trust operating through the trustees, the amended complaint does not include Daniel's employers as defendants. Therefore, this opinion does not consider any possible obligations of employers under the 1933 and 1934 Acts with regard to pension plans.

ably disclose this information, a retiree who does not meet the vesting requirements will have no remedy under the securities acts, even if he subjectively did not comprehend the disclosed information. In addition, other pension funds may be immunized by the applicable statute of limitations. These considerations, as well as others, may arise here in future cases as constraints on plan liability.

Order Affirmed.

TONE, Circuit Judge, concurring.

I am able to agree with much that Judge Cummings says in his scholarly opinion for the court, but certain doubts lead me to write separately.

For me, this is a close and difficult case. I am beset by the same doubts arising from the ordinary meaning of the words "security," "investment contract," and "sale" and from Congress' basic purpose in adopting the Securities Acts that must have influenced the several district judges who have reached conclusions inconsistent with ours. *Hurn v. Retirement Trust Fund, Etc.,* 424 F.Supp. 80 (C.D.Cal. 1976); *Wiens v. International Brotherhood of Teamsters,* BNA Securities and Law Report (No. 397, April 6, 1977, p. A-13) (C.D. Cal. 1977); *Robinson v. United Mine Workers of America Health and Retirement Funds,* 435 F. Supp. 245, (D.D.C. 1977). The series of transactions by which Daniel acquired his interest, or expectancy, such as it was, do not fit neatly into the traditional concept of a sale of a security. In addition, it may well be, as Judge Gesell believes (*see Robinson, supra*), that the *Forman* case [*United Housing Foundation, Inc. v. Forman,* 421 U.S. 837, 95 S.Ct. 2051, 44 L.Ed.2d 621 (1975)]. and other recent Supreme Court decisions indicate "a pronounced disfavor with attempts to stretch the securities laws beyond their traditional scope." Nevertheless, considering the breadth of the definitions of "investment contract" and "sale" in the statutes themselves and the interpretation of those terms in cases we must still regard as authoritative, I believe the balance tips in favor of the plaintiff's position.

In reaching this conclusion, I have found little comfort in the opinion expressed by the SEC, as *amicus curiae.* Apparently for the first time ever, it now takes the position in its brief before us that the employee's interest or expectancy in a plan such as this is subject to the anti-fraud provisions of the securities laws. The Commission has not been as candid as we might have hoped in acknowledging and explaining its change in position. As late as 1971 in its *Institutional Investor Study* submitted to Congress in connection with the consideration of the ERISA legislation, the Commission's view was that although a non-contributory pension plan might well be an investment contract, the element of sale was lacking.[1] Before that, not even the existence of a security was acknowledged. It is true that the Commission's attention seems to have been focused largely on registration requirements rather than the anti-fraud provisions,[2] but there appears to have been no intimation over the years that it viewed the anti-fraud provisions as applicable. The statement in the *Institutional Investor Study* that the Commission staff "has taken the position that the Securities Act [of 1933] does not apply"[3] seemed to refer to all the disclosure provisions of that Act, not merely its registration provisions. It should be added, however, that the SEC's former position appears to have initially been based in large part on the unduly restrictive view that the employer's contribution on behalf of the employee was a gift and that a necessary volitional element was lacking; and, so far as its public statements disclose, the Commission persisted in that position without any real reexamination of its basis.

Members of Congress considering legislative proposals after the adoption of the securities acts who relied on the SEC's interpretation of those acts must have understood that they did not apply to transactions of the kind before us. It is realistic, however, to believe that most members of Congress understood that the SEC is not infallible, that the Supreme Court has been known to disagree with that agency's interpretation of the securities acts, and that the applicability of those acts to various kinds of transactions, including non-contributory pension plans, has yet to be determined by the Supreme Court. It appears likely that Congress has chosen to leave the matter in that posture. I find no persuasive evidence to the contrary in the legislative history subsequent to the adoption of the securities laws.

In *Daniel,* the court applied the *Howey* definition of investment contract to a collectively bargained, noncontributory pension plan. Even though the plan did not require or permit contributions by the employees, the court concluded that there was an investment of money by the employees. The

1. 3 SEC *Institutional Investor Study* 996 (1971).

2. Between which a distinction can rationally be drawn. *See SEC v. National Securities, Inc.,* 393 U.S. 453, 89 S.Ct. 564, 21 L.Ed.2d 668 (1969).

3. Cited at note 1, *supra.*

court felt that the contributions made by the contributing employers otherwise would have been received by the employees in their paychecks thus, in effect, they were making an indirect investment. Because the plan was common to all members of the union local, the court held that the pension plan was a common enterprise.

The more difficult question for the court was whether there were profits. In this regard, the court held that the excess of benefits provided over the contributions made by the contributing employer constituted a profit. Presumably, the realization by the employees that their pension benefits would exceed the amounts contributed by the contributing employer in return for their services was some form of economic inducement to work or to continue to work. The court had little difficulty in determining that this profit would be derived primarily through the effort of others. The pension plan was established in accordance with §302(c)(5) of the Taft-Hartley Act, and the trustees had exclusive authority and control with respect to the administration and management of the plan.

The decision in *Daniel* is not the only decision in this area. Several courts have reached the opposite conclusion. *Wiens v. International Brotherhood of Teamsters,* ____ F.Supp. ____ (C.D. Calif. 1977), like *Daniel,* involved an employee's participation in a collectively bargained, noncontributory pension plan. However, the court in *Wiens* held that an interest in such a plan does not constitute a security since an item is not a security if it does not have the "characteristics that fall within the ordinary concept of a security in our commercial world." A review of the transcript of proceedings, adopted by the parties as findings of fact and conclusions of law, indicates that the court in *Wiens* relies rather heavily on the Supreme Court decision in *United Housing Foundation v. Forman*, 421 U.S. 837 (1975).

WIENS V. INTERNATIONAL BROTHERHOOD OF TEAMSTERS

____ F.Supp. ____ (C.D. Calif. 1977)

THE COURT: Let's now proceed to motion No. 2, which is a motion for judgment on the pleadings.

Now, you can be seated here, sir. There are some preliminary matters I would like to talk about first.

Counts I and II charge the international union, two locals, 290 and 431, and some of the trustees of the pension trust, and also the trust.

I believe that is an accurate statement, is it not?

MR. DICKSTEIN: Yes, your Honor.

THE COURT: All right. The motion, however, is apparently made only by the International. The grounds would seem equally applicable to all defendants, it seems to me.

Would you not agree with that?

MR. DICKSTEIN: Your Honor, I would agree. But as far as we can ascertain, there is no Local 290. In any event, I don't believe a Local 290 has been served.

With respect to the other local union, I would see no reason why the grounds would not be equally applicable to them. And as far as Western Conference is concerned, I suppose Mr. Gregory, having joined in the motion, to the extent it's applicable—

MR. GREGORY: On behalf of the two individual employees of a separate corporation, they do have standing, and I do join in the motion.

THE COURT: Well, let me ask the plaintiff if he would not agree that this motion may be deemed for the benefit of all defendants.

MR. WERNER: Yes, your Honor. I think it would just be a technicality, and I think I would go along.

THE COURT: And force me to hear the same motion over again seriatim, which I am not happy about doing; and I appreciate your agreement.

So that is the situation. The motion is deemed for the benefit of and to be applicable to all defendants.

Now, Counts I and II are based on alleged jurisdiction under the Securities Acts of 1933, 10b-5. Plaintiff is claiming fraud in connection with his share or interest in a pension plan. It's apparently a non-contributory plan, one in which all funds are contributed by the employers.

Right, Mr. Werner?

MR. WERNER: Yes, your Honor.

THE COURT: It's an involuntary plan in that the individual employee does not get to elect whether to join up with the plan or not.

That is your understanding, is it not?

MR. WERNER: To the point that he is a member of that specific union and participates in that specific employment, yes, your Honor.

THE COURT: He is automatically in the plan in the sense that contributions are made for him by the employer, if he is in that union and employment.

Now, this plaintiff was denied the benefits, apparently, on the grounds of a break in continuous service and says he was defrauded into believing that he would not be denied benefits.

I think it's only a Securities Act of '33, 10b-5 theory. Am I right? Or is there a Section 17 in there, too?

MR. WERNER: There is an alleged Section 17 involved.

THE COURT: All right. Then my earlier statement should so reflect.

Both 10b-5 and Section 17 require as a basis for federal jurisdiction the purchase or sale of a security. And the basis for the current motion is that the pension plan is not a security, and an interest in it is not a security; and if, arguendo, it is, there has been no purchase or sale.

I think now that it's clear that Section 17 is involved, the words of art in Section 17 are "offer or sale," and that those words for the purposes of this case are indistinguishable from the words "purchase and sale."

Now, with this motion filed on March 10th is a declaration of Mr. Uranga of the Pension Trust Fund, and attached to that are copies of the pension plan and trust agreements as of 1955 and 1960.

It seems to me that the facts of the matter are not contested and that the preferable procedure treatment is to treat this motion as a summary judgment motion.

Is that agreeable with you, Mr. Werner?

MR. WERNER: It's not quite agreeable, your Honor, because—

THE COURT: Come to the podium.

What is the problem?

MR. WERNER: I think, your Honor, that there are additional facts that may not be stated within the rules, the 1955 rules and other rules that were submitted. And as far as that is concerned, your Honor, those facts were not treated because we were not apprised that this would be a summary judgment motion.

THE COURT: Well, you saw evidence accompanying the motion—

MR. WERNER: Yes, your Honor.

THE COURT:—in the form of the Uranga declaration and the attachment.

MR. WERNER: Yes, your Honor. But I viewed that evidence not in the light of—

THE COURT: What do you think it was doing there?

MR. WERNER: I believed it was there for the purposes of a judgment on the pleadings based on the law rather than on the facts, your Honor; and as evidence that there wasn't any violation of—

THE COURT: What facts would you contest?

MR. WERNER: I am just suggesting, your Honor, that there may be additional evidence as to securities fraud or, you know, as specific evidence rather than in terms of the law.

THE COURT: Well, wait just a second. I have already told you that I am concentrating on two questions, which are, is the plan, and interest therein, a security?

MR. WERNER: Yes.

THE COURT: Now, we know what the plan is, so that leaves no fact problem in dispute. That's a legal question, right?

MR. WERNER: Yes, your Honor.

THE COURT: And, secondly, even if it is, arguendo, is there in this case any possible offer, purchase or sale of a security?

MR. WERNER: Yes, your Honor.

THE COURT: That, too, is a legal question, is it not?

MR. WERNER: Yes, your Honor.

THE COURT: So the facts, insofar as they pose these legal problems, are not in dispute.

MR. WERNER: Yes, your Honor.

THE COURT: Okay. Thank you. That is appreciated.

Do you agree?

MR. DICKSTEIN: Yes, your Honor, I do.

THE COURT: All right. Now, I therefore am going to hold that there are no material facts in dispute and treat it as a summary judgment motion procedurally.

And my tentative view, Mr. Werner, is that the motion ought to be granted on alternative grounds of there being no security involved; and if there is a security, arguendo, that there was no purchase, offer or sale involved.

Let me expound those views a little bit, then I will give you a chance to argue.

As to what is a security, the way is pointed by the teachings of the Supreme Court in *United Housing Foundation v. Forman,* decided in 1975, 421 U.S. 837.

Now, in *Forman* even an item called stock was held not to be a security because it did not have the characteristics that fall within the ordinary concept of a security in our commercial world. The Supreme Court in *Forman* lists those characteristics as the right to receive dividends contingent upon and being a part of profits—that's No. 1. Negotiability, No. 2. Ability to be pledged or hypothecated, No. 3. Voting rights in proportion to number of shares owned, No. 4. And appreciation in value, No. 5.

Now, it seems that all of those facets are lacking with respect to this alleged interest in the pension plan; and certainly the substantial number of them are lacking. These are my tentative views.

I am, of course, aware of the opinion of Judge

Kirkland in the District Court in Illinois in the case of *Daniel v. International Brotherhood of Teamsters,* which Mr. Werner has made available to me. But I cannot agree with its result either on the ground that a security exists or that there was any purchase, offer or sale thereof. In that opinion Judge Kirkland did not consider or deal with the *Forman* case.

I note that there is a decision in this district by my brother Judge Hauk which accords with the tentative decision that I have made here. The case is Hurn, *H-u-r-n, v. Retirement Fund Trust,* Case No. 76-2487, in this district, granting a motion to dismiss.

Now, we have the interesting phenomenon that defendant points out that for forty years the SEC has said that these pension plan interests were not securities; but the SEC may have changed its mind recently as a result of the *Daniel* case. But there is a quick and easy answer to that supplied, I think, by the Supreme Court in *Forman;* and the Supreme Court, I think, teaches us in the *Forman* opinion that the SEC position, past or present, is of minimal importance, and especially of minimal importance when that position has suddenly shifted after a long period in the other direction.

Of greater importance, it seems to me, on this question is a statement in the legislative history of the Act that is commonly called ERISA. Now, in that legislative history the Senate asked for a compendium of present laws covering fraud in pensions and profit-sharing plans: and the Senate committee report, which is Document No. 92-634 of the 92nd Congress, Second Session, says that pension and profit-sharing plans are exempt under the Securities Act of 1933 unless it is a voluntary contribution plan involving the securities of the employer. Which, of course, this is not.

Now, I leave the question of is it a security and I move to the question of whether there has been a purchase, offer or sale even if there was a security. And the only rationale I know for holding that there was one is the one that Judge Kirkland adopts in *Daniel.* And I must say, tentatively at least, I simply do not agree with it.

I don't think that when you vote for a collective bargaining agreement that calls for a pension plan you thereby purchase a security. Nor do I believe that when you work or continue to work for an employer who has an entirely non-contributory plan, you thereby sell your labor in return for a security. I just cannot follow that line of thinking.

Those are my views, tentatively. I will hear you, Mr. Werner, since it appears that the decision may well be adverse to your position.

MR. WERNER: Thank you, your Honor. I know I have an uphill battle to fight here, but—

THE COURT: No pun is intended, I hope. "Uphill?"

(Laughter.)

MR. WERNER: First, I think I would like to distinguish the *Forman* case, your Honor. That case involved a cooperative apartment house, if I remember; and there I think the distinguishing mark is that the court indicated that the purchasers were deriving an immediate benefit, that there wasn't any investment considered. And in the instant case, where you have a pension plan, there is no immediate benefit, as opposed to the *Forman* case; that all benefits would be delayed to the eventual retirement of the plaintiff. And I think on that basis this case should be viewed a little bit differently.

Naturally the court in the *Forman* case outlined a line of requirements, but I think that those requirements were pretty much tailored to that specific case.

THE COURT: Well, they didn't sound like they were being so tailored. They sounded like a list of attributes which were enunciated for the guidance of people like me down the line in a judicial chain. And is it not true that this interest has none of those attributes?

MR. WERNER: I think it's a matter of viewing what attributes there are. There may not be any direct dividends. However, the question becomes whether or not the investments and the money gained from those investments become dividends, except as the dividends remain in the pension fund.

THE COURT: It's awfully hard to call a pension plan interest when drawing a dividend, isn't it?

MR. WERNER: The word "dividends" may not be applicable, your Honor. But it would seem to me that if funds are being invested and profit is made on those funds being invested, and the beneficiary will eventually receive those profits that, in essence, he is receiving dividends; but the dividends are being delayed in terms of payment.

THE COURT: Well, to call those dividends is a usage of that word far different than I have ever heard it used.

MR. WERNER: I don't doubt that, your Honor. What I am suggesting is that there was profit anticipated from investment of funds. And the court here specifically called it dividends. I think they are more concerned with the issue of profits rather than specifically the word "dividends," and that they were using the word "dividends" because they were dealing with something that was called stock at that particular time.

Obviously, the nature of the pension fund, it can't be pledged, and so I would have to agree on that basis. But as far as voting rights are concerned, I think it's a matter of the power of the trustees to determine where funds are to be invested; and I think that with respect to the specific union, they would have the power to select specific pension fund trustees and, therefore, there would be an indirect power to vote. And I would suggest, your Honor, that on that basis it would also fall within the qualifications of requirements afforded.

I think that—does your Honor wish to hear any additional argument? At least, that is what I have on that point.

THE COURT: What do you say about even if it is a security, there hasn't been any purchase or sale or offer?

MR. WERNER: I would say, your Honor, that a union member elects a representative to do bargaining for him. That through that union representative, who acquires an interest or a plan, and acquires benefits for the member, he is basically the hired negotiator for various contracts; and he is the one who is said to go out and be the agent to negotiate, and purchase and sale of the plan. So here you have just a matter of an indirect purchasing agent. Mr. Wiens may not have purchased directly; however, through his purchasing agent—

THE COURT: Well, you say there is a sale, a purchase?

MR. WERNER: A purchase.

THE COURT: What is he paying?

MR. WERNER: The representative, your Honor, is the one who decides to invest in the pension fund. He is the one who negotiated the agreement.

THE COURT: You say the investment is the purchase?

MR. WERNER: No. He is the one who secured the agreement whereby the employer contributes to the pension fund.

THE COURT: Just a second. Under the Securities Acts, as I understand them, the plaintiff must be the purchaser or seller.

MR. WERNER: Yes, your Honor.

THE COURT: Or have offered to purchase—

MR. WERNER: Yes, your Honor.

THE COURT: —of the security. Now, how does this plaintiff become a purchaser, seller, or an offeror of the security, which is the pension interest?

MR. WERNER: Okay. I believe that the elected union officials represent him directly and purchase on his behalf. And what they purchase is they negotiate with the employers to purchase specific benefits. And in this particular case they made an agreement for the investment of money in a pension plan; and that that plan, the investment in that plan was made on behalf of the plaintiff, and that was a purchase in essence on behalf of the plaintiff. That for his labor and services—

THE COURT: Has any court ever followed that theory?

MR. WERNER: Well, your Honor—

THE COURT: The *Daniel* case used the theories I mentioned.

MR. WERNER: I understand that, your Honor, and—

THE COURT: And that is the only case which goes this far that you have been able to find, or that we have been able to find.

MR. WERNER: Yes, your Honor. But in this relatively new area it seems—

THE COURT: The Securities Acts aren't relatively new. They have been around since 1933.

MR. WERNER: However, haven't been litigated, as I understand, until recent years. I would think, your Honor—

THE COURT: Nobody has had the temerity to argue that this was a security.

MR. WERNER: Maybe nobody could afford it, your Honor.

THE COURT: This kind of a plan. But I can't read everybody's mind.

I want to hear from the other side now.

MR. WERNER: Okay.

MR. DICKSTEIN: Your Honor hasn't left me with very much to say.

THE COURT: I am sorry you made the trip out from Washington.

MR. DICKSTEIN: I feel not at all frustrated by it, your Honor, so you don't need to apologize for it.

THE COURT: By the way, is there any other decided litigation that you have heard of recently that is not in the briefs?

MR. DICKSTEIN: No, your Honor, we don't believe there is any.

THE COURT: Judge Hauk's case and the *Daniel* case, and that's it?

MR. DICKSTEIN: And this case, your Honor.

THE COURT: Is either of the other two on appeal?

MR. DICKSTEIN: Yes. *Daniel* is on appeal, your Honor, and will be argued next Monday, as a matter of fact.

THE COURT: Will you be handling that?

MR. DICKSTEIN: Yes, I will.

There is one aspect of the matter, and your Honor has already alluded to it, but it's been referred to by plaintiff's counsel, as well, and that is the question of the purchase or sale. It has always been understood that a purchase or sale turns on somebody making an investment decision. This is why the SEC, at least until recently, always took the position that where there is a compulsory pension plan as an incident of employment, there is nothing which is akin to an investment decision as that term normally would be employed and as that act would normally invoke the provisions of the federal securities laws.

Try as one may to contrive—and I don't use the word in a pejorative sense, but I think it's an accurate description, to find an investment decision out of the act of participating in the ratification of a union contract—under circumstances of which the union permits or requires ratification, that is not always true. But try as one may to find an investment decision out of the act of accepting employment or going to work tomorrow and the day after, or try as one may, as plaintiff's counsel just has, to find it in some vicarious sense, it just doesn't work. And the reason why it doesn't work is because, for one thing, *Forman* and *Blue Chip,* and some other cases which precede them, and have followed in their way, are teaching us that one doesn't stretch, strain to find analogy. The decisions in the Supreme Court—

THE COURT: Well, the high court sure talked about the normal commercial sense and context here.

MR. DICKSTEIN: Of course, your Honor. And as recently as last Monday, in a case which of course is not referred to in our brief, *Santa Fe Industries v. Green,* the Supreme Court again said, "We are not going to construe the federal securities laws in an expansionist mode as if those were the only laws that were intended to regulate commerce."

The question in *Santa Fe* also involved whether or not the state courts should have the role of dealing with the fraud that was contended to exist in that case, and the Supreme Court said, "Yes, indeed. That is the way it should be. We are not going to bring everything within the ambit of the federal securities laws."

And I think that is really the short answer to the plaintiff's claim under Counts I and II, if indeed it was ever possible—ever possible—

THE COURT: Well, I think that I have heard enough argument. I intend to follow the tentative decision. And there will be a couple of other matters I would like to talk about.

What would be left in the case, Mr. Werner, would be Count III, which charges a breach of a duty of fair representation. Now, let me ask you this: How can the International have breached any such duty, since they don't directly represent your client?

MR. WERNER: First off, your Honor,—

THE COURT: Why don't you come to the podium, please.

MR. WERNER: It's my understanding that Count IV is still remaining in the case, which alleges fraud, as well, your Honor.

THE COURT: I don't believe that's correct. My indication is, and my memory is that the only counts alive as of this morning were Counts I, II and III.

And the clerk indicates that that is the effect of the orders that have been entered.

MR. WERNER: Because there had been an order entered to the contrary.

THE COURT: The clerk will show you that the original order had a typographical error.

MR. WERNER: I understand. Okay. Thank you.

THE COURT: And a supplemental nunc pro tunc order was entered.

MR. WERNER: Okay.

THE COURT: So, what do you say, Mr. Werner? We have to be realistic about it. But I put to you a question about whether the International can be dismissed from Count III.

MR. WERNER: Well, the problem with that, your Honor, is, it remains to be seen whether or not there is any involvement of the International in the particular—

THE COURT: Well, just listen to my conceptual problem.

MR. WERNER: Okay. I am sorry.

THE COURT: I know some things remain to be seen, but an international has no duty of fair representation, as far as I know; only the local which directly represents your client.

MR. WERNER: I understand, your Honor.

THE COURT: Do you have any authority or even concept for getting an international into a breach of a duty of fair representation?

MR. WERNER: No, your Honor. I understand.

THE COURT: Can we dismiss the International from Count III?

MR. WERNER: Yes, your Honor.

THE COURT: All right. Then that is ordered by the consent of plaintiff's counsel.

Now, with respect to—well, first, I have been at it a while. Let's take a five-minute recess. Then I want to discuss procedure.

Be thinking about whether a transcript of my remarks, which are rather full and enunciate my reasons, will constitute and can constitute findings of fact and conclusions of law; or whether either of you want more formal findings and conclusions.

Now, we will take a five-minute recess.

(Short recess.)

THE COURT: Well, summary judgment, as per the tentative Court ruling, is granted on Counts I and II.

What about formal findings and conclusions as against a transcript?

MR. WERNER: Plaintiff is prepared to stipulate, your Honor.

THE COURT: To the transcript serving?

MR. WERNER: Yes, your Honor.

THE COURT: Is that agreeable with you?

MR. DICKSTEIN: That is acceptable, your Honor.

THE COURT: Will you order the transcript then?

MR. DICKSTEIN: We already have, your Honor.

THE COURT: All right. And I will write my own judgment.

Interest in Welfare Plan Examined

Unlike *Wiens* and *Daniel, Robinson v. United Mine Workers of America Health and Retirement Funds,* ____ F.Supp. ____ (D.D.C. 1977), did not involve an employee's interest in a pension plan, but rather, an interest in a welfare plan. The court in *Robinson* held that an employee's interest in such a plan was not a security. While the *Robinson* case reflects an analysis of several aspects of the definition of the term "investment contract," probably the most important portion of the decision relates to its holding that there was no expectation of profits. The court found that the employees did not share any "surplus" capital and did not expect to do so in bargaining for the establishment of the plan.

ROBINSON V. UNITED MINE WORKERS OF AMERICA HEALTH AND RETIREMENT FUNDS

____ F.Supp. ____ (D.D.C. 1977)

GESELL, District Judge: In this yet-uncertified class action surviving spouses and dependents of deceased coal miners primarily seek an order declaring their right to permanent health care coverage by the defendant United Mine Workers of America Health and Retirement Funds (the "Funds"). Damages are also sought. Plaintiffs advance several grounds in support of their claim, only one of which—namely whether defendants' actions constitute a violation of the federal securities laws—is encompassed in defendants' motion for partial summary judgment. Finding no dispute as to the material facts, the Court grants defendants' motion.

The United Mine Workers of America Health and Retirement Funds are four irrevocable trusts created pursuant to §302(c) of the Labor Management Relations Act of 1947, 29 U.S.C. §186 (1970 & Supp. V 1975), to provide health and retirement benefits to active and retired miners, their families, dependents, and survivors. One of these trusts—the only one involved in this litigation—is the United Mine Workers of America 1950 Benefit Plan and Trust (the "Trust"). All of the trusts are administered by three trustees, also defendants here, who establish eligibility standards and benefit levels. One trustee is appointed by the union, another by the contributing or "signatory" coal operators; the third, neutral trustee is chosen by the other two. The trusts are funded by fixed, per-tonnage royalties paid by the signatory operators. From the miners' perspective, the Funds are "involuntary" and "noncontributory": payments are made only by the coal operators, and miners have no option to choose higher or lower wages in lieu of lower or higher payments.

Upon the deaths of their coal-miner husbands, each of the named plaintiffs received from the Trust a death benefit in the amount of $5,000 and health care coverage for a period of five years. Plaintiffs allege that the union, which is portrayed as the alter ego or agent of the Funds, represented to them and to their husbands that lifetime health care coverage would be provided. Therefore, plaintiffs claim entitlement to such coverage and to damages from the defendants under §17(a) of the Securities Act of 1933, 15 U.S.C. §77q(a) (1970); §10(b) of the Securities Exchange Act of 1934, *id.* §78j(b); and SEC Rule 10b-5, 17 CFR §240.10(b)-5 (1976).

Although defendants advance several arguments in support of their motion to dismiss the securities acts claims, the Court finds it unnecessary to go beyond the broad contention that an interest in the 1950 Fund is not a "security" as defined in the securities acts.

Section 3(a)(10) of the Securities Exchange Act of 1934, 15 U.S.C. §78c(a)(10) (1970), defines security, in relevant part, as

> any note, stock, treasury stock, bond, debenture, certificate of interest or participation in any profit-

> sharing agreement or in any oil, gas, or other mineral royalty or lease, any collateral-trust certificate, preorganization certificate or subscription, transferable share, *investment contract,* voting-trust certificate, certificate of deposit, for a security, or in general, any instrument commonly known as a "security."
> (Emphasis added.)

The definition under the Securities Act of 1933 is virtually identical. *Id.* §77b(1). Of this list, the only term that could arguably characterize an interest in the 1950 Fund is "investment contract," defined by the Supreme Court as "a contract, transaction or scheme whereby a person invests his money in a common enterprise and is led to expect profits solely from the efforts of the promoter or a third party." *SEC v. W. J. Howey,* 328 U.S. 293, 298-99 (1946). Plaintiffs' brief, and a recent District Court opinion, *Daniel v. International Brotherhood of Teamsters,* 410 F.Supp. 541 (N.D. Ill. 1976), demonstrate the variety of arguments that can be used to stretch the terms of this definition enough to encompass the interest in question. But such a reading, in the Court's opinion, requires a degree of creativity unwarranted by the realities of the transactions and the function and purpose of the securities laws.[1]

Support for this reluctance to expand the scope of the term "investment contract" comes from *United Housing Foundation v. Forman,* 421 U.S. 837 (1975), in which the Court held that shares in a cooperative apartment development are not investment contracts and thus their issuance is not governed by the securities laws. Probing the economic substance of the interest, the Court noted the inalienability of the shares, the lack of any real risk confronting the invested capital, and the fact that the shareowners were deriving immediate benefits through use of the apartments, rather than merely possessing an expectancy of benefits. Any surplus accumulated by the cooperative was distributed as a rebate to shareowners, not invested for profit. These indicia suggested to the Court that "the purchasers were interested in acquiring housing rather than making an investment for profit." *Id.* at 860. The prospect of deriving any "profits" from the investment was simply too speculative and insubstantial to warrant application of the securities laws. Quoting *Howey,* the Court concluded:

> Well-settled principles enunciated by this Court establish that the shares purchased by respondents do not represent any of the "countless and variable schemes devised by those who seek the use of money of others on the promise of profits," . . . and therefore do not fall within "the ordinary concept of a security."
> *Id.* at 848.

A similar conclusion is required here. The miners cannot be said to have "invest[ed] . . . money" within the meaning of *Howey,*[2] for all contributions are made by the operators on a per-tonnage basis, and miners have no power to increase or decrease payments or to convert them to personal use. Since benefits have traditionally been paid mainly out of current contributions from the operators, the Trust capital is subject to very little risk. In addition, Trust participation involves no "expectation of profit" in the sense found necessary in *Howey* and *Forman.* As in *Forman,* interests in the Trust are inalienable, and any surplus will be converted into extended benefits rather than invested for the individual miner's profit. The miners, in bargaining for establishment of the Trust, were obviously interested in creating a sound, comprehensive health plan "rather than making an investment for profit." The Trust simply cannot be characterized as one of the "countless and variable schemes devised by those who seek the use of money of others on the promise of profits."

The securities laws in question, designed to safeguard the integrity of investment decisions, have been in operation for over forty years. Yet until the 1975 decision in *Daniel* (which predated *Forman*) no court had ever held, nor apparently had anyone including the SEC the temerity to argue that an interest in an involuntary, noncontributory pension or health benefit plan was covered by the securities laws. Congress has repeatedly indicated its belief to the contrary. *See, e.g.,* S. Rep. No. 93-127, 93d Cong., 1st Sess. 3 (1975); S. Rep. No. 92-1150, 92d Cong., 2d Sess. 4 (1972); S. Rep. No. 734, 84th Cong., 2d Sess. 60 (1956).[3]

1. Only two other cases have considered whether an interest in a noncontributory pension or health benefits plan is a security. Both have concluded that it is not. *Hurn v. Retirement Fund Trust of Plumbing, Heating and Piping Industry,* 424 F.Supp. 80 (C.D. Cal. 1976); *Wiens v. International Bhd. of Teamsters,* C.A. No. 76-2517 IH (C.D. Cal. Mar. 28, 1977). *Daniel* is distinguishable from the instant case; these differences notwithstanding, the Court disagrees with the reasoning of that opinion.

2. Certainly plaintiffs in this case, miners' spouses, cannot be said to have "invested" any "money" in the Fund. *Cf. Blue Chip Stamps v. Manor Drug Stores,* 421 U.S. 723 (1975).

3. Until *Daniel* the SEC consistently maintained the view that noncontributory pension plans were not cov-

Forman is but one of a series of recent Supreme Court decisions indicating a pronounced disfavor with attempts to stretch the securities laws beyond their traditional scope. *E.g., Santa Fe Industries, Inc. v. Green,* 45 U.S.L.W. 4317 (S.Ct. Mar. 23, 1977); *Blue Chip Stamps v. Manor Drug Stores,* 421 U.S. 723 (1975). This case does not merit departure from the traditional learning. Plaintiffs' participation in the Trust involves nothing akin to the investment decisions the securities laws were enacted to protect. There are other statutes cited in the complaint that are designed to protect any of plaintiffs' rights that may have been infringed. Defendants' motion for partial summary judgment is granted.

SO ORDERED.

The Element of "Sale"

If the conflicting court decisions with respect to whether an employee's interest in a pension or a welfare plan constitutes a security for purposes of the '33 Act are resolved in favor of classifying such interests as securities (not only for purposes of the antifraud provisions, but for purposes of the disclosure or registration provisions as well), the next question is whether the security is sold to employees. It is important to note that the mere finding of a security does not trigger the application of the disclosure requirements. The security must also be sold to someone.

Section 2(3) of the '33 Act defines the term "sale" as:

> Every contract of sale or disposition of a security or interest in a security, for value.

Traditionally, the Securities and Exchange Commission and the courts have construed the statutory definition of the term "sale" broadly in order to effectuate the general remedial nature of the securities laws. However, until recently, the Securities and Exchange Commission and the courts have not taken the position that an interest in a pension or a welfare plan is the subject of a sale (for purposes of the disclosure provisions) to an employee where the plan is a noncontributory plan, or where participation in the plan is compulsory, provided there is no element of volition on the part of employees whether to make contributions or to participate in the plan. Based on this position, those plans which permit employee contributions to be used to purchase employer securities are, for example, subject to the disclosure provisions and the antifraud provisions, but other plans have not been subject to the disclosure requirements.

The position of the Securities and Exchange Commission and the courts may be undergoing modification. The court in the *Daniel* case held that participation by an employee in a collectively bargained, noncontributory pension plan constitutes a "sale" (i.e., a disposition for value) for purposes of the antifraud provisions since the participant acquired an interest in the plan (i.e., a disposition) and the participant gave his services for, among other things, the employer's contribution to the plan on his behalf (i.e., for value). Even though participation in the pension plan was, in effect, compulsory, the court also held that the "element of volition" could be found to the extent that employees vote on the union-negotiated wage package. Since this particular holding is debatable, the court also noted that "voluntariness" is not a requirement for a sale under §2(3) of the '33 Act.

It is important to note that the Securities and Exchange Commission in its *amicus* brief argued in favor of the position ultimately taken by the court. Apparently, the Securities and Exchange Commission takes the rather curious position that, while there may not be a "sale" for purposes of the disclosure provisions, there may be a "sale" for antifraud purposes.

Disclosure or Registration

If an employee's interest in a pension or welfare plan is classified as a security which is sold to the employee, the '33 Act disclosure provisions apply unless an exemption is available. Section 5(a) of the '33 Act provides:

> Unless a registration statement is in effect as to a security, it shall be unlawful for any person, directly or indirectly—
>
> (1) to make use of any means or instruments of transportation or communication in interstate commerce or of the mail to sell such security through the use or medium of any prospectus or otherwise; or
>
> (2) to carry or cause to be carried through the mails or in interstate commerce, by any means or instruments of transportation, any such security for the purpose of sale or for delivery after sale.

This disclosure requirement (through registration)

---

ered by the federal securities laws. *Daniel v. International Bhd. of Teamsters,* 410 F.Supp. at 547. Having suddenly shifted its position in an *amicus* brief in that case, the SEC is no longer entitled on this issue to be accorded the special deference normally granted to an administrative agency interpreting its governing statute. *United Housing Foundation, Inc. v. Forman,* 421 U.S. at 858 n. 25.

is supplemented by a prospectus requirement. Section 5(b) of the '33 Act provides:

> It shall be unlawful for any person, directly or indirectly—
>
> (1) to make use of any means or instruments of transportation or communication in interstate commerce or of the mails to carry or transmit any prospectus relating to any security with respect to which a registration statement has been filed under this title, unless such prospectus meets the requirements of Section 10 prospectus; or
>
> (2) to carry or cause to be carried through the mails or in interstate commerce, any such security for the purpose of sale or for delivery after sale, unless accompanied or preceded by a prospectus that meets the requirements of subsection (a) of Section 10.

Under §10(a)(1) of the '33 Act, the information required to be disclosed through registration and in the prospectus is very similar.

Registration Exemptions

Section 3(a)(2)

The '33 Act contains exemptions from these disclosure requirements for certain securities and transactions. Probably the most important exemption is contained in §3(a)(2), which provides:

> Except as hereinafter expressly provided, the provisions of this title shall not apply to any of the following classes of securities:
>
> . . . . .
>
> . . . any interest or participation in a single or collective trust fund maintained by a bank or in a separate account maintained by an insurance company which interest or participation is issued in connection with (A) a stock bonus, pension or profit-sharing plan which meets the requirements for qualification under §401 of the Internal Revenue Code of 1954 or (B) an annuity plan which meets the requirements for deduction of the employer's contribution under §404(a)(2) of such Code, other than any plan described in clause (A) or (B) of this paragraph (i) the contributions under which are held in a single trust fund maintained by a bank or in a separate account maintained by an insurance company for a single employer and under which an amount in excess of the employer's contribution is allocated to the purchase of securities (other than interests or participations in the trust or separate account itself) issued by the employer or by any company directly or indirectly controlling, controlled by or under common control with the employer or (ii) which covers employees some or all of whom are employees within the meaning of §401(c)(1) of such Code.

While this particular provision seems to exempt most pension plans from the registration requirements, it does not provide an exemption from these requirements for welfare plans.

There are several other problems with this exemption. Particularly troublesome is the requirement that the plan be "maintained by a bank." Plans trusteed by non-bank fiduciaries, such as the employer maintaining the plan, may not be able to satisfy the requirement. More generally, the phrase "maintained by a bank" seems to have different connotations depending on the extent to which the bank exercises discretion with respect to the investment of plan assets and depending on whether there is a single or a collective trust. Presumably, if there is a single trust for a single plan, the bank may be a mere custodian and may rely on others—such as investment managers and non-trustee fiduciaries—to make investment decisions concerning those assets. However, if there is a collective trust for more than one plan or employer, the bank may have to have discretionary authority with respect to the investment of plan assets for the exemption to be available. This distinction is very difficult to justify on the basis of the statutory language, and it may cause particularly acute problems for multiemployer plans where the Taft-Hartley trustees either retain investment discretion or delegate that discretion to an investment adviser other than the bank.

Other Exemptions

The exemption for bank-maintained funds is not the only exemption from the registration requirements. Exemptions for certain transactions are also available, and they should be considered in connection with pension and welfare plans.

For example, §3(a)(11) provides an exemption for any security which is part of an issue offered or sold only to persons resident within a single state or territory, where the issuer of such security is a person resident and doing business within such state or territory. This provision exempts so-called intrastate offerings and it may be available to benefit plans if the employer and the plan are within a single state. Another example is §4(2), which provides an exemption from disclosure for the issue of a security not involving any public offering.

Antifraud

If the establishment of a pension or welfare plan and the distribution of interest therein to employees is classified as the sale of securities, the antifraud provisions of the '33 Act apply even if a registration exemption is available. Section 17(a) of the '33 Act provides:

> It shall be unlawful for any person in the offer or sale of any security by the use of any means or instruments of transportation or communication in interstate commerce or by the use of the mails, directly or indirectly—
> (1) to employ any device, scheme or artifice to defraud, or
> (2) to obtain money or property by means of any untrue statement of a material fact or any omission to state a material fact necessary in order to make the statements made, in light of the circumstances under which they are made, not misleading, or
> (3) to engage in any transaction, practice, or course of business which operates or would operate as a fraud or deceit upon the purchaser.

In and of itself, §17(a) does not impose an affirmative disclosure obligation.[2] Under the '33 Act, affirmative disclosure is primarily a function of the registration and prospectus requirements. This antifraud provision is designed to prevent fraudulent activity in connection with the sale of securities. However, disclosure may be required when the failure to make certain disclosures will render misleading the representations which are made to purchasers. If the distribution of interests in a pension or welfare plan to employees does not constitute the sale of securities for purposes of the registration and prospectus requirements, or if such a distribution does constitute a sale, but is exempt from those requirements by reason of §3(a)(2) or one of the other exemptions, the '33 Act will not require anyone to make oral or written statements relating to the plan to employees. However, once statements are made, they should not be misleading.

For example, in the *Daniel* case, the court premised its conclusion on the finding that the antifraud provisions require disclosure that differs, in both form and substance, from ERISA-required disclosure. The court indicated that the mere distribution of documents required under ERISA to employees might not be sufficient in terms of the '33 Act antifraud provision. The court suggested additional disclosures relating to certain pension terms, and of actuarial probabilities.

Briefly stated, the disclosure requirement under ERISA may trigger disclosure requirements under the antifraud provisions of the '33 Act even if the registration and prospectus requirements are not applicable. If the Securities and Exchange Commission's prospectus requirements for regulated investment companies or mutual funds serve as a useful analogy, the necessary disclosures would include detailed information about pension plan investment practices, including specific information with respect to: borrowing and lending money; investment in real estate; concentration of investments in particular areas; the percentage of plan assets which may be invested in the security of any one issuer; the proportion of assets which may be invested in each type of security proposed to be acquired; and the rate of portfolio turnover. Any material legal proceedings to which a pension or welfare plan was a party would also have to be described. *See* SEC Forms S-5, Item 1(a) and N-8b-1, Items 4, 5 and 9.

The mere failure to make certain disclosures should not result in '33 Act liability, and, to a certain extent, the public may be overreacting to the *Daniel* decision. The court in *Daniel* only held that the plaintiff had stated a cause of action. If the plaintiff in *Daniel* is to prevail on the merits, he will have to show "materiality" and "intent," among other things. The Court's decisions in *TSC Industries v. Northway,* 426 U.S. 438 (1976) (materiality) and *Ernst & Ernst v. Hochfelder,* 425 U.S. 185 (1976) (intent) illustrate these important elements of Daniel's cause of action.

2. The application of the '33 Act antifraud provisions as illustrated here is based primarily on an analysis of the commentary relating to Section 10(b) of the '34 Act, which will be discussed below. The illustration is included here to facilitate analysis.

TSC INDUSTRIES V. NORTHWAY
426 U.S. 438 (1976)

Mr. Justice Marshall delivered the opinion of the Court.

The proxy rules promulgated by the Securities and Exchange Commission under the Securities Exchange Act of 1934 bar the use of proxy statements that are false or misleading with respect to the presentation or omission of material facts. We are called upon to consider the definition of a material fact under those rules, and the appropriateness of resolving the question of materiality by summary judgment in this case.

I

The dispute in this case centers on the acquisition of petitioner TSC Industries, Inc., by petitioner National Industries, Inc. In February 1969 National acquired 34% of TSC's voting securities by purchase from Charles E. Schmidt and his family. Schmidt, who had been TSC's founder and principal shareholder, promptly resigned along with his son from TSC's board of directors. Thereafter, five National nominees were placed on TSC's board; and Stanley R. Yarmuth, National's president and chief executive officer, became chairman of the TSC board, and Charles F. Simonelli, National's executive vice president, became chairman of the TSC executive committee. On October 16, 1969, the TSC board, with the attending National nominees abstaining, approved a proposal to liquidate and sell all of TSC's assets to National. The proposal in substance provided for the exchange of TSC common and Series 1 preferred stock for National Series B preferred stock and warrants.[1] On November 12, 1969, TSC and National issued a joint proxy statement to their shareholders, recommending approval of the proposal. The proxy solicitation was successful, TSC was placed in liquidation and dissolution, and the exchange of shares was effected.

This is an action brought by respondent Northway, a TSC shareholder, against TSC and National, claiming that their joint proxy statement was incomplete and materially misleading in violation of §14(a) of the Securities Exchange Act of 1934, 48 Stat. 895, 15 U.S.C. §78n(a) [15 U.S.C.S. §78n(a)],[2] and Rules 14a-3 and 14a-9 promulgated thereunder. 17 CFR §§240.14a-3, 240.14a-9 (1975).[3] The basis of Northway's claim under Rule 14a-3 is that TSC and National failed to state in the proxy statement that the transfer of the Schmidt interests in TSC to National had given National control of TSC.[4] The Rule 14a-9 claim, insofar as it concerns us,[5] is that TSC and National omitted from the proxy statement material facts relating to the degree of National's control over TSC and the favorability of the terms of the proposal to TSC shareholders.[6]

Northway filed its complaint in the United States District Court for the Northern District of Illinois on December 4, 1969, the day before the

1. Each share of TSC common stock brought .5 share of National Series B preferred stock and 1½ National warrants. Each share of TSC Series 1 preferred stock brought .6 share of National Series B preferred stock and one National warrant. National Series B preferred stock is convertible into .75 share of National common stock. A National warrant entitles the holder to purchase one share of National common stock at a fixed price until October 1978.

2. Section 14(a) provides:

> It shall be unlawful for any person, by the use of the mails or by any means or instrumentality of interstate commerce or of any facility of a national securities exchange or otherwise, in contravention of such rules and regulations as the Commission may prescribe as necessary or appropriate in the public interest or for the protection of investors, to solicit or to permit the use of his name to solicit any proxy or consent or authorization in respect of any security (other than an exempted security) registered pursuant to section 781 of this title.

3. Northway also alleged in its complaint that National pursued a fraudulent plan to acquire TSC for less than its fair value in violation of §10(b) of the Securities Exchange Act, 15 U.S.C. §78j(b) [15 U.S.C.S. §78j(b)], and Rule 10b-5 promulgated thereunder. 17 CFR §240.10 b-5 (1975). Northway has not pursued this claim in the proceedings that we are called upon to review. Northway also brought suit against Charles Schmidt and his family, charging them with aiding and abetting the corporate defendants in violation of §10(b) and Rule 10b-5. The District Court granted summary judgment to the Schmidt defendants, and the Court of Appeals affirmed. That aspect of the original suit is not before us.

4. Rule 14a-3(a) provides that:

> No solicitation subject to this regulation shall be made unless each person solicited is concurrently furnished or has previously been furnished with a written proxy statement containing the information specified in Schedule 14A.

Schedule 14A, Item 5(e), requires:

> If to the knowledge of the persons on whose behalf the solicitation is made a change in control of the issuer has occurred since the beginning of its last fiscal year, state the name of the person or persons who acquired such control, the basis of such control, the date and a description of the transaction or transactions in which control was acquired and the percentage of voting securities of the issuer now owned by such person or persons.

17 CFR §240.14a-101, Item 5(e) (1975).

5. Northway also asserted a claim under Rule 14a-9 that the proxy statement was materially misleading in its assertion that the TSC board of directors had approved the proposed transaction. It contended, first, that the proposal was never legally approved under applicable state law; and, second, that the statement should have in any event disclosed that the proposal received only four affirmative votes, and that the National nominees were cautioned against voting by their legal advisers. The Court of Appeals did not reach the first contention, and it found summary judgment inappropriate on the second. Neither contention is before us.

6. Rule 14a-9(a) provides:

> No solicitation subject to this regulation shall be made by means of any proxy statement, form of proxy, notice of meeting or other communication, written or oral, containing any statement which, at the time and in the light of the circumstances under which it is made, is false or misleading with respect to any material fact, or which omits to state any material fact necessary in order to make the statements therein not false or misleading or necessary to correct any statement in any earlier communication with respect to the solicitation of a proxy for the same meeting or subject matter which has become false or misleading.

shareholder meeting on the proposed transaction, but while it requested injunctive relief it never so moved. In 1972 Northway amended its complaint to seek money damages, restitution, and other equitable relief. Shortly thereafter, Northway moved for summary judgment on the issue of TSC's and National's liability. The District Court denied the motion, but granted leave to appeal pursuant to 28 U.S.C. §1292(b) [28 U.S.C.S. §1292(b)]. The Court of Appeals for the Seventh Circuit agreed with the District Court that there existed a genuine issue of fact as to whether National's acquisition of the Schmidt interests in TSC had resulted in a change of control, and that summary judgment was therefore inappropriate on the Rule 14a-3 claim. But the Court of Appeals reversed the District Court's denial of summary judgment to Northway on its Rule 14a-9 claims, holding that certain omissions of fact were material as a matter of law. 512 F.2d 324 (1975).

We granted certiorari because the standard applied by the Court of Appeals in resolving the question of materiality appeared to conflict with the standard applied by other Courts of Appeals. 423 U.S. 820, 46 L.Ed.2d 37, 96 S.Ct. 33 (1975). We now hold that the Court of Appeals erred in ordering that partial summary judgment be granted to Northway.

II

A

As we have noted on more than one occasion, §14(a) of the Securities Exchange Act "was intended to promote 'the free exercise of the voting rights of stockholders' by ensuring that proxies would be solicited with 'explanation to the stockholder of the real nature of the questions for which authority to cast his vote is sought.'" *Mills v. Electric Auto-Lite Co.* 396 U.S. 375, 381, 24 L.Ed. 2d 593, 90 S.Ct. 616 (1970), quoting HR Rep. No. 1383, 73d Cong. 2d Sess. 14 (1934); S. Rep. No. 792, 73d Cong. 2d Sess. 12 (1934). *See also J. I. Case Co. v. Borak,* 377 U.S. 426, 431, 12 L.Ed.2d 423, 84 S.Ct. 1555 (1964). In *Borak,* the Court held that §14(a)'s broad remedial purposes required recognition under §27 of the Exchange Act, 15 U.S.C. §78aa [15 U.S.C.S. §78aa], of an implied private right of action for violations of the provision. And in *Mills,* we attempted to clarify to some extent the elements of a private cause of action for violation of §14(a). In a suit challenging the sufficiency under §14(a) and Rule 14a-9 of a proxy statement soliciting votes in favor of a merger, we held that there was no need to demonstrate that the alleged defect in the proxy statement actually had a decisive effect on the voting. So long as the misstatement or omission was material, the causal relation between violation and injury is sufficiently established, we concluded, if "the proxy solicitation itself . . . was an essential link in the accomplishment of the transaction." 396 U.S. at 385, 24 L.Ed.2d 593, 90 S.Ct. 616. After *Mills,* then, the content given to the notion of materiality assumes heightened significance.[7]

B

The question of materiality, it is universally agreed, is an objective one, involving the significance of an omitted or misrepresented fact to a reasonable investor. Variations in the formulation of a general test of materiality occur in the articulation of just how significant a fact must be or, put another way, how certain it must be that the fact would affect a reasonable investor's judgment.

The Court of Appeals in this case concluded that material facts include "all facts which a reasonable shareholder *might* consider important." 512 F.2d, at 330 (emphasis added). This formulation of the test of materiality has been explicitly rejected by at least two courts as setting too low a threshold for the imposition of liability under Rule 14a-9. *Gerstle v. Gamble-Skogmo, Inc.* 478 F.2d 1281, 1301-1302 (C.A.2 1973); *Smallwood v. Pearl Brewing Co.* 489 F.2d 579, 603-604 (C.A.5 1974). In these cases, panels of the Second and Fifth Circuits opted for the conventional tort test of materiality—whether a reasonable man *would* attach importance to the fact misrepresented or omitted in determining his course of action. *See* Restatement (Second) of Torts §538(2)(a) (Tent. Draft No. 10, Apr. 20, 1964). *See also* American Law Institute, Federal Securities Code §256(a) (Tent. Draft No. 2, 1973).[8] *Gerstle v. Gamble-*

---

7. Our cases have not considered, and we have no occasion in this case to consider, what showing of culpability is required to establish the liability under §14(a) of a corporation issuing a materially misleading proxy statement, or of a person involved in the preparation of a materially misleading proxy statement. *See Gerstle v. Gamble-Skogmo, Inc.* 478 F.2d 1281, 1298-1301 (C.A.2 1973); *Richland v. Crandall,* 262 F.Supp. 538, 553 n. 12 (S.D.N.Y. 1967); R. Jennings & H. Marsh, Securities Regulation: Cases and Materials 1358-1359 (3d ed. 1972). *See also Ernst & Ernst v. Hochfelder,* 425 U.S. 185, 209 n. 28, 47 L.Ed.2d 668, 96 S.Ct. 1375 (1976).

8. This standard, or a close approximation, has been widely recited in cases involving various sections of the securities laws. *See, e.g., Chris-Craft Industries,*

Skogmo, supra, at 1302, also approved the following standard, which had been formulated with reference to statements issued in a contested election: "whether, taking a properly realistic view, there is a substantial likelihood that the misstatement or omission may have led a stockholder to grant a proxy to the solicitor or to withhold one from the other side, whereas in the absence of this he would have taken a contrary course." *General Time Corp. v. Talley Industries, Inc*. 403 F.2d 159, 162 (C.A.2 1968), *cert. denied,* 393 U.S. 1026, 21 L.Ed.2d 570, 89 S.Ct. 631 (1969).

In arriving at its broad definition of a material fact as one that a reasonable shareholder *might* consider important, the Court of Appeals in this case relied heavily upon language of this Court in *Mills v. Electric Auto-Lite Co., supra.* That reliance was misplaced. The *Mills* Court did characterize a determination of materiality as at least "embod[ying] a conclusion that the defect was of such character that it might have been considered important by a reasonable shareholder who was in the process of deciding how to vote." 396 U.S., at 384, 24 L.Ed.2d 593, 90 S.Ct. 616. But if any language in *Mills* is to be read as suggesting a general notion of materiality, it can only be the opinion's subsequent reference to materiality as a "requirement that the defect have a significant *propensity* to affect the voting process." *Ibid.* (emphasis in original). For it was that requirement that the Court said "adequately serves the purpose of ensuring that a cause of action cannot be established by proof of a defect so trivial, or so unrelated to the transaction for which approval is sought, that correction of the defect or imposition of liability would not further the interests protected by §14(a)." *Ibid.* Even this language must be read, however, with appreciation that the Court specifically declined to consider the materiality of the omissions in *Mills. Id.,* at 381 n. 4, L.Ed.2d 593, 90 S.Ct. 616. The references to materiality were simply preliminary to our consideration of the sole question in the case—whether proof of the materiality of an omission from a proxy statement must be supplemented by a showing that the defect actually caused the outcome of the vote. It is clear, then, that Mills did not intend to foreclose futher inquiry into the meaning of materiality under Rule 14a-9.[9]

C

In formulating a standard of materiality under Rule 14a-9, we are guided, of course, by the recognition in *Borak* and *Mills* of the Rule's broad remedial purpose. That purpose is not merely to ensure by judicial means that the transaction, when judged by its real terms, is fair and otherwise adequate, but to ensure disclosures by corporate management in order to enable the shareholders to make an informed choice. *See Mills,* 396 U.S., at 381, 24 L.Ed.2d 593, 90 S.Ct. 616. As an abstract proposition, the most desirable role for a court in a suit of this sort, coming after the consummation of the proposed transaction, would perhaps be to determine whether in fact the proposal would have been favored by the shareholders and consummated in the absence of any misstatement or omission. But as we recognized in *Mills, supra,* at 382 n. 5, 24 L.Ed.2d 593, 90 S.Ct.

Inc. v. Piper Aircraft Corp. 480 F.2d 341, 363 (C.A.2 1973) (§14(e)); *John R. Lewis, Inc. v. Newman,* 446 F.2d 800, 804 (C.A.5 1971) (§10(b)); *Gilbert v. Nixon,* 429 F.2d 348, 355-356 (C.A.10 1970) (§10(b) of the Securities Exchange Act and §12(2) of the Securities Act of 1933, 48 Stat. 84, 15 U.S.C. §781 [15 U.S.C.S. §781]; *Rogen v. Ilikon Corp.* 361 F.2d 260, 266 (C.A.1 1966) (§10(b)); *SEC v. Texas Gulf Sulphur Co.* 401 F.2d 833, 849 (C.A.2 1968), *cert. denied sub nom Coates v. SEC,* 394 U.S. 976, 22 L.Ed.2d 756, 89 S.Ct. 1454 (1969) (§10(b)); *List v. Fashion Park, Inc.* 340 F.2d 457, 462 (C.A.2), *cert. denied, sub nom List v. Lerner,* 382 U.S. 811, 15 L.Ed.2d 60, 86 S.Ct. 23 (1965) (§10(b)); *Kohler v. Kohler Co.* 319 F.2d 634, 642 (C.A.7 1963) (§10(b)). But *see Sonesta Int'l Hotels Corp. v. Wellington Associates,* 483 F.2d 247, 251 (C.A.2 1973). In several of these cases, the courts have also defined materiality to encompass those facts "which in reasonable and objective contemplation might affect the value" of the securities involved, *Rogen v. Ilikon, supra; SEC v. Texas Gulf Sulphur, supra; List v. Fashion Park, Inc., supra; Kohler v. Kohler Co., supra.* The standard adopted by the Court of Appeals in this case has been applied in *Kohn v. American Metal Climax, Inc.* 458 F.2d 255, 269 (C.A.3 1972) (§10(b)), and *Ronson Corp. v. Liquifin Aktiengesellschaft,* 483 F.2d 846, 851 (C.A.3 1973) (§14(e)).

9. Nor is *Affiliated Ute Citizens v. United States,* 406 U.S. 128, 31 L.Ed.2d 741, 92 S.Ct. 1456 (1972), also relied upon by the Court of Appeals, dispositive. There we held that when a Rule 10b-5 violation involves a failure to disclose, "positive proof of reliance is not a prerequisite to recovery. All that is necessary is that the facts withheld be material in the sense that a reasonable investor might have considered them important in the making of this decision." *Id.,* at 153-154, 31 L.Ed.2d 741, 92 S.Ct. 1456. The conclusion embodied in the quoted language was simply that positive proof of reliance is unnecessary when materiality is established, and in order to reach that conclusion it was not necessary to articulate a precise definition of materiality, but only to give a "sense" of the notion. The quoted language did not purport to do more.

616, such matters are not subject to determination with certainty. Doubts as to the critical nature of information misstated or omitted will be commonplace. And particularly in view of the prophylactic purpose of the Rule and the fact that the content of the proxy statement is within management's control, it is appropriate that these doubts be resolved in favor of those the statute is designed to protect. *Mills, supra,* at 385, 24 L.Ed.2d 593, S.Ct. 616.

We are aware, however, that the disclosure policy embodied in the proxy regulations is not without limit. *See id.,* at 384, 24 L.Ed.2d 593, 90 S.Ct. 616. Some information is of such dubious significance that insistence on its disclosure may accomplish more harm than good. The potential liability for a Rule 14a-9 violation can be great indeed, and if the standard of materiality is unnecessarily low, not only may the corporation and its management be subjected to liability for insignificant omissions or misstatements, but also management's fear of exposing itself to substantial liability may cause it simply to bury the shareholders in an avalanche of trivial information—a result that is hardly conducive to informed decision making. Precisely these dangers are presented, we think, by the definition of a material fact adopted by the Court of Appeals in this case —a fact which a reasonable shareholder *might* consider important. We agree with Judge Friendly, speaking for the Court of Appeals in *Gerstle,* that the "might" formulation is "too suggestive of mere possibility, however unlikely." 478 F.2d, at 1302.

The general standard of materiality that we think best comports with the policies of Rule 14a-9 is as follows: An omitted fact is material if there is a substantial likelihood that a reasonable shareholder would consider it important in deciding how to vote. This standard is fully consistent with *Mills'* general description of materiality as a requirement that "the defect have a significant *propensity* to affect the voting process." It does not require proof of a substantial likelihood that disclosure of the omitted fact would have caused the reasonable investor to change his vote. What the standard does contemplate is a showing of a substantial likelihood that, under all the circumstances, the omitted fact would have assumed actual significance in the deliberations of the reasonable shareholder. Put another way, there must be a substantial likelihood that the disclosure of the omitted fact would have been viewed by the reasonable investor as having significantly altered the "total mix" of information made available.[10]

D

The issue of materiality may be characterized as a mixed question of law and fact, involving as it does the application of a legal standard to a particular set of facts. In considering whether summary judgment on the issue is appropriate,[11] we must bear in mind that the underlying objective facts, which will often be free from dispute, are merely the starting point for the ultimate determination of materiality. The determination requires delicate assessments of the inferences a "reasonable shareholder" would draw from a given set of facts and the significance of those inferences to him, and these assessments are peculiarly ones for the trier of fact.[12] Only if the established omissions are "so obviously important to an investor, that reasonable minds cannot differ on the question of materiality" is the ultimate issue of materiality appropriately resolved "as a matter of law" by summary judgment. *Johns Hopkins University v. Hutton,* 422 F.2d 1124, 1129 (C.A.4 1970). *See Smallwood v. Pearl Brewing Co.* 489 F.2d, at 604; *Rogen v. Ilikon Corp.* 361 F.2d 260, 265-267 (C.A.1 1966).

III

The omissions found by the Court of Appeals to have been materially misleading as a matter of law involved two general issues—the degree of National's control over TSC at the time of the

10. In defining materiality under Rule 14a-9, we are, of course, giving content to a rule promulgated by the SEC pursuant to broad statutory authority to promote "the public interest" and "the protection of investors." *See* n. 2, *supra. Cf. Ernst & Ernst v. Hochfelder,* 425 U.S. at 212-214, 47 L.Ed.2d 668, 96 S.Ct. 1375 (Mar. 30, 1976). Under these circumstances, the SEC's view of the proper balance between the need to insure adequate disclosure and the need to avoid the adverse consequences of setting too low a threshold for civil liability is entitled to consideration. *Cf. Northern Indiana Public Service Co. v. Izaac Walton League,* 423 U.S. 12, 15, 46 L.Ed.2d 156, 96 S.Ct. 172 (1975); *Udall v. Tallman,* 380 U.S. 1, 16-17, 13 L.Ed.2d 616, 85 S.Ct. 792 (1965). The standard we adopt is supported by the SEC. Brief for the Securities and Exchange Commission as Amicus Curiae 13.

11. Federal Rule Civ. Proc. 56(c) permits summary judgment only when "there is no genuine issue as to any material fact."

12. In an analogous context, the jury's unique competence in applying the "reasonable man" standard is thought ordinarily to preclude summary judgment in negligence cases. *See* 10 C. Wright & A. Miller, Federal Practice and Procedure: Civil §2729 (1973).

proxy solicitation, and the favorability of the terms of the proposed transaction to TSC shareholders.

A. National's Control of TSC

The Court of Appeals concluded that two omitted facts relating to National's potential influence, or control, over the management of TSC were material as a matter of law. First, the proxy statement failed to state that at the time the statement was issued, the chairman of the TSC board of directors was Stanley Yarmuth, National's president and chief executive officer, and the chairman of the TSC executive committee was Charles Simonelli, National's executive vice president. Second, the statement did not disclose that in filing reports required by the SEC, both TSC and National had indicated that National "may be deemed to be a 'parent' of TSC as that term is defined in the Rules and Regulations under the Securities Act of 1933." App. 490, 512, 517.[13] The Court of Appeals noted that TSC shareholders were relying on the TSC board of directors to negotiate on their behalf for the best possible rate of exchange with National. It then concluded that the omitted facts were material because they were "persuasive indicators that the TSC board was in fact under the control of National, and that National thus 'sat on both sides of the table' in setting the terms of the exchange." 512 F.2d, at 333.

We do not agree that the omission of these facts, when viewed against the disclosures contained in the proxy statement, warrants the entry of summary judgment against TSC and National on this record. Our conclusion is the same whether the omissions are considered separately or together.

The proxy statement prominently displayed the facts that National owned 34% of the outstanding shares in TSC, and that no other person owned more than 10%. App. 262-263, 267. It also prominently revealed that five out of ten TSC directors were National nominees, and it recited the positions of those National nominees with National—indicating, among other things, that Stanley Yarmuth was president and a director of National, and that Charles Simonelli was executive vice president and a director of National. *Id.,* at 267. These disclosures clearly revealed the nature of National's relationship with TSC and alerted the reasonable shareholder to the fact that National exercised a degree of influence over TSC. In view of these disclosures, we certainly cannot say that the additional facts that Yarmuth was chairman of the TSC board of directors and Simonelli chairman of its executive committee were, on this record, so obviously important that reasonable minds could not differ on their materiality.

Nor can we say that it was materially misleading as a matter of law for TSC and National to have omitted reference to SEC filings indicating that National "may be deemed to be a parent of TSC." As we have already noted, both the District Court and the Court of Appeals concluded, in denying summary judgment on the Rule 14a-3 claim, that there was a genuine issue of fact as to whether National actually controlled TSC at the time of the proxy solicitation. We must assume for present purposes, then, that National did not control TSC. On that assumption, TSC and National obviously had no duty to state without qualification that control did exist. If the proxy statements were to disclose the conclusory statements in the SEC filings that National "may be deemed to be a parent of TSC," then it would have been appropriate, if not necessary, for the statement to have

---

13. The quoted language is from National's Form 13D, filed in compliance with §13(d) of the Securities Exchange Act, 15 U.S.C. §78m(d) [15 U.S.C.S. §78 m(d)]. *See* 17 CFR §240.13d-1 (1975). Substantially identical language appeared in TSC's Form 10-K, and was incorporated by reference into its Form 8-K, both filed in compliance with §13(a) of the Securities Exchange Act, 15 U.S.C. §78m(a) [15 U.S.C.S. §78 m(a)]. *See* 17 CFR §§240.13a-10-11 (1975). The term "parent" is defined in SEC Rule 12b-2(a), (f), (k), 17 CFR §§240.12b-2(a), (f), (k) (1975):

> Unless the context otherwise requires, the following terms, when used in the rules contained in this regulation or in Regulation 13A or 15D or in the forms for statements and reports filed pursuant to sections 12, 13 or 15(d) of the [Securities Exchange] Act, shall have the respective meanings indicated in this rule:
>
> (a) *Affiliate*. An "affiliate" of, or a person "affiliated" with, a specified person, is a person that directly, or indirectly through one or more intermediaries, controls, or is controlled by, or is under common control with, the person specified.
>
> ......
>
> (f) *Control*. The term "control" (including the terms "controlling," "controlled by" and "under common control with") means the possession, directly or indirectly, of the power to direct or cause the direction of the management and policies of a person, whether through the ownership of voting securities, by contract, or otherwise.
>
> ......
>
> (k) *Parent*. A "parent" of a specified person is an affiliate controlling such person directly, or indirectly through one or more intermediaries.

The Rules and Regulations under the Securities Act of 1933 contain the identical definitions. 17 CFR §§230. 405(a), (f), (n) (1975).

included a disclaimer of National control over TSC or a disclaimer of knowledge as to whether National controlled TSC.[14] The net contribution of including the contents of the SEC filings accompanied by such disclaimers is not of such obvious significance, in view of the other facts contained in the proxy statement, that their exclusion renders the statement materially misleading as a matter of law.[15]

B. Favorability of the Terms to TSC Shareholders

The Court of Appeals also found that the failure to disclose two sets of facts rendered the proxy statement materially deficient in its presentation of the favorability of the terms of the proposed transaction to TSC shareholders. The first omission was of information, described by the Court of Appeals as "bad news" for TSC shareholders, contained in a letter from an investment banking firm whose earlier favorable opinion of the fairness of the proposed transaction was reported in the proxy statement. The second omission related to purchases of National common stock by National and by Madison Fund, Inc., a large mutual fund, during the two years prior to the issuance of the proxy statement.

1

The proxy statement revealed that the investment banking firm of Hornblower & Weeks-Hemphill, Noyes had rendered a favorable opinion on the fairness to TSC shareholders of the terms for the exchange of TSC shares for National securities. In that opinion, the proxy statement explained, the firm had considered, "among other things, the current market prices of the securities of both corporations, the high redemption price of the National Series B preferred stock, the dividend and debt service requirements of both corporations, the substantial premium over current market values represented by the securities being offered to TSC stockholders, and the increased dividend income." App. 267.

The Court of Appeals focused upon the reference to the "substantial premium over current market values represented by the securities being offered to TSC stockholders," and noted that any TSC shareholder could calculate the apparent premium by reference to the table of current market prices that appeared four pages later in the proxy statement. *Id.,* at 271. On the basis of the recited closing prices for November 7, 1969, five days before the issuance of the proxy statement, the apparent premiums were as follows. Each share of TSC Series 1 preferred, which closed at $12, would bring National Series B preferred stock and National warrants worth $15.23—for a premium of $3.23, or 27% of the market value of the TSC Series 1 preferred. Each share of TSC common stock, which closed at $13.25, would bring National Series B preferred stock and National warrants worth $16.19—for a premium of $2.94, or 22% of the market value of TSC common.[16]

The closing price of the National warrants on November 7, 1969, was, as indicated in the proxy statement, $5.25. The TSC shareholders were misled, the Court of Appeals concluded, by the proxy statement's failure to disclose that in a communication two weeks after its favorable

14. It is the position of National and TSC that "[s]ince National and the old TSC management . . . never drew any clear-cut battle lines, no one ever really knew who could ultimately control TSC during the entire period between the Schmidt purchase and consummation of the shareholder-approved purchase of TSC's assets." Brief for Petitioners 33.

15. We emphasize that we do not intend to imply that facts suggestive of control need be disclosed only if in fact there was control. If, for example, the proxy statement in this case had failed to reveal National's 34% stock interest in TSC and the presence of five National nominees on TSC's board, these omissions would have rendered the statement materially misleading as a matter of law, regardless of whether National can be said with certainty to have been in "control" of TSC. The reasons for this are twofold. First, to the extent that the existence of control was, at the time of the proxy statement's issuance, a matter of doubt to those responsible for preparing the statement, we would be unwilling to resolve that doubt against disclosure of facts so obviously suggestive of control. Second, and perhaps more to the point, even if National did not "control" TSC, its stock ownership and position on the TSC board make it quite clear that it enjoyed some influence over TSC, which would be of obvious importance to TSC shareholders.

16. The premium based upon November 7, 1969, closing prices is calculated as follows:

	TSC Preferred	TSC Common
National B pfd.		
(at 16-5/8) . . .	$ 9.98 (.6 sh.)	$ 8.31 (.5 sh.)
National warrant		
(at 5-1/4)	5.25	7.88 (1½ war.)
Total.	$15.23	$16.19
Less TSC market		
(pfd. 12)		
(com. 13-1/4) .	12.00	13.25
Premium. . .	3.23	2.94
Premium expressed as a percentage of TSC market . .		27% 22%

opinion letter, the Hornblower firm revealed that its determination of the fairness of the offer to TSC was based on the conclusion that the value of the warrants involved in the transaction would not be their current market price, but approximately $3.50. If the warrants were valued at $3.50 rather than $5.25, and the other securities valued at the November 7 closing price, the court figured, the apparent premium would be substantially reduced—from $3.23 (27%) to $1.48 (12%) in the case of the TSC preferred, and from $2.94 (22%) to $0.31 (2%) in the case of TSC common. "In simple terms," the Court concluded: "TSC and National had received some good news and some bad news from the Hornblower firm. They chose to publish the good news and omit the bad news." 512 F.2d, at 335.

It would appear, however, that the subsequent communication from the Hornblower firm, which the Court of Appeals felt contained "bad news," contained nothing new at all. At the TSC board of directors meeting held on October 16, 1969, the date of the initial Hornblower opinion letter, Blancke Noyes, a TSC director and a partner in the Hornblower firm, had pointed out the likelihood of a decline in the market price of National warrants with the issuance of the additional warrants involved in the exchange, and reaffirmed his conclusion that the exchange offer was a fair one nevertheless. The subsequent Hornblower letter, signed by Mr. Noyes, purported merely to explain the basis of the calculations underlying the favorable opinion rendered in the October 16 letter. "In advising TSC as to the fairness of the offer from [National]," Mr. Noyes wrote, "we concluded that the warrants in question had a value of approximately $3.50."[17] On its face, then, the subsequent letter from Hornblower does not appear to have contained anything to alter the favorable opinion rendered in the October 16 letter—including the conclusion that the securities being offered to TSC shareholders represented a "substantial premium over current market values."

The real question, though, is not whether the subsequent Hornblower letter contained anything that altered the Hornblower opinion in any way. It is, rather, whether the advice given at the October 16 meeting, and reduced to more precise terms in the subsequent Hornblower letter—that there might be a decline in the market price of the National warrants—had to be disclosed in order to clarify the import of the proxy statement's reference to "the substantial premium over current market values represented by the securities being offered to TSC stockholders." We note initially that the proxy statement referred to the substantial premium as but one of several factors considered by Hornblower in rendering its favorable opinion of the terms of exchange. Still, we cannot assume that a TSC shareholder would focus only on the "bottom line" of the opinion to the exclusion of the considerations that produced it.

TSC and National insist that the reference to a substantial premium required no clarification or supplementation, for the reason that there was a substantial premium even if the National warrants are assumed to have been worth $3.50. In reaching the contrary conclusion, the Court of Appeals, they contend, ignored the rise in price of TSC securities between early October 1969, when the exchange ratio was set, and November 7, 1969—a rise in price that they suggest was a result of the favorable exchange ratio's becoming public knowledge. When the proxy statement was mailed, TSC and National contend, the market price of TSC securities already reflected a portion of the premium to which Hornblower had referred in rendering its favorable opinion of the terms of exchange. Thus, they note that Hornblower assessed the

17. The body of the subsequent Hornblower letter, dated October 31, 1969, from Mr. Noyes to Stanley Yarmuth, president of National, reads in full:

> You have asked for our opinion as to the value of warrants to be issued in connection with your proposed acquisition of TSC Industries. We understand that these warrants have terms identical to the National Industries (NII) warrants listed on the American Stock Exchange which allow the holder to purchase one NII Common at the price of $21.40 until October 31, 1978. We further understand that you desire our determination as of October 9, 1969.
>
> Our evaluation of these warrants was made from the point of view of the stockholders of TSC Industries, of which I am a director. In advising TSC as to the fairness of the offer from NII it was necessary to determine whether the value of the warrants was reflected by the market price of the outstanding 487,000 warrants on the day in question. We did so in the light of the fact that approximately 2.6 million additional warrants would be issued in connection with the acquisition.
>
> After studying price relationships of other warrants traded publicly, referring to customary systems of warrant evaluation, and considering the particulars of the proposed acquisition, we concluded that the warrants in question had a value of approximately $3.50.
>
> If you have any questions concerning our evaluation, please feel free to call.
>
> App. 519.

fairness of the proposed transaction by reference to early October market prices of TSC preferred, TSC common, and National preferred. On the basis of those prices and a $3.50 value for the National warrants involved in the exchange, TSC and National contend that the premium was substantial. Each share of TSC preferred, selling in early October at $11, would bring National preferred stock and warrants worth $13.10—for a premium of $2.10, or 19%. And each share of TSC common, selling in early October at $11.63, would bring National preferred stock and warrants worth $13.25—for a premium of $1.62, or 14%.[18] We certainly cannot say as a matter of law that these premiums were not substantial. And if, as we must assume in considering the appropriateness of summary judgment, the increase in price of TSC's securities from early October to November 7 reflected in large part the market's reaction to the terms of the proposed exchange, it was not materially misleading as a matter of law for the proxy statement to refer to the existence of a substantial premium.

There remains the possibility, however, that although TSC and National may be correct in urging the existence of a substantial premium based upon a $3.50 value for the National warrants and the early October market prices of the other securities involved in the transaction, the proxy statement misled the TSC shareholder to calculate a premium substantially in excess of that premium. The premiums apparent from early October market prices and a $3.50 value for the National warrants—19% on TSC preferred and 14% on TSC common—are certainly less than those that would be derived through use of the November 7 closing prices listed in the proxy statement—27% on TSC preferred and 22% on TSC common. But we are unwilling to sustain a grant of summary judgment to Northway on that basis. To do so we would have to conclude as a matter of law, first, that the proxy statement would have misled the TSC shareholder to calculate his premium on the basis of November 7 market prices, and second, that the difference between that premium and that which would be apparent from early October prices and a $3.50 value for the National warrants was material. These are questions we think best left to the trier of fact.

2

The final omission that concerns us relates to purchases of National common stock by National and by Madison Fund, Inc., a mutual fund. Northway notes that National's board chairman was a director of Madison, and that Madison's president and chief executive, Edward Merkle, was employed by National pursuant to an agreement obligating him to provide at least one day per month for such duties as National might request.[19] Northway contends that the proxy statement, having called the TSC shareholders' attention to the market prices of the securities involved in the proposed transaction, should have revealed substantial purchases of National common stock made by National and Madison during the two years prior to the issuance of the proxy statement.[20] In particular, Northway contends that the TSC shareholders should, as a matter of law, have been informed that National and Madison purchases accounted for 8.5% of all reported transactions in National common stock during the period between National's acquisition of the Schmidt interests and the proxy solicitation. The theory behind Northway's contention is that disclosure of these purchases would have pointed to the existence, or at least the possible existence,

18. The premium based upon a $3.50 value for the National warrants and the closing prices of the other securities involved on October 9, 1969, the day the exchange ratio was set, is calculated as follows:

	TSC Preferred	TSC Common
National B pfd. (at 16)	$ 9.60 (.6 sh.)	$ 8.00 (.5 sh.)
National warrant (at 3.50)	3.50	5.25 (1 ½ war.)
Total......	$13.10	$13.25
Less TSC market (pfd. 11) (com. 11-5/8)	11.00	11.63
Premium...	2.10	1.62
Premium expressed as a percentage of TSC market	19%	14%

19. Employed in 1967, Merkle initially received a salary of $2,500 per year (increased in 1968 to $12,000) and an option to purchase 10,000 shares of National common stock. App. 520, 522.

20. In a table entitled "Statements of Consolidated Stockholders' Equity," the proxy statement indicated that National acquired approximately 83,000 shares of its own common stock in 1968 and 1969, while it sold approximately 67,000 shares under stock option plans, employment agreements, and warrants. *Id.,* at 324, 330. The proxy statement did not disclose that Madison acquired approximately 170,000 shares of National common during the two-year period, or that approximately one year prior to the proxy solicitation Madison acquired $2 million in National debentures convertible to common.

of conspiratorial manipulation of the price of National common stock, which would have had an effect on the market price of the National preferred stock and warrants involved in the proposed transaction.[21]

Before the District Court, Northway attempted to demonstrate that the National and Madison purchases were coordinated. The District Court concluded, however, that there was a genuine issue of fact as to whether there was coordination. Finding that a showing of coordination was essential to Northway's theory, the District Court denied summary judgment.

The Court of Appeals agreed with the District Court that "collusion is not conclusively established." 512 F.2d, at 336. But observing that "it is certainly suggested," *ibid.,* the court concluded that the failure to disclose the purchases was materially misleading as a matter of law. The court explained:

> Stockholders contemplating an offer involving preferred shares convertible to common stock and warrants for the purchase of common stock must be informed of circumstances which tend to indicate that the current selling price of the common stock involved may be affected by apparent market manipulations. It was for the shareholders to determine whether the market price of the common shares was relevant to their evaluation of the convertible preferred shares and warrants, or whether the activities of Madison and National actually amounted to manipulation at all.
>
> *Ibid.*

In short, while the Court of Appeals viewed the purchases as significant only insofar as they suggested manipulation of the price of National securities, and acknowledged the existence of a genuine issue of fact as to whether there was any manipulation, the court nevertheless required disclosure to enable the shareholders to decide whether there was manipulation or not.

The Court of Appeals' approach would sanction the imposition of civil liability on a theory that undisclosed information may *suggest* the existence of market manipulation, even if the responsible corporate officials knew that there was in fact no market manipulation. We do not agree that Rule 14a-9 requires such a result. Rule 14a-9 is concerned only with whether a proxy statement is misleading with respect to its presentation of material facts. If, as we must assume on a motion for summary judgment, there was no collusion or manipulation whatsoever in the National and Madison purchases—that is, if the purchases were made wholly independently for proper corporate and investment purposes, then by Northway's implicit acknowledgment they had no bearing on the soundness and reliability of the market prices listed in the proxy statement,[22] and it cannot have been materially misleading to fail to disclose them.[23]

That is not to say, of course, that the SEC could not enact a rule specifically requiring the disclosure of purchases such as were involved in this case, without regard to whether the purchases can be shown to have been collusive or manipulative. We simply hold that if liability is to be imposed in this case upon a theory that it was misleading to fail to disclose purchases suggestive of market manipulation, there must be some showing that there was in fact market manipulation.[24]

IV

In summary, none of the omissions claimed to have been in violation of Rule 14a-9 were, so far as the record reveals, materially misleading as a matter of law, and Northway was not entitled to partial summary judgment. The judgment of the Court of Appeals is reversed, and the case is remanded for further proceedings consistent with this opinion.

It is so ordered.

---

21. *See* n. 1, *supra.*

22. There has been no suggestion that the purchases in question would have any significance if there was in fact no manipulation or collusion, although there may perhaps be such a claim in another case. Nor is there any indication that manipulation or collusion are matters as to whose existence National might have been left in doubt at the time the proxy statement was issued. *Cf.* n. 16, *supra.*

23. In holding that the failure to disclose the National and Madison purchases violated Rule 14a-9 as a matter of law, the Court of Appeals not only found it unnecessary to consider whether there was in fact any collusion or manipulation, but also found it unnecessary to consider whether the purchases had any significant effect on the price of National common stock or, more pertinently, the price of the National preferred stock and warrants involved in the proposed transaction. Since we find the existence of a genuine issue of fact with respect to whether there was manipulation sufficient to bar summary judgment, it is unnecessary to consider the remaining aspects of the Court of Appeals' decision.

24. Of course, such a showing may be by circumstantial as well as direct evidence, and the purchases themselves may be considered.

ERNST & ERNST V. HOCHFELDER
425 U.S. 185 (1976)

Mr. Justice Powell delivered the opinion of the Court.

The issue in this case is whether an action for civil damages may lie under §10(b) of the Securities Exchange Act of 1934 (1934 Act), 48 Stat. 891, 15 U.S.C. §78j(b) [15 U.S.C.S. §78j(b)], and Securities and Exchange Commission Rule 10b-5, 17 CFR §240.10b-5 (1975), in the absence of an allegation of intent to deceive, manipulate, or defraud on the part of the defendant.

I

Petitioner, Ernst & Ernst, is an accounting firm. From 1946 through 1967 it was retained by First Securities Company of Chicago (First Securities), a small brokerage firm and member of the Midwest Stock Exchange and of the National Association of Securities Dealers, to perform periodic audits of the firm's books and records. In connection with these audits Ernst & Ernst prepared for filing with the Securities and Exchange Commission (Commission) the annual reports required of First Securities under §17(a) of the 1934 Act, 15 U.S.C. §78q(a) [15 U.S.C.S. §78q(a)].[1] It also prepared for First Securities responses to the financial questionnaires of the Midwest Stock Exchange (Exchange).

Respondents were customers of First Securities who invested in a fraudulent securities scheme perpetrated by Leston B. Nay, president of the firm and owner of 92% of its stock. Nay induced the respondents to invest funds in "escrow" accounts that he represented would yield a high rate of return. Respondents did so from 1942 through 1966, with the majority of the transactions occurring in the 1950's. In fact, there were no escrow accounts as Nay converted respondents' funds to his own use immediately upon receipt. These transactions were not in the customary form of dealings between First Securities and its customers. The respondents drew their personal checks payable to Nay or a designated bank for his account. No such escrow accounts were reflected on the books and records of First Securities, and none was shown on its periodic accounting to respondents in connection with their other investments. Nor were they included in First Securities' filings with the Commission or the Exchange.

This fraud came to light in 1968 when Nay committed suicide, leaving a note that described First Securities as bankrupt and the escrow accounts as "spurious." Respondents, subsequently filed this action[2] for damages against Ernst & Ernst[3] in the United States District Court for the Northern District of Illinois under §10(b) of the 1934 Act. The complaint charged that Nay's escrow scheme violated §10(b) and Commission Rule 10b-5,[4] and that Ernst & Ernst had "aided and abetted" Nay's violations by its "failure" to conduct proper audits of First Securities. As revealed through discovery, respondents' cause of action rested on a

1. Section 17(a) requires that securities brokers or dealers "make . . . and preserve . . . such accounts . . . books, and other records, and make such reports, as the Commission by its rules and regulations may prescribe as necessary or appropriate in the public interest or for the protection of investors." During the period relevant here, Commission Rule 17a-5, 17 CFR §240.17a-5 (1975), required that First Securities file an annual report of its financial condition that included a certificate stating "clearly the opinion of the accountant with respect to the financial statement covered by the certificate and the accounting principles and practices reflected therein." *See* SEC Release No. 3338 (Nov. 28, 1942), X-17A-5 (h). The Rule required Ernst & Ernst to state in its certificate, *inter alia,* "whether the audit was made in accordance with generally accepted auditing standards applicable in the circumstances" and provided that nothing in the Rule should "be construed to imply authority for the omission of any procedure which independent accountants would ordinarily employ in the course of an audit for the purpose of expressing the opinions required" by the Rule.

2. Two separate, but substantially identical, complaints initially were filed by different members of the present group of respondents. Subsequently the respondents jointly filed a First Amended Complaint. The two cases were treated by the District Court as if they were consolidated, and they were consolidated formally on appeal.

3. The first count of the complaint was directed against the Exchange, charging that through its acts and omissions it had aided and abetted Nay's fraud. Summary judgment in favor of the Exchange was affirmed on appeal. *Hochfelder v. Midwest Stock Exchange,* 503 F.2d 364 (C.A.7), *cert. denied,* 419 U.S. 875, 42 L.Ed.2d 114, 95 S.Ct. 137 (1974).

4. Immediately after Nay's suicide the Commission commenced receivership proceedings against First Securities. In those proceedings all of the respondents except two asserted claims based on the fraudulent escrow accounts. These claims ultimately were allowed in *SEC v. First Securities Co.* 463 F.2d 981, 986 (C.A.7), *cert. denied,* 406 U.S. 880, 34 L.Ed.2d 134, 93 S.Ct. 85 (1972), where the court held that Nay's conduct violated §10(b) and Rule 10b-5, and that First Securities was liable for Nay's fraud as an aider and abettor. The question of Ernst & Ernst's liability was not considered in that case.

theory of negligent nonfeasance. The premise was that Ernst & Ernst had failed to utilize "appropriate auditing procedures" in its audits of First Securities, thereby failing to discover internal practices of the firm said to prevent an effective audit. The practice principally relied on was Nay's rule that only he could open mail addressed to him at First Securities or addressed to First Securities to his attention, even if it arrived in his absence. Respondents contended that if Ernst & Ernst had conducted a proper audit, it would have discovered this "mail rule." The existence of the rule then would have been disclosed in reports to the Exchange and to the Commission by Ernst & Ernst as an irregular procedure that prevented an effective audit. This would have led to an investigation of Nay that would have revealed the fraudulent scheme. Respondents specifically disclaimed the existence of fraud or intentional misconduct on the part of Ernst & Ernst.[5]

After extensive discovery the District Court granted Ernst & Ernst's motion for summary judgment and dismissed the action. The court rejected Ernst & Ernst's contention that a cause of action for aiding and abetting a securities fraud could not be maintained under §10(b) and Rule 10b-5 merely on allegations of negligence. It concluded, however, that there was no genuine issue of material fact with respect to whether Ernst & Ernst had conducted its audits in accordance with generally accepted auditing standards.[6]

The Court of Appeals for the Seventh Circuit reversed and remanded, holding that one who breaches a duty of inquiry and disclosure owed another is liable in damages for aiding and abetting a third party's violation of Rule 10b-5 if the fraud would have been discovered or prevented but for the breach. 503 F.2d 1100 (1974).[7]

The court reasoned that Ernst & Ernst had a common-law and statutory duty of inquiry into the adequacy of First Securities' internal control system because it had contracted to audit First Securities and to prepare for filing with the Commission the annual report of First Securities' financial condition required under §17 of the 1934 Act and Rule 17a-5, 17 C.F.R. §240.17a-5.[8] The court further reasoned that respondents were beneficiaries of the statutory duty to inquire[9] and the re-

5. In their response to interrogatories in the District Court respondents conceded that they did "not accuse Ernst & Ernst of deliberate, intentional fraud," merely with "inexcusable negligence." App. 81.

6. The District Court also held that respondents' action was barred by the doctrine of equitable estoppel and the applicable Illinois statute of limitations of three years. *See* n. 29, *infra.* As customers of First Securities respondents were sent confirmation forms as required under §17(a) and Rule 17a-5 requesting that they verify the accuracy of the statements and notify Ernst & Ernst as to any exceptions. Although the confirmation forms contained no reference to the escrow accounts, Ernst & Ernst was not notified of this fact. The last audit of First Securities by Ernst & Ernst was completed in December 1967 and the first complaint in this action was not filed until February 1971.

7. In support of this holding, the Court of Appeals cited its decision in *Hochfelder v. Midwest Stock Exchange, supra,* where it detailed the elements necessary to establish a claim under Rule 10b-5 based on a defendant's aiding and abetting a securities fraud solely by inaction. *See* n. 3 *supra.* In such a case the plaintiff must show "that the party charged with aiding and abetting had knowledge of or, but for a breach of duty of inquiry, should have had knowledge of the fraud, and that possessing such knowledge the party failed to act due to an improper motive or breach of a duty of disclosure." 503 F.2d, at 374. The court explained in the instant case that these "elements comprise a flexible standard of liability which should be amplified according to the peculiarities of each case." 503 F.2d, at 1104. In view of our holding that an intent to deceive, manipulate, or defraud is required for civil liability under §10(b) and Rule 10b-5, we need not consider whether civil liability for aiding and abetting is appropriate under the section and the Rule, nor the elements necessary to establish such a cause of action. *See, e.g., Brennan v. Midwestern United Life Ins. Co.* 259 F.Supp. 673 (1966) and 286 F.Supp. 702 (N.D. Ind. 1968), *affd,* 417 F.2d 147 (C.A.7 1969), *cert. denied,* 397 U.S. 989, 25 L.Ed.2d 397, 90 S.Ct. 1122 (1970) (defendant held liable for giving active and knowing assistance to a third party engaged in violations of the securities laws). *See generally* Ruder, Multiple Defendants in Securities Law Fraud Cases: Aiding and Abetting, Conspiracy, In Pari Delicto, Indemnification and Contribution, 120 U. Pa. L. Rev. 597, 620-645 (1972).

8. *See* n. 1, *supra.*

9. The court concluded that the duty of inquiry imposed on Ernst & Ernst under §17(a) was "grounded on a concern for the protection of investors such as [respondents]," without reaching the question whether the statute imposed a "direct duty" to the respondents. 503 F.2d, at 1105. The court held that Ernst & Ernst owed no common-law duty of inquiry to respondents arising from its contract with First Securities since Ernst & Ernst did not specifically foresee that respondents' limited class might suffer from a negligent audit, compare *Glanzer v. Shepard,* 233 N.Y. 236, 135 N.E. 275 (1922), with *Ultramares Corp. v. Touche,* 255 N.Y. 170, 174 N.E. 441 (1931); *see. e.g., Rhode Island Hospital Trust Nat. Bank v. Swartz,* 455 F.2d 847, 851 (C.A.4 1972). Moreover, respondents conceded that they did not rely on the financial statements and reports prepared by Ernst & Ernst or on its certificate of opinion. 503 F.2d, at 1107.

lated duty to disclose any material irregularities that were discovered. 503 F.2d, at 1105-1111. The court concluded that there were genuine issues of fact as to whether Ernst & Ernst's failure to discover and comment upon Nay's mail rule[10] constituted a breach of its duties of inquiry and disclosure, *id.,* at 1111, and whether inquiry and disclosure would have led to the discovery or prevention of Nay's fraud. *Id.,* at 1115.[11]

We granted certiorari to resolve the question whether a private cause of action for damages will lie under §10(b) and Rule 10b-5 in the absence of any allegation of "scienter"—intent to deceive, manipulate, or defraud.[12] 421 U.S. 909, 43 L.Ed.2d 773, 95 S.Ct. 1557 (1975). We conclude that it will not and therefore we reverse.[13]

II

Federal regulation of transactions in securities emerged as part of the aftermath of the market crash in 1929. The Securities Act of 1933 (1933 Act), 48 Stat. 74, as amended, 15 U.S.C. §§77a *et seq.* [15 U.S.C.S. §§77a *et seq.*] was designed to provide investors with full disclosure of material information concerning public offerings of securities in commerce, to protect investors against fraud and, through the imposition of specified civil liabilities, to promote ethical standards of honesty and fair dealing. *See* H.R. Rep. No. 85, 73d Cong., 1st Sess., 1-5 (1933). The 1934 Act was intended principally to protect investors against manipulation of stock prices through regulation of transactions upon securities exchanges and in over-the-counter markets, and to impose regular reporting requirements on companies whose stock is listed on national securities exchanges. *See* S. Rep. No. 792, 73d Cong., 2d Sess., 1-5 (1934). Although the Acts contain numerous carefully drawn express civil remedies and criminal penalties, Congress recognized that efficient regulation of securities trading could not be accomplished under a rigid statutory program. As part of the

10. In their briefs respondents allude to several other alleged failings by Ernst & Ernst in its audit of First Securities, principally its failure to inquire into the collectibility of certain loans by First Securities to Nay and its failure to follow up on a 1965 memorandum that characterized First Securities' overall system of internal control as weak because of the centralization of functions in the cashier. The Court of Appeals mentioned none of these alleged deficiencies in its opinion in this case, although it did discuss the loans to Nay and certain other related matters in its opinion in *Hochfelder v. Midwest Stock Exchange,* 503 F.2d, at 370-371, holding that the existence of these facts was insufficient to put the Exchange on notice that further inquiry into First Securities' financial affairs was required.

11. The Court of Appeals also reversed the District Court's holding with respect to equitable estoppel and the statute of limitations. *See* n. 6, *supra.* In view of our disposition of the case we need not address these issues.

12. Although the verbal formulations of the standard to be applied have varied, several Courts of Appeals have held in substance that negligence alone is sufficient for civil liability under §10(b) and Rule 10b-5. *See, e.g., White v. Abrams,* 495 F.2d 724, 730 (C.A.9 1974) ("flexible duty" standard); *Myzel v. Fields,* 386 F.2d 718, 735 (C.A.8 1967), *cert. denied,* 390 U.S. 951, 19 L.Ed.2d 1143, 88 S.Ct. 1043 (1968) (negligence sufficient); *Kohler v. Kohler Co.* 319 F.2d 634, 637 (C.A.7 1963) (knowledge not required). Other Courts of Appeals have held that some type of scienter—i.e., intent to defraud, reckless disregard for the truth, or knowing use of some practice to defraud—is necessary in such an action. *See, e.g., Clegg v. Conk,* 507 F.2d 1351, 1361-1362 (C.A.10 1974), *cert. denied,* 422 U.S. 1007, 45 L.Ed.2d 669, 95 S.Ct. 2628 (1975) (an element of "scienter or conscious fault"); *Lanza v. Drexel & Co.* 479 F.2d 1277, 1306 (C.A.2 1973) ("willful or reckless disregard" of the truth). But few of the decisions announcing that some form of negligence suffices for civil liability under §10(b) and Rule 10b-5 actually have involved only negligent conduct. *Smallwood v. Pearl Brewing Co.* 489 F.2d 579, 606 (C.A.5), *cert. denied,* 419 U.S. 873, 42 L.Ed.2d 113, 95 S.Ct. 134 (1974); *Kohn v. American Metal Climax, Inc.* 458 F.2d 255, 286 (C.A.3 1972) (Adams, J., concurring and dissenting); Bucklo, Scienter and Rule 10b-5, 67 Nw. U.L.Rev.562, 568-570 (1972).

In this opinion the term "scienter" refers to a mental state embracing intent to deceive, manipulate, or defraud. In certain areas of the law recklessness is considered to be a form of intentional conduct for purposes of imposing liability for some act. We need not address here the question whether, in some circumstances, reckless behavior is sufficient for civil liability under §10(b) and Rule 10b-5.

Since this case concerns an action for damages we also need not consider the question whether scienter is a necessary element in an action for injunctive relief under §10(b) and Rule 10b-5. *Cf. SEC v. Capital Gains Research Bureau,* 375 U.S. 180, 11 L.Ed.2d 237, 84 S.Ct. 275 (1963).

13. Respondents further contend that Ernst & Ernst owed them a direct duty under §17(a) of the 1934 Act and Rule 17a-5 to conduct a proper audit of First Securities and that they may base a private cause of action against Ernst & Ernst for violation of that duty. Respondents' cause of action, however, was premised solely on the alleged violation of §10(b) and Rule 10b-5. During the lengthy history of this litigation they have not amended their original complaint to aver a cause of action under §17(a) and Rule 17a-5. We therefore do not consider that a claim of liability under §17(a) is properly before us even assuming respondents could assert such a claim independently of §10(b).

1934 Act Congress created the Commission, which is provided with an arsenal of flexible enforcement powers. *See, e.g.,* 1933 Act §§8, 19, 20, 15 U.S.C. §§77h, 77s, 77t [15 U.S.C.S. §§77h, 77s, 77t], 1934 Act §§9, 19, 21, 15 U.S.C. §§78i, 78s, 78u [15 U.S.C.S. §§78i, 78s, 78u].

Section 10 of the 1934 Act makes it "unlawful for any person . . . (b) [t]o use or employ, in connection with the purchase or sale of any security . . . any manipulative or deceptive device or contrivance in contravention of such rules and regulations as the Commission may prescribe as necessary or appropriate in the public interest or for the protection of investors." 15 U.S.C. §78j [15 U.S.C.S. §78j]. In 1942, acting pursuant to the power conferred by §10(b), the Commission promulgated Rule 10b-5, which now provides:

> Employment of manipulative and deceptive devices.
>
> It shall be unlawful for any person, directly or indirectly, by the use of any means or instrumentality of interstate commerce, or of the mails, or of any facility of any national securities exchange,
>
> (a) To employ any device, scheme, or artifice to defraud,
>
> (b) To make any untrue statement of a material fact or to omit to state a material fact necessary in order to make the statements made, in the light of the circumstances under which they were made, not misleading, or
>
> (c) To engage in any act, practice, or course of business which operates or would operate as a fraud or deceit upon any person in connection with the purchase or sale of any security.

Although §10(b) does not by its terms create an express civil remedy for its violation, and there is no indication that Congress,[14] or the Commission when adopting Rule 10b-5,[15] contemplated such a remedy, the existence of a private cause of action for violations of the statute and the Rule is now well established. *Blue Chip Stamps v. Manor Drug Stores,* 421 U.S. 723, 730, 44 L.Ed.2d 539, 95 S.Ct. 1917 (1975); *Affiliated Ute Citizens v. United States,* 406 U.S. 128, 150-154, 31 L.Ed.2d 741, 92 S.Ct. 1456 (1972); *Superintendent of Insurance v. Bankers Life & Cas. Co.* 404 U.S. 6, 13 n. 9, 30 L.Ed.2d 128, 92 S.Ct. 165 (1971). During the 30-year period since a private cause of action was first implied under §10(b) and Rule 10b-5,[16] a substantial body of case law and commentary has developed as to its elements. Courts and commentators long have differed with regard to whether scienter is a necessary element of such a cause of action, or whether negligent conduct alone is sufficient.[17] In addressing this question, we turn first to the language of §10(b), for "[t]he starting point in every case involving construction of a statute is the language itself." *Blue Chip Stamps, supra,* at 756, 44 L.Ed.2d 539, 95 S.Ct. 1917 (Powell, J., concurring); *see FTC v. Bunte Bros. Inc.* 312 U.S. 349, 350, 85 L.Ed. 881, 61 S.Ct. 580 (1941).

A

Section 10(b) makes unlawful the use or employment of "any manipulative or deceptive device or contrivance" in contravention of Commission rules. The words "manipulative or deceptive" used in conjunction with "device or contrivance" strongly suggest that §10(b) was intended to proscribe knowing or intentional misconduct. *See SEC v. Texas Gulf Sulphur Co.* 401 F.2d 833, 868 (C.A.2 1968) (Friendly, J., concurring), *cert. denied sub nom Coates v. SEC,* 394 U.S. 976, 22 L.Ed.2d 756, 89 S.Ct. 1454 (1969); Loss, Summary Remarks, 30 Bus. Law 163, 165 (Special Issue 1975). *See also Kohn v. American Metal Climax, Inc.* 458 F.2d 255, 280 (C.A.3 1972) (Adams, J., concurring and dissenting).

In its amicus curiae brief, however, the Commission contends that nothing in the language "manipulative or deceptive device or contrivance" limits its operation to knowing or intentional practices.[18] In support of its view, the Commission

14. *See, e.g.,* S. Rep. No. 792, 73d Cong., 2d Sess., 5-6 (1934); Note, Implied Liability Under the Securities Exchange Act, 61 Harv. L. Rev. 858, 860 (1948).

15. SEC Release No. 3230 (May 21, 1942); *Birnbaum v. Newport Steel Corp.* 193 F.2d 461, 463 (C.A.2), *cert. denied,* 343 U.S. 956, 96 L.Ed. 1356, 72 S.Ct. 1051 (1952).

16. *Kardon v. National Gypsum Co.* 69 F.Supp. 512 (E.D. Pa 1946).

17. *See* cases cited in n. 12, *supra.* Compare, e.g., Comment, Scienter and Rule 10b-5, 69 Col. L. Rev. 1057, 1080-1081 (1969); Note, Negligent Misrepresentations under Rule 10b-5, 32 U. Chi. L. Rev. 824, 839-844 (1965); Note, Securities Acts, 82 Harv. L. Rev. 938, 947 (1969); Note, Civil Liability Under Section 10B and Rule 10B-5: A Suggestion for Replacing the Doctrine of Privity, 74 Yale L.J. 658, 682-689 (1965), with, e.g., 3 L. Loss, Securities Regulation 1766 (2d ed 1961); 6 *id.,* at 3883-3885 (1969).

18. The Commission would not permit recovery upon proof of negligence in all cases. In order to harmonize civil liability under §10(b) with the express civil remedies contained in the 1933 and 1934 Acts, the Commission would limit the circumstances in which civil liability could be imposed for negligent violation of Rule 10b-5 to situations in which (i) the defendant knew or reasonably

cites the overall congressional purpose in the 1933 and 1934 Acts to protect investors against false and deceptive practices that might injure them. *See Affiliated Ute Citizens v. United States, supra,* at 151, 31 L.Ed.2d 741, 92 S.Ct. 1456; *Superintendent of Insurance v. Bankers Life & Cas. Co. supra,* at 11-12, 30 L.Ed.2d 128, 92 S.Ct. 165; *J. I. Case Co. v. Borak,* 377 U.S. 426, 432-433, 12 L.Ed. 2d 423, 84 S.Ct. 1555 (1964). *See also SEC v. Capital Gains Res. Bur.* 375 U.S. 180, 195, 11 L.Ed.2d 237, 84 S.Ct. 275 (1963). The Commission then reasons that since the "effect" upon investors of given conduct is the same regardless of whether the conduct is negligent or intentional, Congress must have intended to bar all such practices and not just those done knowingly or intentionally. The logic of this effect-oriented approach would impose liability for wholly faultless conduct where such conduct results in harm to investors, a result the Commission would be unlikely to support. But apart from where its logic might lead, the Commission would add a gloss to the operative language of the statute quite different from its commonly accepted meaning. *See, e.g., Addison v. Holly Hill Fruit Products, Inc.* 322 U.S. 607, 617-618, 88 L.Ed. 1488, 64 S.Ct. 1215, 153 A.L.R. 1007 (1944).[19] The argument simply ignores the use of the words "manipulative," "device," and "contrivance"—terms that make unmistakable a congressional intent to proscribe a type of conduct quite different from negligence.[20] Use of the word "manipulative" is especially significant. It is and was virtually a term of art when used in connection with securities markets. It connotes intentional or willful conduct designed to deceive or defraud investors by controlling or artificially affecting the price of securities.[21]

In addition to relying upon the Commission's argument with respect to the operative language of the statute, respondents contend that since we are dealing with "remedial legislation," *Tcherepnin v. Knight,* 389 U.S. 332, 336, 19 L.Ed.2d 564, 88 S.Ct. 548 (1967), it must be construed " 'not technically and restrictively, but flexibly to effectuate its remedial purposes.' " *Affiliated Ute Citizens v. United States,* 406 U.S., at 151, 31 L.Ed.2d 741, 92 S.Ct. 1456, quoting *SEC v. Capital Gains Res. Bur., supra,* at 195, 11 L.Ed.2d 237, 84 S.Ct. 275. They argue that the "remedial purposes" of the Acts demand a construction of §10(b) that embraces negligence as a standard of liability. But in seeking to accomplish its broad remedial goals, Congress did not adopt uniformly a negligence standard even as to express civil remedies. In some circumstances and with respect to certain classes of defendants, Congress did create express liability predicated upon a failure to exercise reasonable care. E.g., 1933 Act §11(b)(3)(B), 48 Stat. 82, as amended, 15 U.S.C. §77k(b)(3)(B) [15 U.S.C.S. §77k(b)(3)(B)] (liability of "experts," such as accountants, for misleading statements in portions of registration statements for which they are responsible).[22] But in other situations good faith is an absolute defense. 1934 Act §18, 48 Stat. 897, as amended, 15 U.S.C. §78r [15 U.S.C.S. §78r] (misleading statements in

---

could foresee that the plaintiff would rely on his conduct, (ii) the plaintiff did in fact so rely, and (iii) the amount of the plaintiff's damages caused by the defendant's conduct was definite and ascertainable. Brief for SEC as Amicus Curiae 23-33. The Commission concludes that the present record does not establish these conditions since Ernst & Ernst could not reasonably have foreseen that the financial statements of First Securities would induce respondents to invest in the escrow accounts, respondents in fact did not rely on Ernst & Ernst's audits, and the amount of respondents' damages was unascertainable. *Id.,* at 33-36. Respondents accept the Commission's basic analysis of the operative language of the statute and Rule, but reject these additional requirements for recovery for negligent violations.

19. "To let general words draw nourishment from their purpose is one thing. To draw on some unexpressed spirit outside the bounds of the normal meaning of words is quite another. . . . After all, legislation when not expressed in technical terms is addressed to the common run of men and is therefore to be understood according to the sense of the thing, as the ordinary man has a right to rely on ordinary words addressed to him." *Addison v. Holly Hill Fruit Products, Inc.* 322 U.S., at 617-618, 88 L.Ed. 1488, 64 S.Ct. 1215, 153 A.L.R. 1007. *See* Frankfurter, Some Reflections on the Reading of Statutes, 47 Col. L. Rev. 527, 536-537 (1947).

20. Webster's International Dictionary (2d ed 1934) defines "device" as "[t]hat which is devised, or formed by design; a contrivance; an invention; project; scheme; often, a scheme to deceive; a stratagem; an artifice," and "contrivance" in pertinent part as "[a] thing contrived or used in contriving; a scheme, plan, or artifice." In turn, "contrive" in pertinent part is defined as "[t]o devise; to plan; to plot . . . [t]o fabricate . . . design; invent . . . to scheme. . . ." The Commission also ignores the use of the terms "[t]o use or employ," language that is supportive of the view that Congress did not intend §10(b) to embrace negligent conduct.

21. Webster's International Dictionary, *supra,* defines "manipulate" as "to manage or treat artfully or fraudulently; as to *manipulate* accounts. . . . 4. Exchanges. To force (prices) up or down, as by matched orders, wash sales, fictitious reports . . .; to rig."

22. *See infra,* at 208, and n. 26, 47 L.Ed.2d 685.

any document filed pursuant to the 1934 Act). And in still other circumstances Congress created express liability regardless of the defendant's fault, 1933 Act §11(a), 15 U.S.C. §77k(a) [15 U.S.C.S. §77k(a)] (issuer liability for misleading statements in the registration statement).

It is thus evident that Congress fashioned standards of fault in the express civil remedies in the 1933 and 1934 Acts on a particularized basis. Ascertainment of congressional intent with respect to the standard of liability created by a particular section of the Acts must therefore rest primarily on the language of that section. Where, as here, we deal with a judicially implied liability, the statutory language certainly is no less important. In view of the language of §10(b), which so clearly connotes intentional misconduct, and mindful that the language of a statute controls when sufficiently clear in its context, *United States v. Oregon,* 366 U.S. 643, 648, 6 L.Ed.2d 575, 81 S.Ct. 1278 (1961); *Packard Motor Car Co. v. N.L.R.B.,* 330 U.S. 485, 492, 91 L.Ed. 1040, 67 S.Ct. 789 (1947), further inquiry may be unnecessary. We turn now, nevertheless, to the legislative history of the 1934 Act to ascertain whether there is support for the meaning attributed to §10(b) by the Commission and respondents.

B

Although the extensive legislative history of the 1934 Act is bereft of any explicit explanation of Congress' intent, we think the relevant portions of that history support our conclusion that §10(b) was addressed to practices that involve some element of scienter and cannot be read to impose liability for negligent conduct alone.

The original version of what would develop into the 1934 Act was contained in identical bills introduced by Senator Fletcher and Representative Rayburn. S. 2693, 73d Cong., 2d Sess. (1934); H.R. 7852, 73d Cong., 2d Sess. (1934). Section 9 (c) of the bills, from which present §10(b) evolved, proscribed as unlawful the use of "any device or contrivance which, or any device or contrivance in a way or manner which the Commission may by its rules and regulations find detrimental to the public interest or to the proper protection of investors." The other subsections of proposed §9 listed specific practices that Congress empowered the Commission to regulate through its rulemaking power. *See* §§9(a) (short sale), (b) ("stop-loss order"). Soon after the hearings on the House bill were held, a substitute bill was introduced in both Houses which abbreviated and modified §9(c)'s operative language to read "any manipulative device or contrivance." H.R. 8720, 73d Cong., 2d Sess. §9(c) (1934); see S. 3420, 73d Cong., 2d Sess. §10(b)(1934). Still a third bill, retaining the Commission's power to regulate the specific practices enumerated in the prior bills, and omitting all reference to the Commission's authority to prescribe rules concerning manipulative or deceptive devices in general, was introduced and passed in the House. H.R. 9323, 73d Cong., 2d Sess., §9 (1934). The final language of §10 is a modified version of a Senate amendment to this last House bill. *See* H.R. Conf. Rep. No. 1838, 73d Cong., 2d Sess. 32-33 (1934).

Neither the intended scope of §10(b) nor the reasons for the changes in its operative language are revealed explicitly in the legislative history of the 1934 Act, which deals primarily with other aspects of the legislation. There is no indication, however, that §10(b) was intended to proscribe conduct not involving scienter. The extensive hearings that preceded passage of the 1934 Act touched only briefly on §10, and most of the discussion was devoted to the enumerated devices that the Commission is empowered to proscribe under §10(a). The most relevant exposition of the provision that was to become §10(b) was by Thomas G. Corcoran, a spokesman for the drafters. Corcoran indicated:

> Subsection (c) [§9(c) of H.R. 7852—later §10 (b)] says, "Thou shalt not devise any other cunning devices."
>
> . . . . .
>
> Of course subsection (c) is a catch-all clause to prevent manipulative devices. I do not think there is any objection to that kind of clause. The Commission should have the authority to deal with new manipulative devices.
>
> Hearings on H.R. 7852 and H.R. 8720 before the House Committee on Interstate and Foreign Commerce, 73d Cong., 2d Sess., 115 (1934).

This brief explanation of §10(b) by a spokesman for its drafters is significant. The section was described rightly as a "catchall" clause to enable the Commission "to deal with new manipulative [or cunning] devices." It is difficult to believe that any lawyer, legislative draftsman, or legislator would use these words if the intent was to create liability for merely negligent acts or omissions.[23] Neither the legislative history nor the briefs supporting respondents identify any usage or author-

23. *See* n. 21, *supra.*

ity for construing "manipulative [or cunning] devices" to include negligence.[24]

The legislative reports do not address the scope of §10(b) or its catchall function directly. In considering specific manipulative practices left to Commission regulation, however, the reports indicate that liability would not attach absent scienter, supporting the conclusion that Congress intended no lesser standard under §10(b). The Senate Report of S. 3420 discusses generally the various abuses that precipitated the need for the legislation and the inadequacy of self-regulation by the stock exchanges. The Report then analyzes the component provisions of the statute, but does not parse §10. The only specific reference to §10 is the following:

> In addition to the discretionary and elastic powers conferred on the administrative authority, effective regulation must include several clear statutory provisions reinforced by penal and civil sanctions, aimed at those manipulative and deceptive practices which have been demonstrated to fulfill no useful function. These sanctions are found in sections 9, 10 and 16.

S. Rep. No. 792, 73d Cong., 2d Sess., 6 (1934).

In the portion of the general-analysis section of the Report entitled Manipulative Practices, however, there is a discussion of specific practices that were considered so inimical to the public interest as to require express prohibition, such as "wash" sales and "matched" orders,[25] and of other practices that might in some cases serve legitimate purposes, such as stabilization of security prices and grants of options. *Id.,* at 7-9. These latter practices were left to regulation by the Commission. 1934 Act §§9(a)(6), (c), 48 Stat. 890, 15 U.S.C. §§78i(a)(6), (c) [15 U.S.C.S. §§78i (a)(6), (c)]. Significantly, we think, in the discussion of the need to regulate even the latter category of practices when they are manipulative, there is no indication that any type of criminal or civil liability is to attach in the absence of scienter. Furthermore, in commenting on the express civil liabilities provided in the 1934 Act, the Report explains:

24. In support of its position the Commission cites statements by Corcoran in the Senate hearings that "in modern society there are many things you have to make crimes which are sheer matters of negligence" and "intent is not necessary for every crime." Hearings before the Subcommittee on Stock Exchange Practices before the Senate Committee on Banking and Currency, 73d Cong., 2d Sess., 6509-6510 (1934). The comments, taken in context, shed no light on the meaning of §10(b). Corcoran's remarks were made during a discussion of whether criminal violations could arise under §8(a)(3) of S. 2693, 73d Cong., 2d Sess., which in material part was incorporated in §9 of the 1934 Act, 15 U.S.C. §78i [15 U.S.C.S. §78i], in the absence of specific intent to influence security prices for personal gain. The remarks, moreover, were not addressed to the scope of §8, but were general observations concerning activity society might proscribe under criminal law. Ferdinand Pecora, counsel to the committee and a draftsman of S. 2693, *Foremost-McKesson, Inc. v. Provident Securities Co.* 423 U.S. 232, 249-250, n. 24, 46 L.Ed.2d 464, 96 S.Ct. 508 (1976), described the language as "[e]xcluding from its scope an act that is not done with any ulterior motives or purposes, as set forth in the act." Hearings before the Subcommittee on Stock Exchange Practices, *supra,* at 6510. Further, prior to the passage of the 1934 Act, proposed §8 was amended to require willful behavior as a prerequisite to civil liability for violations. Compare §9(e) of the 1934 Act with §8(c) of S. 2693. *See* H.R. Rep. No. 1383, 73d Cong., 2d Sess., 21 (1934).

The Commission also relies on objections to a draft version of §10(b)—§9(c) of S. 2693 and H.R. 7852, *see,* at 201-202, *supra,* 47 L.Ed.2d 681,—raised by representatives of the securities industry in the House and Senate hearings. They warned that the language was so vague that the Commission might outlaw anything. *E.g.,* Hearings before the Subcommittee on Stock Exchange Practices, *supra,* at 6988; Hearings on H.R. 7852 and H.R. 8720 before the House Committee on Interstate and Foreign Commerce, 73d Cong., 2d Sess., 258 (1934). Remarks of this kind made in the course of legislative debate or hearings other than by persons responsible for the preparation or the drafting of a bill, are entitled to little weight. *See, e.g., United States v. United Mine Workers,* 330 U.S. 258, 276-277, 91 L.Ed. 884, 67 S.Ct. 677 (1947); *United States v. Wrightwood Dairy Co.* 315 U.S. 110, 125, 86 L.Ed. 726, 62 S.Ct. 523 (1942). This is especially so with regard to the statements of legislative opponents who "[i]n their zeal to defeat a bill . . . understandably tend to overstate its reach." *N.L.R.B. v. Fruit Packers,* 377 U.S. 58, 66, 12 L.Ed.2d 129, 84 S.Ct. 1063 (1964). *See Schwegmann Bros. v. Calvert Distillers Corp.* 341 U.S. 384, 394-395, 95 L.Ed. 1035, 71 S.Ct. 745, 19 A.L.R.2d 1119, 60 Ohio L. Abs. 81, 44 Ohio. Ops. 395 (1951).

25. "Wash" sales are transactions involving no change in beneficial ownership. "Matched" orders are orders for the purchase/sale of a security that are entered with the knowledge that orders of substantially the same size, at substantially the same time and price, have been or will be entered by the same or different persons for the sale/purchase of such security. Section 9(a)(1) of the 1934 Act, 15 U.S.C. §78i(a)(1) [15 U.S.C.S. §78i(a)(1)], proscribes wash sales and matched orders when effectuated "[f]or the purpose of creating a false or misleading appearance of active trading in any security registered on a national securities exchange, or . . . with respect to the market for any such security." *See In re J. A. Latimer & Co.* 38 SEC 790 (1958); *In re Thornton & Co.* 28 SEC 208 (1948).

> [I]f an investor has suffered loss by reason of illicit practices, it is equitable that he should be allowed to recover damages from the guilty party. . . . [T]he bill provides that any person who unlawfully manipulates the price of a security, or who induces transactions in a security by means of false or misleading statements, or who makes a false or misleading statement in the report of a corporation, shall be liable in damages to those who have bought or sold the security at prices affected by such violation or statement. In such case the burden is on the plaintiff to show the violation or the fact that the statement was false or misleading, and that he relied thereon to his damage. The defendant may escape liability by showing that the statement was made in *good faith.*
>
> S. Rep. No. 792, *supra,* at 12-13 (emphasis supplied).

The Report therefore reveals with respect to the specified practices, an overall congressional intent to prevent "manipulative and deceptive practices which . . . fulfill no useful function" and to create private actions for damages stemming from "illicit practices," where the defendant has not acted in good faith. The views expressed in the House Report are consistent with this interpretation. H.R. Rep. No. 1383, 73d Cong., 2d Sess., 10-11, 20-21 (1934) (H.R. 9323). There is no indication that Congress intended anyone to be made liable for such practices unless he acted other than in good faith. The catchall provision of §10(b) should be interpreted no more broadly.

C

The 1933 and 1934 Acts constitute interrelated components of the federal regulatory scheme governing transactions in securities. *See Blue Chip Stamps,* 421 U.S., at 727-730, 44 L.Ed.2d 539, 95 S.Ct. 1917. As the Court indicated in *SEC v. National Securities, Inc.,* 393 U.S. 453, 466, 21 L.Ed. 2d 668, 89 S.Ct. 564 (1969), "the interdependence of the various sections of the securities laws is certainly a relevant factor in any interpretation of the language Congress has chosen. . . ." Recognizing this, respondents and the Commission contrast §10(b) to other sections of the Acts to support their contention that civil liability may be imposed upon proof of negligent conduct. We think they misconceive the significance of the other provisions of the Acts.

The Commission argues that Congress has been explicit in requiring willful conduct when that was the standard of fault intended, citing §9 of the 1934 Act, 48 Stat. 889, 15 U.S.C. §78i [15 U.S.C.S. §78i], which generally proscribes manipulation of securities prices. Sections 9(a)(1) and (a)(2), for example, respectively prohibit manipulation of security prices "[f]or the purpose of creating a false or misleading appearance of active trading in any security . . . or . . . with respect to the market for any such security," and "for the purpose of inducing the purchase or sale of such security by others." *See also* §9(a)(4). Section 9(e) then imposes upon "[a]ny person who willfully participates in any act or transaction in violation of" other provisions of §9 civil liability to anyone who purchased or sold a security at a price affected by the manipulative activities. From this the Commission concludes that since §10(b) is not by its terms explicitly restricted to willful, knowing, or purposeful conduct, it should not be construed in all cases to require more than negligent action or inaction as a precondition for civil liability.

The structure of the Acts does not support the Commission's argument. In each instance that Congress created express civil liability in favor of purchasers or sellers of securities it clearly specified whether recovery was to be premised on knowing or intentional conduct, negligence, or entirely innocent mistake. *See* 1933 Act, §§11, 12, 15, 48 Stat. 82, 84, as amended, 15 U.S.C. §§77k, 77l, 77o [15 U.S.C.S. §§77k, 77l, 77o]; 1934 Act §§9, 18, 20, 48 Stat. 889, 897, 899, as amended, 15 U.S.C. §§78i, 78r, 78t [15 U.S.C.S. §§78i, 78r, 78t]. For example, §11 of the 1933 Act unambiguously creates a private action for damages when a registration statement includes untrue statements of material facts or fails to state material facts necessary to make the statements therein not misleading. Within the limits specified by §11(e), the issuer of the securities is held absolutely liable for any damages resulting from such misstatement or omission. But experts such as accountants who have prepared portions of the registration statement are accorded a "due diligence" defense. In effect, this is a negligence standard. An expert may avoid civil liability with respect to the portions of the registration statement for which he was responsible by showing that "after reasonable investigation" he had "reasonable ground[s] to believe" that the statements for which he was responsible were true and there was no omission of a material fact.[26] §11(b) (3)(B)(i). *See, e.g., Escott v. Bar-*

26. Other individuals who sign the registration statement, directors of the issuer, and the underwriter of the securities similarly are accorded a complete defense against civil liability based on the exercise of reasonable investigation and a reasonable belief that the reg-

chris Const. Corp. 283 F.Supp. 643, 697-703 (S.D.N.Y. 1968). The express recognition of a cause of action premised on negligent behavior in §11 stands in sharp contrast to the language of §10(b), and significantly undercuts the Commission's argument.

We also consider it significant that each of the express civil remedies in the 1933 Act allowing recovery for negligent conduct, *see* §§11, 12(2), 15, 15 U.S.C. §§77k, 77l(2), 77o [15 U.S.C.S. §§77k, 77l, 77o],[27] is subject to significant procedural restrictions not applicable under §10(b).[28] Section 11(e) of the 1933 Act, for example, authorizes the court to require a plaintiff bringing a suit under §11, §12(2), or §15 thereof to post a bond for costs, including attorneys' fees, and in specified circumstances to assess costs at the conclusion of the litigation. Section 13 specifies a statute of limitations of one year from the time the violation was or should have been discovered, in no event to exceed three years from the time of offer or sale, applicable to actions brought under §11, §12(2), or §15. These restrictions, significantly, were imposed by amendments to the 1933 Act adopted as part of the 1934 Act. Prior to amendment §11(e) contained no provision for payment of costs. 48 Stat. 83. Act of May 27, 1933, c. 38, §11(e). *See* Act of June 6, 1934, c. 404, §206(e), 48 Stat. 907. The amendments also substantially shortened the statute of limitations provided by §13. Compare §13, 48 Stat. 84, with 15 U.S.C. §77m [15 U.S.C.S. §77m]. *See* 1934 Act, §207, 48 Stat. 908. We think these procedural limitations indicate that the judicially created private damages remedy under §10(b)—which has no comparable restrictions[29]—cannot be extended, consistently with the intent of Congress, to actions premised on negligent wrongdoing. Such extension would allow causes of action covered by §§11, 12(2), and 15 to be brought instead under §10(b) and thereby nullify the effectiveness of the carefully drawn procedural restrictions on these express actions.[30] *See, e.g., Fischman v. Raytheon*

istration statement was not misleading. §§11(b)(3)(A), (C), (D), (c). *See, e.g., Feit v. Leasco Data Processing Equipment Corp.* 332 F.Supp. 544, 575-583 (E.D.N.Y. 1971) (underwriters, but not officer-directors, established their due-diligence defense). *See generally* R. Jennings & H. Marsh, Securities Regulation 1018-1027 (3d ed. 1972), and sources cited therein; Folk, Civil Liabilities Under the Federal Securities Acts: The Barchris Case, 55 Va. L. Rev. 199 (1969).

27. Section 12(2) creates potential civil liability for a seller of securities in favor of the purchaser for misleading statements or omissions in connection with the transaction. The seller is exculpated if he proves that he did not know, or in the exercise of reasonable care, could not have known of the untruth or omission. Section 15 of the 1933 Act, as amended by §208 of Title II of the 1934 Act, makes persons who "control" any person liable under §11 or §12 liable jointly and severally to the same extent as the controlled person, unless he "had no knowledge of or reasonable ground to believe in the existence of the facts by reason of which the liability of the controlled person is alleged to exist." 15 U.S.C. §77o [15 U.S.C.S. §77o]. *See* Act of June 6, 1934, c. 404, §208, 48 Stat. 908.

28. Each of the provisions of the 1934 Act that expressly create civil liability, except those directed to specific classes of individuals such as directors, officers, or 10% beneficial holders of securities, *see* §16(b), 15 U.S.C. §78p(b) [15 U.S.C.S. §78p(b)], *Foremost-McKesson, Inc. v. Provident Securities Co.* 423 U.S. 232, 46 L.Ed.2d 464, 96 S.Ct. 508 (1976); *Kern County Land Co. v. Occidental Petroleum Corp.* 411 U.S. 582, 36 L.Ed.2d 503, 93 S.Ct. 1736 (1973), contains a state-of-mind condition requiring something more than negligence. Section 9(e) creates potential civil liability for any person who "willfully participates" in the manipulation of securities on a national exchange. 15 U.S.C. §78i(e) [15 U.S.C.S. §78i(e)]. Section 18 creates potential civil liability for misleading statements filed with the Commission, but provides the defendant with the defense that "he acted in good faith and had no knowledge that such statement was false or misleading." 15 U.S.C. §78r [15 U.S.C.S. §78r]. And §20, which imposes liability upon "controlling person[s]" for violations of the Act by those they control, exculpates a defendant who "acted in good faith and did not . . . induce the act . . . constituting the violation. . . ." 15 U.S.C. §78t [15 U.S.C.S. §78t]. Emphasizing the important difference between the operative language and purpose of §14(a) of the 1934 Act, 15 U.S.C. §78n(a), 15 U.S.C.S. §78n(a), as contrasted with §10(b), however, some courts have concluded that proof of scienter is unnecessary in an action for damages by the shareholder recipients of a materially misleading proxy statement against the issuer corporation. *Gerstle v. Gamble-Skogmo, Inc.* 478 F.2d 1281, 1299 (C.A.2 1973). *See also Kohn v. American Metal Climax, Inc.* 458 F.2d, at 289-290 (Adams, J., concurring and dissenting).

29. Since no statute of limitations is provided for civil actions under §10(b), the law of limitations of the forum State is followed as in other cases of judicially implied remedies. *See Holmberg v. Armbrecht,* 327 U.S. 392, 395, 90 L.Ed. 743, 66 S.Ct. 582, 162 A.L.R. 719 (1946), and cases cited therein. Although it is not always certain which state statute of limitations should be followed, such statutes of limitations usually are longer than the period provided under §13. 3 L. Loss, *supra,* n. 17, at 1773-1774. As to costs *see* n. 30, *infra.*

30. Congress regarded these restrictions on private damage actions as significant. In introducing Title II of

Mfg. Co. 188 F.2d 783, 786-787 (C.A.2 1951); *SEC v. Texas Gulf Sulphur Co.* 401 F.2d, at 867-868 (Friendly, J., concurring); *Rosenberg v. Globe Aircraft Corp.* 80 F.Supp. 123, 124 (E.D. Pa. 1948); 3 L. Loss, Securities Regulation 1787-1788 (2d ed. 1961); R. Jennings & H. Marsh, Securities Regulation 1070-1074 (3d ed. 1972). We would be unwilling to bring about this result absent substantial support in the legislative history, and there is none.[31]

D

We have addressed, to this point, primarily the language and history of §10(b). The Commission contends, however, that subsections (b) and (c) of Rule 10b-5 are cast in language which—if standing alone—could encompass both intentional and negligent behavior. These subsections respectively provide that it is unlawful "[t]o make any untrue statement of a material fact or to omit to state a material fact necessary in order to make the statements made, in the light of the circumstances under which they were made, not misleading . . ." and "[t]o engage in any act, practice, or course of business which operates or would operate as a fraud or deceit upon any person . . ." Viewed in isolation the language of subsection (b), and arguably that of subsection (c), could be read as proscribing, respectively, any type of material misstatement or omission, and any course of conduct, that has the effect of defrauding investors, whether the wrongdoing was intentional or not.

We note first that such a reading cannot be harmonized with the administrative history of the Rule, a history making clear that when the Commission adopted the Rule it was intended to apply only to activities that involved scienter.[32] More

the 1934 Act, Senator Fletcher indicated that the amendment to §11(e) of the 1933 Act, providing for potential payment of costs, including attorneys' fees, "is the most important [amendment] of all." 78 Cong. Rec. 8669 (1934). One of its purposes was to deter actions brought solely for their potential settlement value. *See ibid;* H.R. Conf. Rep. No. 1838, 73d Cong., 2d Sess., 42 (1934); *Blue Chip Stamps v. Manor Drug Stores,* 423 U.S. 723, 740-741, 44 L.Ed.2d 539, 95 S.Ct. 1917(1975). This deterrent is lacking in the §10(b) context, in which a district court's power to award attorneys' fees is sharply circumscribed. *See Alyeska Pipeline Service Co. v. Wilderness Society,* 421 U.S. 240, 44 L.Ed.2d 141, 95 S.Ct. 1612 (1975) ("bad faith" requirement); *F. D. Rich Co. v. United States ex rel. Industrial Lumber Co.* 417 U.S. 116, 129, 40 L.Ed.2d 703, 94 S.Ct. 2157 (1974).

31. Section 18 of the 1934 Act creates a private cause of action against persons, such as accountants, who "make or cause to be made" materially misleading statements in reports or other documents filed with the Commission. 15 U.S.C. §78r [15 U.S.C.S. §78r]. We need not consider the question whether a cause of action may be maintained under §10(b) on the basis of actions that would constitute a violation of §18. Under §18 liability extends to persons who, in reliance on such statements, purchased or sold a security whose price was affected by the statements. Liability is limited, however, in the important respect that the defendant is accorded the defense that he acted in "good faith and had no knowledge that such statement was false or misleading." Consistent with this language the legislative history of the section suggests something more than negligence on the part of the defendant is required for recovery. The original version of §18(a), §17(a) of S. 2693, H.R. 7852 and H.R. 7855, *see supra,* at 201-202, 47 L.Ed.2d 681, provided that the defendant would not be liable if "he acted in good faith and in the exercise of reasonable care had no ground to believe that such statement was false or misleading." The accounting profession objected to this provision on the ground that liability would be created for honest errors in judgment. *See* Senate Hearings on Stock Exchange Practices, *supra,* n. 24, at 7175-7183; House Hearings on H.R. 7852 and H.R. 8720, *supra,* n. 24, at 653. In subsequent drafts the current formulation was adopted. It is also significant that actions under §18 are limited by a relatively short statute of limitations similar to that provided in §13 of the 1933 Act. §18(c). Moreover, as under §11(e) of the 1933 Act the District Court is authorized to require the plaintiff to post a bond for costs, including attorneys' fees, and to assess such costs at the conclusion of the litigation. §18(a).

32. Apparently the Rule was a hastily drafted response to a situation clearly involving intentional misconduct. The Commission's Regional Administrator in Boston had reported to the Director of the Trading and Exchange Division that the president of a corporation was telling the other shareholders that the corporation was doing poorly and purchasing their shares at the resultant depressed prices, when in fact the business was doing exceptionally well. The Rule was drafted and approved on the day this report was received. *See* Conference on Codification of the Federal Securities Laws, 22 Bus. Law. 793, 922 (1967) (remarks of Milton Freeman, one of the Rule's codrafters); *Blue Chip Stamps, supra,* at 767, 44 L.Ed.2d 539, 95 S.Ct. 1917 (Blackmun, J., dissenting). Although adopted pursuant to §10(b), the language of the Rule appears to have been derived in significant part from §17 of the 1933 Act, 15 U.S.C. §77q [15 U.S.C.S. §77q]. *E.g., Blue Chip Stamps, supra,* at 767, 44 L.Ed.2d 539, 95 S.Ct. 1917 (Blackmun, J., dissenting). *SEC v. Texas Gulf Sulphur Co.* 401 F.2d, 833, 867 (C.A.2 1968) (Friendly, J., concurring), *cert. denied sub nom Coates v. SEC,* 394 U.S. 976, 22 L.Ed.2d 756, 89 S.Ct. 1454 (1969). There is no indication in the administrative history of the Rule that any of the subsections was intended to proscribe conduct not involving scienter. Indeed the Commission's release issued contemporaneously with the Rule explained:

importantly, Rule 10b-5 was adopted pursuant to authority granted the Commission under §10(b). The rulemaking power granted to an administrative agency charged with the administration of a federal statute is not the power to make law. Rather, it is " 'the power to adopt regulations to carry into effect the will of Congress as expressed by the statute.' " *Dixon v. United States,* 381 U.S. 68, 74, 14 L.Ed.2d 223, 85 S.Ct. 1301 (1965), quoting *Manhattan General Equipment Co. v. Commissioner,* 297 U.S. 129, 134, 80 L.Ed. 528, 56 S.Ct. 397 (1936). Thus, despite the broad view of the Rule advanced by the Commission in this case, its scope cannot exceed the power granted the Commission by Congress under §10(b). For the reasons stated above, we think the Commission's original interpretation of Rule 10b-5 was compelled by the language and history of §10(b) and related sections of the Acts. *See, e.g., Gerstle v. Gamble-Skogmo, Inc.* 478 F.2d 1281, 1299 (C.A.2 1973); *Lanza v. Drexel & Co.* 479 F.2d 1277, 1304-1305 (C.A.2 1973); *SEC v. Texas Gulf Sulphur Co.* 401 F.2d, at 868 (Friendly, J., concurring); 3 L. Loss, Securities Regulation 1766; 6 *id.,* at 3883-3885 (1969). When a statute speaks so specifically in terms of manipulation and deception, and of implementing devices and contrivances—the commonly understood terminology of intentional wrongdoing—and when its history reflects no more expansive intent, we are quite unwilling to extend the scope of the statute to negligent conduct.[33]

III

Recognizing that §10(b) and Rule 10b-5 might be held to require proof of more than negligent nonfeasance by Ernst & Ernst as a precondition to the imposition of civil liability, respondents further contend that the case should be remanded for trial under whatever standard is adopted. Throughout the lengthy history of this case respondents have proceeded on a theory of liability premised on negligence, specifically disclaiming that Ernst & Ernst had engaged in fraud or intentional misconduct.[34] In these circumstances, we think it inappropriate to remand the action for further proceedings.

The judgment of the Court of Appeals is reversed.

> The Securities and Exchange Commission today announced the adoption of a rule prohibiting fraud by any person in connection with the purchase of securities. The previously existing rules against fraud in the purchase of securities applied only to brokers and dealers. The new rule closes a loophole in the protections against fraud administered by the Commission by prohibiting individuals or companies from buying securities if they engage in fraud in their purchase.
>
> SEC Release No. 3230 (May 21, 1942).

That same year, in its Annual Report, the Commission again stated that the purpose of the Rule was to protect investors against "fraud":

> During the fiscal year the Commission adopted Rule X-10B-5 as an additional protection to investors. The new rule prohibits fraud by any person in connection with the purchase of securities, while the previously existing rules against fraud in the purchase of securities applied only to brokers and dealers.
>
> 1942 Annual Report of the Securities Exchange Commission 10.

33. As we find the language and history of §10(b) dispositive of the appropriate standard of liability, there is no occasion to examine the additional considerations of "policy," set forth by the parties, that may have influenced the lawmakers in their formulation of the statute. We do note that the standard urged by respondents would significantly broaden the class of plaintiffs who may seek to impose liability upon accountants and other experts who perform services or express opinions with respect to matters under the Acts. Last Term, in *Blue Chip Stamps,* 421 U.S., at 747-748, 44 L.Ed.2d 539, 95 S.Ct. 1917, the Court pertinently observed:

> While much of the development of the law of deceit has been the elimination of artificial barriers to recovery on just claims, we are not the first court to express concern that the inexorable broadening of the class of plaintiff who may sue in this area of the law will ultimately result in more harm than good. In *Ultramares Corp. v. Touche,* 255 N.Y. 170, 174 N.E. 441 (1931), Chief Judge Cardozo observed with respect to "a liability in an indeterminate amount for an indeterminate time to an indeterminate class":
>
> > The hazards of a business conducted on these terms are so extreme as to enkindle doubt whether a flaw may not exist in the implication of a duty that exposes to these consequences.
> >
> > *Id.,* at 179-180, 174 N.E., at 444.

This case, on its facts, illustrates the extreme reach of the standard urged by respondents. As investors in transactions initiated by Nay, not First Securities, they were not foreseeable users of the financial statements prepared by Ernst & Ernst. Respondents conceded that they did not rely on either these financial statements or Ernst & Ernst's certificates of opinion. *See* n. 9, *supra.* The class of persons eligible to benefit from such a standard, though small in this case, could be numbered in the thousands in other cases. Acceptance of respondents' view would extend to new frontiers the "hazards" of rendering expert advice under the Acts, raising serious policy questions not yet addressed by Congress.

34. *See* 503 F.2d, at 1104, 1119; n. 5, *supra.*

SECURITIES EXCHANGE ACT OF 1934

Scope

The Securities Exchange Act of 1934 (the '34 Act), 15 U.S.C. §78a, *et seq.*, regulates transactions in securities commonly conducted on national securities exchanges and in the over-the-counter markets. Section 12(a) of the '34 Act prohibits a broker or dealer from trading securities on a national securities exchange unless a registration is effective with respect to such securities with both the Securities and Exchange Commission and the exchange. (Any person engaging in the business of effecting transactions in securities for the account of another person is a broker. A dealer is any person engaging in the business of buying and selling securities for his own account, through a broker or otherwise.) Certain securities are excepted from the registration requirements.

Registration on an exchange is voluntary with the issuer of the securities, but the '34 Act makes it unlawful for an exchange member or broker or dealer to effect a transaction in an unregistered security on a national exchange. Although an issuer is not required to register securities on a national exchange, and the securities may be sold in the over-the-counter market, OTC-traded securities meeting certain shareholder and asset requirements are required to be registered under §12(g) of the '34 Act.

The issuer of securities which are listed on an exchange and registered automatically becomes subject to other requirements of the '34 Act. Registration of securities requires compliance with certain reporting requirements, proxy solicitation requirements, and "insider" reporting and trading requirements. Each of these requirements is applicable to issuers of securities which are registered under the '34 Act, and the "insider" requirements are applicable to their officers, directors and certain shareholders. The primary purpose of the '34 Act is to ensure a fair and honest market, a market which will reflect an evaluation of securities in light of all available material and pertinent data with respect to such securities.

Like the '33 Act, the '34 Act contains provisions that affect the administration of plans and the interaction of pension and welfare plans with the other components of the plan complex. Numerous activities engaged in by pension and welfare plans may be subject to the '34 Act. Registration and reporting requirements must be considered, as well as the involvement of the plan in the securities market generally. The application of the '34 Act to pension and welfare plans is more readily understood if the reader thinks of a pension or welfare plan as an "issuer" of securities.

Disclosure or Registration

One of the first questions to consider is whether the establishment of a pension or welfare plan and the distribution of interest therein to employees through their participation will trigger the application of the registration requirements. Section 12(g)(1) provides:

> every issuer which is engaged in interstate commerce, or in a business affecting interstate commerce, or whose securities are traded by use of the mails or any means or instrumentality of interstate commerce shall—
>
> (A) within 120 days after the last day of its first fiscal year ended after the effective date [July 1, 1964] of this subsection on which the issuer has total assets exceeding $1,000,000 and a class of equity security (other than an exempted security) held of record by seven hundred and fifty or more persons; and
>
> (B) within 120 days after the last day of its first fiscal year ended after two years from the effective date [July 1, 1964] of this subsection on which the issuer has total assets exceeding one million dollars and a class of equity security (other than an exempted security) held of record by 500 or more or less than 750 persons,
>
> register such security by filing with the [Securities and Exchange Commission] a registration statement . . . with respect to such security containing such information and documents as the [Securities and Exchange Commission] may specify comparable to that which is required in an application to register a security pursuant to [Section 12(b)].

An interest in a plan which constitutes a security under §2(1) of the '33 Act generally will constitute a security under §3(a)(10) of the '34 Act. Section 3(a)(10) of the '34 Act defines the term as:

> Any . . . certificate of interest or participation in any profit-sharing agreement . . . investment contract . . . or in general, any instrument commonly known as a "security". . . .

Like the '33 Act, the '34 Act exempts certain securities from its provisions. Section 12(g)(2)(H), which is available for issuers subject to Section 12(g), provides:

> The provisions of [subsection 12(g)(1)] do not apply in respect of . . . any interest or participation in any collective trust funds maintained by a bank or in a separate account maintained by an insurance company which interest or participation is issued in connection with (i) a stock bonus, pension, or profit-sharing plan which meets the requirements for qualification under Section 401 of the Internal Revenue Code of 1954, or (ii) an an-

> nuity plan which meets the requirements for the deduction of the employer's contribution under §404(a)(2) of such Code.

Section 3(a)(12) of the '34 Act, which is available for other than 12(g) issuers, is similar to Section 3(a)(2) of the '33 Act. Section 12(g)(1) does not apply to securities within Section 12(g)(2)(H), but it is important to note that this exemption [and the Section 3(a)(12) exemption] is narrower than the '33 Act exemption. Section 3(a)(2) of the '33 Act extends to interests in a "*single* or collective trust fund maintained by a bank" (emphasis added), while §12(g)(2)(H) of the '34 Act only extends to interests in a "collective trust fund maintained by a bank."

However, the Securities and Exchange Commission has published a regulatory exemption for both tax-qualified and non-qualified plans where the interests are non-transferable except on death or incompetence. Regulation §240.12h-2(a) provides:

> Issuers shall be exempt from the provisions of Section 12(g) of the ['34 Act] with respect to the following securities:
>
> (a) Any interest or participation in an employee stock bonus, stock purchase, profit-sharing, pension, retirement, incentive, thrift, savings or similar plan which is not transferable by the holder except in the event of death or mental incompetency, or any security issued solely to fund such plan....

This exemption should cover most pension plans, but it would not extend to the distribution of interests (through participation) in welfare plans. However, it seems unlikely that any type of registration would be required.

Reporting Requirements

Once issues relating to registration have been considered, it is important to focus on the various reporting requirements, some of which will be discussed here. Section 13(d) provides:

> Any person who, after acquiring directly or indirectly the beneficial ownership of any equity security of a class which is registered pursuant to §12 of this title,... is directly or indirectly the beneficial owner of more than five percentum of such class shall, within 10 days after such acquisition, send to the issuer of the security at its principal office, by registered or certified mail, send to each exchange where the security is traded, and file with the [Securities and Exchange Commission], a statement [containing certain information]....

Reporting may be required if the employer maintaining a pension plan contributes its securities to the plan or if the employer contributes cash which is used by the plan to purchase employer securities. For purposes of §13(d), each person with the power to vote or to control the disposition of stock is the beneficial owner. If a plan such as a profit-sharing or stock bonus plan acquires 5% of the securities of the employer maintaining the plan, the plan or its trustees will have to file the necessary report.

In addition to the reporting required under §13 (d), reporting may be required under §16(a). *See also* '34 Act §16(b) (insider trading). This section requires 10% shareholders to file certain reports relating to their beneficial ownership of securities of the issuer and reports of changes in their ownership. If a profit-sharing plan acquires 10% of the stock of the employer maintaining the plan, the plan or its trustees will have to file this report. However, according to the Securities and Exchange Commission, plan participants probably will not have to report their interests in the plan if the plan's acquisitions of employer securities are without their prior approval. *See* Reg. §16a-8(b).

Another regulation exempts a participant otherwise required to report from reporting "indirect" interests in a "pension or retirement plan." In a "no action" letter, the staff of the Securities and Exchange Commission has interpreted the term "indirect" to mean interests which are substantially restricted as to the participant's right of withdrawal.

Antifraud Provisions

The '34 Act contains antifraud prohibitions similar to those contained in the '33 Act. As under the '33 Act, the various exemptions contained in the '34 Act do not extend to the antifraud provisions. Section 10(b) of the '34 Act provides:

> It shall be unlawful for any person, directly or indirectly, by use of any means or instrumentality of interstate commerce or of the mails, or of any facility of any national securities exchange—
>
> .....
>
> (b) To use or employ, in connection with the purchase or sale of any security registered on a national securities exchange or any security not so registered, any manipulative or deceptive device or contrivance in contravention of such rules and regulations as the (Securities and Exchange Commission) may prescribe as necessary or appropriate in the public interest or for the protection of investors.

This subsection of Section 10 has been amplified by regulations issued by the Securities and Exchange Commission. Regulation §240.10(b)-5 provides that:

> It shall be unlawful for any person, directly or indirectly, by the use of any means or instrumen-

tality of interstate commerce, or of the mails, or of any facility of any national securities exchange,

(a) to employ any device, scheme, or artifice to defraud,

(b) to make any untrue statement of a material fact or to omit to state a material fact necessary in order to make the statements made, in the light of the circumstances under which they were made, not misleading, or

(c) to engage in any act, practice, or course of business which operates or would operate as a fraud or deceit upon any person, in connection with the purchase or sale of any security.

Section 10(b) and Rule 10b-5 have had an impact on the administration of pension plans and on the relationship of plans to the other components of the private employee benefit complex. Of particular interest is the application of the '34 Act to, among other things, the investment of plan assets. The court's decision in *Shapiro v. Merrill Lynch, Pierce, Fenner & Smith, Inc.*, 495 F.2d 228 (2d Cir. 1974), illustrates the application of the antifraud provision. In the *Merrill Lynch* case, the court held that a pension plan could be liable as a "tippee" if it purchased or sold securities based on inside information which it failed to disclose prior to the transaction.

SHAPIRO V. MERRILL LYNCH
495 F.2d 228 (2d Cir. 1974)

TIMBERS, Circuit Judge:

This appeal presents important questions, some of first impression, involving the scope of the antifraud provisions of the federal securities laws in their application to transactions on a national securities exchange when material inside information has not been disclosed.

Specifically, the questions presented are (1) whether Section 10(b) of the Securities Exchange Act of 1934 and Rule 10b-5 were violated by a prospective managing underwriter of a debenture issue and the underwriter's officers, directors and employees when they divulged material inside information to the underwriter's customers for the purpose of protecting the latters' investments in the stock of the issuer; (2) whether the same antifraud provisions of the securities laws were violated by the underwriter's customers when they traded in the stock of the issuer without disclosing the material inside information which had been divulged to them by the underwriter; and (3) whether those referred to above, if they did violate the antifraud provisions of the securities laws, are liable in damages to those persons who during the same period purchased stock in the same company in the open market without knowledge of the material inside information. In short, this case involves the liability of non-trading "tippers" and trading "tippees" under Section 10(b) and Rule 10b-5.

Defendants appeal, pursuant to 28 U.S.C. § 1292(b) (1970), from an order entered in the Southern District of New York, Charles H. Tenney, District Judge, 353 F.Supp. 264 (S.D.N.Y. 1972), denying their motion for judgment on the pleadings on the ground that the complaint failed to state a claim upon which relief can be granted.

The action was brought to recover damages claimed to have been sustained as the result of defendants' trading or recommending trading of common stock of Douglas Aircraft Company, Inc. (Douglas) on the New York Stock Exchange (NY SE) in 1966. Such acts or transactions are alleged to have violated Sections 10(b) and 15(c)(1) of the Securities Exchange Act of 1934, 15 U.S.C. §§78j (b) and 78o(c)(1) (1970); Rules 10b-5 and 15c-1 and 2, 17 C.F.R. §§240.106-5 and 240.156-1 and 2 (1973), promulgated by the Securities and Exchange Commission (SEC); and Section 17(a) of the Securities Act of 1933, 15 U.S.C. §77q(a) (1970).[1]

Applying to the admitted facts before us what we believe to be controlling principles of law as enunciated by the Supreme Court and by our Court, we affirm.

I

In summarizing here the facts necessary to a determination of the legal issues raised on this appeal, we must take as admitted the well-pleaded material facts alleged in the complaint, as the district court did, 353 F.Supp. at 268, since the order under review denied defendants' motion for judg-

1. Jurisdiction is grounded upon Section 27 of the 1934 Act, 15 U.S.C. §78aa (1970), and Section 22(a) of the 1933 Act, 15 U.S.C. §77v(a) (1970). Both acts give to the district courts jurisdiction over all actions brought to enforce any liability or duty created by the respective acts "irrespective of the amount in controversy or the citizenship of the parties." III Loss, Securities Regulation 2005 (2d ed. 1961), citing *Deckert v. Independence Shares Corp.,* 311 U.S. 282, 289 (1940), and *Wilko v. Swan,* 346 U.S. 427, 431 (1953).

Section 27 of the 1934 Act, moreover, is unique in that it gives *exclusive* jurisdiction to the district courts of violations of that act or the rules and regulations thereunder, whereas the state courts are given concurrent jurisdiction over private actions under the other federal securities acts. III Loss, *supra,* at 2005.

ment on the pleadings pursuant to Fed.R.Civ.P. 12(c).[2]

The course of events which culminated in the instant action occurred during the period April 1966 through July 1966. During this period, Merrill Lynch, Pierce, Fenner & Smith Inc. (Merrill Lynch) was engaged as the prospective managing underwriter of a proposed Douglas offering of $75,000,000 principal amount of a new issue of 4¾% convertible subordinated debentures. A registration statement for this offering was filed with the SEC on June 7; it became effective on July 12, with Merrill Lynch the managing underwriter. On June 7, Douglas had released an earnings statement which reported the results of operations for the first five months of its 1966 fiscal year, i.e., through April 30, 1966.[3] This statement indicated that Douglas had earned 85 cents per share on its common stock during that period.

During the period June 17 through June 22, Merrill Lynch and certain of its officers, directors and employees (the individual defendants)[4] were advised by Douglas' management of certain material adverse inside information regarding Douglas' earnings.[5] This information was essentially that (a) Douglas would report substantially lower earnings for the entire first six months than it had reported for the first five months of its 1966 fiscal year; (b) Douglas had sharply lowered its estimate of earnings for its full 1966 fiscal year in that it now expected to have little or no profit for that year; and (c) Douglas had substantially reduced its projection of earnings for its 1967 fiscal year. This information was given to Merrill Lynch solely because of its position as the prospective underwriter for the Douglas debenture issue. The individual defendants and Merrill Lynch knew or should have known that the information had not yet been publicly announced.

During the period June 20 through June 24, Merrill Lynch and the individual defendants disclosed this confidential information to the following Merrill Lynch customers (the selling defendants), most of whom were institutional investors: Investors Management Co., Inc. (a wholly owned subsidiary of Anchor Corporation), Madison Fund, Inc., J. M. Hartwell & Co. (predecessor of J. M. Hartwell & Co., Inc.), Hartwell Associates, Park Westlake Associates, Van Strum & Towne, Inc., Fleschner Becker Associates, A. W. Jones & Co., A. W. Jones Associates, City Associates, Fairfield Partners, Burden Investors Services, Inc. and William A. M. Burden & Co. The selling defendants knew or should have known that this information had not yet been publicly announced.

During the period June 20 through June 23, the selling defendants either sold from existing positions or made short sales of more than 165,000 shares of Douglas common on the NYSE. This was approximately one-half of the total number of Douglas shares sold on the NYSE during this period. These sales were made prior to Douglas' public disclosure of the revised earnings information on June 24[6] and without the sellers having disclosed this information to the investing public, including plaintiffs. As a result of these sales, the individual defendants and Merrill Lynch received

2. 2A Moore, Federal Practice ¶12.08 (2d ed. 1972).

This is so despite defendants' assertion of a Rule 12(b)(6) defense of failure to state a claim upon which relief can be granted in their Rule 12(c) motion, as permitted by Rule 12(h)(2). 5 Wright & Miller, Federal Practice and Procedure: Civil §1367, at 688-89 (1969).

3. Douglas' fiscal year begins December 1 and ends November 30.

4. Of the twelve "individual defendants," referred to in the district court opinion and in the briefs as "employees" of Merrill Lynch, five were salesmen in the New York institutional sales office of Merrill Lynch (i.e., defendants Lee W. Idleman, Lawrence Zicklin, James A. McCarthy, Elias A. Lazor and Chester T. Smith, Jr.).

The other seven individual defendants were vice presidents of Merrill Lynch (i.e., defendants Winthrop Lenz, Julius II. Sedlmayer, Gillette K. Martin, Dean S. Woodman, Edward N. McMillan, Phillip F. Bilbao and Norman H. Heindel, Jr.).

Of the latter, three were directors of Merrill Lynch (i.e., Lenz, Sedlmayer and McMillan).

Each of the vice presidents occupied positions of special significance in the Merrill Lynch organization in the context of the issues in this case. Lenz was chairman of Merrill Lynch's executive committee and was in charge of underwriting; Sedlmayer was director of the underwriting division; Martin was head of the corporate buying department of the underwriting division; Woodman was in charge of the west coast underwriting office; McMillan was director of the institutional and equity sales division; Bilbao was manager of the institutional sales department and municipal sales division; and Heindel was manager of the New York institutional sales office.

5. This information, sometimes described as "nonpublic information," is referred to in this opinion as "inside information."

6. On the morning of June 24, Douglas issued a press release which reported that its earnings for the first six months of its 1966 fiscal year, i.e. through May 31, were 12 cents per share and that it expected that its earnings for the full 1966 fiscal year would be nominal, if any.

commissions from the execution of the selling defendants' orders and also received compensation in the form of customer directed "give ups"—i.e. division of commissions earned by other brokers who executed orders for the selling defendants.

On June 23, plaintiff Gibson purchased an unspecified number of shares of Douglas common on the NYSE; his purchase was prior to the public release on June 24 of Douglas' revised earnings report. The other four plaintiffs—Maurice Shapiro, Isadore Shapiro, Naigles and Saxe—purchased an unspecified number of shares of Douglas common on the NYSE on June 24; their purchases were made without knowledge of the material adverse earnings information released by Douglas that day.[7]

Beginning about June 22 or 23, the market price of Douglas common on the NYSE took a sudden and substantial drop.[8] This coincided with and, according to the complaint, was caused by the substantial sales by the selling defendants on the basis of material inside information, the disclosure of which after plaintiffs' purchases precipitated a further severe drop in the market price of Douglas common.

On August 21, 1970, plaintiffs commenced the instant action in the Southern District of New York. They sued on behalf of themselves and all others similarly situated who purchased Douglas common during the period June 21 through June 24, 1966. Essentially the complaint alleges that defendants were under a duty to disclose to the general investing public, including plaintiffs, the material inside information regarding Douglas' earnings; that defendants defrauded plaintiffs by not disclosing such information, in violation of the antifraud provisions of the securities laws; that plaintiffs would not have purchased Douglas stock if they had known of the information withheld by defendants; and that plaintiffs sustained substantial damages as a result of the acts of defendants. Plaintiffs do not claim to have purchased specific shares of Douglas stock sold by any of the selling defendants. The complaint demands damages sustained by plaintiffs and an accounting of profits realized by defendants.[9]

After the pleadings were closed and certain limited discovery proceedings had taken place, both sides brought on motions before Judge Tenney. Plaintiffs moved, pursuant to Fed.R.Civ.P. 23(c), for an order declaring that the action be maintained as a class action. Defendants moved for judgment on the pleadings on the ground that the complaint failed to state a claim upon which relief can be granted. In support of their motion, defendants contended that plaintiffs lacked standing to sue; that the information defendants withheld was not material; that there was no privity between plaintiffs and defendants; that scienter was absent; and that plaintiffs had failed to allege facts sufficient to establish causation and reliance.

On December 26, 1972, Judge Tenney filed a well reasoned opinion, 353 F.Supp. 264, denying the motions by both sides.[10] In denying defen-

7. The subject matter of Douglas' press release of June 24 appeared in articles in the *New York Times* on June 25 and in the *Wall Street Journal* on June 27.

8. The following is a table of prices of Douglas common stock on the NYSE during the relevant period:

Date	*Volume*	*High*	*Low*	*Closing Price*
June 21. .	66,200	90	86	86¼
June 22. .	66,500	90½	87½	87½
June 23. .	261,500	88¾	77 5/8	78¾
June 24. .	211,100	77	74½	76
June 25		SATURDAY		
June 26		SUNDAY		
June 27. .	121,300	74 3/8	69	69
June 28. .	135,300	70	66¼	68½
June 29. .	102,200	69 7/8	64 1/8	64 3/8
June 30. .	180,900	65¼	61	63 1/8
July 1. .	100,400	64 7/8	61	61¾

9. Based on substantially the same transactions alleged in the complaint in the instant action, the SEC brought administrative proceedings to determine whether certain of the defendants herein had violated the antifraud provisions of the securities laws in connection with the trading of Douglas common stock during the period June 17-June 24, 1966. The upshot of these proceedings was that the SEC accepted the offer of settlement of Merrill Lynch and its employees pursuant to which, for purposes of the administrative proceedings, they consented to findings that they had violated the antifraud provisions, including Section 10(b) and Rule 10b-5. The SEC suspended Merrill Lynch's New York institutional sales office for 15 days and imposed other administrative sanctions on certain of the individual defendants. Merrill Lynch, Pierce, Fenner & Smith, Inc., Securities Exchange Act Release No. 8459 (1968).

With respect to the selling defendants, the SEC in a separate decision, Investors Management Co., Inc., Securities Exchange Act Release No. 9267 (1971), affirmed the initial decision of the hearing examiner who, after a lengthy hearing, found that all of the selling defendants had violated the antifraud provisions, including Section 10(b) and Rule 10b-5, and ordered that they be censured.

10. Plaintiffs' motion for a class action determination was denied because it was impossible on the facts presented by the pleadings to determine the parameters of the class; but leave was granted to renew the motion

dants' motion for judgment on the pleadings, the judge carefully considered but rejected each of the defendants' contentions. He held in substance that Merrill Lynch and the individual defendants violated a duty which they owed to plaintiffs when these defendants disclosed material inside information to the selling defendants; that the selling defendants in turn violated a duty which they owed to plaintiffs when they sold the Douglas stock without disclosing the material inside information which had been divulged to them; that the conduct of all defendants had caused plaintiffs to sustain damages; and that accordingly the complaint stated a claim upon which relief can be granted against all defendants under Section 10(b) and Rule 10b-5.

Since there was no issue before Judge Tenney on defendants' motion for judgment on the pleadings with respect to the measure of damages to which plaintiffs would be entitled or other appropriate relief to be fashioned in the event plaintiffs were successful after trial on the merits, he made no determination on that issue.

On February 22, 1973, upon motion by defendants, Judge Tenney amended his earlier order by adding the certification[11] required by 28 U.S.C. §1292(b) (1970) to permit appeal from an interlocutory order. On March 27, 1973, we granted leave to appeal.

---

when sufficient facts could be presented. 353 F.Supp. at 280. Since a class action determination was not made, we are not presented with those issues discussed in *Eisen v. Carlisle & Jacquelin,* 479 F.2d 1005 (2 Cir.), *vacated and remanded,* ____ U.S. ____ (1974).

The district court denied without comment defendants' motion insofar as it applied to plaintiffs' claims asserted under Section 15(c)(1) of the 1934 Act or Section 17(a) of the 1933 Act, since neither side had briefed those issues. They are not before us on this appeal.

11. Judge Tenney's Section 1292(b) certification reads as follows:

> The undersigned is of the opinion that this order involves a controlling question of law as to which there is substantial ground for difference of opinion, i.e., whether one who allegedly receives material non-public adverse information about a company, and thereafter sells stock in the company on a national securities exchange without disclosing said information, is civilly liable, regardless of the amount sold, to all persons who during the same period purchased securities in the same company in the open market without knowledge of the adverse information, and the Court is further of the opinion that an immediate appeal from this order may materially advance the ultimate determination of the litigation.

II

Upon the basis of the foregoing summary of the facts and prior proceedings, we turn directly to the legal questions presented. They are essentially whether defendants violated Section 10(b) and Rule 10b-5 and, if so, whether they are liable in damages to plaintiffs for such violations. The district court held as a matter of pleading that both questions must be answered in the affirmative. We agree.

Our starting point is the statute and the implementing rule. Section 10(b) of the 1934 Act in relevant part makes it unlawful for any person, directly or indirectly, by the use of any facility of any national securities exchange "[t]o use or employ, in connection with the purchase or sale of any security . . . any manipulative or deceptive device or contrivance in contravention of such rules and regulations as the Commission [SEC] may prescribe as necessary or appropriate in the public interest or for the protection of investors." One such prescription is Rule 10b-5 which provides in relevant part that "in connection with the purchase or sale of any security," it shall be unlawful for any person, directly or indirectly, by the use of any facility of any national securities exchange "(a) [t]o employ any device, scheme, or artifice to defraud, (b) [t]o make any untrue statement of a material fact or to omit to state a material fact necessary in order to make the statements made, in the light of the circumstances under which they were made, not misleading, or (c) [t]o engage in any act, practice, or course of business which operates or would operate as a fraud or deceit upon any person. . . ."

As we have stated time and again, the purpose behind Section 10(b) and Rule 10b-5 is to protect the investing public and to secure fair dealing in the securities markets by promoting full disclosure of inside information so that an informed judgment can be made by all investors who trade in such markets. *E.g., Crane Co. v. Westinghouse Air Brake Co.,* 419 F.2d 787, 793 (2 Cir. 1969), *cert. denied,* 400 U.S. 822 (1970); *SEC v. Texas Gulf Sulphur Co.,* 401 F.2d 833, 848 (2 Cir. 1968), *cert. denied sub nom. Kline v. SEC,* 394 U.S. 976 (1969). We recently held in *Radiation Dynamics, Inc. v. Goldmuntz,* 464 F.2d 876, 890 (2 Cir. 1972), that "[t]he essential purpose of Rule 10b-5 . . . is to prevent corporate insiders and their tippees from taking unfair advantage of the uninformed outsiders."

Moreover, in applying the antifraud provisions of the securities laws to the facts of this case, it is important to bear in mind that "Congress intended securities legislation enacted for the purpose of avoiding frauds to be construed 'not technically and restrictively, but flexibly to effectuate its remedial purposes.' " *Affiliated Ute Citizens v. United States,* 406 U.S. 128, 151 (1972), quoting from *SEC v. Capital Gains Research Bureau, Inc.,* 375 U.S. 180, 195 (1963). This policy of flexible, nontechnical construction of the securities laws has provided the underpinning for the results in recent cases involving specific violations of the antifraud provisions of the securities laws. *E.g., Superintendent of Insurance v. Bankers Life & Casualty Co.,* 404 U.S. 6, 12 (1971); *SEC v. Glen-Arden Commodities, Inc.,* 493 F.2d 1027, 1033-34 (2 Cir. 1974); *International Controls Corp. v. Vesco,* 490 F.2d 1334, 1345 (2 Cir. 1974). *See Chris-Craft Industries, Inc. v. Piper Aircraft Corp.,* 480 F.2d 341, 357, 363 (2 Cir.), *cert. denied,* 414 U.S. 910 (1973).[12]

Here, upon the question of whether Section 10 (b) and Rule 10b-5 were violated, the critical facts —admitted for purposes of this appeal—are that Merrill Lynch, a prospective managing underwriter of a Douglas debenture issue, and some of the officers, directors and employees of Merrill Lynch, divulged to certain of its customers, the selling defendants, material adverse inside information regarding Douglas' earnings; the selling defendants, without disclosing to the investing public this inside information, sold Douglas common stock on a national securities exchange; and as a result of such trading Merrill Lynch and the individual defendants received commissions and other compensation, the selling defendants minimized their losses, but the investing public comprised of uninformed outsiders, including plaintiffs, who purchased Douglas stock during the same period sustained substantial losses.

Our holding that such conduct on the part of all defendants violated Section 10(b) and Rule 10b-5 is based chiefly on our decision in *SEC v. Texas Gulf Sulphur Co., supra,* where we stated that:

> anyone in possession of material inside information must either disclose it to the investing public, or, if he is disabled from disclosing it . . ., must abstain from trading in or recommending the securities concerned while such inside information remains undisclosed.
>
> 401 F.2d at 848.

Defendants argue, however, that *Texas Gulf* is inapplicable here because, first, that was an SEC injunction action and not a private damage action and, second, Rule 10b-5 does not impose upon these defendants a duty to disclose the material inside information in question to these plaintiffs who did not purchase the actual stock sold by defendants.

Although *Texas Gulf* was an SEC injunction action, the strong public policy considerations behind our "disclose or abstain" rule there are equally applicable here. In short, whether invoked in an SEC injunction action or in a private damage action, "the Rule is based in policy on the justifiable expectation of the securities marketplace that all investors trading on impersonal exchanges have relatively equal access to material information. . . ." *SEC v. Texas Gulf Sulphur Co., supra,* 401 F.2d at 848.[13] *See Crane Co. v. Westinghouse Air Brake Co., supra,* 419 F.2d at 796. Since one of the primary goals of the antifraud provisions of the securities laws would be frustrated if our "disclose or abstain" rule enunciated in *Texas Gulf* were to be limited to SEC injunction actions and held inapplicable to private damage actions, we reject such ground of distinction.

---

12. While the antifraud provisions here involved are Section 10(b) and Rule 10b-5, many of the controlling principles applicable thereto have been enunciated in cases arising under other provisions of the 1934 Act. *E.g., Mills v. Electric Auto-Lite Co.,* 396 U.S. 375 (1970) (§14(a)); *J. I. Case Co. v. Borak,* 377 U.S. 426 (1964) (§14(a)); *Chris-Craft Industries, Inc. v. Piper Aircraft Corp., supra* (§14(e)). The standard of causation in fact (dispensing with any requirement of proof of reliance as a prequisite to recovery) as stated by Mr. Justice Harlan in *Mills,* 396 U.S. at 385, has been held applicable by the Supreme Court to a Rule 10b-5 damage action in *Ute,* 406 U.S. at 153-54. In *Chris-Craft,* 480 F.2d at 362, we noted that "the underlying proscription of §14(e) is virtually identical to that of Rule 10b-5," and we stated that "[i]n determining whether §14(e) violations were committed in the instant case, we shall follow the principles developed under Rule 10b-5 regarding the elements of such violations." Accord, *Gulf & Western Industries, Inc. v. Great Atlantic & Pacific Tea Company, Inc.,* 476 F.2d 687, 695-96 (2 Cir. 1973) (§14(e)). *See* 1 Bromberg, Securities Law: Fraud—SEC Rule 10b-5 §4.7, at 86-86.1 (Supp. 1972-73).

13. We further noted in *Texas Gulf* the Congressional purpose to be implemented by Rule 10b-5:

> The core of Rule 10b-5 is the implementation of the Congressional purpose that all investors should have equal access to the rewards of participation in securities transactions. It was the intent of Congress that all members of the investing public should be subject to identical market risks. . . . [And] inequities based upon unequal access to knowledge should not be shrugged off as inevitable in our way of life, or, in view of the congressional concern in the area, remain uncorrected.
>
> 401 F.2d at 851-52.

We also reject defendants' second asserted ground for distinguishing *Texas Gulf*—that our "disclose or abstain" rule is not applicable here because the only duty owed by defendants was to purchasers of the specific shares of Douglas stock sold by defendants and the transactions here involved were not face-to-face sales to plaintiffs. This argument totally misconstrues our *Texas Gulf* rule. 401 F.2d at 848. It also ignores the fact that these transactions occurred on an anonymous national securities exchange where as a practical matter it would be impossible to identify a particular defendant's sale with a particular plaintiff's purchase. And it would make a mockery of the "disclose or abstain" rule if we were to permit the fortuitous matching of buy and sell orders to determine whether a duty to disclose had been violated. See Painter, Inside Information: Growing Pains For The Development Of Federal Corporation Law Under Rule 10b-5, 65 Colum.L.Rev. 1361, 1372, 1377-78 (1965).[14] On this very point, we stated in *Radiation Dynamics, Inc. v. Goldmuntz, supra,* that our "disclose or abstain" rule enunciated in *Texas Gulf* "applies whether the securities are traded on a public stock exchange or sold through private placement." 464 F.2d at 887. To hold that Section 10(b) and Rule 10b-5 impose a duty to disclose material inside information only in face-to-face transactions or to the actual purchasers or sellers on an anonymous public stock exchange, would be to frustrate a major purpose of the antifraud provisions of the securities laws: to insure the integrity and efficiency of the securities markets. *Chris-Craft Industries, Inc. v. Piper Aircraft Corp., supra,* 480 F.2d at 357. We decline defendants' invitation to sanction a result which Section 10(b) and Rule 10b-5 clearly were intended to foreclose. *See Astor v. Texas Gulf Sulphur Co.,* 306 F.Supp. 1333, 1340-42 (S.D.N.Y. 1969). We hold that defendants owed a duty—for the breach of which they may be held liable in this private action for damages—not only to the purchasers of the actual shares sold by defendants (in the unlikely event they can be identified) but to all persons who during the same period purchased Douglas stock in the open market without knowledge of the material inside information which was in the possession of defendants.

14. As the author recognizes, "Since in any active market disclosure to a particular individual is not feasible, the duty to disclose, if such a duty exists, must be owed to all members of that ill-defined class of stockholders who, with the benefit of inside information, would alter their intention to [buy]." Painter, 65 Colum.L.Rev. at 1378.

We find untenable the contentions of the respective defendants that, upon the issue of whether they violated the antifraud provisions of the securities laws, a distinction should be drawn between their roles as non-trading "tippers" and trading "tippees."

With respect to Merrill Lynch and the individual defendants (the non-trading "tippers"), their divulging of confidential material inside information to their customers who sold Douglas stock on the basis of such information clearly violated Section 10(b) and Rule 10b-5. In *SEC v. Texas Gulf Sulphur Co., supra,* 401 F.2d at 852, 856, we held that two "tippers" violated the antifraud provisions of the securities laws by disclosing material inside information to individuals who subsequently entered into transactions on the basis of that information, and we remanded to the district court for determination of an appropriate remedy. Upon remand, the district court held one of these "tippers" liable for "tipping" and awarded appropriate relief. *SEC v. Texas Gulf Sulphur Co.,* 312 F.Supp. 77, 95 (S.D.N.Y. 1970), *modified on other grounds,* 446 F.2d 1301, 1307-08 (2 Cir.), *cert. denied,* 404 U.S. 1005 (1971). We find *Texas Gulf* controlling with respect to the liability of the non-trading "tippers" here.

With respect to the selling defendants (the trading "tippees"), *Texas Gulf* strongly suggests that the same duty to "abstain or disclose" should be imposed upon them. Although the issue of "tippee" liability was not squarely before us in *Texas Gulf,* we did say:

> As Darke's "tippees" are not defendants in this action, we need not decide whether, if they acted with actual or constructive knowledge that the material information was undisclosed, their conduct is as equally violative of the Rule as the conduct of their insider source, though we note that it certainly could be equally reprehensible.
> 401 F.2d at 852-53.

In *Ross v. Licht,* 263 F.Supp. 395, 410 (S.D.N.Y. 1967), the court observed, "If [defendants] were not insiders, they would seem to have been 'tippees' . . . and subject to the same duty as insiders." *See Radiation Dynamics, Inc. v. Goldmuntz, supra,* 464 F.2d at 887, 890; *Cady Roberts & Co.,* 40 S.E.C. 907, 912-13 (1961). *Cf. Kuehnert v. Texstar Corp.,* 412 F.2d 700, 702-05 (5 Cir. 1969). We are not persuaded by the selling defendants' argument that as tippees they were not able to make effective public disclosure of information about a company with which they were not associated; for the duty imposed is not a naked one to disclose, but a duty to abstain from trading unless they do disclose. Since upon the admitted facts before us the selling defendants knew or should have known of the confidential corporate source of the revised earnings information and they knew of its non-public nature, they were under a duty not to trade in Douglas stock without publicly disclosing such information.

In short, for the reasons set forth above, we hold that all defendants violated Section 10(b) and Rule 10b-5.

III

We turn next to the remaining major legal question presented: assuming that defendants did violate the antifraud provisions of the securities laws by trading in or recommending trading in Douglas common stock (as we have held above), whether they are liable in a private action for damages to plaintiffs who during the same period purchased Douglas stock in the open market without knowledge of the material inside information which was in the possession of defendants.

The essential argument of defendants on this question is that, even if they did violate Section 10(b) and Rule 10b-5, their conduct did not "cause" damage to plaintiffs;[15] that it was Douglas' precarious financial condition, not defendants' securities law violations, which precipitated the sudden, substantial drop in the market price of Douglas stock and hence the losses sustained by plaintiffs; that, since plaintiffs had no prior or contemporaneous knowledge of defendants' actions, they would have purchased Douglas stock regardless of defendants' securities law violations; and that, since defendants' sales were unrelated to plaintiffs' purchases and all transactions took place on anonymous public stock exchanges,[16] there is lacking the requisite connection between defendants' alleged violations and the alleged losses sustained by plaintiffs.

The short, and we believe conclusive, answer to defendants' assertion that their conduct did not "cause" damage to plaintiffs is the "causation in fact" holding by the Supreme Court in *Affiliated Ute Citizens v. United States,* 406 U.S. 128, 153-54 (1972), upon the authority of which we conclude that the requisite element of causation in fact has been established here by the uncontroverted facts that defendants traded in or recommended trading in Douglas stock without disclosing material inside information which plaintiffs as reasonable investors might have considered important in making their decision to purchase Douglas stock.

In order more fully to deal with the arguments which have been vigorously urged upon us by defendants' counsel, however, we believe it may be helpful to back up a bit from our conclusion based on *Affiliated Ute* and particularly to indicate briefly the decisional law regarding the requisite element of causation that preceded the Supreme Court's opinion in that case.

We consistently have held that causation is a necessary element of a private action for damages under Rule 10b-5. *E.g., Chasins v. Smith, Barney & Co.,* 438 F.2d 1167, 1172 (2 Cir. 1970); *Crane Co. v. Westinghouse Air Brake Co.,* 419 F.2d 787, 797 (2 Cir. 1969), *cert. denied,* 400 U.S. 822 (1970). Indeed, we have refused "to facilitate outsiders' proof of insiders' fraud" by "reading out of [Rule 10b-5] so basic an element of tort law as the principle of causation in fact." *List v. Fashion Park, Inc.,* 340 F.2d 457, 463 (2 Cir.), *cert. denied,* 382 U.S. 811 (1965). This is consistent with "the basic concept that causation must be proved else defendants could be held liable to all the world." *Globus v. Law Research Service, Inc.,* 418 F.2d 1276, 1292 (2 Cir. 1969), *cert. denied,* 397 U.S. 913 (1970). And we have recognized that the aim of Rule 10b-5 "is to qualify, as between insiders and outsiders, the doctrine of *caveat emptor*—not to establish a scheme of investors' insurance." *List v. Fashion Park, Inc., supra,* 340 F.2d at 463.

As one branch of their absence of causation argument, defendants contend that there was no privity between themselves and plaintiffs. We hold here, as we have held before, that privity between plaintiffs and defendants is not a requisite element of a Rule 10b-5 cause of action for damages. For example, we have upheld Rule 10b-5 claims for relief where there have been no direct transactions between plaintiffs and defendants. *Crane Co. v. Westinghouse Air Brake Co., supra,* 419 F.2d at 796-98; *Heit v. Weitzen,* 402 F.2d 909, 913 (2 Cir. 1968), *cert. denied,* 395 U.S. 903 (1969).

15. While defendants urged upon the district court the absence of other elements of a Rule 10b-5 cause of action—e.g., standing, materiality and scienter, 353 F. Supp. at 270-73, their chief emphasis on this appeal is directed at the asserted absence of causation and reliance and the absence of privity between plaintiffs and defendants.

16. The similarity between certain arguments made here and some discussed above under part II of this opinion is recognized. The issue here is the existence of the essential elements of a private action for damages—whether these plaintiffs may recover damages—while the issue under part II was whether violations of Section 10(b) and Rule 10b-5 had been established. We shall assume familiarity here with our discussion of similar arguments above.

See Astor v. Texas Gulf Sulphur Co., 306 F.Supp. 1333, 1341-42 (S.D.N.Y. 1969). As the Tenth Circuit stated in *Mitchell v. Texas Gulf Sulphur Co.,* 446 F.2d 90, 101 (10 Cir.), *cert. denied,* 404 U.S. 1004 (1971), "[p]erhaps the first step is to realize that the common law requirement of privity has all but vanished from 10b-5 proceedings while the distinguishable 'connection' element is retained." And we recognized in *Globus v. Law Research Service, Inc., supra,* 418 F.2d at 1291, that "[b]efore there may be a violation of the securities acts there need not be present all of the same elements essential to a common law fraud. . . ." *See* Ruder, Texas Gulf Sulphur—The Second Round: Privity and State of Mind in Rule 10b-5 Purchase and Sale Cases, 63 Nw.U.L.Rev. 423, 432-33 (1968). In short, causation as an element of a Rule 10b-5 cause of action can be established notwithstanding lack of privity.

As a further refinement of their absence of causation argument, defendants contend that, even if privity between plaintiffs and defendants is not required, it is still necessary to show a "connection" between defendants' non-disclosure conduct and plaintiffs' purchase of Douglas stock —in the sense that the former induced the latter— before a Rule 10b-5 claim can be established. It is true that prior to the Supreme Court decision in *Affiliated Ute* the so-called connection requirement was stated in terms of causation and reliance. For example, we have noted that the reason for the requirement of reliance "is to certify that the conduct of the defendant actually caused the plaintiff's injury," *List v. Fashion Park, Inc., supra,* 340 F.2d at 462, and we have held that "[t]o the extent that reliance is necessary for a finding of a 10b-5 violation in a non-disclosure case . . ., the test is properly one of tort 'causation in fact.' "*Chasins v. Smith, Barney & Co., supra,* 438 F.2d at 1172. *See Crane Co. v. Westinghouse Air Brake Co., supra,* 419 F.2d at 797. *Cf. SEC v. Texas Gulf Sulphur Co., supra,* 401 F.2d at 860. While the concepts of reliance and causation have been used interchangeably in the context of a Rule 10b-5 claim, the proper test to determine whether causation in fact has been established in a non-disclosure case is "whether the plaintiff would have been influenced to act differently than he did act if the defendant had disclosed to him the undisclosed fact." *List v. Fashion Park, Inc., supra,* 340 F.2d at 463. *See Chasins v. Smith, Barney & Co., supra,* 438 F.2d at 1172. *Cf. Chris-Craft Industries, Inc. v. Piper Aircraft Corp.,* 480 F.2d 341, 373-75 (2 Cir.), *cert. denied,* 414 U.S. 910 (1973).

Even on the basis of the pre-*Affiliated Ute* decisions discussed above, therefore, we would reject defendants' essential causation argument, namely, that, absent an allegation that plaintiffs' purchase of Douglas stock was induced by defendants' non-disclosure of material inside information, the requisite element of causation is lacking. On the contrary, the Rule 10b-5 causation in fact requirement is satisfied by plaintiffs' allegation that they would not have purchased Douglas stock if they had known of the information withheld by defendants.

As must be apparent from our discussion above, we believe that the Supreme Court's decision in *Affiliated Ute*—which we regard as controlling on the issue of causation in the instant case—is a logical sequel to our prior decisions in such cases as *List, Heit, Globus, Crane,* and *Chasins.* Moreover, *Affiliated Ute* specifically applied to a Rule 10b-5 damage action the causation in fact standard enunciated by Mr. Justice Harlan in *Mills v. Electric Auto-Lite Co.,* 396 U.S. 375, 385 (1970), where, in a case involving a cognate provision of the 1934 Act [Section 14(a)], the Court approved dispensing with any requirement of proof of reliance as a prerequisite to recovery in a private damage action. *See* note 12, *supra.*

In *Affiliated Ute,* members of a large class of holders of stock deposited in a bank alleged that two employees of the bank in arranging for sales of this stock had failed to disclose to plaintiffs facts regarding the bank's and the employees' positions as market makers and facts regarding the true value of the stock, in violation of Rule 10b-5. The Supreme Court, in reversing the Court of Appeals which had held that there could be no recovery under Section 10(b) and Rule 10b-5 without a showing of reliance, stated:

> Under the circumstances of this case, involving primarily a failure to disclose, positive proof of reliance is not a prerequisite to recovery. *All that is necessary is that the facts withheld be material in the sense that a reasonable investor might have considered them important in the making of this decision. . . .* This obligation to disclose and this withholding of a material fact establish the requisite element of causation in fact.
>
> 406 U.S. at 153-54. (citations omitted) (emphasis added).

As applied to the instant case, this holding in *Affiliated Ute* surely warrants our conclusion that the requisite element of causation in fact has been established by the admitted withholding by defendants of material inside information which they were under an obligation to disclose, such information being clearly material in the sense that plaintiffs as reasonable investors might have considered it important in making their decision to purchase Douglas stock.

Defendants argue that the *Affiliated Ute* rule of causation in fact should be confined to the facts of that case which involved face-to-face transactions. We disagree. That rule is dependent not upon the character of the transaction—face-to-face versus national securities exchange—but rather upon whether the defendant is obligated to disclose the inside information. Here, as we have held above, defendants were under a duty to the investing public, including plaintiffs, not to trade in or to recommend trading in Douglas stock without publicly disclosing the revised earnings information which was in their possession. They breached that duty. Causation in fact therefore has been established.

Our holding that causation in fact has been established despite the fact that all transactions took place on a national securities exchange is consistent with the underlying purpose of Section 10(b) and Rule 10b-5 "to prevent inequitable and unfair practices and to insure fairness in securities transactions generally, whether conducted face-to-face, over the counter, or on the exchanges. . . . The Act and the Rule apply to the transactions here, all of which were consummated on exchanges." *SEC v. Texas Gulf Sulphur Co.,* 401 F.2d 833, 847-48 (2 Cir. 1968), *cert. denied sub nom. Kline v. SEC,* 394 U.S. 976 (1969) (citations omitted).[17]

For the reasons set forth above, we hold that defendants are liable in this private action for damages to plaintiffs who, during the same period that defendants traded in or recommended trading in Douglas common stock, purchased Douglas stock in the open market without knowledge of the material inside information which was in the possession of defendants.[18]

IV

Finally, having held that all defendants violated Section 10(b) and Rule 10b-5 and that they are liable to plaintiffs in this private action for damages, we leave to the district court the appropriate form of relief to be granted, including the proper measure of damages. This comports with the procedure followed in other cases where appellate courts have determined issues of liability for violations of the securities laws. *Mills v. Electric Auto-Lite Co.,* 396 U.S. 375, 386-89 (1970); *J. I. Case v. Borak,* 377 U.S. 426, 433-35 (1964); *Chris-Craft Industries, Inc. v. Piper Aircraft Corp.,* 480 F.2d 341, 379-80 (2 Cir.), *cert. denied,* 414 U.S. 910 (1973); *Crane Co. v. Westinghouse Air Brake Co.,* 419 F.2d 787, 803-04 (2 Cir. 1969), *cert. denied,* 400 U.S. 822 (1970).

17. Following our remand in *Texas Gulf, supra,* 401 F.2d at 864, the district court ruled on motions for summary judgment by certain defendants in a related shareholders' action. *Astor v. Texas Gulf Sulphur Co.,* 306 F.Supp. 1333 (S.D.N.Y. 1969). Shareholders of Texas Gulf had brought a Rule 10b-5 action against defendants who had purchased Texas Gulf stock on the basis of material inside information during the same period that plaintiffs had sold. Plaintiffs alleged that they would not have sold their stock had they known of the undisclosed information. No privity existed between plaintiff-sellers and defendant-buyers. Defendants had made no affirmative misrepresentations. The transactions were executed on an essentially anonymous market. 306 F.Supp. at 1341. On the basis of these facts, the court, applying the *List* test, found that plaintiffs' complaint stated a claim for relief under Rule 10b-5 and accordingly denied defendants' motions for summary judgment. *Id.* at 1342.

18. Defendants argue that, rather than the instant private action for damages, there are adequate sanctions against those who violate Section 10(b) and Rule 10b-5 in the form of administrative and injunctive proceedings which can be brought by the SEC. *See* note 9, *supra.* The short answer is that such proceedings and the private action for damages are not mutually exclusive remedies. As we recently stated in *Chris-Craft Industries, Inc. v. Piper Aircraft Corp., supra,* 480 F.2d at 356:

> The Supreme Court, as well as other federal courts including our own, have recognized that vigorous enforcement of the federal securities laws, particularly the antifraud provisions, can be accomplished effectively only when implemented by private damage actions. In *J. I. Case Co. v. Borak,* 377 U.S. 426 (1964), the Supreme Court emphasized that private actions provide "a necessary supplement to Commission action" and that "the possibility of civil damages or injunctive relief serves as a most effective weapon in the enforcement" of the securities laws. 377 U.S. at 432. *See Fischman v. Raytheon Mfg. Co.,* 188 F.2d 783 (2 Cir. 1951); *Speed v. Transamerica Corp.,* 235 F.2d 369 (3 Cir. 1956).

In like vein, defendants contend that the recovery of illegal profits resulting from an insider's misuse of corporate information should be left to derivative stockholders actions as in *Schein v. Chasen,* 478 F.2d 817 (2 Cir. 1973), *remanded on other grounds sub nom. Lehman Bros. v. Schein,* ____ U.S. ____ (1974), and *Diamond v. Oreamuno,* 24 N.Y.2d 494, 248 N.E.2d 910, 301 N.Y.S.2d 78 (1969). What we said above regarding the role of the private action for damages in the overall program for vigorous enforcement of the federal securities laws applies with equal force here. Moreover, derivative actions for such relief are not uniformly available in all states.

In the instant case there are especially compelling reasons for following this procedure. Since the appeal comes to us from an interlocutory order denying defendants' motion for judgment on the pleadings, there was no issue before the district court and of course no adjudication below on the form of relief to be granted. Among the questions to be determined which will have an important bearing on the form of relief is whether the action is to be maintained as a class action and, if so, the parameters of the class; as to this, the district court understandably was unable to make a determination on the facts presented by the pleadings. 353 F.Supp. at 280. *See* note 10, *supra.* Another closely related question bearing upon the relief to be granted as to which the district court had insufficient data upon which to make a determination, 353 F.Supp at 279-80, is just when Douglas' news release regarding its revised earnings forecast on the morning of June 24, 1966 became effectively disseminated, especially in the light of *SEC v. Texas Gulf Sulphur Co.,* 401 F.2d 833, 854 n. 18 (2 Cir. 1968), *cert. denied sub nom. Kline v. SEC,* 394 U.S. 976 (1969). Other questions bearing upon the appropriate form of relief which must await trial include the extent of the selling defendants' trading in Douglas stock, whether such trading effectively impaired the integrity of the market, what compensation if any was paid by the selling defendants to Merrill Lynch for the inside information, what profits or other benefits were realized by defendants, what expenses were incurred and what losses were sustained by plaintiffs, and what should be the difference, if any, in the extent of liability imposed on the individual defendants and the selling defendants, respectively. Moreover, we do not foreclose the possibility that an analysis by the district court of the nature and character of the Rule 10b-5 violations committed may require limiting the extent of liability imposed on either class of defendants.

In leaving to the district court the fashioning of appropriate relief, including the proper measure of damages, we are not unmindful of the arguments pressed upon us by all defendants that the resulting judgment for damages may be very substantial in amount—in the words of defendants' counsel, a "Draconian liability." This is an additional reason for leaving to the district court the appropriate form of relief to be granted—a determination that can best be made after an evidentiary hearing and on the basis of appropriate findings of fact.

In short, we decide today only those legal questions properly before us on this appeal from the interlocutory order denying defendants' motion for judgment on the pleadings. We leave all other issues to the district court, including the fashioning of appropriate relief.

Affirmed.

Rule 10(b)-6 is also applicable to pension plans. Regulation §240.10b-6 provides:

> (A) It shall constitute a "manipulative or deceptive device or contrivance" as used in section 10(b) of the ('34) Act for any person;
>
> (1) who is an underwriter or prospective underwriter in a particular distribution of securities, or
>
> (2) who is the issuer or other person on whose behalf such a distribution is being made, or
>
> (3) who is a broker, dealer, or other person who has agreed to participate or is participating in such a distribution,
>
> directly or indirectly, by the use of any means or instrumentality of interstate commerce, or of the mails, or of any facility of any national securities exchange, either alone or with one or more other persons, to bid for a purchase for any account in which he has a beneficial interest, any security which is the subject of such distribution, or any security of the same class and series, or any right to purchase any such security, or any attempt to induce any person to purchase any such security or right until he has completed his participation in such distribution. . . .

The Securities and Exchange Commission applied this rule to purchases of a corporation's shares in the over-the-counter market by a profit-sharing plan during a distribution of securities by the corporation. The staff of the Securities and Exchange Commission took the position that the purchase of such securities constituted a violation of Rule 10b-6 since the profit-sharing plan was deemed to be an "affiliate" of the corporation.

PIPER INDUSTRIES, INC.
(March 6, 1972)
SEC Reply

This is in response to your letter of January 6, 1972 in which you request advice as to certain matters concerning the profit-sharing plan of Piper Industries, Inc. ("the Company").

Regarding the necessity for, or exemption from, filing a Form S-8 covering the Profit-Sharing Plan and Trust ("PSP & T" or "the Plan"), in the absence of an exemption under Section 3(a)(11) or some other section of the Securities Act of 1933 ("the Act"), it would appear that registration of Piper stock is required in connection with (1) an employee's election to have the Company's contribution invested in Piper stock to be held in the Piper Stock Account, and (2) an employee's election to transfer his interest in the Regular Pooled Investment Account to the Piper Stock Account. Moreover, interests of participation in the Piper Stock Account should also be registered along with the Piper stock. (*See* Section 2(1) of the Act.)

As to whether the PSP & T is an "affiliate" of the Company, it should first be recognized that by the very words of the Profit-Sharing Plan and Trust Agreement, PSP & T is designated "The Piper Industries, Inc., Consolidated Profit-Sharing Plan." (Article I). The Company has created PSP & T, has the power and authority to amend the Plan, and can designate the members of the administrative committee (*see* page 13 of Registration statement 2-41129, effective September 15, 1971). By the terms of Rule 405 of the Rules and Regulations under the Act, "affiliate" is defined as "a person that directly, or indirectly through one or more intermediaries, controls, or is controlled by, or is under common control with, the person specified." It would seem to follow that PSP & T is indeed an affiliate of the Company.

As an affiliate of the Company, PSP & T is bound by the same restrictions and limitations as the Company regarding the purchase of the Company's shares in the over-the-counter market for the benefit of its employees. Purchases by the trustee and/or the Company by means of the PSP & T come under the purview of Rule 10b-6 of the Rules and Regulations under the Securities Exchange Act of 1934. As to potential problems thereunder, we refer you to Mr. Robert King of the Division of Trading and Markets who has suggested that you telephone him (202-755-1260).

If you have any additional questions, please do not hesitate to contact the staff.

Inquiry

At the suggestion of Mr. Morton Koeppel, Branch Chief, Branch of Corporate Analysis and Examination, we are requesting advice and guidance as to the following matter.

Exhibit 11 in Volume 2 of 2 exhibits filed with Form S-1 is copy of relevant document pertaining to a Profit-Sharing Plan and Agreement in effect for the employees of the above registrant company. Said Profit-Sharing Plan and Agreement is referred to under the heading "Employees" at page 13 of Form S-1 filed July 9, 1971 as amended August 16, 1971 and September 15, 1971.

On December 16, 1971, amendments were adopted to the above Profit-Sharing Plan and Agreement which permit the employees participating in the plan to direct the Trustee, The First National Bank of Memphis, Memphis, Tennessee, to invest part or all of their existing allocation and part or all of their annual allocation in stock of Piper Industries, Inc.

Also attached are the following additional materials [not reproduced]:

(a) list of members of Administrative Committee showing those who are directors or officers of registrant

(b) statement showing financial status of the Profit-Sharing Fund prepared by The First National Bank of Memphis, Corporate Trustee

(c) statement showing employees who have voluntarily elected to direct the Trustee to invest some part or all of their allocated fund in Piper Industries, Inc. shares showing amount to be so invested

(d) copy of the amendments to the Profit-Sharing Plan and Trust and the corporate action taken thereon

(e) copy of a form for a proposed press release and notice to all stockholders of the registrant

(f) latest available quotation Piper Industries, Inc. common stock.

Mr. Koeppel has suggested that your office can advise as to the necessity for, or exemption from, filing a Form S-8 on behalf of the Profit-Sharing Plan and Trust, and also as to whether under the circumstances the Profit-Sharing Plan and Trust is an "affiliate" of Piper Industries, Inc. and, as such, what limitations, if any, are to be applied to the purchase of Piper Industries, Inc. shares in the over-the-counter market. The total funds available for such investment were $333,090.66, whereas only $195,615.20 have been voluntarily requested as investment in Piper Industries, Inc. shares by the employees participating in the plan.

A prompt response to this request would be appreciated.

Commission Rates and Practices

Section 28(e) is another provision of the '34 Act which has a significant impact on pension plan administration and the relationship of plans to the other components of the plan complex. Section 28(e), which was added to the '34 Act by the Securities Reform Act of 1975, was enacted to protect fiduciaries by permitting them to pay more than the lowest commission to obtain research and certain other services from broker dealers, among others. A historical perspective is necessary before proceeding to the particulars of Section 28(e).

The "Best Execution" Standard

After the Securities and Exchange Commission eliminated "fixed" commission rates in favor of "negotiated" rates, but before the addition of Section 28(e), a fiduciary under ERISA was probably required to negotiate the "best execution" on each securities transaction. The best execution standard requires that the total proceeds or cost in each securities transaction is the most favorable (to the plan) under the circumstances. The best total cost or proceeds from a securities transaction is the most favorable combination of commission rate and purchase or sale price for the security. The fiduciary may even have been required to provide research itself. Briefly stated, an argument could have been made that receipt by a pension or welfare plan fiduciary of research services for a commission paid out of plan assets was inconsistent with the exclusive benefit rule and the prudent man rule, both of which were discussed in Chapter 1.

The obligation of a pension or welfare plan fiduciary to negotiate the best execution was changed by the addition of Section 28(e) to the '34 Act. Subsection (1) of Section 28(e) provides that:

> No person using the mails, or any means or instrumentality of interstate commerce, in the exercise of investment discretion with respect to an account shall be deemed to have acted unlawfully or to have breached a fiduciary duty under State or Federal law unless expressly provided to the contrary by a law enacted by the Congress or by State subsequent to June 4, 1975, solely by reason of his having caused the account to pay a member of an exchange, broker or dealer an amount of commission for effecting a securities transaction in excess of the amount of commission another member of an exchange, broker, or dealer would have charged for effecting that transaction, if such person determined in good faith that such amount of commission was reasonable in relation to the value of the brokerage and research services provided by such member, broker, or dealer, viewed in terms of either that particular transaction or his overall responsibilities with respect to the accounts as to which he exercises investment discretion. This subsection is exclusive and plenary insofar as conduct is covered by the foregoing, unless otherwise expressly provided by contract: Provided, however, that nothing in this subsection shall be construed to impair or limit the power of the [Securities Exchange Commission] under any other provision of this chapter or otherwise.

Section 28(e) of the '34 Act preempts all federal or state common or statutory law unless the law was enacted *after* Section 28(e) and such law expressly provides that it is not superseded. Since ERISA was enacted *before* Section 28(e), ERISA is superseded if, and to the extent that, Section 28(e) and ERISA are inconsistent.

Section 28(e) permits a fiduciary to pay a broker-dealer a commission in excess of the commission that another broker-dealer would have charged for executing the transaction or transactions in question. If, for example, a pension plan fiduciary obtains execution and research and other services from the same broker-dealer and the broker-dealer includes the cost of research and the charge for executing the trade, the fiduciary may pass on the entire charge to the account of the plan for which the trade was executed.

The Decision to "Pay Up"

The addition of Section 28(e) to the '34 Act does not mean, however, that a pension or welfare plan fiduciary may purchase or sell a security or securities at any price and pay any charge for effecting the transaction and obtaining research. A plan fiduciary still has an obligation to purchase and sell securities to be held or disposed of by the pension or welfare plan at the best total proceeds or cost.

In terms of obtaining the best execution, an argument can be made that a plan fiduciary should consider the purchase or sale price of a security or securities in the available markets and compare such prices to determine the lowest purchase cost or highest sale proceeds. In terms of the commission, a pension or welfare plan fiduciary may "pay up" for brokerage and research services provided the fiduciary determines, in good faith, that any commission paid is reasonable in relation to the value of the brokerage and research services provided by the broker-dealer. It should be recognized that Section 28(e) of the '34 Act only protects the fiduciary if he can make such a determination.

It can be argued that a fiduciary should determine the amount of the commission for effecting the transaction without receiving research services. If the fiduciary does not make an attempt to break down the charge in this manner, an argument can be made that the fiduciary did not know what he was paying for brokerage and what he was paying for research services. In the absence of such knowledge, it may be difficult for a fiduciary to demonstrate that he made a determination that the charge was reasonable.

It is important to note that Section 28(e) also requires the disclosure of policies and practices with respect to commissions that will be paid for effecting securities transactions.

INVESTMENT COMPANY ACT OF 1940

The Investment Company Act of 1940 (the '40 Act), 15 U.S.C. §80(a), *et seq.*, relates to the activities of investment companies. Regulation under the '40 Act is in the form of reporting and disclosure, and through regulation of the structure, content and administration of investment companies.

The threshold issue in connection with the '40 Act as it relates to the private employee benefit complex is whether a pension or welfare plan is an investment company. If a pension or welfare plan is an investment company, the '40 Act regulatory provisions are applicable.

The term "investment company" is defined in §3(a) of the '40 Act to include any issuer which, among other things:

> (1) Is or holds itself out as being engaged primarily, or proposes to engage primarily, in the business of investing, reinvesting, or trading in securities; or
>
> . . . . .
>
> (3) Is engaged or proposes to engage in the business of investing, reinvesting, owning, holding, or trading in securities, and owns or proposes to acquire investment securities having a value exceeding 40 percentum of the value of such issuers' total assets. . . .

This definition would seem to encompass most pension plans, since they generally are engaged in the business of "investing, reinvesting, owning, holding, or trading in securities" with respect to a significant portion of the assets held by the plan.

This conclusion is implicit in the specific exclusion from the definition of investment company in Section 3(c)(11) of the '40 Act, which provides an exclusion for:

> Any employees' stock bonus, pension, or profit-sharing trust which meets the requirements for qualification under §401 of the Internal Revenue Code of 1954 . . .

By exempting certain employee benefit plans from the investment company definition if certain conditions are met, Section 3(c)(11) raises the implication that these plans (and at least some other pension and welfare plans) constitute investment companies under Section 3(a). This implication is reinforced by the "no action" letter in *Cheapside Dollar Fund, Inc.* (1977), in which the staff of the Securities and Exchange Commission stated that a plan organized under the laws of a foreign country, but doing business in the United States, constituted an investment company under the '40 Act since it was not a plan satisfying the requirements for qualification under §401 of the Code.

Although the '40 Act contains exemptions from the definition of investment company other than §3(c)(11), the exemption generally utilized by employee benefit plans is contained in §6(b). This section permits the Securities and Exchange Commission to grant exemptions from any and all of the provisions of the '40 Act for any "employee security company" if and to the extent that such an exemption is consistent with the protection of investors. The term "employee security company" is defined in §32(a)(13) of the '40 Act to mean:

> (A)ny investment company or similar issuer of all of the outstanding securities of which . . . are beneficially owned (A) by the employees or persons on a retainer of a single employer or of two or more employers each of which is an affiliated company of the other, (B) by former employees of such employer or employers, (C) by members of the immediate family of such employees, persons on retainer, or former employees, (D) by any two or more of the foregoing classes of persons, ...

The Securities and Exchange Commission also has authority to grant exemptions from some or all of the requirements of the '40 Act under §6(c) of the '40 Act.

If any employee benefit plan constitutes an "investment company" which does not fall within the §3(c)(11) exception and which is not granted an exemption by the SEC under §6(b) or (c), the requirements imposed under the '40 Act must be complied with. These requirements include reporting and disclosure (such as registration with the Securities and Exchange Commission, and quarterly, semiannual and annual reporting), and requirements relating to the structure and content and administration of plans, such as prohibited transactions under Section 17 and fiduciary responsibility under Section 36.

It is important to note that registered investment companies are accorded special treatment under ERISA in recognition of the extensive regulatory requirements under the '40 Act. For example, under §3(21) and §401(b)(1) of ERISA, if an employee benefit plan invests its assets in a registered investment company, the registered investment company's investment adviser is not a plan fiduciary. This treatment is more favorable than the treatment accorded under ERISA to similar investment vehicles, such as common or collective trusts maintained by a bank or separate accounts maintained by an insurance company.

For essentially the same reasons, several class exemptions from the prohibited transaction provisions contained in ERISA have been granted to permit the continuation of certain practices involving employee benefit plans and registered investment companies.

INVESTMENT ADVISERS ACT OF 1940

The Investment Advisers Act of 1940 (the Advisers Act) 15 U.S.C. §80(b), *et seq.*, relates to the activities of investment advisers. The Advisers Act provides substantive regulations with respect to fraudulent and deceptive practices, principal transactions, the approval of investment advisory agreements, investment advisory fees and recordkeeping.

The Advisers Act contains provisions which affect the relationship of plans to other components of the plan complex. For example, plan trustees are generally supposed to have the exclusive authority and responsibility to manage the assets of employee benefit plans, but ERISA permits that authority to be delegated to an "investment manager." Under such circumstances, a trustee generally will have limited responsibility and liability with respect to the management of plan assets. *See* ERISA §405 (c). Section 3(38) of ERISA defines the term "investment manager" to include only banks, insurance companies and investment advisers registered under the Advisers Act.

"Investment Advisers" Defined

The term "investment adviser" is defined in §202(a)(11) of the Advisers Act to mean:

> Any person who, for compensation, engages in the business of advising others, either directly or through publications or writings, as to the value of securities or as to the advisability of investing in, purchasing, or selling securities, or who, for compensation and as part of a regular business, issues or promulgates analyses or reports concerning securities. . . .

There are certain exceptions to this definition of investment adviser. These exceptions include a bank or any bank holding company (as defined in the Bank Holding Company Act of 1956), attorneys, accountants, engineers, or teachers whose investment advice is solely incidental to the practice of their profession, and any broker-dealer whose performance of investment advisory services is solely incidental to the conduct of his business as a broker-dealer and who receives no special compensation for his investment advice.

The Securities and Exchange Commission is also authorized to specify other groups of persons to be excluded from the definition of investment adviser. The Securities and Exchange Commission has exercised this authority in one instance to resolve a problem that arose as a result of ERISA. Shortly after ERISA's enactment, the Securities and Exchange Commission found that individuals were attempting to register under the Advisers Act for the sole purpose of becoming "investment managers" of their employer's pension and welfare plans. Accordingly, the Securities and Exchange Commission adopted Rule 202-1 under the Advisers Act, which provides that:

> The term "investment adviser," in Section 202(a)(11) of the Act, shall not include any person who offers investment advice to an employee benefit plan, as defined in the Employee Retirement Income Security Act of 1974, sponsored by an employer of such person, if such person is not engaged in the business of providing investment advice or management to others and does not hold himself out generally to the public as an investment adviser. For purposes of this rule, "person" shall include a natural person or a company which is controlled by or under common control with the employer and "employer" shall include any company controlling, controlled by or under common control with a person.

The effect of this Rule is to preclude persons from registering as investment advisers for the sole purpose of absolving employers from fiduciary responsibility and liability under ERISA.

Subsection 203(a) of the Advisers Act requires all persons who come within the definition of investment adviser to register with the Securities and Exchange Commission, unless an exemption from registration is available.[2] The Advisers Act also permits the Securities and Exchange Commission to revoke an investment adviser's registration on several grounds; for example, a registration statement containing false or misleading statements constitutes grounds for revocation.

It is important to note that whether or not a person is excluded from the definition of the term "investment adviser" under Section 202(a)(11) of the Advisers Act and whether or not an exemption from registration as an investment adviser is avail-

---

2. In general, persons who do not provide advice with respect to listed securities, and all of whose clients are located in, or are residents of, the state in which such adviser maintains his principal office and place of business, are exempted from registration. Persons who have fewer than 15 clients and do not hold themselves out to the public as investment advisers also do not have to be registered.

able, a qualified "investment manager" under Section 3(38) of ERISA must be a qualified bank, insurance company, or *registered* investment adviser.

Provisions and Requirements

An investment adviser registered under the Advisers Act becomes subject to several substantive provisions of the Act, including requirements to maintain accurate books and records and requirements for the terms of investment advisory contracts and permissible compensation arrangements.

All investment advisers, whether or not registered, are subject to the provisions of Section 206 of the Advisers Act which, generally, preclude investment advisers from engaging in fraudulent and deceptive practices, and require disclosure to clients in certain conflict of interest situations involving transactions between the investment adviser and a client, or agency transactions executed by the adviser between two clients. For example, Section 206(3) permits an investment adviser, among other things, to effect a purchase or sale of securities between two investment advisory clients or between an investment advisory client and a brokerage client, if, prior to the completion of the transaction, disclosure is made to the adviser's client(s) in writing of the adviser's "dual role," and the adviser's client(s) have consented to such transaction. The SEC has recently adopted Rule 206(3)-2 which prescribes a simplified (non-exclusive) disclosure procedure for such transactions. If the client is an employee benefit plan, these disclosures will normally be made to the plan trustee.

CHAPTER 5

Equal Employment Laws

CIVIL RIGHTS ACT OF 1964

Title VII of the Civil Rights Act of 1964, as amended by the Equal Employment Opportunity Act of 1972 (Title VII), 42 U.S.C. §2000(e), *et seq.*, relates to the terms and conditions of employment. Under Title VII, it is an unlawful employment practice to discriminate with respect to the terms, conditions, or privileges of employment on the grounds of race, color, religion, sex, or national origin.

Section 2000e-2(a) provides:

> It shall be an unlawful employment practice for any employer—
>
> (1) to fire or refuse to hire or to discharge any individual, or otherwise to discriminate against any individual with respect to his compensation, terms, conditions, or privileges of employment, because of such individual's race, color, religion, sex, or national origin; or
>
> (2) to limit, segregate, or classify his employees or applicants for employment in any way which would deprive or tend to deprive any individual of employment opportunities or otherwise adversely affect his status as an employee, because of such individual's race, color, religion, sex, or national origin.

The purpose of Title VII in outlawing discrimination in employment is to achieve equality of employment opportunities with respect to individuals, and to remove existing barriers which have operated in favor of certain groups of employees.

The interpretation of Title VII by the Equal Employment Opportunity Commission (EEOC) and the courts has had an impact on the structure and content of pension and welfare plans. For example, the EEOC Guidelines on Sex Discrimination provide that discrimination between men and women with regard to "fringe benefits" constitutes an unlawful employment practice. *See* 29 C.F.R. §1604.9. The term "fringe benefits," as used in these Guidelines, is defined as including:

> medical, hospital, accident, life insurance, and retirement benefits; profit sharing and bonus plans; leave; and other terms, conditions, and privileges of employment. 29 C.F.R. §1604.9(a).

The breadth of this definition generally prohibits discrimination in employee benefits provided pursuant to pension and health and welfare plans.

Pension Plan "Equality"

In EEOC Decision No. 70-513 (1970),[1] the EEOC ruled that the benefits provided under employee benefit plans such as pension and profit-sharing plans are a form of compensation and, therefore, the terms of the plans must be free of the discrimination prohibited under Section 2000e-2. For example, a sex discrimination issue is presented by the payment of benefits in the form of an annuity based on sex-differentiated actuarial tables. In EEOC Decision No. 74-118, the EEOC ruled that sex-differentiated actuarial tables violate Title VII because periodic pension payments for males and females in equivalent circumstances would not be equal: the longer assumed life expectancy for females as a group results in periodic payments to females which are less than the periodic payments to males.

The standard of equality is the amount of monthly benefits rather than the level of contributions to the plan or the aggregate amount of benefits expected to be paid during a man's or woman's lifetime. The courts have ruled, however, that this standard of equality cannot be achieved by re-

1. EEOC Decisions are interpretations of Title VII by the EEOC; they are not adjudications.

quiring females to make contributions to the plan in an amount exceeding contributions required by males. In *Manhart v. City of Los Angeles, Dept. of Water & Power,* 387 F.Supp. 980 (C.D. Calif. 1975), the court held that requiring females to make higher monthly contributions based on actuarially demonstrated longer female longevity is unlawful sex discrimination which cannot be justified under Title VII. This decision was affirmed by the Ninth Circuit Court of Appeals and the Ninth Circuit declined to reconsider in light of the Supreme Court's decision in *Gilbert v. General Electric Company*, 429 U.S. 125, 97 Sup. Ct. 401 (1976), which is discussed below. The Supreme Court has granted certiorari in the *Manhart* case.

MANHART V. CITY OF LOS ANGELES
553 F.2d 581 (9th Cir. 1976)

DUNIWAY, C. J.: The question presented in this case is whether a retirement plan which requires women employees to contribute from their wages 15% more than similarly situated male employees because of the longer average life expectancy of women violates the Civil Rights Act of 1964, Title VII, as amended by the Equal Employment Opportunity Act of 1972, 42 U.S.C. §2000e-2. The district court held that the plan violated Title VII,[1] enjoined the employer from charging the higher contribution rate against women, and awarded a refund of all excess contributions made on or after April 5, 1972.

This is a class action brought by women employees and retirees of the City of Los Angeles, Department of Water and Power [hereinafter "Department"]. The defendants are the Department, the members of the Board of Commissioners of the Department, the members of the Board of Administration of the Department's Employees' Retirement, Disability, and Death Benefit Insurance Plan, the Department's chief accounting officer, and the Department's general manager.

All employees of the Department are required to participate in the established retirement plan which is funded and managed solely within the Department. Each employee must make a monthly contribution to the retirement plan, and the Department matches that contribution 110%. These funds are deposited with the city treasurer but are kept separate and apart from all other monies of the city. The chief accounting employee of the Department is the only person authorized to withdraw money from the retirement account.

The aspect of this program which gives rise to this case is that women employees are required to contribute approximately 15% more than men employees who are identically situated. The Department's justification is that because women get the same monthly benefits upon retiring and because, on the average, they live approximately five years longer, they must, as a group, contribute more.

In June of 1973, the International Brotherhood of Electrical Workers, Local #18, representing the named plaintiffs, filed a charge with the Equal Employment Opportunity Commission [EEOC] alleging that the higher contribution requirement for women was sex discrimination in violation of the Civil Rights Acts of 1871 and 1964. The United States Department of Justice issued a Notice of Right to Sue letter in September of 1973, and this action was filed during that same month.

In their second amended complaint, filed on July 18, 1974, the plaintiffs stated four separate claims for relief, each of which, however, was based upon the same set of facts. The first claim was based upon Title VII, the second upon the Civil Rights Act of 1871, 42 U.S.C. §1983, the third upon the Fourteenth Amendment to the Constitution, and the fourth, a pendent claim, upon Article 1, §§1 and 21, of the Constitution of California.

The plaintiffs' first amended complaint had also asserted claims resting on the same four theories, but had not set them up as separate claims. On March 26, 1974, the court granted in part and denied in part the defendants' motion to dismiss. It granted the motion of the Department, the two boards, and their members in their capacities as members, to dismiss the claim that was based upon 42 U.S.C. §1983, on the ground that the Department and the Board are not "persons" within the meaning of that section. It denied the motion of the Board members in their individual capacities to dismiss the §1983 claim, holding that they are "persons," and that they are not immune from suit under §1983. It granted the motion of all defendants to dismiss the §1983 claim insofar as any of it accrued more than three years before the

1. The relevant provision of Title VII reads:
§2000e-2
(a) It shall be an unlawful employment practice for an employer—
(1) to fail or refuse to hire or to discharge any individual, or otherwise to discriminate against any individual with respect to his compensation, terms, conditions, or privileges of employment, because of such individual's race, color, religion, sex, or national origin.

action was filed on September 26, 1973. It denied the motion to dismiss the Title VII claim, except that it granted the motion as to any claim arising before March 24, 1972. It dismissed the claim under the California Constitution. It did not rule on the claim under the Fourteenth Amendment. And it allowed 20 days for the filing of a second amended complaint. After the second amended complaint was filed, no motion was made by any of the defendants to strike or otherwise dispose of those of the allegations that were inconsistent with the court's order of March 26, 1974.

On June 20, 1975, the court granted the plaintiffs' motion for summary judgment, holding that the plan violated Title VII. On the same day it entered a judgment, declaring that the plan, insofar as it requires larger contributions from female employees than from their male counterparts, violates Title VII, and specifically §701(a)(1) [42 U.S.C. §2000e-2(a)]. The judgment also enjoins requiring larger contributions from females and orders that the Department refund the excess contributions collected on and after April 5, 1972, plus interest at 7%, and that defendants pay counsel for plaintiffs' reasonable attorneys' fees. The judgments say nothing about the claims based on §1983, the Fourteenth Amendment, or the California Constitution.

On July 7, 1975, the defendants appealed from the judgment. This appeal is our No. 75-2729. On July 11, 1975, the plaintiffs appealed from "that portion of the judgment . . . which denies relief to the plaintiffs based on the causes of action and defendants dismissed by the Court in its Order Granting and Denying in Part Defendants Motion to Dismiss, entered on or about March 26, 1974." This appeal is our No. 75-2807. On July 17, the district judge denied a motion by the defendants for a stay of the judgment. They appealed on July 30, 1975. This is our No. 75-2905. We later entered an order staying the judgment pending appeal, insofar as it requires the refund of contributions.

After oral argument before us, and in response to an inquiry from the bench, counsel for plaintiffs stipulated, and we ordered, that the plaintiffs "have heretofore abandoned all claims under 42 U.S.C. §1983 against individual officials in their individual capacities."

I. Our Jurisdiction

A. No. 75-2729. The judgment of June 20, 1975, embodies an injunction against requiring larger contributions from women than from men, and requiring restitution of excess contributions previously paid. As an injunction, it is appealable under 28 U.S.C. §1292(a)(1). It is not appealable as a final judgment under 28 U.S.C. §1291. It does not dispose of any claim except the claim under Title VII. It runs only against the defendants, the Department, the two Boards, and their members as such, but not the defendant members individually. It says nothing about the claims or defendants dismissed in the district court's order of March 26, 1974. There is no "express determination that there is no just reason for delay" nor "express direction for the entry of judgment." [F.R. Civ.P. 54(b)].

B. No. 75-2807. We have no jurisdiction of this appeal. The judgment does not do what the notice of appeal says that it does. The order of March 26, 1974, was interlocutory. It did not purport to determine any issue finally. It permitted amendment of the complaint, and the amendment restated, separately, all of the claims asserted but commingled in the original complaint. The court was not required to reconsider the various questions that it had decided in its March 26, 1974 order. But it should at least have embodied what it then decided in its subsequent judgment. The plaintiffs had attempted to replead all of their claims in their second amended complaint. This they were entitled to do, and those claims remain pending because the district court never disposed of them. We have no jurisdiction in No. 75-2807.

It is no answer to say that the plaintiffs have voluntarily abandoned their claims under 42 U.S.C. §1983 against the individual defendants. That abandonment binds the plaintiffs, but it does not affect their claims against the Department and its Boards and their members and employees in their official capacities under §1983. Those claims are still pending in the district court and are not properly before us.

C. No. 75-2905. Because we have granted a stay, and because we are now affirming the judgment in No. 75-2729, this appeal is moot.

II. The Merits of the Judgment

The basis of the defendants' appeal is that, while requiring women to make larger contributions discriminates against women, there is a sound basis for the requirement, making it a discrimination based on longevity, not sex, and therefore not the kind of invidious discrimination that Title VII was intended to abolish. We disagree.

It is undisputed that the overriding purpose of Title VII is to require employers to treat each employee (or prospective employee) as an individual, and to make job related decisions about each employee on the basis of relevant individual characteristics, so that the employee's membership in a racial, ethnic, religious, or sexual group is irrelevant to the decisions. *See Griggs v. Duke Power Co.,* 1971, [3 EPD ¶8137] 401 U.S. 424, 436. To require every individual woman to contribute 15% more into the retirement fund than her male counterpart must contribute because women "on the average" live longer than men is just the kind of abstract generalization, applied to individual women because of their being women, which Title VII was designed to abolish. Not all women live longer than all men, yet each individual woman is required to contribute more, not because she as an individual will live longer, but because the members of her sexual group, on the average, live longer.

The Department argues, however, that Congress did not intend Title VII to prohibit drawing sexual distinctions when there is a statistically valid basis for doing so and when it is impossible to determine ahead of time when the individual employee is going to die. Thus it is argued that, because it is undisputed that women on the average do live longer, and because it is not possible to predict which women will actually live longer, Title VII ought to permit a higher contribution requirement for all women.

The problem raised by this case is unique. There have been two basic policies which have guided the courts in prior Title VII litigation: (1) the policy against attributing general group characteristics to each individual member of the group, the major thrust of the statute, and (2) the policy allowing relevant employment factors to be considered in differentiating among individuals. *See* Bernstein & Williams, *Title VII and the Problem of Sex Classifications in Pension Programs,* 74 Col. L. Rev. 1203, 1219 (1974). Heretofore, these two policies have not conflicted because in cases where general group characterizations were attributed to the individual employee, the relevant employment characteristics were capable of being individually measured. *Id.* at 1220. For example, in *Rosenfeld v. So. Pacific Co.,* 9 Cir., 1971, [3 EPD ¶8247] 444 F.2d 1219, we held that refusing to hire women for positions which entailed long hours and heavy physical effort violated Title VII because it entailed attributing the generally weaker physique of women to all women. An important basis of our decision was the fact that each individual woman applicant could actually be tested to see whether the relevant characteristic of strength was or was not in fact lacking.

This same consideration has been present in cases finding illegal: (1) the refusal to allow women to work overtime because of a belief that women as a group cannot work the long hours that men can, *Schaeffer v. San Diego Yellow Cabs, Inc.,* 9 Cir., 1972, [4 EPD ¶7882] 462 F.2d 1002; (2) the forced retirement of all women at an earlier age than men because of a belief that, on the average, men were capable of adequate performance longer than women, *Rosen v. Public Service Electric and Gas Co.,* 3 Cir., 1973, [5 EPD ¶8499] 477 F.2d 90, *Bartness v. Drewrys U.S.A., Inc.,* 7 Cir., 1971, [3 EPD ¶8217] 444 F.2d 1186; (3) the termination of women employees who married because of a belief that, on the average, women could not work effectively and keep an adequate home life, *Sprogis v. United Air Lines, Inc.,* 7 Cir., 1971, [3 EPD ¶8239] 444 F.2d 1194; (4) the refusal to hire men as flight attendants because men, on the average, are said to be emotionally unsuited for that type of work, *Diaz v. Pan Am. World Airways, Inc.,* 5 Cir., 1971, [3 EPD ¶8166] 441 F.2d 385; (5) the refusal to hire women as telephone switchmen because of a belief that, on the average, women are incapable of working the long hours and doing the heavy lifting involved, *Weeks v. Southern Bell Telephone & Telegraph Co.,* 5 Cir., 1969, [1 EPD ¶9970] 408 F.2d 228; (6) requiring pregnant women to take mandatory leave after six months of pregnancy because, on the average, pregnant women are supposed to be incapable of working adequately after that point, *Berg v. Richmond Unified School Dist.,* 9 Cir., 1975, [10 EPD ¶10,553] 528 F.2d 1208; (7) the refusal to hire women with preschool children because of a belief that family responsibilities would interfere with their job performance, *Phillips v. Martin Marietta Corp.,* 1971, [3 EPD ¶8088] 400 U.S. 542.

In the present case a relevant characteristic in determining how large an individual's retirement contribution should be is an informed prediction as to how long the person will live. But this characteristic, unlike those in the prior cases, is impossible to determine on an individual basis at the time when the contribution must be made. Thus, the policy of allowing relevant factors to be considered can be met only by allowing the group longevity statistics to be attributed to the individual members of the group. Yet this is exactly what the thrust of Title VII prohibits. We are therefore faced with the unique case in which the policy against per se discrimination directly conflicts with the policy of allowing relevant factors to be considered.

To support its argument that the actuarial distinctions are permitted under Title VII, the Department points to both the "bona fide occupational qualification exception" in 42 U.S.C. §2000 e-2(e) and the Bennett Amendment to Title VII, 42 U.S.C. §2000e-2(h). Reconciliation of the conflicting policies noted above would be easy if Congress had specifically covered the kind of actuarial distinction that is before us in one of the exceptions which the Department cites. Both, however, are very general and have no language relating to actuarially determined discrimination, much less to pension plans.

A. The Bona Fide Occupational Qualification [BFOQ] Exception. Title 42 U.S.C. §2000e-2(e) states that an employer may discriminate on the basis of religion, sex, or national origin "where religion, sex, or national origin is a bona fide occupational qualification reasonably necessary to the normal operation of that particular business or enterprise." EEOC, which is charged with administering and enforcing Title VII and whose interpretations of that statute are entitled to great deference, *Griggs v. Duke Power Co., supra,* 401 U.S. at 433-34; *Hutchison v. Lake Oswego School Dist. #7,* 9 Cir., 1975, [10 EPD ¶10,325] 519 F.2d 961, 965, has issued guidelines directing that the BFOQ exception "be interpreted narrowly." 29 C.F.R. §1604.2(a). In one of the few cases ruling on this exception, the Fifth Circuit has said:

> the use of the word "necessary" in [§2000e-2(e)] requires that we apply a business *necessity* test, not a business *convenience* test. That is to say, discrimination based on sex is valid only when the *essence* of the business operation would be undermined. . . .
>
> *Diaz v. Pan Am. World Airways, Inc., supra,* 442 F.2d at 388 [italics in original]. *See also Weeks v. Southern Bell Telephone & Telegraph Co., supra,* 408 F.2d at 232.

Discriminating against women in setting the amount of retirement contributions in no way affects the ability of the Department to provide water and power to the citizens of Los Angeles. Even if it could be said that the relevant business function here involved is that of providing employees with a stable and secure pension program there is no showing that sexual discrimination is necessary to protect the essence of that function. Actuarial distinctions arguably enhance the ability of the employer and the pension administrators to predict costs and benefits more accurately, but it cannot be said that providing a financially sound pension plan requires an actuarial classification based wholly on sex. This is especially true when distinctions based on many other longevity factors (*e.g.,* smoking and drinking habits, normality of weight, prior medical history, family longevity history) are not used in determining contribution levels. Thus, we find that the BFOQ exception does not permit the sexual classification challenged in this case.

B. The Bennett Amendment. In its original proposed form, 42 U.S.C. §2000e-2(h) stated that discrimination among employees was permitted if based on a bona fide seniority or merit system, a system rewarding quantity or quality of production, different work locations, or professionally developed tests. Because the inclusion of "sex" as one of the categories of discrimination made illegal by Title VII was done by last minute amendment, received almost no attention, and produced no legislative history, *see* 110 Cong. Rec. 2720 (Rep. Green's remarks, Feb. 10, 1964); Bernstein & Williams, *supra,* 74 Col. L. Rev. at 1216-17, Senator Bennett became concerned that the Act might inadvertently conflict with the Equal Pay Act of 1963, which had received careful attention the year before. Therefore, he proposed, and Congress approved, an amendment to §2000e-2(h), which reads:

> It shall not be an unlawful employment practice under this subchapter for any employer to differentiate upon the basis of sex in determining the amount of the wages or compensation paid or to be paid to employees of such employer if such differentiation is authorized by the provisions of section 206(d) of Title 29 [the Equal Pay Act].

Title 29 U.S.C. §206(d)(1), which was thus incorporated into the Civil Rights Act of 1964 by the Bennett Amendment, says that it shall be unlawful to discriminate on the basis of sex in paying wages:

> . . . except where such payment is made pursuant to (i) a seniority system; (ii) a merit system; (iii) a system which measures earnings by quantity or quality of production; or (iv) a differential based on any other factor other than sex.

It is exception iv which the Department says permits the kind of actuarially based discrimination that is in question here. However, it does not seem reasonable to us to say that an actuarial distinction based entirely on sex is "based on any other factor other than sex." Sex is exactly what it is based on.

Additionally, the legislative history of the Equal Pay Act indicates that the general language of §206(d)(1) was not intended to exempt pension plans, or any actuarially based employee program, from its coverage. The House Committee on Education and Labor, which reported out the Equal Pay Act, commented on the exceptions as follows:

> Three specific exceptions and one broad general

> exception are also listed. It is the intent of this committee that any discrimination based upon any of these exceptions shall be exempted from the operation of this statute. As it is impossible to list each and every exception, the broad general exclusion has been also included. Thus, among other things, shift differentials, restrictions on or differences based on time of day worked, hours of work, lifting or moving heavy objects, differences based on experience, training, or ability would also be excluded. It also recognizes certain special circumstances, such as "red circle rates." This term is borrowed from War Labor Board parlance and describes certain unusual, higher than normal wage rates which are maintained for many valid reasons. For instance, it is not uncommon for an employer who must reduce help in a skilled job to transfer employees to other less demanding jobs but to continue to pay them a premium rate in order to have them available when they are again needed for their former jobs.
> House Report #309 to accompany H.R. 6060, May 20, 1963, Committee on Labor and Education, reprinted in 1963 *U.S. Code Cong. & Admin. News* 687, 689 (88th Cong., 1st Sess.).

This is the only legislative history coming from the House concerning the exceptions upon which the Department relies. It seems clear that, at least in the House, exception iv was seen only as a catch-all category which would permit distinctions similar to those based on seniority, merit, or production but which do not literally fall into any of those categories, and not a disguised grant of legitimacy for pension plan discrimination based on sex.[2]

The report of the Senate Committee on Labor and Public Welfare indicates that, unlike the House committee, the Senate committee did specifically consider how pension and insurance plans would fit into the scheme of the Equal Pay Act. It commented:

> Furthermore, questions can legitimately be raised as to the accuracy of defining such costs as pension and welfare payments as related to sex. It has been pointed out that the higher susceptibility of men to disabling injury can result in a greater cost to the employer, and that these figures as to health and welfare costs can only be applied plant-wide. It may be that it is more expensive to hire women in one department but it is more expensive to hire men in another, and overall cost figures may demonstrate conclusively that the employer has made a sound decision to hire women and pay them on an equal basis.
>
> It is the intention of the committee that where it can be shown that, on the basis of all of the elements of the employment costs of both men and women, an employer will be economically penalized by the elimination of a wage differential, the Secretary can permit an exception similar to those he can permit for a bona fide seniority system or other exception mentioned above.
> Senate Report #176 to accompany S. 1409, May 13, 1963, Committee on Labor and Public Welfare, at p. 4 (88th Cong., 1st Sess.).

This seems to indicate that the Senate had a broader view of exception iv than did the House in that, when an employer can demonstrate that he incurs significant costs because of employing a particular sex, exception iv would allow the Secretary of Labor, through the Wage-Hour Administrator, to grant an exception from the provisions of the Act.

However, in this case there is nothing in the record to show, and the Department does not claim, that it requires higher contributions from women because it would be economically penalized if it did not; it requires the higher contributions only because it believes that the pension fund itself will thereby be better funded and easier to administer. Thus, whatever the Senate committee had in mind about the Equal Pay Act, it would not, when grafted onto the provisions of Title VII, be the kind of broad exception to the rule against per se discrimination which the Department needs to justify the contribution rate differential here involved. Neither the clear language of the statute, §206(d)(1), nor the legislative history supports the Department's position.

Nonetheless, the Department points to a dialogue between Senator Humphrey, the floor manager of the 1964 Civil Rights Act, and Senator Randolph, which occurred during the floor debate on the 1964 Act (not the Equal Pay Act) and Title VII.

> Sen. Randolph: Mr. President, I wish to ask of the Senator from Minnesota [Mr. Humphrey], who is the effective manager of the pending bill, a clarifying question on the provisions of Title VII.
>
> I have in mind that the Social Security system, in certain respects, treats men and women differently. For example, widows' benefits are paid automatically; but a widower qualifies only if he is disabled or if he was actually supported by his

---

2. It is especially significant that the Committee made no mention of pension plans, because the problem was specifically brought to its attention during the hearing conducted on the Equal Pay Act. Hearings before the House Special Subcommittee on Education & Labor, 88th Cong., 1st Sess., 1963 (Equal Pay Act, H.R. 3861) at p. 103.

> deceased wife. Also, the wife of a retired employee entitled to Social Security receives an additional old age benefit; but the husband of such an employee does not. These differences in treatment as I recall, are of long standing. Am I correct, I ask the Senator from Minnesota, in assuming that similar differences of treatment in industrial benefit plans, including earlier retirement options for women, may continue in operation under this bill, if it becomes law?
>
> Sen. Humphrey: Yes. That point was made unmistakably clear earlier today by the adoption of the Bennett amendment; so there can be no doubt about it.
>
> 110 Cong. Rec. 13663-64, June 12, 1964.

Although this does seem to give support to the Department's position, we do not find it to be persuasive legislative history. The discussion occurred hours after passage of the Bennett Amendment and cannot be said to be part of the legislative history of that amendment. The Department claims that although the statement was made after the Bennett Amendment was adopted, it was still made before the Senate voted on the entire Civil Rights Act. Thus, it claims that Senator Randolph and others who may have wanted to preserve such distinctions were misled into not offering a further amendment for that purpose. This argument might have some merit were it not for the fact that the same Congress (the 88th) passed both the Civil Rights Act and the Equal Pay Act, and it seems unlikely that Senator Humphrey's erroneous interpretation of the latter misled many, if any, senators. It certainly misled no members of the House. So far as appears, members of the House never heard of it.

We note, too, that every case that has considered whether sex-based early retirement options violate Title VII has held that they do, although it does not appear that the colloquy between Senators Randolph and Humphrey was called to the attention of the courts. *See Chastang v. Flynn and Emrich Co.,* 4 Cir., 1976, [12 EPD ¶11,003] ____ F.2d ____ (slip op. June 10, 1976); *Rosen v. Public Service Electric & Gas Co., supra; Bartness v. Drewrys U.S.A., Inc., supra; Fitzpatrick v. Bitzer,* D. Conn., 1974, [8 EPD ¶9685] 390 F.Supp. 278, 287-88, *aff'd,* 2 Cir., 1975, [10 EPD ¶10,270] 519 F.2d 559, *rev'd on other grounds,* 1976, [12 EPD ¶10,999] ____ U.S. ____. *See also Peters v. Missouri Pacific R. Co.,* 5 Cir., 1973, [5 EPD ¶8550] 483 F.2d 490, 492, n. 3.

As we have noted, Senator Humphrey's remark reflects an erroneous interpretation of the Equal Pay Act. Because all that the Bennett Amendment did was to incorporate the exemptions of the Equal Pay Act into Title VII, it is questionable whether the Senator's statement, made during the debates on the incorporating statute, would be significant when it erroneously interprets the incorporated statute.

The Department cites as additional authority interpretations of the Equal Pay Act by the Administrator of the Wage and Hour Division of the Department of Labor. As the official charged with enforcing and interpreting the Equal Pay Act, his interpretations of that Act are entitled to great deference. *Udall v. Talman,* 1965, 380 U.S. 1. However, the interpretation relied on by the Department, appearing at 29 C.F.R. §800.116(d), merely states that in providing benefit plans for employees through outside insurers an employer does not violate the Equal Pay Act if either the amount contributed by the employer for each employee is the same and the resulting benefits are different or if the amount of the benefit is the same while the employer contributions differ. While this reflects the Wage-Hour Administrator's general thinking, it does not deal directly with our case of an employer requiring greater pension plan contributions from women employees when the plan is funded and administered by the employer and its employees.

We note, too, that to the extent that the Wage-Hour Administrator's interpretation does deal with the present case, his interpretation conflicts with that of EEOC, which administers Title VII and whose interpretations of Title VII must be given great deference. Therefore, the EEOC interpretations of the Bennett Amendment are worthy of more deference than are those of the Wage-Hour Administrator relating to the Equal Pay Act. The EEOC regulation, 29 C.F.R. §1604.9 (e & f), makes it a violation of Title VII where a benefit plan provides unequal benefits to employees even if employer contributions are equal. However, like the Wage-Hour Administrator's, these regulations do not squarely cover the present case. Thus, the Department's reliance on administrative interpretation is misplaced.

Our opinion of the effect of Title VII in this case is reinforced by the fact that following the passage of Title VII Congress did expressly exempt actuarially based pension and retirement funds from the provisions of the Age Discrimination Act of 1967, 29 U.S.C. §623(f)(2). In fact, during deliberations on the 1964 Civil Rights Act, Senator Smathers moved to add "age" as one of the types of discrimination made illegal by Title VII, but the amendment was defeated in part because of a concern that inclusion of "age" as a Title VII protected category might have "tremendous implications" on industrial group insurance and pensions. *Equal Employment Opportunity Commission, Legislative History of Titles VII and IX of Civil Rights Act of 1964,* at 3174 (1968). This tends to indicate that Congress did foresee that actuarially based plans would fall under the provisions of Title VII, and that it felt that age discrimination, but not sex discrimination, on such a basis was proper. Thus, by not adding "age" to Title VII in 1964 and not making a pension plan exception to its terms for "sex," and by later prohibiting age discrimination in a separate bill which does make a pension plan exception to its terms for age, Congress gave a strong indication that it did intend to place sex discrimination in pension and retirement plans, even when based on actuarially sound tables, within the type of discrimination forbidden by Title VII.

We emphasize that our holding rests on the clear policy behind Title VII of requiring that each employee be treated as an individual. Setting retirement contribution rates solely on the basis of sex is a failure to treat each employee as an individual; it treats each employee only as a member of one sex. We do not pass judgment on the legality of a plan which determines contribution rates based on a significant number of actuarially determined characteristics, one of which is sex. Our holding is limited to the proposition that when sex is singled out as the only, or as a predominant, factor, the employee is being treated in the manner which Title VII forbids.

One district court case has dealt with a situation very similar to ours. In *Henderson v. Oregon,* D. Ore., 1975, 405 F.Supp. 1271, the court relied heavily on the lower court decision in the present case in holding a scheme similar to that involved here illegal under Title VII.

Our holding agrees with the only administrative ruling dealing with the exact question before us, one made by the EEOC. EEOC Dec. #75-146, Jan. 13, 1975, 2 *CCH Employment Practices* 4190, ¶6447. Relying in part on its earlier interpretation, noted *supra,* the Commission held:

> An inescapable corollary to this principle is that an employer may not require a higher contribution from members of one sex where benefits to members of both sexes are the same.
>
> [This] is based upon the fundamental Title VII precept that generalizations relating to sex, race, religion, and national origin cannot be permitted to influence the terms and conditions of an *individual's* employment, even where the generalizations are statistically valid.

III. The Reimbursement Issue

The Department finally argues that even if the higher contribution required of women violates Title VII, it would be unfair to refund to the plaintiffs the amounts that they contributed in excess of the amounts that similarly situated male employees contributed. The Department says that it was acting in good faith in that it believed that state law requiring that retirement plans be run on a "sound actuarial basis" (Cal. Gov't Code §45342) mandated the use of sex-based actuarial tables, and that paying these contributions back to the women employees would leave the retirement fund underfunded.

The rule that we have adopted relating to monetary awards for past violations of Title VII is stated in *Schaeffer v. San Diego Yellow Cabs, Inc.,* 9 Cir., 1972, [4 EPD ¶7882] 462 F.2d 1002.

> In the case of damages of this nature, a court must balance the various equities between the parties and decide upon a result which is consistent with the purposes of the Equal Employment Opportunities Act, and the fundamental concepts of fairness. *Id.* at 1006.

The defendant in *Schaeffer* argued that in denying women overtime work it has relied in good faith on a state statute requiring that women not work more than eight hours a day, and that therefore it was unfair to make it pay damages for an unwitting violation. We reject that defense with the following comment:

> Rather than drawing any hard and fast rule concerning the defense of good faith reliance on a state statute, we believe that in each case the merits of the plaintiff's claim and the public policy behind it must be balanced against the hardship on a good faith employer. *Id.* at 1007.

Applying this test to the case at bar, we find that the district court did not abuse its discretion in awarding plaintiffs a refund of their excess contributions.

In the first place, the state statute requiring that such plans be administered on a sound actuarial basis by no means requires that the Department use sex-based, and only sex-based, distinctions. In *Schaeffer,* where we found a back pay award proper, the statute prohibiting women from working more than eight hours a day placed a much greater compulsion on the employer to refuse women overtime work than the statute in the present case placed on the Department to require higher retirement contributions.

Second, *Schaeffer* was a case where back pay was awarded to women for work that they did not perform but which they had sought. The plaintiffs did not earn the award; they were merely denied the opportunity to earn it. This case involves *restitution,* a situation where the plaintiffs actually earned the amount in question, but then had it taken from them in violation of Title VII. It is one of the primary purposes of Title VII to "make persons whole for injuries suffered on account of unlawful employment discrimination." *Albemarle Paper Co. v. Moody,* 1975, [9 EPD ¶10,230] 422 U.S. 405, 418. In light of this purpose we find plaintiffs' claim to recover money rightfully theirs to be very compelling.

In contrast to the plaintiffs' compelling claim, we find the Department's "good faith" defense to be less than compelling. The Supreme Court has recently commented on the "good faith" defense as follows:

> But, under Title VII, the mere absence of bad faith simply opens the door to equity; it does not depress the scales in the employer's favor. If backpay were awardable only upon a showing of bad faith, the remedy would become a punishment for moral turpitude rather than a compensation for workers' injuries. This would read the "make whole" purpose right out of Title VII, for a worker's injury is no less real simply because his employer did not inflict it in "bad faith."
>
> *Albemarle Paper Co. v. Moody, supra,* 422 U.S. at 422.

The impact of returning the excess contributions to the plaintiffs in this case is far from oppressive. The amount involved is only 15% of the contributions made by a minority of the Department's employees for the 33-month period from April 5, 1972, to December 31, 1974. This might leave the plan somewhat underfunded, but a number of solutions to that problem are readily available. Benefits could be lowered. Current contributions from all employees could be increased. The Department could raise its matching percentage on current contributions, or it could make a lump sum payment into the fund to offset the reimbursement. However, whatever the adjustments that would have to be made, we do not find that the burden on the pension plan or the Department is sufficient to offset the compelling claim of the plaintiffs to recover the money which they were wrongfully required to contribute. *See also Rosen v. Public Service Electric and Gas Co., supra,* 477 F.2d at 95-96.

In No. 75-2729, the judgment is affirmed.

In No. 75-2807, the appeal is dismissed.

In No. 75-2905, the appeal is dismissed as moot. The stay heretofore granted by this court will expire when the mandate issues.

Other situations involving sex discrimination under pension plans also have been addressed by the courts. In *Chestang v. Flynn & Emrich Co.*, 541 F.2d 1040 (4th Cir. 1976), the court held that a sex-based vesting schedule which provided for 100% vesting of female employees at early retirement before age 65 but provided only 50% vesting for male employees retiring prior to age 65, was unlawful sex discrimination under Title VII. This decision with regard to early retirement reflects principles extending to mandatory retirement. In *Bartness v. Drewrys U.S.A., Inc.,* 44 F.2d 1186 (7th Cir. 1971), the court held that a mandatory retirement age of 62 for females and of 65 for males violated Title VII. Both of these decisions are consistent with the EEOC sex discrimination guidelines.

Health and Welfare Issues

Sex and other discrimination issues can also arise in connection with health and welfare plans. Section 1604.9(e) of the EEOC Sex Discrimination Guidelines provides that the benefits received under certain welfare plans must be equal between the sexes, notwithstanding that the costs of such benefits may be greater with respect to one sex than the other. This position has been upheld by the courts in the case of *Taylor v. Goodyear Tire & Rubber Co.*, 6 FEP 50 (N.D. Ala. 1972). In *Taylor*, the court held that Title VII is violated if actual benefits for sickness and health are unequal between the sexes.

Similarly, under Section 1604.9(b) of the EEOC Sex Discrimination Guidelines, the provision of insurance or similar benefits for either only males or females is impermissible under Title VII. For example, in EEOC Decision No. 70-513 (1970), the EEOC decided that making death benefits available to surviving spouses of deceased male workers but not to surviving spouses of deceased female workers violates Title VII.

EEOC DECISION 70-513

Case No. at 7-3-224

Facts

Charging party, the surviving spouse of a deceased female employee of respondent employer, alleges that employer is committing an unlawful employment practice in violation of Title VII of the Civil Rights Act of 1964, by refusing to pay death benefits to the surviving spouse of deceased female employees, while paying said benefits to the surviving spouse of male employees, because of sex.

Charging party is the surviving husband of a deceased employee of employer who died on October 13, 1966, after having been in service for twenty years. Pursuant to the terms of the death benefits provisions of employer's employer-paid "Plan for Employees' Pensions, Disability Benefits and Death Benefits," employer refused charging party's claim for death benefits on the grounds that charging party was not a dependent of the deceased at the time of her death and was not physically disabled. Employer admits that, under the terms of the plan, had the deceased employee been male the surviving spouse's claim for death benefits would have been honored and an amount equal to one year's wages (here amounting to $6,205.54) would have been paid to charging party.

Charging party alleges that the sex-based difference in death benefits is an unlawful employment practice and that he is aggrieved by such practice to the extent of $6,205.54.

Employer's answer to the charge incorporates by reference a statement of position submitted by employer at a public hearing held by the Commission on May 3, and 4, 1967 on proposed interpretive rules dealing with the effect of Title VII on differentials based on sex in pension and retirement plans. There employer set forth its view that Title VII was not intended by Congress to do more than protect "employment opportunities" for women; and that pension and retirement benefits, properly considered, are not "employment opportunities" because "they have primary effect at the end rather than at the beginning of one's employment." Employer's statement also set forth sociological and economic considerations which in its view argue against elimination of sex-based differences in its own plan's benefits, including differences in benefits paid to survivors.

Text

On February 24, 1968, the Commission published in the *Federal Register* an amendment to Chapter XIV of Title 29 of the Code of Federal Regulations to add a new section entitled Pension and Retirement Plans, Section 1604.31, which reads as follows:

> 1604.31 Pension and retirement plans.
>
> (a) A difference in optional or compulsory retirement ages based on sex violates Title VII.
>
> (b) Other differences based on sex, such as differences in benefits for survivors, will be decided by the issuance of Commission decisions in cases raising such issues.

In deciding the effect of Title VII on sex-based differences in survivor (or death) benefits, the Commission first looks to the language of Sections 703(a)(1) and 703(a)(2) which, in part, state as follows:

> Section 703(a) It shall be an unlawful employment practice for an employer—(1) to . . . discriminate against any individual with respect to his compensation, terms, conditions or privileges of employment, because of such individual's . . . sex . . .; or
>
> (2) to limit, segregate, or classify his employees in any way which would deprive or tend to deprive any individual of employment opportunities or otherwise adversely affect his status as an employee, because of such individual's . . . sex . . .

Title VII explicitly defines employment opportunity to include "compensation" and "privileges," *inter alia,* and there can be no doubt that death benefits, as well as pension and retirement benefits, are examples of both. There is nothing in the language of the statute to support the view that a benefit must both be earned and enjoyed during the active employment, in order to qualify as "compensation" or "privileges" within the meaning of Title VII, rather than merely be earned during that time and enjoyed thereafter. Deferred compensation is compensation nonetheless. Here the difference in death benefits constitutes less compensation, in effect, for females than for similarly placed males and for that reason is prohibited by the language of Sections 703(a)(1) and 703(a)(2).

Nor is the challenged death benefits difference saved by the provisions in Section 703(h) which states that it shall not be an unlawful employment practice under Title VII for an employer to differentiate upon the basis of sex in determining the amount of wages or compensation paid or to be paid to employees of such employer if such differentiation is authorized by the provisions of Section 6(d) of the Fair Labor Standards Act of 1938, as amended [29 U.S.C. 20 6(d)]. A December 19, 1966 opinion letter (24 AB 707.34) issued by the United States Department of Labor in answer to an inquiry as to the effect of the Fair Labor Standards Act upon sex-based differences in pension plan benefits, states (in part) that where an employer makes such benefits available to employees of one sex but not to employees of the opposite sex, a violation would result.

The sex-based differences in the death benefits provisions of Respondent's Plan clearly are prohibited by the language of Title VII and constitute an unlawful employment practice of which Charging Party stands aggrieved, as alleged.

Conclusion

Reasonable cause exists to believe that the employer is committing an unlawful employment practice in violation of Title VII of the Civil Rights Act of 1964, by maintaining differences in death benefits-compensation based on sex.

Pregnancy as a Disability

Recently, there has been a Supreme Court decision that arguably represents a departure from this thinking. In *General Electric Company v. Gilbert*, 429 U.S. 125, 97 Sup. Ct. 401 (1976), the Court held that disabilities caused or contributed to by pregnancy need not be treated the same as other temporary disabilities. *But see Nashville Gas. Co. v. Satty*, ___ U.S. ___ (1977). According to the Court, a classification which differentiates between pregnant and nonpregnant persons has no disproportionate effect on women as a protected class. The class of nonpregnant persons includes women as well as men and is not an invidious sex classification for purposes of Title VII.

The *Gilbert* decision overrules the portion of the EEOC Sex Discrimination Guidelines requiring disability coverage for pregnancy-related disabilities. *See* 29 C.F.R. §1604.10(b).

[It is important to note that in several states, authorities have refused to adopt the approach taken by the Supreme Court in the *Gilbert* case. *See, e.g., Brooklyn Union Gas Co. v. N.Y. State Division of Human Rights*, 14 FEP 42 (1976). In addition, a bill, S. 995, has been passed by the Senate and a similar bill, H.R. 6075, has been reported to the House of Representatives by the House Labor Committee, both of which, in effect, would reverse the *Gilbert* case.]

GENERAL ELECTRIC CO. V. GILBERT
429 U.S. 125 (1976)
Appearances of Counsel

Theophil C. Kammholz argued the cause for General Electric Company.

Ruth Weyand argued the cause for Gilbert *et al.*

J. Stanley Pottinger argued the cause for the United States, as amicus curiae.

Briefs of Counsel, p. 891, *infra*.

OPINION OF THE COURT

[429 US 127]

Mr. Justice Rehnquist delivered the opinion of the Court.

[1a] Petitioner, General Electric Co.,[1] provides for all of its employees a disability plan which pays weekly nonoccupational sickness and accident benefits. Excluded from the plan's coverage, however, are disabilities arising from pregnancy. Respondents, on behalf of a class of women employees, brought this action seeking, *inter alia,*[2] a declaration

[429 US 128]

that this exclusion constitutes sex discrimination in violation of Title VII of the Civil Rights Act of 1964, 78 Stat. 253, as amended, 42 U.S.C. §§2000e *et seq.,* [42 U.S.C.S. §§2000e *et seq.*]. The District Court for the Eastern District of Virginia, following a trial on the merits, held that the exclusion of such pregnancy-related disability benefits from General Electric's employee disability plan violated Title VII, 375 F. Supp. 367. The Court of Appeals affirmed, 519 F.2d 661, and we granted certiorari, 423 U.S. 822, 46 L.Ed.2d 39, 96 S.Ct. 36. We now reverse.

I

As part of its total compensation package, General Electric provides nonoccupational sickness and accident benefits to all employees under its Weekly Sickness and Accident Insurance Plan (the Plan) in an amount equal to 60% of an employee's normal straight-time weekly earnings. These payments are paid to employees who become totally disabled as a result of a nonoccupational sickness or accident. Benefit payments normally start with the eighth day of an employee's total disability (although if an employee is earlier confined to a hospital as a bed patient, benefit payments will start immediately), and continue up to a maximum of 26 weeks for any one continuous period of disability or successive periods of disability due to the same or related causes.[3]

---

1. All the parties to the suit joined in petitioning for a writ of certiorari. General Electric was the moving party before the Court of Appeals, where the judgment of the District Court was affirmed. The parties have agreed that General Electric is to be deemed the petitioner for purposes of briefing and oral argument, a convention we adopt for the writing of this opinion.

2. Respondents also represent a class of women employees who have been denied such benefits since September 14, 1971, and seek damages arising from this denial.

3. With respect to the Plan, General Electric is, in effect, a self-insurer. While General Electric has obtained, for employees outside California, an insurance policy from the Metropolitan Life Insurance Co., this policy involves the payment of a tentative premium only, subject to adjustment in the light of actual experience.

The individual named respondents are present or former hourly paid production employees at General Electric's plant in Salem, Va. Each of these employees was pregnant during

[429 US 129]

1971 or 1972, while employed by General Electric, and each presented a claim to the company for disability benefits under the Plan to cover the period while absent from work as a result of the pregnancy. These claims were routinely denied on the ground that the Plan did not provide disability-benefit payments for any absence due to pregnancy.[4] Each of the respondents thereafter filed charges with the Equal Employment Opportunity Commission (EEOC) alleging that the refusal of General Electric to pay disability benefits under the Plan for time lost due to pregnancy and childbirth discriminated against her because of sex. Upon waiting the requisite number of days, the instant action was commenced in the District Court.[5] The complaint asserted a violation of Title VII. Damages were sought as well as an injunction directing General Electric to include pregnancy disabilities within the Plan on the same terms and conditions as other nonoccupational disabilities.

[429 US 130]

Following trial, the District Court made findings of fact and conclusions of law, and entered an order in which it determined that General Electric, by excluding pregnancy disabilities from the coverage of the Plan, had engaged in sex discrimination in violation of §703(a)(1) of Title VII, 42 U.S.C. §2000e-2(a)(1) [42 U.S.C.S. §2000e-2(a)(1)]. The District Court found that normal pregnancy, while not necessarily either a "disease" or an "accident," was disabling for a period of six to eight weeks;[6] that approximately "[t]en percent of pregnancies are terminated by miscarriage, which is disabling;"[7] and that approximately 10% of pregnancies are complicated by diseases which may lead to additional disability.[8] The District Court noted the evidence introduced during the trial, a good deal of it stipulated, concerning the relative cost to General Electric of providing benefits under the Plan to male and female employees,[9] all of which indi-

---

Pretrial Stipulation of Facts, ¶11 App. 175-176. In effect, therefore, the Metropolitan Life Insurance Co. is used to provide the administrative service of processing claims, while General Electric remains, for all practical purposes, a self-insurer.

4. Additionally, benefit payment coverage under the Plan for all disabilities, whether or not related to pregnancy, terminates "on the date you cease active work because of total disability or pregnancy, except that if you are entitled to Weekly Benefits for a disability existing on such date of cessation" benefit payments will be continued in accordance with the provisions of the Plan. In cases of personal leave, layoff, or strike, however, the coverage for future nonoccupational sickness or accident disability is continued for 31 days, *ibid.*

In the case of respondent Emma Furch, who took a pregnancy leave on April 7, 1972, and who was hospitalized with a non-pregnancy-related pulmonary embolism on April 21, 1972, a claim was filed for disability benefits under the Plan solely for the period of absence due to the pulmonary embolism. The claim was rejected "since such benefits have been discontinued in accordance with the provisions of the General Electric Insurance Plan."

5. Plaintiffs in the action were seven female employees; the International Union of Electrical, Radio and Machine Workers, AFL-CIO-CLC (IUE); and the latter's affiliate, Local 161, which is a joint collective-bargaining representative, with the IUE, of the hourly paid production and maintenance employees at General Electric's Salem, Va., plant.

6. The District Court made the following "specific findings":

1. While pregnancy is perhaps most often voluntary, a substantial incidence of negligent or accidental conception also occurs.

2. Pregnancy, per se, is not a disease.

3. A pregnancy without complications is normally disabling for a period of six to eight weeks, which time includes the period from labor and delivery, or slightly before, through several weeks of recuperation. 375 F.Supp. 367, 377.

7. *Ibid.*

8. "Five percent of pregnancies are complicated by diseases which are found in nonpregnant persons but which may have been stimulated by pregnancy. Five percent of pregnancies are complicated by pregnancy-related diseases. These complications are diseases which may lead to disability." *Ibid.*

9. The District Court included in its opinion the following charts from a stipulation dated July 24, 1973:

143. During 1970, GE's experience, by sex, with respect to claims under its weekly sickness and accident disability insurance coverage was as follows:

	Male	Female
No. of claims (new)	19,045	15,509
Average duration of claim	48 days	52 days
No. of new claims per thousand employees	77	173
Average No. of employees covered.	246,492	89,705
Total benefits paid	$11,279,110	$7,405,790
Average cost per insured employee of total benefits paid	$45.76	$82.57

cated that, with pregnancy-related disabilities excluded, the cost of the Plan to General Electric per female employee was at least as high as, if not substantially higher than, the cost per male employee.[10]

[429 US 131]

The District Court found that the inclusion of pregnancy-related disabilities within the scope of the Plan would "increase G.E.'s [disability benefits plan] costs by an amount which, though large, is at this time underterminable." 375 F. Supp. at 378. The District Court declined to find that the present actuarial value of the coverage was equal as between men and women,[11] but went on to decide that even

[429 US 132]

had it found economic equivalence, such a finding would not in any case have justified the exclusion of pregnancy-related disabilities from an otherwise comprehensive nonoccupational sickness and accident disability plan. Regardless of whether the cost of including such benefits might make the Plan more costly for women than for men, the District Court determined that "[i]f Title VII intends to sexually equalize employment opportunity, there must be this one exception to the cost differential defense." *Id.,* at 383.

The ultimate conclusion of the District Court was that petitioner had discriminated on the basis of sex in the operation of its disability program in violation of Title VII, *id.*, at 385-386. An order was entered enjoining petitioner from continuing to exclude pregnancy-related disabilities from the coverage of the Plan, and providing for the future award of monetary relief to individual members of the class affected. Petitioner appealed to the Court of Appeals for the Fourth Circuit, and that court by a divided vote affirmed the judgment of the District Court.

Between the date on which the District Court's judgment was rendered and the time this case was decided by the Court of Appeals, we decided *Geduldig v. Aiello*, 417 U.S. 484, 41 L.Ed.2d 256, 94 S.Ct. 2485 (1974), where we rejected a claim that a very similar disability program established under California law violated the Equal Protection Clause of the Fourteenth Amendment because that plan's exclusion of pregnancy disabilities represented sex discrimination. The majority of the Court of Appeals felt that *Geduldig* was not controlling because it

[429 US 133]

arose under the Equal Protection Clause of the Fourteenth Amendment, and not under Title VII, 519 F.2d, at 666-667. The dissenting opinion disagreed with the majority as to the impact of *Geduldig,* 519 F.2d, at 668-669. We granted certiorari to consider this important issue in the construction of Title VII.[12]

II

Section 703(a)(1) provides in relevant part that it shall be an unlawful employment practice for an employer

> to discriminate against any individual with respect to his compensation, terms, conditions, or privileges of employment, because of such individual's race, color, religion, sex, or national origin . . . 42 U.S.C. §2000e-2(a)(1) [42 U.S.C.S. §2000e-2(a)(1)].

144. During 1971, GE's experience, by sex, with respect to claims under its weekly sickness and accident disability insurance coverage was as follows:

	Male	Female
No. of claims (new)	22,987	17,719
Average duration of claim	47 days	52 days
No. of new claims per thousand employees	99	217
Average No. of employees covered.	231,026	81,469
Total benefits paid	$14,343,000	$9,191,195
Average cost per insured employee of total benefits paid	$62.08	$112.91
	Male	Female

Id., at 377.

10. At trial, General Electric introduced, in addition to the material cited in n. 9, *supra,* the testimony of Paul Jackson, an actuary, who calculated that the Plan presently "costs 170% more for females than males. . . ." *Id.,* at 378.

11. "The present plan is objectionable in that it excludes from coverage a unique disability which affects only members of the female sex, while no suggestion is made to exclude disabilities which can be said to affect only males. Additionally, the Court gives no weight to the suggestion that the actuarial value of the coverage now provided is equalized as between men and women. Defenses must be bottomed on evidence, and such, in this regard, is lacking here.

"Whatever inferences may be suggested by the statistical data presented, the Court simply cannot presume to draw any precise conclusions as to the actuarial value of the coverage provided under the present plan, or the effect of including pregnancy related disabilities on the basis of that limited data." *Id.,* at 382-383.

12. As noted, *supra,* at 127 n.1, 50 L.Ed.2d 349, this is a joint petition. Respondents have presented several additional questions, not all of which merit treatment in this opinion. We have concluded that they are all without merit.

While there is no necessary inference that Congress, in choosing this language, intended to incorporate into Title VII the concepts of discrimination which have evolved from court decisions construing the Equal Protection Clause of the Fourteenth Amendment, the similarities between the Congressional language and some of those decisions surely indicate that the latter are a useful starting point in interpreting the former. Particularly in the case of defining the term "discrimination," which Congress has nowhere in Title VII defined, those cases afford an existing body of law analyzing and discussing that term in a legal context not wholly dissimilar to the concerns which Congress manifested in enacting Title VII. We think, therefore, that our decision in *Geduldig v. Aiello, supra,* dealing with a strikingly similar disability plan, is quite relevant in determining whether or not the pregnancy exclusion did discriminate on the basis of sex. In *Geduldig,* the disability insurance system was

[429 US 134]

funded entirely from contributions deducted from the wages of participating employees, at a rate of 1% of the employee's salary up to an annual maximum of $85. In other relevant respects, the operation of the program was similar to General Electric's disability benefits plan, *see* 417 U.S. at 487-489, 41 L.Ed.2d 256, 94 S.Ct. 2485.

We rejected appellee's equal protection challenge to this statutory scheme. We first noted:

> We cannot agree that the exclusion of this disability from coverage amounts to invidious discrimination under the Equal Protection Clause. California does not discriminate with respect to the persons or groups which are eligible for disability insurance protection under the program. The classification challenged in this case relates to the asserted underinclusiveness of the set of risks that the State has selected to insure.
>
> *Id.,* at 494, 41 L.Ed.2d 256, 94 S.Ct. 2485.

This point was emphasized again, when later in the opinion we noted:

> [T]his case is thus a far cry from cases like *Reed v. Reed,* 404 U.S. 71, [30 L.Ed.2d 225, 92 S. Ct. 251] (1971), and *Frontiero v. Richardson,* 411 U.S. 677, [36 L.Ed.2d 583, 93 S.Ct. 1764] (1973), involving discrimination based upon gender as such. The California insurance program does not exclude anyone from benefit eligibility because of gender but merely removes one physical condition—pregnancy—from the list of compensable disabilities. While it is true that only women can become pregnant, it does not follow that every legislative classification concerning pregnancy is a sex-based classification like those considered in *Reed, supra,* and *Frontiero, supra.* Normal pregnancy is an objectively identifiable physical condition with unique characteristics. Absent a showing that distinctions involving pregnancy are mere pretexts designed to effect an invidious discrimination against the members of one sex or the other, lawmakers are constitutionally free to include or exclude pregnancy from the coverage of legislation such as this on any reasonable
>
> [429 US 135]
>
> basis, just as with respect to any other physical condition.
>
> The lack of identity between the excluded disability and gender as such under this insurance program becomes clear upon the most cursory analysis. The program divides potential recipients into two groups—pregnant women and non-pregnant persons. While the first group is exclusively female, the second includes members of both sexes.
>
> *Id.,* at 496-497, n. 20, 41 L.Ed.2d 256, 94 S.Ct. 2485.

The quoted language from *Geduldig* leaves no doubt that our reason for rejecting appellee's equal protection claim in that case was that the exclusion of pregnancy from coverage under California's disability-benefits plan was not in itself discrimination based on sex.

We recognized in *Geduldig,* of course, that the fact that there was no sex-based discrimination as such was not the end of the analysis, should it be shown "that distinctions involving pregnancy are mere pretexts designed to effect an invidious discrimination against the members of one sex or the other," *ibid.* But we noted that no semblance of such a showing had been made:

> There is no evidence in the record that the selection of the risks insured by the program worked to discriminate against any definable group or class in terms of the aggregate risk protection derived by that group or class from the program. There is no risk from which men are protected and women are not. Likewise, there is no risk from which women are protected and men are not.
>
> *Id.,* at 496-497, 41 L.Ed.2d 256, 94 S. Ct. 2485.

Since gender-based discrimination had not been shown to exist either by the terms of the plan or by its effect, there was no need to reach the question of what sort of standard would govern our review had there been such a showing. *See Frontiero v. Richardson,* 411 U.S. 677, 36 L.Ed.2d 583, 93 S. Ct. 1764 (1973); *Reed v. Reed,* 404 U.S. 71, 30 L.Ed.2d 225, 92 S. Ct. 251 (1971).

[429 US 136]

[1b] The Court of Appeals was therefore wrong in concluding that the reasoning of *Ged-*

uldig was not applicable to an action under Title VII. Since it is a finding of sex-based discrimination that must trigger, in a case such as this, the finding of an unlawful employment practice under §703(a)(1), *Geduldig* is precisely in point in its holding that an exclusion of pregnancy from a disability-benefits plan providing general coverage is not a gender-based discrimination at all.

[2] There is no more showing in this case than there was in *Geduldig* that the exclusion of pregnancy benefits is a mere "[pretext] designed to effect an invidious discrimination against the members of one sex or the other." The Court of Appeals expressed the view that the decision in *Geduldig* had actually turned on whether or not a conceded discrimination was "invidious" but we think that in so doing it misread the quoted language from our opinion. As we noted in that opinion, a distinction which on its face is not sex related might nonetheless violate the Equal Protection Clause if it were in fact a subterfuge to accomplish a forbidden discrimination. But we have here no question of excluding a disease or disability comparable in all other respects to covered diseases or disabilities and yet confined to the members of one race or sex. Pregnancy is, of course, confined to women, but it is in other ways significantly different from the typical covered disease or disability. The District Court found that it is not a "disease" at all, and is often a voluntarily undertaken and desired condition, 375 F.Supp. at 375, 377. We do not therefore infer that the exclusion of pregnancy disability benefits from petitioner's plan is a simple pretext for discriminating against women. The contrary arguments adopted by the lower courts and expounded by our dissenting Brethren were largely rejected in *Geduldig.*

[3, 4a] The instant suit was grounded on Title VII rather than the Equal Protection Clause, and our cases recognize that

[429 US 137]

a prima facie violation of Title VII can be established in some circumstances upon proof that the *effect* of an otherwise facially neutral plan or classification is to discriminate against members of one class or another. *See Washington v. Davis,* 426 U.S. 229, 246-248, 48 L.Ed.2d 597, 96 S. Ct. 2040, 2051 (1976). For example, in the context of a challenge, under the provisions of §703(a)(2),[13] to a facially neutral employment test, this Court held that a prima facie case of discrimination would be established if, even absent proof of intent, the consequences of the test were "invidiously to discriminate on the basis of racial or other impermissible classification," *Griggs v. Duke Power Co.* 401 U.S. 424, 431, 28 L.Ed.2d 158, 91 S. Ct. 849 (1971). Even assuming that it is not necessary in this case to prove intent to establish a prima facie violation of §703(a)(1), but *cf. McDonnell Douglas Corp. v. Green,* 411 U.S. 792, 802-806, 36 L.Ed.2d 668, 93 S. Ct. 1817 (1973), the respondents have not made the requisite showing of gender-based effects.[14]

[5a, 6, 7a, 8] As in *Geduldig,* respondents have not attempted to meet the burden of demonstrating a gender-based discriminatory effect resulting from the exclusion of pregnancy-related disabilities from coverage.[15] Whatever the ultimate

[429 US 138]

probative value of the evidence introduced before the District Court on this subject in the instant case, at the very least it tended to illustrate that the selection of risks covered by the Plan did not operate, in fact, to discriminate against women. As in *Geduldig,* we start from the indisputable baseline that "[t]he fiscal and actuarial benefits of the program . . . accrue to members of both sexes," 417 U.S. at 497 n. 20, 41 L.Ed.2d 256, 94 S. Ct. 2485. We need not disturb the findings of the District Court to note that neither is

13. This subsection provides that it shall be an unlawful employment practice for an employer

(2) to limit, segregate, or classify his employees in any way which would deprive or tend to deprive any individual of employment opportunities or otherwise adversely affect his status as an employee, because of such individual's race, color, religion, sex, or national origin.

42 U.S.C. §2000e-2(a)(2) [42 U.S.C.S. §2000e-2(a)(2)].

14. [4b] Respondents, who seek to establish discrimination, have the traditional civil litigation burden of establishing that the acts they complain of constituted discrimination in violation of Title VII. *Albemarle Paper Co. v. Moody,* 422 U.S. 405, 425, 45 L.Ed.2d 280, 95 S. Ct. 2362 (1975); *McDonnell Douglas Corp. v. Green,* 411 U.S. at 802, 36 L.Ed.2d 668, 93 S. Ct. 1817. In *Griggs,* the burden placed on the employer "of showing that any given requirement must have a manifest relationship to the employment in question," 401 U.S. at 432, 28 L.Ed. 2d 158, 91 S. Ct. 849, did not arise until discriminatory effect had been shown, *Albemarle, supra,* at 425, 45 L.Ed.2d 280, 95 S. Ct. 2362.

15. [5b] Absent a showing of gender-based discrimination, as that term is defined in *Geduldig,* or a showing of gender-based effect, there can be no violation of §703(a)(1).

there a finding, nor was there any evidence which would support a finding, that the financial benefits of the Plan "worked to discriminate against any definable group or class in terms of the aggregate risk protection derived by that group or class from the program," *id.,* at 496, L.Ed.2d 256, 94 S. Ct. 2485. The Plan, in effect (and for all that appears), is nothing more than an insurance package, which covers some risks, but excludes others, *see id.,* at 494, 496-497, 41 L.Ed.2d 256, 94 S. Ct. 2485.[16] The "package" going to relevant identifiable groups we are presently concerned with—General Electric's male and female employees—covers exactly the same categories of risk, and is facially nondiscriminatory in the sense that "[t]here is no risk from which men are protected and women are not. Likewise, there is no risk from which women are protected and men are not." *Id.,* at 496-497, 41 L.Ed.2d 256, 94 S. Ct. 2485. As there is no proof that the package is in fact worth more to men than to women, it is impossible to find any gender-based discriminatory effect in this scheme simply because women disabled as a result of pregnancy do not receive benefits; that is to say, gender-based discrimination does not result simply because an employer's disability-benefits plan is less

[429 US 139]

than all-inclusive.[17] For all that appears, pregnancy-related disabilities constitute an *additional* risk, unique to women, and the failure to compensate them for this risk does not destroy the presumed parity of the benefits, accruing to men and women alike, which results from the facially evenhanded *inclusion* of risks. To hold otherwise would endanger the commonsense notion that an employer who has no disability benefits program at all does not violate Title VII even though the "underinclusion" of risks impacts, as a result

[429 US 140]

of pregnancy-related disabilities, more heavily upon one gender than upon the other.[18] Just as there is no facial gender-based discrimination in that case, so, too, there is none here.

16. That General Electric self-insures does not change the fact that it is, in effect, acting as an insurer, just as the State of California was acting in *Geduldig,* 417 U.S. at 492, 41 L.Ed.2d 256, 94 S. Ct. 2485.

17. [7b] Absent proof of different values, the cost to "insure" against the risks is, in essence, nothing more than extra compensation to the employees, in the form of fringe benefits. If the employer were to remove the insurance fringe benefits and, instead, increase wages by an amount equal to the cost of the "insurance," there would clearly be no gender-based discrimination, even though a female employee who wished to purchase disability insurance that covered all risks would have to pay more than would a male employee who purchased identical disability insurance, due to the fact that her insurance had to cover the "extra" disabilities due to pregnancy. While respondents seem to acknowledge that the failure to provide any benefit plan at all would not constitute sex-based discrimination in violation of Title VII, *see* n. 18, *infra,* they illogically also suggest that the present scheme does violate Title VII because:

> A female must spend her own money to buy a personal disability policy covering pregnancy disability if she wants to be fully insured against a period of disability without income, whereas a male without extra expenditure is fully insured by GE against every period of disability.

Supplemental Brief for Respondents on Reargument 11.

Yet, in both cases—the instant case and the case where there is no disability coverage at all—the ultimate result is that a woman who wished to be fully insured would have to pay an incremental amount over her male counterpart due solely to the possibility of pregnancy-related disabilities. Title VII's proscription on discrimination does not, in either case, require the employer to pay that incremental amount. The District Court was wrong in assuming, as it did, 375 F.Supp. at 383, that Title VII's ban on employment discrimination necessarily means that "greater economic benefit[s]" must be required to be paid to one sex or the other because of their differing roles in "the scheme of human existence."

18. Respondents tacitly admit that this situation would not violate Title VII. They acknowledge that "GE had no obligation to establish any fringe benefit program," Brief for Respondents 143. Moreover, the difficulty with their contention that General Electric engaged in impermissible sex discrimination is vividly portrayed in their closing suggestion that "[i]f paying for pregnancy discriminates within the sphere of classification by sex, so does the failure to pay," Response of Respondents to Reply Brief for Petitioners on Reargument 7. As that statement, and its converse, indicate, perceiving the issue in terms of "sex discrimination" quickly places resolution of this issue into a no-win situation. *See also* Supplemental Brief for Respondents on Reargument 59 ("we believe that imposing on employees either unequal costs when benefits are equal or unequal benefits when costs are equal violates the right of each individual employee to be treated equally with each individual employee of the opposite sex . . ."). Troublesome interpretive problems such as this reinforce our belief that Congress, in prohibiting sex-based discrimination in Title VII, did not intend to depart from the longstanding meaning of "discrimination," *cf. Jefferson v. Hackney,* 406 U.S. 535, 548-549, 32 L.Ed.2d 285, 92 S.Ct. 1724 (1972).

III

[9a] We are told, however, that this analysis of the Congressional purpose underlying Title VII is inconsistent with the guidelines of the EEOC, which, it is asserted, are entitled to "great deference" in the construction of the Act, *Griggs,* 401 U.S. at 433-434, 28 L.Ed.2d 158, 91 S. Ct. 849; *Phillips v. Martin Marietta Corp.* 400 U.S. 542, 545, 27 L.Ed.2d 613, 91 S. Ct. 496 (1971) (Marshall, J., concurring). The guideline upon which respondents rely most heavily was promulgated in 1972, and states in pertinent part:

> Disabilities caused or contributed to by pregnancy, miscarriage, abortion, childbirth, and recovery therefrom are, for all job-related purposes, temporary disabilities and should be treated as such under any health or temporary disability insurance or sick leave plan available
>
> [429 US 141]
>
> in connection with employment. . . . [Benefits] shall be applied to disability due to pregnancy or childbirth on the same terms and conditions as they are applied to other temporary disabilities.
>
> 29 C.F.R. §1604.10(b) (1975).[19]

[10, 11] In evaluating this contention it should first be noted that Congress, in enacting Title VII, did not confer upon the EEOC authority to promulgate rules or regulations pursuant to that Title. *Albemarle Paper Co. v. Moody,* 422 U.S. 405, 431, 45 L.Ed.2d 280, 95 S.Ct. 2362 (1975).[20] This does not mean that EEOC Guidelines are not entitled to consideration in determining legislative intent, *see Albermarle, supra; Griggs v. Duke Power Co. supra,* at 433-434, 28 L.Ed.2d 158, 91 S.Ct. 849; *Espinoza v. Farah Mfg. Co.* 414 U.S. 86, 94, 38 L.Ed.2d 287, 94 S.Ct. 334 (1973). But it does mean that courts properly may accord less weight to such guidelines than to administrative regulations which Congress has declared shall have the force of law, *see Standard Oil Co. v. Johnson,* 316 U.S. 481, 484, 86 L.Ed. 1611, 62 S.Ct. 1168 (1942), or to regulations which under the enabling statute may themselves supply the basis for imposition of liability, *see, e.g.,* §23(a), Securities Exchange Act of 1934, 15 U.S.C. §78w(a) [15 U.S.C.S. §78w(a)]. The most comprehensive statement of the role of interpretive rulings such as the EEOC guidelines is found in *Skidmore v. Swift & Co.* 323 U.S. 134, 140, 89 L.Ed. 124, 65 S. Ct. 161 (1944), where the Court said:

> We consider that the rulings, interpretations and opinions of the Administrator under this Act, while not
>
> [429 US 142]
>
> controlling upon the counts by reason of their authority, do constitute a body of experience and informed judgment to which courts and litigants may properly resort for guidance. The weight of such a judgment in a particular case will depend upon the thoroughness evident in its consideration, the validity of its reasoning, its consistency with earlier and later pronouncements, and all those factors which give it power to persuade, if lacking power to control.

[9b] The EEOC guideline in question does not fare well under these standards. It is not a contemporaneous interpretation of Title VII, since it was first promulgated eight years after the enactment of that Title. More importantly, the 1972 guideline flatly contradicts the position which the agency had enunciated at an earlier date, closer to the enactment of the governing statute. An opinion letter by the General Counsel of the EEOC, dated October 17, 1966, states:

> You have requested our opinion whether the above exclusion of pregnancy and childbirth as a disability under the long-term salary continuation plan would be in violation of Title VII of the Civil Rights Act of 1964.
>
> In a recent opinion letter regarding pregnancy, we have stated, "The Commission policy in this area does not seek to compare an employer's treatment of illness or injury with his treatment of maternity since maternity is a temporary disability unique to the female sex and more or less to be anticipated during the working life of most women employees." Therefore, it is our opinion that according to the facts stated above, a company's group insurance program which covers hospital and medical expenses for the delivery of employees' children, but excludes from its long-term salary continuation program those disabilities which result from pregnancy and childbirth would not be in violation of Title VIII. App. 721-722.

[429 US 143]

A few weeks later, in an opinion letter expressly issued pursuant to 29 C.F.R. §1601.30 (1975), the EEOC's position was that "an insurance or other benefit plan may simply exclude maternity as a covered risk, and such an exclusion would not

19. The other regulation cited by respondents, 29 C.F.R. §1604.9(b) (1975), simply restates the statutory proposition that it is an unlawful employment practice to discriminate "between men and women with regard to fringe benefits."

20. The EEOC has been given "authority from time to time to issue . . . suitable procedural regulations to carry out the provisions of this subchapter," §713(a), 42 U.S.C. §2000e-12(a) [42 U.S.C.S. §2000e-12(a)]. No one contends, however, that the above-quoted regulation is procedural in nature or in effect.

in our view be discriminatory." App. 735.

We have declined to follow administrative guidelines in the past where they conflicted with earlier pronouncements of the agency. *United Housing Foundation, Inc., v. Forman,* 421 U.S. 837, 858-859, n. 25, 44 L.Ed.2d 621, 95 S.Ct. 2051 (1975); *Espinoza v. Farah Mfg. Co., supra,* at 92-96, 38 L.Ed.2d 287, 94 S.Ct. 334. In short, while we do not wholly discount the weight to be given the 1972 guideline, it does not receive high marks when judged by the standards enunciated in *Skidmore, supra.*

There are also persuasive indications that the more recent EEOC guideline sharply conflicts with other indicia of the proper interpretation of the sex-discrimination provisions of Title VII. The legislative history of Title VII's prohibition of sex discrimination is notable primarily for its brevity. Even so, however, Congress paid especial attention to the provisions of the Equal Pay Act, 29 U.S.C. §206(d) [29 U.S.C.S. §206(d)],[21] when it amended §703(h) of Title VII by adding the following sentence:

> It shall not be an unlawful employment practice under
>
> [429 US 144]
>
> this subchapter for any employer to differentiate upon the basis of sex in determining the amount of the wages or compensation paid or to be paid to employees of such employer if such differentiation is authorized by the provisions of section 206(d) of Title 29.
>
> 42 U.S.C.S. 2000e-2(h) [42 U.S.C.S. §2000e-2(h)].

This sentence was proposed as the Bennett Amendment to the Senate bill, 110 Cong. Rec. 13647 (1964), and Senator Humphrey, the floor manager of the bill, stated that the purpose of the amendment was to make it "unmistakably clear" that "differences of treatment in industrial benefit plans, including earlier retirement options for women, may continue in operation under this bill, if it becomes law," *id.,* at 13663-13664. Because of this amendment, interpretations of §6(d) of the Equal Pay Act are applicable to Title VII as well, and an interpretive regulation promulgated by the Wage and Hour Administrator under the Equal Pay Act explicitly states:

> If employer contributions to a plan providing insurance or similar benefits to employees are equal for both men and women, no wage differential prohibited by the equal pay provisions will result from such payments, even though the benefits which accrue to the employees in question are greater for one sex than for the other. The mere fact that the employer may make unequal contributions for employees of opposite sexes in such a situation will not, however, be considered to indicate that the employer's payments are in violation of section 6(d), if the resulting benefits are equal for such employees.
>
> 29 C.F.R. §800.116(d) (1975).

Thus, even if we were to depend for our construction of the critical language of Title VII solely on the basis of "deference" to interpretive regulations by the appropriate

[429 US 145]

administrative agencies, we would find ourselves pointed in diametrically opposite directions by the conflicting regulations of the EEOC, on the one hand, and the Wage and Hour Administrator, on the other. Petitioner's exclusion of benefits for pregnancy disability would be declared an unlawful employment practice under §703(a)(1), but would be declared not to be an unlawful employment practice under §703(h).

[9c] We are not reduced to such total abdication in construing the statute. The EEOC guideline of 1972, conflicting as it does with earlier pronouncements of that agency, and containing no suggestion that some new source of legislative history had been discovered in the intervening eight years, stands virtually alone. Contrary to it are the consistent interpretation of the Wage and Hour Administrator, and the quoted language of Senator Humphrey, the floor manager of Title VII in the Senate. They support what seems to us to be the "plain meaning" of the language used by Congress when it enacted §703(a)(1).

[12] The concept of "discrimination," of course, was well known at the time of the enactment of Title VII, having been associated with the Fourteenth Amendment for nearly a century, and carrying with it a long history of judicial con-

---

21. Section 6(d)(1) of the Equal Pay Act, 29 U.S.C. §206(d)(1) [29 U.S.C.S. §206(d)(1)], provides, in pertinent part:

> No employer having employees subject to any provisions of this section shall discriminate, within any establishment in which such employees are employed, between employees on the basis of sex by paying wages to employees in such establishment at a rate less than the rate at which he pays wages to employees of the opposite sex in such establishment for equal work on jobs the performance of which requires equal skill, effort, and responsibility, and which are performed under similar working conditions, except where such payment is made pursuant to (i) a seniority system; (ii) a merit system; (iii) a system which measures earnings by quantity or quality of production; or (iv) a differential based on any other factor other than sex. . . .

struction. When Congress makes it unlawful for an employer to "discriminate . . . because of . . . sex . . .," without further explanation of its meaning, we should not readily infer that it meant something different from what the concept of discrimination has traditionally meant, *cf. Morton v. Mancari,* 417 U.S. 535, 549, 41 L.Ed.2d 290, 94 S. Ct. 2474 (1974); *Ozawa v. United States,* 260 U.S. 178, 193, 67 L.Ed. 199, 43 S. Ct. 65 (1922). There is surely no reason for any such inference here, *see Gemsco v. Walling,* 324 U.S. 244, 260, 89 L.Ed. 921, 65 S. Ct. 605 (1945).

[1c] We therefore agree with petitioner that its disability-benefits plan does not violate Title VII because of its failure

[429 US 146]

to cover pregnancy-related disabilities. The judgment of the Court of Appeals is reversed.

SEPARATE OPINIONS

Mr. Justice Stewart, concurring.

I join the opinion of the Court holding that General Electric's exclusion of benefits for disability during pregnancy is not a per se violation of §703 (a)(1) of Title VII, and that the respondents have failed to prove a discriminatory effect. Unlike my Brother Blackmun, I do not understand the opinion to question either *Griggs v. Duke Power Co.* 401 U.S. 424, 28 L.Ed.2d 158, 91 S. Ct. 849, specifically, or the significance generally of proving a discriminatory effect in a Title VII case.

Mr. Justice Blackmun, concurring in part.

I join the judgment of the Court and concur in its opinion insofar as it holds (a) that General Electric's exclusion of disability due to pregnancy is not, per se, a violation of §703(a)(1) of Title VII; (b) that the plaintiffs in this case therefore had at least the burden of proving discriminatory effect; and (c) that they failed in that proof. I do not join any inference or suggestion in the Court's opinion—if any such inference or suggestion is there—that effect may never be a controlling factor in a Title VII case, or that *Griggs v. Duke Power Co.* 401 U.S. 424, 28 L.Ed.2d 158, 91 S. Ct. 849 (1971), is no longer good law.

Mr. Justice Brennan, with whom Mr. Justice Marshall concurs, dissenting.

The Court holds today that without violating Title VII of the Civil Rights Act of 1964, 42 U.S.C. §§2000e *et seq.,* [42 U.S.C.S. §§2000e *et seq.*], a private employer may adopt a disability plan that compensates employees for all temporary disabilities except one affecting exclusively women, pregnancy. I respectfully dissent. Today's holding not only repudiates the applicable administrative guideline promulgated by the agency charged by Congress

[429 US 147]

with implementation of the Act, but also rejects the unanimous conclusion of all six Courts of Appeals that have addressed this question. *See Communications Workers v. American Tel. & Tel.* 513 F.2d 1024 (C.A.2 1975), *cert. pending,* No. 74-1601; *Wetzel v. Liberty Mut. Ins. Co.* 511 F.2d 199 (C.A.3 1975), *vacated on jurisdictional grounds,* 424 U.S. 737, 47 L.Ed.2d 435, 96 S. Ct. 1202 (1976); *Gilbert v. General Electric Co.* 519 F.2d 661 (C.A.4 1975), this case; *Tyler v. Vickery,* 517 F.2d 1089, 1097-1099 (C.A.5 1975); *Satty v. Nashville Gas Co.* 522 F.2d 850 (C.A.6 1975), *cert. pending,* No. 75-536; *Hutchison v. Lake Oswego School Dist. No. 7,* 519 F.2d 961 (C.A.9 1975), *cert. pending,* No. 75-1049.

I

This case is unusual in that it presents a question the resolution of which at first glance turns largely upon the conceptual framework chosen to identify and describe the operational features of the challenged disability program. By directing their focus upon the risks excluded from the otherwise comprehensive program, and upon the purported justifications for such exclusions, the Equal Employment Opportunity Commission, the women plaintiffs, and the lower courts reason that the pregnancy exclusion constitutes a prima facie violation of Title VII. This violation is triggered, they argue, because the omission of pregnancy from the program has the intent and effect of providing that "only women [are subjected] to a substantial risk of total loss of income because of temporary medical disability." Brief for EEOC as Amicus Curiae 12.

The Court's framework is diametrically different. It views General Electric's plan as representing a gender-free assignment of risks in accordance with normal actuarial techniques. From this perspective the lone exclusion of pregnancy is not a violation of Title VII insofar as all other disabilities are mutually covered for both sexes. This reasoning relies primarily upon the descriptive statement borrowed from

[429 US 148]

Geduldig v. Aiello, 417 U.S. 484, 496-497, 41 L.Ed.2d 256, 94 S.Ct. 2485 (1974): "There is no risk from which men are protected and women are not. Likewise, there is no risk from which women are protected and men are not." *Ante*, at 138, 50 L.Ed.2d 356. According to the Court, this assertedly neutral sorting process precludes the pregnancy omission from constituting a violation of Title VII.

Presumably, it is not self-evident that either conceptual framework is more appropriate than the other, which can only mean that further inquiry is necessary to select the more accurate and realistic analytical approach. At the outset, the soundness of the Court's underlying assumption that the plan is the untainted product of a gender-neutral risk-assignment process can be examined against the historical backdrop of General Electric's employment practices and the existence or nonexistence of gender-free policies governing the inclusion of compensable risks. Secondly, the resulting pattern of risks insured by General Electric can then be evaluated in terms of the broad social objectives promoted by Title VII. I believe that the first inquiry compels the conclusion that the Court's assumption that General Electric engaged in a gender-neutral risk-assignment process is purely fanciful. The second demonstrates that the EEOC's interpretation that the exclusion of pregnancy from a disability insurance plan is incompatible with the overall objectives of Title VII has been unjustifiably rejected.

II

Geduldig v. Aiello, supra, purports to be the starting point for the Court's analysis. There a state-operated disability insurance system containing a pregnancy exclusion was held not to violate the Equal Protection Clause. Although it quotes primarily from one footnote of that opinion at some length, *ante,* at 134-135, 50 L.Ed.2d 353, the Court finally does not grapple with *Geduldig* on its own terms.

Considered most favorably to the Court's view, *Geduldig* established the proposition that a pregnancy classification

[429 US 149]

standing alone cannot be said to fall into the category of classifications that rest explicitly on "gender as such," 417 U.S. at 496 n. 20, 41 L.Ed.2d 256, 94 S.Ct. 2485. Beyond that, *Geduldig* offers little analysis helpful to decision of this case. Surely it offends common sense to suggest, *ante*, at 136, 50 L.Ed.2d 354, that a classification revolving around pregnancy is not, at the minimum, strongly "sex related." *See, e.g., Cleveland Board of Education v. LaFleur,* 414 U.S. 632, 652, 39 L.Ed.2d 52, 94 S. Ct. 791, 67 Ohio Ops. 2d 126 (1974) (Powell, J., concurring). Indeed, even in the insurance context where neutral actuarial principles were found to have provided a legitimate and independent input into the decision-making process, *Geduldig's* outcome was qualified by the explicit reservation of a case where it could be demonstrated that a pregnancy-centered differentiation is used as a "mere pretext . . . designed to effect an invidious discrimination against the members of one sex. . . ." 417 U.S. at 496-497, n. 20, 41 L.Ed.2d 256, 94 S. Ct. 2485.

Thus, *Geduldig* itself obliges the Court to determine whether the exclusion of a sex-linked disability from the universe of compensable disabilities was actually the product of neutral, persuasive actuarial considerations, or rather stemmed from a policy that purposefully downgraded women's role in the labor force. In *Geduldig,* that inquiry coupled with the normal presumption favoring legislative action satisfied the Court that the pregnancy exclusion in fact was prompted by California's legitimate fiscal concerns, and therefore that California did not deny equal protection in effectuating reforms " 'one step at a time.' " *Id.,* at 495, 41 L.Ed.2d 256, 94 S. Ct. 2485. But the record in this case makes such deference impossible here. Instead, in reaching its conclusion that a showing of purposeful discrimination has not been made, *ante,* at 136, 50 L.Ed.2d 354, the Court simply disregards a history of General Electric practices that have served to undercut the employment opportunities of women who become pregnant while employed.[1] Moreover,

[429 US 150]

the Court studiously

1. General Electric's disability program was developed in an earlier era when women openly were presumed to play only a minor and temporary role in the labor force. As originally conceived in 1926, General Electric offered no benefit plan to its female employees because " 'women did not recognize the responsibilities of life, for they probably were hoping to get married soon and leave the company.' " App. 958, excerpted from D. Loth, Swope of G.E.: Story of Gerard Swope and General Electric in American Business (1958). It was not until the 1930's and 1940's that the Company made female employees eligible to participate in the disability program. In common with general business practice, however, General Electric continued to pursue a policy of taking pregnancy and other factors into account in order to scale women's wages at ⅔ the level of men's. *Id.,* at 1002. More recent company policies reflect common stereotypes concerning the potentialities of pregnant women, *see, e.g., Cleveland Board of Education v. LaFleur,* 414 U.S. 632, 644, 39 L.Ed.2d 52, 94 S.Ct. 791, 67 Ohio Ops. 2d 126 (1974), and have coupled forced maternity leave with the nonpayment of disability payments. Thus, the District Court found: "In certain instances it appears that the pregnant employee was re-

ignores the undisturbed conclusion of the District Court that General Electric's " 'discriminatory attitude' toward women was "a motivating factor in its policy," 375 F.Supp. 367, 383 (E.D. Va. 1974), and that the pregnancy exclusion was " 'neutral [neither] on its face' nor 'in its intent.' " *Id.,* at 382.[2]

Plainly then, the Court's appraisal of General Electric's policy as a neutral process of sorting risks and "not a gender-based discrimination at all," *ante,* at 136, 50 L.Ed.2d 345, cannot easily be squared with the historical record in this case. The Court,

[429 US 151]

therefore, proceeds to a discussion of purported neutral criteria that suffice to explain the lone exclusion of pregnancy from the program. The Court argues that pregnancy is not "comparable" to other disabilities since it is a "voluntary" condition rather than a "disease." *Ibid.* The fallacy of this argument is that even if "non-voluntariness" and "disease" are to be construed as the operational criteria for inclusion of a disability in General Electric's program, application of these criteria is inconsistent with the Court's gender-neutral interpretation of the company's policy.

For example, the characterization of pregnancy as "voluntary"[3] is not a persuasive factor, for as the Court of Appeals correctly noted, "other than for childbirth disability, [General Electric] had never construed its plan as eliminating *all* so-called 'voluntary' disabilities," including sport injuries, attempted suicides, venereal disease, disabilities incurred in the commission of a crime or during a fight, and elective cosmetic surgery. 519 F.2d, at 665. Similarly, the label "disease" rather than "disability" cannot be deemed determinative since General Electric's pregnancy disqualification also excludes the 10% of pregnancies that end in debilitating miscarriages, 375 F.Supp. at 377, the 10% of cases where pregnancies are complicated by "diseases" in the intuitive sense of the word, *ibid.,* and cases where women recovering from childbirth are stricken by severe diseases unrelated to pregnancy.[4]

[429 US 152]

Moreover, even the Court's principal argument for the plan's supposed gender neutrality cannot withstand analysis. The central analytical framework relied upon to demonstrate the absence of discrimination is the principle described in Geduldig: "There is no risk from which men are protected and women are not . . . [and] no risk from which women are protected and men are not." 417 U.S. at 496-497, 41 L.Ed.2d 256, 94 S.Ct. 2485, quoted, *ante,* at 138, 50 L.Ed.2d 356. In fostering the impression that it is faced with a mere underinclusive assignment of risks in a gender-neutral fashion—that is, all other disabilities are insured irrespective of gender—the Court's analysis proves to be simplistic and misleading. For although all mutually contractible risks are covered irrespective of gender, but *see* n. 4 *supra,* the plan also insures risks such as prostatectomies, vasectomies, and circumcisions that are specific to the reproductive system of men and for which there exist no female counterparts covered by the plan. Again, pregnancy affords the only disability, sex-specific or other-

quired to take leave of her position three months prior to birth and not permitted to return until six weeks after the birth. In other instances the periods varied. . . . In short, of all the employees it is only pregnant women who have been required to cease work regardless of their desire and physical ability to work and only they have been required to remain off their job for an arbitrary period after the birth of their child." 375 F.Supp. 367, 385. In February 1973, approximately coinciding with commencement of this suit, the company abandoned its forced-maternity-leave policy by formal directive.

2. The Court of Appeals did not affirm on the basis of this finding, since it concluded that "the statute looks to 'consequences,' not intent," and "[a]ny discrimination, such as that here, which is 'inextricably sex-linked' in consequences and result is violative of the Act." 519 F.2d 661, 664.

3. Of course, even the proposition that pregnancy is a voluntary condition is overbroad, for the District Court found that "a substantial incidence of negligent or accidental conception also occurs." 375 F.Supp. at 377. I may assume, however, for purposes of this argument, that the high incidence of voluntary pregnancies and the inability to differentiate between voluntary and involuntary conceptions, except perhaps through obnoxious, intrusive means, could justify the decision-maker's treating pregnancies as voluntarily induced.

4. The experience of one of the class plaintiffs is instructive of the reach of the pregnancy exclusion. On April 5, 1972, she took a pregnancy leave, delivering a stillborn baby some nine days later. Upon her return home, she suffered a blood clot in the lung, a condition unrelated to her pregnancy, and was rehospitalized. The company declined her claim for disability payments on the ground that pregnancy severed her eligibility under the plan. *See id.,* at 372. Had she been separated from work for any other reason—for example, during a work stoppage—the plan would have fully covered the embolism.

wise, that is excluded from coverage.[5] Accordingly, the District Court appropriately remarked:

[429 US 153]

> [T]he concern of defendants in reference to pregnancy risks, coupled with the apparent lack of concern regarding the balancing of other statistically sex-linked disabilities, buttresses the Court's conclusion that the discriminatory attitude characterized elsewhere in the Court's findings was in fact a motivating factor in its policy.
>
> 375 F.Supp. at 383.

If decision of this case, therefore, turns upon acceptance of the Court's view of General Electric's disability plan as a sex-neutral assignment of risks, or plaintiffs' perception of the plan as a sex-conscious process expressive of the secondary status of women in the company's labor force, the history of General Electric's employment practices and the absence of definable gender-neutral sorting criteria under the plan warrants rejection of the Court's view in deference to the plaintiffs'. Indeed, the fact that the Court's frame of reference lends itself to such intentional, sex-laden decisionmaking makes clear the wisdom and propriety of the EEOC's contrary approach to employment disability programs.

III

Of course, the demonstration of purposeful discrimination is not the only ground for recovery under Title VII. Notwithstanding unexplained and inexplicable implications to the contrary in the majority opinion,[6] this Court, *see Washington*

[429 US 154]

v. Davis, 426 U.S. 229, 238-239, 48 L.Ed.2d 597, 96 S.Ct. 2040 (1976); *Albemarle Paper Co. v. Moody,* 422 U.S. 405, 422, 45 L.Ed.2d 280, 95 S.Ct. 2362 (1975); *McDonnell Douglas Corp. v. Green,* 411 U.S. 792, 802, 36 L.Ed.2d 668, 93 S.Ct. 1817 (1973); *Griggs v. Duke Power Co.,* 401 U.S. 424, 432, 28 L.Ed.2d 158, 91 S.Ct. 849 (1971), and every Court of Appeals[7] now have firmly settled that a

5. Indeed, the shallowness of the Court's "underinclusive" analysis is transparent. Had General Electric assembled a catalogue of all ailments that befall humanity, and then systematically proceeded to exclude from coverage *every* disability that is female-specific or predominantly afflicts women, the Court could still reason as here that the plan operates equally: Women, like men, would be entitled to draw disability payments for their circumcisions and prostatectomies, and neither sex could claim payment for pregnancies, breast cancer, and the other excluded female-dominated disabilities. Along similar lines, any disability that occurs disproportionately in a particular group—sickle-cell anemia, for example—could be freely excluded from the plan without troubling the Court's analytical approach.

6. The cryptic "but *cf.*" citation to *McDonnell Douglas Corp. v. Green,* 411 U.S. 792, 36 L.Ed.2d 668, 93 S.Ct. 1817 (1973), *ante,* at 137, 50 L.Ed.2d 355, is perhaps the most mystifying. McDonnell involved a private non-class action under §703(a)(1) of Title VII in which the plaintiff explicitly complained that he was discharged from employment for racial, rather than licit, motives. 411 U.S. 796, 36 L.Ed.2d 668, 93 S.Ct. 1817. In such a case, where questions of motivation openly form the thrust of an individual plaintiff's complaint, the "effects" that company policies may have had on an entire class of persons understandably are only tangentially placed in issue, *see id.,* at 805 n. 19, 36 L.Ed.2d 668, 93 S.Ct. 1817. Even so, the Court expressly held that a prima facie violation of Title VII could be proved without affirmatively demonstrating that purposeful discrimination had occurred. Instead, the Court concluded that such an illicit purpose is inferable from the interplay of four factors which together reveal that the employers' policies have worked to disadvantage the complainant vis-a-vis other prospective employees. *See id.,* at 802, 36 L.Ed.2d 668, 93 S.Ct. 1817. Only if the employer then satisfies the burden of articulating "some legitimate, nondiscriminatory reason for the employee's rejection," *ibid.,* must the latter actually seek to establish an intent to discriminate. *Id.,* at 804, 36 L.Ed.2d 668, 93 S.Ct. 1817. Even at this juncture, however, *McDonnell* makes clear that statistical evidence of the racial composition of the labor force—that is, a statistical showing of adverse impact on the protected group of which the individual plaintiff is part—will be persuasive evidence that the failure to rehire the particular complainant "conformed to a general pattern of discrimination against" his group. *Id.,* at 805, 36 L.Ed.2d 668, 93 S.Ct. 1817. Thus, *McDonnell* went far in allowing proof of "effect," even in the setting of an individualized rather than group claim of discrimination.

Equally unacceptable is the implication in the penultimate paragraph of the opinion, *ante,* at 145, 50 L.Ed. 2d 360, that the Fourteenth Amendment standard of discrimination is coterminous with that applicable to Title VII. Not only is this fleeting dictum irrelevant to the reasoning that precedes it, not only does it conflict with a long line of cases to the contrary, *infra,* at 153 and this page, 50 L.Ed.2d 365, but it is flatly contradicted by the central holding of last Term's *Washington v. Davis,* 426 U.S. 229, 239, 48 L.Ed.2d 597, 96 S.Ct. 2040 (1976): "We have never held that the constitutional standard for adjudicating claims of invidious racial discrimination is identical to the standards applicable under Title VII, and we decline to do so today."

7. *See Boston Chapter NAACP v. Beecher,* 504 F.2d 1017, 1020 (C.A.1 1974); *United States v. Wood, Wire & Metal Lathers, Local Union 46,* 471 F.2d 408, 414 n. 11 (C.A.2 1973); *Pennsylvania v. O'Neill,* 473 F.2d 1029 (C.A.3 1973) (en banc); *United States v. Chesapeake*

[429 US 155]

prima facie violation of Title VII, whether under §703(a)(1) or §703(a)(2), also is established by demonstrating that a facially neutral classification has the *effect* of discriminating against members of a defined class.

General Electric's disability program has three divisible sets of effects. First, the plan covers all disabilities that mutually afflict both sexes. But *see* n. 4 *supra.* Second, the plan insures against all disabilities that are male-specific or have a predominant impact on males. Finally, all female-specific and female-impacted disabilities are covered, except for the most prevalent, pregnancy. The Court focuses on the first factor—the equal inclusion of mutual risks—and therefore understandably can identify no discriminatory effect arising from the plan. In contrast, the EEOC and plaintiffs rely upon the unequal exclusion manifested in effects two and three to pinpoint an adverse impact on women. However one defines the profile of risks protected by General Electric, the determinative question must be whether the social policies and aims to be furthered by Title VII and filtered through the phrase "to discriminate" contained in §703(a)(1) fairly forbid an ultimate pattern of coverage that insures all risks except a commonplace one that is applicable to women but not to men.

As a matter of law and policy, this is a paradigm example of the type of complex economic and social inquiry that Congress wisely left to resolution by the EEOC pursuant to its Title VII mandate. *See* H.R. Rep. No. 92-238, p. 8 (1972). And, accordingly, prior Title VII decisions have consistently acknowledged the unique persuasiveness of EEOC

[429 US 156]

interpretations in this area. These prior decisions, rather than providing merely that Commission guidelines are "entitled to consideration," as the Court allows, *ante,* at 141, 50 L.Ed.2d 357 hold that the EEOC's interpretations should receive "great deference." ***Albemarle Paper Co. v. Moody, supra,*** at 431, 45 L.Ed.2d 280, 95 S.Ct. 2362; ***Griggs v. Duke Power Co., supra,*** at 433-434, 28 L.Ed.2d 158, 91 S.Ct. 849; ***Phillips v. Martin Marietta Corp.*** 400 U.S. 542, 545, 27 L.Ed.2d 613, 91 S.Ct. 496 (1971) (Marshall, J., concurring). Nonetheless, the Court today abandons this standard in order squarely to repudiate the 1972 Commission guideline providing that "[d]isabilities caused or contributed to by pregnancy . . . are, for all job-related purposes, temporary disabilities . . . [under] any health or temporary disability insurance or sick leave plan. . . ." 29 C.F.R. §1604.10 (b) (1975). This rejection is attributed to two interrelated events: an eight-year delay between Title VII's enactment and the promulgation of the Commission's guideline, and interim letters by the EEOC's General Counsel expressing the view that pregnancy is not necessarily includable as a compensable disability. Neither event supports the Court's refusal to accord "great deference" to the EEOC's interpretation.

It is true, as noted, *ante*, at 143 50 L.Ed.2d 358, that only brief mention of sex discrimination appears in the early legislative history of Title VII. It should not be surprising, therefore, that the EEOC, charged with a fresh and uncharted mandate, candidly acknowledged that further study was required before the contours of sex discrimination as proscribed by Congress could be defined. *See* 30 *Fed. Reg.* 14927 (1965). Although proceeding cautiously, the Commission from the outset acknowledged the relationship between sex discrimination and pregnancy, announcing that "policies would have to be devised which afforded female employees reasonable job protection during periods of pregnancy." EEOC First Annual Report to Congress, fiscal year 1965-1966, p. 40 (1967). During the succeeding seven years, the EEOC worked to develop a coherent policy toward pregnancy-oriented employment practices

[429 US 157]

both through the pursuit of its normal adjudicatory functions[8] and by engaging in comprehensive

---

& Ohio R. Co. 471 F.2d 582, 586 (C.A.4 1972); *United States v. Hayes Int'l Corp.* 456 F.2d 112, 120 (C.A.5 1972); *United States v. Masonry Contractors Assn. of Memphis, Inc.* 497 F.2d 871, 875 (C.A.6 1974); *United States v. Carpenters,* 457 F.2d 210, 214 (C.A.7 1972); *United States v. N. L. Industries, Inc.* 479 F.2d 354, 368 (C.A.8 1973); *United States v. Ironworkers Local 86,* 443 F.2d 544, 550-551 (C.A.9 1971); *Muller v. United States Steel Corp.* 509 F.2d 923, 927 (C.A.10 1975); *Davis v. Washington,* 168 U.S. App. D.C. 42, 46, 512 F.2d 956, 960 (1975), *revd. on constitutional grounds,* 426 U.S. 229, 48 L.Ed.2d 597, 96 S.Ct 2040 (1976).

Indeed, following Griggs, Congress in 1972 revised Title VII, and expressly endorsed use of the "effect only" test outlined therein in identifying "increasingly complex" "forms and incidents of discrimination" that "may not appear obvious at first glance." *See H.R.* Rep. No. 92-238, p. 8 (1972).

8. For synopses of the Commission's positions regarding pregnancy and sex discrimination adopted in the course of administrative decisionmaking and litigation activities, *see* the EEOC's Annual Reports to Congress.

studies with such organizations as the President's Citizens' Advisory Council on the Status of Women. *See, e.g.,* Address of Jacqueline G. Gutwillig, Chairwoman, Citizens' Advisory Council, cited in App. 1159. These investigations on the role of pregnancy in the labor market coupled with the Commission's "review . . . [of] its case decisions on maternity preparatory to issuing formal guidelines," *id.,* at 1161, culminated in the 1972 guideline, the agency's first formalized, systematic statement on "[e]mployment policies relating to pregnancy and childbirth."

Therefore, while some eight years had elapsed prior to the issuance of the 1972 guideline, and earlier opinion letters had refused to impose liability on employers during this period of deliberation, no one can or does deny that the final EEOC determination followed thorough and well-informed consideration. Indeed, realistically viewed, this extended evaluation of an admittedly complex problem and an unwillingness to impose additional, potentially premature costs on employers during the decisionmaking stages ought to be perceived as a practice to be commended. It is bitter irony that the care preceded promulgation of the 1972 guideline is today condemned by the Court as tardy indecisiveness, its unwillingness irresponsibly to challenge employers' practices during the formative period is labeled as evidence of inconsistency, and this indecisiveness and inconsistency are bootstrapped into reasons for denying the Commission's interpretation its due deference.

For me, the 1972 guideline represents a particularly conscientious and reasonable product of EEOC deliberations and, therefore, merits our "great deference." Certainly, I can find (U.S.) [429 U.S. 158] no basis for concluding that the guideline is out of step with Congressional intent. *See Espinoza v. Farah Mfg. Co.* 414 U.S. 86, 94, 38 L.Ed.2d 287, 94 S. Ct. 334 (1973). On the contrary, prior to 1972, Congress enacted just such a pregnancy-inclusive rule to govern the distribution of benefits for "sickness" under the Railroad Unemployment Insurance Act, 45 U.S.C. §351 (k)(2) [45 U.S.C.S. §351(k)(2)]. Furthermore, shortly following the announcement of the EEOC's rule, Congress approved and the President signed an essentially identical promulgation by the Department of Health, Education, and Welfare under Title IX of the Education Amendments of 1972, 20 U.S.C. §1681(a) (1970 ed. Supp. II) [20 U.S.C.S. §1681(a)]. *See* 45 C.F.R. §86.57(c) (1976). Moreover, federal workers subject to the jurisdiction of the Civil Service Commission now are eligible for maternity and pregnancy coverage under their sick leave program. *See* Federal Personnel Manual, c. 630, subch. 13, S13-2 (FPM Supp. 990-2, May 6, 1975).

These policy formulations are reasonable responses to the uniform testimony of governmental investigations which show that pregnancy exclusions built into disability programs both financially burden women workers and act to break down the continuity of the employment relationship, thereby exacerbating women's comparatively transient role in the labor force. *See, e.g.,* U.S. Dept. of Commerce, Consumer Income (Series P-60, No. 93, July 1974); Women's Bureau, U.S. Dept. of Labor, Underutilization of Women Workers (rev. ed. 1971). In dictating pregnancy coverage under Title VII, the EEOC's guideline merely settled upon a solution now accepted by every other Western industrial country. Dept. of Health, Education, and Welfare, Social Security Programs Throughout the World, 1971, pp. ix, xviii, xix (Research Report No. 40). I find it difficult to comprehend that such a construction can be anything but a "sufficiently reasonable" one to be "accepted by the reviewing courts." *Train v. Natural Resources Def. Council,* 421 U.S. 60, 75, 43 L.Ed.2d 731, 95 S.Ct. 1470 (1975).

[429 US 159]

The Court's belief that the concept of discrimination cannot reach disability policies effecting "an *additional* risk, unique to women . . .," *ante,* at 139, 50 L.Ed.2d 356, is plainly out of step with the decision three Terms ago in *Lau v. Nichols,* 414 U.S. 563, 39 L.Ed.2d 1, 94 S.Ct. 786 (1974), interpreting another provision of the Civil Rights Act. There a unanimous Court recognized that discrimination is a social phenomenon encased in a social context and, therefore, unavoidably takes its meaning from the desired end products of the relevant legislative enactment, end products that may demand due consideration to the uniqueness of "disadvantaged" individuals.[9] A realistic un-

9. *Lau* held that the failure to provide special language instruction to Chinese-speaking students in San Francisco schools violated the ban against racial or national origin discrimination contained in §601 of the Civil Rights Act of 1964. The Court concluded that the Act, as interpreted by the administrative regulations promulgated by the Department of Health, Education, and Welfare addressed *"effect*[*s*] [to discriminate] even though no purposeful design is present," and ultimately sought to further the broad goal of insuring "a meaningful opportunity to participate in the [schools'] educational program. . . ." 414 U.S. at 568, 39 L.Ed.2d 1,

derstanding of conditions found in today's labor environment warrants taking pregnancy into account in fashioning disability policies. Unlike the hypothetical situations conjectured by the Court, *ante,* at 139-140, and n. 17, 50 L.Ed.2d 356, contemporary disability

[429 US 160]

programs are not creatures of a social or cultural vacuum devoid of stereotypes and signals concerning the pregnant woman employee. Indeed, no one seriously contends that General Electric or other companies actually conceptualized or developed their comprehensive insurance programs disability-by-disability in a strictly sex-neutral fashion.[10] Instead, the company has devised a policy that, but for pregnancy, offers protection for all risks, even those that are "unique to" men or heavily male dominated. In light of this social experience, the history of General Electric's employment practices, the otherwise all-inclusive design of its disability program, and the burdened role of the contemporary working woman, the EEOC's construction of sex discrimination under §703(a)(1) is fully consonant with the ultimate objective of Title VII, "to assure equality of employment opportunities and to eliminate those discriminatory practices and devices which have fostered [sexually] stratified job environments to the disadvantage of [women]." *McDonnell Douglas Corp. v. Green,* 411 U.S. at 800, 36 L.Ed.2d 668, 93 S.Ct. 1817.

I would affirm the judgment of the Court of Appeals.

Mr. Justice Stevens, dissenting.

The word "discriminate" does not appear in the Equal Protection Clause.[1] Since the plaintiffs' burden of proving a prima facie violation of that constitutional provision is significantly heavier than the burden of proving a prima facie violation of a statutory prohibition against discrimination,[2] the constitutional holding in *Geduldig v. Aiello,* 417

[429 US 161]

U.S. 484, 41 L.Ed.2d 256, 94 S.Ct. 2485 (1974), does not control the question of statutory interpretation presented by this case. And, of course, when it enacted Title VII of the Civil Rights Act of 1964, Congress could not possibly have relied on language which this Court was to use a decade later in the Geduldig opinion.[3] We are, therefore, presented with a fresh, and rather simple, question of statutory construction: Does a contract between a company and its employees which treats the risk of absenteeism caused by pregnancy differently from any other kind of absence discriminate against certain individuals because of their sex?

An affirmative answer to that question would not necessarily lead to a conclusion of illegality, because a statutory affirmative defense might justify the disparate treatment of pregnant women in certain situations. In this case, however, the company has not established any such justification. On the other hand, a negative answer to the threshold question would not necessarily defeat plaintiffs' claim because facially neutral criteria may be illegal if they have a discriminatory effect.[4] An analysis of the effect of a company's rules relating to absenteeism would be appropriate if those rules referred only to neutral criteria,

94 S.Ct. 786. Faced with such a generalized objective, the Court repudiated the analysis of the Court of Appeals which had relied upon San Francisco's commitment of equal educational offerings and resources to every child as the basis for concluding that Chinese students have suffered no discrimination due to the failure to adjust the school program to remedy their unique language deficiencies. Instead, the Court agreed that the anti-discrimination language fairly can be read "to require affirmative remedial efforts to give special attention to linguistically deprived children." *Id.,* at 571, 39 L.Ed.2d 1, 94 S.Ct. 786 (Stewart, J., concurring). Similarly, given the broad social objectives that underlie Title VII, *see infra,* at 160, 50 L.Ed.2d 369, and General Electric's apparent unhesitancy to take into account the unique physical characteristics of their male workers in defining the breadth of disability coverage, *see supra,* at 152, 50 L.Ed.2d 364, ample support appears for upholding the EEOC's view that pregnancy must be treated accordingly.

10. *See, e.g.,* n. 1, *supra.*

1. The word does, however, appear in a number of statutes, but has by no means been given a uniform interpretation in those statutes. *Compare FTC v. Morton Salt Co.* 334 U.S. 37, 44-45, 92 L.Ed. 1196, 68 S.Ct. 822, 1 A.L.R.2d 260 (1948) (Robinson-Patman Act) with *N.L.R.B. v. Great Dane Trailers,* 388 U.S. 26, 32-35, 18 L.Ed.2d 1027, 87 S.Ct. 1792 (1967) (National Labor Relations Act).

2. *Washington v. Davis,* 426 U.S. 229, 238-248, 48 L.Ed.2d 597, 96 S.Ct. 2040 (1976).

3. Quite clearly Congress could not have intended to adopt this Court's analysis of sex discrimination because it was seven years after the statute was passed that the Court first intimated that the concept of sex discrimination might have some relevance to equal protection analysis. *See Reed v. Reed,* 404 U.S. 71, 30 L.Ed.2d 225, 92 S.Ct. 251 (1971).

4. *Griggs v. Duke Power Co.* 401 U.S. 424, 429-432, 28 L.Ed.2d 158, 91 S.Ct. 849.

such as whether an absence was voluntary or involuntary, or perhaps particularly costly. This case, however, does not involve rules of that kind.

Rather, the rule at issue places the risk of absence caused by pregnancy in a class by itself.[5] By definition, such a

[429 US 162]

rule discriminates on account of sex; for it is the capacity to become pregnant which primarily differentiates the female from the male. The analysis is the same whether the rule relates to hiring, promotion, the acceptability of an excuse for absence, or an exclusion from a disability insurance plan. Accordingly, without reaching the questions of motive, administrative expertise, and policy, which Mr. Justice Brennan so persuasively exposes, or the question of effect to which Mr. Justice Stewart and Mr. Justice Blackmun refer, I conclude that the language of the statute plainly requires the result which the Courts of Appeals have reached unanimously.

EQUAL PAY ACT OF 1963

The Equal Pay Act of 1963 (the Equal Pay Act), 29 U.S.C. §206(d), which amended the Fair Labor Standards Act of 1938, 29 U.S.C. §1, *et seq.*, relates to wage differentials based on sex. Section 206(d) makes it unlawful for an employer to discriminate between the sexes in the payment of wages for equal work. Section 206(d)(1) provides that:

> No employer having employees subject to any provisions of this section shall discriminate, within any establishment in which such employees are employed, between employees on the basis of sex by paying *wages* to employees in such establishment at a rate less than the rate at which he pays wages to employees of the opposite sex in such establishment for equal work on jobs the performance of which requires equal skill, effort, and responsibility, and which are performed under similar working conditions, except where such payment is made pursuant to (i) a seniority system; (ii) a merit system; (iii) a system which measures earnings by quantity or quality of production; or (iv) a differential based on any other factor other than sex. . . .
>
> (Emphasis added).

The Equal Pay Act was enacted for the purpose of correcting sex-based wage differentials which existed in industries engaged in commerce or in the production of goods for commerce. Any employer covered by the Fair Labor Standards Act is subject to this requirement.

The Equal Pay Act, like Title VII, has had an impact on the structure and content of pension and welfare plans.

Wages, Remuneration Defined

The term "wages" as used in Section 206(d)(1) has the same meaning as it has elsewhere in the Fair Labor Standards Act. (The Fair Labor Standards Act requires employers to pay non-exempt employees for overtime at one and one-half times their regular rate.) For purposes of determining an employee's regular rate of pay, wages paid to an employee generally include all payments made to or on behalf of an employee as remuneration for employment. Section 207(e) provides that wages include:

> all remuneration for employment paid to, or on behalf of, the employee. . . .

This definition would seem to encompass at least some benefits provided pursuant to plans.

This implication is reinforced by Section 207(e) (3)(b) and (4). Section 207(e)(3)(b) and (4) provide that "remuneration" does *not* include:

> (3) sums paid in recognition of service performed during a given period if . . . (b) the payments are made pursuant to a bona fide profit-sharing plan or trust or bona fide thrift or savings plan, meeting the requirements of the Administrator set forth in appropriate regulations which he shall issue, having due regard among other relevant factors, to the extent to which the amounts paid to the employee are determined without regard to hours of work, production, or efficiency;
>
> . . . . .
>
> (4) contributions irrevocably made by an employer to a trustee or third person pursuant to a bona fide plan for providing old-age, retirement, life, accident, or health insurance or similar benefit for the employees. . . .

---

5. It is not accurate to describe the program as dividing "'potential recipients into two groups—pregnant women and nonpregnant persons.'" *Ante,* at 135, 50 L.Ed.2d 353. Insurance programs, company policies, and employment contracts all deal with future *risks* rather than historic facts. The classification is between persons who face a risk of pregnancy and those who do not.

Nor is it accurate to state that under the plan "'[t]here is no risk from which men are protected and women are not.'" *Ibid.* If the word "risk" is used narrowly, men are protected against the risks associated with a prostate operation whereas women are not. If the word is used more broadly to describe the risk of uncompensated unemployment caused by physical disability, men receive total protection (subject to the 60% and 26-week limitations) against that risk whereas women receive only partial protection.

By exempting certain benefits from the definition of "remuneration" if specified conditions are met, Sections 207(c)(3)(b) and (4) raise the clear implication that employee benefits constitute remuneration.

Requirements for Plan Qualification

Both Sections 207(e)(3)(b) and (4) have been interpreted by the Wage and Hour Division of the Department of Labor's Employment Standards Administration. Regulations set forth the requirements of a "bona fide thrift or savings plan" under Section 207(e)(3)(b). These regulations delineate both the essential requirements for qualification under this subsection and the disqualifying provisions. For example, a qualified plan must specifically set forth the category or categories of employees participating in the plan and the basis of their eligibility. *See* 29 C.F.R. §547.1(c). Another requirement for qualification is a definite (as opposed to a discretionary) contribution formula. *See* 29 C.F.R. §547.1(d). It is interesting to note that under the Internal Revenue Code of 1954 (discussed in Chapter 2), either a definite or discretionary formula is acceptable.

An example of a disqualifying provision is the requirement that the amounts contributed by the employer under the plan may not be based on the employee's hours of work, production or efficiency. *See* 29 C.F.R. §547.2(c).

Regulations also set forth the requirements for qualification under Section 207(e)(4), which includes several conditions for the exclusion of pension and health and welfare plan contributions from the definition of "remuneration." Plans satisfying the requirements for qualification delineated in Section 401(a) of the Code (i.e., tax-qualified plans) are deemed to have met some of these conditions. *See* 29 C.F.R. §778.215(b). In addition, tax-qualified plans must satisfy other conditions, and other plans, e.g., non-qualified plans and health and welfare plans, must satisfy all of the requirements. For example, the primary purpose of the plan must be to provide systematically for the payment of benefits to employees on account of death, disability, advanced age, retirement, illness, medical expenses, hospitalization and other similar reasons. *See* 29 C.F.R. §778.215(a)(2). The employer's contributions must be paid irrevocably to a trustee who assumes the usual fiduciary responsibilities imposed upon trustees under the applicable law.

As under Title VII, numerous interpretations under the Equal Pay Act have applied its antidiscrimination provisions to both pension and welfare benefit plans. For example, the Wage and Hour Division has interpreted the Equal Pay Act exclusions from the definition of "remuneration" as requiring *either* equal employer contributions *or* equal benefits paid from a plan providing insurance coverage or similar benefits. *See* 29 C.F.R. §§800.116(d), 800.151. (It is important to note that the EEOC has interpreted Title VII as requiring equal benefits.) Similarly, the provision of group insurance for one sex only is impermissible. *See* 29 C.F.R. §§800.116, 800.142.

AGE DISCRIMINATION IN EMPLOYMENT ACT OF 1967

The Age Discrimination in Employment Act of 1967 (the '67 Act), 29 U.S.C. §621, *et seq.*, prohibits discrimination in the terms and conditions of employment on the basis of age. Section 4(a)(1) of the '67 Act provides that it is unlawful for an employer:

> (1) To fail or refuse to hire or to discharge any individual or otherwise discriminate against any individual with respect to his compensation, terms, conditions, or privileges of employment, because of such individual's age;
>
> (2) To limit, segregate, or classify his employees in any way which would deprive or tend to deprive any individual of employment opportunities or otherwise adversely affect his status as an employee, because of such individual's age; or
>
> (3) To reduce the wage rate of any employee in order to comply with this Chapter.

Provisions Examined

These provisions were designed to promote employment of older persons based on their ability rather than their age, and to prohibit arbitrary age discrimination in employment. The '67 Act applies to "employers" (and to certain "employment agencies"), and its provisions protect individuals who are at least 40 years of age but less than 65 years of age. (It is important to note that the '67 Act does not preempt state laws. For example, California and Alaska have enacted laws with no upper age limit and the '67 Act does not preempt these more liberal laws.)

The term "employer" is defined in the '67 Act as "any person engaged in an industry effecting commerce who has 25 or more employees," and it also includes "any agent of such a person." The limitation of the protected category to individuals who are at least 40 years of age but less than 65 years of age means that it is unlawful for an employer to discriminate in hiring or in any other employment practice by giving preference because of age to an individual outside of the protected category—e.g., an individual 30 years old—over another individual who is within the 40-65 age bracket. Similarly, an employer may violate the '67 Act, in situations where it applies, when one individual within the age bracket of 40-65 is given job preference in hiring, assigning, promotion or any other term, condition or privilege of employment, on the basis of age, over another individual within the same age bracket.

It is important to note that the term "compensation" includes almost all remuneration paid to an employee for his services. It is also important to note that the phrase "terms, conditions, or privileges of employment" encompasses a broad range of job-related factors including pension and welfare benefits. An employer will be considered to have violated the '67 Act if he discriminates against any individual within its protection because of age with respect to these and other fringe benefits, unless a statutory exception from the broad prohibitions is available.

While §4(a)(1) is quite broad, §4(f)(2) specifically provides that it is not unlawful:

> To observe the terms of any bona fide seniority system or any bona fide employee benefit plan such as a retirement, pension, or insurance plan, which is not a subterfuge to evade the purpose of this Act, except that no such employee benefit plan shall excuse the failure to hire any individual. . . .

The interpretation of this language by both the Wage and Hour Division of the Department of Labor's Employment Standards Administration and the courts has had an impact on the structure and content of pension and welfare plans. The two areas of most significant impact relate to involuntary retirement before age 65 and costs and benefits under pension and welfare plans.

Involuntary Retirement

While most pension plans provide that age 65 is the "normal retirement age," some plans provide for an earlier retirement age. In some of these plans the earlier retirement age, e.g., age 60, is not only the "normal" retirement age but also the mandatory or compulsory retirement age.

The Department of Labor originally took the position that the '67 Act authorized "involuntary retirement irrespective of age, provided that such retirement is pursuant to the terms of a retirement or pension plan meeting the requirements of §4(f)(2)." 29 C.F.R. §860.110. However, with the *McMann* case, the Department seems to have changed its position.

In 1941, United Airlines established a pension plan providing for "normal retirement" at age 60. McMann was employed by United Airlines in 1944, became a participant in the plan in 1964, and was involuntarily retired at age 60 in 1973. He applied for and received an opinion from the Department of Labor that United's plan was bona fide and did not appear to be a subterfuge to evade the purposes of the '67 Act, but he still decided to file suit against United. McMann lost in District Court, but won at the Court of Appeals level. The Fourth Circuit held that a pre-age 65 retirement falls within the meaning of "subterfuge" unless the employer can show that the "early retirement provision . . . has some economic or business purpose other than arbitrary age discrimination." *McMann v. United Airlines, Inc.*, 542 F.2d 217, 221 (4th Cir. 1976). McMann's success was in part attributable to the support he received from the Secretary of Labor. In the Court of Appeals, the Secretary of Labor filed a "friend of the court" brief contending that enforcement of the age 60 retirement provision, even under a bona fide plan instituted in good faith in 1941, was subterfuge to evade the '67 Act.

The Supreme Court reversed the Court of Appeals, and held that United's pension plan fell within the §4(f)(2) exception.

UNITED AIRLINES V. McMANN

____ U.S. ____ (1977)

MR. CHIEF JUSTICE BURGER, delivered the opinion of the Court.

The question presented in this case is whether, under the Age Discrimination in Employment Act of 1967, retirement of an employee over his objection and prior to reaching age 65 is permissible under the provisions of a bona fide retirement plan established by the employer in 1941 and joined by the employee in 1964. We granted certiorari to resolve a conflict between the holdings of the Fifth Circuit in *Brennan v. Taft Broadcasting Co.,* 500 F.2d 212 (1974), and the Fourth Circuit now before us. *See Zinger v. Blanchette,* 549 F.2d 901 (C.A.3 1977), *petition for cert. filed,* April 7, 1977 (No. 76-1375).

I

The operative facts were stipulated by the parties in the District Court and are not controverted here. McMann joined United Air Lines, Inc. in 1944, and continued as an employee until his retirement at age 60 in 1973. Over the years he held various positions with United and at retirement held that of technical specialist-aircraft systems. At the time McMann was first employed, United maintained a formal retirement income plan it had inaugurated in 1941, in which McMann was eligible to participate, but was not compelled to join.[1] He voluntarily joined the plan in January of 1964. The application form McMann signed showed the normal retirement age for participants in his category was 60 years.

McMann reached his 60th birthday on January 23, 1973, and was retired on February 1, 1973, over his objection. He then filed a notice of intent to sue United for violation of the Act pursuant to 29 U.S.C. §626(d). Although he received an opinion from the Department of Labor that United's plan was bona fide and did not appear to be a subterfuge to evade the purposes of the Act, he brought this suit.

McMann's suit in the District Court seeking injunctive relief, reinstatement and backpay alleged his forced retirement was solely because of his age and was unlawful under the Act. United's response was that McMann was retired in compliance with the provisions of a bona fide retirement plan which he had voluntarily joined. On facts as stipulated, the District Court granted United's motion for summary judgment.

In the Court of Appeals it was conceded the plan was bona fide "in the sense that it exists and pays benefits."[2] But McMann, supported by a brief *amicus curiae* filed in that court by the Secretary of Labor, contended the enforcement of the age 60 retirement provision, even under a bona fide plan instituted in good faith in 1941, was a subterfuge to evade the Act.[3]

The Court of Appeals agreed, holding that a pre-age 65 retirement falls within the meaning of "subterfuge" unless the employer can show that the "early retirement provision . . . has some economic or business purpose other than arbitrary age discrimination." *McMann v. United Air Lines, Inc.,* 542 F.2d 217, 221 (1976). The Court of Appeals remanded the case to the District Court to allow United an opportunity to show an economic or business purpose and United sought review here.

We reverse.

II

Section 2(b) of the Age Discrimination in Employment Act of 1967 recites that its purpose is

> to promote employment of older persons based on their ability rather than age; to prohibit arbitrary age discrimination in employment; to help employers and workers find ways of meeting problems arising from the impact of age on employment.
>
> 29 U.S.C. §621(b).

Section 4(a)(1) of the Act makes it unlawful for an employer

> to discharge any individual or otherwise discriminate against any individual with respect to his compensation, terms, conditions, or privileges of employment, because of such individual's age. . . .
>
> 29 U.S.C. §623(a)(1).

The Act covers individuals between ages 40 and 65, 29 U.S.C. §631, but does not prohibit all enforced retirements prior to age 65; some are permitted under §4(f)(2) which provides:

> It shall not be unlawful for an employer . . . or labor organization to observe the terms of a bona fide seniority system or any bona fide employee benefit plan such as a retirement, pension, or insurance plan which is not a subterfuge to evade the purposes of this [Act], except that no such employee benefit plan shall excuse the failure to hire any individual. . . .
>
> 29 U.S.C. §623(f)(2). *See infra,* at 6-10.

McMann argues the term "normal retirement age" is not defined in the plan other than in a provision that "A Participant's Normal Retirement Date is the first day of the month following his 60th birthday." From this he contends normal retirement age does not mean mandatory or compelled retirement at age 60, and United therefore did not retire him "to observe the terms" of the plan as required by §4(f)(2). As to this claim, however, we accept the analysis of the plan by the Court of Appeals, Fourth Circuit:

> While the meaning of the word "normal" in this context is not free from doubt, counsel agreed in oral argument on the manner in which the plan is operated in practice. The employee has no discretion whether to continue beyond the "normal" retirement age. United legally may retain employees such as McMann past age 60, but has never done so; its policy has been to retire all employees at the "normal" age. Given these facts, we conclude that *for purposes of this decision, the plan should be regarded as one requiring re-*

1. The plan paid retirement benefits pursuant to a group annuity contract between United and two life insurance companies.

2. The same concession was made in this Court.

3. No brief *amicus* was filed on behalf of the Department of Labor in this Court, but after submission of the case following oral argument the Solicitor General wrote a letter to the Clerk of this Court stating that the Government agreed with the Fourth Circuit and was prepared to file a brief *amicus* within three weeks. The Rules of this Court do not allow the filing of briefs *amicus* after oral argument. See Rule 42. No motion for leave to file a brief *amicus* was filed.

tirement at age 60 rather than one permitting it at the option of the employer.

542 F.2d, at 219. (Emphasis supplied.)

McMann had filed a grievance challenging his retirement since, as a former pilot, he held a position on the pilots' seniority roster. In that arbitration proceeding he urged that "normal" means "average" and so long as a participant is in good health and fit for duty he should be retained past age 60. The ruling in the arbitration proceeding was that " '[n]ormal' means regular or standard, not average, not only as a matter of linguistics but also in the general context of retirement and pension plans and the settled practice at United." It was also ruled that the involuntary retirement of McMann "was taken in accordance with an established practice uniformly applied to all members of the bargaining unit."

Though the District Court made no separate finding as to the meaning of "normal" in this context, it had before it the definition ascribed in the arbitration proceeding and that award was incorporated by reference in the court's findings and conclusions. In light of the facts stipulated by the parties and found by the District Court, we also accept the Court of Appeals' view as to the meaning of "normal."[4]

In *Brennan v. Taft Broadcasting Co., supra,* at 215, the Fifth Circuit held that establishment of a bona fide retirement plan long before enactment of the Act "eliminat[ed] any notion that it was adopted as a subterfuge for evasion."[5] In rejecting the *Taft* reasoning, the Fourth Circuit emphasized that it distinguished between the Act and the *purposes* of the Act. The distinction relied on is untenable because the Act is the vehicle by which its purposes are expressed and carried out; it is difficult to conceive of a subterfuge to evade the one which does not also evade the other.

McMann argues that §4(f)(2) was not intended to authorize involuntary retirement before age 65, but was only intended to make it economically feasible for employers to hire older employees by permitting the employers to give such older employees lesser retirement and other benefits than provided for younger employees. We are persuaded that the language of §4(f)(2) was not intended to have such a limited effect.

In *Zinger v. Blanchette,* 549 F.2d 901 (1977), *petition for cert. filed,* April 7, 1977 (No. 76-1375), the Third Circuit had before it both the *Taft* and *McMann* decisions. It accepted *McMann's* distinction between the Act and its purposes, which, in this setting, we do not, but nevertheless concluded:

> The primary purpose of the Act is to prevent age discrimination in *hiring* and *discharging* workers. There is, however, a clear, measurable difference between outright discharge and retirement, a distinction that cannot be overlooked in analyzing the Act. While discharge without compensation is obviously undesirable, retirement on an adequate pension is generally regarded with favor. A careful examination of the legislative history demonstrates that, while cognizant of the disruptive effect retirement may have on individuals, Congress continued to regard retirement plans favorably and chose therefore to legislate only with respect to discharge.

549 F.2d at 905. (Emphasis supplied.)

The dissent relies heavily upon the legislative history, which by traditional canons of interpretation is irrelevant to an unambiguous statute. However, in view of the recourse to the legislative history we turn to that aspect to demonstrate the absence of any indication of Congressional intent to undermine the countless bona fide retirement plans existing in 1967 when the Act was passed.

---

4. We note, too, that the Department of Labor's interpretation of §4(f)(2), issued nearly contemporaneously with the effective date of the Act, was that the meaning did not turn on whether or not all employees under a plan are required to retire at the same age:

> . . . The fact that an employer may decide to permit certain employees to continue working beyond the age stipulated in the formal retirement program does not, in and of itself, render an otherwise bona fide plan invalid insofar as the exception provided in Section 4(f)(2) is concerned.

29 C.F.R. §860.110(a) (as amended).

The Department's more recent position on the section is that pre-65 retirements "are unlawful unless the mandatory retirement provision . . . is required by the terms of the plan and is not optional. . . ." Dept. of Labor Ann. Rep. on Age Discrimination in Employment Act of 1967, at 17 (1975). Having concluded, as did the Court of Appeals, that the United plan calls for mandatory retirement at age 60, however, we need not consider this further.

5. Similarly, in *de Loraine v. MEBA Pension Trust,* 499 F.2d 49 (C.A.2), *cert. denied,* 419 U.S. 1009 (1974), the court said a bona fide pension plan established in 1955 was not a subterfuge. That case did not properly present the question of whether the Act forbade involuntary retirement before age 65 and the court did not purport to decide it. 499 F.2d. at 51 n. 7. *Steiner v. National League of Professional Baseball Clubs,* 377 F.Supp. 945, 948 (C.D. Cal. 1974), *aff'd* No. 74-2604 (C.A.9 1975), likewise rejected the idea that a pension plan established long before the Act could be a subterfuge saying, "Obviously it could not have been evolved in an attempt to circumvent any public policy or law."

Such a pervasive impact on bona fide existing plans should not be read into the Act without a clear, unambiguous expression in the statute.

When the Senate Subcommittee was considering the bill, the then Secretary of Labor, Willard Wirtz, was asked what effect the Act would have on existing pension plans. His response was:

> It would be my judgment . . . that the effect of the provisions in 4(f)(2) [of the original bill] . . . is to protect the application of almost all plans which I know anything about. . . . It is intended to protect retirement plans.
>
> Hearings on S. 830 before the Subcommittee on Labor of the Senate Committee on Labor and Public Welfare, 90th Cong., 1st Sess., at 53 (1967).[6]

When the present language of §4(f)(2) was later proposed by amendments, Mr. Wirtz again commented that established pension plans would be protected. Hearings on H.R. 4221 before the General Subcommittee on Labor of the House Committee on Education and Labor, 90th Cong., 1st Sess., at 40 (1967).

Senator Javits' concern with the Administration version of §4(f)(2), expressed in 1967 when the legislation was being debated, was that it did not appear to give employers flexibility to hire older employees without incurring extraordinary expenses because of their inclusion in existing retirement plans. His concern was not, as inferred by the dissent, that involuntary retirement programs would still be allowed. He said,

> The administration bill, which permits involuntary separation under bona fide retirement plans meets only part of the problem. It does not provide any flexibility in the amount of pension benefits payable to older workers depending upon their age when hired, and thus may actually encourage employers, faced with the necessity of paying greatly increased premiums, to look for an excuse not to hire older workers when they might have hired them under a law granting them a degree of flexibility with respect to such matters.
>
> That flexibility is what we recommend.
>
> We also recommend that the age discrimination law should not be used as the place to fight the pension battle but that we ought to subordinate the importance of adequate pension benefits for older workers in favor of the employment of such older workers and not make the equal treatment under pension plans a condition of that employment.
>
> Senate Hearings, *supra,* at 27.[7]

In keeping with this objective Senator Javits proposed the amendment, which was incorporated into the 1967 Act, calling for "a fairly broad exemption . . . for bona fide retirement and seniority systems which will facilitate hiring rather than deter it and make it possible for older workers to be employed without the necessity of disrupting those systems." *Id.,* at 28.

The true intent behind §4(f)(2) was not lost on the representatives of organized labor; they viewed it as protecting an employer's right to require pre-65 retirement pursuant to a bona fide retirement plan and objected to it on that basis. The legislative director for the AFL-CIO testified:

> We likewise do not see any reason why the legislation should, as is provided in section 4(f)(2) of the Administration bill, permit involuntary retirement of employees under 65. . . . Involuntary retirement could be forced, regardless of the age of the employee, subject only to the limitation that the retirement policy or system in effect may not be merely a subterfuge to evade the Act.
>
> Senate Hearings, *supra,* at 96.

In order to protect workers against involuntary retirement, the AFL-CIO suggested an "Amendment to Eliminate Provision Permitting Involuntary Retirement From the Age Discrimination in Employment Act, and to Substitute Therefore Provision Safeguarding Bona Fide Seniority or Merit Systems," which would have deleted any reference to retirement plans in the exception. *Id.,* at 100. This amendment was rejected.

But as noted in *Zinger,* 549 F.2d, at 907, the exemption of benefit plans remained in the bill as enacted notwithstanding Labor's objection, and the Labor proposed exemption for seniority systems was added. There is no basis to view the final version of §4(f)(2) as an acceptance of Labor's request that the benefit plan provision be deleted; the plain language of the statute shows it is still there, albeit in different terms.

Also added to the section when it emerged from the Senate Subcommittee is the language "except that no such employee benefit plan shall excuse the failure to hire any such individual." Rather than reading this addendum as a redundancy as does the dissent, *post,* at 5, and 5 n. 5, it is clear this is the result of Senator Javits' con-

6. Section 4(f)(2) of the original, Administration bill provided, "It shall not be unlawful for an employer . . . to separate involuntarily an employee under a retirement policy or system where such policy or system is not merely a subterfuge to evade the purposes of this Act. . . ."

7. Legislative observations 10 years after passage of the Act are in no sense part of the legislative history. See *post,* at 12.

cern that observance of existing retirement plan terms might discourage hiring of older workers. *Supra,* at 8. Giving meaning to each of these provisions leads inescapably to the conclusion they were intended to permit observance of the mandatory retirement terms of bona fide retirement plans, but that the existence of such plans could not be used as an excuse not to hire any person because of age.

There is no reason to doubt that Secretary Wirtz fully appreciated the difference between the Administration and Senate bills. He was aware of Senator Javits' concerns, and knew the Senator sought to amend the original bill to focus on the *hiring* of older persons notwithstanding the existence of pension plans which they might not economically be permitted to join. *See* Senate Hearings, *supra,* at 40. Senator Javits' view was enacted into law making it possible to employ such older persons without compulsion to include them in pre-existing plans.

The dissent misconceives what was said in the Senate debate. The dialogue between Senators Javits and Yarborough, the minority and majority managers of the bill, respectively, is set out below[8] and clearly shows awareness of the continued vitality of pre-age 65 retirements.

III

In this case, of course, our function is narrowly confined to discerning the meaning of the statutory language; we do not pass on the wisdom of fixed mandatory retirements at a particular age. So limited we find nothing to indicate Congress intended wholesale invalidation of retirement plans instituted in good faith before its passage, or intended to require employers to bear the burden of showing a business or economic purpose to justify bona fide pre-existing plans as the Fourth Circuit concluded. In ordinary parlance, and in dictionary definitions as well, a subterfuge is a scheme, plan, stratagem or artifice of evasion. In the context of this statute, "subterfuge" must be given its ordinary meaning and we must assume Congress intended it in that sense. So read, a plan established in 1941, if bona fide, as is conceded here, cannot be a subterfuge to evade an Act passed 26 years later. To spell out an intent in 1941 to evade a statutory requirement not enacted until 1967 attributes, at the very least, a remarkable prescience to the employer. We reject any such *per se* rule requiring an employer to show an economic or business purpose in order to satisfy the subterfuge language of the Act.[9]

Accordingly, the judgment of the Court of Appeals is reversed and the case is remanded for further proceedings consistent with this opinion.

Reversed.

MR. JUSTICE STEWART, concurring in the judgment.

The Age Discrimination in Employment Act, 29 U.S.C. §621 *et seq.,* forbids any employer to discharge or otherwise discriminate against any employee between the ages of 40 and 65 because of his age. 29 U.S.C. §623(a)(1). But the Act also expressly provides that it is not unlawful for an employer to observe the terms of a bona fide employee benefit plan, such as a retirement plan, so

8. "Mr. YARBOROUGH. I wish to say to the Senator that that is basically my understanding of the provision in line 22, page 20 of the bill, clause 2, subsection (f) of section 4, when it refers to retirement, pension, or insurance plan, it means that a man who would not have been employed except for this law does not have to receive the benefits of the plan. Say an applicant for employment is 55, comes in and seeks employment, and the company has bargained for a plan with its labor union that provides that certain moneys will be put up for a pension plan for anyone who worked for the employer for 20 years so that a 55-year-old employee would not be employed past 10 years. This means he cannot be denied employment because he is 55, but he will not be able to participate in that pension plan because unlike a man hired at 44, he has no chance to earn 20 years retirement. In other words, this will not disrupt the bargained-for pension plan. This will not deny an individual employment or prospective employment but will limit his rights to obtain full consideration in the pension, retirement, or insurance plan.

Mr. JAVITS. I thank my colleague. That is important to business.

113 Cong. Rec. 31255 (1967).

9. Reference is made by the dissent, *post,* at 12 n. 13, to a recital on §4(f)(2) in the House Report. The House Report states that §4(f)(2)

> applies to new and existing employee benefit plans, and to both the establishment and maintenance of such plans. *This exception serves to emphasize the primary purpose of the bill—hiring of older workers—by permitting employment without necessarily including such workers in employee benefit plans.* The specific exception was an amendment to the original bill, is considered vita[l] to the legislation, and was favorably received by witnesses at the hearings.
>
> H. R. Rep. No. 805, 90th Cong., 1st Sess., 4 (1967).

The italicized portion shows quite clearly that the primary purpose of the bill was the hiring of older workers. A quite different question would be presented if a preexisting bona fide plan were used as a reason for refusing to *hire* an older applicant for employment.

long as the plan is not a "subterfuge to evade the purposes" of the Act. 29 U.S.C. §623(f)(2).

It is conceded that United's retirement plan is bona fide. The only issue, then, is whether it is a "subterfuge to evade the purposes" of the Act. I think it is simply not possible for a bona fide retirement plan adopted long before the Act was even contemplated to be a "subterfuge" to "evade" either its terms or its purposes.

Since §623(f)(2) on its face makes United's action under the retirement plan lawful, it is unnecessary to address any of the other questions discussed in the Court's opinion or by MR. JUSTICE WHITE.

MR. JUSTICE WHITE, concurring in the judgment.

I

While I agree with the Court and with MR. JUSTICE STEWART that McMann's forced retirement at age 60 pursuant to United's retirement income plan does not violate the Age Discrimination in Employment Act, 29 U.S.C. §621 *et seq.,* I disagree with the proposition that this bona fide plan necessarily is made lawful under §4(f)(2) of the Act, 29 U.S.C. §623(f)(2), merely because it was adopted long before the Act's passage. Even conceding that the retirement plan could not have been a subterfuge to evade the purposes of the Act when it was adopted by United in 1941, I believe that the decision by United to continue the mandatory aspects of the plan after the Act became effective in 1968 must be separately examined to determine whether it is proscribed by the Act.

The legislative history indicates that the exception contained within §4(f)(2) "applies to new and *existing* employee benefit plans, and to both the establishment and *maintenance* of such plans." H.R. Rep. No. 805, 90th Cong., 1st Sess., 4 (1967); S. Rep. No. 723, 90th Cong., 1st Sess., 4 (1967) (emphasis added). This statement in both the House and Senate reports demonstrates that there is no magic in the fact that United's retirement plan was adopted prior to the Act, for not only the plan's establishment but also its maintenance must be scrutinized. For that reason, unless United was legally bound to continue the mandatory retirement aspect of its plan, its decision to continue to require employees to retire at age 60 after the Act became effective must be viewed in the same light as a post-Act decision to adopt such a plan.

No one has suggested in this case that United did not have the legal option of altering its plan to allow employees who desired to continue working beyond age 60 to do so; at the most it has been concluded that United simply elected to apply its retirement policy uniformly. *See ante,* at 4. Because United chose to continue its mandatory retirement policy beyond the effective date of the Act, I would not terminate the inquiry with the observation that the plan was adopted long before Congress considered the age discrimination act but rather would proceed to what I consider to be the crucial question: does the Act prohibit the mandatory retirement pursuant to a bona fide retirement plan of an employee before he reaches age 65? My reading of the legislative history, set out in Part II of the Court's opinion, convinces me that it does not.

II

As the opinion of the Court demonstrates, Congress in passing the Act did not intend to make involuntary retirements unlawful. In recommending the legislation to Congress, President Johnson specifically suggested an exception for those "special situations . . . where the employee is separated under a regular retirement system." 113 Cong. Rec. 1089-1090 (1967).[1] Pursuant to this recommendation, the House and Senate bills that were referred to committee expressly excepted involuntary retirements from the Act's prohibition,[2] an exception which, with only slight changes remained in the final version enacted by Congress. As the Court correctly concludes, the changes that were made in §4(f)(2) were intended, not to eliminate the protection for retirement plans, but rather to meet the additional concern expressed by Senator Javits concerning the applicability of retirement plans to older workers who are hired. While the discussion in Congress concerning the language change was not extensive, it indicated that the change was intended to broaden the exception for retirement plans. I thus find unacceptable the dissent's view that Congress acceded to labor's suggestion that the protection for involuntary retirement be eliminated.

III

In this case, the Fourth Circuit recognized the fact that United's retirement plan is "bona fide"

1. Other exceptions recommended by the President, which were included within the final version of the Act, covered "special situations where age is a reasonable occupational qualification, [and] where an employee is discharged for good cause. . . ." 113 Cong. rec. 1089-1090 (1967).

2. S. 830, 90th Cong., 1st Sess. (1967); H.R. 4221, 90th Cong., 1st Sess. (1967).

in the sense that it provides McMann with substantial benefits. The court, however, viewed as separate and additional the requirement that the plan not be a subterfuge to evade the purposes of the Act. I find no support in the legislative history for the interpretation of that language as requiring "some economic or business purpose." 542 F.2d 217, 221 (C.A.4 1976). Rather, as I read the history, Congress intended to exempt from the Act's prohibition all retirement plans—even those whose only purpose is to terminate the services of older workers—as long as the benefits they pay are not so unreasonably small as to make the "retirements" nothing short of discharges.

What little discussion there was in Congress concerning the meaning of the §4(f)(2) exception indicates that the no-subterfuge requirement was merely a restatement of the requirement that the plan be bona fide. *See* 113 Cong. Rec. 31255 (1967). It is significant that the subterfuge language was contained in the original Administration bill, for that version was recognized as being "intended to protect retirement plans." *See ante,* at 7. Because all retirement plans necessarily make distinctions based on age, I fail to see how the subterfuge language, which was included in the original version of the bill and was carried all the way through, could have been intended to impose a requirement which almost no retirement plan could meet. For that reason I would interpret the §4(f)(2) exception as protecting actions taken pursuant to a retirement plan which is designed to pay substantial benefits.

Because the Court relies exclusively upon the adoption date of United's retirement plan as a basis for concluding that McMann's forced retirement was not unlawful, I cannot join its opinion. Instead, I would adopt the approach taken by the Third Circuit in *Zinger v. Blanchette,* 549 F.2d 901 (C.A.3 1977) *petition for cert. filed,* April 7, 1977 (No. 76-1375), and would hold that his retirement was valid under the Act, not because the retirement plan was adopted by United prior to the Act's passage, but because the Act does not prohibit involuntary retirements pursuant to bona fide plans.

MR. JUSTICE MARSHALL, with whom MR. JUSTICE BRENNAN joins, dissenting.

Today the Court, in its first encounter with the Age Discrimination in Employment Act of 1967, Pub. L. 90-202. 81 Stat. 602, 29 U.S.C. §621 *et seq.,* sharply limits the reach of that important law. In apparent disregard of settled principles of statutory construction, it gives an unduly narrow interpretation to a Congressional enactment designed to remedy arbitrary discrimination in the workplace. Because I believe that the Court misinterprets the Act, I respectfully dissent.

But for §4(f)(2) of the Act, 29 U.S.C. §623(f)(2), petitioner's decision to discharge respondent because he reached the age of 60 would violate §4(a)(1), 29 U.S.C. §623(a)(1). This latter section makes it unlawful for an employer "to fail or refuse to hire or to discharge or otherwise discriminate against any individual [between 40 and 65] with respect to his compensation, terms, conditions, or privileges of employment, because of such individual's age."

The language used in §4(a)(1) tracks the language of §703(a)(1) of the Civil Rights Act of 1964, 42 U.S.C. §2000e-2(a)(1).[1] This section has been interpreted as forbidding involuntary retirement when improper criteria, such as race or sex, are used in selecting those to be retired. With reference to the statutory language, courts have reasoned that forced retirement is "tantamount to a discharge." *Bartness v. Drewrys U.S.A., Inc.,* 444 F.2d 1186, 1189 (C.A.7), *cert. denied.* 404 U.S. 939 (1971), or that the employer requiring retirement is "discriminat[ing] against" the retired employee "with respect to . . . [a] condition . . . of employment." *See Peters v. Missouri Pacific Railroad Co.,* 483 F.2d 490, 492 n. 3 (C.A.5), *cert. denied,* 414 U.S. 1002 (1973); *Rosen v. Public Service Electric & Gas Co.,* 477 F.2d 90, 94-95 (C.A.3 1973); *Bartness v. Drewrys U.S.A., Inc., supra,* 444 F.2d at 1188-1189.[2]

Given these constructions of §703(a)(1) of the Civil Rights Act and the absence of any indication that Congress intended §4(a)(1) of the Age Discrimination in Employment Act to be interpreted differently, I would construe the identical lan-

1. Section 703(a)(1) provides that it is unlawful for an employer "to fail or refuse to hire or to discharge any individual or otherwise to discriminate against any individual with respect to his compensation, terms, conditions, or privileges of employment, because of such individual's race, color, religion, sex, or national origin." 42 U.S.C. §2000e-2(a)(1).

2. Courts have also suggested that involuntary retirement of an employee on a discriminatory basis might violate §703(a)(2) of the Civil Rights Act, which proscribes classification by an employer of an employee in a way which would "adversely affect his status as an employee." 42 U.S.C. §2000e-2(a)(2). *Bartness v. Drewrys U.S.C., Inc., supra,* at 1189; *Peters v. Missouri-Pacific Railroad Co., supra,* at 495. Section 4(a)(2) of the Age Discrimination in Employment Act, 29 U.S.C. §6232 (a)(2), includes an identical prohibition.

guage of the two statutes in an identical manner. The question that remains is whether §4(f)(2) sanctions this otherwise unlawful act. That section provides:

> It shall not be unlawful for an employer . . . to observe the terms of a bona fide seniority system or any bona fide employee benefit plan such as a retirement, pension, or insurance plan, which is not a subterfuge to evade the purposes of [the Act]. . . .

The opinion of the Court assumes that this language is clear on its face. *Ante*, 3. 6. I cannot agree with this premise. In my view, the statutory language is susceptible of at least two interpretations, and the only reading consonant with Congressional intent would preclude involuntary retirement of employees covered by the Act.

On this latter reading, §4(f)(2) allows different treatment of older employees only with respect to the benefits paid or available under certain employee benefit plans, including pension and retirement plans.[3] Alternatively, the section may be read, as the Court has, also to permit involuntary retirement of older employees prior to age 65 pursuant to a pension or retirement benefit plan. *Ante,* at 3. The critical question, then, is whether the phrase "employee benefit plan," as used by Congress here to include a "retirement, pension or insurance plan," encompasses only the rules defining what benefits retirees receive, or whether it also encompasses rules mandating retirement at a particular age.

We need not decide on a strictly grammatical basis which reading is preferable. We are judges, not linguists, and our task is to divine Congressional intent, using all available evidence. "[W]ords are inexact tools at best and for that reason there is wisely no rule of law forbidding resort to explanatory legislative history no matter how 'clear the words may appear on "superficial examination." ' " *Harrison v. Northern Trust Co.,* 317 U.S. 476, 479 (1943), quoting *United States v. American Trucking Assn.,* 310 U.S. 534, 544 (1940). *See Train v. Colorado Public Interest Research Group,* 426 U.S. 1, 10 (1976).

The Court's analysis of the legislative history establishes that the primary purpose of the Act was to facilitate the hiring of older workers. I have no quarrel with that proposition. Understanding this primary purpose, however, aids not at all in determining whether Congress also intended to prohibit forced retirement of those already employed. The Court's analysis of the legislative history on this issue, *ante,* at 6-9, on which MR. JUSTICE WHITE relies, *ante,* at 2-3, is unpersuasive, since it relies primarily on references to an exception that was not enacted.

There can be no question, that had Congress enacted §4(f)(2) in the form in which it was proposed by the Administration, forced retirement would be permissible. That section of the initial bill quite specifically allowed such retirement. It provided:

> It shall not be unlawful for an employer . . . to separate involuntarily an employee under a retirement policy or system where such policy or system is not merely a subterfuge to evade the purposes of this Act. . . .
>
> S. 830. H.R. 4221. §4(f)(2), 90th Cong., 1st Sess.

Thus the remarks of Secretary Wirtz, Senator Javits and the representative of the AFL-CIO on which the Court relies, *see ante,* at 7-9, quite properly reflect that the bill as it then existed would have authorized involuntary retirement. But the present benefit-plan exception to the §4(a) prohibition on age discrimination differs significantly from that contained in the original bill. The specific authorization for involuntary retirement was deleted. That this deletion was made may of itself suggest that Congress concluded such an exception was unwise; a review of the legislative history strongly supports this view.

Two sets of objections were made to the bill during the Senate and House hearings.[4] Many persons, including members of the Committees,

---

3. This reading is illustrated by Senator Yarborough's example of the effect of §4(f)(2):

> Say an applicant for employment is 55, comes in and seeks employment, and the company has bargained for a plan with its labor union that provides that certain moneys will be put up for a pension plan for anyone who worked for the employer for 20 years so that a 55-year-old employee would not be employed past 10 years. This means he cannot be denied employment because he is 55, but he will not be able to participate in that pension plan because unlike a man hired at 44, he has no chance to earn 20 years retirement. In other words, this will not disrupt the bargained-for pension plan. This will not deny an individual employment or prospective employment but will limit his rights to obtain full consideration in the pension, retirement or insurance plan. 113 Cong. Rec. 31255 (1967).

4. Hearings on S. 830 et al. before the Subcommittee on Labor of the Senate Committee on Labor and Public Welfare, 90th Cong., 1st Sess. (1967); Hearings on H.R. 4221 et al. before the General Subcommittee on Labor of the House Committee on Education and Labor, 90th Cong., 1st Sess. (1967).

expressed concern that the Act "does not provide any flexibility in the amount of pension benefits payable to older workers depending on their age when hired, and thus may actually encourage employers, faced with the necessity of paying greatly increased premiums, to look for excuses not to hire older workers when they might have hired them under a law granting them a degree of flexibility with respect to such matters." Statement of Sen. Javits, Senate Hearing, *supra,* n. 4. at 27; *see also, e.g.,* House Hearings, *supra,* n. 4. at 62-63 (Statement of Labor Counsel, Chamber of Commerce of the United States). Representatives of organized labor voiced totally different objections to the initial version of §4(f)(2); they argued against permitting any involuntary retirement based on age for those within the coverage of the bill, whether or not pursuant to a bona fide plan. Senate Hearings, *supra*, n. 4. at 98; House Hearings, *supra,* n. 4. at 413. In addition, they suggested that bona fide seniority systems should receive express protection under §4(f). *Ibid.*

After the hearings, the House and Senate Committees changed the exemption section to its present form. By adding to §4(f)(2) a provision permitting observance of bona fide seniority systems, Congress acceded to organized labor's concern that seniority systems not be abrogated. The addition of language permitting observance of the terms of a benefit plan was plainly responsive to the numerous criticisms that the bill would deter employment of older workers.[5] But the third change that was made—the deletion of the specific language permitting involuntary retirement—was not responsive to either of those criticisms, since deletion of that language could have no effect on the hiring of older workers or on seniority systems. A reasonable inference to be drawn from the deletion, therefore, is that Congress was responding to labor's other objection by removing the authorization for involuntary retirement from the exceptions to the statute's prohibitions. While, as the Court notes, *ante,* at 9, the specific language proposed by labor was not adopted, the Court offers no alternative explanation for the deletion of the explicit authorization for involuntary retirement.[6]

In contrast to the hearings on the original version of the §4(f)(2) exception, where there are repeated references to the fact that the bill permitted involuntary retirement, there are no similar statements in the Committee Reports or in the House and Senate debates with respect to the amended version of §4(f)(a). For example, the House and Senate Committee Reports explain the purpose and effect of §4(f)(2) as follows:

> This exception serves to emphasize the primary purpose of the bill—hiring of older workers—by permitting employment without necessarily including such workers in employee benefit plans. The specific exception was an amendment to the original bill, is considered vita[l] to the legislation, and was favorably received by witnesses at the hearings.
>
> H. R. Rep. No. 90-805, 90th Cong., 1st Sess. (1967), at 4; *see* S. Rep. No. 90-723, 90th Cong., 1st Sess. (1967), at 4.[7]

Nowhere did the Committees suggest that the exemption permitted involuntary retirements. Indeed, their emphasis on encouraging the employment of older workers by allowing employers to make distinctions based on age in the provision of certain ancillary employment benefits, fully accords with the view that §4(f)(2) was intended only to permit those variations. Moreover, when the sponsors of the legislation explained the bill to the House and Senate during the debates preceeding its passage, they made no mention of the possibility that §4(f)(2) permitted involuntary retirement and discussed it in terms incompatible with any such interpretation.[8] The following ex-

5. The Committees' concern that the Act not deter employers from hiring older employees is also reflected in the amendment to the section providing that "no such employee benefit plan shall excuse the failure to hire any individual." §4(f)(2), 29 U.S.C. §623(f)(2).

6. The Committees were certainly aware that Congress could retain the provision specifically authorizing involuntary retirement and add to it a provision permitting variation in the coverage of insurance and benefit plans. Many of the state statutes at which the Committees looked employed that approach. Senate Hearings, *supra,* n. 4, at 298-315; House Hearings, *supra,* n. 4, at 501-518 (*e.g.,* Connecticut, Indiana, Maine, Pennsylvania). That they deleted the specific authorization rather than following the model of those state statutes is not without significance.

7. The Senate Committee Report's description, although otherwise identical, did not include the statement that the amendment was considered vital. *Supra,* at 4.

8. During the hearings, Senator Javits indicated that the Administration bill might raise problems concerning existing pension plans. He stated that the involuntary retirement provision did not adequately address whether variations in benefits based on age would be permitted. Senate Hearings, *supra,* n. 4, at 27. Although as the Court notes he offered no objection during the hearings to the provision allowing involuntary retirement, it is significant that at no point in his statements on the floor of the Senate did he even hint that the bill as revised permitted involuntary retirement. Since Senator Javits had

change between Senator Javits, the minority floor manager of the bill and Senator Yarborough, the majority floor manager, is illustrative:

> MR. JAVITS. The meaning of this provision is as follows: An employer will not be compelled under this section to afford to older workers exactly the same pension, retirement, or insurance benefits as he affords to younger workers. If the older worker chooses to waive all of those provisions, then the older worker can obtain the benefits of this act, but the older worker cannot compel an employer through the use of this act to undertake some special relationship, course, or other condition with respect to a retirement, pension, or insurance plan which is not merely a subterfuge to evade the purposes of the act—and we understand that—in order to give that older employee employment on the same terms as others.
>
> I would like to ask the manager of the bill whether he agrees with that interpretation, because I think it is very necessary to make its meaning clear to both employers and employees. . . .
>
> MR. YARBOROUGH. I wish to say to the Senator that that is basically my understanding of the provision in line 22, page 20 of the bill, clause 2, subsection (f) of section 4, when it refers to retirement, pension, or insurance plan, it means that a man who would not have been employed except for this law does not have to receive the benefits of the plan. Say an applicant for employment is 55, comes in and seeks employment, and the company has bargained for a plan with its labor union that provides that certain moneys will be put up for a pension plan for anyone who worked for the employer for 20 years so that a 55-year-old employee would not be employed past 10 years. This means he cannot be denied employment because he is 55, but he will not be able to participate in that pension plan because unlike a man hired at 44, he has no chance to earn 20 years retirement. In other words, this will not disrupt the bargained-for pension plan. *This will not deny an individual employment or prospective employment but will limit his rights to obtain full consideration in the pension, retirement, or insurance plan.*
>
> MR. JAVITS. I thank my colleague. That is important to business.

113 Cong. Rec. 31255 (1967) (emphasis added).[9]

The statements of those who criticized the bill for not going far enough lend still further support to the interpretation of the Act that would preclude forced retirement of persons covered by the Act. Senator Young spoke eloquently against subjecting those aged 65 or older to "compulsory retirement programs" which, he proclaimed, "have forged an iron collar" for those Americans "ready, willing and able" to work past 65. 113 Cong. Rec. 31256 (1967). Senator Young never alluded to the possibility that compulsory retirement of those under 65 and thus covered by the Act would be permitted, since the unmistakable premise of his argument was that, under the law being considered, compulsory retirement of covered employees was prohibited. *Ibid.* Others criticized §4(f)(2) because it authorized employers to deny older employees various benefits in accordance with benefit plans, but again made no reference to the possibility of forced retirement of covered employees. *Id.,* at 34745 (remarks of Rep. Smith); *id.,* at 34750 (remarks of Rep. Randall). In view of the tenor and substance of those objections to the Act, it is inconceivable that these Congressmen would have remained silent had they understood §4(f)(2) to allow involuntary retirement before the age of 65.[10]

---

expressly acknowledged the permissibility of involuntary retirement under the Administration's bill at the hearings, in explaining at length the meaning of §4(f)(2) as revised by the Committee he would surely have adverted to involuntary retirement if it were still allowed.

9. The Court somehow finds that the above dialogue indicates approval by Senators Yarborough and Javits of mandatory retirement before age 65. *Ante,* at 10. I see nothing in this dialogue to suggest that the Senators thought involuntary retirement before age 65 was permissible.

10. In contrast to this history which demonstrates forcefully that §4(f)(2) was not intended to provide for involuntary retirement, there are only two pieces of legislative history that provide even a modicum of support for the Court's interpretation. First, when he testified during the hearings on the House bill which then specifically permitted involuntary retirement, Secretary Wirtz was asked about the effect of the Senate Committee's modification of §4(f)(2). He responded that "[w]e count that change as not going to the substance and involving matters going to clarification which would present no problem." House Hearings, *supra,* n. 4, at 40. Since no exemption for benefit plans had been provided in the original bill, it is difficult to understand how Secretary Wirtz could reasonably have called the change only a "clarification." In any event, his statement at the hearing is entitled to far less weight than the Committee reports and the statements by the floor managers and sponsors of the Act. *See Brotherhood of Maintenance of Way Employees v. United States,* 366 U.S. 169, 176-177 (1961); *Leedom v. International Union of Mine, Mill, and Smelter Workers,* 352 U.S. 145, 149-150 (1956).

Second, on the House floor, Representatives Eilberg and Olson, in voicing their support for the bill, stated that one reason the bill was necessary was that people who were retired needed to have opportunities for other

Any doubt as to the correctness of reading the Act to prohibit forced retirement is dispelled by considering the anomaly that results from the Court's contrary interpretation. Under §§4(a) and 4(f)(2), *see* n. 5, *supra,* it is unlawful for an employer to refuse to hire a job applicant under the age of 65 because of his age. If, as the Court holds, involuntary retirement before age 65 is permissible under §4(f)(2), the individual so retired has a simple route to regain his job: he need only reapply for the vacancy created by his retirement. As a new applicant, the individual plainly cannot be denied the job because of his age. And as someone with experience in performing the tasks of the "vacant" job he once held, the individual likely will be better qualified than any other applicant. Thus the individual retired one day would have to be hired the next. We should be loathe to attribute to Congress an intention to produce such a bizarre result.

One final reason exists for rejecting the Court's broad interpretation of the Act's exemption. The Age Discrimination in Employment Act is a remedial statute designed, in the Act's own words, "to promote employment of older persons based on their ability rather than age; to prohibit arbitrary age discrimination in employment; [and] to help employers and workers find ways of meeting problems arising from the impact of age on employment." §1(b), 29 U.S.C. §621(b). It is well settled that such legislation should "be given a liberal interpretation . . . [and] exemptions from its sweep should be narrowed and limited to effect the remedy intended." *Piedmont & Northern R. Co. v. ICC,* 286 U.S. 299, 311-312 (1932). *See also, e.g., Phillips v. Walling,* 324 U.S. 490, 493 (1945). To construe the §4(f)(2) exemption broadly to authorize involuntary retirement when no statement in the committee reports or by the Act's floor managers or sponsors in the debates supports that interpretation flouts this fundamental principle of construction.

The mischief the Court fashions today may be short lived. Both the House and Senate have passed amendments to the Act. 123 Cong. Rec. H9984-9985 (Daily ed. Sept. 23, 1977); *id.,* at S17303 (Daily ed. Oct. 19, 1977). The amendments to §4(f)(2) expressly provide that the involuntary retirement of employees shall not be permitted or required pursuant to any employee benefit plan. Thus, today's decision may have virtually no prospective effect.[11] But the Committee reports of both Houses make plain that, properly understood, the existing Act already prohibits involuntary retirement, and that the amendment is only a clarification necessitated by court decisions misconstruing Congressional intent. H.R. Rep. No. 95-527, 95th Cong., 1st Sess. (1977), at 5-6; *id.,* at 27 (additional views of Rep. Weiss, quoting statement of Sen. Javits); S. Rep. No. 95-493, 95th Cong., 1st Sess. (1977), at 9-10.[12] Because the Court today has also misconstrued Congressional intent and has thereby deprived many older workers of the protection which Congress sought to afford, I must dissent.[13]

---

employment open to them. 113 Cong. Rec. 34745 (1967); *id.,* at 34746. It is not entirely clear whether they were referring to people who would be involuntarily retired in the future, or only to those who had been retired prior to enactment of the Act. But even if they were implicitly expressing the view that the Act permits involuntary retirement, their statements stand in opposition to the clear import of every other statement on the floor of each House, as well as to the Committee reports. Such a conflict must be resolved in favor of "the statements of those most intimately connected with the final version of the statute." *Brotherhood of Maintenance of Way Employees v. United States, supra,* at 117. *See* remarks of Sen. Yarborough, quoted *supra,* at 8-9.

11. Indeed both the House and Senate bills provide that, because the addition to §4(f)(2) is only a clarification, it is to be effective immediately; by contrast, the effective date for other changes regarded as alterations of the 1967 Act has been deferred.

12. The Committee Reports cite and discuss *Zinger v. Blanchette,* 549 F.2d 901 (C.A.3 1977), *petition for cert. filed* April 7, 1977 (No. 76-1375) *Brennan v. Taft Broadcasting Co.,* 500 F.2d 212 (C.A.5 1974); and the instant case. H.R. Rep., *supra,* at 5; S. Rep., *supra,* at 10.

13. Because I do not interpret §4(f)(2) to authorize involuntary retirement, I have no occasion to address the questions discussed by the Court, *ante,* at ____, and by MR. JUSTICE STEWART, *ante,* at ____, as to whether the plan involved here is "a subterfuge to evade the purposes of [the Act]." 29 U.S.C. §623(f)(2). I am compelled to note, however, my emphatic disagreement with their suggestion that a pre-Act plan cannot be a subterfuge to avoid the purposes of the Act. The 1967 Committee Reports of both Houses expressly state: "It is important to note that [§4(f)(2)] applies to new and existing employee benefit plans, and to both the establishment and maintenance of such plans. This exception serves to emphasize the primary purpose of the bill—hiring of older workers—by permitting employment without necessarily including such workers in employee benefit plans. The specific exception was an amendment to the original bill, is considered vita[l] to the legislation, and was favorably received by witnesses at the hearings." H.R. Rep. No. 90-805, *supra,* at 4; *see* S. Rep. No. 90-723, *supra,* at 4.

Read broadly, the Supreme Court's decision in *McMann* implies that mandatory pre-age 65 retirement pursuant to the terms of a pension plan will not constitute a violation of the '67 Act. However, the Court seemed to place great weight on the fact that United's pension plan was established approximately 36 years prior to the enactment of the '67 Act. The Court may not be inclined to extend its holding to plans established after 1967. In addition, the *McMann* case involved a pension plan and its rationale may not extend to other plans, such as profit-sharing plans. *See* 29 C.F.R. §860. 120; WH Opinion Letter (March 2, 1977).

Costs of Benefits

Other issues relating to the §4(f)(2) exception have arisen in connection with costs and benefits under pension and welfare plans. The Department of Labor has stated that an employer is not required to provide older workers (i.e., individuals within the age 40-65 bracket) with the same pension, retirement or insurance benefits as he provides to younger workers if any differential between them is in accordance with a bona fide pension or welfare plan. *See* 29 C.F.R. §860.120(a). For example, in certain cases, an employer may provide lesser amounts of insurance coverage under a group insurance plan to older workers than he does to younger workers.

A pension or welfare plan may be considered in compliance with the '67 Act in cases where the actual amount of costs incurred for older workers is equal to that incurred for younger workers, even though the older worker may actually receive a smaller benefit. However, according to the Department of Labor, only pension plans similar to the kind enumerated in §4(f)(2) of the '67 Act fall within this provision. For example, a profit-sharing plan may not be within the §4(f)(2) exception. The most important question would seem to be whether such a plan is designed to provide "retirement" benefits as opposed to some other type of benefits.

Recent Legislation

In connection with the '67 Act, it is important to note that in late 1977 the House of Representatives and the Senate passed legislation amending this law. The amendments increase the protected category to include individuals who are at least 40 years of age but less than 70 years of age (as opposed to less than 65 years of age). More importantly, the legislation amends §4(f)(2). If this legislation is enacted, §4(f)(2) will provide:

> It shall not be unlawful . . . to observe the terms of a bona fide seniority system or any bona fide employee benefit plan such as a retirement, pension, or insurance plan, which is not a subterfuge to evade the purposes of this Act, except that no such employee benefit plan shall excuse the failure to hire any individual *and except that the involuntary retirement of any employee shall not be required or permitted by any seniority system or any such employee benefit plan because of the age of such employee. . . .*
> (Emphasis added.)

This amendment will, in effect, reverse the Supreme Court's decision in the *McMann* case. If enacted, this legislation will probably permit pre-age 70 "normal retirement age" provisions, but it will be unlawful to involuntarily retire employees pursuant to these provisions.

While employers will be unable to fire employees prior to age 70 pursuant to the terms of a pension plan, the plans may provide that the accrual of benefits ceases at "normal retirement age," which, under ERISA would probably be age 65. There does not appear to be anything in the '67 Act or in the pending amendments that would require an employer to credit, for purposes of benefit accrual, those years of service which occur after an employee's normal retirement age. Similarly, ERISA would not seem to require such accrual. Section 204 of ERISA and §411(b) of the Internal Revenue Code of 1954 limit the extent to which a pension plan may provide for the accrual of benefits at a higher rate during later and presumably higher paid years of service. These sections set forth alternative accrual requirements, and two of these requirements permit a plan to cease benefit accrual after normal retirement age.

AGE DISCRIMINATION ACT OF 1975

The Age Discrimination Act of 1975 (the '75 Act) 29 U.S.C. §6101, *et seq.*, prohibits "unreasonable discrimination on the basis of age in programs which receive federal financial assistance." Unlike the '67 Act, the '75 Act is not limited in its application to employees between the ages of 40 and 65.

EXECUTIVE ORDER 11141

Executive Order 11141 provides that federal contractors and subcontractors may not discriminate "in connection with the terms, conditions, or privileges" of employment against employees on the basis of age "except on the basis of a bona fide occupational qualification, retirement plan, or statutory requirement."

EXECUTIVE ORDER 11246

Executive Order 11246 relates to contracts between the U.S. government and private contractors. Such contracts must contain an "equal opportunity clause," providing that the contractor will not discriminate against any employee because of race, color, religion, sex or national origin.

This statement has been interpreted by the Office of Federal Contract Compliance Programs of the Department of Labor's Employment Standards Administration in §60-20.3(c) of their Sex Discrimination Guidelines, which provides:

> In the area of employer contributions for insurance, pensions, welfare programs and other similar "fringe benefits" the employer will not be considered to have violated these guidelines if his contributions are the same for men and women *or* if the resulting benefits are equal.
> (Emphasis added.)

It is important to note that, while the OFCCP requires *either* equal contributions or equal benefits, the EEOC requires equal benefits under Title VII. The OFCCP requirement, however, is similar to the requirement of the Wage and Hour Division relating to the standard of equality required under the Equal Pay Act.

CHAPTER 6

Banking Laws

NATIONAL BANK ACT

Scope

The National Bank Act (the Glass-Steagall Act), 12 U.S.C. §38 *et seq.*, regulates national or federally chartered banks and the activities engaged in by these entities. The Glass-Steagall Act authorizes the Comptroller of the Currency (and formerly, the Board of Governors of the Federal Reserve System) to permit national banks to act as trustees or in any other fiduciary capacity in which state banks or trust companies are permitted to act under the laws of the state in which the national bank is located. *See* 12 U.S.C. §92a. The purpose of this law is to create "competitive equality" between state and national banks, which, in the absence of legislation such as the Glass-Steagall Act, could not exercise fiduciary or other authority. *See American Trust Co., Inc. v. South Carolina State Bd. of Bank Control*, 381 F.Supp. 313 (D. S.C. 1974). Pursuant to this authority, the Comptroller has issued regulations governing the activities of national banks as fiduciaries, e.g., as trustees.

Since banks often act as fiduciaries with respect to pension and welfare plans, the Glass-Steagall Act and, in particular, the Comptroller's Regulations, affect the private employee benefit complex. The regulations of the Comptroller establish procedures by which national banks may apply for authority to exercise "fiduciary powers," and the Comptroller determines whether to approve such applications. *See* 12 U.S.C. §§4.7b, 9.2.

The Comptroller's regulations also relate to the bank's administration of its fiduciary powers generally, as well as the administration of collective investment funds. Through these regulations, the Comptroller has an impact on plan administration and the interaction of the plan with the other components of the plan complex.

Exercise of Fiduciary Powers

Application to Exercise Fiduciary Powers

Prior to exercising fiduciary powers, a national bank must file an application with the Comptroller of the Currency. *See* 12 C.F.R. §§4.7b, 9.2. The term "fiduciary powers" is defined in the regulations as the power to act, when not in contravention of local law, as a trustee or in any other fiduciary capacity in which state banks and trust companies may act under local law. *See* 12 C.F.R. §9.1(d).

Once this application is filed, the Comptroller of the Currency may conduct an investigation before determining whether to exercise its authority to grant the application. The decision to grant or deny an application is based on a number of factors. *See* 12 C.F.R. §9.3. For example, the Comptroller of the Currency will consider whether the bank has sufficient capital and surplus to exercise the fiduciary powers applied for, which capital and surplus must not be less than that which state law requires of state banks.

The Comptroller of the Currency will also consider the general condition of the bank, including the adequacy of its capital and surplus in relation to the character and condition of its assets and to its deposit liabilities and other corporate responsibilities (e.g., the exercise of fiduciary powers). Furthermore, before determining whether to grant or deny an application, the Comptroller will consider the nature of the supervision to be given to the fiduciary activities, including the qualifications, experience and character of the proposed officer or officers of the bank's trust department.

Administration of Fiduciary Powers

Once an application to exercise fiduciary powers has been granted, the bank must comply with additional rules and regulations issued by the Comptroller of the Currency. These rules and regulations relate to a bank's administration of its fiduciary powers and its investment of assets held in a fiduciary capacity.

Responsibility Assigned. Regulation 9.7 places the responsibility for the bank's proper exercise of its fiduciary powers with the bank's board of directors, and provides that "... no fiduciary account shall be accepted without the prior approval of the board, or of the director(s), officer(s), or committee(s) to whom the board may have designated the performance of that responsibility." *See* 12 C.F.R. §9.7(a). Once the bank accepts a fiduciary account for which the bank has investment discretion, it must review the assets immediately. It must also review investments periodically thereafter to determine the advisability of retaining or disposing of certain investments.

Of course, all officers and employees of the bank participating in the operation of the trust department must be adequately bonded. This bonding requirement is similar to the bonding requirements contained in §412 of ERISA.

"Chinese Wall." One of the more important provisions relating to the administration of the bank's fiduciary powers is contained in §9.7(d) of the Comptroller's regulations. This section provides that:

> The Trust Department may utilize personnel and facilities of other departments of the bank, and other departments of the bank may utilize the personnel and facilities of the trust department only to the extent not prohibited by law. Every national bank exercising fiduciary powers shall adopt written policies and procedures to ensure that the Federal Securities Laws are complied with in connection with any decision or recommendation to purchase or sell any security. Such policies and procedures, in particular, shall ensure the (sic) national bank trust departments shall not use any material inside information in connection with any decision or recommendation to purchase or sell any security.

Section 9.7(d) is important since banks frequently have both trust and commercial departments, and the trust department may have access to confidential information generated by the commercial department. A significant amount of financial data is generated by a bank's commercial department in its capacity as a creditor. The knowledge gathered by loan officers in their contacts with officers of borrowers (such as corporations) may be important sources of investment information.

In the past, this information moved along established lines of communication throughout the bank, increasing the efficient utilization of information resources. Practices of this nature were arguably consistent with the common law of trusts. A number of court decisions support the proposition that the acquisition of "inside information" constituted evidence of the trustee's prudence. *See, e.g., In re Estate of McCafferty,* 147 Misc. 179, 264 N.Y.S. 38 (Sur. Ct. 1933). More importantly, the court in *In re Estate of McCafferty* stated that a fiduciary was under an obligation to take advantage of all sources of information reasonably available to him.

However, these decisions and the interdepartmental relationships between bank trust and commercial departments have been modified, in effect, by the development of the law under §10b of the Securities Exchange Act of 1933 and, in particular, by Regulation 10b-5. (The Securities Exchange Act of 1933 was discussed in Chapter 4.) In *in re Cady, Roberts & Co.,* 40 SEC 907 (1961), the Securities and Exchange Commission held that Regulation 10b-5 prohibited a broker-dealer from trading for a discretionary account on the basis of inside information obtained by a member of the firm through a commercial relationship. This decision stands for the proposition that investment recommendations developed on the basis of material inside information are contrary to public policy. The Securities and Exchange Commission focused on the inherent inequity involved where one investor takes advantage of such inside information knowing that the information is not available to the investing public. Under this principle, the argument can be made that the information flow between the trust and the commercial department is permissible only to the extent that material inside information is not involved.

This principle (as well as other related principles) is much easier to state than to apply. Both the use and the non-use of material inside information by a bank trust department arguably expose the bank to 10b-5 liabilities.

The bank's response to this dilemma has resulted in the creation of "Chinese Walls," whereby the source of the information, usually the commercial department, is separated by a wall of non-communication from the investment decisions of the trust department. While the effectiveness of the wall is beyond the scope of this book, it is important to note that there is likely to be a significant amount of litigation in this area. The court's decision in *O'Brien v. Continental Illinois National Bank and*

Trust Company of Chicago, 431 F.Supp. 292 (N.D. Ill. 1977), illustrates some of the problems.

O'BRIEN V. CONTINENTAL ILLINOIS NATIONAL BANK & TRUST COMPANY OF CHICAGO

431 F.Supp. 292 (N.D. Ill. 1977)

FLAUM, District Judge:

Before the court is defendant's motion to reconsider Judge McGarr's May 10, 1974 order denying defendant's motion to dismiss plaintiffs' complaints in causes 72-C-2551, 73-C-46, 73-C-660, 73-C-772, and 73-C-3132. Defendant has also moved to dismiss in cases 74-C-2899 and 73-C-1755, which have been consolidated with the aforementioned actions.

The relevant facts are as follows: In all seven cases,[1] plaintiffs are either beneficiaries of trusts, or principals in agency relationships, in which defendant, Continental National Bank and Trust Company of Chicago ("Continental") is the trustee or agent.[2] All the complaints allege that the trust agreements between the parties are "discretionary" in nature with the trustee given complete discretion in making all investment decisions for the trust res, subject, of course, to a fiduciary's duty of due care. Plaintiffs allege that Continental has committed various violations of the Securities Exchange Act of 1934, §10(b), 15 U.S.C. §78j(b), and rule 10b-5, 17 C.F.R. §240.10b-5, promulgated thereunder, as well as violations of state common law. These violations are premised on plaintiffs' allegations that Continental, in administering the different trusts, breached its fiduciary duty as trustee to the beneficiaries/plaintiffs by investing substantial sums of the trusts' funds in securities issued by corporations to which Continental, in its capacity as a commercial lender, had loaned large amounts of money. Plaintiffs contend that Continental, in its capacity as a commercial lender, obtained inside information concerning the aforementioned corporations which indicated that investment in their securities would be unwise. Plaintiffs claim that the purchases and retention for the trusts of securities issued by corporations to which Continental had outstanding loans were improper because they were made:

> (1) without disclosure to plaintiffs by Continental of its conflict of interest;
>
> (2) without disclosure of inside information Continental obtained indicating the financial difficulties of the corporations issuing the securities; and
>
> (3) with the knowledge of Continental that the securities were poor risks and with the intention of protecting its own investments in the financially troubled companies.[3]

Plaintiffs further allege that had they been aware of this material information, and but for defendant's fraudulent scheme, they would have ended their trust arrangements with defendant and not purchased or retained the securities in issue.

In support of its request for dismissal of plaintiffs' complaints, Continental relies primarily on the Supreme Court's decision in *Blue Chip Stamps v. Manor Drug Stores,* 421 U.S. 723, 95 S.Ct. 1917, 44 L.Ed.2d 539 (1975), and the recent decision in *Santa Fe Indus., Inc. v. Green,* ____ U.S. ____, 97 S.Ct. 1292, 51 L.Ed.2d 480 (1977). Defendant argues first that, as trust beneficiaries, plaintiffs are not "purchasers or sellers" of securities and therefore lack "standing" to claim that defendant's operation of plaintiffs' trust accounts violated section 10(b) and rule 10b-5.[4] Second, defendant contends that plaintiffs' complaints merely allege breaches of Continental's fiduciary duty to plaintiffs and that these claims are not cognizable under rule 10b-5. And, since there is no independent subject matter jurisdiction over plaintiffs' state law claims, Continental contends that plaintiffs' complaints must be dismissed in their entirety.

While this court does not agree with defendant's position that *Blue Chip Stamps* mandates that in all situations a trust beneficiary lacks standing to sue his trustee under rule 10b-5, *see James v. Gerber Products Co.,* 483 F.2d 944 (6th Cir.

1. The cases before the court involve the same general factual situations although they differ in certain irrelevant particulars. *See* Judge McGarr's May 10, 1974 order reported in [1973-74 Transfer Binder] CCH Fed.Sec.L.Rep. ¶94,565, at 95,956-58 (N.D.Ill.1974).

2. The fact that some complaints allege trust relationships, while the others allege agencies is irrelevant to the determination of the pending motions. Although the labels of the relationships differ, they all resemble trust arrangements and this court shall hereinafter refer to plaintiffs as beneficiaries and to defendant as trustee.

3. For example, in the *Kenco* case, 73-C-1755, plaintiffs allege that Continental had made a $20 million loan to Interway Corporation and thereupon bought a $3.5 million note for the account of plaintiffs which was subordinated to Continental's loan. *See* Complaint ¶8, in 73-C-1755.

4. Defendant also argues that this court lacks jurisdiction over plaintiffs' securities laws claims because of the "primary jurisdiction" doctrine. However, this court does not have to reach this issue in the cases at bar.

1973) (standing granted); *Klamberg v. Roth,* 425 F.Supp. 440 (S.D.N.Y. 1976) (post-*Blue Chip Stamps;* standing granted), this court is compelled to agree with defendant's contention that *Blue Chip Stamps* and *Green* bar plaintiffs from proceeding with their 10b-5 allegations in their complaints. These decisions[5] place a new gloss on section 10(b) and rule 10b-5 actions requiring the courts to scrutinize with great care the appropriateness of federal securities law remedy for certain conduct by defendants. The Supreme Court in recent decisions has adopted a more limited approach to section 10(b) and rule 10b-5, and this limited approach leads this court to the conclusion that plaintiffs' allegations fail to state claims for relief under rule 10b-5. Therefore, defendant's motion to reconsider the May 10, 1974 order in this cause and its motion to dismiss plaintiffs' 10b-5 claims must be granted.

In their complaints, plaintiffs raise three types of claims under the federal securities laws: (1) that Continental fraudulently "retained" securities it knew it should have sold; (2) that Continental failed to "disclose" to plaintiffs certain inside information it had obtained and the existence of the conflict of interest defendant faced as trustee and commercial lender prior to Continental's purchase of securities for plaintiffs' accounts;[6] and (3) that Continental defrauded plaintiffs by purchasing securities for plaintiffs' accounts knowing the securities to be of high risk and unworthy of investment in order to protect defendant's own interests in the corporate issuers of the securities.

[1] First, *Blue Chip Stamps* has made it clear that plaintiffs may not maintain their 10b-5 claims of fraudulent "retention" of securities since as to these allegations plaintiffs are not the "purchasers or sellers" of securities. In adopting the "purchaser or seller" requirement for 10b-5 actions first enunciated in *Birnbaum v. Newport Steel Corp.,* 193 F.2d 461 (2d Cir.), *cert. denied,* 343 U.S. 956, 72 S.Ct. 1051, 96 L.Ed. 1356 (1952), the Supreme Court delineated three categories of 10b-5 plaintiffs who did not have standing to proceed with their claims. 421 U.S. at 737-38, 95 S.Ct. 1917. The second category consisted of

> actual shareholders in the issuer who allege that they decided not to sell their shares because of an unduly rosy representation or a failure to disclose unfavorable material.

Id. Plaintiffs' allegations of fraudulent retention fall within this second category and therefore must be dismissed. *See Marsh v. Armada Corp.,* 533 F.2d 978 (6th Cir. 1976), *cert. denied,* ____ U.S. ____, 97 S.Ct. 1598, 51 L.Ed.2d ____ (1976); *Williams v. Sinclair,* 529 F.2d 1383 (9th Cir. 1975).

[2] Second, as to plaintiffs' allegations of "nondisclosure" of material information, plaintiffs have failed to allege that these nondisclosures were in fact "in connection with" or material to their purchases of the securities in issue as required by rule 10b-5. *See Superintendent of Ins. of New York v. Bankers Life & Casualty Co.,* 404 U.S. 6, 12, 92 S.Ct. 165, 30 L.Ed.2d 128 (1971). As plaintiffs admit in their complaints, the trusts established with the defendant are "discretionary" in nature, vesting complete investment decision authority in Continental. Under the trust agreements, Continental was under no obligation to consult with plaintiffs prior to making any investment. While plaintiffs did retain the right to ratify or disapprove defendant's decisions, any information obtained by plaintiffs relative to these decisions to purchase would be *ex post* the actual purchase and give rise to complaints concerning improper "retention" of securities, claims, as stated previously, plaintiffs cannot raise under rule 10b-5.[7] Even if the plaintiffs were aware of all the facts, the defendant still could have purchased the securities in issue. Thus, plaintiffs' claims of "nondisclosure" are really "in connection with" plaintiffs' decision to retain or remove Continental as trustee, and have no relation to the plaintiffs becoming the owners of securities.

[3, 4] This result and analysis is in accord with the purpose of rule 10b-5 to insure that all persons making investment decisions have full and accurate information concerning the securities subject to a transaction. *See Affiliated Ute*

5. *See also Piper v. Chris-Craft Indus., Inc.,* ____ U.S. ____, 97 S.Ct. 926, 51 L.Ed.2d 124 (1977); *Ernst & Ernst v. Hochfelder,* 425 U.S. 185, 96 S.Ct. 1375, 47 L.Ed.2d 668 (1976); *TSC Indus., Inc. v. Northway, Inc.,* 426 U.S. 438, 96 S.Ct. 2126, 48 L.Ed.2d 757 (1976).

6. Plaintiffs have not sought to claim that the mere existence of the conflict of interest defendant faced states a 10b-5 cause of action. Plaintiffs' Memorandum in Opposition to Defendant's Motion to Reconsider at 49-50. In light of *Ernst & Ernst v. Hochfelder,* 425 U.S. 185, 96 S.Ct. 1375, 47 L.Ed.2d 668 (1976), and its rejection of a mere negligence 10b-5 action, it appears such a claim would fail as not adequately alleging an intentional "fraud."

7. *See Rich v. Touche Ross & Co.,* 415 F.Supp. 95 (S.D.N.Y. 1976), in which the district court held that an accountant's fraud in getting plaintiff to leave its securities with a certain broker was not "in connection with" the purchase or sale of a security but in connection with the plaintiff's decision to continue the bailment.

Citizens v. United States, 406 U.S. 128, 151, 92 S.Ct. 1456, 31 L.Ed.2d 741 (1972). Unlike *Chasins v. Smith, Barney & Co.,* 438 F.2d 1167 (2d Cir. 1970), in which the Second Circuit recognized a 10b-5 action against a stock broker for failure to disclose to plaintiff to whom it sold securities that the broker was "making market" in the securities,[8] in the cases at bar, there was no investment decision to be made by plaintiffs and no such investments were affected by any lack of information on plaintiffs part. The "market transactions" in the cases at bar were pure,[9] the trust relationships allegedly were not. Rule 10b-5, however, protects the former and not the latter.

[5] Therefore, this court refuses to read into all discretionary trusts, pursuant to rule 10b-5, a requirement that trustees inform their beneficiaries of information prior to making investments totally within the trustees' discretion. In such situations, failure to disclose material information is simply not "in connection with" any purchase or sale of a security and is not material to any investment decision made by plaintiffs. *Santa Fe Indus., Inc. v. Green,* ___ U.S. ___, ___ n.14, 97 S.Ct. 1292, 51 L.Ed.2d 480 (1977).

[6] Finally, in regard to plaintiffs' allegations that Continental defrauded them by knowingly purchasing high risk securities for their trust accounts and in order to protect its own interests as a commercial lender, the landmark decision in *Santa Fe Indus., Inc. v. Green, supra,* compels the conclusion that plaintiffs' fraud counts fail to state claims for relief under section 10(b) since they merely allege breaches by Continental of its fiduciary duty of care in purchasing securities for plaintiffs. In *Green,* the Supreme Court held that a "short-form merger," in which minority shareholders were forced to sell their shares even though there was no valid reason for the merger, was not the type of fraud on the seller of securities cognizable under rule 10b-5. In addressing the facts before it, the Court stated that in order for a fraud in connection with the purchase or sale of a security to state a 10b-5 claim, the fraud has to constitute a "deceptive" or "manipulative" device. ___ U.S. at ___ – ___, 97 S.Ct. 1292. Thus, the Court held that frauds which constituted mere breaches of fiduciary duties would not violate rule 10b-5 unless they involved "omissions" or "misstatements" of information constituting a deception, or "manipulations" which the Court defined as "practices, such as wash sales, matched orders, or rigged prices, that are intended to mislead investors by artificially affecting market activity." *Id.* at ___, 97 S.Ct. at 1302.

[7-9] In the cases at bar, plaintiffs' allegations of fraud do not constitute deceptions or manipulations as those terms are defined above. No "deceptions" are alleged since in plaintiffs' allegations of Continental's purchase of high risk securities to protect its own interests, there are no allegations of omissions or misstatements of information. As stated previously, prior to Continental's purchase of securities for plaintiffs' accounts, Continental was under no requirement to communicate to plaintiffs concerning its investment decisions. Moreover, no manipulative devices are alleged since the knowing purchase of high risk securities by a fiduciary to protect its own interests in the issuer of the securities is not that type of device which artificially affects market activity. "Manipulation," as the Court states, is a "term of art," *id.* at ___, 97 S.Ct. 1292, and its narrow scope does not include ordinary types of breaches of fiduciary duties by trustees in purchasing securities for their beneficiaries' accounts.

This court recognizes that the facts in the cases at bar differ from the "short-form merger" situation before the Supreme Court in *Green.* Nevertheless, the Court in *Green* has made it clear that especially when a state court remedy exists for the type of fraud alleged by a 10b-5 plaintiff, *id.* at ___, 97 S.Ct. 1292, and where the type of fraud alleged is not unique to the operation of the securities market, that courts should be hesitant in expanding rule 10b-5's reach. The Court has simply stated that Congress, in enacting section 10(b), and the courts, in interpreting the scope of a private right of action thereunder, do not mean for that statute to have such a broad and pervasive scope.

Accordingly, plaintiffs' section 10(b) and rule 10b-5 claims must be dismissed and the May 10, 1974 order vacated. Moreover, pursuant to Fed. R.Civ.P. 54(b), there being no just cause for delay, final judgment is entered on plaintiffs' dismissed 10b-5 claims. This court does not, however, dismiss these causes in their entirety since the parties have requested an opportunity to brief the issue of whether under the doctrine of "pendent jurisdiction" this court should continue to hear the state law claims raised by plaintiffs. Therefore,

8. In *Chasins,* a nondiscretionary account was involved leaving all investment decisions to plaintiff.

9. There is no allegation that the corporations failed to disclose to plaintiffs' trustee, the defendant, all material information concerning the securities in issue. Thus, both actual parties to the sale were privy to all relevant information.

defendant is granted ten (10) days to file a brief in support of dismissal of the state claims, and plaintiffs are given ten (10) days to respond with five (5) days to reply by defendant. Until this issue is decided, this court shall stay its ruling on plaintiffs' motion to strike defendant's affirmative defenses.

It is so ordered.

The court's decision in the *O'Brien* case preceded the amendment of Section 9.7(d) to read as quoted above. Section 9.7(d) now requires trust departments to adopt written policies and procedures with respect to their use of other departments; such policies and procedures must be designed to ensure that the trust department's use of another department will not lead to violations of the federal securities laws. They must preclude the trust department from using any material inside information of which it may become aware to make recommendations or decisions to sell or purchase securities for the account of a pension and welfare plan. These policies and procedures do not have to be disclosed to current or potential trust accounts (such as pension plans), but banks should consider some form of disclosure.

It is important to note that, according to the Comptroller, the mere knowledge of material inside information is not necessarily illegal or improper; it is the intent to defraud and the actual use of such information in connection with the purchase or sale of securities which may lead to 10b-5 liability. *See Ernst & Ernst v. Hochfelder,* 425 U.S. 185 (1976). (The *Ernst & Ernst* case was discussed in Chapter 4.)

Investment of Assets

Interim Investment. The rules and regulations relating to a bank's administration of its fiduciary powers are supplemented by regulations relating to the bank's investment of assets held in a fiduciary capacity. For example, Regulation 9.10 provides that assets held by a bank in its capacity as a fiduciary must not be held uninvested any longer than is reasonable for the proper management of the assets. However, this section also provides that assets awaiting investment or distribution may be deposited in the savings or commercial department of the bank, unless the instrument which creates the trust or local law prohibits such an investment. [It is important to note the relationship between this section of the Comptroller's Regulations and Section 408(b)(4) of ERISA and Section 4975(d)(4) of the Internal Revenue Code, both of which contain an exemption from the prohibited transaction provisions for similar investments. The prohibited transaction provisions were discussed in Chapters 1 and 2.]

Before such an investment can be made, the bank must provide collateral security for the assets to be invested, in the form of United States obligations or readily marketable securities, but only to the extent that the assets to be invested exceed the amount insured by the Federal Deposit Insurance Corporation. (The Federal Deposit Insurance Act is discussed below.) The collateral provided by the bank as security for the assets must be held under the control of the trust department.

Nature of Investments. Regulation 9.11 also governs the investment of assets held by a bank in a fiduciary capacity. The principal requirement is that "... funds held by a national bank in a fiduciary capacity shall be invested in accordance with the instrument establishing the fiduciary relationship and local law." If the trust instrument does not specify the class or character of investments to be made and does not give the bank discretion to determine such investments, the assets may be invested in any instrument in which corporate fiduciaries may invest under local law.

The Comptroller of the Currency has taken a number of positions with respect to investment policy governing trust investments. For example, the Comptroller will object to a bank investing in partnerships unless state law limits liability. Likewise, the Comptroller will object to investment in limited partnerships unless such investments are specifically authorized by the trust agreement. *See Comptroller's Handbook for National Trust Examiners.*

The Comptroller has also taken the position that, under the prudent man rule, investment in speculative assets is not proper, and might expose the bank to liability in the event a loss should be sustained unless such investment is specifically authorized by the terms of the governing instrument. The Comptroller feels that the following investments usually can be deemed speculative: (1) art objects, (2) commodity futures, (3) Euro-dollars, (4) foreign companies, (5) foreign currency, (6) jewels, (7) oil and gas exploration, (8) paintings, (9) precious metals, (10) rare coins, (11) selling short, (12) venture companies, (13) warrants, and (14) stock options. However, the Comptroller will not object to the writing of call options on securities held in trust department accounts where specific authority for such transactions is contained in the governing instrument of the particular account, such as the trust agreement, and where the particular transaction is appropriate for the account. In addition, the Comptroller will not object to transactions in other forms of options which are directly related to a covered call option which the bank has outstanding. For example, the bank could protect its position by purchasing a call on the same security as is presently subject to a call, to provide protection in a declining market. However, the Comptroller also notes that these other forms of options are improper when engaged in as an original investment.

Regulation 9.12 relates to self-dealing and other conflicts of interest. This section specifically prohibits a bank acting as a fiduciary from investing assets in stock or obligations of the bank or of its directors, officers or employees, unless the trust department specifically provides for such investments. This means that the authority to make such investments must be specific as to the conflict of interest involved, and may be permissive in nature. According to the Comptroller, no general investment powers, however broad, would be authority for the bank to invest in its own stock. This opinion would include not only the outright purchases of bank stock, but also bank stock acquired through exchanges or debt retirement.

Collective Investment Funds

The assets held by a bank in a fiduciary capacity may be invested collectively. *See* 12 C.F.R. §§9.11(c), 9.18. However, collective investment funds, which are usually referred to as common or pooled funds, must satisfy certain structure and content requirements.

If the bank establishes a common fund, it must be done in accordance with a written plan approved by its board of directors and filed with the Comptroller of the Currency. The plan is required to include numerous provisions relating to the investment and management of such a fund, including the manner in which the fund is to be operated, a general statement of the investment policy to be followed by the bank in investing the fund's assets, the method for valuing the fund and for allocating income, gains and losses; and (of particular interest to individual trusts participating in the fund) the terms and conditions for admission to and withdrawal from the fund itself. Common funds must also be administered pursuant to the rules and regulations of the Comptroller. Moreover, the Comptroller's Regulations specifically govern the investment of assets held collectively.

Common Funds vs. "Investment Companies"

It is important to note the similarities between common funds and investment companies or mutual funds. (Investment companies were discussed in Chapter 4.) However, certain common funds are exempted from the definition of the term "investment company" contained in the Investment Company Act of 1940. *See* '40 Act §3(c)(3), 3(c)(11).

These exemptions, particularly the exemption contained in Section 3(c)(11) of the '40 Act, do not mean that banks may engage in securities activities without restriction. The Court's decision in *Investment Company Institute v. Camp,* 401 U.S. 617 (1971) illustrates some of the restrictions. Of particular importance is the Court's statement that ". . . no provision of the banking law suggests that it is improper for a national bank to pool trust assets, or to act as the managing agent for individual customers, or to purchase stock for the account of its customers. But the union of these powers gives birth to an investment fund whose activities are of a different character."

INVESTMENT COMPANY INSTITUTE V. CAMP
401 U.S. 617 (1971)

Mr. Justice Stewart delivered the opinion of the Court.

These companion cases involve a double-barreled assault upon the efforts of a national bank to go into the business of operating a mutual investment fund. The petitioners in No. 61 are an association of open-end investment companies and several individual such companies. They brought an action in the United States District Court for the District of Columbia, attacking portions of Regulation 9 issued by the Comptroller of the Currency,[1] on the ground that this Regulation, in purporting to authorize banks to establish and operate collective investment funds, sought to permit activities prohibited to national banks or their affiliates by various provisions of the Glass-Steagall Banking Act of 1933, 48 Stat. 162.[2] The petitioners also specifically attacked the Comptroller's approval of the application of First National City Bank of New York for permission to establish and operate a collective investment fund. In No. 59 the National Association of Securities Dealers filed a petition in the United States Court of Appeals for the District of Columbia

1. 12 C.F.R. Pt. 9 (1970).

2. The provisions of the Glass-Steagall Act are codified in various sections scattered through Title 12 of the United States Code.

Circuit seeking review of an order of the Securities and Exchange Commission that partially exempted the collective investment fund of First National City Bank of New York from various provisions of the Investment Company Act of 1940.[3]

In No. 61 the District Court concluded that the challenged provisions of Regulation 9 were invalid under the Glass-Steagall Act.[4] The Comptroller and First National City Bank appealed from this decision, and the appeal was consolidated with the petition for review in No. 59. The Court of Appeals held that the actions taken by the Securities and Exchange Commission and the Comptroller were fully consonant with the statutes committed to their regulatory supervision. Accordingly, it affirmed the order of the Commission and reversed the judgment of the District Court.[5] We granted certiorari to consider important questions presented under federal regulatory statutes.[6] For the reasons that follow, we hold Regulation 9 invalid insofar as it authorizes the sale of interests in an investment fund of the type established by First National City Bank pursuant to the Comptroller's approval. This disposition makes it unnecessary to consider the propriety of the action of the Securities and Exchange Commission in affording this fund exemption from certain of the provisions of the Investment Company Act of 1940.

I

In No. 61 it is urged at the outset that petitioners lack standing to question whether national banks may legally enter a field in competition with them. This contention is foreclosed by *Data Processing Service v. Camp,* 397 U.S. 150, 25 L.Ed.2d 184, 90 S.Ct. 827. There we held that companies that offered data processing services to the general business community had standing to seek judicial review of a ruling by the Comptroller that national banks could make data processing services available to other banks and to bank customers. We held that data processing companies were sufficiently injured by the competition that the Comptroller had authorized to create a case or controversy. The injury to the petitioners in the instant case is indistinguishable. We also concluded that Congress did not intend "to preclude judicial review of administrative rulings by the Comptroller as to the legitimate scope of activities available to national banks under [the National Bank Act]." 397 U.S. at 157, 25 L.Ed.2d at 190. This is precisely the review that the petitioners have sought in this case. Finally, we concluded that Congress had arguably legislated against the competition that the petitioners sought to challenge, and from which flowed their injury. We noted that whether Congress had indeed prohibited such competition was a question for the merits. In the discussion that follows in the balance of this opinion we deal with the merits of the petitioners' contentions and conclude that Congress did legislate against the competition that the petitioners challenge. There can be no real question, therefore, of the petitioners' standing in the light of the *Data Processing* case. *See also Arnold Tours v. Camp,* 400 U.S. 45, 27 L.Ed.2d 179, 91 S.Ct. 158.

II

The issue before us is whether the Comptroller of the Currency may, consistently with the banking laws, authorize a national bank to offer its customers the opportunity to invest in a stock fund created and maintained by the bank. Before 1963 national banks were prohibited by administrative regulation from offering this service. The Board of Governors of the Federal Reserve System, which until 1962 had regulatory jurisdiction over all the trust activities of national banks, allowed the collective investment of trust assets only for "the investment of funds held for true fiduciary purposes." The applicable regulation, Regulation F, specified that "the operation of such Common Trust Funds as investment trusts for other than strictly fiduciary purposes is hereby prohibited." The Board consistently ruled that it was improper for a bank to use "a Common Trust Fund as an investment trust attracting money seeking investment alone and to embark upon what would be in effect the sale of participations in a Common Trust Fund to the public as investments." 26 Fed. Reserve Bull. 393 (1940); *see also* 42 Fed. Reserve Bull. 228 (1956); 41 Fed. Reserve Bull. 142 (1955).

In 1962 Congress transferred jurisdiction over most of the trust activities of national banks from the Board of Governors of the Federal Reserve System to the Comptroller of the Currency, without modifying any provision of substantive law. Pub. L. 87-722, 76 Stat. 668, 12 U.S.C. §92a. The Comptroller thereupon solicited suggestions for improving the regulations applicable to trust ac-

3. The exemption was granted in response to an application filed pursuant to §6(c) of the Act, 54 Stat. 802, 15 U.S.C. §80a-6(c).

4. 274 F.Supp. 624.

5. 136 U.S. App. D.C. 241, 420 F.2d 83.

6. 397 U.S. 986, 25 L.Ed.2d 394, 90 S.Ct. 1114.

tivities. Subsequently, new regulations were proposed which expressly authorized the collective investment of monies delivered to the bank for investment management, so-called managing agency accounts. These proposed regulations were officially promulgated in 1963 with changes not material here.[7] In 1965 the First National City Bank of New York submitted for the Comptroller's approval a plan for the collective investment of managing agency accounts. The Comptroller promptly approved the plan, and it is now in operation. This plan, which departs in some respects from the plan envisaged by the Comptroller's Regulation, is expected, the briefs tell us, to be a model for other banks which decide to offer their customers a collective investment service.[8]

Under the plan the bank customer tenders between $10,000 and $500,000 to the bank, together with an authorization making the bank the customer's managing agent. The customer's investment is added to the fund, and a written evidence of participation is issued which expresses in "units of participation" the customer's proportionate interest in fund assets. Units of participation are freely redeemable, and transferable to anyone who has executed a managing agency agreement with the bank. The fund is registered as an investment company under the Investment Company Act of 1940. The bank is the underwriter of the fund's units of participation within the meaning of that Act. The fund has filed a registration statement pursuant to the Securities Act of 1933. The fund is supervised by a five-member committee elected annually by the participants pursuant to the Investment Company Act of 1940. The Securities and Exchange Commission has exempted the fund from the Investment Company Act to the extent that a majority of this committee may be affiliated with the bank, and it is expected that a majority always will be officers in the bank's trust and investment division.[9] The actual custody and investment of fund assets is carried out by the bank as investment advisor pursuant to a management agreement. Although the Investment Company Act requires that this management agreement be approved annually by the committee, including a majority of the unaffiliated members, or by the participants, it is expected that the bank will continue to be investment advisor.

III

Section 16 of the Glass-Steagall Act as amended, 12 U.S.C. §24, Seventh, provides that the "business of dealing in securities and stock [by a national bank] shall be limited to purchasing and selling such securities and stock without recourse, solely upon the order, and for the account of, customers, and in no case for its own account. . . . Except as hereinafter provided or otherwise permitted by law, nothing herein contained shall authorize the purchase by [a national bank] for its own account of any shares of stock of any corporation."[10] The petitioners contend that a purchase of stock by a bank's investment fund is a purchase of stock by a bank for its own account in violation of this section.

Section 16 also provides that a national bank "shall not underwrite any issue of securities or stock." And §21 of the same Act, 12 U.S.C. §378 (a), provides that "it shall be unlawful—(1) for any person, firm, corporation, association, business trust, or other similar organization, engaged in the business of issuing, underwriting, selling, or distributing, at wholesale or retail, or through syndicate participation, stocks, bonds, debentures, notes, or other securities, to engage at the same time to any extent whatever in the business of [deposit banking]." The petitioners contend that the creation and operation of an investment fund by a bank which offers to its customers the opportunity to purchase an interest in the fund's assets constitutes the issuing, underwriting, selling, or distributing of securities or stocks in violation of these sections.

The questions raised by the petitioners are novel and substantial. National banks were granted trust powers in 1913. Federal Reserve Act, §11, 38 Stat. 261. The first common trust fund was or-

7. 12 C.F.R. §9.18(a) provides that:

Where not in contravention of local law, funds held by a national bank as fiduciary may be invested collectively: . . . (3) In a common trust fund, maintained by the bank exclusively for the collective investment and reimbursement of monies contributed thereto by the bank in its capacity as managing agent under a managing agency agreement expressly providing that such monies are received by the bank in trust. . . .

8. For example, the investment fund plan as established does not provide that the bank receives the investor's money in trust.

9. The opinion of the Commission and the dissent of Commissioner Budge are unofficially reported at CCH Fed.Sec.L.Rep. 1964-1966 Decisions, ¶77,332.

10. Section 16, as enacted in 1933, granted no authority to purchase stock for the account of customers and prohibited any purchase of stock by a national bank. The 1935 Amendments to the National Bank Act included a provision intended to make it clear that a national bank may buy stock for the account of customers but not for its own account. S.Rep.No. 1007, 74th Cong., 1st Sess., 17; H.R. Rep. No. 742, 74th Cong., 1st Sess., 18.

ganized in 1927, and such funds were expressly authorized by the Federal Reserve Board by Regulation F promulgated in 1937. Report on Commingled or Common Trust Funds Administered by Banks and Trust Companies. H.R. Doc. No. 476, 76th Cong., 2d Sess., 4-5 (1939). For at least a generation, therefore, there has been no reason to doubt that a national bank can, consistently with the banking laws, commingle trust funds on the one hand, and act as a managing agent on the other. No provision of the banking law suggests that it is improper for a national bank to pool trust assets, or to act as a managing agent for individual customers, or to purchase stock for the account of its customers. But the union of these powers gives birth to an investment fund whose activities are of a different character. The differences between the investment fund that the Comptroller has authorized and a conventional open-end mutual fund are subtle at best, and it is undisputed that this bank investment fund finds itself in direct competition with the mutual fund industry. One would suppose that the business of a mutual fund consists of buying stock "for its own account" and of "issuing" and "selling" "stock" or "other securities" evidencing an undivided and redeemable interest in the assets of the fund.[11] On their face, §§16 and 21 of the Glass-Steagall Act appear clearly to prohibit this activity by national banks.[12]

But we cannot come lightly to the conclusion that the Comptroller has authorized activity that violates the banking laws. It is settled that courts should give great weight to any reasonable construction of a regulatory statute adopted by the agency charged with the enforcement of that statute. The Comptroller of Currency is charged with the enforcement of the banking laws to an extent that warrants the invocation of this principle with respect to his deliberative conclusions as to the meaning of these laws. *See First National Bank v. Missouri,* 263 U.S. 640, 658, 68 L.Ed. 486, 493, 44 S.Ct. 213.

The difficulty here is that the Comptroller adopted no expressly articulated position at the administrative level as to the meaning and impact of the provisions of §§16 and 21 as they affect bank investment funds. The Comptroller promulgated Regulation 9 without opinion or accompanying

11. A mutual fund is an open-end investment company. The Investment Company Act of 1940 defines an investment company as an "issuer" of "any security" which "is or holds itself out as being engaged primarily . . . in the business of investing . . . in securities. . . ." 15 U.S.C. §§80a-2(a)(21), 80a-3(a)(1). An open-end company is one "which is offering for sale or has outstanding any redeemable security of which it is the issuer." 15 U.S.C. §80a-5(a)(1). An investment company also includes a "unit investment trust": an investment company which, among other things, "is organized under a . . . contract of . . . agency . . . and . . . issues only redeemable securities, each of which represents an undivided interest in a unit of specified securities. . . ." 15 U.S.C. §80a-4(2).

12. Section 20 of the Act, 12 U.S.C. §377, prohibits affiliations between banks that are members of the Federal Reserve System and organizations "engaged principally in the issue, flotation, underwriting, public sale, or distribution at wholesale or retail or through syndicate participation of stocks, bonds, debentures, notes, or other securities. . . ." And §32, 12 U.S.C. §78, provides that no officer, director, or employee of a bank in the Federal Reserve System may serve at the same time as officer, director, or employee of an association primarily engaged in the activity described in §20. The petitioners contend that if a bank's investment fund be conceived as an entity distinct from the bank, then its affiliation with the investment fund is in violation of these sections.

The Board of Governors has had occasion to consider whether an investment fund of the type operated by First National City Bank involves a violation of §32 of the Glass-Steagall Act. 12 C.F.R. §218.111 (1970). The Board concluded, based on "general principles that have been developed in respect to the application of section 32," that it would not violate that section for officers of the bank's trust department to serve at the same time as officers of the investment fund because the fund and the bank "constitute a single entity," and the fund "would be regarded as nothing more than an arm or department of the bank." The Board called attention to §21 whose provisions it summarized as forbidding "a securities firm or organization to engage in the business of receiving deposits, subject to certain exceptions." The Board, however, declined to express a position because of its policy not to express views as to the meaning of statutes that carry criminal penalties. Nor has the Board expressed its views on the application of any other provision of the banking law to the creation and operation of a bank investment fund.

We have no doubt but that the Board's construction and application of §32 is both reasonable and rational. The investment fund service authorized by the Comptroller's regulation and as provided by the First National City Bank is a service available only to customers of the bank. It is held out as a service provided by the bank, and the investment fund bears the bank's name. The bank has effective control over the activities of the investment fund. Moreover, there is no danger that to characterize the bank and its fund as a single entity will disserve the purpose of Congress. The limitations that the banking laws place on the activities of national banks are at least as great as the limitations placed on the activities of their affiliates. For example, §32 refers to the "public sale" of stocks or securities while §21 proscribes the "selling" of stocks or securities.

statement. His subsequent report to Congress did not advert to the prohibitions of the Glass-Steagall Act. Comptroller of the Currency, 101st Annual Report 14-15 (1963).[13] To be sure, counsel for the Comptroller in the course of this litigation, and specifically in his briefs and oral argument in this Court, has rationalized the basis of Regulation 9 with great professional competence. But this is hardly tantamount to an administrative interpretation of §§16 and 21. In *Burlington Truck Lines v. United States,* 371 U.S. 156, 9 L.Ed.2d 207, 83 S.Ct. 239, we said, "The courts may not accept appellate counsel's post hoc rationalizations for agency action. . . . For the courts to substitute their or counsel's discretion for that of the [agency] is incompatible with the orderly functioning of the process of judicial review." *Id.,* at 168-169, 9 L.Ed.2d at 216, Congress has delegated to the administrative official and not to appellate counsel the responsibility for elaborating and enforcing statutory commands. It is the administrative official and not appellate counsel who possesses the expertise that can enlighten and rationalize the search for the meaning and intent of Congress. Quite obviously the Comptroller should not grant new authority to national banks until he is satisfied that the exercise of this authority will not violate the intent of the banking laws. If he faces such questions only after he has acted, there is substantial danger that the momentum generated by initial approval may seriously impair the enforcement of the banking laws that Congress enacted.

IV

There is no dispute that one of the objectives of the Glass-Steagall Act was to prohibit commercial banks, banks that receive deposits subject to repayment, lend money, discount and negotiate promissory notes and the like, from going into the investment banking business. Many commercial banks were indirectly engaged in the investment banking business when the Act was passed in 1933. Even before the passage of the Act it was generally believed that it was improper for a commercial bank to engage in investment banking directly.[14] But in 1908 banks began the practice of establishing security affiliates that engaged in, *inter alia,* the business of floating bond issues and, less frequently, underwriting stock issues.[15] The Glass-Steagall Act confirmed that national banks could not engage in investment banking directly, and in addition made affiliation with an organization so engaged illegal. One effect of the Act was to abolish the security affiliates of commercial banks.[16]

It is apparent from the legislative history of the Act why Congress felt that this drastic step was necessary. The failure of the Bank of United States in 1930 was widely attributed to that bank's activities with respect to its numerous securities

13. A law review article written by Comptroller Saxon and Deputy Comptroller Miller in 1965 did take the position that the Glass-Steagall Act is inapplicable to bank common trust funds. Saxon & Miller, Common Trust Funds, 53 Geo. LJ 994 (1965). But this view was predicated on the argument that when Congress in 1936 provided a tax exemption for common trust funds maintained by a bank, now 26 U.S.C. §584, it contemplated the exemption of common trust funds created for strictly investment purposes, and that consequently Congress must have assumed that the banking laws, which otherwise appear to proscribe such funds, were not applicable. *Id.,* at 1008-1010. Whatever the merits of this argument, it has no bearing on the instant litigation. It is clear that the collective investment funds authorized by Regulation 9 need not qualify for tax exemption under §584; the First National City Bank Fund does not so qualify. Moreover, the position advanced in the brief filed on behalf of the Comptroller in this litigation is not that the banking laws are inapplicable to bank investment funds, but rather that the creation and operation of such funds are consistent with the banking laws.

It is noteworthy that the §584 exemption is available to common trust funds "maintained by a bank . . . exclusively for the collective investment and reinvestment of moneys contributed thereto by the bank in its capacity as a *trustee, executor, administrator, or guardian. . . .*" (Emphasis added.) This language, which makes no reference to contributions by the bank in its capacity as managing agent, is identical to that exempting such common trust funds from the Investment Company Act of 1940, 15 U.S.C. §80a-3(c)(3). The Securities and Exchange Commission has taken the position that commingled managing agency accounts do not come within §80a-3(c)(3). *See* Statement of Commissioner Cary, Hearings on Common Trust Funds—Overlapping Responsibility and Conflict in Regulation, before a Subcommittee of the House Committee on Government Operations, 88th Cong., 1st Sess., 3 (1963).

14. Hearings Pursuant to S. Res. 71 before a Subcommittee of the Senate Committee on Banking and Currency (hereafter 1931 Hearings), 71st Cong., 3d Sess., 40 (1931); 1920 Report of the Comptroller of the Currency, quoted *id.,* at 1067, 1068. Senator Glass, commenting on earlier banking legislation, said, "We tried to, and thought at the time we had, removed the system as far as possible from the influence of the stock market." *Id.,* at 262.

15. *Id.,* at 1052.

16. Report on Investment Trusts and Investment Companies, pt. 2, H.R. Doc. No. 70, 76th Cong., 1st Sess., 59 (1939).

affiliates.[17] Moreover, Congress was concerned that commercial banks in general and member banks of the Federal Reserve System in particular had both aggravated and been damaged by stock market decline partly because of their direct and indirect involvement in the trading and ownership of speculative securities.[18] The Glass-Steagall Act reflected a determination that policies of competition, convenience, or expertise which might otherwise support the entry of commercial banks into the investment banking business were outweighed by the "hazards" and "financial dangers" that arise when commercial banks engage in the activities proscribed by the Act.[19]

The hazards that Congress had in mind were not limited to the obvious danger that a bank might invest its own assets in frozen or otherwise imprudent stock or security investments. For often securities affiliates had operated without direct access to the assets of the bank. This was because securities affiliates had frequently been established with capital paid in by the bank's stockholders, or by the public, or through the allocation of a legal dividend on bank stock for this purpose.[20] The legislative history of the Glass-Steagall Act shows that Congress also had in mind and repeatedly focused on the more subtle hazards that arise when a commercial bank goes beyond the business of acting as fiduciary or managing agent and enters the investment banking business either directly or by establishing an affiliate to hold and sell particular investments. This course places new promotional and other pressures on the bank which in turn create new temptations. For example, pressures are created because the bank and the affiliate are closely associated in the public mind, and should the affiliate fare badly, public confidence in the bank might be impaired. And since public confidence is essential to the solvency of a bank, there might exist a natural temptation to shore up the affiliate through unsound loans or other aid.[21] Moreover, the pressure to sell a particular investment and to make the affiliate successful might create a risk that the bank would make its credit facilities more freely available to those companies in whose stock or securities the affiliate has invested or become otherwise involved. Congress feared that banks might even go so far as to make unsound loans to such companies.[22] In any event, it was thought that the bank's salesman's interest might impair its ability to function as an impartial source of credit.[23]

Congress was also concerned that bank depositors might suffer losses on investments that they purchased in reliance on the relationship between the bank and its affiliate.[24] This loss of customer good will might "become an important handicap to a bank during a major period of security market deflation."[25] More broadly, Congress feared that the promotional needs of investment banking might lead commercial banks to lend their reputation for prudence and restraint to the enterprise of selling particular stocks and securities, and that this could not be done without that reputation being undercut by the risks necessarily incident to the investment banking business.[26] There was also perceived the danger that when commercial banks were subject to the promotional demands of investment banking, they might be tempted to make loans to customers with the expectation that the loan would facilitate the purchase of stocks and securities.[27] There was evidence before Congress that loans for investment written by commercial banks had done much to feed the speculative fever of the late 1920's.[28] Senator Glass made it plain that it was "the fixed purpose of Congress" not to see the facilities of commercial

17. 1931 Hearings, 116-117, 1017, 1068.

18. *See* S.Rep.No. 77, 73d Cong., 1st Sess., 6, 8, 10.

19. *Id.,* at 18; *see* 1931 Hearings 365; 75 Cong. Rec. 9911 (remarks of Sen. Bulkley).

20. 1931 Hearings 41, 192, 1056; 1920 Report of the Comptroller of the Currency, quoted *id.,* at 1067.

21. 1931 Hearings 20, 237, 1063. *See also id.,* at 1058, where it is said:

> Activities of a bank's security affiliate as a holding or finance company or an investment trust are also fraught with the danger of large losses during a deflation period. Bank affiliates of this kind show a much greater tendency to operate with borrowed funds than do organizations of this type which are independent of banks, the reason being that the identity of control and management which prevails between the bank and its affiliate tends to encourage reliance upon the lending facilities of the former.

22. *See id.,* at 1064; 75 Cong. Rec. 9912 (remarks of Sen. Bulkley).

23. *See* 1931 Hearings 87 (remarks of Chairman Glass).

24. *See* 77 Cong. Rec. 4028 (remarks of Rep. Fish).

25. 1931 Hearings 1064.

26. *See* 75 Cong. Rec. 9912:

> And although such a loss would possibly not result in any substantial impairment of the resources of the banking institution owning that affiliate . . . there can be no doubt that the whole transaction tends to discredit the bank and impair the confidence of its depositors. (Remarks of Sen. Bulkley.)

27. S.Rep. No. 77, 73d Cong., 1st Sess., 9-10.

28. 1931 Hearings 1006-1029; S.Rep. No. 77, 73d Cong., 1st Sess., 8-9.

banking diverted into speculative operations by the aggressive and promotional character of the investment banking business.[29]

Another potential hazard that very much concerned Congress arose from the plain conflict between the promotional interest of the investment banker and the obligation of the commercial banker to render disinterested investment advice. Senator Bulkley stated:

> Obviously, the banker who has nothing to sell to his depositors is much better qualified to advise disinterestedly and to regard diligently the safety of depositors than the banker who uses the list of depositors in his savings department to distribute circulars concerning the advantages of this, that, or the other investment on which the bank is to receive an originating profit or an underwriting profit or a distribution profit or a trading profit or any combination of such profits.[30]

Congress had before it evidence that security affiliates might be driven to unload excessive holdings through the trust department of the sponsor bank.[31] Some witnesses at the hearings expressed the view that this practice constituted self-dealing in violation of the trustee's obligation of loyalty, and indeed that it would be improper for a bank's trust department to purchase anything from the bank's securities affiliate.[32]

In sum, Congress acted to keep commercial banks out of the investment banking business largely because it believed that the promotional incentives of investment banking and the investment banker's pecuniary stake in the success of particular investment opportunities was destructive of prudent and disinterested commercial banking and of public confidence in the commercial banking system. As Senator Bulkley put it:

> If we want banking service to be strictly banking service, without the expectation of additional profits in selling something to customers, we must keep the banks out of the investment security business.[33]

V

The language that Congress chose to achieve this purpose includes the prohibitions of §16 that a national bank "shall not underwrite any issue of securities or stock" and shall not purchase "for its own account . . . any shares of stock of any corporation," and the prohibition of §21 against engaging in "the business of issuing, underwriting, selling, or distributing . . . stocks, bonds, debentures, notes, or other securities." In this litigation the Comptroller takes the position that the operation of a bank investment fund is consistent with these provisions, because participating interests in such a fund are not "securities" within the meaning of the Act. It is argued that a bank investment fund simply makes available to the small investor the benefit of investment management by a bank trust department which would otherwise be available only to large investors, and that the operation of an investment fund creates no problems that are not present whenever a bank invests in securities for the account of customers.

But there is nothing in the phrasing of either §16 or §21 that suggests a narrow reading of the word "securities." To the contrary, the breadth of the term is implicit in the fact that the antecedent statutory language encompasses not only equity securities but also securities representing debt. And certainly there is nothing in the language of these provisions to suggest that the sale of an interest in the business of buying, holding, and selling stocks for investment is to be distinguished from the sale of an interest in a commercial or industrial enterprise.

Indeed, there is direct evidence that Congress specifically contemplated that the word "security" includes an interest in an investment fund. The Glass-Steagall Act was the product of hearings conducted pursuant to Senate Resolution 71 which included among the topics to be investi-

---

29. 75 Cong. Rec. 9884. *See also* S.Rep. No. 77, 73d Cong., 1st Sess., 8:

> The outstanding development in the commercial banking system during the prepanic period was the appearance of excessive security loans, and of over-investment in securities of all kinds. The effects of this situation in changing the whole character of the banking problem can hardly be overemphasized. National banks were never intended to undertake investment banking business on a large scale, and the whole tenor of legislation and administrative rulings concerning them has been away from recognition of such a growth in the direction of investment banking as legitimate.

In the same vein Representative Steagall said:

> Our great banking system was diverted from its original purposes into investment activities. . . .
>
> . . . . .
>
> The purpose of the regulatory provisions of this bill is to call back to the service of agriculture and commerce and industry the bank credit and the bank service designed by the framers of the Federal Reserve Act.

77 Cong. Rec. 3835.

30. 75 Cong. Rec. 9912.

31. 1931 Hearings 237; *cf. id.*, at 1064.

32. *Id.*, at 266, 300, 311.

33. 75 Cong. Rec. 9912.

gated the impact on the banking system of the formation of investment and security trusts.[34] The subcommittee found that one of the activities in which bank security affiliates engaged was that of an investment trust: "buying and selling securities acquired purely for investment or speculative purposes."[35] Since Congress generally intended to divorce commercial banking from the kinds of activities in which bank security affiliates engaged, there is reason to believe that Congress explicitly intended to prohibit a national bank from operating an investment trust.[36]

But, in any event, we are persuaded that the purposes for which Congress enacted the Glass-Steagall Act leave no room for the conclusion that a participation in a bank investment fund is not a "security" within the meaning of the Act. From the perspective of competition, convenience, and expertise, there are arguments to be made in support of allowing commercial banks to enter the investment banking business. But Congress determined that the hazards outlined above made it necessary to prohibit this activity to commercial banks. Those same hazards are clearly present when a bank undertakes to operate an investment fund.

A bank that operates an investment fund has a particular investment to sell. It is not a matter of indifference to the bank whether the customer buys an interest in the fund or makes some other investment. If its customers cannot be persuaded to invest in the bank's investment fund, the bank will lose their investment business and the fee which that business would have brought in. Even as to accounts large enough to qualify for individual investment management, there might be a potential for a greater profit if the investment were placed in the fund rather than in individually selected securities, because of fixed costs and economies of scale. The mechanics of operating an investment fund might also create promotional pressure. When interests in the fund were redeemed, the bank would be effectively faced with the choice of selling stocks from the fund's portfolio or of selling new participations to cover redemptions. The bank might have a pecuniary incentive to choose the latter course in order to avoid the cost of stock transactions undertaken solely for redemption purposes.

Promotional incentives might also be created by the circumstance that the bank's fund would be in direct competition with mutual funds that, from the point of view of the investor, offered an investment opportunity comparable to that offered by the bank. The bank would want to be in a position to show to the prospective customer that its fund was more attractive than the mutual funds offered by others. The bank would have a salesman's stake in the performance of the fund, for if the fund were less successful than the competition the bank would lose business and the resulting fees.

A bank that operated an investment fund would necessarily put its reputation and facilities squarely behind that fund and the investment opportunity that the fund offered. The investments of the fund might be conservative or speculative, but in any event the success or failure of the fund would be a matter of public record. Imprudent or unsuccessful management of the bank's investment fund could bring about a perhaps unjustified loss of public confidence in the bank itself. If imprudent management should place the fund in distress, a bank might find itself under pressure to rescue the fund through measures inconsistent with sound banking.

The promotional and other pressures incidental to the operation of an investment fund, in other words, involve the same kinds of potential abuses that Congress intended to guard against when it legislated against bank security affiliates. It is not the slightest reflection on the integrity of the mutual fund industry to say that the traditions of that industry are not necessarily the conservative traditions of commercial banking. The needs and interests of a mutual fund enterprise more nearly approximate those of securities underwriting, the activity in which bank security affiliates were primarily engaged. When a bank puts itself in competition with mutual funds, the bank must make an accommodation to the kind of ground rules that Congress firmly concluded could not be prudently mixed with the business of commercial banking.

And there are other potential hazards of the kind Congress sought to eliminate with the passage of the Glass-Steagall Act. The bank's stake in the investment fund might distort its credit decisions or lead to unsound loans to the companies in which the fund had invested. The bank might exploit its confidential relationship with its commercial and industrial creditors for the benefit of the fund. The bank might undertake, directly or indirectly, to make its credit facilities available to the fund or to render other aid to the fund incon-

34. S. Res. 71, 71st Cong., 2d Sess., is reprinted in S. Rep. No. 77, 73d Cong., 1st Sess., 1.

35. 1931 Hearings 1057. *See also id.,* at 307.

36. *See also supra,* n. 21.

sistent with the best interests of the bank's depositors. The bank might make loans to facilitate the purchase of interests in the fund. The bank might divert talent and resources from its commercial banking operation to the promotion of the fund. Moreover, because the bank would have a stake in a customer's making a particular investment decision—the decision to invest in the bank's investment fund—the customer might doubt the motivation behind the bank's recommendation that he make such an investment. If the fund investment should turn out badly there would be a danger that the bank would lose the good will of those customers who had invested in the fund. It might be unlikely that disenchantment would go so far as to threaten the solvency of the bank. But because banks are dependent of the confidence of their customers, the risk would not be unreal.

These are all hazards that are not present when a bank undertakes to purchase stock for the account of its individual customers or to commingle assets which it has received for a true fiduciary purpose rather than for investment. These activities, unlike the operation of an investment fund, do not give rise to a promotional or salesman's stake in a particular investment; they do not involve an enterprise in direct competition with aggressively promoted funds offered by other investment companies; they do not entail a threat to public confidence in the bank itself; and they do not impair the bank's ability to give disinterested service as a fiduciary or managing agent. In short, there is a plain difference between the sale of fiduciary services and the sale of investments.[37]

VI

The Glass-Steagall Act was a prophylactic measure directed against conditions that the experience of the 1920's showed to be great potentials for abuse. The literal terms of that Act clearly prevent what the Comptroller has sought to authorize here. Because the potential hazards and abuses that flow from a bank's entry into the mutual investment business are the same basic hazards and abuses that Congress intended to eliminate almost 40 years ago, we cannot but apply the terms of the federal statute as they were written. We conclude that the operation of an investment fund of the kind approved by the Comptroller involves a bank in the underwriting, issuing, selling, and distributing of securities in violation of §§16 and 21 of the Glass-Steagall Act. Accordingly, we reverse the judgment in No. 61 and vacate the judgment in No. 59.

It is so ordered.

37. *See* 26 Fed. Reserve Bull. 393 (1940), quoted *supra,* at 621, 28 L.Ed.2d at 373.

Tax Rulings

The Court's decision in the *Camp* case resulted in the amendment of the Comptroller's Regulations, but the assets held by a bank in a fiduciary capacity may still be invested collectively either in a common fund maintained by the bank exclusively for the collective investment and reinvestment of monies contributed by the bank in its capacity as trustee, or in a common fund consisting solely of assets of qualified trusts maintained in connection with tax-qualified plans. *See* 12 C.F.R. §9.18(a)(1). Assets held by a bank in its capacity as trustee for a tax-exempt trust may be invested in either type of common fund, and the common fund itself will be tax exempt. *See* 12 C.F.R. 9.18(b)(2). Of equal importance, such investment will not result in the disqualification of the pension trust.

In Revenue Ruling 56-267, 1956-1 Cum. Bull. 206, the Internal Revenue Service stated that qualified trusts, which are tax exempt under §501 of the Code, forming part of a tax-qualified plan, will not be disqualified by reason of the pooling of those trusts in a group trust fund created solely for the purpose of providing a satisfactory diversification of investments for the individual participating trusts. However, certain conditions must be satisfied.

First, the group trust must be adopted as part of each tax-qualified plan. Second, the group trust agreement must expressly limit participation to qualified trusts which are tax exempt under §501 of the Code by reason of §401 of the Code. Third, the group trust agreement must prohibit that part of its corpus of income which equitably belongs to any participating trust from being used for or diverted to any purpose other than for the exclusive benefit of the employees who are entitled to benefits under the participating trust. Fourth, the group trust instrument must prohibit assignment by a participating trust of any part of its equity or interest in the group trust. Fifth, the group trust must be created and maintained at all times as a domestic trust in the United States.

In Revenue Ruling 66-297, 1966-2 Cum. Bull. 234, the Internal Revenue Service distinguished group trusts from common funds. A common trust fund is defined in §584 of the Code as:

> a fund maintained by a bank . . . exclusively for the collective investment and reinvestment of

> monies contributed thereto by the bank in its capacity as trustee . . . in conformity with the rules and regulations, prevailing from time to time, of the Board of Governors of the Federal Reserve System or the Comptroller of the Currency pertaining to the collective investment of trust funds maintained by national banks.

This section permits banks to maintain common trust funds consisting solely of assets of tax-qualified plans without regard to requirements for tax exemption relating to a group trust under Revenue Ruling 56-267. *See also* Rev. Rul. 67-301, 1967-2 Cum. Bull. 146. Therefore, a common fund may commingle the assets of tax-qualified plans with any other funds held by the bank as a trustee, but a group trust fund must consist solely of assets of tax-qualified plans. *See* Rev. Rul. 75-530, 1975-2 Cum. Bull. 208.

REVENUE RULING 66-297
1966-2 Cum. Bull. 234

Advice has been requested whether a collective investment fund, established by a bank and consisting solely of property held by the bank in its capacity as trustee of qualified pension and profit-sharing trusts which are exempt from Federal income tax, may be exempt from Federal income tax as a common trust fund within the meaning of section 584 of the Internal Revenue Code of 1954 irrespective of the requirements of Revenue Ruling 56-267, C. B. 1956-1, 206, pertaining to group trust funds.

Section 584(a) of the Code provides, in part, that the term "common trust fund" means a fund maintained by a bank (1) exclusively for the collective investment and reinvestment of moneys contributed thereto by the bank in its capacity as a trustee, executor, administrator, or guardian; and (2) in conformity with the rules and regulations, prevailing from time to time, of the Comptroller of the Currency pertaining to the collective investment of trust funds by national banks.

Section 1.584-1(b) of the Income Tax Regulations provides, in part, that (2) above applies whether or not the bank maintaining the fund is a national bank or a member of the Federal Reserve System.

Section 584(b) of the Code provides that a common trust fund shall not be subject to Federal income tax and shall not be considered a corporation.

Section 9.18(a) of Title 12 of the Code of Federal Regulations relating to fiduciary powers of national banks and collective investment funds, provides that, where not in contravention of local law, funds held by a national bank as fiduciary may be invested collectively (1) in a common trust fund maintained by the bank exclusively for the collective investment and reinvestment of moneys contributed thereto by the bank in its capacity as executor, administrator, guardian or trustee under a will or deed; (2) in a fund consisting solely of assets of retirement, pension, profit-sharing, stock bonus, or other trusts which are exempt from Federal income taxation under the Internal Revenue Code; (3) in a common trust fund, maintained by the bank exclusively for the collective investment and reinvestment of moneys contributed thereto by the bank in its capacity as managing agent under a managing agency agreement expressly providing that such moneys are received by the bank in trust. See Revenue Ruling 64-59, C. B. 1964-1 (Part 1), 193, as it pertains to (3) above.

Section 9.18(b)(2) of Title 12 provides that property held by the bank in its capacity as trustee of retirement, pension, profit-sharing, stock bonus or other trusts which are exempt from Federal income taxation under the Internal Revenue Code may be invested in collective investment funds established under the provisions of subparagraph (1) or (2) of section 9.18(a) of Title 12.

Revenue Ruling 56-267 holds that where, under certain specified conditions, separate tax-exempt trusts, forming parts of employers' qualified pension or profit-sharing plans, pool their funds in a group trust created to provide diversification of investments, the group trust may qualify as a tax-exempt trust and the exempt status of the separate trusts will not be adversely affected.

There is no requirement that a common trust fund maintained by a bank and consisting solely of property contributed by the bank in its capacity as trustee of exempt pension and profit-sharing trusts comply with Revenue Ruling 56-267 in order to qualify as a "common trust fund" under section 584 of the Code. If the common trust fund is maintained by the bank exclusively for the collective investment and reinvestment of moneys contributed thereto by the bank in its capacity as trustee and this is done in conformity with the rules and regulations, prevailing from time to time, of the Comptroller of the Currency pertaining to the collective investment of trust funds by national banks, it qualifies as a "common trust fund." The fact that the common trust fund may consist solely of property held by the bank in its capacity as trustee of qualified pension and profit-sharing trusts which are exempt from Federal income tax does not alter the rule, since such trust funds may be invested in a collective investment fund under the provisions of either subparagraph (1) or (2) of section 9.18(a) of Title 12.

Accordingly, a common trust fund, maintained by a bank and consisting solely of property held by the bank in its capacity as trustee of pension and profit-sharing trusts exempt from Federal income tax, will continue to be exempt from Federal income tax as a common trust fund within the meaning of section 584 of the Code, independently of the requirements for exemption of a group trust fund under Revenue Ruling 56-267.

Further, a group trust fund, maintained by a bank, consisting solely of assets of exempt pension and profit-sharing trusts, and complying with Revenue Ruling 56-267, will continue to be exempt from Federal income tax under section 501(a) of the Code, independently of the requirements for exemption of a common trust fund under section 584 of the Code. However, a group trust which commingles the funds of qualified employees' trusts with the funds of other exempt organizations will not be a trust described in section 401(a) or section 501(c) or section 501(d) of the Code and therefore cannot qualify for exemption from Federal income tax under section 501(a) of the Code.

Participation

The administration of these common funds is also regulated by the Comptroller. *See* 12 C.F.R. §9.18(b). For example, the bank is required to value the assets in the fund at least once every three months, and participations in the fund cannot be admitted or withdrawn except on the basis of those valuations and on the date that such valuations are made. A request for admittance to or withdrawal from a common fund must have been entered in the fiduciary records of the bank and approved prior to any valuation date. After such valuation date has passed, a request or notice of admittance or withdrawal cannot be cancelled.

Participation in a collective investment fund is on a proportionate basis, and each participant in the fund has an undivided interest equal to the ratio that the value of its account bears to the total market value of the fund, which valuations are to be determined as of any valuation date of the fund itself. This means that if a particular investment of the fund is withdrawn in kind for the benefit of all participants in the fund and is not distributed, each participant in the fund must have a proportionate interest in the asset which has been withdrawn. The asset must be administered or realized upon for the benefit ratably of all participants in the collective investment fund at the time of withdrawal.

Financial Report

A bank administering a collective investment fund must also cause the fund to be audited at least once every 12 months. If the audit is performed by independent public accountants, the expense of the audit may be charged to the fund to the extent it is reasonable. This charge will be prorated among the individual participants in the fund, as an expense of administration.

The fiduciary bank then must prepare a financial report of the fund, based on the audit and containing specific information on the investments in the fund, the fund's activity during the 12 months following the last financial report, and other detailed information. The bank is specifically prohibited from including in the financial report any representations as to the future results of the fund, or comparisons of the performance of that particular fund with any other fund that is not administered by the bank. However, the Comptroller has authorized comparisons of common fund performance with that of general market indices, such as the Dow Jones and the S&P 500, to be included in the report. A copy of the financial report must be given to each trust participating in the fund, or notice must be given that a copy of the report is available and will be furnished without charge. Comparisons with established indices should assist in evaluating the results of the bank's management.

Conflicts of Interest

The rules and regulations discussed above, which relate to the administration of common trust funds, are supplemented by rules and regulations governing the investment of assets held in common funds. For example, the bank must avoid conflicts of interest. *See* 12 C.F.R. §9.18(b)(8). The only interest a bank may have in a common fund is in its fiduciary capacity.

No assets of a common fund may be invested in stock or obligations, including time or savings deposits, of the bank or any of its affiliates. However, such deposits may be made with assets awaiting investment or distribution. Certain creditor relationships that may cause a conflict of interest must also be avoided. For example, if the bank acquires an interest in a participation in a common fund through a creditor relationship, the participation must be withdrawn on the first date on which such withdrawal can be effected.

Comptroller's Handbook

Guidelines Given

In connection with the Comptroller's responsibility for supervising the national bank system and monitoring its soundness, the Office of the Comptroller of Currency has published the *Comptroller's Handbook for National Trust Examiners*, which replaces the previously published *Comptroller's Manual for Representatives of Trusts*. The *Handbook* provides guidelines for the examination of banks exercising fiduciary powers, and serves as a means for banks to assess the soundness of their trust departments and their compliance with the rules and regulations issued by the Comptroller.

The *Handbook* cites, as the basis of evaluation for examiners, certain goals which are desirable for banks to achieve in the operation of their trust departments. The primary goal is compliance with law, Regulation 9 and sound fiduciary principles. In addition, a bank's practices and policies are expected to result in the safeguarding of fiduciary assets and the maintenance of reliable accounting records.

The Questionnaire as Checklist

The *Handbook* further provides that examiners should evaluate the management, condition, and future prospects of the trust department. The *Handbook* also reproduces Regulation 9, and contains a questionnaire to be used by bank examiners in conducting their examination of bank trust departments. This questionnaire can be utilized by banks in assessing whether or not the policies and practices of their trust departments and of the bank as a whole result in compliance with Regulation 9—and, of at least equal importance, with the applicable provisions of ERISA and the Code.

The questionnaire contained in the *Handbook* is divided into separate areas of investigation for bank examiners, one of which deals solely with the management and administration of employee benefit accounts. The questionnaire asks if the bank, when acting as a trustee, ascertains that the instrument governing the employee benefit plan contains certain information which, in the opinion of the Comptroller, is necessary to properly administer the trust. The checklist also sets forth the standards for fiduciary conduct embodied in ERISA, and asks if the bank complies with those standards in discharging its fiduciary duties. In addition, the questionnaire asks if the bank when acting as trustee monitors transactions so that neither it nor other fiduciaries engage in self-dealing or use plan assets to profit for their own account.

In completing the questionnaire, a "no" answer will generally indicate that the bank is weak in that area of its trust department and should review its policies and procedures to ensure that the trust department is functioning in compliance with Regulation 9 as well as any other law which may relate to the bank's exercise of fiduciary powers. The questionnaire thus serves as a valuable internal aid to bank trust departments in determining whether the bank's performance as trustee of an employee benefit plan is in conformance with the requirements of ERISA; that the bank protects itself from liabilities which may arise under ERISA as a result of the actions of other parties; and that the bank acts in the best interests of employee benefit plan participants and beneficiaries.

FEDERAL RESERVE ACT

Scope

The Federal Reserve Act, 12 U.S.C. 221 *et seq.*, established the Federal Reserve System and made membership in that system mandatory for all national banks. State banks and trust companies may also be members of the Federal Reserve System.

The purpose of the Federal Reserve Act was to place all national banks and certain other financial institutions under federal control, and to allow the governing body of the Federal Reserve System, the Board of Governors, to exercise certain powers with regard to banks which are members of the System. The Board of Governors is empowered to examine banks and their accounts, to regulate the issuance of currency to banks through the Comptroller of the Currency and generally to establish monetary policies and regulate the availability of credit in the national economy. Several of the Board's regulations affect pension and welfare plans.

Specific Provisions

Regulation G

Regulation G relates to the extension of credit in certain securities transactions by persons other than banks, brokers or dealers. *See* 12 C.F.R. §207. This regulation affects pension and welfare plans and the other components of the plan complex because a plan may be either a borrower or a lender, as may the employer or employers maintaining the plan. Alternatively, an employer or union may guarantee the extension of credit to a plan.

Section 207.1 requires persons who in the ordinary course of their business extend credit which is secured by collateral consisting wholly or partly of margin securities to register with the Board of Governors. Such a person must register if the total credit extended or arranged for during any calendar quarter is $100,000 or more, or if the total credit outstanding at any time in a calendar quarter is $500,000 or more. Registration is accomplished by filing Form G-1 with the Federal Reserve Bank for the district in which the extender of the credit's principal office is located.

A person who has registered previously but has not extended or arranged for the extension of credit for six months, or who during a six month period has not had more than $200,000 of credit outstanding at any time, may apply for a termination of a previous registration by filing Federal Reserve Form G-2. This application must be approved by the Board of Governors before a previous registration can be terminated.

Section 207.1 also restricts the amount of credit which may be extended by a person subject to the registration requirements for the purpose of purchasing or carrying a margin security. If the credit extended is secured wholly or partly by collateral that includes a margin security, the person extending the credit is a "lender" and may not arrange for or extend credit for the purpose of purchasing margin securities which would exceed the maximum loan value of the collateral. As defined in Section 207.5, the maximum loan value of any margin security is 50% of its current market value.

Any person who extends credit which is secured directly or indirectly, in whole or in part, by a collateral that includes a margin security must obtain a statement from the customer to which the credit will be extended, which statement conforms with Federal Reserve Form G-3. The term "margin security" is defined as an equity security which is a registered equity security, an over-the-counter margin stock, a debt security which is convertible into a margin security or carries any warrant or right to subscribe to or purchase a margin security, any such warrant or right, or a security issued by an investment company which is registered under the Investment Company Act of 1940. (The Investment Company Act of 1940 is discussed in Chapter 4.)

Regulation U

Regulation U relates to the extension of credit by banks for the purpose of purchasing or carrying margin stocks. *See* 12 C.F.R. §221. This regulation also affects pension plans.

Section 221.112 of Regulation U is a response to a request for advice as to whether or not the provisions of Regulation U relate to the administration by a bank of an employees' savings plan. The situation discussed in Section 221.112 involves a plan that permits an employee to authorize his employer to make deductions from his salary and transmit the amount deducted to a bank which serves as trustee. Under the plan, a participant has the right to direct the investment of funds held for his benefit: he can choose from insurance or annuity contracts or Series E savings bonds, or can direct that his account be invested in one or more of three specific securities which are listed on a stock exchange. The plan also provides that participants may obtain loans from the trust funds to purchase the stocks, which loans are then secured by the balance of the participant's account in the savings fund, excluding insurance and annuity contracts and government securities. Loans are only made from the trust fund and are not made from bank funds.

Those requesting the advice on this matter contended that loans made from the trust fund to purchase stock should not cause the bank, in its capacity as trustee, to be subject to the restrictions of Regulation U. However, the Board of Governors took the position that, although the bank had little discretion with regard to loans from the trust fund, the provisions of Regulation U which restrict the extension of credit for the purpose of purchasing securities apply to a bank which is acting as a trustee. The effect of Regulation U is to restrict the amount of credit which may be extended by a bank for the purpose of purchasing margin stocks to the maximum loan value of the stocks, which is generally 50% of its current market value.

Regulation Q

Regulation Q regulates the interest payable on deposits in banks which are members of the Federal Reserve System. This regulation has a direct effect on individual retirement accounts and on Keogh (H.R. 10) plans. *See* 12 C.F.R. §217.

Section 217 establishes the maximum allowable interest rate on time and savings deposits, depending on the date of maturity and the amount to be deposited. This section has established a new category of time deposit for individual retirement account and Keogh plan assets in order to encourage the maintenance of those accounts with commercial banks which are members of the Federal Reserve System. This new category of time deposit is designed to be competitive with the time periods and interest rates offered to depositors by mutual savings banks and by savings and loan associations.

Because a participant in an individual retirement account may roll over contributions from one financial institution to another once every three years without paying a tax penalty, Section 217.7 provides that participants in individual retirement accounts or Keogh plans may invest in time deposits of under $100,000 which will mature in a minimum of three years. These time deposits will pay the highest permissible interest at a rate which is normally allowed only on deposits with a maturity date of six years or more. In addition, the $1,000 minimum amount which is usually required in order to earn the highest rate of interest does not apply to deposits of individual retirement account and Keogh plan funds.

Section 217 also provides that individual retirement accounts and Keogh plan assets deposited in a member bank may be withdrawn without being subject to the penalty for early withdrawal which would normally be imposed, provided that the withdrawal is due to the depositor's attainment of age 59½ or disability. Regulation Q therefore impacts on both the investment of individual retirement account and Keogh plan funds, and on the time of payment of benefits from those funds.

FEDERAL DEPOSIT INSURANCE ACT

Insured Banks

The Federal Deposit Insurance Act, 12 U.S.C. 1812 *et seq*., established the Federal Deposit Insurance Corporation for the purpose of insuring the deposits of all banks which qualified for insurance under the provisions of that act. Section 1817(i) of the Federal Deposit Insurance Act provides that trust funds which are held by an insured bank in its capacity as fiduciary will be insured up to $40,000 for each trust estate, regardless of whether the owners of the trust or the beneficiaries are similarly insured for other deposits or accounts.

Any bank may apply to become an insured bank under the provisions of this act, and must report its condition each calendar quarter to the Board of Directors, the Comptroller of the Currency or a Federal Reserve Bank, depending upon the type of financial institution. The Federal Deposit Insurance Act also describes the method of reporting an insured bank's condition and the information which is required to be included in each report.

IRAs and H.R. 10 Plans

The Board of Directors of the Federal Deposit Insurance Corporation has issued regulations which specify the maximum rates of interest payable on time and savings deposits in insured banks and specify certain penalties for a premature withdrawal of those deposits. *See* 12 C.F.R. §329. Part 329 is of particular interest to participants in IRAs and Keogh (H.R. 10) plans where those funds have been invested in time deposits in an insured bank.

Section 329 exempts individual retirement accounts and Keogh plan assets from the penalty ordinarily imposed for an early withdrawal of time deposits, if the individual making the withdrawal has attained age 59½ or has become disabled. Section 329 also allows deposits of IRA and Keogh plan assets which total less than $100,000 to earn interest at a rate higher than the highest rate of interest permissible for time and savings deposits of other types of funds in an insured commercial bank.

Formerly, individual retirement accounts and Keogh plan funds were unable to earn the maximum interest unless those funds were deposited in a mutual savings bank or savings and loan association. In addition, the maximum rate of interest could only be earned if the deposit was for a period of six years or more. Section 329 now allows those deposits to earn interest at the maximum rate if they are held in a time deposit with a maturity of three or more years. This applies to accounts where the entire interest is held in an individual retirement account or in a Keogh plan established pursuant to Section 501 of the Internal Revenue Code.

FEDERAL HOME LOAN BANK ACT

Scope

The Federal Home Loan Bank Act, 12 U.S.C. 1421 *et seq*., creates the Federal Home Loan Bank Board and divides the United States into districts, establishing a Federal Home Loan Bank at a city in each district. The act allows financial institutions which meet certain requirements to become members, or non-member borrowers, of a Federal Home Loan Bank by investing in the stock of that bank. The United States Government then purchases any remaining stock which has not been acquired by financial institutions desiring to become members or non-member borrowers. Each Federal Home Loan Bank is managed by a board of directors consisting of 12 members, who must be residents of the district in which the Federal Home Loan Bank is located.

A Federal Home Loan Bank has the authority to make advances to its members upon the security of home mortgages, United States obligations and obligations 100% guaranteed by the United States. The Federal Home Loan Bank Board makes rules, regulations and orders, and places restrictions and limitations on advances to member institutions and the terms of repayment and security for those advances. The Federal Home Loan Bank Board also generally supervises the operation of Federal Home Loan Banks.

Specific Regulations

The impact of the Federal Home Loan Bank Act on pension plans is primarily in the area of investments. Regulation Section 545.17-1, promulgated by the Federal Home Loan Bank Board, gives federally chartered savings and loan associations the authority to serve as trustees for trusts which form part of a tax-qualified stock bonus, pension or profit-sharing plan, and to receive reasonable compensation for services as a trustee. This section also authorizes savings and loan associations to act as a custodian for an individual retirement account under Section 408 of ERISA, and to receive compensation for their services as such. The savings and loan association may only act as a trustee or custodian if the funds of such trusts or accounts are invested solely in savings accounts or deposits of the savings and loan, or in obligations or securities which are issued by the savings and loan association. This regulation generally affects who may act as a trustee or custodian for a qualified trust maintained in connection with a tax-qualified plan or individual retirement account, and restricts the investment of those funds if a savings and loan association is acting as trustee or custodian.

Regulation Section 563.3-1 provides that there will be no penalty for early withdrawal on fixed-time, fixed-rate certificates of deposit of a savings and loan association, if the withdrawal is made by reason of the death, disability or attainment of age 59½ by a participant in an individual retirement account. This regulation impacts on the time of payment of benefits to participants and beneficiaries.

CHAPTER 7

Departments and Agencies Involved in Regulation

EMPLOYEE RETIREMENT INCOME SECURITY ACT OF 1974

Department of Labor

The Department of Labor has responsibility for administering and enforcing portions of ERISA. Within the Department, the principal unit which is responsible for carrying out the Secretary's duties under ERISA is the Labor Management Services Administration (LMSA).

LMSA is headed by the Assistant Secretary for Labor-Management Relations, who has overall responsibility for the Department's labor-management relations activities. Most of this person's day-to-day activities related to ERISA, however, are conducted by the Administrator of Pension and Welfare Benefit Programs, a program within LMSA. This program is divided into five functional offices and receives legal services from the Solicitor of Labor and, in particular, from the Associate Solicitor for the Plan Benefits Security Division. The Associate Solicitor and his staff are responsible for legal analyses and other services of a legal nature, while the Administrator and his staff are responsible for policy and operational matters.

Department of the Treasury

The Department of the Treasury also has responsibility for administering and enforcing portions of ERISA. Treasury's responsibilities under ERISA are principally carried out by the Internal Revenue Service. The unit within the Internal Revenue Service which acts by and on behalf of the Commissioner of Internal Revenue is the unit under the Assistant Commissioner for Employee Plans and Exempt Organizations (EPEO). Legal services for EPEO are provided by the Chief Counsel of the Internal Revenue Service.

Other offices within the Department of Treasury may also provide views on matters under consideration by the Internal Revenue Service. For example, the Office of the Assistant Secretary for Tax Policy reviews and signs-off on all regulations. In addition, the Office of the Assistant Secretary for Capital Markets and Debt Management, the Office of the Assistant Secretary for Economic Policy and the Office of the General Counsel may review regulations prior to proposal and adoption by the Internal Revenue Service.

Pension Benefit Guaranty Corporation

The Pension Benefit Guaranty Corporation, a self-financed, wholly owned government corporation subject to the provisions of the Government Corporation Control Act, was established under ERISA to administer the plan termination insurance program. A Board of Directors consisting of the Secretaries of Labor, Commerce and the Treasury, with the Secretary of Labor acting as Chairman of the Board, governs the PBGC. The PBGC itself is headed by an Executive Director who is responsible for administering the Corporation in accordance with policies established by the Board. In carrying out his functions, the Executive Director is supported by five offices.

Department of Justice

In the absence of a special provision contained in ERISA, the Department of Justice would represent the Secretary of Labor in all litigation relating to ERISA in the same manner as the Department of Justice represents other Secretaries. Section 502(j) of ERISA, however, provides that attorneys appointed by the Secretary of Labor (i.e., attorneys within the Office of the Solicitor of Labor and, particularly the Plan Benefits Security Division) may represent the Secretary in all civil actions; however, such litigation is still subject to the direction and control of the Attorney General. This provision permits Department of Labor attorneys to conduct employee benefits litigation. The respective roles of the Labor and Justice Departments are set forth in a Memorandum of Understanding executed by the two departments. Within the Justice Department, the principal unit responsible for directing ERISA litigation is the Civil Division, which is headed by an Assistant Attorney General.

The enforcement of all criminal laws, such as the criminal penalties contained in Section 501 of ERISA, is also the responsibility of the Department of Justice. The principal unit which discharges this responsibility is the Criminal Division, which is headed by an Assistant Attorney General.

The other unit within the Department of Justice with responsibilities under ERISA is the Parole Commission. Under Section 411(a) of ERISA, no person who has been convicted of certain crimes may hold certain positions with respect to an employee benefit plan during the five year period immediately following the later of the conviction or the end of any imprisonment, unless the Parole Commission determines that the person's service with respect to the plan would not be contrary to the purposes of ERISA. The Parole Commission consists of nine members, appointed by the President by and with the advice and consent of the Senate. It has sole authority to grant, modify or revoke the paroles of all prisoners.

Department of Health, Education and Welfare

The Department of Health, Education and Welfare, in particular, the Social Security Administration, has limited responsibilities under ERISA. Under Section 1031 of ERISA, which added Section 6057 to the Code, certain information relating to employee pension benefit plans must be filed with the Department of Treasury, which transmits it to the Secretary of HEW. In certain cases, this information must be provided by the Department of HEW to certain individuals. This function is carried out by the Social Security Administration. The Social Security Administration is headed by the Office of the Commissioner of Social Security, who is directly responsible to the Secretary for all programs administered by SSA.

TAX LAWS

Department of the Treasury

Most of the tax laws including, but not limited to, the Internal Revenue Code of 1954, as amended, the Tax Reduction Act of 1975 and the Tax Reform Act of 1976, are administered and enforced by the Department of the Treasury. This department is headed by the Secretary of Treasury, a cabinet-level (Executive Level I) political appointee who has responsibilities in numerous areas. In carrying out these responsibilities, the Secretary is supported by a Deputy Secretary, two Under Secretaries, eight Assistant Secretaries, the Comptroller of the Currency, the General Counsel and the Commissioner of Internal Revenue.

With relatively few exceptions, the administration and enforcement of the tax laws relating to the private employee benefit complex have been delegated to the Commissioner of Internal Revenue. The Commissioner of Internal Revenue is supported by a number of Assistant Commissioners. One of these Assistant Commissioners is the Assistant Commissioner for Employee Plans and Exempt Organizations. The Office of the Assistant Commissioner for Employee Plans and Exempt Organizations includes three divisions, two of which perform functions relating to employee benefits. These divisions are the Employee Plans Division and the Actuarial Division. (The third division, the Exempt Organizations Division, does not get involved in matters relating to the regulation of the private employee benefit complex.) The Chief Counsel of the Internal Revenue Service, who is also an Assistant General Counsel of the Treasury, provides legal services to the Commissioner and the Assistant Commissioners.

Although the Secretary of the Treasury has delegated most of his employee benefit functions to the Commissioner of Internal Revenue, the Department of the Treasury is still involved in employee benefit regulation. The Office of the Assistant Secretary for Tax Policy, among other activities, advises and assists the Secretary in the formulation and execution of domestic tax policies and programs. His functions include the development and review of regulations and rulings under the tax laws. For example, the Commissioner of Internal Revenue signs regulations prior to publication in the *Federal Register*, but the regulations must be approved by the Assistant Secretary for Tax Policy. The Assistant Secretary's functions are carried out by supporting staff offices, and the principal office providing support relating to employee benefits is the Office of the Tax Legislative Counsel.

Other offices within the Department of the Treasury may also provide views on matters under consideration by the Internal Revenue Service and the Office of the Assistant Secretary for Tax Policy. For example, the Office of the Assistant Secretary for Capital Markets and Debt Management, the Office of the Assistant Secretary for Economic Policy, and the Office of the General Counsel may review regulations prior to publication by the Internal Revenue Service. The nature and extent of the involvement of these offices varies with the particular matter under consideration.

Department of Commerce

Most of the laws affecting industry and commerce including, but not limited to, the Trade Act of 1974, are administered and enforced by the Department of Commerce. The Department of Commerce is headed by the Secretary of Commerce, a cabinet-level (Executive Level I) political appointee. The Secretary of Commerce, like the Secretary of Treasury, has numerous responsibilities. Support for the Secretary is provided by an Under Secretary, nine Assistant Secretaries and the General Counsel.

The administration and enforcement of the Trade Act of 1974 is the responsibility of the Assistant Secretary for Domestic and International Business. This person is also the head of the Domestic and International Business Administration.

The Assistant Secretary for Policy, the General Counsel and the Chief Economist may also provide views on matters under consideration by the Domestic and International Business Administration and the Economic Development Administration. Their involvement in matters relating to employee benefits depends on the nature of the matter under consideration.

LABOR LAWS

Department of Labor

Most of the labor laws including, but not limited to, the Labor-Management Reporting and Disclosure Act, the Vietnam Era Veterans Readjustment Assistance Act, the Service Contract Act and the Davis-Bacon Act, are administered by the Department of Labor. The Secretary of Labor, a cabinet-level (Executive Level 1) political appointee, is the head of the Department of Labor. In carrying out his responsibilities, the Secretary of Labor is supported by an Under Secretary, six Assistant Secretaries, the Commissioner of Labor Statistics and the Solicitor of Labor.

The administration of the Labor-Management Reporting and Disclosure Act and the Vietnam Era Veterans Readjustment Assistance Act is the responsibility of the Assistant Secretary for Labor-Management Relations, who is the head of the Labor-Management Services Administration. The Assistant Secretary's day-to-day responsibilities relating to the Labor-Management Reporting and Disclosure Act are carried out by the Director of the Office of Labor-Management Standards Enforcement. The Director of the Office of Veterans Reemployment Rights performs the Assistant Secretary's daily functions relating to the Vietnam Era Veterans Readjustment Assistance Act.

The administration of the Service Contract Act and the Davis-Bacon Act is the responsibility of the Assistant Secretary of the Employment Standards Administration, who is the titular head of the ESA. The Assistant Secretary's functions under these laws are carried out by the Wage and Hour Division.

Since the Solicitor of Labor has responsibility for all the legal activities of the Department, the Solicitor, through a subordinate staff of attorneys, provides legal advice to the persons discussed above. The relationship between the Solicitor and, for example, the Assistant Secretary for Labor-Management Relations is similar to the relationship between a lawyer and his client.

Other offices within the Department of Labor also may provide views on matters under consideration by these Assistant Secretaries and the Solicitor. For example, the Office of the Assistant Secretary for Policy, Evaluation and Research and the Office of the Commissioner of Labor Statistics may provide advice relating to the development of regulations.

Department of Justice

Most of the litigation involving the United States is conducted by attorneys with the Department of Justice. The Department is headed by the Attorney General, a cabinet-level (Executive Level I) political appointee. In carrying out his responsibilities, the Attorney General is supported by a Deputy Attorney General, nine Assistant Attorney Generals, the Solicitor General and numerous other officials.

The Department of Justice has responsibility for the enforcement of Section 302 of the Taft-Hartley Act and Section 501 of the LMRDA. The enforcement of this law is primarily the responsibility of the Assistant Attorney General of the Criminal Division, particularly the Labor-Management Laws Section.

National Labor Relations Board

The National Labor Relations Board is an independent agency created by the National Labor Relations Act, as amended by Taft-Hartley. The

Board is composed of five members, one of whom is the Chairman of the National Labor Relations Board. The Board is supported by the Executive Secretary and the Solicitor. In addition, certain legal functions are performed by the General Counsel. The General Counsel has final authority in certain matters.

Two principal functions have been delegated to the National Labor Relations Board under the National Labor Relations Act: preventing and remedying unfair labor practices by employers and employee organizations, and conducting secret ballot elections among employees in appropriate collective bargaining units to determine whether they desire to be represented by an employee organization.

SECURITIES LAWS

The Securities and Exchange Commission (SEC) was created under the authority of the '34 Act. The '33 Act, the '34 Act, the '40 Act and the Advisers Act are administered and enforced by the SEC.

The SEC is headed by a five member Commission, one of whom is the Chairman of the SEC. The Commission is supported by an Executive Director and five operating divisions, as well as by regional offices. The two most important divisions in terms of pension and welfare plans are the Division of Corporate Finance and the Division of Investment Management Regulation. Legal and accounting services are provided to the Commission and the operating divisions by the Commission's General Counsel and Chief Accountant, respectively.

EQUAL EMPLOYMENT LAWS

Department of Labor

The Department of Labor has responsibility for the administration and enforcement of the Equal Pay Act, the Age Discrimination in Employment Act of 1967 (the '67 Act), Executive Order 11141 and Executive Order 11246.

The principal unit within the Department of Labor which is responsible for carrying out the Department's duties under these laws is the Employment Standards Administration (ESA). ESA is headed by the Assistant Secretary for Employment Standards, who has overall responsibility for the Department's employment standards programs. Most of the day-to-day activities relating to the Equal Pay Act and the '67 Act are conducted by the Administrator of the Wage and Hour Division, within ESA. This Division is composed of several offices, and receives legal services from the Solicitor of Labor.

Most of the Assistant Secretary's day-to-day activities relating to Executive Order 11141 and Executive Order 11246 are conducted by the Deputy Assistant Secretary for Employment Standards, who is also the Director of the Office of Federal Contract Compliance Programs, a program within ESA. Like the Wage and Hour Division, this program is divided into several offices and receives legal services from the Solicitor of Labor.

Department of Health, Education and Welfare

The Department of Health, Education and Welfare is responsible for the administration and enforcement of the Age Discrimination Act of 1975 (the '75 Act), and also has certain responsibilities under Executive Order 11246. The Secretary of Health, Education and Welfare, a cabinet-level (Executive Level I) political appointee, is the head of the Department.

The principal unit within the Department of Health, Education and Welfare responsible for carrying out the Secretary's duties under the '75 Act is the Office of Human Development. The Office of Human Development is headed by an Assistant Secretary for Human Development, who organizes the Department's planning and resources to focus on and assist certain groups with special needs. Most of this person's day-to-day activities relating to the '75 Act, however, are conducted by the Commissioner of the Administration on Aging. As the title suggests, the Commissioner is the titular head of the Administration on Aging, an administration within OHD.

The principal unit within the Department of Health, Education and Welfare which has the responsibility for carrying out the Secretary's duties under Executive Order 11246 is the Office for Civil Rights. The Office for Civil Rights is headed by a Director, who provides staff support to the Secretary.

Equal Employment Opportunity Commission

The Equal Employment Opportunity Commission was created by Title VII, and became operational in 1965. The EEOC is headed by a five-member commission, one of whom is the Chairman of the EEOC. The EEOC is supported by an Executive Director and a General Counsel. While EEOC attorneys represent the EEOC in all litigation relating to Title VII, the EEOC does not have authority to issue regulations, only guidelines.

BANKING LAWS

Federal Reserve Board

The Federal Reserve Act created the Federal Reserve System, which consists of five parts: the Board of Governors; the 12 Federal Reserve Banks and their 25 branches and other facilities; the Federal Open Market Committee; the Federal Advisory Council; and the member commercial banks, which include all national banks and state-chartered banks that have voluntarily joined the System.

Broad supervisory powers are vested in the Board of Governors. The Board is composed of seven members including the Chairman. By Executive Order, the Chairman of the Board of Governors is a member of the National Advisory Council on International Monetary and Financial Policies. The Board determines general monetary, credit and operating policies for the Federal Reserve System as a whole, and formulates the rules and regulations necessary to carry out the purposes of the Federal Reserve Act. The Board's principal duties consist of exerting an influence over credit conditions and supervising the Federal Reserve Banks and member banks.

Department of the Treasury

The Department of the Treasury has responsibility for administering and enforcing portions of the National Bank Act. The principal unit within the Department which has this responsibility is the Comptroller of the Currency. The Comptroller, as the Administrator of National Banks, is responsible for the execution of laws relating to national banks, and promulgates rules and regulations governing the operations of approximately 4,600 national and District of Columbia banks.

Index

I

K

L

M

N